# Dietary Reference Intakes (DRIs): Recommended Dietary Allowances and Adequate Intakes, Vitamins
## Food and Nutrition Board, Institute of Medicine, National Academies

| Life Stage Group | Vitamin A (µg/d)[a] | Vitamin C (mg/d) | Vitamin D (µg/d)[b,c] | Vitamin E (mg/d)[d] | Vitamin K (µg/d) | Thiamin (mg/d) | Riboflavin (mg/d) | Niacin (mg/d)[e] | Vitamin B6 (mg/d) | Folate (µg/d)[f] | Vitamin B12 (µg/d) | Pantothenic Acid (mg/d) | Biotin (µg/d) | Choline (mg/d)[g] |
|---|---|---|---|---|---|---|---|---|---|---|---|---|---|---|
| **Infants** | | | | | | | | | | | | | | |
| 0 to 6 mo | 400* | 40* | 15 | 4* | 2.0* | 0.2* | 0.3* | 2* | 0.1* | 65* | 0.4* | 1.7* | 5* | 125* |
| 6 to 12 mo | 500* | 50* | 15 | 5* | 2.5* | 0.3* | 0.4* | 4* | 0.3* | 80* | 0.5* | 1.8* | 6* | 150* |
| **Children** | | | | | | | | | | | | | | |
| 1–3 y | **300** | **15** | **15** | **6** | 30* | **0.5** | **0.5** | **6** | **0.5** | **150** | **0.9** | 2* | 8* | 200* |
| 4–8 y | **400** | **25** | **15** | **7** | 55* | **0.6** | **0.6** | **8** | **0.6** | **200** | **1.2** | 3* | 12* | 250* |
| **Males** | | | | | | | | | | | | | | |
| 9–13 y | **600** | **45** | **15** | **11** | 60* | **0.9** | **0.9** | **12** | **1.0** | **300** | **1.8** | 4* | 20* | 375* |
| 14–18 y | **900** | **75** | **15** | **15** | 75* | **1.2** | **1.3** | **16** | **1.3** | **400** | **2.4** | 5* | 25* | 550* |
| 19–30 y | **900** | **90** | **15** | **15** | 120* | **1.2** | **1.3** | **16** | **1.3** | **400** | **2.4** | 5* | 30* | 550* |
| 31–50 y | **900** | **90** | **15** | **15** | 120* | **1.2** | **1.3** | **16** | **1.3** | **400** | **2.4** | 5* | 30* | 550* |
| 51–70 y | **900** | **90** | **15** | **15** | 120* | **1.2** | **1.3** | **16** | **1.7** | **400** | **2.4**[h] | 5* | 30* | 550* |
| > 70 y | **900** | **90** | **20** | **15** | 120* | **1.2** | **1.3** | **16** | **1.7** | **400** | **2.4**[h] | 5* | 30* | 550* |
| **Females** | | | | | | | | | | | | | | |
| 9–13 y | **600** | **45** | **15** | **11** | 60* | **0.9** | **0.9** | **12** | **1.0** | **300** | **1.8** | 4* | 20* | 375* |
| 14–18 y | **700** | **65** | **15** | **15** | 75* | **1.0** | **1.0** | **14** | **1.2** | **400**[i] | **2.4** | 5* | 25* | 400* |
| 19–30 y | **700** | **75** | **15** | **15** | 90* | **1.1** | **1.1** | **14** | **1.3** | **400**[i] | **2.4** | 5* | 30* | 425* |
| 31–50 y | **700** | **75** | **15** | **15** | 90* | **1.1** | **1.1** | **14** | **1.3** | **400**[i] | **2.4** | 5* | 30* | 425* |
| 51–70 y | **700** | **75** | **15** | **15** | 90* | **1.1** | **1.1** | **14** | **1.5** | **400** | **2.4**[h] | 5* | 30* | 425* |
| > 70 y | **700** | **75** | **20** | **15** | 90* | **1.1** | **1.1** | **14** | **1.5** | **400** | **2.4**[h] | 5* | 30* | 425* |
| **Pregnancy** | | | | | | | | | | | | | | |
| 14–18 y | **750** | **80** | **15** | **15** | 75* | **1.4** | **1.4** | **18** | **1.9** | **600**[j] | **2.6** | 6* | 30* | 450* |
| 19–30 y | **770** | **85** | **15** | **15** | 90* | **1.4** | **1.4** | **18** | **1.9** | **600**[j] | **2.6** | 6* | 30* | 450* |
| 31–50 y | **770** | **85** | **15** | **15** | 90* | **1.4** | **1.4** | **18** | **1.9** | **600**[j] | **2.6** | 6* | 30* | 450* |
| **Lactation** | | | | | | | | | | | | | | |
| 14–18 y | **1,200** | **115** | **15** | **19** | 75* | **1.4** | **1.6** | **17** | **2.0** | **500** | **2.8** | 7* | 35* | 550* |
| 19–30 y | **1,300** | **120** | **15** | **19** | 90* | **1.4** | **1.6** | **17** | **2.0** | **500** | **2.8** | 7* | 35* | 550* |
| 31–50 y | **1,300** | **120** | **15** | **19** | 90* | **1.4** | **1.6** | **17** | **2.0** | **500** | **2.8** | 7* | 35* | 550* |

**NOTE:** This table (taken from the DRI reports, see www.nap.edu) presents Recommended Dietary Allowances (RDAs) in **bold type** and Adequate Intakes (AIs) in ordinary type followed by an asterisk (*). An RDA is the average daily dietary intake level; sufficient to meet the nutrient requirements of nearly all (97-98 percent) healthy individuals in a group. It is calculated from an Estimated Average Requirement (EAR). If sufficient scientific evidence is not available to establish an EAR, and thus calculate an RDA, an AI is usually developed. For healthy breastfed infants, an AI is the mean intake. The AI for other life stage and gender groups is believed to cover the needs of all healthy individuals in the groups, but lack of data or uncertainty in the data prevent being able to specify with confidence the percentage of individuals covered by this intake.

[a] As retinol activity equivalents (RAEs). 1 RAE = 1 µg retinol, 12 µg β-carotene, 24 µg α-carotene, or 24 µg β-cryptoxanthin. The RAE for dietary provitamin A carotenoids is two-fold greater than retinol equivalents (RE), whereas the RAE for preformed vitamin A is the same as RE.

[b] As cholecalciferol. 1 µg cholecalciferol = 40 IU vitamin D.

[c] Under the assumption of minimal sunlight.

[d] As α-tocopherol. α-Tocopherol includes *RRR*-α-tocopherol, the only form of α-tocopherol that occurs naturally in foods, and the 2*R*-stereoisomeric forms of α-tocopherol (*RRR*-, *RSR*-, *RRS*-, and *RSS*-α-tocopherol) that occur in fortified foods and supplements. It does not include the 2*S*-stereoisomeric forms of α-tocopherol (*SRR*-, *SSR*-, *SRS*-, and *SSS*-α-tocopherol), also found in fortified foods and supplements.

[e] As niacin equivalents (NE). 1 mg of niacin = 60 mg of tryptophan; 0–6 months = preformed niacin (not NE).

[f] As dietary folate equivalents (DFE). 1 DFE = 1 µg food folate = 0.6 µg of folic acid from fortified food or as a supplement consumed with food = 0.5 µg of a supplement taken on an empty stomach.

[g] Although AIs have been set for choline, there are few data to assess whether a dietary supply of choline is needed at all stages of the life cycle, and it may be that the choline requirement can be met by endogenous synthesis at some of these stages.

[h] Because 10 to 30 percent of older people may malabsorb food-bound B12, it is advisable for those older than 50 years to meet their RDA mainly by consuming foods fortified with B12 or a supplement containing B12.

[i] In view of evidence linking folate intake with neural tube defects in the fetus, it is recommended that all women capable of becoming pregnant consume 400 µg from supplements or fortified foods in addition to intake of food folate from a varied diet.

[j] It is assumed that women will continue consuming 400 µg from supplements or fortified food until their pregnancy is confirmed and they enter prenatal care, which ordinarily occurs after the end of the periconceptional period—the critical time for formation of the neural tube.

**SOURCES**: *Dietary Reference Intakes for Calcium, Phosphorous, Magnesium, Vitamin D, and Fluoride* (1997); *Dietary Reference Intakes for Thiamin, Riboflavin, Niacin, Vitamin B6, Folate, Vitamin B12, Pantothenic Acid, Biotin, and Choline* (1998); *Dietary Reference Intakes for Vitamin C, Vitamin E, Selenium, and Carotenoids* (2000); *Dietary Reference Intakes for Vitamin A, Vitamin K, Arsenic, Boron, Chromium, Copper, Iodine, Iron, Manganese, Molybdenum, Nickel, Silicon, Vanadium, and Zinc* (2001); *Dietary Reference Intakes for Water, Potassium, Sodium, Chloride, and Sulfate* (2005); and *Dietary Reference Intakes for Calcium and Vitamin D* (2011). These reports may be accessed via www.nap.edu.

## Dietary Reference Intakes (DRIs): Recommended Dietary Allowances and Adequate Intakes, Elements
### Food and Nutrition Board, Institute of Medicine, National Academies

| Life Stage Group | Calcium (mg/d) | Chromium (µg/d) | Copper (µg/d) | Fluoride (mg/d) | Iodine (µg/d) | Iron (mg/d) | Magnesium (mg/d) | Manganese (mg/d) | Molybdenum (µg/d) | Phosphorus (mg/d) | Selenium (µg/d) | Zinc (mg/d) | Potassium (g/d) | Sodium (g/d) | Chloride (g/d) |
|---|---|---|---|---|---|---|---|---|---|---|---|---|---|---|---|
| **Infants** | | | | | | | | | | | | | | | |
| 0 to 6 mo | 200* | 0.2* | 200* | 0.01* | 110* | 0.27* | 30* | 0.003* | 2* | 100* | 15* | 2* | 0.4* | 0.12* | 0.18* |
| 6 to 12 mo | 260* | 5.5* | 220* | 0.5* | 130* | **11** | 75* | 0.6* | 3* | 275* | 20* | **3** | 0.7* | 0.37* | 0.57* |
| **Children** | | | | | | | | | | | | | | | |
| 1–3 y | **700** | 11* | **340** | 0.7* | **90** | **7** | **80** | 1.2* | **17** | **460** | **20** | **3** | 3.0* | 1.0* | 1.5* |
| 4–8 y | **1,000** | 15* | **440** | 1* | **90** | **10** | **130** | 1.5* | **22** | **500** | **30** | **5** | 3.8* | 1.2* | 1.9* |
| **Males** | | | | | | | | | | | | | | | |
| 9–13 y | **1,300** | 25* | **700** | 2* | **120** | **8** | **240** | 1.9* | **34** | **1,250** | **40** | **8** | 4.5* | 1.5* | 2.3* |
| 14–18 y | **1,300** | 35* | **890** | 3* | **150** | **11** | **410** | 2.2* | **43** | **1,250** | **55** | **11** | 4.7* | 1.5* | 2.3* |
| 19–30 y | **1,000** | 35* | **900** | 4* | **150** | **8** | **400** | 2.3* | **45** | **700** | **55** | **11** | 4.7* | 1.5* | 2.3* |
| 31–50 y | **1,000** | 35* | **900** | 4* | **150** | **8** | **420** | 2.3* | **45** | **700** | **55** | **11** | 4.7* | 1.5* | 2.3* |
| 51–70 y | **1,000** | 30* | **900** | 4* | **150** | **8** | **420** | 2.3* | **45** | **700** | **55** | **11** | 4.7* | 1.3* | 2.0* |
| > 70 y | **1,200** | 30* | **900** | 4* | **150** | **8** | **420** | 2.3* | **45** | **700** | **55** | **11** | 4.7* | 1.2* | 1.8* |
| **Females** | | | | | | | | | | | | | | | |
| 9–13 y | **1,300** | 21* | **700** | 2* | **120** | **8** | **240** | 1.6* | **34** | **1,250** | **40** | **8** | 4.5* | 1.5* | 2.3* |
| 14–18 y | **1,300** | 24* | **890** | 3* | **150** | **15** | **360** | 1.6* | **43** | **1,250** | **55** | **9** | 4.7* | 1.5* | 2.3* |
| 19–30 y | **1,000** | 25* | **900** | 3* | **150** | **18** | **310** | 1.8* | **45** | **700** | **55** | **8** | 4.7* | 1.5* | 2.3* |
| 31–50 y | **1,000** | 25* | **900** | 3* | **150** | **18** | **320** | 1.8* | **45** | **700** | **55** | **8** | 4.7* | 1.5* | 2.3* |
| 51–70 y | **1,200** | 20* | **900** | 3* | **150** | **8** | **320** | 1.8* | **45** | **700** | **55** | **8** | 4.7* | 1.3* | 2.0* |
| > 70 y | **1,200** | 20* | **900** | 3* | **150** | **8** | **320** | 1.8* | **45** | **700** | **55** | **8** | 4.7* | 1.2* | 1.8* |
| **Pregnancy** | | | | | | | | | | | | | | | |
| 14–18 y | **1,300** | 29* | **1,000** | 3* | **220** | **27** | **400** | 2.0* | **50** | **1,250** | **60** | **12** | 4.7* | 1.5* | 2.3* |
| 19–30 y | **1,000** | 30* | **1,000** | 3* | **220** | **27** | **350** | 2.0* | **50** | **700** | **60** | **11** | 4.7* | 1.5* | 2.3* |
| 31–50 y | **1,000** | 30* | **1,000** | 3* | **220** | **27** | **360** | 2.0* | **50** | **700** | **60** | **11** | 4.7* | 1.5* | 2.3* |
| **Lactation** | | | | | | | | | | | | | | | |
| 14–18 y | **1,300** | 44* | **1,300** | 3* | **290** | **10** | **360** | 2.6* | **50** | **1,250** | **70** | **13** | 5.1* | 1.5* | 2.3* |
| 19–30 y | **1,000** | 45* | **1,300** | 3* | **290** | **9** | **310** | 2.6* | **50** | **700** | **70** | **12** | 5.1* | 1.5* | 2.3* |
| 31–50 y | **1,000** | 45* | **1,300** | 3* | **290** | **9** | **320** | 2.6* | **50** | **700** | **70** | **12** | 5.1* | 1.5* | 2.3* |

**NOTE:** This table (taken from the DRI reports, see www.nap. edu) presents Recommended Dietary Allowances (RDAs) in **bold type** and Adequate Intakes (AIs) in ordinary type followed by an asterisk (*). An RDA is the average daily dietary intake level; sufficient to meet the nutrient requirements of nearly all (97–98 percent) healthy individuals in a group. It is calculated from an Estimated Average Requirement (EAR). If sufficient scientific evidence is not available to establish an EAR, and thus calculate an RDA, an AI is usually developed. For healthy breastfed infants, an AI is the mean intake. The AI for other life stage and gender groups is believed to cover the needs of all healthy individuals in the groups, but lack of data or uncertainty in the data prevent being able to specify with confidence the percentage of individuals covered by this intake.

**SOURCES**: *Dietary Reference Intakes for Calcium, Phosphorous, Magnesium, Vitamin D, and Fluoride* (1997); *Dietary Reference Intakes for Thiamin, Riboflavin, Niacin, Vitamin B6, Folate, Vitamin B12, Pantothenic Acid, Biotin, and Choline* (1998); *Dietary Reference Intakes for Vitamin C, Vitamin E, Selenium, and Carotenoids* (2000); and *Dietary Reference Intakes for Vitamin A, Vitamin K, Arsenic, Boron, Chromium, Copper, Iodine, Iron, Manganese, Molybdenum, Nickel, Silicon, Vanadium, and Zinc* (2001); *Dietary Reference Intakes for Water, Potassium, Sodium, Chloride, and* Sulfate (2005); and *Dietary Reference Intakes for Calcium and Vitamin D* (2011). These reports may be accessed via www.nap.edu.

# Dietary Reference Intakes (DRIs): Tolerable Upper Intake Levels (UL[a])
### Food and Nutrition Board, Institute of Medicine, National Academies

## Vitamins

| Life-Stage Group | Vitamin A (µg/d)[b] | Vitamin C (mg/d) | Vitamin D (µg/d) | Vitamin E (mg/d)[c, d] | Vitamin K | Thiamin | Riboflavin | Niacin (mg/d)[d] | Vitamin B₆ (mg/d) | Folate (µg/d)[e] | Vitamin B₁₂ | Pantothenic Acid | Biotin | Choline (g/d) |
|---|---|---|---|---|---|---|---|---|---|---|---|---|---|---|
| **Infants** | | | | | | | | | | | | | | |
| 0–6 mo | 600 | ND[f] | 25 | ND | ND | ND | ND | ND | ND | ND | ND | ND | ND | ND |
| 7–12 mo | 600 | ND | 25 | ND | ND | ND | ND | ND | ND | ND | ND | ND | ND | ND |
| **Children** | | | | | | | | | | | | | | |
| 1–3 y | 600 | 400 | 50 | 200 | ND | ND | ND | 10 | 30 | 300 | ND | ND | ND | 1.0 |
| 4–8 y | 900 | 650 | 50 | 300 | ND | ND | ND | 15 | 40 | 400 | ND | ND | ND | 1.0 |
| **Males, Females** | | | | | | | | | | | | | | |
| 9–13 y | 1,700 | 1,200 | 50 | 600 | ND | ND | ND | 20 | 60 | 600 | ND | ND | ND | 2.0 |
| 14–18 y | 2,800 | 1,800 | 50 | 800 | ND | ND | ND | 30 | 80 | 800 | ND | ND | ND | 3.0 |
| 19–70 y | 3,000 | 2,000 | 50 | 1,000 | ND | ND | ND | 25 | 100 | 1,000 | ND | ND | ND | 3.5 |
| >70 y | 3,000 | 2,000 | 50 | 1,000 | ND | ND | ND | 35 | 100 | 1,000 | ND | ND | ND | 3.5 |
| **Pregnancy** | | | | | | | | | | | | | | |
| 14–18 y | 2,800 | 1,800 | 50 | 800 | ND | ND | ND | 30 | 80 | 800 | ND | ND | ND | 3.0 |
| 19–50 y | 3,000 | 2,000 | 50 | 1,000 | ND | ND | ND | 35 | 100 | 1,000 | ND | ND | ND | 3.5 |
| **Lactation** | | | | | | | | | | | | | | |
| 14–18 y | 2,800 | 1,800 | 50 | 800 | ND | ND | ND | 30 | 80 | 800 | ND | ND | ND | 3.0 |
| 19–50 y | 3,000 | 2,000 | 50 | 1,000 | ND | ND | ND | 35 | 100 | 1,000 | ND | ND | ND | 3.5 |

[a] UL = The maximum level of daily nutrient intake that is likely to pose no risk of adverse effects. Unless otherwise specified, the UL represents total intake from food, water, and supplements. Due to lack of suitable data, ULs could not be established for vitamin K, thiamin, riboflavin, vitamin B₁₂, pantothenic acid, biotin, carotenoids. In the absence of ULs, extra caution may be warranted in consuming levels above recommended intakes.
[b] As preformed vitamin A only.
[c] As α-tocopherol; applies to any form of supplemental α-tocopherol.
[d] The ULs for vitamin E, niacin, and folate apply to synthetic forms obtained from supplements, fortified foods, or a combination of the two.
[e] β-Carotene supplements are advised only to serve as a provitamin A source for individuals at risk of vitamin A deficiency.
[f] ND = Not determinable due to lack of data of adverse effects in this age group and concern with regard to lack of ability to handle excess amounts. Source of intake should be from food only to prevent high levels of intake.

## Elements

| Life-Stage Group | Boron (mg/d) | Calcium (g/d) | Copper (µg/d) | Fluoride (mg/d) | Iodine (µg/d) | Iron (mg/d) | Magnesium (mg/d)[c] | Manganese (mg/d) | Molybdenum (µg/d) | Nickel (mg/d)[e] | Phosphorus (g/d) | Selenium (µg/d) | Vanadium (mg/d)[e] | Zinc (mg/d) |
|---|---|---|---|---|---|---|---|---|---|---|---|---|---|---|
| **Infants** | | | | | | | | | | | | | | |
| 0–6 mo. | ND | ND | ND | 0.7 | ND | 40 | ND | ND | ND | ND | ND | 45 | ND | 4 |
| 7–12 mo. | ND | ND | ND | 0.9 | ND | 40 | ND | ND | ND | ND | ND | 60 | ND | 5 |
| **Children:** | | | | | | | | | | | | | | |
| 1–3 y | 3 | 2.5 | 1,000 | 1.3 | 200 | 40 | 65 | 2 | 300 | 0.2 | 3 | 90 | ND | 7 |
| 4–8 y | 6 | 2.5 | 3,000 | 2.2 | 300 | 40 | 110 | 3 | 600 | 0.3 | 3 | 150 | ND | 12 |
| **Males, Females** | | | | | | | | | | | | | | |
| 9–13 y | 11 | 2.5 | 5,000 | 10 | 600 | 40 | 350 | 6 | 1,100 | 0.6 | 4 | 280 | ND | 23 |
| 14–18 y | 17 | 2.5 | 8,000 | 10 | 900 | 45 | 350 | 9 | 1,700 | 1.0 | 4 | 400 | ND | 34 |
| 19–70 y | 20 | 2.5 | 10,000 | 10 | 1,100 | 45 | 350 | 11 | 2,000 | 1.0 | 4 | 400 | 1.8 | 40 |
| >70 y | 20 | 2.5 | 10,000 | 10 | 1,100 | 45 | 350 | 11 | 2,000 | 1.0 | 3 | 400 | 1.8 | 40 |
| **Pregnancy** | | | | | | | | | | | | | | |
| 14–18 y | 17 | 2.5 | 8,000 | 10 | 900 | 45 | 350 | 9 | 1,700 | 1.0 | 3.5 | 400 | ND | 34 |
| 19–50 y | 20 | 2.5 | 10,000 | 10 | 1,100 | 45 | 350 | 11 | 2,000 | 1.0 | 3.5 | 400 | ND | 40 |
| **Lactation** | | | | | | | | | | | | | | |
| 14–18 y | 17 | 2.5 | 8,000 | 10 | 900 | 45 | 350 | 9 | 1,700 | 1.0 | 4 | 400 | ND | 34 |
| 19–50 y | 20 | 2.5 | 10,000 | 10 | 1,100 | 45 | 350 | 11 | 2,000 | 1.0 | 4 | 400 | ND | 40 |

[c] The ULs for magnesium represent intake from a pharmacological agent only and do not include intake from food and water.
[e] Although vanadium in food has not been shown to cause adverse effects in humans, there is no justification for adding vanadium to food and vanadium supplements should be used with caution. The UL is based on adverse effects in laboratory animals and this data could be used to set a UL for adults but not children and adolescents.
[f] ND = Not determinable due to lack of data of adverse effects in this age group and concern with regard to lack of ability to handle excess amounts. Source of intake should be from food only to prevent high levels of intake.

SOURCES: Dietary Reference Intakes for Calcium, Phosphorous, Magnesium, Vitamin D, and Fluoride (1997); Dietary Reference Intakes for Thiamin, Riboflavin, Niacin, Vitamin B6, Folate, Vitamin B₁₂, Pantothenic Acid, Biotin, and Choline (1998); Dietary Reference Intakes for Vitamin C, Vitamin E, Selenium, and Carotenoids (2000); Dietary Reference Intakes for Vitamin A, Vitamin K, Arsenic, Boron, Chromium, Copper, Iodine, Iron, Manganese, Molybdenum, Nickel, Silicon, Vanadium, and Zinc (2001); and Dietary Reference Intakes for Water, Potassium, Sodium, Chloride, and Sulfate (2004). These reports may be accessed via http://www.nap.edu.

# Dietary Reference Intakes (DRIs):
# Estimated Average Requirements for Groups

### Food and Nutrition Board, Institute of Medicine, National Academies

| Life-Stage Group | CHO (g/d) | Protien (g/d)a | Vitamin A (µg/d)b | Vitamin C (mg/d) | Vitamin E (mg/d)c | Thiamin (mg/d) | Riboflavin (mg/d) | Niacin (mg/d)d | Vitamin B6 (mg/d) | Folate (µg/d)e | Vitamin B12 (µg/d) | Copper (µg/d) | Iodine (µg/d) | Iron (mg/d) | Magnesium (mg/d) | Molybdenum (µg/d) | Phosphorus (mg/d) | Selenium (µg/d) | Zinc (mg/d) |
|---|---|---|---|---|---|---|---|---|---|---|---|---|---|---|---|---|---|---|---|
| **Infants** | | | | | | | | | | | | | | | | | | | |
| 7–12 mo. | 9* | | | | | | | | | | | | | 6.9 | | | | | 2.5 |
| **Children:** | | | | | | | | | | | | | | | | | | | |
| 1–3 y | 100 | 11 | 210 | 13 | 5 | 0.4 | 0.4 | 5 | 0.4 | 120 | 0.7 | 260 | 65 | 3.0 | 65 | 13 | 380 | ·17 | 2.5 |
| 4–8 y | 100 | 15 | 275 | 22 | 6 | 0.5 | 0.5 | 6 | 0.5 | 160 | 1.0 | 340 | 65 | 4.1 | 110 | 17 | 405 | 23 | 4.0 |
| **Males** | | | | | | | | | | | | | | | | | | | |
| 9–13 y | 100 | 27 | 445 | 39 | 9 | 0.7 | 0.8 | 9 | 0.8 | 250 | 1.5 | 540 | 73 | 5.9 | 200 | 26 | 1,055 | 35 | 7.0 |
| 14–18 y | 100 | 44 | 630 | 63 | 12 | 1.0 | 1.1 | 12 | 1.1 | 330 | 2.0 | 685 | 95 | 7.7 | 340 | 33 | 1,055 | 45 | 8.5 |
| 19–30 y | 100 | 46 | 625 | 75 | 12 | 1.0 | 1.1 | 12 | 1.1 | 320 | 2.0 | 700 | 95 | 6 | 330 | 34 | 580 | 45 | 9.4 |
| 31–50 y | 100 | 46 | 625 | 75 | 12 | 1.0 | 1.1 | 12 | 1.1 | 320 | 2.0 | 700 | 95 | 6 | 350 | 34 | 580 | 45 | 9.4 |
| 51–70 y | 100 | 46 | 625 | 75 | 12 | 1.0 | 1.1 | 12 | 1.4 | 320 | 2.0 | 700 | 95 | 6 | 350 | 34 | 580 | 45 | 9.4 |
| >70 y | 100 | 46 | 625 | 75 | 12 | 1.0 | 1.1 | 12 | 1.4 | 320 | 2.0 | 700 | 95 | 6 | 350 | 34 | 580 | 45 | 9.4 |
| **Females** | | | | | | | | | | | | | | | | | | | |
| 9–13 y | 100 | 28 | 420 | 39 | 9 | 0.7 | 0.7 | 9 | 0.8 | 250 | 1.5 | 540 | 73 | 5.7 | 200 | 26 | 1,055 | 35 | 7.0 |
| 14–18 y | 100 | 38 | 485 | 56 | 12 | 0.9 | 0.9 | 11 | 1.0 | 330 | 2.0 | 685 | 95 | 7.9 | 300 | 33 | 1,055 | 45 | 7.3 |
| 19–30 y | 100 | 38 | 500 | 60 | 12 | 0.9 | 0.9 | 11 | 1.1 | 320 | 2.0 | 700 | 95 | 8.1 | 255 | 34 | 580 | 45 | 6.8 |
| 31–50 y | 100 | 38 | 500 | 60 | 12 | 0.9 | 0.9 | 11 | 1.1 | 320 | 2.0 | 700 | 95 | 8.1 | 265 | 34 | 580 | 45 | 6.8 |
| 51–70 y | 100 | 38 | 500 | 60 | 12 | 0.9 | 0.9 | 11 | 1.3 | 320 | 2.0 | 700 | 95 | 5 | 265 | 34 | 580 | 45 | 6.8 |
| >70 y | 100 | 38 | 500 | 60 | 12 | 0.9 | 0.9 | 11 | 1.3 | 320 | 2.0 | 700 | 95 | 5 | 265 | 34 | 580 | 45 | 6.8 |
| **Pregnancy** | | | | | | | | | | | | | | | | | | | |
| 14–18 y | 135 | 50 | 530 | 66 | 12 | 1.2 | 1.2 | 14 | 1.6 | 520 | 2.2 | 785 | 160 | 23 | 335 | 40 | 1,055 | 49 | 10.5 |
| 19–30 y | 135 | 50 | 530 | 70 | 12 | 1.2 | 1.2 | 14 | 1.6 | 520 | 2.2 | 800 | 160 | 22 | 290 | 40 | 580 | 49 | 9.5 |
| 31–50 y | 135 | 50 | 550 | 70 | 12 | 1.2 | 1.2 | 14 | 1.6 | 520 | 2.2 | 800 | 160 | 22 | 300 | 40 | 580 | 49 | 9.5 |
| **Lactation** | | | | | | | | | | | | | | | | | | | |
| 14–18 y | 160 | 60 | 885 | 96 | 16 | 1.3 | 1.3 | 13 | 1.7 | 450 | 2.4 | 985 | 209 | 35 | 300 | 35 | 1,055 | 59 | 10.9 |
| 19–30 y | 160 | 60 | 900 | 100 | 16 | 1.3 | 1.3 | 13 | 1.7 | 450 | 2.4 | 1,000 | 209 | 36 | 255 | 36 | 580 | 59 | 10.4 |
| 31–50 y | 160 | 60 | 900 | 100 | 16 | 1.3 | 1.3 | 13 | 1.7 | 450 | 2.4 | 1,000 | 209 | 36 | 265 | 36 | 580 | 59 | 10.4 |

NOTE: This table presents Estimated Average Requirements (EARs), which serve two purposes: for assessing adequacy of population intakes, and as the basis for calculating Recommended Dietary Allowances (RDAs) for individuals for those nutrients. EARs have not been established for vitamin D, vitamin K, pantothenic acid, biotin, choline, calcium, chromium, fluoride, manganese, or other nutrients not yet evaluated via the DRI process.

a For individual at reference weight (Table 1-1). *indicates change from prepublication copy due to calculation error.

b As retinol activity equivalents (RAEs). 1 RAE = 1 µg retinol, 12 µg β-carotene, 24 µg α-carotene, or 24 µg β-cryptoxanthin. The RAE for dietary provitamin A carotenoids is twofold greater than retinol equivalents (RE), whereas the RAE for preformed vitamin A is the same as RE.

c As α-tocopherol. α-tocopherol includes RRR-α-tocopherol, the only form of α-tocopherol that occurs naturally in foods, and the 2R-stereoisomeric forms of α-tocopherol (RRR-, RSR-, RRS-, and RSS-α-tocopherol) that occur in fortified foods and supplements. It does not include the 2S-stereoisomeric forms of α-tocopherol (SRR-, SSR-, SRS-, and SSS-α-tocopherol), also found in fortified foods and supplements.

d As niacin equivalents (NE). 1 mg of niacin = 60 mg of tryptophan.

e As dietary folate equivalents (DFE). 1 DFE = 1 µg food folate = 0.6 µg of folic acid from fortified food or as a supplement consumed with food = 0.5 µg of a supplement taken on an empty stomach.

*SOURCES:* Dietary Reference Intakes for Calcium, Phosphorous, Magnesium, Vitamin D, and Fluoride (1997); Dietary Reference Intakes for Thiamin, Riboflavin, Niacin, Vitamin B6, Folate, Vitamin B12, Pantothenic Acid, Biotin, and Choline (1998); Dietary Reference Intakes for Vitamin C, Vitamin E, Selenium, and Carotenoids (2000); Dietary Reference Intakes for Vitamin A, Vitamin K, Arsenic, Boron, Chromium, Copper, Iodine, Iron, Manganese, Molybdenum, Nickel, Silicon, Vanadium, and Zinc (2001), and Dietary Reference Intakes for Energy, Carbohydrate, Fiber, Fat, Fatty Acids, Cholesterol, Protein, and Amino Acids (2002). These reports may be accessed via www.nap.edu.

# Dietary Reference Intakes (DRIs):
## Estimated Energy Requirements (EER) for Men and Women
### Food and Nutrition Board, Institute of Medicine, National Academies

| Height (m [in]) | PAL* | Weight for BMI[c] of 18.5 kg/m$^2$ (kg [lb]) | Weight for BMI of 24.99 kg/m$^2$ (kg [lb]) | EER, Men[d] (kcal/day) BMI of 18.5 kg/m$^2$ | (kcal/day) BMI of 24.99 kg/m$^2$ | EER, Women[d] (kcal/day) BMI of 18.5 kg/m$^2$ | (kcal/day) BMI of 24.99 kg/m$^2$ |
|---|---|---|---|---|---|---|---|
| 1.50 (59) | Sedentary | 41.6 (92) | 56.2 (124) | 1,848 | 2,080 | 1,625 | 1,762 |
| | Low active | | | 2,009 | 2,267 | 1,803 | 1,956 |
| | Active | | | 2,215 | 2,506 | 2,025 | 2,198 |
| | Very active | | | 2,554 | 2,898 | 2,291 | 2,489 |
| 1.65 (65) | Sedentary | 50.4 (111) | 68.0 (150) | 2,068 | 2,349 | 1,816 | 1,982 |
| | Low active | | | 2,254 | 2,566 | 2,016 | 2,202 |
| | Active | | | 2,490 | 2,842 | 2,267 | 2,477 |
| | Very active | | | 2,880 | 3,296 | 2,567 | 2,807 |
| 1.80 (71) | Sedentary | 59,9 (132) | 81.0 (178) | 2,301 | 2,635 | 2,015 | 2,211 |
| | Low active | | | 2,513 | 2,884 | 2,239 | 2,459 |
| | Active | | | 2,782 | 3,200 | 2,519 | 2,769 |
| | Very active | | | 3,225 | 3,720 | 2,855 | 3,141 |

[a] For each year below 30, add 7 kcal/day for women and 10 kcal /day for men. For each year above 30, subtract 7 kcal/day for women and 10 kcal/day for men.

[b] PAL = physical activity level.

[c] BMI = body mass index.

[d] Derived from the following regression equations based on doubly labeled water data:

Adult man: EER = 662 − 9.53 x age (y) + PA x (15.91 ? wt [kg] + 539.6 x ht [m])

Adult woman: EER = 354 − 6.91 x age (y) + PA x (9.36 ? wt [kg] + 726 x ht [m])
Where PA refers to coefficient for PAL
PAL = total energy expenditure ÷ basal energy expenditure
PA = 1.0 if PAL ? 1.0 < 1.4 (sedentary)
PA = 1.12 if PAL ? 1.4 < 1.6 (low active)
PA = 1.27 if PAL ? 1.6 < 1.9 (active)
PA = 1.45 if PAL ? 1.9 < 2.5 (very active)

# Dietary Reference Intakes (DRIs):
## Acceptable Macronutrient Distribution Ranges
### Food and Nutrition Board, Institute of Medicine, National Academies

| Macronutrient | Range (percent of energy) Children, 1–3 y | Children, 4–18 y | Adults |
|---|---|---|---|
| Fat | 30–40 | 25–35 | 20–35 |
|     *n*-6 polyunsaturated fatty acidsa (linoleic acid) | 5–10 | 5–10 | 5–10 |
|     *n*-3 ployunsaturated fatty acidsa ( -linolenic acid) | 0.6–1.2 | 0.6–1.2 | 0.6–1.2 |
| Carbohydrate | 45–65 | 45–65 | 45–65 |
| Protien | 5–20 | 10–30 | 10–35 |

[a] Approximately 10% of the total can come from longer -chain *n*-3 or *n*-6 fatty acids

SOURCE: Dietary Reference Intakes for Energy, Carbohydrate, Fiber, Fat, Fatty Acids, Cholesterol, Protein, and Amino Acids (2002).

# Dietary Reference Intakes (DRIs):
## Recommended Intakes for Individuals, Macronutrients
Food and Nutrition Board, Institute of Medicine, National Academies

| Life-Stage Group | Water[a] (L/d) | Carbohydrates (g/d) | Fiber (g/d) | Fat (g/d) | Linoleic Acid (g/d) | * Linolenic Acid (g/d) | Protien[b] (g/d) |
|---|---|---|---|---|---|---|---|
| **Infants** | | | | | | | |
| 0–6 mo | 0.7* | 60* | ND | 31* | 4.4* | 0.5* | 9.1* |
| 7–12 mo | 0.8* | 95* | ND | 30* | 4.6* | 0.5* | **11.0**[c] |
| **Children** | | | | | | | |
| 1–3 y | 1.3* | **130** | 19* | ND | 7* | 0.7* | 13 |
| 4–8 y | 1.7* | **130** | 25* | ND | 10* | 0.9* | 19 |
| **Males** | | | | | | | |
| 9–13 y | 2.4* | **130** | 31* | ND | 12* | 1.2* | **34** |
| 14–18 y | 3.3* | **130** | 38* | ND | 16* | 1.6* | 52 |
| 19–30 y | 3.7* | **130** | 38* | ND | 17* | 1.6* | **56** |
| 31–50 y | 3.7* | **130** | 38* | ND | 17* | 1.6* | **56** |
| 51–70 y | 3.7* | **130** | 30* | ND | 14* | 1.6* | **56** |
| >70 y | 3.7* | **130** | 30* | ND | 14* | 1.6* | **56** |
| **Females** | | | | | | | |
| 9–13 y | 2.1* | **130** | 26* | ND | 10* | 1.0* | **34** |
| 14–18 y | 2.3* | **130** | 26* | ND | 11* | 1.1* | **46** |
| 19–30 y | 2.7* | **130** | 25* | ND | 12* | 1.1* | **46** |
| 31–50 y | 2.7* | **130** | 25* | ND | 12* | 1.1* | **46** |
| 51–70 y | 2.7* | **130** | 21* | ND | 11* | 1.1* | **46** |
| >70 y | 2.7* | **130** | 21* | ND | 11* | 1.1* | **46** |
| **Pregnancy** | | | | | | | |
| 14–18 y | 3.0* | **175** | 28* | ND | 13* | 1.4* | **71** |
| 19–30 y | 3.0* | **175** | 28* | ND | 13* | 1.4* | **71** |
| 31–50 y | 3.0* | **175** | 28* | ND | 13* | 1.4* | **71** |
| **Lactation** | | | | | | | |
| 14–18 y | 3.8* | **210** | 29* | ND | 13* | 1.3* | **71** |
| 19–30 y | 3.8* | **210** | 29* | ND | 13* | 1.3* | **71** |
| 31–50 y | 3.8* | **210** | 29* | ND | 13* | 1.3* | **71** |

*NOTE:* This table presents Recommended Dietary Allowances (RDAs) in bold type and Adequate Intakes (AIs) in ordinary type followed by an asterisk (*). RDAs and AIs may both be used as goals for individual intake. RDAs are set to meet the needs of almost all (97 to 98 percent) individuals in a group. For healthy infants fed human milk, the AI is the mean intake. The AI for other life stage and gender groups is believed to cover the needs of all individuals in the group, but lack of data or uncertainty in the data prevent being able to specify with confidence the percentage of individuals covered by this intake.

[a] Total water includes all water contained in food, beverages, and drinking water.

[b] Based on 0.8 g/kg body weight for the reference body weight.

[c] Change from 13.5 in prepublication copy due to calculation error.

# Dietary Reference Intakes (DRIs):
## Additional Macronutrient Recommendations
Food and Nutrition Board, Institute of Medicine, National Academies

| Macronutrient | Recommendation |
|---|---|
| Dietary cholesterol | As low as possible while consuming a nutritionally adequate diet |
| Trans fatty acids | As low as possible while consuming a nutritionally adequate diet |
| Saturated fatty acids | As low as possible while consuming a nutritionally adequate diet |
| Added sugars | Limit to no more than 25% of total energy |

*SOURCE:* Dietary Reference Intakes for Energy, Carbohydrate, Fiber, Fat, Fatty Acids, Cholesterol, Protein, and Amino Acids (2002).

# NUTRITION
## Real People, Real Choices

**Second Edition**

**Susan J. Hewlings**
University of Central Florida College of Medicine

**Denis M. Medeiros**
Kansas State University

**Kendall Hunt**
publishing company

Cover images © 2011 Shutterstock, Inc.

www.kendallhunt.com
*Send all inquiries to:*
4050 Westmark Drive
Dubuque, IA 52004-1840

Printed in the United States of America
10 9 8 7 6 5 4 3 2 1

# Dedication

I dedicate this project, as I do all of my accomplishments, to my parents, Joan and Chuck Hewlings. Their unconditional love and support of me and of each other have given me the foundation and the strength to persevere through every challenge I have encountered. I thank my partner in the adventure race of life, Dave Shuman, for always being there to listen. The love and support of the entire Hewlings and Runkle families are greatly appreciated. To my four-legged loves, your unconditional love has no human equal.

*—Susan J. Hewlings*

I dedicate this book to several inspirational people in my life: to my mother Rita Wilkie, for always being a driving force in my life and encouraging me to seek a higher education and to never give up. To my loving wife, Susan, whose love, encouragement, and suggestions throughout this project made its completion possible. To my loving daughter Kathryn, who has always marched to the beat of a different drum and who has made me proud. And to my late father, Joseph Medeiros, and my late stepfather, William Wilkie. All of these people have, in some measure, made me who I am.

*—Denis M. Medeiros*

# Brief Contents

# Contents

# Quick Reference To Want To Know More? Features

Following, by chapter, are the topics of the *Want to know more?* features. This unique resource facilitates assignable coverage of additional topics, expansion of other topics, and/or voluntary exploration by students who want to go beyond the text.

# Preface

## What's Different and Why

**N**utrition: Real People, Real Choices was created as a result of a close working partnership with instructors across the country who teach the introductory nutrition course. *Our overriding goal was to produce a thoroughly modern text that represents a clear and positive alternative to existing texts. We accomplished this through the research process, during which we were able to identify and then respond to needs that are not currently being met. We're confident that our goal has been achieved, but the only confirmation that ultimately matters is yours.*

### Research Driven

As have authors of other texts, we began our project with several clearly defined goals and objectives. Based on our own teaching experience, we identified several features and benefits we believed would successfully differentiate our text. Fortunately, we were associated with a publisher willing to allow us to interact with and receive input from more than 100 instructors across the country in order to thoroughly test and refine our initial assumptions and to benefit from countless suggestions for enhancing our text both substantively and pedagogically.

It was through this process of focus groups (which we attended), reviews, a three-day reviewer conference, more reviews, and three comprehensive drafts of the manuscript that this partnership was formed and carried out. The published text and ancillaries that accompany it represent a collaborative and research/instructor-driven text in every way possible. We are confident that this partnership with nutrition instructors and students (via surveys and class testing) has produced a unique learning tool and one that, above all else, responds to what you and your colleagues say is needed to meet the demands of the modern nutrition course.

### What Do Nutrition Instructors Want in a Nutrition Text?

Our extensive research and dialog with instructors led to six major conclusions:

1. Instructors lack *sufficient time* to cover all of the essential and important topics. Instructors, on average, assign and cover only 12 chapters, reluctantly leaving out topics such as lifespan nutrition, food safety, global nutrition, and supplementation. The instructors we worked with stressed that when topics are omitted due to time constraints, students are shortchanged and their expectations go partially unmet.
2. Although all existing texts attempt to provide *practical information,* more than 80 percent of instructors believe that those texts do not meet students' needs and expectations in this respect.
3. To satisfy the science requirement—the reason why many students enroll in this course—any new introductory text must be *scientifically sound, accurate, and contemporary*. It must also serve nonmajors and majors alike.
4. Certain topics—*dietary supplements, alcohol, sports nutrition,* and *eating disorders*—deserve full-chapter treatment because of their importance and to satisfy the interests and expectations of students. Other topics, such as *ethnic foods, vegetarianism,* and *disease and nutrition,* need more coverage and emphasis than is currently reflected in existing texts.
5. *Readability* matters, now more than ever. Reading skills have declined and many students are non-native English speakers. Existing texts frequently fail to reflect these circumstances. Additionally, most texts are written in a passive voice and fall short in continuously relating topics to the reader, thereby missing the opportunity to provide interest and generate motivation.
6. *Ancillaries,* especially those used most frequently, such as the Test Bank, PowerPoints, Instructor's Manual, and Diet Analysis Software, need to be well conceived, accurate, and easy to use.

# How We Responded

As we've noted, in any introductory or survey text, not all relevant topics can be assigned and covered or covered in the desired depth, especially for majors. In many instances instructors differ as to what topics should be covered and to what extent. Until now, authors have been forced to choose among these topics, with unsatisfactory results for many instructors. Our text is the first to overcome this limitation through development of a unique combination of solutions.

## Unequaled Flexibility in Breadth and Depth of Coverage

*Integrated Topics.* Instructors identified several topics that they would like to cover but frequently are unable to cover due to time constraints. To do so with existing texts would require assignment of a full chapter for each. We solved this challenge—thanks to some brainstorming in focus group discussions and our invaluable conference with reviewers—by integrating coverage of the following topics (listed alphabetically), where appropriate, throughout:

- Culture and Ethnic Foods
- Culture and Nutrition
- Dietary Supplements
- Disease and Nutrition
- Sustainable Nutrition
- Global Nutrition
- Lifestages and Nutrition
- Vegetarianism

Accordingly, regardless of the chapters you choose for inclusion in your syllabus, your students will receive exposure to these topics. We have accomplished this via *integrated* features (as opposed to setting off content in boxes or appending them to the ends of chapters) that focus on these topics precisely *when and where they are directly related to the chapter's coverage.* Although each is identified by its own icon, the content flows within the narrative so that the reader is not signaled that this content is "optional" (see pages 10, 11, and 13 for examples). Because of the importance of this coverage, our *test bank* provides specifically designated questions for each feature's content.

**Scope of Coverage.** Although the typical instructor assigns only twelve chapters, our research shows that there is significant variation in the topics chosen. Thus, our approach for establishing the scope of our table of contents (TOC) was to identify those topics that at least two-thirds of instructors thought should be given full-chapter coverage. The result is a TOC of 17 chapters. In the cases of Chapter 11 on dietary supplements and Chapter 12 on alcohol, more than 80 percent and 70 percent of respondents, respectively, asked for full-chapter coverage.

**Expandable Scope and Depth of Coverage.** Another *unique* aspect of our text (and one that was universally popular with reviewers) responds directly to the variations that exist among nutrition instructors in terms of the *range and depth* of topics assigned. Every chapter contains annotated references in the margin to the Hewlings/Medeiros companion website. This feature, titled **Want to Know More?,** directs students to the website where they can (1) explore in greater detail selected topics introduced in the text and/or (2) investigate related topics that many instructors would like to assign but can't unless they use handouts. There are 129 *Want to Know More?* references interspersed throughout the text. Examples include principles of kosher and Islamic food laws, bioengineered foods, warning signs of diabetes, the role of vitamin $B_{12}$ in mental disorders and Alzheimer's disease, nutritional guidelines in other countries, nutrients to focus on when planning a vegetarian diet, and calcium intake and weight control. We authored the majority of this information, and its appearance on the website matches its presentation in the text; a full listing of these features appears, by chapter, on pages xiv, and xv. In other instances, the student can click on a direct link to the related website.

Whether assigned or explored voluntarily, this feature provides instructors and students with a much broader resource than the traditional print text, and one that gives instructors considerable flexibility in content, scope, and breadth. And for those majoring in nutrition, this feature provides an immediate and easy-access resource for broader and more in-depth study.

## Unequaled Emphasis on Practicality and Relevance

The number one goal of instructors teaching this class is to engage students and to motivate them to care about nutrition and the impact it has on their health and everyday lives. Most instructors suggested that the best way to accomplish that is to present information with a constant, captivating, and cutting-edge approach that addresses not only what students need to know, but what they want to know. Many texts attempt to meet this expectation but fall short by varying degrees in terms of thoroughly addressing nutrition pop culture and edgy topics such as agribusiness, food imports, and food processing. We do not shy away from these topics or cover them superficially. They are relevant, and our students both need and expect to learn about each of them in order to be informed consumers. Furthermore, as our reviewers advised, we don't simply sprinkle practical information in here and there or orphan it at the end of the chapter or in an offset box—which many students ignore. We address hot and controversial topics head-on in every chapter and *provide more practical and applied information than any other text.*

Overall, we want students to apply what they learn through this course and to be able to make informed choices every time they decide what to eat for any meal or snack. Therefore, in every chapter we include several applications to assist students in turning knowledge into action through features such as ***Application Tips, Make It a Practice, Self-Assessment***, and ***You Decide***. For example, in Chapter 5, Proteins, one of the application tips is *"Sources of protein that are low in fat."*

In addition to the aforementioned application features, we have integrated in every chapter a ***Real People, Real Choices*** case to which students can relate. All chapters begin with a topic-appropriate real person who is facing real choices regarding a particular nutrition issue. Later in the chapter, suggestions and potential strategies are provided by real students, registered dietitians (RDs), and nutrition instructors in the ***Real People, Other Voices*** portion of the case. The solution is provided at the end of the chapter in the ***Real People, Real Strategies*** segment. Inclusion of a proposed solution to the case by a real student demonstrates firsthand the value and applicability of the chapter's content. Furthermore, it empowers students by demonstrating that information obtained in this course will provide them with the knowledge to make real choices. The cases were selected after asking instructors which nutrition issues and challenges their students most frequently identify.

Another key feature in our quest to provide students with a text they can relate to is the ***In the Student's Voice*** questions. We surveyed both students and instructors on a chapter-by-chapter basis to identify the questions students ask most frequently. These questions are interspersed throughout and placed in the margins adjacent to the narrative portion of the text that provides the answer.

To fully demonstrate the application of concepts covered throughout, Chapter 2 provides a set of cooking tips and some quick, easy, healthy recipes that students can prepare in minutes in their dorms, apartments, or homes. This highly practical and applied information was endorsed by numerous reviewers who want their students to recognize the critical link between knowledge and everyday application.

Overall, we selectively utilize *nine* different elements to meet instructor and student expectations for relevant, applicable information.

1. *Real People, Real Choices* case in every chapter with involvement by nutrition students, RDs, and instructors via the *Real People, Other Voices* component (see pages 19, 46, and 91)
2. *Application Tips* (over 100—see pages 7, 8
3. *In the Student's Voice Questions* (interspersed throughout—more than 60)
4. *Make It a Practice* (feature)
5. *Self-Assessment* (feature)
6. *To Supplement or Not* (feature)
7. *You Decide* (feature)
8. *Want to Know More?*
9. *Cooking tips and recipes for quick, easy, healthy meals students can prepare*

## Scientifically Sound and Contemporary

The increasing awareness and ensuing interest in the impact of nutrition on health, weight management, and overall quality of life have brought nutrition to the forefront of science and pop culture. One of our primary goals in writing this text is to provide students with scientifically based information that will enable them to separate fact from fiction.

In our *Myths and Legends* feature, we provide students with examples of how to apply science as they sort through many nutritional myths. For example, in Chapter 6, Digestion, Absorption, and Metabolism, we discuss the myth that *"If you swallow chewing gum it will stay in your stomach for seven years."*

To assist students in addressing current issues related to nutrition, we incorporate *What's Hot* topics such as *"Energy drinks: Do they give you wings or leave you hangin'?"* Throughout the text we challenge students to question myths and misinformation through a basic understanding of scientific principles. Given this scientific base, students will be more informed consumers and will have some defense against the constant bombardment of nutrition misinformation in advertisements, fad diets, and television commercials. This base will also enable students to interpret professional and government recommendations pertaining to dietary changes.

## Readability

We believe the best way to ensure a readable text is to choose content that is constantly interesting and useful. We're well aware that if students don't find the content stimulating and relevant, then ease of reading becomes a moot issue. Based on instructor and student feedback, we're extremely confident we've produced a user-friendly text that will motivate and reward the reader on every page with relevance and practicality. The second task in producing a readable text is to subject every sentence and page to extensive reading and scrutiny by numerous students and instructors. In addition to being reviewed by more than 100 instructors through three full drafts, we thoroughly class-tested the manuscript and continuously surveyed students regarding readability, interest level, and what's really useful to them in terms of in-text learning and study aids.

## Unequaled Ancillaries

In many cases the ancillaries that accompany nutrition texts are an afterthought: They are poorly conceived, poorly developed, and error-prone. Instructors in our focus groups frequently cited ancillaries that provided so little quality as to be of no use. We were determined to ensure that the ancillaries accompanying *Nutrition: Real People, Real Choices* are exceptional in their quality, utility, and original content. As with the text, they are based on research with instructors across the country. The Instructor's Manual, Test Bank, PowerPoints, and Student Assessment and Learning Guide all contain *unique* features. They have been reviewed by several instructors in a fashion similar to the text manuscript, have been revised based on that feedback, and then have been carefully edited and checked for accuracy. In short, *they're different*. Descriptions of each appear later in this preface under the heading You Asked for Them: Better Ancillaries.

# Approach and Organization: From Farm to Fork

In addition to providing information that students can immediately adapt to everyday practices, we want to challenge them to think of issues they never thought of as being related to nutrition. One such example is our integrated feature *Food Technology and the Environment*. We have included this feature to stimulate students to broaden their appreciation of food and where it comes from, to think of food as an agricultural act—to encourage them to make food choices based not only on their health as an individual, but to consider the impact that their food choices have on the environment. In other words, we want them to think of food from "farm to fork."

During discussion with instructors who teach this course, we reinforced our sense that many find teaching the concepts related to chemistry and anatomy and physiology difficult considering that, as in our own experience, the majority of the students taking this course have little or no science background. These concepts are most relevant when discussing digestion, absorption, and metabolism. In response to this common challenge, we have designed this book utilizing a unique concept for organization and discussion of the nutrients. *The organization encourages students to visualize the nutrients as they would experience them: from the plate to their mouth; through the digestive system; and then metabolized for energy, stored for energy, or excreted as waste.* This is why we discuss the macronutrients in Chapters 3, 4, and 5 before we discuss digestion and metabolism in Chapter 6. We believe it is important for students to have a thorough understanding of what the nutrients are and how they affect health before we discuss how they are broken down and utilized inside the body. Pedagogically, this is a meaningful departure from the way many other texts present this material. Some discuss the digestive system in a chapter on anatomy and physiology before going into detail about the macronutrients. Digestion is then covered again for each macronutrient in the relevant chapter. Based on extensive research, we concluded that many instructors find this an awkward and often redundant way to cover these crucial topics. Moreover, all other texts leave metabolism out entirely. We asked instructors if they were satisfied with this omission of a challenging topic. More than 70 percent agreed that, although a challenging topic for introductory level students, metabolism needs to be covered. Therefore, we introduce metabolism in Chapter 6 as a natural flow of the nutrients from plate to usable energy. We cover the material in a meaningful, level-appropriate manner. Reviewers were enthusiastic and indicated that our presentation would facilitate and justify adding coverage of metabolism to their course. And they agreed that this organization will allow students to truly understand and internalize "What is a carbohydrate?" and "How much should I eat?" before they move on to understanding how it is digested, absorbed, and metabolized. These concepts frequently seem abstract to students if presented too early.

## Unique Chapters

During development of this text, we continuously asked instructors to answer this question: What topics do students seem most interested in and ask the most questions about? Not surprisingly, instructors agreed that students ask about *dietary supplements* more than anything else. We have, therefore, devoted an entire chapter to this topic. However, if you choose not to assign the full chapter, your students will still be exposed to the topic because we have interspersed it as a feature (***To Supplement or Not***) throughout the text.

The majority of instructors indicated that *eating disorders, alcohol,* and *sports nutrition* are the other topics that students most frequently ask about and want more information on. The majority of instructors favored full-chapter treatment of each. Accordingly, we offer separate but optional chapters on these topics.

## Coverage of Vitamins and Minerals

*Separate* or *combined* coverage of vitamins and minerals? Our research confirmed that instructors across the country agree that vitamins and minerals is one of the most challenging of all topics to teach in the introductory course. Most believe it is very difficult to cover this material while keeping students engaged. Other texts have attempted to address this issue by combining the coverage into one chapter or by approaching the material by physiological system in what is described as a functional approach. The idea is appealing, but it can be difficult in practice because few students have a background to make the connection to the physiological systems. For that reason, we elected to cover the vitamins and minerals in two separate chapters. *Unlike other texts, however, we have presented the information with a practical, applied approach.* To keep students engaged, it is necessary to continuously show them how this information can influence their lives. We accomplish this goal right from the start in Chapter 9 in the *Real People, Real Choices case.* We present Anthony Pulz, a student who is taking mega-doses of vitamins because he believes that they will make him healthier. We then ask students to assess their own vitamin intake in the Self-Assessment feature. Continuing, we encourage them to add as many fruits and vegetables to their diet as possible. Many students say they don't like fruits and vegetables, so we suggest they "hide" them in smoothies and sauces. It is just this type of practical application that students and instructors indicate is lacking from other texts.

For those who have adjusted their course to teach from a *systems or functional approach* to vitamins and minerals, we have authored a single chapter featuring combined coverage. It is available as a customized version of the text.

## Nutrition and Disease

Consistent with our effort to produce an introductory text suitable for use in classes populated with both majors and nonmajors, we've given special attention to our coverage of nutrition and disease. In many nonmajors texts, these topics are either under- or overemphasized. Rather than go into great detail on obscure metabolic diseases that most nonmajor students have never heard of and probably never will outside of class, we focus on the most common lifestyle and nutrition-related diseases. We then introduce students to the connection of nutrition and disease. In the interspersed *Nutrition and Disease* features, we present the idea of nutrition as treatment. For example, in Chapter 17, which covers lifestages, we focus on *"Obesity in children: an epidemic?"*

## Appreciation for Cultural Diversity

American culture and the makeup of student bodies in the United States have changed and evolved in recent years. Many accrediting agencies now require student learning outcomes for their courses, and one of today's most prevalent learning outcomes is attention to diversity. In our research, instructors repeatedly mentioned that many college-age students are uninformed about cultural differences in health, nutrition, the importance of food, and food supply. For this reason, we established a goal to connect cultural differences and similarities throughout the book. We have done this by providing an emphasis on culture throughout: through *Nutrition and Culture, Culture and Ethnic Foods, and Global Nutrition* features. For example, in Chapter 3, Carbohydrates, we discuss *"Okinawans have the world's longest life expectancy. Is it their diet?"* We have also made a point of including pictures of foods from different cultures throughout, as well as illustrating and discussing the food pyramids of several different populations and cultures.

## The Continuum of Nutrition across the Lifespan

In addition to enhancing students' cultural connections, we want to connect students with various lifestages and their associated nutritional concerns. We think it is important to teach students about the needs of those in other stages of life and to demonstrate the continuum of nutrition and the role it plays in health throughout the lifecycle. However, many instructors run out of time before reaching these later chapters. In order to address this circumstance and to keep students connected to the concept of the nutrition continuum, we provide a *Nutrition and Lifestages* feature in several chapters throughout the text. For example, in Chapter 3, Carbohydrates, we discuss what's so bad about soda in schools; and in Chapter 11, Nutrition and Lifestages, we discuss *"DHEA: The fountain of youth in a bottle?"*

# Student-Driven Study Features

In addition to a focus on readability, one of our goals was to provide students with *in-text* learning and study aids that *they* would endorse—components they evaluated and sanctioned as having the highest utility and making the text as user-friendly as possible. The end result is a logical set of study aids that clearly identify what's important and facilitates comprehension.

1. A *Here's Where You've Been* and *Here's Where You're Going* feature begins each chapter, identifying the upcoming key concepts and linking them to related content in prior chapters.
2. *Before you go on* . . . questions at the end of each major section of a chapter are designed to test reading comprehension and encourage students to read with a purpose and focus.
3. *Key terms* are set in **boldface,** defined in the narrative, and listed with page references at the end of the chapter.
4. *New and unfamiliar terms* that are not considered "key" but require definitions for reading comprehension are included in the end-of-text glossary of additional terms.
5. *Critical thinking questions* are periodically embedded in the narrative and illustration captions.

6. *Summary tables* are interspersed in chapters where needed to consolidate a large volume of information. Examples are the tables for vitamins and minerals in Chapters 9 and 10, respectively. Many of these use a "What it is," "What it does," and "Why it's important" format that students find extremely useful during study and review.

7. *End-of-chapter summaries* are formatted as bulleted lists that concisely recap the main concepts.

8. *Chapter quizzes* appear at the conclusion of each chapter and provide students with another tool to help them quickly test their comprehension.

# Why Should You Adopt This Text?

1. *We listened.* As a research-driven text, every feature and nuance has been developed and tested in response to and in partnership with more than 100 instructors across the country. Our text has also had the benefits of class-testing and insights provided in survey data completed by hundreds of students.

2. Unequaled flexibility in terms of topic selection, scope, and depth of coverage.

3. Unequaled emphasis on practicality, relevance, and application.

4. Integrated coverage throughout of topics that instructors frequently don't have time to cover such as *food technology, lifestages, diseases, global nutrition,* and *vegetarianism.*

5. In addition to the core chapters, full-chapter presentations are provided on topics that the majority of instructors and students think are important: *dietary supplements, alcohol, eating disorders,* and *sports nutrition.*

6. Innovative organization that follows nutrients as students encounter them, from food on your plate to energy in your cells.

7. Metabolism is presented in an applicable, easy-to-understand manner.

8. Unequaled emphasis on culture, diversity, and ethnic foods—integrated throughout.

9. Emphasis throughout on giving students the knowledge and tools they need to separate nutrition fact from fiction.

10. Students are empowered by seeing *real* students apply chapter concepts in the *Real People, Other Voices* segment of the Real People, Real Choices cases.

11. Through a unique feature, *In the Student's Voice,* the questions most frequently asked by students are posed and answered.

12. Highly readable narrative that is user-friendly without oversimplification and watered-down science.

13. Unequaled and *student-endorsed* in-text learning and study aids.

14. Carefully crafted ancillaries that are unequaled in scope, quality, and utility.

15. Chapter 2 provides tips and simple recipes that apply concepts students will learn throughout.

# You Asked for Them: Better Ancillaries

Based on our research and feedback from the focus groups involving users of every major competing textbook, we can state without hesitation that no package of ancillaries published for the introductory nutrition course is as market-responsive and as fully integrated as those described below. Whether you are a course coordinator, an adjunct or first-time instructor, or an experienced teacher frustrated by poorly developed supplements that are characterized by a lack of utility and quality control, you can consign that view and those negative experiences to the past.

## Instructor's Manual (IM)

The IM is unique in its resources, layout, and integration with both the text and ancillaries. Authored by Sarah Thompson and Alexa Schmidt of Binghamton University, each chapter opens with a comprehensive listing of *instructor resources* available for use in presenting that chapter's content. Consequently, you do not have to search through numerous sources to discover which supplementary materials are available for use with each chapter.

The next set of elements for each chapter are a *chapter outline,* list of *key terms* with definitions, followed by a detailed set of *lecture notes* in large type that always appear on the left-hand facing pages. To promote awareness of their availability and to make all resources easier to use, each right-hand page contains *notes recommending where to use PowerPoints* (each with its own lecture notes), *lecture enhancers* (supplemental lecture topics), *critical thinking questions, critical thinking exercises, supplemental activities, supplemental group exercises, supplemental Internet exercises,* and *commentary on the chapter's Real People, Real Choices case* and *strategies.* Additionally, the "Before you go on . . ." questions are repeated and answers are provided.

## Test Bank

For many instructors this is *the* most important ancillary. We are keenly aware that for any test bank to be successful it must be comprehensive, balanced in terms of its coverage of key concepts and range of difficulty, *and above all—accurate*! Our test bank is unique in its utility, meets all of these criteria, and goes well beyond.

Co-authored by Sarah Thompson of Binghamton University and Holly Morris of Lehigh Carbon Community College, it contains more than 2,000 questions, each of which is classified in a *test table* by three levels of learning (1—*factual,* 2—*conceptual,* and 3—*applied*) and arranged by learning objective/key concept. Questions are included for all text content, including the integrated features.

All questions have been reviewed by five instructors, including the text authors, revised accordingly, and carefully edited and checked for accuracy.

## Computerized Test Bank

Over 100 true/false, fill-in-the-blank, multiple choice, and short answer questions for each chapter (more than 2,000 total) are compiled.

## PowerPoints®

Based on instructor preferences, we have produced PowerPoint lecture slides. Authored by Susan Hewlings, these images are designed to augment the key concepts and topics in the text and they allow you to enrich and visually enhance your lectures. Detailed annotations regarding content and recommended uses for each slide are included. Scaled-down images of each PowerPoint, along with its lecture uses and notes, are reproduced in the Instructor's Manual. All content has been class-tested, carefully reviewed by three nutrition instructors, and edited for clarity and accuracy.

## Transparency Acetates

This set of transparency acetates features selected figures and tables from the text, including figure numbers and captions.

## Student Assessment and Learning Guide

Authored by Carol W. Turner of New Mexico State University, the *Student Assessment and Learning Guide* contains a unique and rich set of learning tools designed to both assess and enhance students' understanding and application of each chapter's key concepts. Each chapter includes the following components: *chapter overview and outline, list of key concepts* (learning objectives), *key terms exercise, list of commonly used acronyms, study questions, true/false exercise, self-assessment exercise, diet analysis exercise,* a *Can You Do It? exercise,* and *Real People, Real Choices* case analysis. Similar to the test bank, it has been reviewed by five instructors, including the text authors, and carefully revised based on their input.

## Companion Website

The companion website includes the "Want to Know More" features from the text, "Before You Go On" videos featuring the authors, "Real People, Real Choices" videos that bring each chapter's character to life, Key Terms from the textbook under the glossary section, Study Questions and True/False Questions from the *Student Assessment and Learning Guide,* and Chapter Outlines.

# Acknowledgments

It is overwhelming to consider the number of talented people who have contributed to this project. This book is truly a collaborative effort. Everything you see on these pages is a reflection of the people we mention below.

As instructors of nutrition, foremost we acknowledge the significant influence that our students have had upon us in making us better instructors and getting a sense of what works and what doesn't. We have taught so many and they have influenced us in countless ways, but especially in terms of teaching style and understanding of the various approaches to learning. We would like to thank those that helped by class-testing and reviewing various drafts of the manuscript.

As we stressed earlier in this preface, this book is truly a collaborative effort with instructors across the country. We cannot begin to express our gratitude for the ideas and input of these passionate reviewers and contributors:

**Nancy Adamowitz**
University of Arizona

**Kwaku Addo**
University of Kentucky

**Ryan Andrews, RD**
Lutherville, MD

**Sharon Antonelli**
San Jose City College

**Michelle Bartell**
Monroe Community College

**Claire Berg**
Brookdale Community College

**Michael Bizeau**
Colorado State University

**Susan Bohanan, RD**
Orinda, CA

**Emily Boldrin**
Oklahoma State University

**Patricia Brevard**
James Madison University

**Anne Bridges**
University of Alaska-Anchorage

**Cindy Brison, RD**
Omaha, NE

**Melanie Burns**
Eastern Illinois University

**Thomas Castonguay**
University of Maryland

**Erin Caudill**
Southeast Community College

**Melissa Chabot**
University of Buffalo (SUNY)

**Roberto Chamul**
California State University-Los Angeles

**J. J. Chen**
University of Nevada-Las Vegas

**Dorothy Chen-Maynard**
California State University-San
  Bernardino

**Sai Chidambaram**
Canisius College

**Carolyn Conn**
University of New Mexico

**Marcia Costello**
Villanova University

**Helen Curhan, RD**
Santa Barbara, CA

**Earlene Davis**
Bakersfield College

**Maggi Dorsett**
Butte College

**Sara Ducey**
Montgomery College-Rockville, MD

**Linda S. Eck Mills, RD**
Bernville, PA

**Mary Emerson, RD**
Gorham, ME

**Alyson Escobar, MD**
Montgomery College-Rockville

**Claudia Fajardo-Lira**
California State University-Northridge

**Stacy Fisher, RD**
Cedar Park, TX

**Cindy Fitch**
West Virginia University

**Gary Fosmire**
Pennsylvania State University

**Bernard Frye**
University of Texas at Arlington

**Cynthia Gossage**
Prince George's Community College

**Margaret Gunther**
Palomar College

**Timaree Hagenburger**
Cosumnes River College

**Patricia Heacock**
CUNY-Brooklyn College

**Susan Heinrich**
Pima Community College

**Benjamin Heinz, RD**
Bloomington, MN

**Tawni Holmes**
University of Central Oklahoma

**Carolyn Impara**
Mt. San Antonio College

**James Kahora**
Middlesex County College

**Lalita Kaul, RD**
Rockville, MD

**Nicole Kerneen-Fasules, RD**
Milwaukee, WI

**Lydia Kloiber**
Texas Tech University

**Terri Lisagor**
California State University-Northridge

**Edralin Lucas**
Oklahoma State University

**Sharon McWhinney**
Prairie View A&M University

**Juliet Mevi-Shiflett**
Diablo Valley College

**Allison Miner**
Prince George's Community College

**Cherie Moore**
Cuesta College

**Holly Morris**
Lehigh Carbon Community College

**Michelle Neymann**
California State University-Chico

**Anne O'Donnell**
Santa Rosa Junior College

**Jack Osman**
Towson University

**Kandi Perrazzo, RD**
Allentown, PA

**Rebecca Pobocik**
Bowling Green State University

**Ruth Reilly**
University of New Hampshire

**Barbara Reynolds**
College of the Sequoias

**Patricia Rhea**
Community College of Baltimore
County-Catonsville

**Jennifer Ricketts**
University of Arizona

**Heather (Lynne) Rothenberg**
Mission College

**David Rowell, RD**
Garrison, MT

**Tammy Sakanashi**
Santa Rosa Junior College

**Tiffany Schlinke**
University of Central Oklahoma

**Alexa Schmidt**
Binghamton University

**Ann-Marie Scott**
University of North Carolina-
Greensboro

**Claudia Sealey-Potts**
Sam Houston State University

**Peachy Seiden, RD**
Cincinnati, OH

**Terry Shaw**
Austin Community College

**Christina Shepard**
Arizona State University

**Sarah Short**
Syracuse University

**James Siniscalchi**
New Jersey City University

**Lorraine Sirota**
CUNY-Brooklyn College

**Mollie Smith**
California State University-Fresno

**John Snyder, RD**
Harrisburg, PA

**LuAnn Soliah**
Baylor University

**Tammy Stephenson**
University of Kentucky

**Jo Taylor**
Southeast Community College

**Sarah Thompson**
Binghamton University

**Norm Trezek**
Pima Community College

**Carol W. Turner**
New Mexico State University

**Sherry Valente-Gaspari, RD**
Haddon Township, NJ

**Dana Wassmer**
Cosumnes River College

**Elizabeth Watanabe, RD**
Sitka, AK

**Jennifer Weddig**
Metropolitan State College of Denver

**Rick S. Weissinger, RD**
Middletown, DE

**Christopher Wendtland**
Monroe Community College

**Thomas Wilson**
University of Massachusetts-Lowell

**Fred Wolfe**
University of Arizona

**Jean York**
Mt. San Antonio College

**Donna Zoss**
Purdue University

We must separately recognize and thank the following instructors who, in addition to reviewing the entire manuscript, gave up three days from their busy schedules to attend our reviewer conference. During this session they tirelessly endured extensive brainstorming sessions and cheerfully gave advice that had an enormous impact on the final text: Nancy Adamowicz, University of Arizona; Cindy Fitch, West Virginia University; Carolyn Impara, Mt. San Antonio College; Lydia Kloiber, Texas Technical University; Allison Miner, Prince George's Community College; Ann-Marie Scott, University of North Carolina-Greensboro; and Sarah Thompson, Binghamton University.

We would especially like to recognize Sarah Thompson of Binghamton University, Alexa Schmidt of Binghamton University, Holly Morris of Lehigh Carbon Community College, and Carol W. Turner of New Mexico State University as authors of key ancillaries, and Sherri Hewlings from Pennsylvania Institute of Technology and Jeffrey Cara for their assistance with the PowerPoint slides. All have gone above and beyond in terms of generating the unique utility and exceptional quality we sought. Instructors who use our Test Bank, Instructor's Manual, *Student Assessment and Learning Guide,* and PowerPoints will recognize the excellence of their work.

We would also like to recognize our family, friends, and colleagues who supported us and listened to us every step of the way. In particular, we thank Dr. Robert Wildman for introducing both of us and recommending us as a writing team.

From Susan: The support and encouragement of my family cannot be overstated: Mom, Dad, Gram, Sherri, Brother, Dottie, Delaney, Avery, Tad, and Cody, who make being overly-enmeshed a good thing. Eric taught me the depth of my perseverance. Dave, you deserve a medal for having to live with me through the ups and downs of this endeavor.

From Denis: I would like to thank my wife Susan for her love and for her encouragement throughout the project; her patience with me when I had to work on the manuscript; and her active role in proofreading the manuscript and helping to compile the food composition tables. I also want to thank the faculty and staff at Kansas State University for acting as a sounding board throughout the writing process and for their generosity in offering so many worthwhile suggestions. Special thanks go to Janet Finney and Pam Gudjohnsen for helping in numerous ways in the processing of the manuscript.

### Susan J Hewlings Ph.D., RD, CSCS, CSSD

Susan Hewlings received her Ph.D. in Nutrition from the Department of Nutrition, Food, and Exercise Sciences at Florida State University. Her dissertation research was titled "Eating Disorder Prevention Program for Pre-Adolescent Children." She received her BS in Nutrition and her MS in Exercise Physiology also from Florida State. Susan is a Registered and Licensed Dietitian, a Board Certified Specialist in Sports Dietetics, and a Certified Strength and Conditioning Specialist. She has been involved in the food and nutrition industry for more than ten years. She is currently an Assistant Professor at the University of Central Florida College of Medicine. Susan completed a summer fellowship studying protein and fat metabolism at The University of Texas Medical Branch/Shriners Burn Institute. She authored the Eating Disorders section for the American Dietetics Association's online *Clinical Care Manual.* In addition, she is self-employed as a nutrition and wellness consultant, in which capacity she provides speaking, group workshops, individual nutrition counseling, and various nutrition related services. Susan incorporates an integrative, balanced approach to health and nutrition while specializing in clients with disordered eating, sports nutrition, and weight loss issues. She is also a competitive adventure racer and distance runner. Susan also runs a non-profit dog rescue.

### Denis M. Medeiros, Ph.D., RD

Denis M. Medeiros is currently the Department Head of Human Nutrition and Associate Dean for Scholarship and Research at Kansas State University. He received his Ph.D. from Clemson University. He received his BS degree in Biology from Central Connecticut State University and his MS from Illinois State University. Denis has taught at several major universities, including Mississippi State University, The University of Wyoming, The Ohio State University, and currently Kansas State University. He has taught nonmajors introductory nutrition for many years. His research has been supported by federal grants and has focused primarily on minerals, heart disease, and general mineral metabolism. Denis also received fellowships to study at the University of California-Davis and Washington University School of Medicine. He has developed programs for underrepresented minority students to be trained in the biomedical sciences working with the National Institutes of Health. He has authored or co-authored 120 publications in professional peer-referreed journals. Denis is also a Registered and Licensed Dietitian.

# Text Features

*Nutrition: Real People, Real Choices* presents nutrition in a flexible format that provides scientifically sound and accurate coverage.

## The Right Depth of Coverage for Introductory Nutrition

The science of nutrition is presented at the appropriate level for introductory students with this innovative organization and coverage.

With over *120 Want to Know More* references interspersed throughout the book, you can go to the website to explore and investigate selected topics.

## Brief Contents

"Plate to Mouth" format encourages you to visualize nutrients as you experience them: from plate to mouth, followed by digestion.

Metabolism is covered as a natural flow of the nutrients from plate to usable energy in a level-appropriate, applicable manner.

Unique chapter on Dietary Supplements provides added depth on this important topic.

v

# Breadth of Coverage in Every Chapter

## To Supplement or Not?

### What are fat blockers and do they work?

There are several types of fat blockers on the market. Some work and some do not. There are different ways in which some of these products work to block fat absorption. One common blocker is marketed over-the-counter as Alli,® sometimes referred to as Xenicol,® which is available through prescription. The chemical name for both is Orlistat. The drug works by inhibiting an enzyme produced by the pancreas that breaks shrimp and crabs. It is thought to lower fat absorption in the small intestine. Is it effective? Some animal studies suggest it is and that it can even raise HDL-cholesterol and lower LDL-cholesterol, which is beneficial in combating heart disease. However, studies with humans have yielded negative results. A study at the University of California-Davis reported there was not a greater excretion of fat in the feces of people taking the chitosan supplements. If fat absorption were being blocked you would have expected to see more fat in the feces. Furthermore, there was no reduction in body weight with the use of these products. For these types of fat blocker the best advice is to save your money and block fat by not eating excessive amounts to begin with! ■

## Integration of Cutting-Edge Features within the Text

Cutting-edge content on hot topics such as Sustainable Nutrition, To Supplement or Not, Culture and Ethnic Foods, What's Hot, Global Nutrition, and Vegetarianism are integrated into the text (rather than placed in separate boxes), giving you the opportunity to learn about things that are important to your daily life throughout the course.

## Sustainable Nutrition

### Cage-free or free-roaming—what do they really mean?

Did you know that most commercial egg-laying chickens are kept in small cages? Producers contend that caging hens has benefits for the birds, consumers, and their workers. The cages help separate the birds from their feces, which is said to help reduce the risk of disease and infections. Producers also contend that working conditions for their farmers and employees are better with caged hens than with other systems. Moreover, by using cages producers can employ automation, which decreases labor time, costs, and the prevalence of dust and ammonia. Eggs are laid on the sloping floor of the cage so that there is minimal contact between the egg and the hen, which producers say decreases the possibility of bacterial contamination of the egg.

Stimulates you to think of food as an agricultural act.

Connects cultural differences and similarities by providing an emphasis throughout the book.

## Global Nutrition

### Obesity as a global issue

Contrary to popular belief, the obesity epidemic is not just an issue for the United States and other industrialized societies. According to the World Health Organization, more than 1 billion adults worldwide are overweight, and at least 300 million of them are clinically obese. Current obesity levels range from less than 5 percent in China, Japan, and certain African nations to more than 75 percent in urban Samoa. But even in relatively low-prevalence countries such as China, rates have risen to almost 20 percent in some cities.

Childhood obesity is already an epidemic in some areas of the world and on the rise in others. An estimated 22 million children under age 5 are estimated to be overweight worldwide. The problem is global and increasingly extends into the developing world; for example, in Thailand the prevalence of obesity in 5-to-12-year-olds rose from 12.2 percent to 15.6 percent in just two years. ■

# What You Really Want to Know for Everyday Choices

## Nutrition: Real People, Real Choices

gives you real, practical information you can apply to your daily life, and tools for telling nutrition fact from fiction.

 ■ **Self-Assessment**

*Are you practicing heart-healthy eating?*

How does your personal diet relate to and compare with the several diet recommendations we have discussed in previous chapters? Is it heart healthy, or do you need to make some adjustments? Using the self-assessment tool that follows, you can see how your current diet stacks up.

For each category listed in the following table, check the column that most closely applies to you and then record your score for that food category in the left column. For example, if you consume 2 to 3 servings of vegetables per day, enter the number 3 in the "Score" space at the bottom of the "3 points" column. Add up your score for all categories and compare it to the ranges shown in the Interpretation section below the table.

**Rate Your Plate**

| Category | 5 Points | 3 Points | 0 Points |
|---|---|---|---|
| **Grains: Bread, Cereal, Pasta, Rice, Dry Beans, and Peas** | Avoid all high-fat breads/cereals, such as croissants, sweet rolls, pastries, snack crackers, granola-type cereals. Eat at least 8 servings daily. | Avoid most high-fat breads/cereals. Eat at least 6 servings daily. | Do not limit high-fat breads/cereals. Eat less than 6 servings daily or do not know how many servings you are eating. |
| Score: ——— | ——— | ——— | ——— |
| **Vegetables** | Eat 4 or more servings daily. Avoid all vegetables prepared in butter, creams, or sauces. | Eat 2 or 3 servings daily. Avoid most vegetables prepared in butter, cream, or sauces. | Eat 1 serving or less daily. |
| Score: ——— | ——— | ——— | ——— |
| **Fruit** | Eat 4 servings daily. | Eat 2 to 3 servings daily. | Eat 1 serving or less daily. |
| Score: ——— | ——— | ——— | ——— |
| **Eggs** | Eat 0 to 2 egg yolks per week. *Remember to cou eggs used in cooki | Eat 3 to 4 egg yolks per week. | Eat more than 4 egg yolks per week. |
| Score: ——— | | | |

## Self-Assessments and Application Tips

These tools help you to examine your nutritional practices and to determine steps towards behavior change, while over 100 Application Tips provide helpful ways to put better eating practices into action.

## Real People, Real Choices Case Studies

Chosen by experts in human nutrition, these case studies open the chapter to help you learn to apply the science of nutrition. These case studies are revisited twice more within the chapter to emphasize good strategies and decision-making and to provide a helpful conclusion.

### Real People, Other Voices

**Student:**
**Etheline Cimatu**
San Jose City College, San Jose, CA

I can understand Marisol's anxiety stemming from the challenges of change—being a freshman in college and away from home. She will need to make initial assessments to give herself a starting point. Having recorded her diet for several days, she needs to deal with the issue of being homesick, which is driving a lot of her "bad" food choices. To help in her transition, she could join a club or group, which will give her a sense of a family support system.

I noticed that Marisol has a busy schedule, gets little physical activity, and eats a diet lacking nutritious foods. To jump-start her day, she should wake up about an hour earlier to get at least thirty minutes of physical activity; she can start with moderate walking. She

**Instructor:**
**Jau-Jiin Chen, PHD, RD**
University of Nevada, Las Vegas

Even a person with a busy schedule has time for a healthy meal. Marisol has access to the school cafeteria with many food choices. Her current meals contain large amounts of concentrated sugar and saturated fat, not enough variety, and minimal fruits and vegetables. If she thinks before she eats and follows the principles outlined in the *Dietary Guidelines* and MyPyramid to include five food groups, she can develop her own healthy meal plan. Initially, it might be difficult to satisfy all the recommendations, but as she practices it will become easier.

The easiest way to get started is to have two-thirds of her foods come from plant sources (such as vegetables, fruits, and grain products) and one-third from

**Registered dietitian:**
**Linda S. Eck Mills, MBA, RD, LDN, FADA**
Bernville, PA

First, it's great that Marisol realizes the need to do something to improve her eating habits and has taken this nutrition course as an elective early in her college career. This course will provide her with a great foundation for a healthy, independent lifestyle.

Planning healthy eating can seem like a daunting task, so she needs to start with the basics and progress from there. I would recommend she start with the MyPyramid website—www.MyPyramid .gov—and enter her personal information to see how much she should be eating from each food group. Then she should take the three-day food record she did for class and put that information into the MyPyramid Tracker. Next Marisol needs to look at where she is falling

# CHAPTER 1

# The Food on Your Plate

## Here's Where You're Going >

*The following topics and concepts are the ones we'll emphasize in Chapter 1.*

- There are six classes of nutrients; three of them (carbohydrates, fats, and proteins) yield energy and the rest (vitamins, minerals, and water) perform other vital functions.
- The reasons we choose the foods we eat range from taste, convenience, and cost to culture, among many factors.
- Our diets are connected to obesity and several diseases prominent in our culture.
- Lack of sufficient food in diets continues to be a worldwide problem.
- There are ways in which you can identify reputable sources of nutrition information.

## Real People, Real Choices

Twenty-one-year-old Andrew Kreider lives in a suburb of Philadelphia and is a sophomore at a local community college, where he is taking three classes. He commutes daily to his classes and his job at the Wegmans supermarket, where he works thirty-two hours per week. He lives at home with his single mom and a couple of younger sisters. He tries to help out at home when time allows, but it rarely does. Normally he is up by 6:30 A.M. and out the door at 7:00 A.M. in order to get in a couple of hours of work before traveling to campus for his first class at 10:00 A.M. He has a half-hour break around 1:00 P.M., goes back to class at 1:30 P.M., and gets out at 3:00 P.M. From there he is off to his job again starting at 4:00 P.M. He takes a late dinner around 7:00 P.M., when he gets off work.

Given his schedule, his meals consist mostly of anything that's convenient. In the morning he scouts the kitchen to see what looks good and often ends up having only a glass of orange juice and a pastry. At 1:00 P.M., he usually goes to the vending machines on campus. He can consider a sit-down meal in the evening after work. This usually consists of visiting a fast-food restaurant near Wegmans or on his way home. His other alternative is to return home and pop something into the microwave, typically a frozen dinner. He works eight hours on Saturdays, but has Sundays off.

Because Andrew is a health sciences major, he knows that his current dietary habits should not continue. Although he's in his early twenties, he feels tired, rushed, and stressed. To compensate for his poor eating habits he recently started taking a vitamin and mineral supplement, yet he isn't getting the extra energy from it that he expected. Because he doesn't see any immediate prospects for change in the demands of his schedule, he decides to discuss his situation and diet with his nutrition instructor. What advice do you think she will give him?

## Why Study Nutrition?

Is your situation similar to Andrew's? Do the demands of a typical day lead you to neglect aspects of your personal care, including nutrition? Many students taking their first course in nutrition arrive in the class with misconceptions and myths about what the food they eat can do to their bodies. Claims of miracle cures through the use of dietary supplements, the notion that vitamin and mineral supplements will give you energy, or the idea that certain diets allow you to eat all you want and still lose weight are just a few common misconceptions about nutrition. Distinguishing credible information from incorrect claims continues to be a challenge.

Look familiar? With all the nutrition information available, how do you make good decisions about what to purchase at the grocery store?

Many of us are interested in how food and nutrients can promote better health and prevent and treat certain diseases. Much of the interest and some of the myths about nutrition stem from the potential role of nutrients as medicine. For instance, can certain nutrients cure a disease that you already have? You will discover in this chapter and throughout this book that much of what we know about nutrition has evolved from studies of disease. You will discover that nutrition is not only a young science, but one founded in many disciplines: physiology, organic chemistry, biochemistry, anthropology, psychology, and food science and technology, to name a few. You will find that the science of nutrition involves its share of politics from a legislative perspective as well as in public policy.

## How Nutrition Has Evolved

The science of nutrition originated from the study of nutrient deficiencies, but today the field has evolved to include other factors such as toxicology, behavioral and sociological aspects, and chronic disease. Nutrients not only prevent deficiencies, but optimize health. Nutrition is an ever-evolving and quickly changing science.

Well into the twentieth century, the federal government's role in nutrition was non-existent. In the 1940s many men who were drafted to serve in World War II were rejected because of nutritional ailments such as deficiencies of specific nutrients. This led to the creation of the first **Recommended Dietary Allowances (RDAs)** in 1941. This is simply the recommended nutrient intake required to meet the known nutrient needs of the healthy population. After the war, the RDAs continued to be revised periodically by the Food and Nutrition Board under the National Research Council of the National Academy of Sciences. However, new information emerged in the 1970s as a result of congressional hearings on nutrition and health, generating a rebirth of nutrition science. Charles Butterworth, a physician and nutritionist, wrote an important article, "The Skeleton in the Hospital Closet," in which he documented how some patients entering a hospital for even minor ailments were leaving malnourished and afflicted with many nutrient deficiencies that had long been considered conquered in the United States. The article also revealed that medical students were not receiving any nutrition education, and most physicians were unable to give sound nutrition advice. Obesity and overweight conditions among Americans also began to receive more attention from health professionals and policy advocates. In response to these nutritional issues, the federal government published the first *Dietary Guidelines for Americans*.

The types of foods that Americans consume have changed since the early twentieth century. Americans eat more refined foods and take in more calories than their bodies need. Additionally, Americans participate in less physical activity. The combination of our less-than-ideal nutritional intake and decreasing physical activity is harmful to our health as a nation.

## How Do We Define Nutrition?

Food contains substances that we call nutrients. The study of nutrients has led to the science of nutrition. A **nutrient** is a substance that the body needs for energy, growth, and development. Traditionally, nutrients have been defined as *essential* or *non-essential*. An *essential nutrient* is one that is necessary for life and one that the body cannot make at all or cannot make in sufficient amounts to sustain its functions; therefore, it must be included in the diet. A *non-essential nutrient* is one that the body can make in sufficient amounts if it is lacking in the diet, or one that may deliver a health benefit when added to the diet.

*What's so important about nutrition?*

An essential nutrient for one organism may not be essential for another. Let's take vitamin C, for example. You have probably heard that vitamin C is good for you and is needed in your diet. This is true; without vitamin C in your diet you would not be able to live. However, did you know that many other animals make their own vitamin C and do not require it in their diets? Cats, dogs, rats, and rabbits all make enough vitamin C for normal health and thus do not need an extra source. Humans, monkeys, apes, catfish, bats, and guinea pigs are among the animals that need vitamin C in their diets to survive.

Non-essential nutrients are constantly being discovered. For example, there are many plant chemicals in fruits and vegetables that are now recognized as healthy whereas years ago we did not even know of their existence. These plant chemicals are being isolated and studied to determine if they protect against chronic diseases such as heart disease, cancer, and diabetes.

## Classifying Nutrients

We can simplify the discussion of nutrients by dividing them into two broad classes: (1) nutrients that provide energy and (2) nutrients that don't provide energy but do support metabolism or basic bodily functions (Table 1.1). We introduce them as general concepts here, and in subsequent chapters we expand on each.

### Nutrients That Provide Energy

The nutrients that provide energy for the body are referred to as **macronutrients** simply because relative to other compounds, they are required and consumed in large amounts. This is not to suggest

### Table 1.1     Summary of Nutrient Classes

| Class | Nutrient | Energy (kcal/g) | Function |
|---|---|---|---|
| Nutrients that provide energy | Carbohydrate | 4 | Provides energy |
| | Fat (lipids) | 9 | Provides energy, stores energy |
| | Protein | 4 | Promotes growth and maintenance |
| Nutrients that support metabolism | Vitamins | 0 | Regulate biochemical reactions, antioxidants |
| | Minerals | 0 | Regulate biochemical reactions, provide structure |
| | Water | 0 | Regulates temperature, provides lubrication |

We will discuss two substance classes that are not in the table. *Alcohol* is not a nutrient, but it supplies calories (Chapter 12). *Phytochemicals* (plant chemicals) are found in food and have antioxidant and other functions, but organisms can survive without them.

that the **micronutrients** are less important; they are just needed in much smaller quantities. The energy-yielding macronutrients are carbohydrate, fat, and protein. Water is a macronutrient, but it does not yield energy; it is discussed separately.

A *calorie* is scientific unit of energy; the calories used to measure food energy are actually *kilocalories* (kcal). One kilocalorie, or food calorie, equals 1,000 calories; in this book, when we use the term **calorie** we are referring to a kilocalorie. The scientific definition of a kilocalorie is the amount of energy needed to raise the temperature of 1 kilogram of water 1 degree Celsius. When we discuss how many calories are in a particular food, we are referring to how much energy is released by the nutrients in that food once it has been digested and absorbed by your gastrointestinal tract.

**Carbohydrates.** A **carbohydrate** consists of energy-yielding nutrients such as sugars and starches and non-energy-yielding nutrients such as fiber. Carbohydrates are composed of the elements carbon, oxygen, and hydrogen. As a general rule, for every gram of carbohydrate consumed, 4 kcal of energy are released (except for fiber, which has little energy).

**Fats.** The more technical word for **fat** is *lipid*. Foods such as oils and butter are common sources of fat. Fat provides 9 kcal per gram, or more than twice the amount of energy in carbohydrates. Fat, like carbohydrate, is composed of carbon, oxygen, and hydrogen, but contains twice as many hydrogen atoms as a carbohydrate. This property of having lots of hydrogen is one reason why fats yield more energy when broken down.[1] Thus foods that have a much higher fat content deliver more energy.

**Protein.** **Protein** is an energy-yielding nutrient that contains nitrogen; its primary purpose is to support growth, maintenance, and repair of tissue. It provides 4 kcal per gram.

*How do you calculate calories in food?*

**How to Calculate Calories in Your Food.** Now that you know the energy content of the macronutrients, you can easily calculate the energy content of a food. You need to know the portion size and how many grams of carbohydrate, fat,

[1]Fatty acids have more carbons, but the bonds between the hydrogen and carbon atoms provide extra energy.

and/or protein are in the portion. Suppose the label on a food product indicates that it has 15 g of carbohydrate, 5 g of fat, and 8 g of protein. The total energy content of that food is as follows:

$$15 \text{ g carbohydrate} \times 4 \text{ kcal/g} = 60 \text{ kcal}$$
$$5 \text{ g fat} \times 9 \text{ kcal/g} = 45 \text{ kcal}$$
$$8 \text{ g protein} \times 4 \text{ kcal/g} = 32 \text{ kcal}$$
$$\text{Total kcal} = 137 \text{ kcal}$$

Notice that even though the food contains only 5 g of fat, they contribute more total calories than the 8 g of protein.

## What Substances Are Needed to Support Your Metabolism?

**Metabolism** is the biochemical activity that occurs in cells, releasing energy from nutrients or using energy to create other substances such as proteins. We have briefly discussed the roles of carbohydrate, fat, and protein in this process. Now let's consider the roles of vitamins, minerals and water. Many consumers believe that vitamins and minerals will "give you energy" or act as a "pick-me-up." After all, that is how they are marketed. However, what vitamins and minerals do is help the macronutrients, such as carbohydrates, fats, and proteins, release their energy; but vitamins cannot be broken down to provide energy themselves. Some think that if a vitamin or mineral assists in a certain bodily function, consuming more of it may be better for you. For example, many people think that because vitamin C boosts the body's immune function, taking increased amounts will help treat or prevent colds. But consuming vitamins and minerals in excess can actually be harmful to your health, as they may reach a toxic level when consumed in large amounts. Vitamins and minerals have many other roles in the body besides supporting metabolism, including providing structure. For example, calcium helps build bones. We'll focus on nutrients that support metabolism by dividing them into vitamins, minerals, and water.

Beware! Many over-the-counter supplement products make false claims regarding their role as an energy source.

**Vitamins.** **Vitamins** are a group of nutrients that contain carbon and are required in small amounts to maintain normal body function. Vitamins are classified into two broad categories: (1) fat-soluble and (2) water-soluble (Table 1.2). The **fat-soluble vitamins** are insoluble in water, can be stored in the body for long periods of time, and do not need to be consumed daily. On the other hand, because they can be stored, they can build up and become toxic if consumed in excess. The **water-soluble vitamins** dissolve in water, are not stored in the body to any extent, and are excreted mostly through the urine. These normally must be consumed daily to replenish the lost vitamins. Compared to those that are fat soluble, the risk of toxicity is not as great with the water-soluble vitamins; however, this does not mean that you cannot consume toxic amounts of water-soluble vitamins. Some water-soluble vitamins can be toxic if taken in large amounts, such as vitamin C, which can cause kidney problems. Both groups of vitamins play significant roles in regulating metabolism and maintaining health.

**Minerals.** Minerals can be considered body-building and body-regulating nutrients. They are classified into two groups: **macrominerals** (or major elements) and **microminerals** (or trace elements). This classification is based on

| Table 1.2 | Vitamins and Minerals in Human Nutrition | |
|---|---|
| **Vitamins** | **Minerals** |
| Fat soluble: | Macrominerals: |
| Vitamin A | Sodium |
| Vitamin D | Potassium |
| Vitamin E | Chlorine |
| Vitamin K | Calcium |
| Water soluble: | Phosphorus |
| Thiamin (vitamin $B_1$) | Magnesium |
| Riboflavin (vitamin $B_2$) | Sulfur |
| Niacin (vitamin $B_3$) | Microminerals (trace elements): |
| Pyridoxine (vitamin $B_6$) | Iron |
| Cobalamin (vitamin $B_{12}$) | Zinc |
| Folic acid | Copper |
| Pantothenic acid | Iodine |
| Biotin | Selenium |
| Vitamin C | Manganese |
| | Molybdenum |
| | Chromium |
| | Vanadium |
| | Boron |
| | Nickel |

the relative requirements of each mineral. Macrominerals are required by the body in amounts equal to or in excess of 100 milligrams (mg) per day; microminerals are required by the body in an amount less than 100 mg per day.

Macrominerals such as sodium, potassium, and chlorine are macrominerals that are often called **electrolytes.** An electrolyte is a mineral that assumes a charge when dissolved in water. Once electrolytes are dissolved, one of their primary roles is to maintain the body's water balance. Water balance is important for controlling temperature and lubricating joints.

Almost all of the minerals can be toxic if consumed in excess. This is particularly true of the microminerals such as iron, zinc, copper, selenium, etc. (see Table 1.2 for complete list). Non-essential microminerals such as lead, mercury, and cadmium, sometimes referred to as "heavy metals," have long been known for their toxicities.

**Water.** Water does not yield energy but is listed as a macronutrient. Life as we know it cannot exist without water. It is the largest single component of living organisms, making up 56–64 percent of their tissues. Water balance is important for controlling temperature and lubricating joints, as well as other important functions. We will discuss water more thoroughly in Chapter 8.

## Other Food Components That Have a Role in Food and Nutrition

There are two compounds left that we present separately. Neither is considered a nutrient, but each impacts our health either positively or negatively. It is important to recognize that alcohol is not a nutrient, but it supplies energy. Phytochemicals (plant chemicals) promote health and are found in food.

**Alcohol. Alcohol** provides 7 kcal per gram and therefore contributes to energy intake. When metabolized by the body, alcohol yields energy but does not provide vitamins and minerals, and it has other characteristics that can damage your health and well-being.

**Phytochemicals. Phytochemicals**, while not nutrients in the classical sense, are chemical compounds in plants that have various effects on body functions. They are not considered essential but play an important role in health; we discuss them in several chapters, such as Chapters 2, 9 and 12. Many of these compounds have powerful health benefits, with supporting evidence of their roles in combating heart disease, cancer, diabetes, and other serious degenerative diseases.

Many of these phytochemicals are being used in the formulation of "**functional foods**" discussed in Chapter 10. Simply defined, functional foods are

Plant foods, such as tea, olives, and tomatoes often have chemicals that improve your health, although they may not be considered essential.

those foods that when added to or present in a diet provide a health benefit beyond normal nutrition.

***Note to Student.*** Periodically within each chapter you will encounter a series of reading comprehension questions under the "Before you go on . . ." heading. You should review and answer these questions prior to reading the next section.

> **Before you go on . . .**
> 1. Briefly describe the evolution of nutrition as a science.
> 2. Define *nutrient.*
> 3. Which substances supply your body with energy?
> 4. What is the major difference between the macrominerals and the microminerals?
> 5. Why are minerals such as sodium and potassium called electrolytes?

## Why Do We Make the Food Choices We Do?

Have you ever wondered why you eat the foods you do or why a friend of yours may eat foods that are unfamiliar to you? Think about it for a while and list the reasons why you eat certain foods for breakfast, lunch, dinner, and snacks, or even how often you eat per day. Some of these reasons are as follows:

- Environment
- Culture and tradition
- Taste, likes, and dislikes
- Family
- Finances
- Convenience
- The media
- Age
- Health issues

### Environment

The term *environment* as we use it here refers to where one eats food or a meal. Teenagers may eat differently when they are away from home. Older people living alone and even young college students living on their own and cooking for themselves may not prepare meals that are as healthy as they would be if they cooked for a group. Within a household, even the type of available utensils and cookware can have an influence.

### Culture and Tradition

Cultural differences within our communities as well as between different parts of the world typically influence what we eat. For example, many Asian communities have a diet high in fish compared to that of the United States. Asian communities consume a lot of rice, and even Asians living in the United States tend to consume more rice than non-Asians.

Some regional dietary differences in the United States originally may have had a cultural basis. For instance, in the South grits and collard greens are not

The Cui family of Weitaiwu village, Beijing Province, in their living room with a week's worth of food, for which they paid the equivalent of $57.27 U.S. dollars. Note the abundance of vegetables and the lack of meat and seafood.

Red beans and rice are commonly consumed by some cultures, such as Cajuns in the southern United States. Other cultures also have their favorite dishes.

 **Want to know more?**
If you would like to explore the general principles of Kosher food and Islamic food laws, go to the text website at http://webcom8.grtxle.com/nutrition and click on the Chapters button. Select Chapter 1.

uncommon in diets. Seafood gumbo and red beans and rice are dishes found among Cajun communities in Louisiana. Many Hispanics living in the United States and Central America are apt to have greater levels of legumes (beans) or spices in their diets than people of northern and central European decent. Many of these cultural aspects turn into traditions. In other words, many people eat certain foods because that's the way it has been done for a long time.

### ■ Culture and Ethnic Foods

*What does religion have to do with diets?*

Culture and religion can have a profound impact on what we eat. We have already briefly discussed the relationship between food choices and cultural influence; religious doctrines may be a determinant as well. For example, Mormons avoid coffee, tea, alcoholic beverages, and tobacco. Many Hindus are vegetarian. At one time Catholics could not eat meat on Fridays, and many still refrain from eating meat on Fridays during Lent. Some Jews follow a *kosher* diet. Kosher laws deal with both foods that can and cannot be eaten and how they are to be prepared. Muslims follow Islamic dietary laws and do not ordinarily consume pork. ■

## Taste, Likes, and Dislikes

Food likes and dislikes are typically based on the sensory attributes of food. These can be learned traits in that we develop a certain taste for food early on. For instance, early introduction of salty foods may allow some to develop a taste preference for them. Mouthfeel, texture, smell, and aftertaste are all attributes that affect our like or dislike of a food.

## Family

Closely linked to culture is family; most families have food preferences based on their cultures. As children, what we eat with our family typically influences us

The family unit typically plays a prominent role in influencing what we eat. The traditional family Thanksgiving meal is a good example of culture and family combining to determine our food choices. Do all Americans eat turkey at Thanksgiving? Why?

throughout our lives. For instance, as adults we often consume the same foods we did as children because they remind us of a time when we were younger and among family and friends. Many times these foods are referred to as *comfort foods*.

## Finances

Cost is, of course, a major factor in deciding what we consume. Plant foods, especially grain-based foods such as bread and rice, are most commonly consumed worldwide because of their relatively low cost. Meat and milk are more expensive in most cultures because of the higher costs of raising cattle, hogs, and other livestock. Even in the United States many families cannot afford meat, or they may be able to purchase only smaller and cheaper cuts that have a higher fat content. Fruits and vegetables that are fresh rather than frozen are also typically more expensive.

## Convenience

Convenience can also play a large role for everyone, but especially for single consumers who prepare their own food. Two-income households or busy families with hectic lifestyles may want easy-to-prepare foods when their available time for cooking is limited. Convenience may also mean local access to specific foods such as fresh fruit. In many parts of the world, including the United States, some foods are more convenient and available at certain times of the year; examples include peaches in Michigan and Georgia, strawberries in California, lobster in Maine, and shrimp along the Gulf Coast.

### ▪ Sustainable Nutrition
#### What is Sustainable Nutrition?
There is no agreed-upon definition of Sustainable Nutrition. However, the most widely quoted definition of sustainability in general is that of the Brundtland Commission of the United Nations: "sustainable development is development that meets the needs of the present

The seasonal availability of food can influence what we eat. Some foods pictured here may be available only at certain times of the year, depending on where you live.

**Want to know more?**

For more information on the general principles of sustainable nutrition go to the text website at http://webcom8.grtxle .com/nutrition and click on the Chapters button. Select Chapter 1.

**Want to know more?**

For more facts about organic food, go to the text website at http://webcom8 .grtxle.com/nutrition and click on the Chapters button. Select Chapter 1.

United States Department of Agriculture label showing that the product is 95% organic.

*Source:* United States Department of Agriculture.

without compromising the ability of future generations to meet their own needs." Most who encourage living a sustainable lifestyle suggest that it includes three major concepts: ecology, economy and health. In reference to nutrition, it can be thought of as a way of choosing and eating foods that benefit the health and well-being of the individual, of the community (socially and economically), of the food producer, and of the environment. Therefore, sustainable nutrition emphasizes the benefits of eating local, seasonal, organic foods, minimizing waste, and growing your own foods whenever possible. Throughout the text we will be discussing issues related to sustainable nutrition. For more information on the basic concepts related to sustainable nutrition, please see the "Want to Know More?" item.

Advocates for organic food claim that is healthier than conventional food because it is grown without the use of chemical fertilizers and pesticides. Others feel that it tastes better. Despite the claims of advocates, most independent studies that compare the nutritional value and health benefits of conventional foods with organic products remain open-ended about the differences between the two. However, a 2008 study by Chensheng Lu and colleagues reported lower signs of pesticides in the urine of children when switched from conventional foods to their comparable organic counterparts. Results were seen in just 5 days on the organic diet. Many consumers who advocate for organic foods are not as concerned with the individual health benefits of consuming these foods, but choose to eat organic because they feel it is better for the environment and for the animals used for food production. Whatever their reasons, a growing number of consumers are buying organic products. This is particularly true of produce. In fact, according to the Organic Trade Association, organic produce not only represents 38% of all organic food sales, but also 11.4% of all U.S. fruit and vegetable sales. In comparison, in 2000, organic fruit/ vegetable sales totaled $2.55 billion, or just 3% of total fruit/vegetable sales, OTA reports. Therefore without solid scientific evidence to support the benefits of consuming organic foods over conventional foods, it becomes a matter of personal choice. The USDA has not made any health claims for organic foods. The U.S. Department of Health and Human Services, Centers for Disease Control and Prevention, the USDA, and the Environmental Protection Agency are now expanding their research to explore the scientific basis for the health benefits of organic foods. ■

## The Media

The media, through advertisements and coverage of nutrition and health topics, certainly play a role in our food selection process. New food items often must be advertised in order to make us aware of their existence. Soft drinks, beers, and snack foods tend to show increased consumption when pushed by aggressive media campaigns.

## Age

What stage of life we are in may play a role in our choice of foods. Older people may consume foods that were available or popular when they were younger and ignore those that are newer or trendy. Older people may lose their sense of taste and smell. Trouble with chewing may lead to eating less meat and fiber. On the other end of the age spectrum, teenagers are likely to consume more food items independent of the family and succumb to peer pressure to eat or not eat certain foods.

## Health Issues

People with certain illnesses may choose foods to help alleviate the illness. Those with high cholesterol or a history of heart disease may choose low-fat foods. Postmenopausal women may consume extra calcium to prevent fragile bones. As more nutrition information linking diet with disease becomes available, this factor may become more important in influencing what we eat.

### ■ What's Hot?

*Genetically engineered foods—are they a change for the better?*

*Genetically engineered foods* are produced from crops whose DNA (the material in the cell's nucleus that carries genetic information) has been altered in some way to bring about a desirable trait. Genetically engineered foods are also called *bioengineered foods, biotech foods,* and *genetically modified foods*, or just *GE*. A breed of tomato that did not rot as quickly as other tomatoes was the first genetically engineered product; it went on the market in 1994. Since then, many more genetically engineered foods have been developed and marketed. The Grocery Manufacturers of America estimate that between 70 percent and 75 percent of all processed foods available in U.S. grocery stores may contain ingredients from genetically engineered plants. Breads, cereal, frozen pizzas, hot dogs, and soda are just a few of them.

Soybean oil, cottonseed oil, and corn syrup are ingredients used extensively in processed foods. Through genetic engineering, these plants have been designed to ward off pests and to tolerate herbicides used to kill weeds. Their use continues to grow. For example, GE soybeans developed to be resistant to herbicides that kill surrounding weeds represented 91% of the total U.S. soybean acreage in 2009 compared to 68% in 2001. Similarly, in 2009 63% of the U.S. corn acreage was produced by GE strains of corn which were developed to be insect resistant. Other crops, such as squash, potatoes, and papaya, have been engineered to resist various plant diseases. Regulation of genetically modified foods in the United States is shared by several agencies: the Food and Drug Administration (FDA), the USDA, and the Environmental Protection Agency (EPA). The FDA has the responsibility of ensuring that foods made from these plants are safe for humans and animals to eat. Among its various tasks, it is the USDA's duty to make certain that plants are safe to grow. And a key function of the EPA is to ensure that any pesticides introduced into plants are safe for human and animal consumption and for the environment. ■

### Before you go on . . .

1. List at least six factors that can influence what people eat.
2. How might a person's environment affect what they eat?
3. What are genetically modified foods?
4. Define sustainable nutrition.

### Want to know more?

You can learn more about bioengineered foods by going to the text website at http://webcom8 .grtxle.com/nutrition and clicking on the Chapters button. Select Chapter 1.

Fast foods are a reality of our culture. Each year, research shows, more people, especially adolescents, are eating a greater number of their meals away from home.

## How Do the Food Choices We Make Influence Our Health?

During the twentieth century, the United States and many other Western nations underwent a transformation in the types of diseases that afflict us. We still suffer from **malnutrition,** but a different type. In the strict sense of the word, *mal,* means "bad." We can subdivide malnutrition into two categories: **undernutrition,** or lack of specific nutrients, and **overnutrition,** or too much of a specific nutrient. Either of these can involve any of the nutrients we have discussed thus far. In general, as a nation we went from a state of undernutrition to one of overnutrition in less than 100 years. At the beginning of the twentieth century, deficiency diseases such as beriberi (vitamin $B_1$ or thiamin deficiency), scurvy (vitamin C deficiency), and pellagra (vitamin $B_3$ or niacin deficiency) were common. As time progressed the food supply improved, and with fortification and enrichment of foods, along with our continued economic development, the United States became a nation of plenty. However, undernutrition and overnutrition can coexist. As an example, those who are overweight may have iron deficiency if they consume too few iron-rich foods.

Today we face overnutrition as a result of uncontrolled supplementation with vitamins, minerals, and other compounds, or just simply consumption of too many calories and not enough physical activity. Thirty-one percent of Americans are obese; the rate is 65 percent for obesity and overweight combined (see Chapter 7). Obesity is increasing and is now the number one public health nutrition problem in the United States. Most alarming is the rapidly increasing incidence among adolescents. Along with nutrition concerns associated with obesity, health officials continue to express concern with Americans' general lack of physical activity, leading some health agencies to advocate inclusion of the importance of physical activity as a part of the study of nutrition. What makes

this such a problem is the strong link between obesity and heart disease, diabetes, stroke, and cancer. In addition, obesity is costing our nation financially—now more than $117 billion *annually* in direct and indirect health care expenditures, as reported in the U.S. Surgeon General's report titled "Call to Action to Prevent and Decrease Overweight and Obesity."

### ■ Nutrition and Disease

*How common is the connection between diet and disease?*

There is a strong connection between diet and illness. Although nutrient deficiencies are not as common in the United States as they were during the early part of the twentieth century, they are not completely gone. For example, osteoporosis affects postmenopausal women at a higher rate and has been attributed to lack of calcium and vitamin D, among other factors. Iron deficiency is still a problem for some in the United States.

Increasingly, modern science is discovering links between our dietary choices and the occurrence of heart disease, diabetes, and many types of cancer. Many other common illnesses are also diet related. In a condition known as a *hiatal hernia,* a portion of the stomach pushes up through the diaphragm and into the thoracic cavity, pressing up against the heart. The person is likely to feel a lot of heartburn as one symptom. Remarkably, this condition occurs in *one-third* of all U.S. adults. A low-fiber diet is thought to be a major factor. Another common problem related to the Western diet is constipation, which can lead to hemorrhoids and is typically linked to a low-fiber diet. ■

## Obesity's Connection to Major Lifestyle Diseases

As mentioned previously, diet is thought to be related to several prevalent diseases. Heart disease is the number one cause of death in the United States, and diet typically plays a large role in its development. Research has shown that compared to people of normal weight, overweight individuals are at greater risk for many other diseases as well. Some cancers, diabetes, and musculoskeletal problems are strongly related to overweight and obesity. However, even thin people can experience these diseases if they do not eat a healthy diet. Some people have genetic predispositions to these diseases, but diet may modify their risk for certain diseases. Various compounds in the diet may decrease the risk of these diseases regardless of one's weight. We also know that the presence of *antioxidants* (substances that protect food from oxygen damage) in foods helps prevent heart disease and cancer. Finally, along with proper nutrition, frequent exercise is an important factor in decreasing the risk and/or onset of heart disease and cancer.

## What Americans Eat

The link between diet and the increasing incidence of chronic weight-related diseases in Western societies, including the United States, has resulted in numerous studies on the foods consumed and their nutritional content. Changes in industrial food production, changes in lifestyle, and increased availability and consumption of fast food are some aspects that are linked with diet and diseases prevalent in Western society. About thirty years ago, the diets of Americans were composed of 12 percent of calories from protein, 40 percent of calories

*Do Americans eat as unhealthy as everyone says they do?*

Larger portion sizes means more calories. Is this a major cause of obesity?

from fat, and 48 percent of calories from carbohydrate. The typical diet then was composed of twice the amount of saturated and polyunsaturated fat, and much of the carbohydrate consumed was in the form of simple sugars such as sucrose or table sugar. We also had a low fiber intake of about 10–12 grams per day, compared to the recommended intake of 25–38 grams per day.

Since that time many health organizations have recommended that we decrease our level of fat intake to 30 percent of our calories and simultaneously increase the level of carbohydrates (mainly fruits and vegetables) in our diets. Moreover, intake of complex carbohydrates such as starches and fiber (pasta, breads, whole-wheat cereals) are encouraged over simple sugars. Equal amounts of saturated and polyunsaturated fat and monounsaturated fat are recommended (see Chapter 4 for definition). This is important, as saturated fats are thought to promote certain types of heart disease, and monounsaturated and polyunsaturated fats are healthier. As a society we have slightly decreased our intake of fat and saturated fat and increased the amount of fiber. Despite these changes, the incidence of obesity has increased dramatically in the last fifteen years, leading one to ask, "What happened?" While many of us choose low-fat foods, many of them are higher in sugars and other carbohydrates. Portion sizes have increased, substantially in many cases. Fast-food establishments have increased meal sizes, ("super-sized") and the total number of calories consumed has increased. These factors are often ignored. With fewer Americans working in physically demanding jobs, the elimination of physical education from the curricula of many of our schools due to budget cuts, and the fact that we seem to spend more and more time watching television or surfing the Internet, weight balance in our society is clearly not a priority.

While we are primarily afflicted with overnutrition leading to obesity, we still have inadequate intake of specific nutrients. Iron-deficiency anemia, for instance, remains the number two public health nutrition problem in the United States. Women of childbearing age, infants, and even some teenagers are at higher risk for this. Minority and economically disadvantaged populations often have inadequate nutrient intake compared to the rest of the population.

In summary, we have our work cut out for us. Our diet and lack of exercise are causing us to be afflicted with deadly diseases, as well as others that are simply debilitating, such as osteoporosis.

### ■ You Decide

*Is the use of hormones and antibiotics in the production of meat and dairy products harmful?*

The USDA allows the use of several hormones to promote animal growth. Experts debate whether there is residue from such hormones in the meat and milk produced, and whether this residue harms consumers over the long term. Many believe that the residue from the antibiotics may contribute to resistance to antibiotic treatment in humans, thus making some more susceptible to disease. Evidence also suggests that the added hormones may be carcinogenic to humans over the long term. For instance, one type of genetically engineered growth hormone given to cattle has been suggested to increase the risk of colon and breast cancer in humans. Others claim that the milk from organic cows has a greater nutritional value than milk from traditional cows due to the food they consume. In fact, a study by Croissant et al. published in 2007 showed that pasture-fed organic cows produced milk that contained a higher percentage of unsaturated fatty acids compared to the milk from cows fed a traditional diet.

As yet, this debate has no clear-cut answers. All meat will have some hormones, as animals have naturally occurring hormones just like humans do. However, many people do not feel safe consuming meat or dairy products that contains added hormones. Therefore, there has been an increase in sales of organic dairy products and meats, which must come from animals raised hormone and antibiotic free. ■

## The Role of Nutrition in the Treatment of Disease

We can do many things to prevent diseases. However, dietary manipulation sometimes helps treat those who are ill. For example, patients are often placed on a clear liquid diet following surgery and gradually advanced to a soft diet and then a regular diet. People with diabetes must follow a dietary regimen that spreads calories and the energy-yielding macro-nutrients throughout the day to control the disease. People with cancer are often at risk for losing lean muscle mass, and they may drink special high-energy, high-protein beverages to prevent such loss. Beverages designed to rehydrate dehydrated patients or even athletes are commonly used. Many gastrointestinal disorders are treated by modifying dietary fiber and by spreading the patient's food intake among smaller, more frequent meals. Many people with kidney disease must limit their protein and sodium (salt) intake, because their kidneys may not be able to excrete nitrogen, a by-product of protein utilization. Proper nutrition is critical to health care, both for preventing disease and for recovering from illness.

In the clinical setting, the expert assigned to help treat disease through diet is usually the **Registered Dietitian (RD).** These professionals have the education and clinical training to make dietary recommendations and to counsel patients. They work with the attending physician and other health team members to aid in the treatment of the patient in the preceding examples.

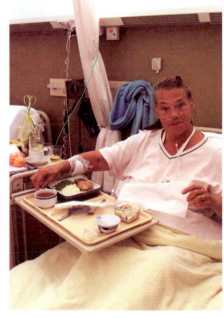

Nutrition is used in the modern medical setting to help the patient recover from illness or surgery.

## The Role of Government in Nutrition

Several government agencies are involved in nutrition recommendations. As we stated earlier, the formulation and issuance of the Recommended Dietary Allowances (RDAs) was the federal government's first entry into nutrition. The initial RDAs were recommendations of known nutrients that were needed on a daily basis to maintain health and to prevent deficiencies. Now these recommendations have expanded to include limits of nutrients. As you will learn in Chapter 2, they are updated periodically.

The U.S. Department of Agriculture (USDA) also plays a major role in food and nutrition policy. The *Dietary Guidelines for Americans,* discussed earlier, are USDA recommendations for the American public on food choices in order to remain healthy. The agency updates them periodically, and we will discuss them throughout the text. The national school lunch and school breakfast programs are both funded by the USDA. The **Expanded Food and Nutrition Education Program (EFNEP),** also USDA-funded, is a community-based

With respect to certain illnesses, the Registered Dietitian (RD) is a key member of the health care team that must consider all angles of the recovery, including nutrition.

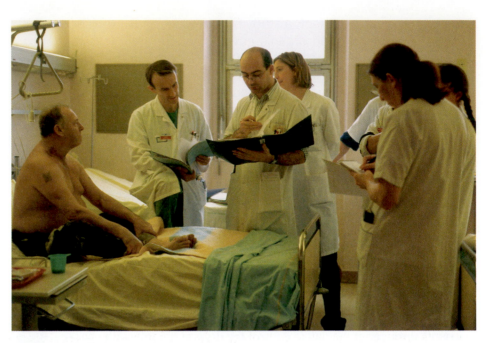

Nutrition is not immune from politics and legislation. Many food and nutrition programs have been developed by national and state governments in attempts to improve the health of our citizens.

program that helps people of limited financial means enhance their food and nutrient intake. Another government program is the **Special Supplemental Nutrition Program for Women, Infants, and Children (WIC),** which is designed to improve the nutrition of pregnant and breastfeeding mothers, infants, and children up to age 5.

The involvement of government institutions in nutrition programs and policies means that knowledge of politics and political networking is important for nutritionists. Even changing the RDA for a specific nutrient can be fraught with politics, as many government-sponsored feeding programs must meet the RDAs in terms of nutrient content. Lowering the RDA for one nutrient may mean less of a particular food required in a meal and less sales by the food producer of the foods rich in that particular nutrient.

### Before you go on . . .

1. How does the U.S. diet today compare to that of thirty years ago?
2. Identify two major nutrition problems in the United States today and describe their primary causes.
3. What are the major concerns with the use of hormones and antibiotics in the production of meat and dairy products?
4. When did the U.S. government first get involved with nutrition policy and why?

## World Nutrition Problems

Thus far, some of our discussion in this chapter has focused on overnutrition and its effects. However, undernutrition is still a huge problem around the world, and there is no simple reason why people don't have enough food to eat. In many cases the reason is not lack of food, but lack of particular nutrients in the foods consumed. Some parts of the world have enough food and calories, but lack sufficient quantities of vitamin A or protein in the foods grown and consumed, which may lead to deficiency.

# Real People, Other Voices

### Student
### Richard Samsky

Prince George's Community College, Largo, MD

In my opinion, Andrew should begin by focusing on the 2,000-calorie diet. Because Andrew works at a supermarket, he could do all of his food shopping for each meal of the day there. He could start learning and understanding the nutritional facts on food labels. If he is taking the vitamin and mineral supplement simply for energy, then he should eliminate it from his diet because they do not provide energy. Cutting out all fast foods, vending machine snacks, and processed food would also greatly improve his health.

Because he only has thirty minutes for lunch, I would recommend that he wake up a little earlier each morning and pack himself a nutritious lunch. For energy he should eat more foods that are high in carbohydrate and protein. Good sources of carbohydrate for Andrew would be whole grains, fruits, and vegetables. Good sources of protein would be meats, dairy, fish, poultry, nuts, and seeds. Important minerals to incorporate into his diet are calcium (milk), iron (meats), potassium (fruits and vegetables), and magnesium (whole grains). Important vitamins are A (fruits and vegetables), B (whole grains), C (fresh fruits and vegetables), D (plenty of sunshine), E (fats and oils), and K (leafy green vegetables). Water is also very important daily. A healthy diet for Andrew should provide adequacy, balance, calorie control, moderation, and variety.

### Instructor
### Sarah Thompson

Binghamton University

Despite Andrew's very busy schedule, he has several things going for him. Having breakfast every day is a plus, and swapping his current breakfast for natural peanut butter on two slices of whole-grain bread and a glass of low-fat milk will be a healthier choice. Another positive aspect to Andrew's schedule is that he works at a great supermarket with an abundance of healthy options. He can easily do grocery shopping for his family. With his Sundays free he can prepare several meals ahead of time for the week, packaging them in small containers. He can bring premade meals to eat during his short lunch breaks. Cooking can be simple. Supermarkets often have sample menus that are easy to prepare. Online recipes are abundant and can provide a wealth of knowledge to the novice cook.

One of Andrew's biggest dietary downfalls is the fast food meals he consumes. Instead of eating fast food or a microwave dinner, he could easily pick up a nutritious sub sandwich at the in-store deli. Opting for a lean source of protein such as turkey or tuna, including a variety of vegetables and adding healthy olive oil, makes a balanced meal on the run. Fresh in-season fruit from the produce section will be a delicious dessert. Overall, Andrew will save money and likely feel a lot better. By making a few small changes to his diet, Andrew will receive his required nutrients and calories, and the multivitamins won't be necessary.

### Registered Dietitian
### Sherry Valente-Gaspari, MA, RD

Haddon Township, NJ

Andrew has the advantage of being an employee of a supermarket, which makes it convenient for him to purchase foods at the end of his shift. A key strategy for Andrew's success in improving his eating habits would be to start planning his meals. He could buy store-roasted turkey breast and whole-grain bread to make a sandwich for his 1:00 P.M. break. He could also try packing nutritious snack bars, carrot sticks, or a container of yogurt for a snack at school. For his dinner at 7:00 P.M. he could consider making a salad from the salad bar at work.

If he has the entire day off on Sunday, he could take advantage of this time to plan and prepare some meals for the week. Some ideas may include making a large pot of soup or chili and breaking it down into individual portions that can be kept in the freezer until ready to use. He could also make a tray of lasagna or rice and beans for evening meals.

Convenience is obviously important for Andrew, and he needs to begin planning a strategy to succeed in improving his eating habits.

One world with haves and have-nots. The issues of too much versus too little food on our planet will continue to be a major one in this century.

## Undernutrition in the World

People may think of famine when they hear about undernutrition, as this is what is often reported in the media. Undernutrition can be defined as inadequate nutrition resulting from lack of food or failure of the body to absorb or digest nutrients properly. Worldwide, the nutrients most likely to be deficient in diets are the macronutrient protein and micronutrients such as iron, iodine, Vitamin A, and zinc.

Undernutrition is often a consequence of inadequate diet and frequent infection, which can lead to deficiencies in calories, protein, vitamins, and minerals. Conversely, frequent infection can be caused by undernutrition that weakens the immune system. Many nonbiological factors are also associated with malnutrition, such as poverty, low educational level, low variety in the diet due to limited purchasing power of nutritious foods, limited or non-existent health services including prenatal care, high population densities, and gender inequalities.

Undernutrition is not evenly distributed around the world. It occurs more often in parts of Asia (Laos and Cambodia) and sub-Saharan Africa (Chad and Sudan). Figure 1.1 presents the percentage of the population that is undernourished in the geographic regions of the world. Children in these regions are particularly vulnerable. For instance, 46 percent of all children in South Asia are moderately to severely underweight, and 44 percent show stunted growth. Similarly, 29 percent of all children in sub-Saharan Africa are moderately to severely underweight, with 38 percent showing stunted growth. Worldwide, 27 percent

**Figure 1.1** Prevalence of undernutrition in various parts of our world. What do you think are the primary causes?
*Source: The State of Food Insecurity in the World 2008,* Food and Agriculture Organization of the United Nation and *FAOSTAT.* © 2009 United Nations World Food Programme

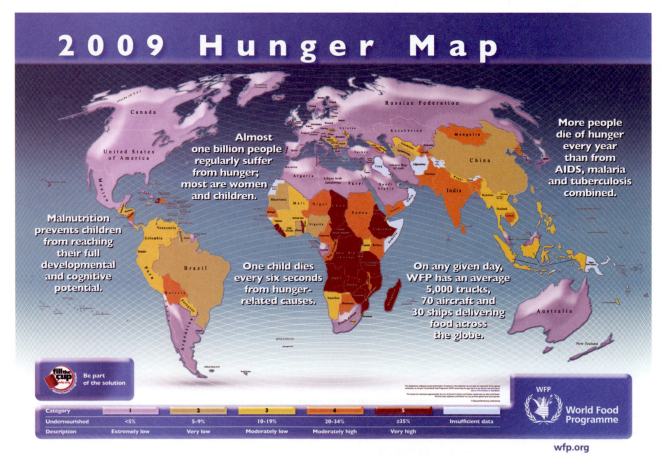

of children under age 5 are moderately to severely underweight, 10 percent are severely underweight, 10 percent show moderate to severe wasting (loss of muscle), and 31 percent show stunted growth.

Undernutrition is common in women of childbearing age (especially those who are pregnant or breastfeeding), infants, and children in many parts of the world. This includes the United States, but most often it occurs in Africa, South America, Central America, and Asia. Such women and children have increased nutritional requirements and are in stages of cell multiplication in growth and reproduction. Thus, their health is more easily compromised when they are nutrient deficient.

Infants of undernourished women begin life undernourished and have a higher risk of disease and death during childhood. Lifelong health disparities are also possible, as undernutrition in infants and children has been linked with the development of chronic conditions such as poor health and lower IQ. Malnourished children may be less productive as adults in job performance.

Pregnant and lactating women need to meet the nutritional requirements of themselves and the baby. Women who have consecutive pregnancies close together have even greater nutritional needs, as the body takes approximately two years to completely recover from pregnancy. Iron and folic acid are particularly important for women. Worldwide, anemia caused by iron deficiency in association with pregnancy and childbirth problems kills around 585,000 women each year. About one-fifth of infant deaths and one-tenth of maternal mortality in developing countries are attributable to iron deficiency. Additionally, women of reproductive age need an increased daily intake of folate, a B vitamin, to prevent the fetus from developing *neural tube defects*. The neural tube is the embryonic structure that gives rise to the brain and spinal cord. A lack of folate has been linked to birth defects of the spinal cord and brain.

Pregnant women are especially vulnerable to undernutrition, even in the United States. Poverty is a leading cause of undernutrition and frequently is responsible for poor health outcomes for both baby and mother.

## Societal Causes of Undernutrition

Let's identify and consider some of the major issues that contribute to global undernutrition problems.

### Limited Access to Food

The persistence of undernutrition in developing countries is not a result of the world's failure to produce enough food to feed its population; it is more a problem of *access*. Access can be inhibited by such things as inadequate development of roads, primitive forms of transportation, lack of safe storage facilities, political corruption, and lack of favorable social policies and reform. Some governments export food grains while thousands of their citizens are undernourished or even starving. Weather, with either too much water or periods of drought, also has a significant impact.

### War

Some undernutrition is human induced. In several countries in central and western Africa, civil strife has disrupted both food production and access to food. Civil war in Sudan has continued to be associated with severe undernutrition among its population.

### Overpopulation

We cannot ignore population expansion, a very important cause of undernutrition in much of the world. Too many people and too little food are produced in some countries and regions. More than 6 billion people inhabit this planet. As recently as the middle of the last century (1950), world population was less than

Natural weather changes greatly influence agricultural productivity. Here we see the poor results from farming in an arid environment without adequate water.

*Who's most at risk for undernutrition?*

Irrigating farm land can make huge differences in productivity. However, irrigation systems require economic resources and access to water from reservoirs and rivers.

3 billion. Humankind has doubled itself in half a century. By 2020 there could be as many as 8 billion people on Earth, all competing for its food and resources.

Unplanned pregnancies, lack of education, lack of access to birth control, the low social position of women in many countries, religious doctrines, and the cultural expectations of women to bear children all account for overpopulation and malnutrition. The notion that families need more children to farm the land or to help the family with income of some type can also contribute to overpopulation; children in these circumstances and cultures are seen as essential economic assets or tools.

Most population growth is occurring in developing parts of the world, which, unfortunately, is where poverty is most prevalent. Poverty, rather than food shortage, is often the cause of hunger. Severe and/or prolonged poverty leads to undernutrition when the means to obtain a nutritionally adequate diet are lacking. Famine even occurs in countries that have enough food available per person—including the United States—so it is not just a "foreign" issue.

Many poor households include large families, and numerous studies show a direct correlation between poverty and family size. Women are disproportionately represented as heads of poor households. Poverty is disproportionately present in rural areas and concentrated among those with less education and nonlandowners. Poverty, of course, typically affects access of the poor to markets for land, labor, and credit.

> **Before you go on . . .**
> 1. If the people of a region consume enough food and calories, how can they be undernourished?
> 2. List the societal causes of undernutrition in the world.
> 3. What individuals are most at risk for undernutrition in the world? Why?
> 4. Why do areas of undernutrition often have overpopulation problems?

## The Science of Nutrition

Compared to other disciplines, nutrition is a young science. It initially formed in the early part of the 1900s from the combination of other sciences. At *land-grant universities,* which are federally funded to promote the agricultural sciences, professors in agricultural chemistry and animal science departments made many important discoveries. Each state has a land-grant institution. In Florida, it is the University of Florida; in Kansas, it is Kansas State University; in California, it is the University of California at Davis; in New York, it is Cornell University; in Michigan, it is Michigan State University; in Ohio, it is the Ohio State University. Do you know what your land-grant university is? See www.higher-ed.org/resources/land_grant_colleges.htm to determine which university is a land-grant institution in your state.

Surprisingly, *modern* nutrition science evolved from many different and sometimes diverse fields, including anthropology, food science and technology, psychology, physiology, economics, public health, sociology, organic chemistry, biochemistry, molecular biology, epidemiology, and law. In the first part of the twentieth century, many "nutritionists" were trained in one of these disciplines but studied issues dealing with food and the nutrients it contains. By the middle of the twentieth century, some schools had begun to develop special degrees in dietetics and nutrition for students wanting to pursue a career in nutrition (see Figure 1.2).

Nutritionists study many different aspects of nutrition, from genes to entire populations. Some focus on the impact of a nutrient at the gene or molecular level in a cell. For instance, much recent work focuses on how vitamin A plays a role in activating certain genes, such as those involved with bone development. Some nutritionists study the whole organism or individual, such as what people eat and why. Clinical researchers may look at certain diets related to particular diseases. Others examine cultural differences in eating behavior or specialize in the important relationship between nutrition and politics. These are just a few examples of the many topics that nutrition researchers explore.

More recently, as the obesity epidemic continues to grow, biobehavioral sciences have taken a more significant role in nutrition. Knowing what motivates people to make diet and physical activity choices, how to modify behavior to promote health, and how to prevent poor lifestyle choices are growing research areas within the field of nutrition. Additionally, **Nutrigenomics** is a newly emerging multi-disciplinary field of medical science and clinical practice. It is an integrated science that attempts to understand a genetic and molecular connection for how dietary compounds alter the expression and/ or structure of an individual's genetic makeup, thus affecting their health and risk of disease.

## Whom Are We to Believe About Diet Advice?

The large number of nutrition books available in bookstores often overwhelms the consumer. Many of these books suggest quick ways to lose weight or to solve a health problem. You as a consumer must be prepared to decide whether you should buy the book and whether it is credible. Unfortunately, just about anyone can call himself or herself a nutritionist without having formal training. Conflicting information, sometimes generated from scientific studies, adds to the uncertainties and confusion surrounding what we should do about the poor state of our diets. In this and the following chapter we will offer summaries of what "experts" advocate. An expert in nutrition is someone with an advanced degree and credentials in the field, such as an MS or PhD degree in nutrition or dietetics from an accredited university, or a health care professional who is an RD. An RD completes a BS or advanced degree covering basic and advanced information on nutrition, food, human metabolism, diet and disease; completes an internship experience; and must pass a national exam to earn his or her credentials. Many states have also required that practitioners be licensed.

## How Can You Identify Reputable Sources of Nutrition Information?

No doubt you have had this problem before—you've read or heard conflicting information about what to eat. You are continually bombarded with claims made by weight-loss programs. Infomercials, radio and newspaper ads, magazines, websites with pop-up ads, diet centers and health-food stores, and even your local grocer all seem to have some type of advice regarding nutrition, and many say, "Studies show. . . ." With all this information, how do you wisely determine

**Want to know more?**
You can learn more about Nutrigenomics by going to the text website at http://webcom8.grtxle .com/nutrition and clicking on the Chapters button. Select Chapter 1.

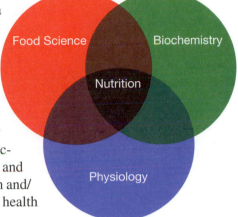

Food Science    Biochemistry

Nutrition

Physiology

**Figure 1.2** The science of nutrition grew out of many different disciplines. As this diagram shows, the fields of biochemistry, physiology, and food science are the primary components that make up the field of modern nutrition.

**Want to know more?**
If you would like more information about becoming a Registered Dietitian, go to the text website at http://webcom8.grtxle .com/nutrition and click on the Chapters button. Select Chapter 1.

whom or what to trust? Are any of these sources believable? Some of the reputable nutrition journals include:

*American Journal of Clinical Nutrition*

*Journal of Food Science*

*Journal of Nutrition*

*Journal of Nutrition Education and Behavior*

*Journal of Nutritional Biochemistry*

*Journal of the American Dietetic Association*

*Nutrition and Cancer*

*Nutrition in the Elderly*

*Nutrition Research*

Many other reputable nutrition journals and science journals also publish articles on nutrition.

Fortunately, the government is becoming more strict about nutrition claims that appear on food products. Any type of health claim appearing on a food product now must be backed up by adherence to a stringent set of guidelines. The FDA has regulatory authority over these claims, and manufacturers of food products making these claims must now provide scientific evidence, including studies on humans, that the product provides the benefits promised. However, keep in mind that in a newspaper or magazine ad these regulations do not apply. Another factor that may surprise you is that dietary supplements are largely unregulated by any government agency. We will discuss this thoroughly in Chapter 11.

Some food producers attempt to take advantage of the consumer's lack of knowledge. For instance, have you noticed the claim on a bottle of vegetable oil that it is "cholesterol free"? If so, you may have concluded that the oil was a superior product, because cholesterol is bad for the heart. The part about the absence of cholesterol being good is true. However, all vegetables and vegetable oils are completely devoid of cholesterol. Only foods of animal origin have cholesterol. So what is so new about vegetable oil not having cholesterol? Absolutely nothing.

Nutrition information (and misinformation) is big business, especially in books relating to weight loss. If these books are so effective, then, why are we a nation of increasingly obese and overweight people?

New knowledge typically evolves from research conducted by scientists in a particular field. The process involves a scientist asking a question and then conducting research on cells, animals, and humans in an effort to answer that question. Therefore, when determining whether a source is reliable, make sure that research was conducted to generate the information and that the research was conducted under rigorous controls and methods. This approach is commonly referred to as the *scientific method*. For instance, if you want to know whether zinc supplements can lower blood cholesterol levels, you need to have one group of human subjects given zinc tablets and another group given a "fake" tablet called a **placebo.** The participants in a study who receive the treatment or substance being studied to determine whether it has an anticipated outcome is called the **experimental group.** We need to have the second or **control group** (the one that receives the placebo) because sometimes people change their diets or other things in their life during the study period that could affect the results. Many times the investigator or researcher does not know who is receiving which treatment; this type of research is called a **double-blind study.** The number of subjects in each group is important. Often a study will be repeated with other groups in order to verify the results of the first.

Nutrition claims are everywhere—from popular fitness magazines to scientific journals. When reading a nutrition claim in a popular fitness magazine, be certain to see if it references a study from a reputable scientific journal.

Typically, after the study is done, the data are analyzed and written up as a manuscript and submitted to a science journal. The journal publisher gives the article to other experts in the field to review the study, judge its validity, and comment on whether the findings warrant publication. This is called the *peer review system.* If the manuscript is accepted and published, other scientists get to read it. The article must have enough information for other scientists to replicate the findings.

At this point, readers can access the article from many university libraries. However, much of what is published in these journals is too technical for the everyday layperson to grasp. Normally, science and health writers from the media then interpret the articles for the public. Eventually, this material may end up in nutrition textbooks and other media. As a by-product of this process, it may become more generalized and end up on the Internet. *The best way to decide if something you are reading is reputable is to see whether it cites a journal where the original research was published.* If no such citation appears, it may not be a reputable source. Always look for the citations.

Another source of credible information is the Registered Dietitian described earlier. RDs have schooling in dietetics and nutrition. Scientists with an MS or doctoral degree in human nutrition from an accredited college or university are also reputable sources and are experts in the subject matter.

On the other end of this spectrum, you should be skeptical about individuals who earn certificates and degrees in nutrition from mail-order or nonaccredited institutions. Surprisingly, many physicians have little training in nutrition, but this is improving as in-service training and medical school curriculums change. If you are unsure of something, ask the experts or consult a legitimate nutrition textbook.

## Before you go on . . .

1. You've just read an article in a weekly magazine that describes how a particular vitamin may help prevent breast cancer. How would you determine whether the claim is valid?
2. What is a double-blind study?
3. Where would you look for accurate information about the effect of copper on the heart?

## Real People, Real Strategies

Andrew met with his nutrition instructor, who agreed that he has a problem. The first thing Andrew realized is that diet is part of a lifestyle, and he might need to look at his eating habits as part of a bigger picture.

His instructor quickly dispelled one myth Andrew held: vitamin and mineral supplements do not give you extra energy. While his schedule is hectic, he does have some time that he could use to plan better. For instance, he has Sundays off. This would be a good time to plan his meals for the week. One suggestion his instructor made was to prepare some simple meals on Sundays that can be refrigerated or frozen and simply heated up during the week. And if he wants to eat out, especially at dinner, she recommended that he select non-fast-food restaurants that serve vegetables and salads as part of a broad array of choices. She also showed him how to select items from a fast-food restaurant menu and have a balanced meal.

His main problem seems to be breakfast and lunch. In the morning, he needs to have something with carbohydrate and protein. Here he can have something as simple as a multigrain cereal with milk and a glass of juice, peanut butter and bread with juice, or a serving of yogurt and a banana. Using his Sunday planning time, he can make up some trail mix or pack pretzels and a piece of fresh fruit to snack on during his 1:00–1:30 P.M. break. He can always add some crackers with cheese or peanut butter if needed. Another option for either breakfast or lunch is to buy some instant-breakfast meals, snack bars, or granola bars.

In summary, Andrew's instructor's primary advice was to (1) figure out what is realistic, (2) set priorities, (3) change his lifestyle, especially with respect to nutrition, and (4) learn that breakfast, lunch, and dinner do not need to be all that complicated and difficult to meet his nutrient needs. (See Chapter 2 for quick and healthy meals.)

## Chapter Summary

- The major classes of nutrients are carbohydrate, fat, protein, water, vitamins, and minerals. The energy-yielding nutrients are carbohydrate, fat, and protein. Vitamins, minerals, and water do not provide energy, but support biochemical reactions and have structural functions in the body. Alcohol and phytochemicals are not nutrients but are important considerations when discussing nutrition and health.
- Carbohydrate and protein supply 4 kcal per gram, and fat supplies 9 kcal per gram. The nonnutrient alcohol supplies 7 kcal per gram.
- Available food choices for any population are typically due to a wide variety of factors. For example, our living and working environment and lifestyle can determine what we eat, such as availability, variety, and convenience of fast-food establishments. Our likes and dislikes with respect to taste, family traditions, finances, media advertisement, and even our age are all contributing factors.
- The study of nutrition involves both undernutrition and overnutrition. In the United States, overnutrition has become a major public health problem as evidenced by the widespread increase in the percentage of the population who are either overweight or clinically obese.

- Chronic diseases have been linked to poor nutrition. Cancer, heart disease, fragile bones as we age (osteoporosis), and diabetes are primary examples.
- Several government programs, such as the Women, Infants, and Children (WIC) program and the Expanded Food and Nutrition Education Program (EFNEP), support better nutrition. Many of these are sponsored by the U.S. Department of Agriculture.
- Undernutrition worldwide is due to many factors, including limited access to food, war, overpopulation, and poverty. Sufficient food is often available, but distribution problems due to poor infrastructure and transportation, lack of safe storage facilities, and political policies can preclude getting it to those in need.
- Nutrition science grew out of many disciplines, including anthropology, food science and technology, psychology, physiology, economics, public health, sociology, organic chemistry, biochemistry, molecular biology, epidemiology, and law.
- Credible information on nutrition arises through use of the scientific method by nutrition experts and subsequent publication of their research in reputable journals. When you read a nutrition article in a lay publication, it is important to determine the source of the information reported and to see whether a specific scientific article is cited.

## Key Terms

**alcohol** A nonnutrient that has 7 kcal per gram. (p. 8)

**calorie** A scientific unit of energy; the calories used to measure food energy are actually *kilocalories* (kcal). One kilocalorie, or food calorie, equals 1,000 calories. (p. 6)

**carbohydrate** A category of macronutrients that includes energy-yielding nutrients such as starches and sugars, as well as non-energy-yielding nutrients such as fiber. (p. 6)

**control group** The participants in an experiment or research study who do not receive the treatment or substance being studied. A control group provides an "untreated" basis of comparison with the *experimental group.* (p. 24)

**double-blind study** A study in which the participating subjects and the scientists conducting the experiment do not know who is receiving which treatment. (p. 24)

**electrolytes** (ee-LEK-tro-lyetz) Minerals such as sodium, potassium, and chlorine that assume a charge when dissolved in water. (p. 8)

**Expanded Food and Nutrition Education Program (EFNEP)** A government program to help people of limited financial means enhance their food and nutrient intake. (p. 17)

**experimental group** The participants in an experiment or research study who receive the treatment or substance being studied to determine whether it has an anticipated outcome. (p. 24)

**fat** An energy-yielding nutrient that is insoluble in water; it provides more than twice as much energy as carbohydrate or protein. (p. 6)

**fat-soluble vitamins** Vitamins that are insoluble in water, can be stored in the body for long periods of time, and do not need to be consumed daily. (p. 7)

**functional food** Foods that when added or present in a diet provide a health benefit beyond normal nutrition. (p. 8)

**macromineral** A mineral required by the body in excess of 100 mg per day; also called a *major element.* (p. 7)

**macronutrients** Nutrients needed in large amounts, such as carbohydrates, proteins, fats, and water. (p. 5)

**malnutrition** Lack of proper nutrition resulting from deficient or excessive food or nutrient intake. (p. 14)

**metabolism** (mu-TAE-bu-lizm) The biochemical activity that occurs in cells, releasing energy from nutrients or using energy to create other substances such as proteins. (p. 7)

**micromineral** A mineral required by the body in an amount less than 100 mg per day. (p. 7)

**micronutrients** Nutrients needed in small amounts, such as vitamins and numerals. (p. 6)

**nutrient** A substance that the body needs for energy, growth, and development. (p. 5)

**overnutrition** A type of malnutrition characterized by too much of a specific nutrient; it is generally associated with excess energy intake and results in overweight or obesity. (p. 14)

**nutrigenomics** An integrated science that attempts to understand a genetic and molecular connection for how dietary compounds alter the expression and/or structure of an individual's genetic makeup, thus affecting their health and risk of disease. (p. 23)

**phytochemicals** (FIE-toe-KEM-i-kulz) Chemical compounds in plants that have various effects on body functions; they are not nutrients in the classical sense. (p. 8)

**placebo** (pluh-SEE-boh) In an experiment or research study, an inert substance or treatment given to subjects in the control group instead of the actual substance or treatment being studied. (p. 24)

**protein** An energy-yielding nutrient that contains nitrogen; its primary purpose is to support growth, maintenance, and repair of tissues. (p. 6)

**Recommended Dietary Allowances (RDAs)** The recommended nutrient intake required to meet the known nutrient needs of the healthy population. (p. 4)

**Registered Dietitian (RD)** A professional who has the education and clinical training to make dietary recommendations and to counsel patients. (p. 17)

**Special Supplemental Nutrition Program for Women, Infants, and Children (WIC)** A nutrition program run by the U.S. Department of Agriculture that is designed to improve the nutrition of pregnant and breastfeeding mothers, infants, and children up to age 5. (p. 18)

**undernutrition** A type of malnutrition characterized by lack of specific nutrients. (p. 14)

**vitamins** A group of nutrients that contain carbon and are required in small amounts to maintain normal body function. (p. 7)

**water-soluble vitamins** Vitamins that dissolve in water, are not stored in the body to any extent, and are excreted mostly through the urine. (p. 7)

# Chapter Quiz

Select the one best answer to each question.

1. All of the following provide energy except
   a. carbohydrate.
   b. trace minerals.
   c. protein.
   d. fat.

2. In a study, subjects who receive a "fake" treatment or inert substance are referred to as
   a. the inattentive group.
   b. the experimental group.
   c. the double-blind group.
   d. the control group.

3. Which of the following is most likely to be at risk for malnutrition?
   a. a young man from Central America
   b. American teenagers who skip breakfast
   c. pregnant or breastfeeding women in sub-Saharan Africa
   d. an elder in a poor village in Mexico

4. Which of the following sources of nutrition information is least likely to be credible?
   a. an article from the *American Journal of Clinical Nutrition*
   b. the National Institutes of Health website

c.  Nancy Frawley's Eating Healthy website

d.  a Registered Dietitian

5.  Food grown without using most pesticides, herbicides, or other synthetic products is called

a.  fresh.

b.  chemical free.

c.  nutritious.

d.  organic.

6.  Which of the following is a source of nitrogen and can promote growth and maintenance?

a.  protein

b.  carbohydrate

c.  alcohol

d.  fat

7.  Which of the following contributes about 7 kcal per gram in energy?

a.  carbohydrate

b.  fat

c.  protein

d.  alcohol

8.  You have just had a snack that contains 9 g of fat, 2 g of protein, and 5 g of carbohydrate. How many calories does it contain?

a.  127

b.  109

c.  67

d.  43

9.  Which of the following areas of the world has the highest rate of undernutrition?

a.  northern Russia

b.  Central America

c.  Sub-Saharan Africa and Southeast Asia

d.  the Deep South of the United States

10.  All of the following conditions may be linked to some extent to the current American diet except

a.  scurvy.

b.  heart disease.

c.  cancer.

d.  obesity.

Chapter Quiz Answer Key
1. b; 2. d; 3. c; 4. c; 5. d; 6. a; 7. d; 8. b; 9. c; 10. a

## CHAPTER 2

# Think Before You Eat

## Developing a Nutrition Plan for Health

## < Here's Where You've Been

*The following topics were introduced in the preceding chapter and are related to concepts we'll discuss in Chapter 2. Be certain that you're familiar with them before proceeding.*

- Different nutrients have different important functions in the body.
- Undernutrition is a major health problem worldwide, particularly in developing nations.
- Obesity rates are growing in Westernized countries. People who are obese are at an increased risk for many diseases.
- The foods we choose influence our current health as well as our long-term risk of disease and disabilities.
- It is important to determine whether nutrition information comes from a reputable source.

## Here's Where You're Going >

*The following topics and concepts are the ones we'll emphasize in Chapter 2.*

- Healthy eating includes balance, variety, and moderation.
- Healthy eating requires that you think before you eat.
- Many guidelines exist to help you make healthy choices when you eat, including the *Dietary Guidelines*, the Dietary Reference Intakes (DRIs), MyPyramid, and the Nutrition Facts label.

## Real People, Real Choices

Marisol Hernandez, like so many other college freshmen, had to adjust to lots of change when she moved away from home for the first time. She is living in a new town, has a roommate, is making new friends, and must balance college coursework with her part-time job. Marisol sort of expected all of this, but did not anticipate what a major change attending college would mean to her eating habits. She is the youngest in a big family, and in her household everyone ate at different times and there was always something to eat. Marisol's college requires freshmen to purchase the meal plan, but she feels overwhelmed when she walks into the cafeteria with so many choices, and the food just does not taste like what she is used to. She finds herself eating more junk food and pizza then she ever did before.

Food and what she eats on a daily basis are not something Marisol really thought about before her first month on campus. However, when considering her classes for the second semester, she discovered that a course in nutrition would satisfy one of her core requirements. Her first assignment in the course was to record everything she ate for three days. After writing it all down, she was astonished at what she discovered. Marisol quickly realized that she is not eating according to the recommendations and guidelines she's studying in class, but she is not sure what to do about it. She knows she needs a plan but does not know how to go about putting one together.

Here is her schedule and what she ate for one of the three days she recorded.

| | |
|---|---|
| 8:00 | Class |
| 9:15 | Breakfast: Bagel with 1 Tbsp. butter, 12-oz. sports drink |
| 10:00 | Class |
| 12:00 | Class |
| 1:30 | Lunch: 1 slice cheese pizza, 1 slice chocolate cake, and a 12-oz. Coke |
| 3:00–7:00 | Work |
| 7:30 | Dinner: Hamburger, about 4 oz., on white bun and 1/2 c. fries from late-night café on campus with 12 oz. sweetened iced tea |
| 8:30–11:30 | Study (about 1-1/2 c. frozen yogurt and a Snickers bar) |
| 11:30 | Go to bed |

How can Marisol eat healthily with such a busy schedule and so much to think about? Where should she start?

Answer the question "What do I need to eat?" before making your choices.

**M**any people feel overwhelmed or confused when trying to plan a healthy diet. After all, there are so many food choices, so much information to consider, so many weight loss and nutrition plans, and so many diets from a variety of sources. As if this weren't confusing enough, everyone tells you something different. "I heard that such-and-such isn't good for you." Or "They say you shouldn't eat anything after five P.M." So how *do* you plan a healthy diet?

Remember that eating is supposed to be pleasant, and having a plan and being aware of what is healthy makes it even more enjoyable. *The key is to have a plan.* Throughout this book we will define a healthy diet. In this chapter we will talk about some guidelines that will help you not only define a healthy diet but also develop a plan for healthy eating. The most important strategy, regardless of what tools you use to devise your plan, is that you think before you eat. This means that when you walk into your kitchen, enter a cafeteria, or open a menu at a restaurant, instead of first thinking, "What do I feel like eating?" you should begin by asking yourself, "What do I need to eat?" In other words, "Have I had enough vegetables today?" "Have I had enough dairy?" You should walk into these environments with a plan. Similarly, when you go grocery shopping, have a list and don't just look at foods in the aisle to see what looks good. After deciding what you need to eat, then you can ask, "What do I feel like eating?" After all, eating would probably be less enjoyable if all you did was eat strictly from the plan. Let's discuss some recommendations and plans that will help you answer these questions.

## Defining a Healthy Diet

*What does it mean to eat a healthy diet?*

Before we can understand how to plan a healthy diet, we need to know what one is. A reporter once asked me to define a "healthy diet" in one sentence. I hesitated, quickly realizing that this is not as easy as it seems. After all, scientists and health experts have spent decades trying to define a healthy diet, and they still haven't reached complete agreement. Nutritional needs change over the life span and can be different for athletes or under special circumstances such as when a person is sick, pregnant, or taking certain medications. But I knew that I could not use an entire textbook to answer the reporter's question. Therefore, after a brief hesitation, I responded by saying, "It is a plan of eating that incorporates balance, variety, and moderation while meeting individual nutritional needs and balancing energy intake to maintain a healthy weight."

**Balance** means incorporating foods from *all* food groups into your daily plan so that you are eating fruits, vegetables, whole grains, dairy (or dairy substitutes), fats, and proteins. It means not relying on or favoring any one food group at the expense of another. **Variety**, of course, means eating different types of foods within each food group. For example, if you eat an adequate number of servings of vegetables every day, but you eat only carrots, then you are not consuming a variety and therefore may be missing some important nutrients found in other vegetables. Plus, you're likely to get bored eating just carrots. **Moderation** means not overconsuming any one food or food group. This term can also refer to *portion sizes*. We discuss the importance of portion sizes and portion control throughout this book, typically in reference to calories, but it can be applied to any food or food group.

While it is important to incorporate the concepts of balance, variety, and moderation when planning a healthy diet, you must also consider the *nutrient*

Nutrient dense foods versus empty calories.

*density* of the foods you are eating. Nutrient density refers to the nutrient content of a food relative to its calories. For example, suppose you are trying to decide what to have for a snack and you have the choice of eating candy such as Skittles® or a banana. You determine that the portions you have both contain about 200 calories, so what's the difference? The Skittles® taste better and you decide to eat them. Although both foods provide 200 calories, the banana provides several nutrients such as vitamins and minerals, whereas the Skittles® are essentially just sugar. The Skittles® represent **empty calories**, or calories with little or no nutrient content. Therefore, the more nutrient-dense and healthier choice would be the banana.

There are many ways to incorporate these basic concepts into a healthy eating plan. The government-supplied guidelines discussed in this chapter—*Dietary Guidelines for Americans,* the Dietary Reference Intakes, MyPyramid, and the Nutrition Facts label—will help you with the basic information and take you a step closer to easily developing your plan. They all incorporate the basic concepts of balance, variety, and moderation.

## Dietary Guidelines

*Dietary Guidelines for Americans* has been published jointly every five years since 1980 by the U.S. Department of Health and Human Services (HHS) and the U.S. Department of Agriculture (USDA). The latest guidelines, shown in Figure 2.1, were released December 2010. They summarize science-based advice to promote health through diet and physical activity and to reduce risk for major *chronic diseases* for healthy people over age 2. The newest guidelines consider the obesity epidemic to be the single greatest threat to public health in this century. Therefore, the report is focused on recommendations considered effective in stopping and reversing the obesity problem. The newest guidelines focus particularly on the obesity epidemic in children. The new report has a chapter devoted to the entire diet in an attempt to integrate all aspects of a healthy diet with hopes that compliance to the guidelines will improve. For the first time, the importance of certain specific behaviors—eating breakfast, drinking sweetened beverages, consuming more plant-based foods, snacking, eating fast foods, and screen time—were addressed. Perhaps two of the most noted changes from the 2005 guidelines are the recommendations to reduce saturated fat intake from 10% to 7% of calories and

**Figure 2.1** The Dietary Guidelines summarize scientific information in order to provide nutritional advice that promotes health and reduces the risk for cancer, diabetes, and major diseases associated with the heart.
*Source:* United States Department of Health and Human Services.

Balance the food you eat with physical activity–maintain or improve your weight

Choose a diet with plenty of grain products, vegetables, and fruits

Choose a diet low in fat, saturated fat, and cholesterol

Eat a variety of foods

Choose a diet moderate in salt and sodium

Choose a diet moderate in sugars

If you drink alcoholic beverages, do so in moderation

**Want to know more?**

For more information on how the guidelines were established, go to the text website at http://webcom8.grtxle.com/nutrition and click on the Chapters button. Select Chapter 2.

**Want to know more?**

To review the complete dietary guidelines and recommendations for the general population, go to the text website at http://webcom8.grtxle.com/nutrition and click on the Chapters button. Select Chapter 2.

**Want to know more?**

If you would like to explore specific nutritional guidelines in other countries and cultures, go to the text website at http://webcom8.grtxle.com/nutrition and click on the Chapters button. Select Chapter 2.

to reduce daily sodium intake from 2300 mg to 1500 mg. They are based on a 2,000-calorie-per-day diet and consist of 9 focus areas, 23 recommendations for the general population, and 18 specific recommendations for the elderly, children, and different ethnic groups. Although the guidelines are designed for Americans, they are very similar to those of other countries (see the Nutrition and Culture feature below).

Eating a healthy balance of nutritious foods is a central point in *Dietary Guidelines for Americans,* but the recommendations also recognize that balancing nutrients is not enough for health. Total calories also count, especially as more Americans are gaining weight. Because almost two-thirds of Americans are now overweight or obese and more than half get too little physical activity, the *Dietary Guidelines* place a strong emphasis on calorie control and physical activity. The guidelines also serve as the foundation for federal food and nutrition education programs. You can use the nutrition labels found on food products to implement these guidelines on a daily basis. The guidelines can also be adapted for special populations such as those with hypertension. The **DASH (Dietary Approaches to Stop Hypertension)** diet plan is a tool to help individuals lower sodium intake and implement the *Dietary Guidelines.*

A basic premise of the *Dietary Guidelines* is that nutrient needs should be met primarily through consuming foods. However, the guidelines recognize that in certain cases **fortified foods**, or foods (such as orange juice fortified with calcium) with nutrients added to them that were not originally present, may help meet nutrient needs, but they cannot replace a healthful diet. Of course, **enriched foods** also contribute to daily nutrient intakes. Enriched foods have had nutrients added back that were removed during processing. For example, enriched white rice has had some nutrients added back that were present before the outer brown husk was removed.

### ■ Nutrition and Culture

*Dietary guidelines around the world—there's much that we share.*

An emerging global transition in dietary guidance is to increasingly address overnutrition and corresponding chronic disease prevention, especially in low-income communities and developing countries. However, undernutrition continues to be the larger problem for certain segments of the population in many developing countries (see Chapter 1 for a more detailed discussion of undernutrition).

Guidelines may vary from culture to culture to reflect various traditions and food patterns specific to the population. For example, Asian countries often recommend a higher level of sodium than Western countries do. Despite these various differences, dietary guidelines have surprising similarities in countries as diverse as Japan, Scandinavia, Guatemala, and the United States. Whether a country has five guidelines or fifteen, they tend to share the same basic recommendations and foundational goals (see Figure 2.2). ■

### Healthy People 2020

Due to the critical role nutrition plays in the prevention of all major diseases, nutrition-related goals have been included in many health promotion initiatives. One such important effort is **Healthy People 2020**, which is yet another set of government objectives that provide dietary and other guidelines for the overall

**Figure 2.2** Dietary Messages Shared Across Cultures

*Eat a variety of foods.* Overwhelmingly, this is the first and most consistent message across dietary guidelines worldwide. This guideline is intended to ensure that people obtain an optimal mix of vitamins and minerals in their daily food intake. Variety also helps reduce the risk of coronary heart disease. Japanese guidelines specifically recommend eating at least thirty different foods every day!

*Moderate your fat intake.* Recommended fat intake varies from country to country. Korea recommends fat consumption of 20 percent of energy (calorie) intake; the Netherlands recommends a higher level of 35 percent of energy. These varied percentages reflect cultural differences and variations in food availability.

*Moderate your salt intake.* Most nutrition guidelines throughout the world advocate a moderate salt intake, although recommended levels are not generally quantified. In countries that do provide guidelines, the level varies. For example, in Singapore it's 5 g/day; in Japan, 10 g/day; and in the United States, 1,500 mg/day (1.5 g/day).

*Moderate your sugar intake.* In some countries, moderation in sugar intake is recommended. The Vietnamese guideline is, "Consume a small amount of sugar." In other countries, including Canada, Korea, Japan, China, and the Philippines, sugars are not mentioned at all.

*Moderate your alcohol consumption.* Moderation of alcohol intake can also be found in the dietary guidelines in most countries. Messages include "If you drink, keep within sensible limits" in the United Kingdom and "Alcohol is forbidden for children and pregnant women" in Hungary. The United States says, "Drink alcohol in moderation" (see Chapter 11 for more information).

*Maintain a healthy body weight.* Many countries recognize the importance of maintaining a healthy body weight in preventing diet-related disease, and thus they take a simple yet proactive position. The United Kingdom, for example, focuses on weight control through continued use of the message, "Eat the right amount to be a healthy weight," while in Indonesia the guideline recommends, "Consume foods to provide sufficient energy."

*Eat clean and safe foods.* This is a common guideline in many Asian countries, where the climate means that many foods can be more easily spoiled. Messages include "Consume food that is hygienically prepared" in Malaysia and "Eat clean and safe food—this will prevent food-borne diseases in the family" in the Philippines.

*Enjoy your meals.* Some guidelines recognize that eating is more than just nourishment—it provides pleasure and has strong links to family, traditions, and culture. The United Kingdom simply says, "Enjoy your food." Vietnamese guidelines recommend "a healthy family meal that is delicious, wholesome, clean, and economical, and served with affection."

*Follow nutrient-specific recommendations.* In countries where deficiencies of vitamins and minerals have been identified as a public health issue, guidelines reflect this. In Australia, women and girls are urged to "eat more calcium-containing foods," while Indonesians are advised to "consume iron-rich foods." The Philippines recommends that its citizens "choose foods fortified with nutrients."

*Source:* www.afic.org

health of the population, hopefully to be achieved by 2020. Although it is managed by the Office of Disease Prevention and Health Promotion, a division of the U.S. Department of Health and Human Services, Healthy People 2020 was created by a collaborative effort of scientists, federal and state agencies, and public feedback. The primary goals are to increase our quality of life through better health and to eliminate health disparities. It identifies the most significant preventable threats to health and establishes national goals to reduce these threats. It sets guidelines and prioritizes health promotion programs for states, communities, and organizations. The objectives are listed according to leading health indicators:

- Physical activity
- Overweight and obesity

The Casales family of Cuernavaca, Mexico, is shown here with a week's worth of food. They spent the equivalent of $189.09, with the largest outlays going for fruits, vegetables, and nuts ($44.21); meat, fish, and eggs ($42.81); beverages ($39.07); and dairy ($26.81). How do you think their total expenditure and allocation of dollars among the various food groups compares to a family of four in the United States?

**Want to know more?**
If you would like to know more about Healthy People 2020, visit the text website at http://webcom8.grtxle.com/nutrition and click on the Chapters button. Select Chapter 2.

- Tobacco use
- Substance abuse
- Responsible sexual behavior
- Mental health
- Injury and violence
- Environmental quality
- Immunization
- Access to health care

**Before you go on . . .**
1. What are the components of a healthy diet?
2. Describe the difference between nutrient-dense calories and empty calories.
3. What does it mean to think before you eat?
4. Who issues *Dietary Guidelines for Americans* and what is their purpose?

## Recommendations for Specific Nutrients

Thus far we have discussed the guidelines for developing a nutrition plan based solely on food and food groups. This plan is intended to be general and therefore does not provide information on the specific requirements of each nutrient. The requirements for each nutrient are listed in **dietary standards**. Dietary standards provide recommended intakes for specific nutrients. They can be used to plan diets for individuals and groups.

### The Dietary Reference Intakes (DRIs)

In 1941, the Food and Nutrition Board published the first dietary standards, called the **Recommended Dietary Allowances (RDAs)** for specific nutrients. These standards have been used by health care workers, educators, and scientists to assess and improve the nutritional status of Americans. They were also used to interpret food consumption records of populations, to establish standards for food assistance programs, to plan menus for schools and the military, and to establish guidelines for nutrition labeling. It is important to note that the original standards were established to prevent diseases caused by nutrient deficiencies; but they have recently been revised to include information on nutrition and disease prevention.

The new standards, the **Dietary Reference Intakes (DRIs)**, are designed for healthy people and have been established to replace the original RDAs in the United States and the *Recommended Nutrient Intakes (RNIs)* in Canada. To establish these new guidelines, seven panels of nutrition experts and two subcommittees assisted the DRI Committee. All members of the DRI Committee, the expert panels, and the subcommittees are leaders from the United States and Canada in their fields of nutrition and food science. The two countries have combined their efforts for the first time.

The current DRIs are listed in the beginning of your text. They differ from the original values in that they are intended to go beyond preventing deficiency to also prevent the onset of chronic diseases such as cancer, heart disease, and osteoporosis. In addition—and as a response to common overconsumption of many nutrients, especially through supplements—the DRIs now include recommendations for maximum intake for any nutrient that has been shown to have toxic levels. Finally, components of food that have not traditionally been considered nutrients have been shown to have health benefits, such as phytochemicals (which we discussed in Chapter 1), are being reviewed. If sufficient evidence becomes available, reference intakes for them will also be established.

The DRIs are a set of four nutrient-based reference values: Recommended Dietary Allowance (RDA), **Adequate Intake (AI)**, **Estimated Average Requirement (EAR)**, and **Tolerable Upper Intake Level (UL)**. See Table 2.1 for a complete description of each value and Figure 2.3 for a graphical representation of the differences.

The DRIs are established for healthy groups of people (not those with chronic or acute disease) who need extra nutrients, or who are recovering from a diagnosed deficiency. For example, a person who smokes may require more than the RDA of vitamin C. DRIs can also be used to ensure that menus for individuals and for institutions such as hospitals and school cafeterias provide adequate nutrition, but not too much of any one nutrient or too many calories.

As noted earlier, you can use these values to assess your personal diet. For example, you can use dietary analysis software to compare your food intake to each of the recommendations we've described. The software will then provide an assessment indicating the percentage you consumed of the recommended intake of vitamin C, iron, calcium, and so on.

## Energy and Macronutrient Requirements

People often ask, "How many calories should I eat?" To help answer that question there is a general recommendation called the **Estimated Energy Requirement (EER)** that can help answer that question. It is based on formulas designed to include individual characteristics such as age, gender, height, weight, and level of physical activity. Because macronutrients contribute to calories consumed, it is important to provide guidelines for how much each macronutrient

**Want to know more?**

You can review a complete listing of the DRIs and how they were developed by going to the text website at http://webcom8 .grtxle.com/nutrition and clicking on the Chapters button. Select Chapter 2.

### APPLICATION TIP

Remember, all of the guidelines for nutrition issued by the federal government are intended to work together. Some are general, others more specific. For instance, the DRIs suggest that adults consume 1,000 mg of calcium per day. This recommendation is reflected in the DASH and MyPyramid guidelines, which suggest that adults consume three servings of dairy (a high source of calcium) per day. Similarly, the guidelines incorporate this information as part of the focus area "Key Food Groups to Encourage" by stating, "Consume 3 cups per day of fat-free or low-fat milk or equivalent milk products."

**Want to know more?**

For more information on the Estimated Energy Requirement and to estimate your individual energy requirement, go to the text web site at http:// webcom8.grtxle.com/nutrition and click on the Chapters button. Select Chapter 2.

## Table 2.1    Dietary Reference Intakes (DRIs)

| Reference Value | What It Is | Why It Is Important |
|---|---|---|
| Recommended Dietary Allowance (RDA) | The recommended intake required to meet the daily nutrient needs for 97–98 percent of all individuals in a given age or gender group. | The RDA is used for diet planning for individuals and is the foundation of the DRI. |
| Adequate Intake (AI) | The value assigned to a nutrient if some scientific evidence is available, but not quite enough to establish a recommendation with certainty. | The AI is used to make recommendations for healthy individuals for nutrients with no RDA. AIs are also used in calculating the nutritional requirements of infants. For all nutrients except vitamin D, the AI for infants is based on intakes of healthy babies that are fed only breast milk. |
| Estimated Average Requirement (EAR) | The value assigned to a nutrient that would meet the needs of 50 percent of the people of a specific age or gender. | The EAR by itself is used only by federal agencies for research and policy making. |
| Tolerable Upper Intake Level (UL) | The highest level of daily nutrient intake that poses little risk of adverse health effects to individuals in a specific age or gender group. As intake increases above the UL, the potential risk for adverse health effects goes up as well. | The UL was established in response to potential toxic levels of nutrients being consumed, particularly by those taking dietary supplements or consuming foods with nutrients added to them. ULs are also used to set safe limits for nutrients added to our food and water, such as the fluoride added to tap water. |

**Figure 2.3** A graphic representation of the three reference values that are the DRI. The graph shows that the risk of adverse effects is greatest when intake is higher or lower than the recommended amounts.

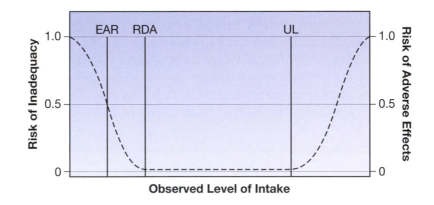

should contribute to overall calorie intake. The recommendations for carbohydrates, fats, and proteins are provided under the **Acceptable Macronutrient Distribution Range (AMDR)**. This is a recommended range of macronutrient requirements based on the total daily calorie needs and balance of nutrients that are associated with a decreased risk of chronic disease:

Protein            10–35 percent of total daily calories
Fat                20–35 percent of total daily calories
Carbohydrates      45–65 percent of total daily calories

**APPLICATION TIP**

According to the AMDR, a person on a 2,000-calorie diet should consume 200–700 calories from protein, 400–700 calories from fat, and 900–1,300 calories from carbohydrates. That might look like this: 50 percent carbohydrate, 20 percent protein, and 30 percent fat. The following is a sample daily menu.

| Breakfast | Lunch | Dinner |
|---|---|---|
| ¾ c. cereal (not sweetened) | 1 c. lettuce | 4 oz. salmon (baked with 1 tsp. olive oil) |
| 8 oz. skim or 1% milk | ½ c. carrots (shredded) | 1 c. rice (brown) |
| 1 slice wheat bread | ¼ c. tomatoes (sliced) | ½ c. broccoli (steamed) |
| 1 Tbsp. peanut butter | ¼ c. cucumbers (sliced) | ½ c. zucchini with 1 tsp. olive oil (sautéed) |
| ½ grapefruit | 2 oz. chicken (grilled) | 1 ¼ c. strawberries |
| Coffee or tea | 2 Tbsp. dressing (low-fat) | 2 Tbsp. whipped topping (fat-free or light) |
|  | 1 wheat pita | Mineral water |
|  | 8 oz. milk (skim) |  |
|  | 1 apple (small) |  |

| Snack 1 | Snack 2 |
|---|---|
| 6 oz. yogurt (low-fat plain or with no calorie sweetener) | 1 c. cantaloupe (in cubes) |
|  | Half of a granola bar |
| 3 graham cracker squares |  |

Adapted from EBSCO Health Libraries.

**Want to know more?**
If you would like to see the menu shown in the Application Tip in Spanish, go to the text website at http://webcom8.grtxle .com/nutrition and click on the Chapters button. Select Chapter 2.

> **Before you go on . . .**
> 1. What is the function of the DRIs, and how do they differ from the RDA standards?
> 2. What standards are established under the DRIs?
> 3. Define the Estimated Energy Requirement (EER) and explain its purpose.
> 4. What is the purpose of the Acceptable Macronutrient Distribution Range (AMDR)?

# MyPyramid

Because we eat foods and not nutrients, it is important to translate the DRIs and the general *Dietary Guidelines* into a daily plan for food intake. The USDA's **MyPyramid** is designed to help you do just that. The most recent version, released in 2005, is pictured in Figure 2.4.

MyPyramid is divided into six different columns, each representing a different food group. The width of the band represents what portion of the total daily intake should come from that group. An important addition to the latest version of the pyramid is the human figure shown running up the stairs, which represents the importance of physical activity and the combination of exercise and nutrition for maintaining health. The first band represents the grain group, the second vegetables, followed by fruits, fats, milk and dairy, and finally meats and beans. Each group has a specific message, listed in Figures 2.5 and 2.6; serving size recommendations are provided for different caloric intakes (Table 2.2).

**Want to know more?**
For instructions on how to use the MyPyramid Tracker, as well as links to more detailed information and the interactive web tools, go to the text website at http://webcom8 .grtxle.com/nutrition and click on the Chapters button. Select Chapter 2.

**Figure 2.4** The USDA's MyPyramid helps to translate the DRIs into an individualized guideline.

# Anatomy of MyPyramid

### One size doesn't fit all

USDA's new MyPyramid symbolizes a personalized approach to healthy eating and physical activity. The symbol has been designed to be simple. It has been developed to remind consumers to make healthy food choices and to be active every day. The different parts of the symbol are described below.

**Activity**
Activity is represented by the steps and the person climbing them, as a reminder of the importance of daily physical activity.

**Moderation**
Moderation is represented by the narrowing of each food group from bottom to top. The wider base stands for foods with little or no solid fats or added sugars. These should be selected more often. The narrower top area stands for foods containing more added sugars and solid fats. The more active you are, the more of these foods can fit into your diet.

**Personalization**
Personalization is shown by the person on the steps, the slogan, and the URL. Find the kinds and amounts of food to eat each day at MyPyramid.gov

**Proportionality**
Proportionality is shown by the different widths of the food group bands. The widths suggest how much food a person should choose from each group. The widths are just a general guide, not exact proportions. Check the Web site for how much is right for you.

**Variety**
Variety is symbolized by the 6 color bands representing the 5 food groups of the Pyramid and oils. This illustrates that foods from all groups are needed each day for good health.

**Gradual Improvement**
Gradual improvement is encouraged by the slogan. It suggests that individuals can benefit from taking small steps to improve their diet and lifestyle each day.

**MyPyramid.gov**
STEPS TO A HEALTHIER YOU

| Grains | Vegetables | Fruits | Oils | Milk | Meat & Beans |
|---|---|---|---|---|---|

**Figure 2.5** Specific recommendations for each group in MyPyramid.

| GRAINS<br>Make half your grains whole | VEGETABLES<br>Vary your veggies | FRUITS<br>Focus on fruits | MILK<br>Get your calcium-rich foods | MEAT & BEANS<br>Go lean with protein |
|---|---|---|---|---|
| Eat at least 3 oz. of whole-grain cereals, breads, crackers, rice, or pasta every day<br><br>1 oz. is about 1 slice of bread, about 1 cup of breakfast cereal, or ½ cup of cooked rice, cereal, or pasta | Eat more dark-green veggies like broccoli, spinach, and other dark leafy greens<br><br>Eat more orange vegetables like carrots and sweet potatoes<br><br>Eat more dry beans and peas like pinto beans, kidney beans, and lentils | Eat a variety of fruit<br><br>Choose fresh, frozen, canned, or dried fruit<br><br>Go easy on fruit juices | Go low-fat or fat-free when you choose milk, yogurt, and other milk products<br><br>If you don't or can't consume milk, choose lactose-free products or other calcium sources such as fortified foods and beverages | Choose low-fat or lean meats and poultry<br><br>Bake it, broil it, or grill it<br><br>Vary your protein routine — choose more fish, beans, peas, nuts, and seeds |

**For a 2,000-calorie diet, you need the amounts below from each food group. To find the amounts that are right for you, go to MyPyramid.gov.**

| Eat 6 oz. every day | Eat 2½ cups every day | Eat 2 cups every day | Get 3 cups every day | Eat 5½ oz. every day |
|---|---|---|---|---|

**Find your balance between food and physical activity**
- Be sure to stay within your daily calorie needs.
- Be physically active for at least 30 minutes most days of the week.
- About 60 minutes a day of physical activity may be needed to prevent weight gain.
- For sustaining weight loss, at least 60 to 90 minutes a day of physical activity may be required.
- Children and teenagers should be physically active for 60 minutes every day, or most days.

**Know the limits on fats, sugars, and salt (sodium)**
- Make most of your fat sources from fish, nuts, and vegetable oils.
- Limit solid fats like butter, margarine, shortening, and lard, as well as foods that contain these.
- Check the Nutrition Facts label to keep saturated fats, *trans* fats, and sodium low.
- Choose food and beverages low in added sugars. Added sugars contribute calories with few, if any, nutrients.

**Figure 2.6** Key food group messages from the Dietary Guidelines and MyPyramid.

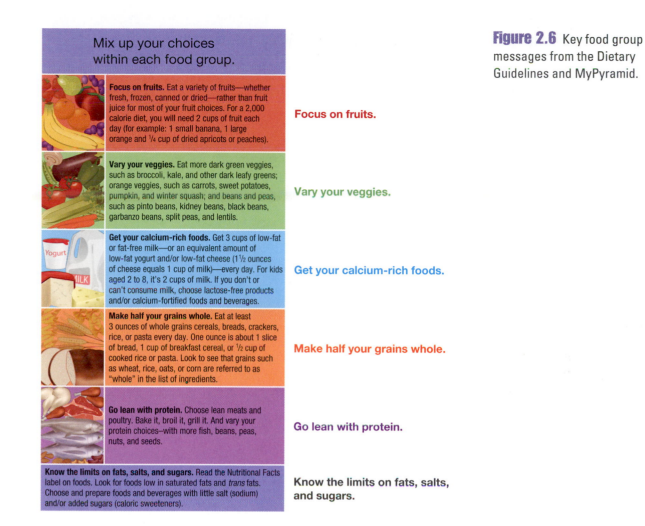

**Mix up your choices within each food group.**

**Focus on fruits.** Eat a variety of fruits—whether fresh, frozen, canned or dried—rather than fruit juice for most of your fruit choices. For a 2,000 calorie diet, you will need 2 cups of fruit each day (for example: 1 small banana, 1 large orange and 1/4 cup of dried apricots or peaches).

**Focus on fruits.**

**Vary your veggies.** Eat more dark green veggies, such as broccoli, kale, and other dark leafy greens; orange veggies, such as carrots, sweet potatoes, pumpkin, and winter squash; and beans and peas, such as pinto beans, kidney beans, black beans, garbanzo beans, split peas, and lentils.

**Vary your veggies.**

**Get your calcium-rich foods.** Get 3 cups of low-fat or fat-free milk—or an equivalent amount of low-fat yogurt and/or low-fat cheese (1½ ounces of cheese equals 1 cup of milk)—every day. For kids aged 2 to 8, it's 2 cups of milk. If you don't or can't consume milk, choose lactose-free products and/or calcium-fortified foods and beverages.

**Get your calcium-rich foods.**

**Make half your grains whole.** Eat at least 3 ounces of whole grains cereals, breads, crackers, rice, or pasta every day. One ounce is about 1 slice of bread, 1 cup of breakfast cereal, or ½ cup of cooked rice or pasta. Look to see that grains such as wheat, rice, oats, or corn are referred to as "whole" in the list of ingredients.

**Make half your grains whole.**

**Go lean with protein.** Choose lean meats and poultry. Bake it, broil it, grill it. And vary your protein choices—with more fish, beans, peas, nuts, and seeds.

**Go lean with protein.**

**Know the limits on fats, salts, and sugars.** Read the Nutritional Facts label on foods. Look for foods low in saturated fats and *trans* fats. Choose and prepare foods and beverages with little salt (sodium) and/or added sugars (caloric sweeteners).

**Know the limits on fats, salts, and sugars.**

MyPyramid translates the concepts of balance, moderation, and variety, along with the information from the *Dietary Guidelines* and the Dietary Reference Intakes, into a usable diet plan. The new symbol is intentionally very simple and is meant to be used with the interactive website and the free handouts found at www.mypyramid.gov.

At this website you can enter your personal information such as height, weight, age, gender, and activity level and receive an individualized plan. In addition, you can track your diet over several days and compare it to recommendations by using the MyPyramid Tracker. The website will also help you design personalized menus to meet your specific dietary requirements. For example, the site provides a vegetarian pyramid and the option to plan vegetarian menus. See the Vegetarianism feature for more information.

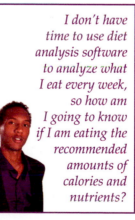

*I don't have time to use diet analysis software to analyze what I eat every week, so how am I going to know if I am eating the recommended amounts of calories and nutrients?*

### ■ Vegetarianism
*Planning a diet*

A vegetarian diet can meet all recommendations and nutrient requirements, and there is a food pyramid dedicated to it (see Figure 2.7). However, a little more effort and thought may be required when planning this type of diet, especially one that's vegan. A vegan diet is perhaps the most restrictive of the different types of vegetarian diets (see Chapter 5 for more information). **Vegans** consume no meat, seafood, eggs, or dairy products. However, many resources provide background information as well as helpful tips for easy menu planning. See Figure 2.8 for the USDA recommendations. ■

**Want to know more?**
For more information on nutrients to focus on when planning a vegetarian diet, go to the text website at http://webcom8.grtxle.com/nutrition and click on the Chapters button. Select Chapter 2.

| Table 2.2 | MyPyramid Recommendations for Specific Caloric Intake |
|---|---|

**Daily Amount of Food from Each Group**

| Calorie Level | 1,000 | 1,200 | 1,400 | 1,600 | 1,800 | 2,000 |
|---|---|---|---|---|---|---|
| Fruits | 1 c. | 1 c. | 1.5 c. | 1.5 c. | 1.5 c. | 2 c. |
| Vegetables | 1 c. | 1.5 c. | 1.5 c. | 2 c. | 2.5 c. | 2.5 c. |
| Grains | 3 oz. eq. | 4 oz. eq. | 5 oz. eq. | 5 oz. eq. | 6 oz. eq. | 6 oz. eq. |
| Meat and Beans | 2 oz. eq. | 3 oz. eq. | 4 oz. eq. | 5 oz. eq. | 5 oz. eq. | 5.5 oz. eq. |
| Milk | 2 c. | 2 c. | 2 c. | 3 c. | 3 c. | 3 c. |
| Oils | 3 tsp. | 4 tsp. | 4 tsp. | 5 tsp. | 5 tsp. | 6 tsp. |
| Discretionary calorie allowance | 165 | 171 | 171 | 132 | 195 | 267 |
| **Calorie Level** | **2,200** | **2,400** | **2,600** | **2,800** | **3,000** | **3,200** |
| Fruits | 2 c. | 2 c. | 2 c. | 2.5 c. | 2.5 c. | 2.5 c. |
| Vegetables | 3 c. | 3 c. | 3.5 c. | 3.5 c. | 4 c. | 4 c. |
| Grains | 7 oz. eq. | 8 oz. eq. | 9 oz. eq. | 10 oz. eq. | 10 oz. eq. | 10 oz. eq. |
| Meat and Beans | 6 oz. eq. | 6.5 oz. eq. | 6.5 oz. eq. | 7 oz. eq. | 7 oz. eq. | 7 oz. eq. |
| Milk | 3 c. | 3 c. | 3 c. | 3 c. | 3 c. | 3 c. |
| Oils | 6 tsp. | 7 tsp. | 8 tsp. | 8 tsp. | 10 tsp. | 11 tsp. |
| Discretionary calorie allowance | 290 | 362 | 410 | 426 | 512 | 648 |

*Source:* United States Department of Agriculture

**Figure 2.7** With proper planning, nutrient needs can be met on a vegetarian diet.

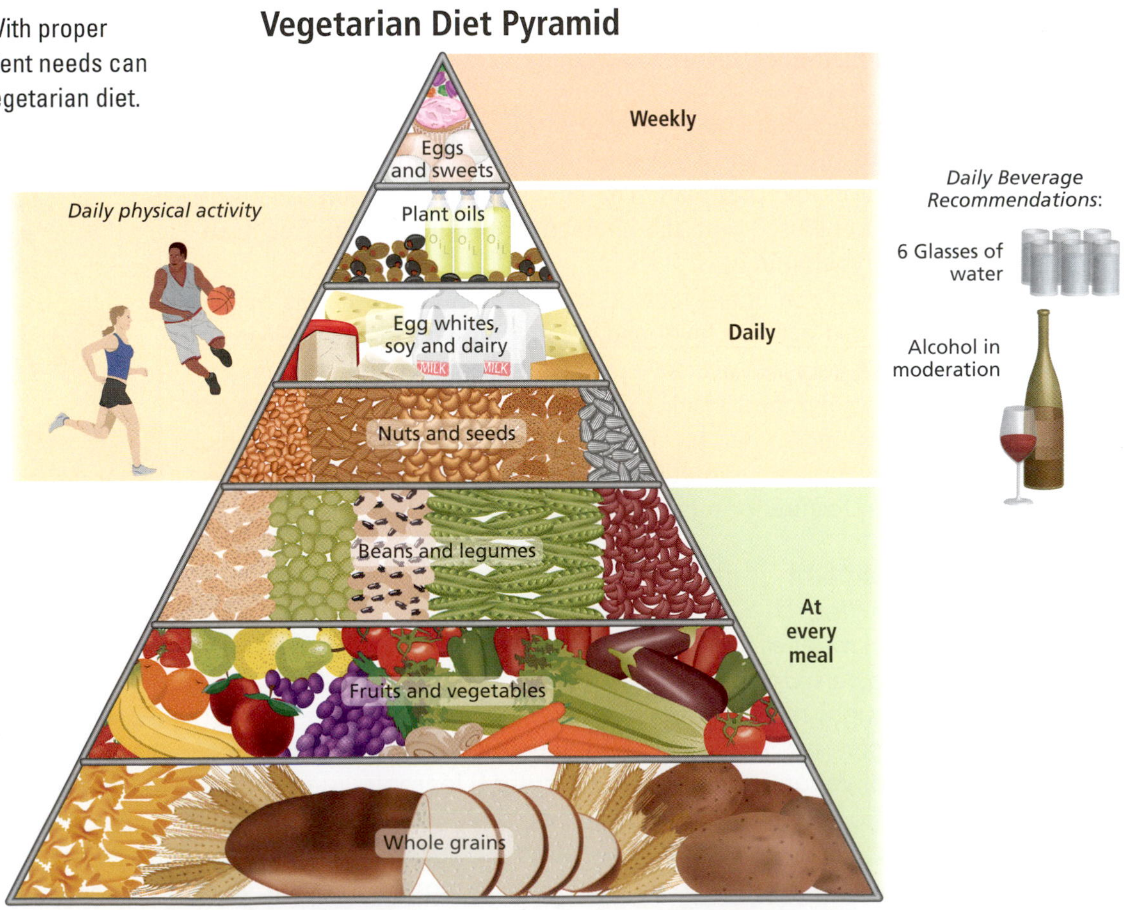

**Vegetarian Diet Pyramid**

Weekly

Daily physical activity

Eggs and sweets

Plant oils

Egg whites, soy and dairy

Daily

Nuts and seeds

Beans and legumes

At every meal

Fruits and vegetables

Whole grains

Daily Beverage Recommendations:

6 Glasses of water

Alcohol in moderation

**Figure 2.8** Tips for Planning Vegetarian Diets from the USDA

- Build meals around protein sources that are naturally low in fat, such as beans, lentils, and rice.
- Don't overload meals with high-fat cheeses to replace the meat.
- Calcium-fortified soy-based beverages can provide calcium in amounts similar to milk. They are usually low in fat and do not contain cholesterol.
- Many foods that typically contain meat or poultry can be made vegetarian. This can increase vegetable intake and cut saturated fat and cholesterol intake. Consider the following:

   Pasta primavera or pasta with marinara or pesto sauce

   Veggie pizza

   Vegetable lasagna

   Tofu-vegetable stir-fry

   Vegetable lo mein

   Vegetable kabobs

   Bean burritos or tacos

- A variety of vegetarian products look (and may taste) like their nonvegetarian counterparts, but are usually lower in saturated fat and contain no cholesterol.

   For breakfast, try soy-based sausage patties or links.

   Rather than hamburgers, try veggie burgers. A variety of kinds are available, made with soybeans, vegetables, and/or rice.

   Add vegetarian meat substitutes to soups and stews to boost protein without adding saturated fat or cholesterol. These include tempeh (cultured soybeans with a chewy texture), tofu, and wheat gluten (seitan).

   For barbecues, try veggie or garden burgers, soy hot dogs, marinated tofu or tempeh, and veggie kabobs.

   Make bean burgers, lentil burgers, or pita halves with falafel (spicy ground chickpea patties).

   Some restaurants offer soy options (texturized vegetable protein, TVP) as a substitute for meat, and soy cheese as a substitute for regular cheese.

- Most restaurants can accommodate vegetarian modifications to menu items by substituting meatless sauces, omitting meat from stir-fries, and adding vegetables or pasta in place of meat. These substitutions are more likely to be available at restaurants that make food to order.

Many Asian and Indian restaurants offer a varied selection of vegetarian dishes.

*Source:* United States Department of Agriculture

## Discretionary Calories

The answer is yes, but sweets, snack foods, and other empty calories tend to be high in sugar and fat and low in vitamins and minerals. Accordingly, they should contribute only a small amount of your total calories for the day. How much that "small amount" should be depends on your total daily calorie needs. This question is addressed in MyPyramid under the concept of **discretionary calories**. These are the calories you can consume after you meet all your nutrient needs, without going over your total calorie target for the day. Discretionary calories allow for an increased intake of foods from any group, such as an extra glass of milk, but they are *not* meant for just sweets and snacks. In making this choice, be aware that most Americans already consume more than their recommended discretionary calories. Of course, if your energy requirements

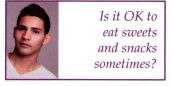

*Is it OK to eat sweets and snacks sometimes?*

are greater due to increased physical activity, the amount of discretionary calories you can consume goes up. For example, if you require 2,000 calories and typically meet your nutrient needs by consuming 1,800 calories in your regular meals, then you have about 200 discretionary calories, while a person who consumes 1,800 calories but needs 2,100 calories can add 300 calories in snacks without gaining weight.

### ■ What's Hot

*The ongoing debate over the Food Guide Pyramid*

Many health professionals criticized the Food Guide Pyramid for being out of date, difficult to use, based on "poor science," and influenced by lobbying efforts of the food industry. This criticism was part of the reason the pyramid was updated and reconstructed. However, the new pyramid is by no means immune to criticism and debate either. In fact, the Harvard School of Public Health criticizes it for being heavily influenced by business interests, unavailable to those without web access, and too simple. Moreover, the school has even suggested that many of the foods the pyramid recommends are not essential to good health and that some may be detrimental to your health if consumed in the quantities suggested. Those who criticize the pyramid suggest that there is inadequate scientific evidence to support the statements made. In response to their conclusions, the experts at Harvard have created their own version called the Healthy Eating Pyramid, pictured in Figure 2.9.

Other groups have criticized the pyramid for not being culturally diverse; they have also suggested that the assignments of meats, beans, poultry, fish, and nuts in the pyramid are incorrect. They contend that the guidelines need to make clear that red meats should be consumed only occasionally, because research indicates that a diet high in these meats increases the risk for certain diseases. Regardless of which side of the debate you are on, it is important to remember that MyPyramid is meant as a guideline to help the public improve health and decrease obesity. ■

**Want to know more?**
To address these and other issues, several alternative pyramids have now been created, such as the Asian Pyramid, the Latin Pyramid, and the Mediterranean Pyramid. To view these pyramids, go to the text website at http://webcom8 .grtxle.com/nutrition and click on the Chapters button. Select Chapter 2.

**Before you go on . . .**
1. What is the purpose of MyPyramid?
2. What does the picture of the figure on the stairs on the side of MyPyramid represent?
3. Define *discretionary calories.*
4. Why did the USDA abandon use of the term *serving size?*
5. What are some of the criticisms of the revised pyramid?

## Serving Size: A Frequent Case of Misinterpretation

In response to criticisms and suggestions from health and nutrition professionals, the pyramid has been updated. One of the main goals of the committees charged with updating the pyramid was to more accurately communicate what a proper serving size is for each food group. Research on consumer understanding of the previous pyramid indicated that most consumers defined a serving size as "the food on my plate," or their portion of food. So when recommended amounts of foods are described as a certain "number of servings," most people

**Want to know more?**
For more information on the Healthy Eating Pyramid visit the text web site at http://webcom8 .grtxle.com/nutrition and click on the chapters button. Select Chapter 2.

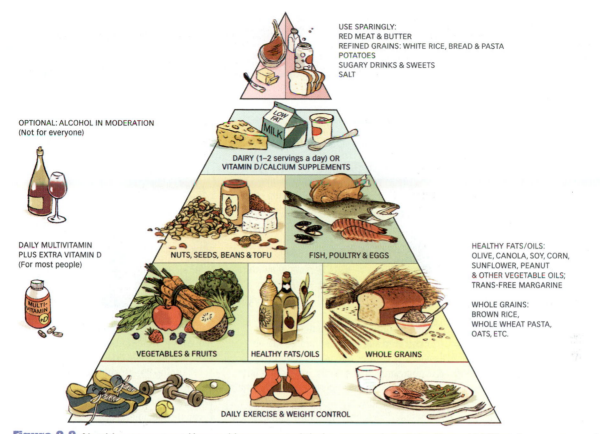

USE SPARINGLY:
RED MEAT & BUTTER
REFINED GRAINS: WHITE RICE, BREAD & PASTA
POTATOES
SUGARY DRINKS & SWEETS
SALT

OPTIONAL: ALCOHOL IN MODERATION
(Not for everyone)

DAIRY (1–2 servings a day) OR
VITAMIN D/CALCIUM SUPPLEMENTS

DAILY MULTIVITAMIN
PLUS EXTRA VITAMIN D
(For most people)

NUTS, SEEDS, BEANS & TOFU          FISH, POULTRY & EGGS

HEALTHY FATS/OILS:
OLIVE, CANOLA, SOY, CORN,
SUNFLOWER, PEANUT
& OTHER VEGETABLE OILS;
TRANS-FREE MARGARINE

WHOLE GRAINS:
BROWN RICE,
WHOLE WHEAT PASTA,
OATS, ETC.

VEGETABLES & FRUITS     HEALTHY FATS/OILS          WHOLE GRAINS

DAILY EXERCISE & WEIGHT CONTROL

**Figure 2.9** Nutrition experts at Harvard have created their own version of the Pyramid. What do you see as the primary differences between it and MyPyramid (Figure 2.4)? Copyright © 2008. For more information about The Healthy Eating Pyramid, please see The Nutrition Source, Department of Nutrition, Harvard School of Public Health, http://www .thenutritionsource.org, and *Eat, Drink, and Be Healthy,* by Walter C. Willett, M.D. and Patrick J. Skerrett (2005), Free Press/Simon & Schuster Inc.

interpret this to mean that they should eat it that many times, even if their typical portion is much larger than the standardized "serving" professionals envisioned. For example, if the recommendations say "2 servings of milk," the average person interprets this to mean two full glasses. A serving is actually 8 oz., but most people do not use glasses that small. The size of your glass can make a big difference in your total calories for the day!

Because larger-than-recommended portion sizes surely contribute to our growing obesity problem, serving sizes need to be clearly defined and emphasized. Therefore, the USDA eliminated the use of the term *servings* to describe how much we should eat. Instead, it describes recommended amounts in cups or ounces for the day, which can be eaten as several portions at different times.

The MyPyramid website provides examples of how much food comprises a cup or ounce equivalent in each food group. For example, on a 2,000-calorie diet the recommended amount of grains is "6 oz. eq." In general, an *ounce equivalent* is equal to one slice of bread; 1 c. of ready-to-eat cereal; or 1/2 c. of cooked rice, cooked pasta, or cooked cereal. On a 2,000-calorie diet the daily recommended intake for grains is a 6 ounce equivalent equal to six slices of bread. Or perhaps more realistically, 1.5 cups of cereal at breakfast, two slices of whole-wheat bread at lunch, and a cup of brown rice at dinner.

Serving size = 8oz.  Portion size = 64 oz.
Calories = 108       Calories = 864
        Caloried difference = 756

The size of your container can make a substantial difference in your calorie intake.

# Real People, Other Voices

**Student:**

## Etheline Cimatu

San Jose City College, San Jose, CA

I can understand Marisol's anxiety stemming from the challenges of change—being a freshman in college and away from home. She will need to make initial assessments to give herself a starting point. Having recorded her diet for several days, she needs to deal with the issue of being homesick, which is driving a lot of her "bad" food choices. To help in her transition, she could join a club or group, which will give her a sense of a family support system.

I noticed that Marisol has a busy schedule, gets little physical activity, and eats a diet lacking nutritious foods. To jump-start her day, she should wake up about an hour earlier to get at least thirty minutes of physical activity; she can start with moderate walking. She should eat breakfast before heading to her first class of the day to avoid getting too hungry later in the day. Because she is very busy throughout the day, the key is to make sure she has prepared healthy snacks for when she doesn't have more than a ten- or fifteen-minute break. She can pack fresh fruits, nuts, and baby carrots. Instead of drinking sweetened beverages, she should have water, which helps in satiety and aids in bodily functions. She can take advantage of the meal plan she has already purchased to choose foods that are healthy.

Aside from Marisol's awareness of her not-so-healthy eating choices, she will need to come to terms with her deeper connection with food and her family back home in order to be successful in changing for the better, eating better, and feeling better about herself.

**Instructor:**

## Jau-Jiin Chen, PHD, RD

University of Nevada, Las Vegas

Even a person with a busy schedule has time for a healthy meal. Marisol has access to the school cafeteria with many food choices. Her current meals contain large amounts of concentrated sugar and saturated fat, not enough variety, and minimal fruits and vegetables. If she thinks before she eats and follows the principles outlined in the *Dietary Guidelines* and MyPyramid to include five food groups, she can develop her own healthy meal plan. Initially, it might be difficult to satisfy all the recommendations, but as she practices it will become easier.

The easiest way to get started is to have two-thirds of her foods come from plant sources (such as vegetables, fruits, and grain products) and one-third from animal sources. Whether she is in a cafeteria or a fast-food restaurant, she should aim for low-fat choices of vegetables and grains, with a small amount of foods containing protein. She can mix or alternate vegetables from different color groups, and substitute milk or 100% juice for soda or sweetened drinks. A piece of fruit (e.g., apple, orange, grapes, strawberries) after the meal or as a snack would not only satisfy her sweet tooth but also supply many micronutrients and phytochemicals. Drinking plenty of water throughout the day will keep her hydrated. Once she gets used to incorporating all five food groups into her diet, practicing portion control may allow her to consume discretionary calories. After all, eating should be enjoyable, and health enhancing as well.

**Registered dietitian:**

## Linda S. Eck Mills, MBA, RD, LDN, FADA

Bernville, PA

First, it's great that Marisol realizes the need to do something to improve her eating habits and has taken this nutrition course as an elective early in her college career. This course will provide her with a great foundation for a healthy, independent lifestyle.

Planning healthy eating can seem like a daunting task, so she needs to start with the basics and progress from there. I would recommend she start with the MyPyramid website—www.MyPyramid .gov—and enter her personal information to see how much she should be eating from each food group. Then she should take the three-day food record she did for class and put that information into the MyPyramid Tracker. Next Marisol needs to look at where she is falling short of meeting her needs and then use that information to start making gradual changes. She needs to make a practice of reading food labels so she understands what she is eating and is aware of the portion size in each package. This is not a diet plan, but rather a way of eating healthy. Remember, the key is to plan for balance, variety, and moderation in the foods she chooses.

It is also important for Marisol to include physical activity in her daily routine. The combination of exercise and nutrition is needed for maintaining health.

If she has any special needs because of a medical condition, she may need individual nutrition counseling. She can locate a Registered Dietitian by going to the American Dietetic Association website—www.eatright.org—and clicking on "Find a Nutrition Professional."

# The Nutrition Facts Label

The **Nutrition Facts label** provides information about the nutritional content of products and is part of the required information on food labels today. Food labels provide one of the easiest and most accessible tools for diet planning. Knowing how to use them can make trips to the grocery store a lot more interesting! Regulations for the contents of food labels are issued by two federal agencies: the Food and Drug Administration (part of HHS) and the Food Safety and Inspection Service of the USDA. The USDA regulates the labeling of meat, poultry, and eggs; the FDA regulates labeling for all other foods. Food labeling is required for most packaged foods, such as breads, cereals, canned and frozen foods, snacks, desserts, and drinks. The USDA has only recently required labeling for meats, poultry, and eggs. Nutrition labeling for fruits, vegetables, and fish is still voluntary but highly encouraged. Also, nutrition information is required for restaurant foods that make health or nutrient claims such as "low-fat" or "heart-healthy." However, labels are not required for any recipes endorsed by medical or dietary groups such as the American Heart Association.

Some foods are exempt from nutrition labeling including the following:

- Food served for immediate consumption, such as that served in hospital cafeterias and airplanes, and that sold by food service vendors—for example, mall cookie counters, sidewalk vendors, and vending machines
- Ready-to-eat food that is not necessarily intended for immediate consumption but is prepared primarily on site—for example, bakery, deli, and candy store items
- Medical foods, such as those used to meet the nutritional needs of patients with certain diseases or supplement drinks used in hospitals
- Coffee and tea, some spices, and other foods that contain no significant amounts of any nutrients

A food label has five mandatory parts:

- A statement of identity: the common name of the product
- The net contents of the package: the accurate weight, volume, measure, or numerical count of the product in the package
- The name and address of the manufacturer
- A list of ingredients: ingredients must be listed by common name in descending order by weight; any food additives or preservatives are to be included here (see You Decide for more information)
- Nutrition information; includes the Nutrition Facts label

 ## ▇ You Decide

*Food additives—do we need them and are they safe?*

Are some of the words in the ingredients list of many food labels unfamiliar to you or hard to pronounce? Most of these ingredients are additives designed to keep foods fresher longer, to maintain their color, and in some cases to enhance their nutritional value. Legally, food additives are "any substance the intended use of which results or may reasonably be expected to result—directly or indirectly—in its becoming a component or otherwise affecting the characteristics of any food." This definition includes any substance used to produce, process, treat, package, transport, or store food.

 **Want to know more?**
For more information on how to read a food label, visit the text web site at http://webcom8.grtxle.com/nutrition and click on the Chapters button. Select Chapter 2.

**Want to know more?**
Do you know where the food you consume originates? You can review additional information regarding concerns related to foods produced outside of the United States and information on buying locally produced foods by visiting the text website at http://webcom8.grtxle.com/nutrition and clicking on the Chapters button. Select Chapter 2.

**Want to know more?**
If you would like to review a list of food additives and what they are used for, go to the text website at http://webcom8.grtxle.com/nutrition and click on the Chapters button. Select Chapter 2.

**Want to know more?**
To read more about the Center for Science in the Public Interest's opinion on food additives and access its list of safe and unsafe additives, go to the text website at http://webcom8.grtxle.com/nutrition and click on the Chapters button. Select Chapter 2.

The FDA oversees substances added to food and is charged with the responsibility of monitoring their safe use. Under the federal Food, Drug, and Cosmetic Act (FDCA), the FDA must review the safety of food and color additives before manufacturers and distributors can market them. The agency also has a notification program for substances that are "Generally Recognized as Safe" (GRAS).

Additives are used in foods to improve taste, texture, appearance, and quality. Food additives also improve the nutritional content as when food is fortified (for example, when iodine is added to salt). They can also be used to color food; they are used to make mint ice cream green, margarines yellow, and colas brown.

Despite the uses of additives in food, many consumer groups such as the Center for Science in the Public Interest question just how safe many of these additives are. They say, "The food and chemical industries have said for decades that all food additives are well tested and safe. And most additives are safe. However, the history of food additives is riddled with [several] that, after many years of use, were found to pose health risks. . . . The moral of the story is that when someone says that all food additives are well tested and safe you should take their assurances with a grain of salt."

How can we trust the food manufacturers and companies that develop these additives, especially when many of them are not based in the United States? This question has come to the forefront of consumer concerns over the safety of our food supply. With reports in the news of contaminated products coming from China and other nations, many Americans are paying more attention to where their food and the additives in their food are coming from. These concerns are leading many consumers to buy more locally produced foods. ■

Under the label's "Nutrition Facts" heading, manufacturers are required to provide information on certain nutrients, which were selected because they address today's health concerns. The order in which they must appear reflects the priority of current dietary recommendations. We will examine and discuss each part of the label, depicted in Figure 2.10.

## Serving Size

The information on a label is based on a serving size, and the number of serving sizes per container is listed. Serving sizes are no longer up to the discretion of the manufacturer. They are now uniform so that one serving of milk is the same regardless of the brand or whether it is whole milk or skim. This standardization makes comparing products a lot easier. Serving sizes must be expressed in both common household and metric measures. The FDA allows the following as common household measures: the cup, tablespoon, teaspoon, piece, slice, and fraction (such as "1/4 pizza"). Ounces may also be used, but only if a common household unit is not

## Nutrition Facts

Serving Size 1 cup (228g)
Servings Per Container 2

**Start here**

**Amount Per Serving**

Calories 250  Calories from Fat 110

**Check calories**

| | % Daily Value* |
|---|---|
| **Total Fat** 12g | 18% |
| Saturated Fat 3g | 15% |
| *Trans* Fat 3g | |
| **Cholesterol** 30mg | 10% |
| **Sodium** 470mg | 20% |
| **Potassium** 700mg | 20% |
| **Total Carbohydrate** 31g | 10% |
| Dietary Fiber 0g | 0% |
| Sugars 5g | |
| **Proteins** 5g | |
| Vitamin A | 4% |
| Vitamin C | 2% |
| Calcium | 20% |
| Iron | 4% |

**Quick guide to % DV**

5% or less is low
20% or more is high

**Limit these**

**Get enough of these**

*Percent Daily Values are based on a 2,000 calorie diet. Your daily values may be higher or lower depending on your calorie needs.

| | Calories: | 2,000 | 2,500 |
|---|---|---|---|
| Total Fat | Less than | 65g | 80g |
| Sat Fat | Less than | 20g | 25g |

**Footnote**

**Figure 2.10** The nutrition facts on food labels provide information regarding a product's nutrient content to enable consumers to make informed choices. Do you think restaurants should be required to provide similar information? Why?

applicable and an appropriate visual unit is given—for example, 1 oz. (28 g/ about 1/2 pickle).

## Calories and Calories from Fat

The total number of calories in a labeled food is always listed first because consumers must be able to match daily calorie intake with calorie expenditure to avoid weight gain. Calories shown are for one serving, so if you eat more than one serving, remember that you are consuming more calories than are listed on the label. The next items list how many and what percentage of the calories come from fat. So our sample label has the total calories and calories from fat, followed by the *total* fat and what a single serving represents in terms of a daily recommendation. This information can help you balance your meals for the day so that you consume the recommended 30 percent or less of your total calories from fat.

## Nutrients

The nutrients listed first are those that Americans tend to eat too much of: total fat, saturated fat, trans fat, cholesterol, and sodium. As we have noted, consuming too much of these nutrients may increase your risk of heart disease and certain cancers. The typical American diet should limit intake of the first five nutrients and strive to increase potassium, dietary fiber, vitamin A, vitamin C, calcium, and iron.

## Daily Value

Perhaps the key to using the Nutrition Facts label for diet planning is the percent Daily Value (%DV). The **Daily Values** are the nutrient standards used on food labels; they are based on a 2,000-calorie diet. Why create yet another set of standards? Because many of the other standards vary for different age and gender groups. For labeling purposes, 2,000 calories has been established as the reference for calculating percent Daily Values. This level was chosen, partly because many health experts say it approximates the maintenance calorie requirements of the groups most often targeted for weight reduction, such as postmenopausal women. The Daily Values are set for the "average person" and are listed in Table 2.3. Because many people need more or less than 2,000 calories, these values are best used to compare one product to another. If you compare products, make sure the serving sizes are similar, especially the weight (grams, milligrams, ounces). The percent Daily Value helps you determine whether a serving of food is high or low in a nutrient. A 5% DV or less is *low* for all nutrients, even those you want to limit (such as fat, saturated fat, cholesterol, and sodium), and of course those that you want to consume in greater amounts (fiber, calcium, and so on). A 20% DV or more is *high* for all nutrients. Note that there is no percent Daily Value for protein, sugar, or trans fats. A percent Daily Value is required to be listed if a claim such as "high in protein" is made. Otherwise, unless the food is meant for use by infants and children under age 4, none is needed. No Daily Value has been established for sugars because no recommendations currently exist for the total amount to eat in a day. Experts have also not provided a Daily Value for trans fat; however, they recommend that you limit trans fats as much as possible.

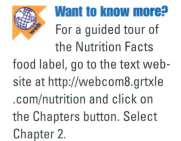

### Table 2.3    Daily Values

| Food Component | Daily Value (DV) |
|---|---|
| Fat (based on 30% of total calories) | 65 g |
| Saturated fat (based on 10% of total calories) | 20 g |
| Cholesterol | 300 mg |
| Total carbohydrate (based on 60% of total calories) | 300 g |
| Fiber (based on 11.5 g fiber per 1,000 calories) | 25 g |
| Sodium | 2,400 mg* |
| Potassium | 3,500 mg |
| Protein (based on 10% of total calories) | 50 g |
| Vitamin A | 5,000 IU |
| Vitamin C | 60 mg |
| Thiamin | 1.5 mg |
| Riboflavin | 1.7 mg |
| Niacin | 20 mg |
| Calcium | 1.0 g |
| Iron | 18 mg |
| Vitamin D | 400 IU |
| Vitamin E | 30 IU |
| Vitamin $B_6$ | 2.0 mg |
| Folic acid | 0.4 mg |
| Vitamin $B_{12}$ | 6 mcg |
| Phosphorus | 1.0 g |
| Iodine | 150 mcg |
| Magnesium | 400 mg |
| Zinc | 15 mg |
| Copper | 2 mg |
| Biotin | 0.3 mg |
| Pantothenic acid | 10 mg |

*To reflect the changes in the dietary guidelines, the daily values may soon change to 1,500 mg.
Note: Daily Values are given in grams (g), milligrams (mg), micrograms (mcg), and international units (IU).

Free-range eggs are produced by hens that are allowed to graze or roam outside for at least some portion of each day. Typically, egg-producing chickens are raised in crowded cages, as shown below.

The regulations for food labeling also define what terms may be used to describe the level of a nutrient in a food and how they can be used. See Figure 2.11 for a list of nutrient content claims.

Even claims that are regulated, may often appear confusing or misleading at first glance. For example, some egg manufacturers sell "free-range" and "cage-free" eggs. These products typically display a picture of a farm or of chickens in a field. The consumer may get the visual of freely grazing, happy chickens. Is this really the case? It is important to understand the definitions and guidelines behind such claims and to understand that some "play on words" can be involved. See Sustainable Nutrition for more information.

**Figure 2.11** Nutrient Content Claims

- *"Free"*: No or trivial amounts of fat, saturated fat, cholesterol, sodium, sugars, or calories. For example, "calorie-free" means less than 5 calories per serving, and "sugar-free" and "fat-free" both mean less than 0.5 g per serving.

- *"Low"*:

    *"low-fat"*: 3 g or less per serving

    *"low-saturated-fat"*: 1 g or less per serving

    *"low-sodium"*: 140 mg or less per serving

    *"very-low-sodium"*: 35 mg or less per serving

    *"low-cholesterol"*: 20 mg or less, and 2 g or less of saturated fat, per serving

    *"low-calorie"*: 40 calories or less per serving

- *"Lean" and "extra lean"*: These terms can be used to describe the fat content of meat, poultry, seafood, and game meats.

- *"Lean"*: Less than 10 g fat, 4.5 g or less saturated fat, and less than 95 mg cholesterol per serving or per 100 g

- *"Extra lean"*: Less than 5 g fat, less than 2 g saturated fat, and less than 95 mg cholesterol per serving or per 100 g

- *"High"*: 20 percent or more of the Daily Value for a particular nutrient in a serving

- *"Good source"*: 10–19 percent of the Daily Value for a particular nutrient.

- *"Reduced" or "Less"*: At least 25 percent less of a nutrient or calories than the regular product. A "reduced" claim can't be made on a product if its reference food already meets the requirement for a "low" claim. In other words, applesauce can't say "reduced in saturated fat" because it never had saturated fat in it to begin with.

- *"Light"*: This term can mean one of three things:

    One-third fewer calories or half the fat of the regular food

    Sodium content of a low-calorie, low-fat food reduced by 50 percent

    Texture and color, as long as the label explains the intent—for example, "light brown sugar" or "light and fluffy"

- *"More"*: At least 10 percent more of the Daily Value than the original food.

- *"Healthy"*: Low in fat, saturated fat, trans fat, cholesterol, and sodium. It must contain 10 percent of the Daily Value of vitamin A or C, iron, calcium, protein, or fiber.

## ■ Sustainable Nutrition

### *Cage-free or free-roaming—what do they really mean?*

Did you know that most commercial egg-laying chickens are kept in small cages? Producers contend that caging hens has benefits for the birds, consumers, and their workers. The cages help separate the birds from their feces, which is said to help reduce the risk of disease and infections. Producers also contend that working conditions for their farmers and employees are better with caged hens than with other systems. Moreover, by using cages producers can employ automation, which decreases labor time, costs, and the prevalence of dust and ammonia. Eggs are laid on the sloping floor of the cage so that there is minimal contact between the egg and the hen, which producers say decreases the possibility of bacterial contamination of the egg.

Despite manufacturers' claims that caging is healthier for the chickens and helps decrease contamination, many organizations such as the Humane Society of the United States and similar European entities believe that caging represents inhumane treatment of the hens. As to the supposed increased risk of bacterial contamination in hens not kept in cages, they say, "In cage-free systems, eggs laid on litter rather than in nests could theoretically pose a higher risk of *Salmonella* [bacterial] contamination. However, a recent study by the UK Food Standards Agency found no significant differences in *Salmonella* contamination of eggs produced in cages, deep litter, free-range, and organic systems. Other studies have found the incidence of *Salmonella* is influenced more by the genetics of the layer hen strain than by housing."

This issue is still being debated, and many consumers prefer to purchase eggs produced from hens that are not kept in cages. In order to meet this growing demand, some producers raise their birds in a *cage-free* or *free-roaming* system. However, "cage free" does not necessarily mean that the birds are raised outdoors. Typically, these birds are maintained on the floor of a poultry house. The higher production costs associated with this type of management system are of course reflected in the price.

Most eggs are obtained from caged hens. However, many consumers prefer to purchase eggs produced by hens that are not kept in cages.

There's even more to consider with this issue on the labeling front. Often the packaging of cage-free eggs can be used to mislead the consumer about the product they are purchasing. Designs on egg cartons often show chickens roaming free outdoors—which many cage-free hens are not allowed to do. Typically, these hens are maintained indoors, just not in cages.

*Free-range* eggs are produced by hens that are allowed to graze or roam outside. They don't have to be allowed outside all of the time, but, if not, they must be kept in a poultry house that has access to the outdoors if they want to go out. They are then usually locked indoors at night to protect the hens from predators. There is no set standard on how much time the hens need to be allowed outdoors, but any producers who claim that their chickens are free-range have to demonstrate to the USDA that the chickens have been allowed access to the outside. ■

## Health Claims on Labels

Every time you turn on the TV or go to the grocery store, you see a new product claiming that it helps prevent a disease or that it is high in a certain nutrient. These claims are often overwhelming and leave the consumer wondering what to believe. In an effort to regulate the use of such health claims, the FDA has established specific guidelines that manufacturers must follow to make certain health claims on their food labels. **Health claims** are statements made about a product that link it or some of its ingredients to a reduced risk of disease, such as a claim that consuming fiber reduces your risk of heart disease. Such claims have to be approved by the FDA and must be supported by scientific evidence. Examples of some of these approved health claims are:

- Calcium—decreased risk of osteoporosis
- Fiber-containing grain products, fruits, and vegetables—decreased risk of cancer

- Folic acid—reduced risk of neural tube defects
- Fruits, vegetables, and grain products that contain fiber—lower risk of heart disease
- Fruits and vegetables—lower risk of cancer
- Lower fat—decreased risk of cancer
- Lower saturated fat and cholesterol—decreased risk of heart disease
- Lower sodium—reduced risk of high blood pressure
- Soluble fiber from certain foods, such as whole oats and psyllium seed husk—decreased risk of heart disease

For a detailed list of all approved health claims, go to the text website at http://webcom8.grtxle.com/nutrition and click on the Chapters button. Select Chapter 2.

## Putting It All Together

So far we have discussed the recommendations and the various tools available to help you plan a healthy diet. Now you have to incorporate this information into a menu of meals that fit your lifestyle, accommodate your schedule, and include foods you like. So the first step is to get out a sheet of paper and start listing the foods you normally eat. Second, make a list of the different categories represented by the pyramid. Third, place the foods you like into the various categories of the pyramid. Do you have foods from each category? Do you have a variety of foods in each group? If not, consider making a list of new foods to try. You can begin to construct a menu plan by incorporating the foods you like in the amounts recommended by the pyramid and other recommendations. See the section on quick easy healthy meals at the end of this chapter for suggestions. Then compare your menu to the checklist provided on the text website at http://webcom8.grtxle.com/nutrition and click on the Chapters button. Select Chapter 2.

**Before you go on . . .**

1. Why are manufacturers required to provide information on selected nutrients on the food product's Nutrition Facts label?
2. What is the difference between the terms "fat-free" and "low-fat"?
3. What are the Daily Values used for?
4. What must occur before a manufacturer can make a health claim about a product?

## Real People, Real Strategies

As part of her class assignment, Marisol had to compare her diet to the established guidelines. She went to www.mypyramid.gov to start the process. She is 19, is 5'4" tall, and weighs 130 lb. When she entered the information, the guidelines suggested the following general plan:

1,965 calories (per day)
6 oz. grains
2.5 c. vegetables
2 c. fruits
3 c. milk and dairy
5.5 oz. meat

On the website Marisol could look up serving sizes and amounts and track her daily intake. She was very excited about using MyPyramid because what she really needed in putting a plan together is a place to start. She decided to compare one of the days she recorded for her class assignment to the guidelines provided.

| | |
|---|---|
| 9:15 | Breakfast: Bagel with 1 Tbsp. butter, 12-oz. sports drink |
| 1:30 | Lunch: 1 slice cheese pizza, 1 slice chocolate cake, and a 12-oz. Coke |
| 7:30 | Dinner: Hamburger, about 4 oz., on white bun and 11/2 c. fries from late-night café on campus with 12 oz. sweetened iced tea |
| 8:30–11:30 | Study (about11/2 c. frozen yogurt and a Snickers bar) |

She was astonished to discover that she ate 2,300 calories (335 more than recommended) and less than half the recommended fiber. Her diet was high in saturated fat and low in both polyunsaturated and monounsaturated fats. It was also low in vitamins A, C, and E; folate; calcium; iron; and magnesium.

Compared to the recommended servings from each part of MyPyramid, she did not consume adequate amounts of any of the food groups except grains. When she looked further, she realized that her caloric intake was high because she ate so much sugar. It also seemed odd to her that she consumed more than the recommended number of calories, yet not enough of any of the food groups except grains. Marisol shared her results and thoughts with her nutrition instructor, who explained that her dietary problem was attributable to her consumption of so many empty calories such as the chocolate cake, the frozen yogurt, the Snickers bar, the sweet tea, and the sports drink. Based on this feedback, she developed a plan for the next day. She knows she has to keep her busy schedule in mind and that she needs to make changes gradually. She created a plan that she believes she can carry out and that when analyzed on MyPyramid is much closer to the recommendations and guidelines for her age, height, and weight. It looks something like this:

| | |
|---|---|
| 9:15 | Breakfast: Whole-grain bagel with 1 Tbsp. all-natural peanut butter, 1 glass of skim milk, 1 banana |
| 1:30 | Lunch: 1 slice pizza with mushrooms and broccoli, a small apple, some baked potato chips, 8-oz. sports drink |

| 3:30 | Snack: Vanilla yogurt |
| 7:30 | Dinner: Grilled chicken breast with brown rice, small salad with Italian salad dressing, small brownie for dessert, 12 oz. water |
| 8:30–11:30 | Study (1 bag of Smart Balance microwave popcorn, 12 oz. water) |

To see Marisol's assessment from MyPyramid.gov, go to the text website at http://webcom8.grtxle.com/nutrition and click on the Chapters button. Select Chapter 2.

## Chapter Summary

- A healthy diet includes balance, variety, and moderation. *Balance* means incorporating foods from all food groups into your plan daily. *Variety* means eating different types of foods within each food group. *Moderation* means not overconsuming any one food or food group.
- It is important to eat mostly nutrient-dense foods, or foods with a lot of nutrients for the number of calories they contain, rather than empty calories or foods that supply calories but not many nutrients.
- Having a plan will help you think before you eat and accomplish your goal of eating a healthy diet.
- Guidelines exist that can help you develop a healthy eating plan, such as *Dietary Guidelines for Americans*, the Dietary Reference Intakes, MyPyramid, and the Nutrition Facts label.
- The *Dietary Guidelines* provide the general recommendations needed for planning a healthy diet.
- The DRIs, which include RDAs, AIs, EARs, and ULs, provide specific recommendations for nutrient intakes. The RDAs and the AIs are most often used.
- MyPyramid translates the concepts of balance, variety, and moderation, along with the information from the *Dietary Guidelines* and the Dietary Reference Intakes, into a usable diet plan. You can individualize it at the interactive MyPyramid website.
- MyPyramid includes discretionary calories. These are the calories you can consume after you meet all your nutrient needs without going over your total calorie target for the day.
- MyPyramid translates servings into understandable portions, such as 1 cup, to help consumers control portion sizes in an effort to control calorie intake.
- The Nutrition Facts label found on many food products is intended to help you make choices regarding individual foods.
- Food labeling is required for most packaged foods such as breads, cereals, canned and frozen foods, snacks, desserts, and drinks. The USDA has only recently required labeling for meats, poultry, and eggs. Nutrition labeling for fruits, vegetables, and fish is voluntary but highly encouraged.
- Nutrition information is required for restaurant foods that make health or nutrient claims such as "low-fat" or "heart-healthy."
- The regulations for food labeling also define what terms may be used to describe the level of a nutrient in a food and how they can be used, such as "fat-free" or "low-sodium."

- Health claims are statements made about a product that link it or some of its ingredients to a reduced risk of disease, such as a claim that consuming fiber reduces your risk of heart disease. Such claims must be approved by the FDA and supported by scientific evidence.
- All of the nutrient guidelines generated by federal agencies and the required Nutrition Facts label are designed to work together to help you plan a healthy diet.

# Key Terms

**Acceptable Macronutrient Distribution Range (AMDR)** A recommended range of requirements for carbohydrates, fats, and proteins based on the total daily calorie needs and balance of nutrients that are associated with a decreased risk of chronic disease. (p. 38)

**Adequate Intake (AI)** The value assigned to a nutrient if some scientific evidence is available, but not quite enough to establish a recommendation with certainty. (p. 37)

**balance** Incorporating foods from all food groups into your daily eating plan. (p. 32)

**Daily Values** The nutrient standards used on food labels; they are based on a 2,000-calorie diet. (p. 49)

**DASH (Dietary Approaches to Stop Hypertension)** A tool to help individuals lower sodium intake and implement the *Dietary Guidelines*. (p. 34)

**Dietary Guidelines for Americans** A summary of science-based advice to promote health through diet and physical activity and to reduce the risk for major chronic diseases in people over age 2. (p. 33)

**Dietary Reference Intakes (DRIs)** Guidelines designed for healthy people, established to replace the original RDAs in the United States and the Recommended Nutrient Intakes (RNIs) in Canada. (p. 37)

**dietary standards** Recommended intakes for specific nutrients. They can be used to plan diets for individuals and groups. (p. 36)

**discretionary calories** The calories you can consume after you meet all your nutrient needs, without going over your total calorie target for the day. (p. 43)

**empty calories** Calories with little or no nutrient content. (p. 33)

**enriched foods** Foods that have had nutrients added back that were removed during processing. For example, enriched white rice has had some nutrients added back that were present before the outer brown husk was removed. (p. 34)

**Estimated Average Requirement (EAR)** The value assigned to a nutrient that would meet the needs of 50 percent of the people of a specific age or gender. It is used only by federal agencies for research and policy making. (p. 37)

**Estimated Energy Requirement (EER)** A general recommendation for energy needs. (p. 37)

**fortified foods** Foods with nutrients added to them that were not originally present. An example is orange juice fortified with calcium. (p. 34)

**health claims** Statements made about a product that link it or some of its ingredients to a reduced risk of disease, such as a claim that consuming fiber reduces your risk of heart disease. (p. 52)

**Healthy People 2020** A list of health objectives for the nation to achieve by 2020. It is designed to identify the most significant preventable threats to health and to establish national goals to reduce these threats. (p. 34)

**moderation** Avoiding overconsumption of any one food or food group. (p. 32)

**MyPyramid** An interactive website and program that can be used to translate the concepts of balance, moderation, and variety, along with the information from the *Dietary Guidelines* and the Dietary Reference Intakes, into a usable diet plan. (p. 39)

**Nutrition Facts label** Part of the required information on a food label that provides the nutritional content of the product. (p. 47)

**Recommended Dietary Allowances (RDAs)** The recommended intake required to meet the daily nutrient needs for 97–98 percent of all individuals in a given age or gender group. It is used for diet planning for individuals and is the foundation of the DRI. (p. 36)

**Tolerable Upper Intake Level (UL)** The highest level of daily nutrient intake that poses little risk of adverse health effects to individuals in a specific age or gender group. (p. 37)

**variety** Eating different types of foods within each food group. (p. 32)

**vegan** (VEE-gun) A person who consumes no meat, seafood, eggs, or dairy products. (p. 41)

# Chapter Quiz

1. According to MyPyramid, which of the following is not an example of a whole grain?
   a. white rice
   b. brown rice
   c. whole-wheat flour
   d. oatmeal

2. According to MyPyramid, frozen yogurt is considered part of the milk group and also part of which of the following?
   a. the protein group
   b. the carbohydrate group
   c. discretionary calories
   d. none of the above

3. According to MyPyramid, beans and nuts count in which two food groups?
   a. the fruit and vegetable groups
   b. the meat and vegetable groups
   c. the meat and fruit groups
   d. none of the above

4. What is the most important strategy, regardless of what tools you use to create a meal plan?
   a. to watch your carbohydrate intake
   b. to limit your saturated fat
   c. to eat enough fiber
   d. to think before you eat

5. Which of the following beverages would be considered a nutrient-dense choice?
   a. skim milk
   b. a sports drink
   c. sweetened tea
   d. Coca-Cola

6. The overall purpose of the *Dietary Guidelines* is:
   a. to create healthy menus.
   b. to support the food industry.
   c. to encourage Americans to make healthier food choices.
   d. to help Americans lose weight.

7. In eating a healthy diet, the concept of balance refers to:
   a. eating different types of foods.
   b. eating less of foods that contain high levels of fat.
   c. not relying on any one food or food group more than another.
   d. eating three meals a day.

8. What tools are available for you to put the *Dietary Guidelines* into practice?
   a. MyPyramid
   b. food labels
   c. any commercial diet
   d. both a and b

9. Why are the *Dietary Guidelines*, the DRIs, and food labels periodically updated?

   a. to keep consumers informed

   b. to include new ingredients

   c. to reflect current scientific information related to food and disease

   d. to combine recommendations from other countries

10. If there is some scientific evidence available about how much of a nutrient we need, but not quite enough to establish a recommendation, then that nutrient is assigned which of the following standards?

    a. an EAR

    b. a UL

    c. a DRI

    d. an AI

# Cooking 101: Quick, Easy, Healthy Meal Planning and Preparation

## It's Easier Than You May Think!

Healthy eating is more than just consuming the right amounts of calories, and fats, carbohydrates, and proteins and a balance of vitamins and minerals. It takes planning and execution, but for most people, especially students, the entire process needs to be quick and easy, too. Add that to adjusting to a new schedule, moving into a dorm or apartment, and juggling academics, family, job, and social life—and it can all be very stressful. Accordingly, it's little wonder that so many college students tend to put healthy eating and food preparation at the bottom of their priority list. But you shouldn't, and it doesn't have to be stressful. With a little bit of planning and very little cooking time, healthy meals can fit easily into your schedule. Preparing some of your own food can also save you money—so add that to its benefits.

## Keeping It Simple: Some Tips to Get You Started

### Tools of the Trade for the Beginner's Kitchen

If you are buying equipment for a kitchen in your first home or just trying to pick up the essentials for preparing quick meals in your apartment or dorm room, some basic tools can be very helpful. The following checklist can help you get started.

- Something to cook on (many dorms have restrictions, so check before buying):
  Microwave
  Toaster and/or toaster oven
  Hot plate (unless you have access to a stove)
  Rice steamer
  Slow cooker

**Figure 2.12** Rice University student Elliot Flannery shows off some of the food he made with a rice steamer in his dorm room.

**Want to know more?**
For tips on what cookware to buy, go to the text website at http://webcom8.grtxle.com/nutrition and click on the Chapters button. Select Chapter 2.

**Want to know more?**
For more tips on measuring techniques for different food items, go to the text website at http://webcom8.grtxle.com/nutrition and click on the Chapters button. Select Chapter 2.

- Silverware
- Cups, plates, bowls
- Spatula
- Dish soap and sponge
- Potholders or oven mitts
- Two knives (utility or chef's knife for cutting and chopping; paring knife for coring, seeding, etc.)
- Vegetable peeler
- Dry measuring cups and spoons
- Liquid measuring cup
- Two thermometers one for your refrigerator and one for measuring the temperature/doneness of cooked poultry and meats)
- Cookware (avoid those with nonstick coatings):
    - Three pots with lids one small; (one medium; and one large or stockpot for cooking pasta)
    - Frying pan
    - Baking sheet
    - Strainer
    - Can opener
    - Blender
    - Basic spices/condiments:
        - Salt
        - Pepper
        - Cinnamon
        - Italian spices (you can usually find a blend of oregano, basil, etc.)
        - Vinegar
        - Vanilla
        - Garlic

**Figure 2.13** You need only a few essential pieces of equipment for a functioning kitchen.

**Figure 2.14** Measuring cups and spoons are important items to include in any kitchen.

## Common Measurements

When reading recipes you may have noticed that the metric system and the U.S. system are both used, depending on what recipe you are following. Therefore, it is helpful to have measuring cups and spoons that use both systems, like those pictured here. If yours do not have both measurements see Table 2.4, which includes some common equivalents.

In addition to conversions, it is helpful to be aware of common abbreviations used in recipes. Table 2.5 includes some of the more common ones.

Following is a list of common cooking terms.

*Bake/Roast:* To cook food uncovered in an oven or similar appliance.
*Beat:* To make a mixture smooth with rapid, regular motion using a wire whisk, spoon, hand beater, or mixer. When using a spoon, lift the mixture up and over with each stroke.
*Blend:* To mix two or more ingredients thoroughly.
*Boil:* To heat a liquid until bubbles break on the surface, or to cook in boiling water.
*Braise:* To slowly cook meat or poultry in a small amount of liquid in a covered pot.
*Broil:* To use direct heat above the food to cook.
*Brown:* To cook quickly until the surface of the food is brown.
*Chop:* To cut food into small pieces.

| Table 2.4 | Common Equivalents | | |
|---|---|---|---|
| dash | = | 1/8 teaspoon |
| 3 teaspoons | = | 1 tablespoon |
| 2 tablespoons | = | 1 fl. oz. |
| 4 tablespoons | = | 1/4 cup (2 fl. oz.) |
| 5 1/3 tablespoons | = | 1/3 cup (2 2/3 fl. oz.) |
| 16 tablespoons | = | 1 cup (8 fl. oz.) |
| 2 cups | = | 1 pint (16 fl. oz.) |
| 2 pints | = | 1 quart (32 fl. oz.) |
| 4 quarts | = | 1 gallon (128 fl. oz.) |
| 2 gallons | = | 1 peck |
| 4 pecks | = | 1 bushel |
| 1 gram | = | 0.035 ounces (1/30 oz.) |
| 1 ounce | = | 28.35 grams (often rounded to 30 for convenience) |
| 454 grams | = | 1 pound |
| 2.2 pounds | = | 1 kilogram (1000 grams) |
| 1 teaspoon | = | 5 milliliters |
| 1 tablespoon | = | 15 milliliters |
| 1 fluid ounce | = | 28.35 milliliters (often rounded to 30 for convenience) |
| 1 cup | = | 0.24 liters |
| 1 gallon | = | 3.80 liters |

| Table 2.5 | Common Abbreviations | | |
|---|---|---|---|
| teaspoon | = | tsp. |
| tablespoon | = | Tbsp. |
| cup | = | c. |
| pint | = | pt. |
| quart | = | qt. |
| gram | = | g |
| milliliter | = | mL |
| liter | = | L |
| ounce | = | oz. |
| fluid ounce | = | fl. oz. |
| pound | = | lb. |
| kilogram | = | kg |

*Coat:* To cover the entire surface of a food with a mixture such as flour or breadcrumbs.

*Core:* To use a sharp knife to remove the core and seeds of fruit/vegetables.

*Cream:* To stir or blend one or more foods until they are soft (in a liquid state).

*Crisp-tender:* The "doneness" of vegetables when they are cooked only until tender and remain slightly crisp or crunchy in texture.

*Crush:* To use a garlic press or a blunt object to smash foods such as garlic until the fibers separate.

*Cube:* To cut food into 1/2-inch cubes (or size noted in recipe).

*Dash:* Less than 1/8 teaspoon.

*Deep-fry:* To cook in hot oil deep enough for food to float.

*Dice:* To cut into small, square pieces.

*Drain:* To put food and liquid into a strainer or colander, or pour liquid out of a pot by keeping the lid slightly away from the edge of the pan and pouring away from you.

*Flute:* To pinch the edges of dough, such as on piecrust.

*Fold:* To mix by gently turning over and over.

*Fork-tender:* The "doneness" of a food when a fork can easily penetrate it.

*Fry:* To pan-fry by cooking in a frying pan, usually over medium heat, using a small amount of oil.

*Grate:* To rub food on a grater, or chop it in a blender or food processor to produce fine, medium, or coarse particles.

*Grease:* To cover or lubricate with oil to keep food from sticking.

*Knead:* To work dough by folding and stretching with the heel of the hand.

*Marinate:* To allow food to soak in liquid before cooking in order to increase flavor and tenderness.

*Mince:* To cut or chop food into very small pieces.

*Mix:* To combine ingredients using a fork, spoon, or whisk.

*Oil:* To apply a thin layer of vegetable oil on a dish or pan. Can substitute vegetable oil spray.

*Peel:* To remove the outer covering of foods by trimming away with a knife or vegetable peeler.

*Poach:* To cook food over low heat in a small amount of hot, simmering liquid.

*Preheat:* To heat the oven to the desired temperature before putting food in to bake.

*Sauté:* To cook in a small amount of oil or water.

*Scald:* To heat milk until bubbles appear. Bubbles should not be "breaking" on the surface.

*Shred:* To rub a food against a grater to divide it into small pieces.

*Sift:* To remove lumps or lighten the dry ingredients by putting them through a strainer or sifter.

*Simmer:* To cook at a temperature just below the boiling point. Bubbles form slowly but do not reach the surface.

*Slice:* To cut food into thin pieces.

*Steam:* To cook over boiling water.

*Stew:* To cook over low heat in a large amount of simmering liquid.

*Stir-fry:* To quickly fry food, usually at high heat, to a crisp-tender state while constantly stirring.

*Stock:* Water in which vegetables and/or meat and meat bones have been cooked; should be stored in the refrigerator.

*Thaw:* To slowly change from a frozen state to a liquid or unfrozen state.

*Toss:* To mix foods lightly with a lifting motion, using forks or spoons.

## Before You Start

- Make sure you read any recipe you are following carefully.
- Check to see that you have all of the ingredients.
- Gather and prep all ingredients; in other words, get them out and ready for cooking (the culinary term for this is *mise en place*).
- Use clear measuring cups for liquid ingredients and opaque (or clear) cups for dry.
- Level all dry ingredients off and measure carefully.

## Meals That Are Quick, Easy, and Healthy

The following are some quick, easy, healthy meals you can prepare anywhere—in an apartment or even a dorm—if you have access to a microwave. Use the Internet, cookbooks, and other

**Figure 2.15** *Mise en place* means getting all the ingredients together before you start cooking.

sources to expand this list. The meals have intentionally not been categorized into breakfast, lunch, and dinner because any of these foods can be eaten at any time!

## Pizza

### Ingredients:

Crust (ready-made (whole-wheat is ideal), pita, or tortilla)

Sauce (spaghetti sauce or canned tomato or pizza sauce)

Vegetables (any are fine; get creative)

Cooked meat or shrimp or extra-firm tofu (optional)

Cheese (soy, low-fat, regular)

### To prepare:

Top your crust, pita, or tortilla with sauce and toppings; finish with cheese. Bake in the oven according to the package directions on the crust, or until the cheese is melted or the crust has reached the desired crispiness (or you can cook it in a toaster oven or microwave).

## Quesadilla

### Ingredients:

2 whole-wheat tortillas

Cheese (soy, low-fat, regular)

Veggies (optional)

Cooked meat, beans, or tofu (optional)

### To prepare:

Turn the stove to medium heat. Spray a frying pan with nonstick spray, place one tortilla in the pan, and fill it with your chosen ingredients. Place the second tortilla on top and carefully flip/turn the quesadilla until the tortillas are slightly browned or the cheese is melted. You can also use a microwave or toaster oven.

**Figure 2.16** Quesadillas can be made with many different ingredients and are quick and healthy.

## Spaghetti

Chopped chicken breast, ground turkey breast, lean ground beef, and black beans are good protein options for this recipe. You can save any extra sauce and use it for pizza.

### Ingredients:

Olive oil

Salt

Whole-wheat spaghetti

Spaghetti sauce

Finely chopped vegetables: broccoli, mushrooms, peppers, onions, carrots, eggplant, etc. (optional)

Cooked meat, canned beans (drained and rinsed), or extra-firm beans, tofu, chopped (optional)

### To prepare:

Fill a large pot with 6 to 8 quarts of water, leaving enough space at the top to prevent boiling over. Add a dash of olive oil and salt, cover the pot, and bring to a full boil. Add the spaghetti, replace the cover, and cook according to the package directions.

Meanwhile, heat the sauce in a separate pot at low to low-medium heat. Add vegetables, meat, beans, and tofu to the sauce as desired and heat through.

Serve the sauce over the cooked spaghetti.

## Bean Dip Meal

To make your own guacamole for this recipe, peel and dice an avocado, mash it with a big spoon or purée it in a blender, and add lime juice and an envelope of seasonings. Add protein to the dip by adding tofu or cooked ground beef or chicken flavored with taco seasoning.

### To prepare the "dipping chips":

Spray an oat bran or whole-wheat pita or tortilla with nonstick spray and season it with garlic or any seasonings you like. Toast in a toaster oven or under the broiler in the oven (watch it closely so it doesn't burn). Cut into serving pieces (slightly larger than tortilla chips).

### To prepare the dip:

Open a can of fat-free refried beans and spoon them into a bowl. Top with shredded cheddar cheese and microwave for about 1 minute, or until the cheese is melted. Top with shredded lettuce, chopped tomatoes, salsa, plain yogurt, guacamole, tofu, or meat as desired. Use toasted pita and dip into bean mixture.

## Burrito

You can get really creative here!

**Figure 2.17** Serving properly cooked scrambled eggs.

### To prepare:

Fill a tortilla with your choice of fillings: chopped or diced vegetables; shredded or crumbled cheese; canned tuna, tofu, scrambled eggs, cooked chicken, beans; plain yogurt (instead of sour cream); or salsa. Roll up burrito-style and serve.

### Egg Burrito

Crack two eggs into a small bowl. Add a teaspoon of milk, shredded cheese and your choice of finely chopped veggies. Whip the mixture with a fork and then pour it into a pan sprayed with non-stick spray. Cook over medium heat, constantly stirring with a spatula to prevent sticking or overcooking, until firm.

Place the cooked eggs into a tortilla. Add any additional ingredients you like, such as beans, salsa, hot peppers, tomatoes, or plain yogurt, and fold over.

### Tuna Sandwich or Wrap

Sandwiches or wraps can also be made with cooked turkey, chicken breast, ham, roast beef, and cheese. Also, cooked beans can be pureed in a blender and used as a spread.

Drain a can of tuna packed in water and rinse. Season as desired (mix with mustard rather than mayonnaise). Add sliced tomato, cucumber, avocado, or cheese as desired. Serve on tortillas, whole-wheat bread, or toast; in pita pockets; or on salad. Have a few raw carrots or soy chips on the side.

**Figure 2.18** Preparing a wrap sandwich in a tortilla.

### MyPyramid Pasta Salad

Cook pasta (tri-colored is ideal) according to package directions. Drain and cool.

As the pasta is cooking, chop your choice of vegetables (carrots, cucumber, broccoli, tomatoes, mushrooms, onions, peppers), Do not add tomatoes to the entire dish if you are planning to store it; just sprinkle them on each serving. Add cooked shredded or cubed chicken, canned tuna, canned beans, or extra-firm tofu if desired.

Combine all ingredients with the cooled pasta. Toss with Italian salad dressing or balsamic vinegar and sprinkle with shaved almonds and dried cranberries or raisins, if desired.

**Figure 2.19** Pasta salad is a quick, easy, healthy way to get all your nutrients in one dish.

### Tossed Salad

Toss dark green lettuce with your choice of chopped vegetables: broccoli, carrots, cucumbers, tomatoes, cauliflower, onions, peppers, mushrooms, and so on. Add canned beans, cooked chicken, canned tuna, shredded cheese, or marinated tofu, if desired. Add a low-fat salad dressing and toss all ingredients. Top with raisins, dried cranberries, nuts, or soy nuts.

### Twice-Baked Potatoes

Pierce a potato several times with a fork (to allow steam to escape) and bake it in the oven at 400° F for 1 hour, or in the microwave (most microwaves will have a setting for them). To tell if it is done, pierce it with a fork, if the inside feels soft, it is ready.

Cut the potato in half and scoop out the pulp, leaving the potato skins intact and reserving them for stuffing. (Wear oven mitts to avoid getting burned!) Mash the potato pulp in a bowl using a fork or hand mixer, and add your choice of fillings: plain yogurt, shredded cheese, minced garlic, chopped veggies, canned beans, or cooked meat.

Put the potato mixture back into the potato skins, sprinkle with uncooked oatmeal or oat bran cereal and your choice of seasonings, and spray with nonstick spray. Bake again for 10–15 minutes, or broil in a toaster oven until the topping is lightly browned.

### Stuffed Tomato or Pepper

Preheat the over to 350° F.

Cut the top off a large, firm tomato or green bell pepper, scoop out the insides with a spoon, and place in a bowl. Be careful not to puncture the sides or the bottom and leave enough on the inside to support the shell.

In a small bowl, combine your choice of spices, minced veggies, shredded cheese, cooked lean ground meat, cooked chicken, tofu, canned beans, cooked brown rice, or soy crumbles.

Place the filling into the shell, top with dry oatmeal or oat bran cereal, and spray with nonstick spray. Bake in a baking dish for 15–20 minutes, or until the shell is tender. (You can also cook it in a microwave or toast it in a toaster oven; just watch closely to make sure it doesn't burn.)

### Outdoor Grilling

Outdoor grilling is a great way to cook a surprising array of foods (including fruits and vegetables) in a quick, easy, and healthy manner. Of course, most dorms do not allow grills, but many fraternity/sorority houses and apartments do. These include various-sized charcoal grills, small electric ones like the popular Foreman brand, and the large propane gas variety. Regardless, a seemingly endless and ever-increasing volume of recipes are available for grilling meats, vegetables, and just about anything else you can cook inside. When selecting meats for grilling, avoid those that are high in fats, such as sausage and pork or beef ribs.

### Stir-Frying

You don't need a wok to achieve the effects of stir-frying. Use any vegetables available (you can get very creative).

Spray a wok or frying pan with nonstick spray and place over medium-high to high heat. Add your choice of chopped vegetables; stir and cook until vegetables are crisp-tender. Keep in mind that some vegetables, such as carrots, green beans, and potatoes, take longer to cook than others, so those will need to be started before softer vegetables such as tomatoes, squash, and eggplant.

Add beans, extra-firm tofu, cooked chicken or beef, or canned tuna, if desired. Add stir-fry sauce and cook a bit longer to heat through.

Top with cashews or almonds and serve with toasted pitas or cooked brown rice.

**Figure 2.20** Grilling can be healthy and quick, inside or out.

**Want to know more?**
For more information on grilling techniques and recipes, go to the text website at http://webcom8 .grtxle.com/nutrition and click on the Chapters button. Select Chapter 2.

**Figure 2.21** Stir-frying can incorporate a variety of ingredients and is a quick way to cook lots of vegetables. It is also one of the most healthful types of frying because it requires the least amount of oil.

## Hummus

One 16-oz. can garbanzo beans, drained (reserve the liquid)

1 tsp. fresh lemon juice

1 clove garlic (or more, if you like)

Pinch of salt

Blend all ingredients in a blender or mash thoroughly with a fork, until smooth. Drizzle with a teaspoon or two of olive oil and some chopped fresh parsley, if desired; serve with tomato, avocado, and toasted pita, or use it as filling for a sandwich or wrap.

## The Old Standby PB&J or PB&B (healthy versions)

Peanut butter (all-natural or freshly ground)

Jelly or preserves, or sliced banana

Spread the peanut butter on a pita, a slice of whole-wheat bread, or a tortilla. Top with the jelly or banana and close the sandwich. Serve with raw carrots and celery or soy chips.

## Cold Day Special—Grilled Cheese

For this recipe, you can use regular, fat-free, or soy cheese in any flavor.

Spray a frying pan with nonstick spray. Place a slice of whole-wheat bread in the pan and top with sliced cheese. Add a thin slice of onion or tomato, if desired. Place the other bread slice on top. Cook over medium heat, flipping back and forth, until the bread is toasted and/or the cheese is melted. Serve with low-sodium tomato soup.

**Figure 2.22** When in doubt (or in a hurry), go for the old standby, peanut butter and jelly (the healthy version) or peanut butter and banana.

## Parfait

Vanilla yogurt (soy or low-fat)

Granola or any cereal

Nuts

Dried fruit (raisins, dried cranberries, dried apricots, etc.)

Sliced bananas or other fresh fruit

Layer the ingredients in a bowl or tall glass and serve.

## Cottage Cheese Surprise

Cottage cheese

Dried or fresh fruit, sliced or diced

Fruit preserves

Mix the ingredients and use as a topping for rice cakes, or add granola or other cereal to add a crunchy texture and serve in a bowl.

## Fast-Food Fool

To save time, buy ready-made burgers or veggie burgers in the frozen-food section or meat department.

Combine lean ground beef, ground turkey breast, or veggie protein crumbles with dry onion soup mix and water to enhance the flavor. Form into a patty and fry over medium heat or bake at 350° F until well done. (If you are using veggie burgers, cook according to package directions.) Top the finished burger with cheese and allow to melt, if desired.

Place the burger on a toasted whole-wheat burger bun or pita and top with ketchup, mustard, tomato, onion, or lettuce as desired. Serve with baked french fries.

## Chili

There are a lot of different ways to make chili, and if you are feeling ambitious you can search online for various options. Here is an easy version. Chili can also be made efficiently and in large quantity in a slow cooker.

Brown lean ground beef, ground turkey breast, or veggie crumbles in a frying pan or skillet. Add a chili seasoning packet and stir thoroughly. Add diced onions, bell peppers, spicy chile peppers, canned kidney or pinto beans (drained and rinsed), and chopped tomatoes, if desired.

Serve over brown rice or whole-wheat pasta; you can also serve as a topping for baked potatoes or stuffed in a whole-wheat pita pocket.

## Joanie's Macaroni and Cheese

You can make a lot of this dish and have plenty left over to mix with different things in order to get a variety of meals out of one recipe.

### Ingredients:

1-lb. box whole-wheat pasta (elbow macaroni, penne, or fusilli)

16 oz. (2 c.) shredded sharp cheddar cheese (low-fat, soy, or rice cheese)

1 1/2 Tbsp. margarine (Smart Balance or Benecol)

1 Tbsp. whole-wheat flour

1 c. skim milk

salt and pepper

1/4 c. Italian bread crumbs or oat bran cereal

### To prepare:

Preheat the oven to 350° F.

Cook the pasta according to package directions; drain and rinse with cold water.

While the pasta is cooking, make a basic cheese sauce. Begin by melting the margarine in a small pot over low heat. Stir in the flour and then slowly pour in the milk, stirring constantly. Add salt and pepper to taste. Bring to a boil over medium-low heat, then add 1 1/2 c. of the cheese; stir until hot and bubbly.

Spray a large baking dish with nonstick spray and pour the cooked pasta into it. Pour the cheese sauce over the pasta and mix evenly; add extra milk if needed to get desired consistency. Sprinkle with the remaining cheese and top with the bread crumbs or cereal. Bake for 30–45 minutes, or until the top is golden brown.

## Smoothies

Smoothies can be made in a variety of ways. You can make them with or without protein powders or meal replacements. If you do purchase these supplements, try a few to find the one you like. Most products supply recipes. You can also make a healthy smoothie without spending money on the powders. Instead, try using dried nonfat milk powder or powdered egg whites. All you need is a blender and some ice. You will need to experiment with the amount of milk and juice to get the consistency and flavor you like best. "Have fun" and "be creative" are the only rules for these recipes. To be creative, experiment with different juices, milks, and soy products. Try adding flax seed, wheat germ, flavorings such as vanilla, and whatever else you think you would like. Simply blend it all together until smooth.

## Basic Smoothie

10 oz. skim or soy milk

1 banana

Frozen fruit (use less ice)

Vanilla yogurt

Ice

Blend all ingredients. Add cinnamon, vanilla, or chocolate to taste (try chocolate soy milk). To increase calories, add peanut butter.

## Five-a-Day the Easy Way Smoothie

1/2 c. yogurt

1 c. fruit and/or vegetable juice

1/2–1 c. fresh, frozen, or canned fruit

Ice (if using fresh or canned fruit)

Blend all ingredients.

## Berry Smoothie

1 c. frozen berries (blackberries, strawberries, raspberries, blueberries, or a mix)

1 c. vanilla soy milk (or skim milk, plus vanilla extract to taste)

1/2 c. soy or vanilla yogurt

1 Tbsp. honey or sugar

Blend all ingredients. You can add a little more milk to thin the smoothie, if desired.

**Figure 2.23** Smoothies are a great way to combat the "I don't have time" excuse.

## < Here's Where You've Been

*The following topics were introduced in preceding chapters and are related to concepts we'll discuss in Chapter 3. Be certain that you're familiar with them before proceeding.*

- The basic nutrients are divided into different classes. (Chapter 1)
- You can obtain reliable or credible nutrition claims from reputable sources in various ways. (Chapter 1)
- Americans are becoming increasingly overweight, and diet composition, portion size, and consumer food choices are major contributing factors. (Chapter 1)
- The U.S. government has developed recommendations for optimizing nutrition to assist in planning diets through the Recommended Dietary Intakes and MyPyramid.gov. (Chapter 2)
- Healthy eating involves balance, variety, and moderation. (Chapter 2)

## Here's Where You're Going >

*The following topics and concepts are the ones we'll emphasize in Chapter 3.*

- Sugars and starches are a major source of calories in our diets.
- When consumed in a balanced diet, carbohydrates provide several benefits.
- Dietary fiber optimizes health and is a healthy carbohydrate.
- Excess sugar in our diets is a major health concern.
- The food industry has developed a number of sweeteners other than simple sugars that may help reduce the caloric content of certain foods.

## Real People, Real Choices

Petros Sampos is in his early thirties, and since graduating from college approximately ten years ago he has gained more than 30 pounds. He works for an investment firm in Dallas, where his typical workday involves sitting and staring at the computer screen. Petros recognizes that without some form of change in his diet or lifestyle, his weight problem will continue to worsen. As many of us are inclined to do, Petros is looking for some easy solutions to his predicament. One of his colleagues mentioned that she recently lost 20 pounds on a low-carb diet. In an article in *Men's Health*, Petros read that there are "good" and "bad" carbs. He then read somewhere else that carbs make you fat. After some research, he compiled a list of carbs that are thought to increase body fat. He also read something about the "glycemic index" of carbohydrates and that it is related to whether you will gain weight. It all sounded extremely complicated.

Petros decided that the best strategy for him would be to just lower his carbohydrate intake. This modification in his diet means that he is consuming more protein and fat than normal. In what represented a radical change for him, he eliminated potatoes, muffins, breads, pastas, and cereals from his diet. As he began to lose weight, he decided to exclude some fruits and vegetables that contain carbohydrates. After two weeks on his new diet he is doing rather well—he has lost about 8 pounds. In fact, along with this diet, he joined a gym to work out. However, Petros has begun to experience unwanted side effects. This low-carbohydrate diet makes him feel really tired, he has trouble concentrating, he is constipated, and his workouts have become difficult. He also feels as if he has no endurance. One of his best friends even commented that his breath smells odd. Frustrated and confused at this point, he wonders what to do. He has decided to seek the advice of an old college friend who is working on a graduate degree in human nutrition. What advice do you think she will give him? What would you do if you had a similar weight problem?

Petros's dilemma is not new to nutritionists. Both the number of and interest in low-carbohydrate diets have increased dramatically in the past decade. Every so often their popularity increases as a method of weight loss. Both "good carbs" and "bad carbs" are believed to exist—some that make you fat and others that do not. For the general public, one of the most misunderstood of all the nutrients is carbohydrates; the range of opinions and misinformation about them is widespread. They are demonized in many weight-loss programs, such as the Atkins Diet. One common myth about carbohydrates is that consumption of simple sugars causes certain behavioral problems in children. Other consumers believe that intake of excessive amounts of sugar can lead to diabetes. On the other side of this spectrum are many athletes who think carbohydrates are important in enhancing endurance.

**Figure 3.1** Photosynthesis. This illustration shows how glucose is produced in plants. It occurs through the biochemical reactions of water from the soil, carbon dioxide from the atmosphere, and energy from the sun. The reaction occurs in the chlorophyll-containing plant organelles called *chloroplasts.*

## Carbohydrates: A Diverse Class of Nutrients

Carbohydrates are a diverse class of nutrients, and each specific carbohydrate has unique health properties. The major function of carbohydrates is to supply energy or calories. Carbohydrates are produced by *photosynthesis* in plants. Photosynthesis is the process in which carbon dioxide from the atmosphere, water from the soil, and energy from the sun interact in a biochemical reaction in plant cells to produce the simplest of all carbohydrates, glucose (Figure 3.1). This process occurs with the assistance of the plant compound (pigment) chlorophyll. The energy from the sun is trapped chemically within the bonds of this sugar. Worldwide, carbohydrates are the most important source of energy and are a cheap source of calories. Many types of carbohydrates exist. Some carbohydrates provide little energy, but have other health benefits. Dietary fiber is a good example of this type of carbohydrate. Although it's not a source of high calories, it promotes gastrointestinal health and may prevent some diseases that are prevalent in Western cultures, such as colon cancer. Other carbohydrates, such as sugar, when consumed in excess have been linked to disease and obesity.

Simple sugar is a major source of carbohydrates in our diets today, though it is not the only one. Wheat is a major source of carbohydrates in North America and Europe. However, this is not the case in other parts of the world. For instance, in Asia, rice is a major source; in South America, corn; and in parts of Africa, cassava (Figure 3.2). Cassava is a shrub whose root is high in starch; this starch is often used to make tapioca. Table 3.1 (see page 74) lists the percentages of carbohydrate content of selected foods.

### Global Nutrition
*Sorghum—the Forgotten Grain*

Ever hear of the grain sorghum, sometimes called milo? Thousands of acres of this grain are grown in the Midwest every year, but few Americans have ever heard of it. In the U.S. it is most often used as an animal feed for livestock. However, in many

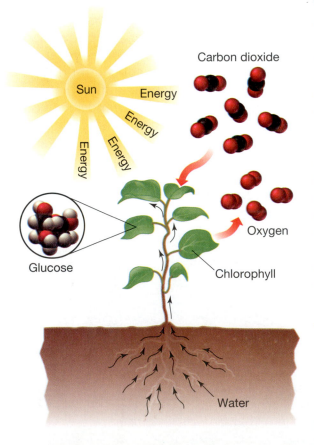

Sun
Energy
Energy
Energy
Energy

Carbon dioxide

Oxygen

Chlorophyll

Glucose

Water

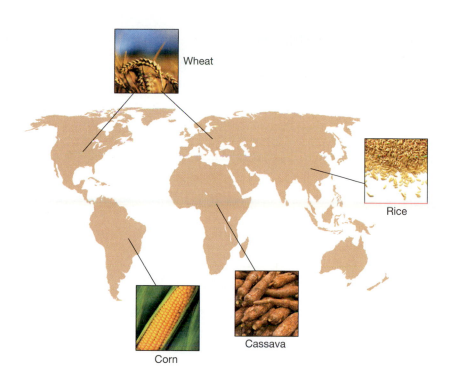

**Figure 3.2** The primary sources of carbohydrates in different parts of the world are rice, corn, wheat, and cassava. The map indicates where many of the world's sources of each are grown.

parts of the world, such as Africa and parts of Asia, sorghum is an important crop and is used in flours, snack foods and alcoholic beverages. It grows well in dry areas because it does not require much water and is therefore a very sustainable crop. There is increasing interest in sorghum in Western countries due to recent discoveries that it may have potential health benefits. Sorghum contains compounds similar to what is present in blueberries, which have strong antioxidant activities. In fact, the antioxidant level in sorghum is much higher than levels in most other grains, fruits and vegetables. Studies in animals reveal that it can lower blood cholesterol. It has been demonstrated to reduce cancer, particularly esophageal cancer. Furthermore, it can result in less weight gain when compared to other carbohydrates largely due to its inhibition of some digestive enzymes. We are likely to hear more about sorghum as part of a healthy diet in the future. ■

## How Do We Define a Carbohydrate?

Scientists coined the term *carbohydrate* based on its chemical composition. Only three elements compose carbohydrates: carbon, hydrogen, and oxygen. For every atom of carbon there is one molecule of water ($H_2O$). Literally, *carbohydrate* means "carbon with water." All carbohydrates supply approximately 4 kcal per gram of energy when digested. We must eat carbohydrates daily because our bodies store limited quantities of carbohydrate in the liver and muscle.

## Types of Carbohydrates

Carbohydrates are categorized as either simple or complex, based on how many sugar units (monosaccharides) compose the nutrients. For example, a carbohydrate with less than ten monosaccharide units is classified as simple; a carbohydrate with more than ten (all the way up to thousands) is classified as complex.

## Table 3.1    Carbohydrate in Selected Foods by Weight

| Food | Household Measure | Weight (g) | Amount of Carbohydrate (g) | (%) |
|------|-------------------|------------|----------------------------|-----|
| Apple, with peel | 1 apple | 138 | 19 | 14 |
| Banana | 1 banana | 118 | 27 | 23 |
| Butter | 1 Tbsp. | 15 | <0.1 | 0 |
| Cheddar cheese | 1 oz. | 28 | 1 | 0.04 |
| Corn oil | 1 tsp. | 14 | 0 | 0 |
| Ice cream | 1/2 c. | 66 | 16 | 24 |
| Lima beans, cooked | 1/2 c. | 85 | 20 | 24 |
| Milk, 2% | 1 c. | 244 | 11 | 4.5 |
| Orange juice | 1/2 c. | 124 | 13 | 11 |
| Peanuts, roasted | 1/2 c. | 37 | 8 | 22 |
| Peanut butter, smooth | 1 Tbsp. | 16 | 3 | 19 |
| Rice, cooked | 1/2 c. | 79 | 22 | 28 |
| Spaghetti noodles | 1/2 c. | 65 | 20 | 31 |
| Tuna, water packed | 2 oz. | 57 | 0 | 0 |
| Table sugar | 1 tsp. | 4 | 4 | 100 |
| White bread | 1 slice | 25 | 13 | 52 |

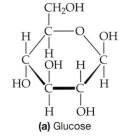

(a) Glucose

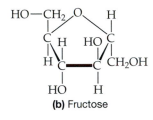

(b) Fructose

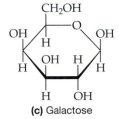

(c) Galactose

**Figure 3.3** Chemical structures of the three basic monosaccharides: glucose, fructose, and galactose.

### Simple Sugars

**Monosaccharides.** *Monosaccharides* are single, simple sugars. They consist of one basic chemical ring (see Figure 3.3). There are three monosaccharides; glucose, fructose, and galactose.

Biologically, the most important and common form of monosaccharides is **glucose**. Glucose is the main source of energy for the body and circulates in the blood. It is often referred to as *blood sugar*. Glucose units, when linked together, make up the more complex carbohydrates such as starches and fibers.

**Fructose** is the sugar found abundantly in fruit, honey, and vegetables such as beets, sweet potatoes, parsnips, and onions. **High-fructose corn syrup** is made from cornstarch and is converted to fructose using enzymes through food processing. In essence, the cornstarch is made into a syrup that is about half fructose and half glucose. You can find high-fructose corn syrup in sodas, desserts, low-fat yogurt, English muffins, ketchup, and other baked goods. It has become a concern for health professionals and consumer interest groups in that its prevalence in our diets is believed to contribute toward obesity by providing excess calories. Because fructose can increase blood lipids, it may be harmful to heart health.

**Galactose** is a third type of monosaccharide that is consumed as a part of the disaccharide lactose found in milk. Galactose rarely exists by itself. It may also be found as a type of fiber component of fruit (pectin). Fruits such as bananas, berries, and cherries are good sources. Vegetables such as broccoli, cabbage, cauliflower, cucumber, mushrooms, pumpkin, and spinach have galactose.

**Disaccharides.** *Disaccharides* are composed of two monosaccharides linked together by a chemical bond. One disaccharide is **sucrose**, which is commonly known as table sugar and is composed of one glucose molecule and one fructose

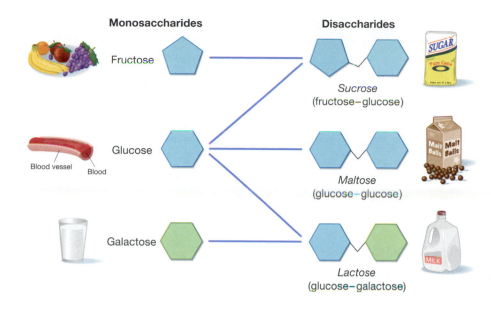

**Monosaccharides**                                    **Disaccharides**

Fructose

Glucose

Galactose

*Sucrose*
(fructose–glucose)

*Maltose*
(glucose–glucose)

*Lactose*
(glucose–galactose)

Blood vessel   Blood

**Figure 3.4** The disaccharides are each composed of two monosaccharides as shown. Sucrose, or table sugar, is composed of glucose and fructose. Maltose is two glucose molecules linked together. Lactose, or milk sugar, is composed of glucose and galactose.

molecule (Figure 3.4). Sucrose comprises 25 percent of the total caloric intake of Western diets, or 500 calories per day of a 2,000-calorie diet!

Another disaccharide is **lactose**, or milk sugar (Figure 3.4), which is composed of glucose and galactose. Only mammals (including humans) produce lactose in mother's milk; it is a major source of calories for young animals and infants. Lactose has other benefits, such as aiding in the absorption of the mineral calcium and favoring the growth of beneficial intestinal bacteria.

**Maltose** (Figure 3.4) is a disaccharide that is composed of two glucose units. Maltose is rather mysterious. In plants, it is found for only a brief time in germinating seeds. In animals, it is found when starches are broken down during digestion. The major source of this sugar in our diets may be malted candies or shakes; it can also be found in malt liquors and beer.

### ■ Myths and Legends

*Is honey healthier for you than table sugar?*

Common, refined table sugar or sucrose is a disaccharide composed of glucose and fructose. Honey is composed of the same two monosaccharides, but they are not bonded together as in the case of sucrose. Fructose is sweeter than glucose and thus is often used to sweeten foods. However, fructose is not converted to energy as efficiently as glucose; this slower metabolic conversion means it is not as likely to raise blood glucose or insulin as readily. Because of this and the notion that honey is natural, many believe it is a healthier form of sweetener than table sugar. Honey, however, is a simple sugar and therefore is not any healthier for you than table sugar. Honey may also accelerate tooth decay due to its sticky nature and adherence to the enamel of teeth. It has 21 kcal per teaspoon compared to 17 kcal for table sugar. One other aspect of honey that's important for parents and child caregivers to know is that it should never be given to infants less than 1 year old. Because it is made by bees, it can contain the spores of the bacterium *Clostridium botulinum*; infants have much less acid in their stomachs, so these spores can germinate and lead to botulism, which is a deadly form of food-borne illness. ■

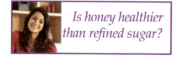
*Is honey healthier than refined sugar?*

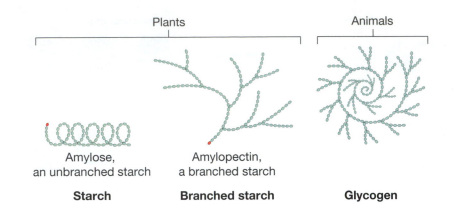

**Figure 3.5** Illustrations of complex carbohydrates from plants (starch) and animals (glycogen). Notice that animal starch is much more highly branched than starch from plants.

Plants

Animals

Amylose,
an unbranched starch

Amylopectin,
a branched starch

**Starch**

**Branched starch**

**Glycogen**

## Complex Carbohydrates

Complex carbohydrates include **polysaccharides** and **dietary fiber**. Polysaccharides are carbohydrates composed of a chain with thousands of glucose molecules linked together. Dietary fiber is composed of repeating units of glucose and other monosaccharides that cannot be digested by human enzymes and thus can't be absorbed and used by body cells.

**Starch** is the storage form of carbohydrate found in plants. Generally starches are either a long, straight chain or branched (Figure 3.5). Both are composed of repeating glucose units. Potatoes and pasta contain appreciable levels of starch. In muscle, starch is also present and is similar to plant starch, but it is more highly branched than the branched starch found in plants. **Glycogen** is the storage form of starch found in the liver and muscle of animals. The body can use glycogen for energy on a carbohydrate-restricted diet or between meals. In fact, the average human stores only approximately 2,000 calories as glycogen. Therefore, glycogen can be depleted within less than a day by fasting, carbohydrate restriction, or exercise. Glycogen is not a major source of dietary carbohydrate and is more important in muscle biochemistry and metabolism.

**Before you go on . . .**

1. Explain the major difference between monosaccharides and disaccharides.
2. What sugars are found only in milk and its products?
3. Define *starch* and *glycogen*.

# What Are the Primary Sources of Carbohydrates?

In the last century, total intake of carbohydrates has declined. Today, they provide about half of the energy in our diets, whereas they once provided as much as 75 percent. On the other hand, from the early 1900s until the 1970s sucrose, or table sugar, intake increased from 12 percent to 25 percent of the total calories in our diets. The average American now consumes more than 45 pounds of sucrose per year. While overall intake of sucrose has declined since the 1970s, consumption of high-fructose corn syrup has increased. Some estimates indicate that 16 percent of our calories now come from fructose.

Where do we get carbohydrates in our diet and what foods contain simple sugars, starches, and fiber? Carbohydrates are naturally present in almost all plant food—fruits, vegetables, grains, legumes—and in milk. Carbohydrates, mostly in the form of simple sugars, are added to a wide variety of foods, some which may surprise you: ketchup, low-fat salad dressing, and tomato sauce. What foods are high in sucrose? Obvious sources of sucrose are table sugar, cakes, cookies, pastries, certain breakfast cereals, and ice cream. Simple carbohydrates such as high-fructose corn syrup and sucrose have been added to low-fat foods to enhance taste. In many ways, doing so has substituted one problem (our high-fat diets) for another problem (overconsumption of simple sugars) (Figure 3.6).

Recommended carbohydrate intake is 45–65 percent of total calories according to the DRIs. It may also be useful to consider the recommendation for carbohydrate in terms of grams. The minimum carbohydrate intake to spare protein and avoid ketosis is about 130 g/day. For a 2,000-calorie diet, about 250–300 g of carbohydrate would mean that 50–60 percent of calories are provided by carbohydrates.

Breads, pastas, potatoes, cassava, vegetables, and legumes are foods that are high in starches. These are examples of complex carbohydrates that are a good source of energy.

Eating whole grains, such as whole-wheat bread or cereal (those not refined by milling), is important for health because the kernels of grains normally lost in processing add many nutrients (including fiber). The germ of a grain kernel (the innermost part of the kernel) is rich in protein, oils, vitamins and minerals (Figure 3.7). The *endosperm* is the middle portion of the kernel; it is very high in starch. The bran part of the grain is high in dietary fiber; the outer husk is not edible. When whole grains of wheat are milled in the production of white flour, the outer husk and bran layer, and even part of the germ layer, are removed, making the product much lower in dietary fiber and other nutrients. The end product is white flour which is high in starch. White bread is typically made from white flour and is thus a good source of starch but nutritionally inferior to whole-wheat bread. Whole-wheat flour is a better source because the kernels have not undergone the same extensive milling process. Bread made with whole-wheat flour is high not only in starch, but also in dietary fiber. Although both wheat and whole-wheat breads are enriched with nutrients, whole-wheat breads have more fiber and other nutrients that white enriched bread lacks. As noted later in this chapter, fiber can help reduce heart disease and colon cancer, among other health benefits.

If you wish to obtain more complex carbohydrates in your diet, including fiber, follow these simple rules:

- When possible, use bread made from whole grains instead of white flour. Be sure to look for "whole grain" on the label.
- Choose high-fiber cereals that have little or no sucrose added (read the label).

### Regular Ranch Salad Dressing

## Nutrition Facts
Serving Size 2 tbsp (29.0 g)

**Amount Per Serving**

**Calories** 148   Calories from Fat 140

|  | % Daily Value* |
|---|---|
| **Total Fat** 15.6g | **24%** |
| Saturated Fat 2.4g | **12%** |
| **Cholesterol** 8mg | **3%** |
| **Sodium** 287mg | **12%** |
| **Total Carbohydrates** 1.3g | **0%** |
| Dietary Fiber 0.1g | **0%** |
| Sugars 1.2g | |
| **Protein** 0.4g | |
| Vitamin A | 0% |
| Vitamin C | 0% |
| Calcium | 1% |
| Iron | 0% |

**Nutritional Units** 4
*Percent Daily Values are based on a 2,000 calorie diet. Your daily values may be higher or lower depending on your calorie needs.

### Fat-Free Ranch Dressing

## Nutrition Facts
Serving Size 2 tbsp (35.0 g)

**Amount Per Serving**

**Calories** 48      Calories from Fat 3

|  | % Daily Value* |
|---|---|
| **Total Fat** 0.4g | **1%** |
| Saturated Fat 0.1g | **0%** |
| **Cholesterol** 0mg | **0%** |
| **Sodium** 354mg | **15%** |
| **Total Carbohydrates** 10.7g | **4%** |
| Dietary Fiber 0.2g | **1%** |
| Sugars 2.1g | |
| **Protein** 0.2g | |
| Vitamin A | 0% |
| Vitamin C | 0% |
| Calcium | 1% |
| Iron | 0% |

**Nutritional Units** 1
*Percent Daily Values are ` ased on a 2,000 calorie diet. Your daily values may be higher or lower depending on your calorie needs.

**Figure 3.6** Two food labels: One from a regular ranch salad dressing and the second from fat-free ranch dressing. Note that the total carbohydrates in the fat-free salad dressing is 10.7 g and in the regular dressing, 1.3 g. Have you ever tried the fat-free version? If so, did you notice a significant difference in the taste?

**Figure 3.7** A kernel of grain showing its various components. There are three main parts of a kernel: germ, bran, and endosperm.

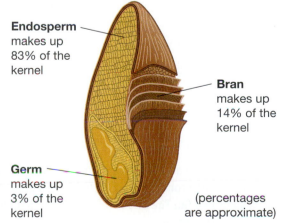

**Wheat Kernel**

**Endosperm** makes up 83% of the kernel

**Bran** makes up 14% of the kernel

**Germ** makes up 3% of the kernel

(percentages are approximate)

**Figure 3.8** Whole-grain stamps that identify products at two levels of whole grain content.

*Source:* Whole Grain Stamps are a trademark of Oldways Preservation Trust and the Whole Grains Council. Reprinted with permission.

- Use brown rice instead of white rice.
- In recipes, use more beans such as navy, kidney, black, or pinto beans. These beans can also be used as a meat substitute.
- Keep the edible peels on your fruits and vegetables, because they are high in dietary fiber.
- Increase your intake of fresh vegetables and fruits.

To lower your intake of simple carbohydrates, follow these suggestions:

- Limit your intake of soda and other sugared drinks such as sports beverages, fruit punch, and other fruit drinks.
- Use canned fruits that are packed in natural juices; better yet, use fresh or frozen fruits for desserts and to sweeten baked goods such as pancakes and waffles, instead of syrup.
- Limit your intake of ice cream, high-sugar breakfast cereals, candy, and desserts.
- Decrease the use of added sugars, honey, and syrups.

### ■ Myths and Legends

*Is there a problem with wheat?*

In the United States, wheat, rye and barley are some of the most widely consumed grains. Cereals made from these grains provide fiber, calories, and some protein. However, some people have an intolerance to the protein in these grains called gluten. Sometimes this disorder is called *celiac disease.* Celiac disease is a genetic condition that causes a range of gastrointestinal problems from cramps and diarrhea to an inability to absorb nutrients. The treatment is to eliminate all wheat products and anything that contains gluten. This is not as easy as it sounds. Think of all the food made with wheat: bread, cereals, artificial coffee creamers (in some cases), crackers, pasta, cookies, and even soy sauce, just to name a few.

Until recently, celiac disease was considered to be relatively uncommon. Previous U.S. figures suggested that it affected one in 6,000 persons. However, population studies published in the past decade suggest a much higher prevalence, particularly in persons of European ancestry. Approximately 1 in 100 to 200 people in the U.S. suffer from celiac disease. Why the increase in prevalence? One explanation is that physicians may be more familiar with this condition and tests to screen for it are more advanced; thus, previously undiagnosed diarrhea and abdominal discomfort conditions are now being diagnosed. It has

**Nutrition Facts**

Serving Size 33g
Servings Per Container about 14

| Amount Per Serving | |
|---|---|
| **Calories** 150   Calories from Fat 70 | |

| | % Daily Value* |
|---|---|
| **Total Fat** 8g | **12%** |
| Saturated Fat 2.5g | **13%** |
| Trans Fat 0g | |
| **Cholesterol** 0mg | **0%** |
| **Sodium** 110mg | **5%** |
| **Total Carbohydrate** 22g | **7%** |
| Dietary Fiber 2g | **8%** |
| Sugars 10g | |
| **Protein** 2g | |

| | |
|---|---|
| Vitamin A | **0%** |
| Vitamin C | **0%** |
| Calcium | **0%** |
| Iron | **4%** |

*Percent Daily Values are based on a 2,000 calorie diet. Your daily values may be higher or lower depending on your calorie needs:

| | Calories: | 2,000 | 2,500 |
|---|---|---|---|
| Total Fat | Less than | 65g | 80g |
| Sat Fat | Less than | 20g | 25g |
| Cholest | Less than | 300mg | 300mg |
| Sodium | Less than | 2,400mg | 2,400mg |
| Total Carb | | 300g | 375g |
| Fiber | | 25g | 30g |

**(a)**

**Nutrition Facts**

Serving Size 1 Bar (35g)
Servings Per Container about 14

| Amount Per Serving | |
|---|---|
| **Calories** 140   Calories from Fat 45 | |

| | % Daily Value* |
|---|---|
| **Total Fat** 5g | **8%** |
| Saturated Fat 0.5g | **3%** |
| Trans Fat 0g | |
| **Cholesterol** 0mg | **0%** |
| **Sodium** 105mg | **4%** |
| **Potassium** 100mg | **3%** |
| **Total Carbohydrate** 20g | **7%** |
| Dietary Fiber 4g | **14%** |
| Soluble Fiber 1g | |
| Insoluble Fiber 3g | |
| Sugars 5g | |
| **Protein** 6g | |

| | |
|---|---|
| Vitamin A | **0%** |
| Vitamin C | **0%** |
| Calcium | **0%** |
| Iron | **6%** |

*Percent Daily Values are based on a 2,000 calorie diet. Your daily values may be higher or lower depending on your calorie needs.

**(b)**

**Figure 3.9** Are all whole-grain products healthier for you? Notice that the product in part (a) has whole grain, but also contains saturated fat. The one in (b) is healthier because of the lower saturated fat content.

also been suggested the increasing number of diagnosed cases could be due to the way grains are grown and processed or due to the fact that gluten is used more frequently as a filler in processed foods and medicines.

Still others suggest that the growing number of people who are saying they are "gluten sensitive" without an official diagnosis may make the growth in diagnosed cases appear larger than it is. Because the gluten-free diet dictates that you stay away from many fatty, fried, and pre-packaged foods, it has caught on in Hollywood and with the media as a fad diet. The increased popularity of a gluten-free diet has led to a greater variety of gluten-free products on the market, but many are just as processed as the foods they replace. According to a report from the market-research group Packaged Facts, sales of gluten-free products in the United States have grown by an average of 28 percent over the past five years. This is good news for true celiac patients who in the past had a difficult time finding gluten-free products and therefore had to make all of their food from scratch. Most people who stick to the gluten-free diet report that they "feel" better doing so, but this is strictly anecdotal and may be due to an increased consumption of fruits and vegetables. Whatever the cause, gluten-free eating has caught on in the mainstream and is no longer just for celiacs. ■

GLUTEN FREE

**Before you go on . . .**

1. What percentage of your calories should come from carbohydrates, according to the DRIs?
2. List some practical ways to increase complex carbohydrates in your diet.
3. What is a whole-grain food, and why is whole grain important for our diets?
4. What is the most common type of carbohydrate we consume?

## The Dietary Role of Carbohydrates

As we've discussed, carbohydrates are an important part of a healthy balanced diet. They provide the body with energy and vital nutrients and perform many other important functions. Most important is that our brain function uses carbohydrates as an energy source. In addition to supplying energy, carbohydrates spare protein, prevent ketosis, enhance the sweetness and flavor of foods, and regulate blood glucose levels. We will discuss each of these functions separately as follows. We will also discuss a concept called the glycemic index, defined below.

### Dietary Energy

We have already mentioned that half of the calories we consume are in the form of carbohydrates. They are an easily digestible form of energy. Most carbohydrates end up in the form of glucose. One gram of carbohydrate supplies 4 kcal per gram. The speed with which we obtain energy from carbohydrates depends on how quickly they are digested. Simple sugars are digested and absorbed quickly to provide a quick source of energy. On the other hand, more slowly digested and absorbed carbohydrates may be better when a more sustained level of energy is needed to get through the day and while we sleep.

**APPLICATION TIP**

The simplest way to cut sugar intake is not to consume regular sodas and other sugar-sweetened drinks. These are the largest source of simple sugars in our diet.

*Why do we need carbohydrates?*

## Protein Sparing

A diet low in carbohydrates causes the body to obtain energy from other sources. If carbohydrates are restricted, the body begins to use protein (muscle protein) as a source of calories. This is not an ideal situation, as we need protein for growth and maintenance of muscle and organs and to maintain an adequate immune system (which we'll discuss in Chapter 5). If sufficient carbohydrates are available, then the protein and amino acids will be spared for use in growth and repair. However, if carbohydrate intake is insufficient, then protein will be broken down to maintain blood glucose levels. This process is called **gluconeogenesis**, which is the synthesis of new glucose from noncarbohydrate sources. Having sufficient dietary carbohydrates is critical for maintaining muscle mass.

## Preventing Ketosis

Another source of calories for energy is stored fat. Fat, carbohydrates, and protein can be broken down into a compound called *acetyl CoA*. From this point, acetyl CoA can be further broken down to obtain energy. However, to fully break fats down, we need a chemical from carbohydrates called *oxaloacetate*. Without carbohydrates, oxaloacetate is not present and the liver responds by making fats into ketone bodies. **Ketone bodies** are acidic fat derivatives that arise from the incomplete breakdown of fat. Although they can be a source of energy for some cells in the body, high levels can damage the acid-base balance of the blood, alter kidney function, and lead to dehydration. This condition is called *ketosis*. Although the brain and nervous system prefer to use glucose as an energy source, they can adapt to using ketones if not enough glucose is available. However, people who do not have sufficient carbohydrates in their diets may show signs of compromised mental function, such as dizziness and even fainting, and their breath may smell fruity or foul because of the natural odor of ketone bodies.

## Regulating Blood Glucose Levels

The body has mechanisms to maintain a stable level of glucose in the blood. Once glucose is absorbed in the bloodstream from the small intestine, it travels to the liver. It will subsequently be re-released into the bloodstream, where other tissues can use it as a source of energy. If it is not used as a source of energy, the body may convert it to glycogen or fat.

When sugar is consumed and enters the bloodstream, a hormone called **insulin** is released from the pancreas. Insulin allows glucose to enter cells and be used for energy. This process results in a decrease of glucose in the blood. Insulin also has other functions. For example, it promotes protein synthesis and the conversion of extra glucose to glycogen and fat. When you have not eaten for three hours and as blood glucose begins to fall, two other hormones are released to raise it:

- glucagon
- epinephrine (adrenalin)

Glucagon is produced by the pancreas; epinephrine is produced by the adrenal glands (which are located on your kidneys). Remember that glucose is stored as glycogen in the liver. Epinephrine and glucagon cause the glucose from the liver glycogen to be released into the blood. In essence, insulin, glucagon, and epinephrine work together to keep your blood glucose levels in the normal range (Figure 3.10).

If you haven't eaten for a few hours and then you drink a soda or eat a candy bar, both of which are high in simple sugars, the quick digestion and absorption of glucose can cause a very large surge of blood sugar and insulin. This surge of insulin causes a rapid drop in blood glucose levels as the glucose is taken up in the cells. In fact, levels can drop very quickly and to such a low point that it can make you feel dizzy or even drowsy. It is known to happen to students who skip a meal and have a cookie or candy bar prior to class. If you consume a snack that includes a complex carbohydrate, or a mixed meal that contains fat and protein, the sugars will take longer to break down and will be released into the blood much more slowly. This slower release of glucose prevents a surge in insulin levels and the resulting rapid drop in blood glucose levels. This does not happen in everyone, and apparently some individuals are more sensitive to this reaction than others.

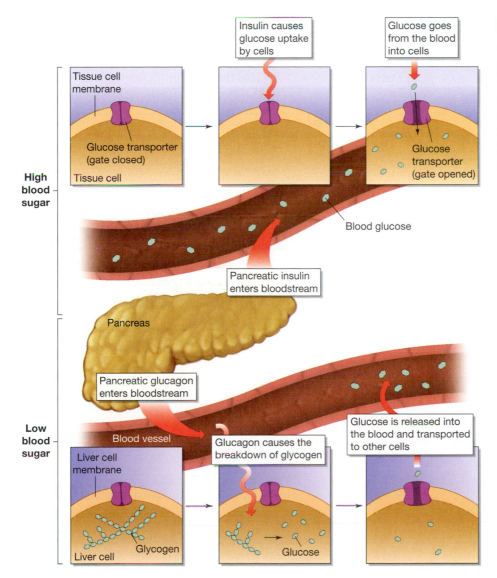

**Figure 3.10** This illustration demonstrates how insulin and glucagon work to regulate blood glucose levels within normal limits. Insulin lowers blood glucose, and glucagon raises blood glucose. Both hormones are produced by the pancreas.

## Flavoring and Sweetening Foods

Beyond our requirement for carbohydrate as a nutrient, the sweetener aspect adds flavor and enjoyment to our diets. Substances added to foods to enhance sweetness may be classified as either **nutritive** or **nonnutritive sweeteners**. **Nutritive sweeteners** can be digested and yield calories. Nonnutritive sweeteners are sometimes referred to as alternative sweeteners or sugar substitutes. They are synthetic and do not provide food energy.

Substances such as fructose and sucrose are nutritive sweeteners. The intensity of the sweetness varies depending on the type of sugar (see Table 3.2 for the sweetness of sugars and sugar alternatives). For example, fructose is the sweetest simple sugar and lactose is the least sweet. Refined or processed sweeteners are also used; examples include molasses and high-fructose corn syrup. We described high-fructose corn syrup earlier in this chapter; it is one and a half times as sweet as sucrose, or table sugar. Molasses is a by-product of refined sugarcane or sugar beets that contains significantly higher levels of the minerals iron and calcium compared to other sweeteners.

*Sugar alcohols* are either natural or derived from industrial processes. Sorbitol, mannitol, and xylitol are examples. These sweeteners are not digested to the same

## Table 3.2    Sweetness of Sugars and Sugar Alternatives

| Type of Sweetener | Relative Sweetness to Sucrose | Typical Sources |
|---|---|---|
| **Sugars** | | |
| Lactose | 0.2 | Dairy |
| Maltose | 0.4 | Sprouted seeds |
| Glucose | 0.7 | Corn syrup |
| Sucrose | 1.0 | Table sugar |
| Fructose | 1.7 | Fruit, honey, soft drinks |
| **Sugar alcohols** | | |
| Sorbitol | 0.6 | Dietetic candies, sugarless gum, frozen desserts, baked goods |
| Mannitol | 0.7 | Dietetic candies, chocolate-flavored coating agents for ice cream and confections |
| Xylitol | 0.9 | Sugarless gums, hard candies, throat lozenges, toothpaste |
| **Natural sweetener** | | |
| Stevia | 30 | Desserts, powdered sweeteners, liquids |
| **Artificial sweeteners** | | |
| Aspartame (Nutrasweet or Equal) | 200 | Diet soft drinks and fruit drinks, powdered sweeteners |
| Acesulfame-K (Sunette) | 150–200 | Chewing gums, desserts, alcoholic beverages, syrups, candies, sauces, yogurt |
| Saccharin (Sweet' n Low) | 500 | Diet soft drinks |
| Sucralose (Splenda) | 600 | Soft drinks, baked goods |

extent as the other simple sugars; they are not as sweet as sucrose, so they are less likely to cause dental caries. Excess intake of these sweeteners can lead to diarrhea and abdominal cramps, as they pass undigested through the intestines. However, they can be metabolized and yield fewer calories. Sorbitol supplies 2.6 kcal per gram, xylitol 2.4 kcal per gram, and mannitol 1.6 kcal per gram. This compares to 4 kcal per gram for sugars. You can find sorbitol in candies, frozen deserts, and baked goods. Xylitol is found in similar foods, but also in mouthwashes and toothpaste. Mannitol is found in candies and the chocolate-flavored coating agent some kids (and adults) want on their ice cream.

Artificial or nonnutritive sweeteners are now quite prevalent in our food supply. Aspartame, acesulfame-K, saccharin, and sucralose are examples. These compounds are much sweeter than natural sugars or sugar alcohols. Many diet sodas use these sweeteners. Also manufacturers often combine nonnutritive sweeteners in their products.

## Glycemic Response

No carbohydrates are really "bad" or "good" for you; carbohydrates simply have different effects on blood sugar levels and therefore on insulin release. This difference is referred to as the **glycemic index**, which measures how fast blood glucose levels increase when a person ingests a particular food, compared to ingestion of glucose. The glycemic index is appropriate only when eating the single food item itself on an empty stomach. This standard is also where the notion of "good carbs" and "bad carbs" comes from. "Good carbs" do not increase body fat, and "bad carbs" do, according to this notion.

The glycemic index has recently been of interest to both health professionals and consumers because of the belief that foods with a high glycemic index have a greater ability to cause weight gain. Therefore, many diet plans have suggested consuming foods with a low glycemic index (good carbs) and avoiding foods with a high glycemic index (bad carbs). As yet, not enough long-term studies have been conducted to determine whether the glycemic index will be a useful weight-loss tool. However, many consumers appear to be keenly interested in learning about the glycemic index of particular foods. The index is really being misused, as it was designed for single food items. When these items are consumed in the form of a meal or mixed with other foods, the glycemic index may not be that accurate. People who choose foods with a lower glycemic index may be cutting excess calories by eliminating high-glycemic-index foods and not replacing them with other foods, thus lowering calories and causing weight loss. Some common foods and their glycemic index are presented in Table 3.3. A glycemic index of 70 or greater is considered high; 56–69 medium; below 55 low.

Another drawback of the glycemic index is that it is based on the consumption of 50 g of the food item. The

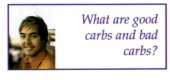

*What are good carbs and bad carbs?*

| Table 3.3 | Glycemic Index of Selected Food Items |
|---|---|
| **Food** | **Glycemic Index** |
| Maltose | 105 |
| Dates | 103 |
| Glucose | 100 |
| Boiled white potato | 85 |
| Cornflakes | 83 |
| Doughnut | 76 |
| Graham crackers | 74 |
| Soda | 72 |
| Corn chips | 72 |
| Watermelon | 72 |
| White bread | 70 |
| Grape-Nuts | 67 |
| Wheat Thins crackers | 67 |
| Raisins | 64 |
| Table sugar | 64 |
| Oatmeal cookies | 57 |
| Banana | 56 |
| Potato chips | 56 |
| All-Bran cereal | 51 |
| Carrots | 47 |
| Orange juice | 46 |
| Grapes | 46 |
| Baked beans | 44 |
| Spaghetti | 44 |
| Orange | 43 |
| Apple | 38 |
| Skim milk | 32 |
| Whole milk | 30 |
| Grapefruit | 25 |
| Plain yogurt | 14 |

Note: These are values for simple food items consumed on an empty stomach and not part of a mixed meal, which gives different results.

*glycemic load* is a mathematical tool used to account for the total carbohydrate in a food to begin with. If you use broccoli to determine the glycemic index, you will need several cups to get the 50 g needed for the test. However, when we consume a serving of broccoli (half a cup), the glycemic load is much lower than when we consume the 50 g needed for the test.

> ### Before you go on . . .
> 1. What do we mean when we say that carbohydrate "spares" protein?
> 2. What is the cause of ketosis?
> 3. If you skip breakfast, go to class, and then snack on a candy bar and soda after class, you may feel dizzy and nervous. What causes this to happen in some people?

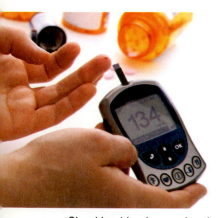

Checking blood sugar levels is important to properly manage diabetes and avoid complications of the disease.

## Diabetes Mellitus

About 25 million Americans (almost one-tenth of the total population) are now afflicted with diabetes mellitus. **Diabetes mellitus** is the inability of the body to regulate blood glucose levels within normal limits. Under normal conditions, after a meal the pancreas releases insulin as glucose is absorbed into the blood. The insulin allows the body's cells to take up the glucose and use it, which brings glucose in the blood down to normal levels. In diabetes, the ability of the body's cells to take up glucose and use it for energy is impaired, which can cause blood glucose levels to be elevated even when the person has not eaten for several hours. This condition is called **hyperglycemia**, which means an elevated blood glucose level. Hyperglycemia can lead to a variety of problems. First, glucose spills over into the urine; when this occurs, water is pulled from the blood to make urine to excrete the glucose. This water loss results in intense thirst and frequent urination. Often, persistent thirst and excessive urination are the first signs of one type of diabetes. Because the body must obtain energy from somewhere other than glucose, the body starts to rely on fat. However, as noted earlier, fat cannot be fully metabolized without the presence of carbohydrates. The result is the production of ketones. Ketones have a sweet and fruity odor to them, so people with diabetes often have a fruity smell to their breath. Ketosis and acidosis are the result. **Acidosis** is the buildup of acids in body fluids such as blood. People who develop acidosis and ketosis become drowsy and lethargic, may feel nauseated, and have rapid breathing. In addition to fat, the body can break down proteins for energy; this increases the demands on the kidney through the increased excretion of nitrogen. If protein breakdown continues, muscle wasting (atrophy) may occur.

People with diabetes are also at an increased risk for coronary heart disease (due to elevated blood lipid levels), kidney disease, high blood pressure, and damage to the eyes and blood vessels. The narrowing of the blood vessels that supply the arms, hands, legs, and feet is much higher in diabetics and is the leading cause of non-accident-caused amputations of the limbs. People with more advanced stages of diabetes mellitus also develop nerve damage due to the elevated levels of glucose in their bodies. The excess glucose needs to go somewhere, and in these more severe cases it clumps to nerve endings, where it forms a hard substance. These deposits interfere with nerve transmission. People with diabetes can also experience dizziness, which results from low levels of blood glucose.

Despite some beliefs, excess sugar intake does *not* cause diabetes mellitus. Several types of diabetes mellitus exist, and their causes are complex. Some variations may be caused by genetic predisposition; others may be related to lifestyle factors. Next we discuss the various forms of diabetes.

## Forms of Diabetes

### Type 1 Diabetes

**Type 1 diabetes**, formerly known as juvenile-onset diabetes or *insulin-dependent diabetes mellitus (IDDM),* is most often diagnosed in children or adolescents. It constitutes about 10 percent of all cases of diabetes mellitus. However, adults may develop this form as well. Type 1 diabetes occurs when the pancreas is unable to produce insulin; it is thought to be an autoimmune disease. An autoimmune disease is one in which the body begins to see its own organs and proteins as foreign, and the immune system attacks its own organs and tissues. The condition develops suddenly and the person loses weight. The patient experiences muscle wasting due to the fact that muscle protein is being broken down to form glucose. Lifelong insulin injections or use of an insulin pump are the usual treatment, along with a carbohydrate-controlled diet to help regulate blood glucose levels and insulin requirements.

### Type 2 Diabetes

**Type 2 diabetes**, formerly known as adult-onset diabetes or *non-insulin-dependent diabetes mellitus (NIDDM),* accounts for more than 90 percent of all cases of diabetes mellitus. In Type 2 diabetes, the individual may be able to produce insulin, even too much, but the insulin does not appear to function; sometimes the term *insulin resistant* is applied to these individuals. People with Type 2 diabetes are typically older than age 40 and overweight or obese when diagnosed. However, many overweight adolescents are now being diagnosed as well, and even children as young as 3 years old. The increase in Type 2 diabetes has been linked with an increase in obesity for people of all ages. This type of diabetes also appears to have a genetic link, so obesity and overweight factors alone may not be totally responsible. Diet and exercise are the first line of treatment, but oral glucose-lowering drugs and insulin may be prescribed. A loss of 5–7 percent of body weight often improves insulin function dramatically. That's only a 10- to 14-lb. weight loss for a 200-lb. individual.

The percentage of a population that develops diabetes varies for different ethnic groups. African Americans, especially women, are twice as likely to develop Type 2 diabetes as non-Hispanic whites. Hispanics also have a much higher risk for diabetes compared to whites (Figure 3.11). Twenty-five percent of African Americans between ages 65 and 74 have diabetes; this group also experiences a higher incidence of complications from diabetes. Researchers also believe that African American children may be at increased risk for Type 2 diabetes due to genetic factors. If you want to know your future risk of diabetes, take the test offered at http://ndep.nih.gov/ddi/resources/risktest.pdf, sponsored by the Centers for Disease Control.

### Gestational Diabetes

Another type of diabetes is **gestational diabetes**, which is diabetes that occurs in some women during pregnancy. Hispanics and Native Americans have higher susceptibility for this. Physicians and dietitians alike must take extra care to

**Want to know more?** If you would like to know more about the warning signs of diabetes and other related information, visit the text website at http://webcom8.grtxle.com/nutrition and click on the Chapters button. Select Chapter 3.

**Figure 3.11** The rates of diabetes among various ethnic or racial groups over the past 24 years. Note that African American females have the highest rate. According to a 2005 study by Mathematica Policy Research, treatment for people with diabetes cost nearly $80 billion and accounted for 12 percent of federal health care spending.

*Source:* CDC.gov

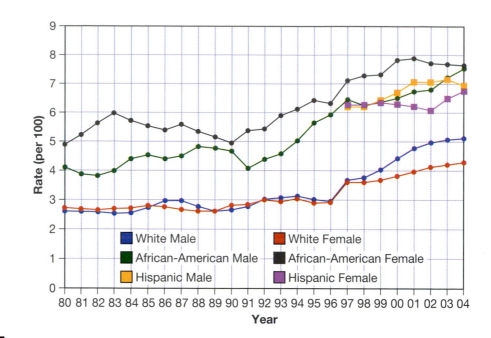

Green, leafy vegetables and fresh and dried fruits—as well as whole-grain pastas, breads, and cereals—are all good sources of fiber.

### APPLICATION TIP

If you want both soluble and insoluble fibers in one food item, try eating those peas your mother told you about when you were younger!

ensure that the fetus is not harmed. This type of diabetes can cause fetal or infant illness or death. The risks of high infant birth weight or surgical birth are higher with gestational diabetes. After birth, the condition typically disappears. However, mothers with gestational diabetes are at higher risk for developing Type 2 diabetes later in life, and their infants are more likely to do so as adults.

**Before you go on . . .**

1. Define *diabetes mellitus* and describe why those who have it are at risk for coronary heart disease.
2. Differentiate between Type 1 and Type 2 diabetes.
3. What is gestational diabetes?

## Health Benefits of Dietary Fiber

In humans, dietary fiber is simply the carbohydrates that resist human digestive enzymes. Dietary fiber is important, as it prevents a number of chronic diseases. Fiber is mostly polysaccharides, although one component of dietary fiber, *lignin,* is technically not a carbohydrate. A more accurate term used instead of *dietary* fiber is *nonstarch polysaccharide.* There are two types of dietary fiber: soluble and insoluble. **Soluble fiber** can dissolve in water. It is composed of many repeating monosaccharides that are acid derivatives of galactose. It is a jellylike material that acts as a cement in plants. **Insoluble fiber** is mainly composed of plant cell walls. It cannot be dissolved in water and is resistant to human digestive enzymes. It is composed of cellulose, hemicellulose, and lignin. Table 3.4 summarizes the types of dietary fiber, what they are composed of, and some food sources. Table 3.5 and the photo on this page give examples of the amounts of soluble and insoluble fibers in foods, showing that both fiber types are normally present.

Each class of dietary fiber has its own health benefits, which we will discuss later in this chapter. Soluble fibers are known for their ability to lower blood cholesterol. Insoluble fibers tend to hold on to water in the gut and may soften

### Table 3.4    Dietary Fiber Types, Composition, Food Sources, and Health Outcomes

| Fiber Type | Soluble | Insoluble |
|---|---|---|
| **Examples** | Pectin, gums, mucilages | Cellulose, hemicellulose, lignin (not a carbohydrate) |
| **What Is It?** | Soluble fiber is composed of many repeating monosaccharides that are acid derivatives of galactose. It is a jellylike material that acts as a cement in plants. *Gums* are normally found in plants at a site of injury and in many ways are similar to scar tissue in humans. *Mucilages* are produced in plants at particular sites to prevent transpiration or evaporation of water. | Insoluble fiber is mainly made up of plant cell walls, and it cannot be dissolved in water. The chemical composition varies widely. Cellulose, which is similar to starch, is composed of repeating glucose units. The chemical bonds in cellulose have a different shape than those found in starch, making it impossible for human digestive enzymes to break cellulose it down. Cellulose is found in the plant cell wall and gives structure to the plant. The *hemicellulose* fiber is confusing because of its name and is really not at all similar to cellulose. This type of fiber has many subtypes and is found in the plant cell wall. *Lignin* is a compound that acts as a cement for cellulose in plants and plant cell walls. |
| **Food Sources** | Fruits (apples, oranges), legumes, oats, oat bran, potatoes, and peas are all good sources of soluble fiber. | Cereals, grains, legumes, kidney beans, green beans, wheat bran cereal, brown rice, carrots, and seeds. |
| **Health Outcomes** | Lowers blood cholesterol levels. Can help in reducing heart disease and controlling diabetes. | Prevents some large intestine problems such as constipation and hemorrhoids. May also protect against cancer of the large intestine. |

### Table 3.5    Soluble and Insoluble Fibers in Selected Foods

| Food | Serving Size | Soluble Fiber (g) | Insoluble Fiber (g) |
|---|---|---|---|
| Apple | 1 small | 2.3 | 1.6 |
| Brown rice | 1/2 c. cooked | 0.1 | 1.6 |
| Corn | 2/3 c. | 0.2 | 1.4 |
| Cornflakes | 1 c. | 0 | 0.5 |
| Green beans | 2/3 c. | 0.6 | 3.3 |
| Kidney beans | 1/2 c. cooked | 0.5 | 4.0 |
| Oatmeal | 1/3 c. uncooked | 1.4 | 1.3 |
| Orange | 1 medium | 1.3 | 1.9 |
| Peas | 1/2 c. | 2.0 | 3.2 |
| Popcorn | 3 c. | 0.8 | 2.0 |
| Potatoes | 1 small | 2.2 | 1.6 |
| Rye bread | 1 slice | 0.8 | 1.9 |
| Whole-wheat bread | 1 slice | 0.3 | 1.2 |

stools and accelerate the passage of contents through the gastrointestinal tract, decreasing what is called *transit time*. Eating foods containing both forms of fiber is important in maintaining good health.

Dietary fiber, although it is classified as a carbohydrate, does not yield energy from breakdown as do the other carbohydrates. However, despite this limitation in providing energy, we know that dietary fiber has many health benefits to the human body and is the focus of much research. Here are some of the currently understood health benefits of dietary fiber:

- Dietary fiber gives bulk to the contents of the digestive tract and improves the ability of the gastrointestinal tract to move food along. The time food takes to pass through the large intestine (transit time) is decreased.
- Dietary fiber dilutes toxic materials, which results in less contact between toxins and the intestinal wall.
- Dietary fiber allows for easier defecation. Fiber tends to hold on to water and makes the stools softer, which results in easier bowel movements.
- Dietary fiber aids in weight control. The water-holding capacity of fiber may give a feeling of fullness. Fiber may also help in weight control as it displaces sugars and fats from the diet. High-dietary-fiber foods are generally also low in fat.
- Dietary fiber can bind with bile acids and enhance their excretion. Typically, bile (or liver) acids secreted into the gastrointestinal tract can be reabsorbed to make cholesterol. Fiber stops this reabsorption, which forces the liver to pull cholesterol from the gastrointestinal tract to make the needed bile, which in turn lowers blood cholesterol levels.
- The effects of dietary fiber typically decrease the following diseases or health problems:

  - Diverticulosis, a condition in which outpockets have formed in the colon due to increased intra-abdominal pressure exerted during defecation. These pockets can trap feces and become inflamed and infected.
  - Constipation and diarrhea
  - Colon cancer
  - Ulcerative colitis, or inflammation of the colon
  - Appendicitis
  - Hiatal hernia, or the pushing of part of the stomach up to the thoracic cavity
  - Hemorrhoids and varicose veins
  - Heart disease (particularly soluble fiber, as it tends to lower blood cholesterol)
  - Insulin requirements (because fiber can help control blood glucose levels)

*How much fiber do we need?*

The current *Dietary Guidelines for Americans* encourage frequent consumption of fiber-rich fruits, vegetables, and whole grains. The current recommended fiber intake ranges from 12 to 15 g/day for most Americans. In the United States, the fecal bulk (weight of feces excreted) per person is around 110 g/day; in underdeveloped nations where people have unrefined plant-based diets and dietary fiber is much greater, it is 500 g/day. The transit time (the time food takes to pass through the entire gastrointestinal system) in Western nations is around seventy hours. However, in some British populations, transit times of two weeks have been recorded! Generally, a shorter transit time is desirable. Fewer incidents of constipation and less contact of toxic compounds with the wall of the gastrointestinal tract are two benefits of a short transit time. In more underdeveloped societies, the average transit time is about thirty-five hours. In order to decrease the incidence of diseases and conditions associated with low fiber consumption, nutrition experts generally agree that 25–38 g or 14 g per 1,000 calories daily is sufficient. Consumption within the recommended range is important for another reason. Eating *too much* fiber (more than 50 g/day) can have negative effects, such as binding diet minerals and preventing their absorption.

## Resistant Starches

Another type of carbohydrate that is often grouped with dietary fiber is called **resistant starches**. This is an area of growing research as more health benefits of this type of starch are emerging. What is a resistant starch? Simply stated, it is a starch that escapes the digestion within the small intestine. There are four classes of these starches: R1, R2, R3, and R4. R1 is the most non-digestible and may be found in seeds, unprocessed whole grains, and legumes. R2 is a more granular type of starch found in, as a couple of examples, uncooked potatoes and green banana flours. R3 is created by first cooking and then cooling rapidly a high-starch food. Breads, cornflakes, and cooked-then-cooled potatoes have this type of starch. R4 is chemically synthesized and not found in nature.

The resistant starches that have been researched the most have been R2 and R3 starches. R3 starches may enhance satiety (feeling of fullness), leading to decreased food intake. Other studies show that R2 and R3 can improve glucose tolerance. These two starch types can also improve large intestinal health by encouraging healthy bacteria to grow. Resistant starch does deliver calories, approximately 2 to 3 kcal per gram as opposed to 4 kcal per gram for typical flour. One benefit of resistant starch is that it tastes less like fiber and more like starch, and perhaps is more acceptable to consumers who want to increase fiber in their diets but don't like the taste of most high-fiber foods. About 3 to 7 grams per day of resistant starch is consumed by Westerners, but more can be consumed without harmful effects. Navy beans are a good source of resistant starch, with ½ cup cooked beans providing almost 10 grams. Other good sources include bananas, cold potatoes, cold pasta, lentils, oatmeal, and whole-grain bread.

### ■ Make It a Practice
*What's the best way to add fiber to your diet?*
Increasing your intake of dietary fiber may not be as difficult as you think, but it does take some knowledge of food composition. A person who simply follows the recommendations of MyPyramid by choosing fruits, vegetables, and whole grains will typically get about 25–30 g of fiber per day.
In general, the following foods are high in fiber:

- Legumes and lentils such as dried beans, peas, baked beans, kidney beans, split peas, garbanzos (chickpeas), lentils, pinto beans, black beans, green beans, snap beans, pole beans, lima beans, and broad beans
- Fruits such as blackberries, strawberries, cherries, plums, pears, apples, kiwifruit, guava, bananas, and dried fruits (dried figs, prunes, and raisins)
- Vegetables such as fresh or frozen green peas, broccoli, Brussels sprouts, sweet corn, beet root, baked potato (with skin), and carrots; green leafy vegetables such as spinach, beet greens, kale, collards, Swiss chard, and turnip greens
- Nuts such as almonds, Brazil nuts, coconut, peanuts, and walnuts (high in fiber but also in fat)
- Whole wheat, barley, rye, oats, buckwheat, and cornmeal

**Want to know more?**
If you would like more information on good sources of dietary fiber in specific foods, go to the text website at http://webcom8 .grtxle.com/nutrition and click on the Chapters button. Select Chapter 3.

Be careful if you go on a high-fiber diet—assuming your current fiber intake is low. Your body will rebel to some extent because it is not accustomed to processing lots of fiber. The best advice is to increase the fiber content slowly, giving your gastrointestinal tract some time to adjust. In addition, be sure to consume plenty of water when making this change. Abruptly and substantially increasing fiber intake often results in diarrhea and other forms of gastrointestinal distress. ■

## Can You Consume Too Much Fiber?

As noted earlier, overconsumption of fiber carries some health risks. Fiber can bind up minerals and interfere with their absorption. An intake of 50 g of fiber per day (compared to the 12–15 g/day that Americans currently consume) has been shown to significantly decrease the absorption of several minerals, including calcium, zinc, copper, and iron. However, one study in which participants consumed 30 g/day, showed little if any evidence of a negative effect on zinc absorption. Zinc is an important cofactor for many enzymes, so a zinc deficiency is dangerous. Excess fiber intake causes an increased number of bowel movements, and some people may experience diarrhea, which can lead to dehydration.

### ■ To Supplement or Not?

*Is supplemental fiber in pill or powder form the same as fiber found in food?*

Many advertisements today urge us to purchase fiber pills to increase the dietary intake of this important nutrient. We have discussed the health benefits of dietary fiber, so why not get it from a pill? One reason to get your fiber from food is that foods high in fiber contain antioxidant compounds. Remember from Chapter 1 that antioxidants protect against free radicals that can damage cells. Sometimes when isolated fibers are put in pill form, they lose their antioxidant potential. Another issue is whether fiber pills can really dissolve in the stomach and intestines and have a significant impact.

Purified sources of fiber may also bind up some minerals, whereas in food the level consumed may not cause such impairment. Some individuals (e.g., older adults) take fiber supplements to increase bowel movements and avoid constipation. These work, but generally people become dependent on them. This is not necessarily bad, except that if you stop taking the supplements you may be more constipated than before you started taking them. In general, getting fiber from food sources is your best choice for health. ■

**Before you go on . . .**

1. Can you distinguish between the health benefits of soluble fiber and insoluble fiber?
2. How does fiber affect the movement of food and waste components along the gastrointestinal tract?
3. How much fiber is recommended and how does this compare to what most Americans typically consume on a daily basis?
4. What pitfalls may occur if you consume too much fiber?
5. What is a resistant starch and what benefits do they have in a diet?

# Real People, Other Voices

### Student:
**Theresa Lindsay**

Eastern Illinois University

Over the past several years, people who yearn to lose weight have turned to a low-carbohydrate diet. Petros must understand that there are no easy and quick ways to lose weight. Any diet that promotes quick and unhealthy weight loss should be questioned. Petros should seek the advice of a physician first to address his health concerns. I would advise him to stop following the low- to no-carbohydrate diet. Introducing fruits and vegetables back into his diet will help with the constipation, because fruits and vegetables are high in fiber, which keeps us regulated.

Petros should seek to develop and maintain a healthy lifestyle and should not focus on the actual amount of weight loss. Because carbohydrates are our main source of energy, this helps explain why he is experiencing a lack of energy. If he adds carbohydrates back into his diet, his energy level will continue to increase. Petros should continue working out on a regular basis as well. I'm confident that if he begins to create a healthier lifestyle, including consuming carbohydrates, he will attain the results he wants.

### Instructor:
**Holly J. Morris,**

PROFESSOR OF BIOLOGY
Lehigh Carbon Community College

The new diet that Petros is trying to follow is a radical change for him, which means it will be difficult to follow in the long run. He should forget "low carb" and bring back fruits, vegetables, and whole grains. If he plans his daily diet around five to nine servings of fruits and vegetables, and six servings of grains, cereals, or bread, along with adequate fluid intake, he will have a healthy base. This should help reduce his tiredness and relieve the constipation. He can then fill in with meat or fish and additional grains, depending on his calorie goal.

Petros will still need to make some adjustments from his old diet, however. Instead of a large blueberry muffin, he might allow himself an occasional medium-sized apple-bran muffin. A baked potato with yogurt or fat-free sour cream is fine. Eliminate french fries. Pasta can still be included, but Petros could try a whole-wheat or high-fiber pasta. If he does not like the heavier taste, he could mix it 50/50 with regular pasta. He may want to spend a week or two weighing and measuring his food so that he has a good idea about portion size.

Working out at a gym is great, but Petros could also incorporate some other activity into his daily routine. Simple adjustments, such as parking farther away, walking for half of his lunch break, and walking to a co-worker's office instead of phoning or e-mailing, will burn more calories.

### Registered dietitian:
**Stacy Fisher,**

RD, LD
Cedar Park, TX

I would begin the consultation with Petros by exploring what is most important to him. He has already identified weight loss as a personal goal, and now he must find some realistic solutions to achieve that goal. After reviewing his history (past diet experiences, current medications, supplements, etc.), evaluation of BMI and other anthropometric data would help assess health risks and determine if weight loss is appropriate.

Because he has revealed that his experience with avoiding carbohydrates has produced some less-than-desirable results (feeling tired, poor concentration, constipation, etc.), he may be ready to hear about other strategies. I would review the benefits and general requirements for carbohydrates, as well as pointing out the correlation between his symptoms and low intake of carbohydrates. I would encourage Petros to slowly begin introducing complex carbohydrates such as whole grains, fruits, and vegetables into his diet, which should also help promote bowel regularity. Explaining that weight gain results when excess calories are consumed—not only carbohydrates, but protein and fat as well—might help Petros understand the importance of a well-balanced diet. I would suggest that he keep a food journal so that we could identify any patterns that might be contributing to his weight gain. Discussing the role of physical activity in weight management would also be useful; it may help reinforce his decision to maintain increased activity levels.

# Your Health and Carbohydrates

## Empty Calories

We should clarify the difference between a food that is nutrient dense and one that generates empty calories. *Nutrient density* is the measure of the relative number of nutrients delivered per calorie in a given food. A candy bar and a banana may each provide 150 calories. However, the banana has other nutrients while the candy bar probably does not. The banana would be considered nutrient dense, whereas the candy bar would be considered an empty-calorie food. A goal should be to consume carbohydrate foods that are rich in micronutrients, such as vitamins and minerals, and to minimize consumption of foods with high calories but few nutrients. Unfortunately, this is not always the case in Western societies, and the issue is becoming much more worrisome. Health professionals are aware of the increased consumption of soft drinks that both are high in sugar and have very little nutritive value. Cakes, cookies, pastries, and ice cream are other foods high in fat as well as sugar. Any positive effects from the presence of calcium in ice cream may be counterbalanced by its high caloric content.

### ■ Nutrition and Lifestages

*What's so bad about soda in schools?*

Soda consumption in the United States increased from 22.2 gal. per person per year in 1970 to 49.2 gal. a year in 2004, a jump of 122%. One 12-oz. can of regular, sugar-sweetened soda contains approximately 140 calories. A recent study of 11- and 12-year-old adolescents monitored both their soda intake and body mass index (BMI). BMI is a measure that is used to determine overweight and obesity. This research revealed that BMI increased with increased sugared soda consumption. In other words, the more sugared soda a person drinks, the greater the risk of becoming overweight or obese. During the period from 1985 to 1997, consumption of soda in our schools increased by 1,200 percent, while

Soda vending machines in schools are controversial. Do you know if they are present in your local schools? Should public schools be obligated to provide or make available only foods that are considered nutritious and healthy? Why?

the purchase of milk by students decreased by 30 percent. In a more recent study using National Health and Nutrition Examination Survey data for 1999–2002, the heaviest consumers of carbonated beverages were white adolescent and young-adult males. They consumed about 1.8 servings of regular carbonated soft drinks per day (1 serving = 12 oz.). White females in the same age brackets were not far behind; they consumed about 1.2 servings per day. However, public concern over soda consumption may have made some impact. Per capita consumption of carbonated soft drinks has declined for 11 straight years, according to data from Beverage Marketing Corporation. It now stands 22 percent below its peak in 1998, according to the trade publication **Beverage Digest** and calculations by the Center for Science in the Public Interest (CSPI).

Even with the declines in consumption in recent years, Coca-Cola, PepsiCo, Dr. Pepper, Snapple, and other companies produced 9.4 billion cases of sugary soda pop and energy drinks in 2009.

At the 1998 peak, when CSPI first published its Liquid Candy report, companies were producing 638 8-ounce servings of non-diet soft drinks per person per year. By 2009, that figure was down to 543 8-ounce servings, which is still 140 empty calories per person in the United States per day!

Health officials are very concerned about increasing soda consumption and its implications for maintenance of good health. The decrease in calcium intake in all ages due to decreased milk consumption, particularly during the adolescent years when peak bone mass is developing, may lead to osteoporosis in adulthood. Increased consumption of soda may also be linked to an upward spike in dental decay. Of course, the connection between obesity and excess caloric intake is a major problem that health officials must confront. In addition to a high level of sugar, most soda beverages contain caffeine, and a concern over potential caffeine dependence, especially in children and adolescents, has also emerged. Those who consume soda may also be decreasing their intake of healthy foods and beverages. The average 12- to 19-year-old in the United States now consumes 868 cans of soda (12 oz. each) yearly, or about 2.3 cans per day—more than 80 gal./year. To make matters worse, many schools have multiple vending machines where students can select snacks that are also high in sugar and fat content. Because vending machines are profitable for schools, some school officials are reluctant to remove them. However, the availability of these food items is contrary to the goals of the federal school lunch program, which is designed to help schools provide nutritious meals and to educate students on proper nutrition. ■

## Sugar Intake and Dental Decay

The association of sugar intake with dental decay or cavities has been documented for some time. The key factor is that a sticky carbohydrate can adhere to the enamel of the teeth and combine with oral bacteria to produce lactic acid. Lactic acid degrades tooth enamel, allowing further infiltration of bacteria into the inner parts of the teeth. Fluoridation of water, practiced for more than forty years in this country,

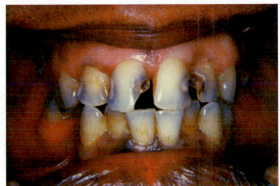

This severe example of dental decay resulted from poor food choices and poor eating habits. Much of this decay is due to the presence of a sticky carbohydrate on teeth. Bacteria adhere to and produce lactic acid, which dissolves the tooth enamel, leading to cavities.

has resulted in a dramatic decrease in the incidence of dental decay, presumably due to the hardening effect of fluoride on tooth enamel. However, if our sugar consumption were decreased, perhaps we would observe an even further decline in dental disease.

## Carbohydrate Intake and Obesity

Previously we discussed the issue of consuming empty calories through sugar intake. In addition to sugared soda, and based on the rapid increase in obesity in U.S. children and teens, nutrition experts are concerned about the availability of candy in our schools. How strong is this link? Obesity has a complex etiology; therefore, the increasing obesity rate cannot be attributed entirely to increased carbohydrate intake. Fat is also very high in calories (9 kcal per gram) and thus a concentrated source of energy. The typical American diet is very high in animal protein, which contains a lot of fat. While genetic predisposition also plays a significant role in a person's weight, physical inactivity and continued consumption of excessive amounts of calories set the stage for weight gain and ultimately obesity. Many consumers are also apparently unaware of how many calories are in the foods they eat. Frequently the caloric contents of foods are much higher than we think (see Chapter 7 for more information).

 ■ **Myths and Legends**
*Does eating sugar really cause obesity?*

It depends on whom you ask. The more calories you consume (and sugar is often a prime source of excess calories) and the less energy you expend, the more weight you will gain. As noted earlier, research studies indicate that the more sugar one consumes, the greater the risk of becoming obese. But does that mean sugar causes the obesity, or simply that it provides extra calories? As low-fat products have become popular in recent years, the public may have been misled about their caloric content. Many of these low-fat products have extra sugar added, such as high-fructose corn syrup, in order to keep the flavor desirable. In a debate among nutrition experts, one group suggests that no more than 10 percent of our calories should come from sugar. Others believe that the current intake of 25 percent of our calories coming from sugar is not a problem with regard to obesity. Even the research can contribute to uncertainty. One study suggested that women who consume soft drinks are more at risk of developing obesity. Remember that soda is the leading source of sugar in the American diet. However, another study failed to confirm a link between soda consumption and the incidence of obesity. The government's *Dietary Guidelines for Americans* is not specific; it says that sugar should only be used in moderation. ■

## Low-Carbohydrate Diets and Weight Loss

Low-carbohydrate diets have been highly and widely touted as a great way to lose weight. The idea is that severely reduced carbohydrate consumption forces the body into ketosis, in which products of fat are broken down and turned into ketone bodies. Ketone bodies cannot be further metabolized by the body and are excreted in the urine. Thus, from a theoretical perspective, one loses calories and weight. Also, on a low-carbohydrate diet, muscle glycogen is broken down to glucose. Glycogen holds on to water, but when it is broken down on a low-carbohydrate diet, the water is released. Water is lost as urine on these diets, which accounts for weight loss.

The Atkins and South Beach diets are probably the two most popular examples of low-carbohydrate diets and have some similarities. Unfortunately, clinical trials on low-carbohydrate diets are not numerous. A recent federal study showed that after six months on an Atkins-like diet, compared to a traditional low-fat diet, the Atkins participants actually lost more weight. However, a lot of this reduced weight was attributable to water loss. Interestingly, as the study progressed further, the earlier difference in weight loss between the two diets was not observed after twelve months. In fact, both groups had a high dropout rate, suggesting the inability of subjects to sustain either type of diet.

One major concern about low-carbohydrate diets is the high intake of fat allowed on these diets, which research has shown can lead to increased risk for heart disease. However, data from the study just mentioned did not indicate that those on the low-carbohydrate, high-fat diet developed or experienced an increased risk for heart disease as compared to those on the conventional low-fat diet. No long-term studies have as yet been reported on the correlation between low-carbohydrate diets and heart disease. In addition to being restrictive and difficult to stick to, low-carbohydrate diets may cause bad breath due to an increase of ketone bodies, constipation due to low intake of dietary fiber, and dehydration from induced water loss.

The controversy over carbohydrate restriction for weight loss is likely to continue for some time. Although many so-called fad diets do lead to weight loss, much of the reduction for many dieters is temporary. This problem of regaining lost weight is an important concern in our struggle against obesity.

## Cancer and Heart Disease

Research continues to show that complex carbohydrates and fiber play a significant role in lowering the incidence of cancer and heart disease. Soluble fiber in the diet can lower blood cholesterol and therefore decrease the risk for heart disease. An increased intake of insoluble fiber has long been thought to decrease the risk of colon and other types of cancer as well. Although no current evidence shows that increased intake of carbohydrates leads to either heart disease or cancer, both diseases occur at a higher rate in those who are obese.

### ■ Culture and Ethnic Foods
*Okinawans have the world's longest life expectancy. Is it their diet?*

Are you familiar with the Okinawa diet? Its popularity in recent years has increased to the point that food guide pyramids have been developed for it. The Okinawa diet is based on the health outcomes and longevity of residents of Okinawa, Japan. Figure 3.12 shows that Okinawans live longer than other Japanese, Swedes, and Americans; they also experience few of the chronic diseases that afflict the populations in most Western societies. Because of this, researchers are studying such factors as genetics, diet, exercise habits, psychological health, and spiritual beliefs and practices of this population.

Naturally, one of the most important questions is how the Okinawan diet differs from or is similar to those of other cultures. Significantly, the diet is low in calories. Okinawans, on average, consume 40 percent fewer calories than typical Americans. In lab animals, caloric restriction increases

**APPLICATION TIP**

Moderate caloric restriction and increased physical activity are still the best methods of losing weight and maintaining weight loss.

**Figure 3.12** The life expectancy of Okinawans compared to other Japanese, Swedes, and Americans. Okinawans' life expectancy has been higher for more than 40 years and is still increasing. How do you think our life expectancy compares to other Asian cultures?

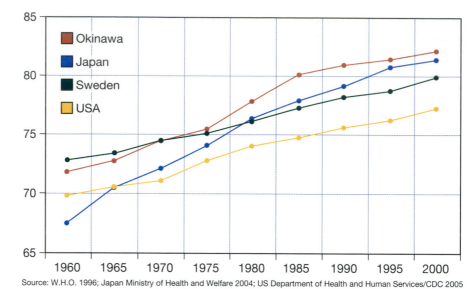

Source: W.H.O. 1996; Japan Ministry of Health and Welfare 2004; US Department of Health and Human Services/CDC 2005

life span, and this phenomenon could be similar to that observed in the Okinawan diet. Remember that in our diets, we get a lot of our energy from carbohydrate, particularly sugar. The Okinawan diet is different, as it includes high levels of soy, vegetables, and fish, and low levels of alcohol. Okinawans also consume 30 percent or less of their calories as fat and keep their salt intake low. Other characteristics of this population, and likely contributors to their exceptional longevity, are a high level of physical activity well into old age and low levels of psychological stress.

Figure 3.13 gives some details on the food guide pyramid developed for this diet. As you can see, rice, noodles, beans, whole grains, and vegetables form the all-important base of the pyramid. These types of complex carbohydrates are emphasized. The Okinawan diet is high in flavonoids, or plant compounds that have potent antioxidant properties, as well as omega-3 fatty acids from fish. *Flavonoids* are a group of plant pigments that give plants their bright colors; a few thousand types exist. Fruits such as cranberries, apples, blueberries, and strawberries are rich in flavonoids. ■

## Lactose Intolerance

The inability of some people to digest milk sugar, or lactose, is commonly known as lactose intolerance. It is most often a genetic condition related to loss of function of the enzyme *lactase;* however, it can also result from aging, abdominal surgery in which part of the small intestine is removed, or use of certain medications. Lactase breaks down lactose into galactose and glucose, both of which can be absorbed. Virtually all infants have the ability to produce sufficient levels of lactase, but as they become older and develop into children, the synthesis or function of this enzyme dramatically decreases in those of African and Asian descent, and even those of southern European ancestry.

Those who are lactose intolerant typically experience side effects such as diarrhea, bloating, and flatulence when they consume milk. These symptoms are caused by lactose entering the large intestine, where it cannot be digested. Its presence causes the bacteria to ferment the lactose, producing lactic acid and gas. The presence of lactose and lactic acid increases osmotic pressure (the pressure

## Okinawa Food Guide Pyramid

Sweets
**0–3 servings**

Meat, poultry and eggs
**0–7 servings**

**Optional weekly**

Vegetable oils and condiments
Sparingly, **1–2 tablespoons**

Omega-3 foods
**1–3 servings**

**Eat daily**

Fruit
**2–4 servings**

Flavonoid foods
**2–4 servings**

Calcium foods
**2–4 servings**

Rice, noodles, beans and
other whole grains
**7–13 servings**

Vegetables
**7–13 servings**

*Daily beverage
recommendations:*

Daily tea

Alcohol in
moderation

**Figure 3.13** The Okinawa Food Guide Pyramid. Note the emphasis on rice, noodles, beans, whole grains, fruits and vegetables, and omega-3 fatty acids. How does this differ from what we eat? Do you think Okinawans consume fewer calories? Eat less fast food?

exerted by water moving into the gastrointestinal tract) and draws water into the large intestine, leading to diarrhea. The fermentation process leads to gas production, which causes bloating and flatulence. Despite this condition, most nutritionists believe that those who are lactose intolerant need not avoid milk and dairy products totally, because a large amount of milk or lactose must be consumed at one time to trigger the symptoms. For those who are more severely lactose intolerant, several options exist. Consuming three 8-oz. glasses of milk spread throughout the day may not result in these symptoms in some people. In other people one 8-oz. glass may produce symptoms. In lactose-hydrolyzed milk, lactase has been added to break down the lactose. Other products such as sweet acidophilus milk, buttermilk, and soy milk are low in lactose and may be safely consumed. However, soy, rice, and almond milk are lower in calcium and may lack other nutrients unless they are fortified. Yogurt is yet another food that can be consumed to retain the nutritional benefits of dairy products. Another way to incorporate milk into a diet of a lactose-intolerant individual is to offer small amounts of milk (2–3 oz.) with a mixed meal.

> ## Before you go on . . .
> 1. What is nutrient density?
> 2. How does sugar consumption contribute to dental decay?
> 3. What are the major differences between the typical American and Okinawan diets?
> 4. Many people are lactose intolerant. Why does this occur?

Examples of some products that can be used by people with lactose intolerance to get the benefit of dairy products.

## Real People, Real Strategies

Through various sources Petros discovered that carbohydrates are an important part of his diet. He realized he needs fiber, B vitamins, and energy for his brain and for exercise. His nutritionist friend informed him that his lack of endurance during exercise and his feeling of tiredness is a condition known as *ketosis*. This diagnosis also explained the fruity smell of his breath—a condition caused by the incomplete metabolism of fat. Another issue he had to confront was that the weight loss he experienced on the low-carbohydrate diet was mostly water. This dehydrating effect led to another factor that he needs to be concerned about as he exercises: his water requirement. He has also depleted his glycogen stores needed for endurance exercises. He now knows why he felt so tired. And finally, his friend educated him that the concept of "good carbs" and "bad carbs" is controversial. The scientific evidence for dividing carbohydrates into two groups is not supported in weight-loss programs. The friend recommended that Petros *moderate* his carbohydrate intake while maintaining a balanced and healthy diet. She also advised him to increase his consumption of fiber by adding whole wheat and grains to his diet, while cutting back on sodas and sweets. After making these changes, he will be able to continue with a slower, gradual weight loss, and his workouts will not exhaust him.

## Chapter Summary

- Carbohydrates are responsible for several major functions, the most important of which is serving as the major source of energy in diets. In addition, carbohydrates spare stored protein from being broken down so that muscle mass is maintained. Having ample carbohydrates in your diet prevents ketosis. Carbohydrates also provide flavoring or sweetness to foods we consume.

- The simple sugars are divided into two categories: monosaccharides and disaccharides. The monosaccharides are glucose, fructose, and galactose; the disaccharides are sucrose, lactose, and maltose. Glucose is sometimes referred to as blood sugar. Fructose is found primarily in fruits; galactose is a component of lactose or milk sugar. Simple table sugar is sucrose.

- Plant starches are composed of complex carbohydrates or polysaccharides. The animal version of stored complex carbohydrate, called glycogen, is found mainly in the liver and muscle.

- Dietary fiber is a complex carbohydrate that has many health benefits and may lower the risk of many types of chronic diseases, such as cancer, heart disease, and diabetes. The DRI recommends 25–38 g/day of dietary fiber. The average American consumes only about half the fiber recommended by several health agencies, or approximately 12–15 g/day.

- Food sources vary in levels of soluble and insoluble fiber. Fruits are excellent sources of soluble fiber, and whole-grain cereals and breads are good sources of insoluble fiber. Soluble fiber can lower blood cholesterol, whereas insoluble fiber is more likely to help prevent colon cancer.

- Resistant starch is another type of carbohydrate grouped with dietary fiber. There are 4 classes designated as R1, R2, R3, and R4, with R1 the most non-digestible and R4 chemically synthesized. R2 and R3 starches provide 2 to 3 Kcal per gram.
- Many diets contain excess sugars and insufficient levels of whole-grain carbohydrate sources. Excess intake of sugars may be one of the primary reasons why obesity has increased in the United States. Low intake of whole grains, fruits, and vegetables may contribute to heart disease, several types of cancer, and diabetes.
- Some people do not produce enough of the enzyme lactase to break down the milk sugar lactose. This can cause them to have gastrointestinal discomfort such as diarrhea, bloating, and flatulence. Despite these issues, lactose-intolerant people may still consume dairy products without ill effects if they ingest small amounts and/or spread their intake of dairy products throughout the day, or choose fermented dairy products that are lower in lactose, such as yogurt.

## Key Terms

**acidosis** A buildup of acids in body fluids such as blood. (p. 84)

**diabetes mellitus** The inability of the body to regulate blood glucose levels within normal limits. (p. 84)

**dietary fiber** A carbohydrate composed of repeating units of glucose and other mono-saccharides that cannot be digested by human enzymes and thus cannot be absorbed and used by the body. (p. 76)

**fructose** A monosaccharide that has a simple ring structure. It is the sugar found abundantly in fruit, honey, and also some vegetables such as beets, sweet potatoes, parsnips, and onions. It is the sweetest sugar. (p. 74)

**galactose** A monosaccharide that is con-sumed as a part of the disaccharide lactose found in milk; it is a basic component of other, more complex carbohydrates. (p. 74)

**gestational diabetes** (jes-TAY-shun-ul die-uh-BEE-tees) Diabetes that occurs in some women during pregnancy. (p. 85)

**gluconeogenesis** (gloo-coh-nee-oh-JEN-eh-sis) Synthesis of new glucose from noncarbohydrate sources. (p. 80)

**glucose** The monosaccharide that circulates in the blood and is often referred to as *blood sugar*. It is the main source of energy for the body. (p. 74)

**glycemic index** A measure of how fast blood glucose increases when a person ingests a particular food, compared to ingestion of glucose. (p. 83)

**glycogen** The storage form of starch found in the liver and muscle of animals. (p. 76)

**high-fructose corn syrup** A carbohydrate derived from cornstarch and converted to fructose using enzymes through food pro-cessing. In essence, cornstarch is made into a syrup that is about half fructose and half glucose. (p. 74)

**hyperglycemia** An elevated blood glucose level. (p. 84)

**insoluble fiber** A type of fiber that is mainly composed of plant cell walls. It cannot be dis-solved in water and resists human digestive enzymes. It is composed of cellulose, hemi-cellulose, and lignin. (p. 86)

**insulin** A hormone released from the pan-creas that allows glucose to enter cells to be used for energy. (p. 80)

**ketone bodies** Acidic fat derivatives that arise from the incomplete breakdown of fat. (p. 80)

**lactose** A disaccharide, commonly known as milk sugar, that is composed of glucose and galactose. (p. 75)

**maltose** A disaccharide that is composed of two glucose units. (p. 75)

**nonnutritive sweeteners** Products that are sometimes referred to as alternative sweeteners or sugar substitutes. They are synthetic and do not provide food energy. (p. 82)

**nutritive sweeteners** Sweeteners that can be digested and yield calories. (p. 82)

**polysaccharide** (pahl-ee-SAK-er-ide) A carbohydrate composed of a chain with thousands of glucose molecules linked together. (p. 76)

**resistant starch** a starch that escapes the digestion in the small intestine. (p. 89)

**soluble fiber** Fiber that can dissolve in water. It is composed of many repeating monosaccharides that are acid derivatives of galactose. It is a jellylike material that acts as a cement in plants. (p. 86)

**starch** The storage form of carbohydrate found in plants. (p. 76)

**sucrose** A disaccharide commonly known as table sugar; it is composed of one glucose molecule and one fructose molecule. (p. 74)

**Type 1 diabetes** A disease that occurs when the pancreas is unable to produce insulin. It was formerly known as juvenile-onset diabetes or insulin-dependent diabetes mellitus (IDDM), because of its frequent diagnosis in children or adolescents. (p. 85)

**Type 2 diabetes** A disease that occurs when the insulin produced by the pancreas does not appear to function. It was formerly known as adult-onset diabetes or non-insulin-dependent diabetes mellitus (NIDDM). (p. 85)

# Chapter Quiz

1. Elevation of blood glucose levels is called
   a. ketosis.
   b. acidosis.
   c. hyperglycemia.
   d. mucilage.

2. Which of the following foods is most likely to be a good source of soluble fiber?
   a. cornflakes
   b. a slice of whole-wheat bread
   c. an orange
   d. a glass of milk

3. All of the following are likely to be a good source of flavonoids except
   a. cranberries.
   b. strawberries.
   c. whole-wheat bread.
   d. apples.

4. In the United States, which of the following foods contributes the largest amount of sugar in our diet?
   a. candy bars
   b. soda
   c. sweetened cereal
   d. pastries

5. Which of the following is considered a nonnutritive sweetener?
   a. sucralose
   b. sorbitol
   c. fructose
   d. none of the above

6. Which of the following is not a health benefit of fiber?
   a. dilutes toxic materials
   b. gives bulk to the diet
   c. takes food a longer time to get through the gastrointestinal tract
   d. binds up bile acids

7. Which of the following is considered a complex carbohydrate?
   a. maltose
   b. glycogen
   c. sorbitol
   d. lactose

8. A low-carbohydrate diet has been shown to
   a. be more effective than other diets.
   b. decrease the risk for heart disease.
   c. result in the production of ketone bodies.
   d. be very effective in the treatment of diabetes.

9. Which of the following hormones will your body produce if your blood glucose levels get too low?

   a. glucagon

   b. insulin

   c. pepsin

   d. xylitol

10. A diet high in fiber may decrease the risk for

    a. dental caries.

    b. osteoporosis.

    c. heart disease and cancer.

    d. stomach ulcers.

## < Here's Where You've Been

*The following topics were introduced in preceding chapters and are related to concepts we'll discuss in Chapter 4. Be certain that you're familiar with them before proceeding.*

- Chronic diseases and poor nutrition are strongly linked with one another. (Chapter 1)
- Many guidelines exist to help you think before you eat. These include the *Dietary Guidelines*, the Dietary Reference Intakes (DRIs), MyPyramid, and the Nutrition Facts label. (Chapter 2)
- Carbohydrates in the form of sugars and starches are a major source of dietary energy. (Chapter 3)
- Our intake of sugars is typically higher than it should be and may lead to health problems. (Chapter 3)
- Dietary fiber has many health benefits and can help prevent some diseases, including colon cancer and heart disease. (Chapter 3)
- Many sweeteners (sugar substitutes) are on the market to help reduce the calorie content of foods. (Chapter 3)

## Here's Where You're Going >

*The following topics and concepts are the ones we'll emphasize in Chapter 4.*

- Several types of fat exist, both in food and in your body.
- Not all fats are created equal; key differences exist between saturated and unsaturated fats.
- Fats provide energy and insulation and perform numerous other functions in the body.
- Foods differ in fat content; therefore interpreting food labels is an important skill.
- Too much fat in the diet can lead to heart disease and various types of cancer.

## Real People, Real Choices

Janine Sullivan is a stay-at-home mom in her early thirties, with two children under age 5 who keep her very busy. She has steadily gained weight since the children were born, and she is now about 30 lb. heavier than she was before her first pregnancy. On a routine physical checkup with her doctor, a blood test revealed that her cholesterol was above the desirable levels. Her physician recommended that she diet and begin an exercise program, but informed her that if these measures were not successful she would have to begin taking medication to lower her blood cholesterol—something Janine found frightening.

Her physician gave her information on various diets and sources where she could obtain more related information. After reading the physician's information and doing some research on the Internet, she discovered a lot of conflicting information about which type of dietary changes are most effective. Because her cholesterol is elevated, she decided to implement a diet specifically aimed at reducing it. However, she encountered some remarkable differences in terms of recommendations among the various diets she's considering—and some suggestions simply don't seem logical. Some online sources say that she should reduce carbohydrates; others indicate that she should eat a very low-fat diet. Yet others suggest that she should change the type of fats and carbohydrates she is eating. Janine is not sure which suggestions are best for someone in her situation. What should be her next step?

anine's story and medical condition are not at all unusual. You may also have elevated blood cholesterol levels, or you have friends or relatives who do. As Janine discovered, a lot of information is available on how to treat elevated blood cholesterol levels. How does Janine make an informed decision?

You hear all the time from health professionals and even hear it on commercials and in food advertising that we should limit how much fat and cholesterol we consume. Does eating cholesterol raise your blood cholesterol or does eating certain types of fats raise it more? We will discuss these topics in this chapter. We're told that eating fat makes you fat—but how true is that statement? We have fat in our diets, and we have fat in our bodies. There's a difference, as we will discuss in this chapter.

## The Lipids in Our Food and Our Bodies

What are fats? Carbohydrates dissolve in water, but fats do not. Just look at what happens when you add a drop of oil to water! It simply sits there on top of the water. Fats, or the more scientific term, *lipids,* are defined as substances that are insoluble in water, but soluble in organic solvents such as ether, acetone, and chloroform. A wide variety of lipids influence human health, such as the following:

Oil and water. Notice how the two do not mix.

- Fatty acids
- Triglycerides
- Phospholipids
- Sterols such as cholesterol

Triglycerides and phospholipids contain fatty acids. We will focus much of our attention on fatty acids, because these compounds affect triglyceride and phospholipid function and ultimately our health. Cholesterol is vital, as it is converted to other important hormones, but it also can lead to heart disease when present in the blood at too high a level.

Lipids are composed of the same elements that compose carbohydrates:

- Carbon (C)
- Hydrogen (H)
- Oxygen (O)

The major difference is that lipids contain almost twice as many hydrogen atoms than do carbohydrates. Why is this important? The number of hydrogen atoms is a good predictor of how much energy a substance has and why lipids provide more energy than the other nutrients.

## Fatty Acids

We will begin our discussion with fatty acids, followed by triglycerides and phospholipids. Fatty acids are not only important lipid compounds by themselves, but also as components of triglycerides and phospholipids. On the other hand, sterols and cholesterol are very different from fatty acids, triglycerides, and phospholipids in terms of structure and how they function in the body.

Fatty acids play important roles in the body by themselves. What is a fatty acid? Fatty acids are simply a chain of carbons linked (or bonded) together. One end of the chain has a *carboxyl group* (see Figure 4.1), which we represent with COOH. This end allows fatty acids to mix a bit with water, and is thus called *hydrophilic*. The other end of the chain has a *methyl group* (Figure 4.1)

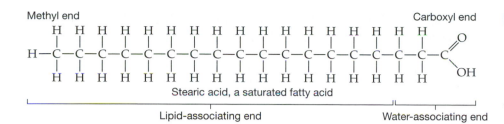

Figure 4.1 Structure of a fatty acid. The carboxyl end associates with water, and the methyl end and long carbon chain associate with lipid.

represented by $CH_3$. This part of the chain does not like to be mixed with water, and is thus called *hydrophobic*. The long chain between the two ends tends to behave like the methyl end and is not soluble in water. This means that the shorter the chain, the more it likes water.

### Fatty Acid Saturation

Health professionals think of saturated fat in terms of its ability to cause heart disease and to increase the risk of developing certain types of cancer. To a chemist it means something different. So let's talk chemistry just a bit more. Fatty acid saturation refers to whether a fatty acid chain is occupied by all of the hydrogen atoms it can hold. If the chain is fully occupied by hydrogen atoms, then it is a **saturated fatty acid** (Figure 4.2). However, not all fatty acids contain carbons that are fully saturated with hydrogens. Some have areas where hydrogen atoms are missing; we refer to these fatty acids as *unsaturated*. These unsaturated fatty acids form a *double bond* when hydrogen atoms are not present between two carbon atoms. A fatty acid with one double bond is called a **monounsaturated fatty acid;** one with two or more double bonds is called a **polyunsaturated fatty acid** (Figure 4.3).

Foods are composed of mixtures of all of these fatty acids, but some fatty acids are higher in some foods than others (Figure 4.4). Saturated fatty acids are usually solid at room temperature. Saturated fats are typically found in dairy products, meats, and some plants and tropical oils such as coconut, palm, and palm kernel oils. Fats from these foods can increase blood cholesterol levels in some people. See the feature on page 119, What's Hot: Is Coconut Oil Bad for you or not? Plant foods are good sources of monounsaturated fatty acids and include oils such as canola and olive oils. Polyunsaturated fatty acids are liquid at room temperature. They can be found in vegetable oils, such as sunflower, flaxseed, corn, and safflower oils, and other foods, including vegetables, flax, and fish oils. Both monounsaturated and polyunsaturated fats can lower blood cholesterol levels in some people.

### Essential and Nonessential Fatty Acids

The concept of what is essential is rather simple. Nutrients that the body's tissues or cells cannot make, either at all or in an amount needed to maintain

*What's a saturated fat?*

### APPLICATION TIP

Read food labels to *avoid* tropical oils that are saturated; look for ingredients such as palm, palm kernel, or coconut oils. Even though they come from plants, they are saturated and unhealthier for you than monounsaturated and polyunsaturated fats.

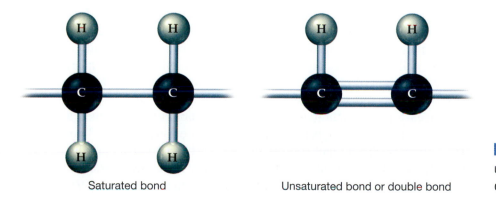

Saturated bond                    Unsaturated bond or double bond

Figure 4.2 Saturated and unsaturated bonds connecting carbon atoms.

**Figure 4.3** Fatty acids that are saturated, monounsaturated, and polyunsaturated.

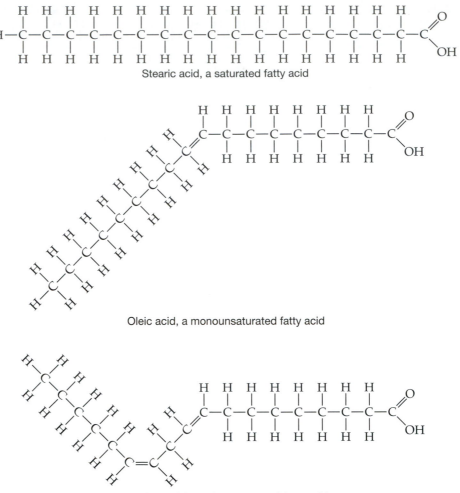

Stearic acid, a saturated fatty acid

Oleic acid, a monounsaturated fatty acid

Linoleic acid, a polyunsaturated fatty acid

health, are said to be essential. Fatty acids that cannot be made by the body and can be provided only by the diet are called **essential fatty acids.** We need to have these in our diets. These essential fatty acids are in two families of fatty acids, *omega-6* and *omega-3*. *Linoleic acid* (omega-6) and *linolenic acid* (omega-3) are the two most prominent essential fatty acids.

### Omega-3 and Omega-6 Fatty Acids

You may have recently heard or read about these two fatty acid families through the media or advertisements. The numbers 3 and 6 refer to where the double bonds are located in the fatty acids (Figure 4.5). The location of the double bonds dramatically affects the function of the fatty acid. Omega-6 fatty acids compose cell membranes and are precursors to powerful biological compounds that can play a role in reproduction and blood flow. Omega-3 fatty acids also compose cell membranes and help prevent tissue inflammation, heart disease, and the formation of blood clots. Most Americans get plenty of omega-6 fatty acids, but not enough omega-3s.

Omega-6 polyunsaturated fatty acids that should be consumed are liquid vegetable oils, such as soybean, corn, and safflower oils. Omega-3 polyunsaturated fatty acids from plant sources include soybean and canola oils, walnuts, and flaxseed. Two other important omega-3 fatty acids in addition to linolenic acid are *eicosapentaenoic acid (EPA)* and *docosahexaenoic acid (DHA)*. These

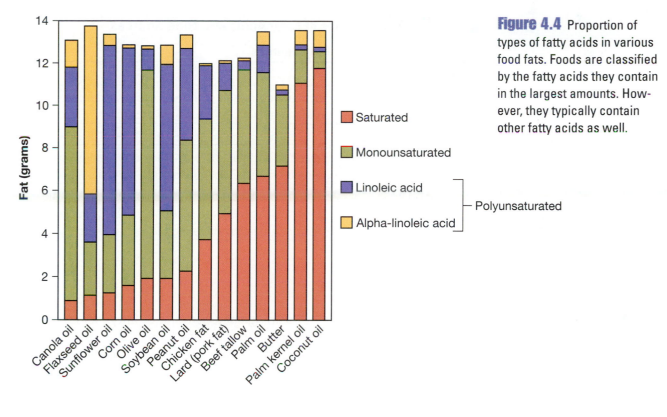

**Figure 4.4** Proportion of types of fatty acids in various food fats. Foods are classified by the fatty acids they contain in the largest amounts. However, they typically contain other fatty acids as well.

Saturated

Monounsaturated

Linoleic acid

Alpha-linoleic acid

Polyunsaturated

Carbon number from CH₃ end

1  2  3  4  5  6  7  8  9  10  11  12  13  14  15  16  17  18
$CH_3-CH_2-CH_2-CH_2-CH_2-CH=CH-CH_2-CH=CH-CH_2-CH-CH-CH_2-CH_2-CH_2-CH_2-COOH$
Omega end                                                                                                  Alpha end

First double bond is on sixth carbon from the omega end
of the fatty acid
**(a)** An omega-6 fatty acid (linolenic acid)

Carbon number from CH₃ end

1  2  3  4  5  6  7  8  9  10  11  12  13  14  15  16  17  18
$CH_3-CH_2-CH=CH-CH_2-CH=CH-CH_2-CH=CH-CH_2-CH_2-CH_2-CH_2-CH_2-CH_2-CH_2-COOH$
Omega end                                                                                                  Alpha end

First double bond is on third carbon from the omega end of the fatty acid
**(b)** An omega-3 fatty acid (linolenic acid)

**Figure 4.5** Differences between omega-6 and omega-3 fatty acids. Note where the double bonds occur.

omega-3 fatty acids are abundant in coldwater fish. Fish that naturally have more oil (e.g., salmon, trout, herring) have higher concentrations of EPA and DHA than leaner fish (e.g., cod, haddock, catfish). Humans can make only small amounts of EPA and DHA from linolenic acid. EPA and DHA are also formed in breast milk. Evidence suggests that for the general population, consumption of fatty acids in fish and reduced risks of cardiovascular disease are related. Other sources of EPA and DHA may provide similar benefits (see Table 4.1). Because very little linolenic acid is converted to EPA and DHA in humans, experts recommend that we consume more fish to get the health benefit of omega-3 fatty acids.

### ■ What's Hot?
*Something fishy—omega-3 fatty acids*
Numerous research studies have validated the positive health benefits of omega-3 fatty acids, and nutritionists continue to advocate an increased consumption of foods that contain them. Consuming omega-3 fatty acids is likely to decrease the risk of developing

| Table 4.1 | Families of Fatty Acids and Food Sources |
|---|---|

| Fatty Acid Family | Food Sources |
|---|---|
| Omega-6 fatty acid | |
| Linoleic acid | Soybean, corn, and safflower oils; vegetables, fruits, seeds, grains. |
| Omega-3 fatty acids | |
| Linolenic acid | Flax seed and flax oil, pumpkin seed, walnut oil, green leafy vegetables, walnuts, canola oil. |
| EPA and DHA* | Fish such as lake trout, herring, sardines, Atlantic salmon, albacore tuna, bluefish, halibut, mackerel. *Caution:* Tuna may have high levels of mercury. |

*Also found in breast milk.

Salmon, sardines, buffalo, walnuts, canola oil, and flax seed are examples of good sources of omega-3 fatty acids.

coronary heart disease. Physiologically, omega-3 fatty acids reduce inflammation, may lower blood pressure, reduce blood clotting, and lower blood triglyceride levels. However, one should be careful about taking excessive fish oil *supplements* because they can thin the blood and inhibit blood clotting. Those who take blood-thinning medications should ask their physician how much dietary omega-3 fatty acid is appropriate. Another important role for omega-3 fatty acids is improved cognition in infants fed formula containing omega-3 fatty acids. There is also some evidence to suggest it may delay the onset of certain dementia associated with aging.

How much omega-3 fatty acid should adults consume daily? It depends on whom you ask. For a typical 2,000-calorie daily intake, about 3 g of omega-3 fatty acids are recommended. Two tablespoons of vegetable oils (flaxseed, canola, or soybean oils) and four meals of fatty fish per week would meet this goal. However, this would mean a dramatic increase in fish intake for most Americans. Others recommend lower levels of omega-3 fatty acids. The American Heart Association recommendations are often used as a guide:

| Population | Recommendation |
|---|---|
| Patients without heart disease | Eat a variety of fatty fish at least twice per week. Include foods rich in linolenic acid (flaxseed, canola, and soybean oils, flaxseed and walnuts). |
| Patients with heart disease | Consume 1 g of EPA + DHA per day, preferably from fatty fish. Use supplements only after consultation with a physician. |
| Patients who need to lower blood triglycerides | Consume 2–4 g of EPA + DHA per day, provided in capsules under a physician's care. |

These recommendations are the best way to get omega-3 fatty acids; food manufacturers are also adding these fatty acids to some products. Tropicana has added DHA to orange juice under the brand name Healthy Heart. ■

## Trans Fatty Acids

Have you ever heard of trans fats and wondered what they are? Look at food labels for snack foods and margarine and you may find information about total fat, saturated fat, and *trans fat*. As of January 1, 2006, the FDA requires that trans fatty acids be listed in nutrition labeling. This law was passed in response to a petition from the Center for Science in the Public Interest and to published human studies that showed that the intake of trans fatty acids increased low-density lipoproteins (LDL or "bad cholesterol") in the blood, very much as the intake of saturated fatty acids does, and that trans fatty acids decreased high-density lipoproteins (HDL or "good cholesterol").

*What's an example of an unhealthy fat?*

What are trans fatty acids? A **trans fatty acid** is an unhealthy fatty acid produced through addition of hydrogen atoms to double bonds of fatty acids, which causes the molecule to assume an unnatural shape. Only a small amount of trans fatty acids are found in milk and meat; they are not found naturally to any great extent. Let's take margarine, for example. Most margarines are made out of vegetable oils, which are liquid, yet most margarines are solids. So how do manufacturers take something that is liquid and make it into something solid? They do this through a process called *hydrogenation*. In hydrogenation, hydrogen atoms are added to the unsaturated fatty acid under intense heat so that there are fewer double bonds. This process serves two purposes: it makes the product into a solid and less susceptible to spoiling. Sounds great, but there is a downside. When you add the hydrogen back to the product, you change the configuration or arrangement of the bond.

Most hydrogen atoms bonded to a carbon atom will be in a *cis* arrangement, but in a hydrogenated product they will be in a *trans* arrangement (see Figure 4.6)—hence the term *trans fatty acids*. When hydrogenation is used for any product you will see the term *partially hydrogenated* on the food label in the ingredients list. The term *partial hydrogenation* is used because only some

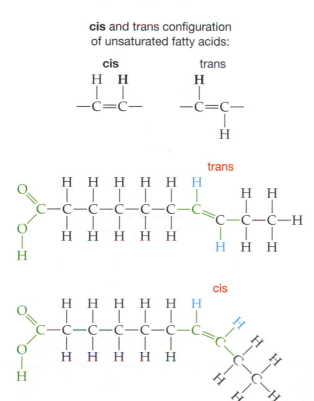

**Figure 4.6** Differences between trans fatty acids and cis fatty acids.

unsaturated fats are converted to saturated fats. Some unsaturated fatty acids remain in the *cis* form; others are converted to the trans form. Therefore, the fatty acids in the product have not become completely saturated, as are the fully saturated fatty acids naturally found in butter. The hydrogenated oils are often preferred for cooking because they don't break down under high cooking temperatures as quickly as other oils, and they are usually cheaper than butter. The higher cooking temperatures tolerated by these processed oils allow a crisp texture to be achieved, and most people crave the taste. As mentioned previously, partially hydrogenated fatty acids behave more like saturated fat and therefore have similar health consequences. Health and nutrition professionals recommend that we limit our intake of trans fatty acids as much as possible. The American Heart Association recommends 2 g of trans fatty acids per day or less. This is less than 1 percent of calories.

Local communities and several states either have banned or are considering legislation to ban trans fat from being used in restaurants. This move started outside the United States, with Denmark banning trans fat in 2003. The New York City Board of Health and the City of Philadelphia have now banned trans fat in their eating establishments. Some states, including New Jersey and California, are considering it, and by the time you read this they may have enacted a ban. Some companies have agreed to eliminate trans fat from some or all of their products; an example is Dunkin' Donuts, which initially removed trans fat from its muffins. Both Wendy's and McDonald's have changed their food preparation methods to do away with trans fats. Some other eateries, such as Kentucky Fried Chicken (KFC), have actually been sued over the use of trans fat in their cooking. KFC has since agreed to halt the practice. A rising proportion of consumers have become more conscious of these artery-clogging fats and report that they check food labels for the presence of trans fat. Interestingly, recent research in Denmark has revealed that consumers as a group were unable to detect a change in the taste of products once trans fats were removed.

## ■ Myths and Legends

*Healthwise, which is better—butter or margarine?*

What's your answer? It may surprise you that nonhydrogenated spreads like Smart Balance or those made from canola and/or olive oil is the answer. Here's why: the essential difference is that butter is an animal fat, while margarine is a fat produced from plants. In fact, margarine was developed as a substitute for butter. Both butter and margarine have the same number of calories per serving. However, butter is high in cholesterol as well as saturated fat, which can raise your body's total blood cholesterol level. Because margarine is derived from a plant source, it does not contain cholesterol. The drawback to margarine is that even though it is a vegetable oil and high in unsaturated fat, it typically becomes liquid at room temperature and therefore is not easy to "spread" on breads and other foods. Thus manufacturers subject it to the hydrogenation process, which yields trans fatty acids.

A new group of spreads that recently entered the market have emulsifiers (substances that facilitate mixture) added to enable unsaturated

Spreadable products that are made with soy or omega-3 fatty acids and are lower in total fat and saturated fat are now available to consumers.

fats to be stable and spreadable in the product. They also have water added, which decreases the caloric content. These alternatives, unlike butter and traditional margarines, have fewer calories, less saturated fat, and no cholesterol. Additionally, other spreads have soy added to help reduce the level of blood cholesterol. Benecol, made from soybeans, is a good example of this; the plant sterols of soy reduce the levels of total and LDL cholesterol (bad cholesterol), while raising HDL cholesterol (good cholesterol). So the answer is that soft, tub margarine is best for you as long as it is not hydrogenated. ■

## Triglycerides

Triglycerides are a form of fat found in food and in the body. Simply stated, a **triglyceride** is a chemical structure composed of a three-carbon compound called *glycerol* in which fatty acids are bonded to each of the carbons (see Figure 4.7). The three fatty acids present are different from each other and often reflect dietary fatty acids consumed.

## Phospholipids

As we mentioned in the beginning of the chapter, fat and water don't mix. Because your blood is mainly composed of water, your body has difficulty transporting fat through this watery substance. It accomplishes this task by synthesizing a unique compound called a **phospholipid.** Chemically, phospholipids are very similar to triglycerides. Phospholipids have a three-carbon glycerol backbone; the first two carbons of the glycerol molecule have fatty acids bound to them, and the third carbon has a phosphate group bonded to it (see Figure 4.8). The presence of this phosphate group changes the physical properties of the structure so that the phosphate end mixes with water while the other end mixes with fat. This allows it to blend with fats in the watery blood. We call the blending of fat and water *emulsification*. In food processing, many manufacturers add the emulsifier *lecithin* found in egg yolks to mix oil and water. An example of this is mayonnaise. Even though it is made from oil and water, it does not separate but stays mixed together because of the phospholipid lecithin.

We do not normally consume a lot of phospholipids in our diet. Only 2 percent of the fat consumed in the typical diet is from phospholipids and most

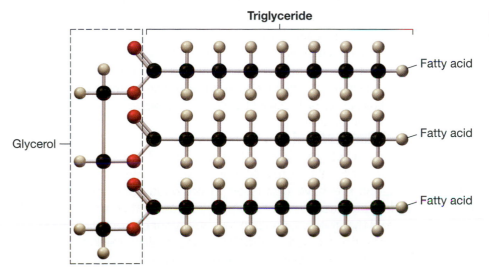

**Triglyceride**

Glycerol

Fatty acid

Fatty acid

Fatty acid

**Figure 4.7** General structure of a triglyceride fat.

**Figure 4.8** General structure of a phospholipid.

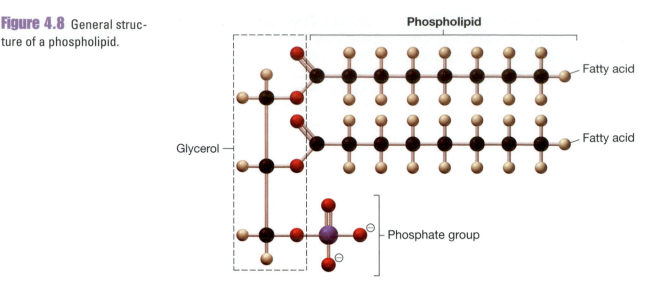

Fatty acid

Fatty acid

Glycerol

Phosphate group

of this comes from meat, poultry, and eggs. This is not a problem because the body can synthesize phospholipids from triglycerides present in cells. In the body phospholipids compose cell membranes and blood **lipoproteins.** Lipoproteins are molecules in the blood that help transport cholesterol and fatty acids to tissues.

## Sterols/Cholesterol

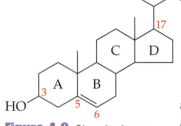

**Figure 4.9** Chemical structure of cholesterol.

Perhaps you have heard relatives or friends talk about their blood cholesterol levels and how they are trying to avoid too much cholesterol in the foods they eat. Most consumers have heard of cholesterol and its relation to heart disease. These groups of lipids are quite different chemically from the other lipids that we have discussed (see Figure 4.9). While cholesterol has received a lot of negative press, sterols are vital to health and basic metabolic functions. In fact, sex hormones such as *testosterone* and *estrogen* are sterols. Even vitamin D is a sterol. Some "stress hormones," such as *cortisol,* are also sterols. Cholesterol is a precursor to these other compounds.

Health professionals caution us to watch the amount of cholesterol we consume. This is because the liver makes most of the cholesterol our bodies contain. In fact, we do not need cholesterol in our diets. The total amount of fat in your diet, especially saturated and trans fat, is more likely to raise your blood cholesterol than the amount of actual cholesterol you consume. Thus, consumption of fatty acids can lead to increased cholesterol production. To help maintain your blood cholesterol levels within acceptable limits, many professionals recommend that you watch your intake of saturated fat, trans fat, and total fat more carefully than your intake of cholesterol, as discussed later in this chapter.

### ■ Self-Assessment

*Are you practicing heart-healthy eating?*

How does your personal diet relate to and compare with the several diet recommendations we have discussed in previous chapters? Is it heart healthy, or do you need to make some adjustments? Using the self-assessment tool that follows, you can see how your current diet stacks up.

For each category listed in the following table, check the column that most closely applies to you and then record your score for that food category in the left column. For example, if you consume 2 to 3 servings of vegetables per day, enter the number 3 in the "Score" space at the bottom of the "3 points" column. Add up your score for all categories and compare it to the ranges shown in the Interpretation section below the table.

## Rate Your Plate

| Category | 5 Points | 3 Points | 0 Points |
|---|---|---|---|
| **Grains: Bread, Cereal, Pasta, Rice, Dry Beans, and Peas** | Avoid all high-fat breads/cereals, such as croissants, sweet rolls, pastries, snack crackers, granola-type cereals.<br><br>Eat at least 8 servings daily. | Avoid most high-fat breads/cereals.<br><br>Eat at least 6 servings daily. | Do not limit high-fat breads/cereals.<br><br>Eat less than 6 servings daily or do not know how many servings you are eating. |
| Score: ——— | ——— | ——— | ——— |
| **Vegetables** | Eat 4 or more servings daily.<br><br>Avoid all vegetables prepared in butter, creams, or sauces. | Eat 2 or 3 servings daily.<br><br>Avoid most vegetables prepared in butter, cream, or sauces. | Eat 1 serving or less daily. |
| Score: ——— | ——— | ——— | ——— |
| **Fruit** | Eat 4 servings daily. | Eat 2 to 3 servings daily. | Eat 1 serving or less daily. |
| Score: ——— | ——— | ——— | ——— |
| **Eggs** | Eat 0 to 2 egg yolks per week.<br><br>*Remember to count eggs used in cooking. | Eat 3 to 4 egg yolks per week. | Eat more than 4 egg yolks per week. |
| Score: ——— | ——— | ——— | ——— |
| **Dairy** | Drink at least 2 cups skim milk daily.<br><br>Use all fat-free or non-fat dairy foods such as cheese, cottage cheese, frozen dairy desserts (fat-free ice cream, frozen yogurt). | Drink no more than 2 cups of 2% milk daily.<br><br>Use all low-fat products, such as cheese, cottage cheese, frozen dairy desserts. | Drink whole milk or more than 2 cups of 2% milk daily.<br><br>Use high-fat products such as cheese, cottage cheese, ice cream. |
| Score: ——— | ——— | ——— | ——— |
| **Meat, Poultry, Fish, Shellfish** | Limit red meat (pork, beef) to a 3-ounce portion 3 times per week.<br><br>Trim all visible fat.<br><br>Remove all poultry skin.<br><br>Eat more than 1 meatless meal per week. | Eat a 3-ounce portion of red meat no more than once a day.<br><br>Select only lean cuts of meat.<br><br>Eat 1 meatless meal per week. | Eat red meat twice a day.<br><br>Eat fried meat/poultry at least twice a week. |
| Score: ——— | ——— | ——— | ——— |

## Rate Your Plate

| Category | 5 Points | 3 Points | 0 Points |
|---|---|---|---|
| **Fats, Oils** | Use margarine, oil, and salad dressings made with only unsaturated oils: corn, olive, peanut, canola, safflower, sesame, soybean, sunflower.<br><br>Limit fats and oils to 3 teaspoons or less daily. | Use margarine, oil, and salad dressings made with only unsaturated oils.<br><br>Limit fats and oils to 4 teaspoons daily. | Eat unlimited amounts of margarine, oil, and salad dressings.<br><br>or<br><br>Do not use margarine, oil, and salad dressings made with only unsaturated oils.<br><br>or<br><br>Don't know what oils are in the margarine, oil, and salad dressings that I consume. |
| Score: ——— | ——— | ——— | ——— |
| **Sweets, Snacks** | Avoid all high-fat frozen desserts; high-fat cakes, snacks, beverages (milkshakes); and store-bought bakery products (cookies, cakes, etc.)<br><br>Eat nonfat or low-fat desserts, snacks, bakery products. | Avoid *most* high-fat frozen desserts; high-fat cakes, snacks, beverages (milkshakes); and store-bought bakery products (cookies, cakes, etc.)<br><br>Eat sparingly homemade cakes, cookies, pies containing unsaturated oils. | Eat high-fat frozen desserts, cakes, snacks, and store-bought bakery products. |
| Score: ——— | ——— | ——— | ——— |
| **Salt** | Use no salt in cooking or at the table.<br><br>Use salt-free seasonings only.<br><br>Make homemade soups without salt. | Use a small amount of salt in cooking, but none at the table.<br><br>Use salt-free seasonings only.<br><br>Use reduced-sodium soups. | Use salt in cooking and at the table.<br><br>Use seasonings that contain salt: garlic salt, onion salt, etc.<br><br>Use regular canned soups. |
| Score: ——— | ——— | ——— | ——— |

TOTAL SCORE ———

Calculate your total score from above and compare to the box below to see how your diet shapes up. How did you do?

| Score | Interpretation |
|---|---|
| 45 | Perfect! You already have a heart-healthy eating lifestyle. |
| 38–44 | Close to perfect! You've made many heart-healthy changes. |
| 30–37 | Good effort! Try to improve in the categories in which you did not score **5 points.** |
| 22–29 | You're trying! Work harder to eat your way to a healthy heart. |
| 21 or less | You could do much better! See a physician or a registered dietitian for assistance on your diet. |

Source: Adapted from the Prairie Heart Institute at St. John's Hospital, Center for Living, 619 E. Mason Street, Springfield, IL 62701, Sara Lopinski, MS, RD, LDN. Reprinted by permission. ■

## Lipid Functions

Lipids perform various functions in human nutrition, including storing energy, supplying essential fatty acids, absorbing and transporting fat-soluble vitamins, protecting and insulating vital organs, providing flavor and satiety in food, providing cell membrane structure, and serving as a precursor to steroid hormones (Figure 4.10).

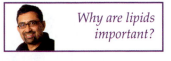

*Why are lipids important?*

### Storage Form of Energy

Fats are the major form of stored energy in the body. The typical adult male of normal weight has 100,000 calories stored as fat. Compare this to glycogen, the storage form of carbohydrates, which stores about 1,500 calories.

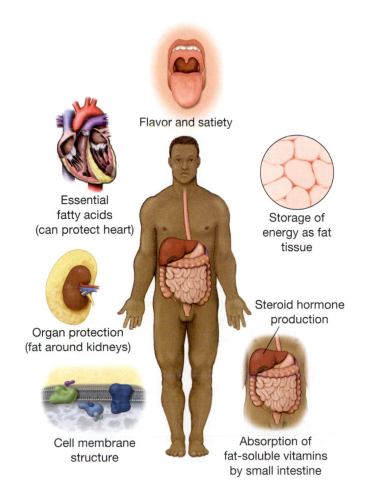

Flavor and satiety

Essential fatty acids (can protect heart)

Storage of energy as fat tissue

Organ protection (fat around kidneys)

Steroid hormone production

Cell membrane structure

Absorption of fat-soluble vitamins by small intestine

**Figure 4.10** Fats carry out a number of functions in the human body.

This amount of fat calories is equal to 30 pounds of fat. Fat is a concentrated energy source; it contains 9 calories per gram, compared with 4 calories per gram for carbohydrate and protein. A tablespoon of almost any type of vegetable oil has 120 calories. With respect to the heart, lipids are significant because the heart uses fatty acids as its preferred source of energy.

## Supply of Essential Fatty Acids

We have already mentioned that dietary fat supplies the body with essential fatty acids—linoleic and linolenic acids. The omega-3 fatty acid linolenic acid gives rise to the longer-chain fatty acids EPA and DHA. These fatty acids are converted to a group of metabolically active chemicals termed **eicosanoids.** Eicosanoids have powerful physiological effects, including relaxing blood vessels and promoting clotting.

## Absorption and Transport of Fat-Soluble Vitamins

Fat is very important for the absorption of fat-soluble vitamins, which are vitamins A, D, E, and K. When conditions cause incomplete fat digestion or fat malabsorption, the amount of these vitamins absorbed decreases dramatically.

## Organ Insulation and Protection

Fat has an important function in protecting and insulating the vital organs of the body, such as the fat deposits surrounding the kidney. The fat layer under the skin can also contribute to the insulating effects of fat. For reproductive reasons adult females have a greater percentage of body fat than males, and thus more insulating capacity as well.

## Flavor and Satiety of Food

*Why does food high in fat always taste so good?*

It would be difficult to overstate the contribution of fat to the taste of food. The most important aspect of fat in foods from a consumer perspective is sensory. Foods with fat have superior mouthfeel and texture, and the taste lingers in the mouth after swallowing. Have you noticed that regular ice cream has a smooth and creamy mouthfeel and the flavors linger longer than in the reduced-fat version? The flavor compounds in foods are generally interacting with the fat portion of food.

Fat in foods causes you to feel full longer. This means that you tend to be more satisfied and less hungry after consuming fat in a meal. This is called **satiety.** Satiety is the feeling of being satisfied after consuming food. One of the reasons for this effect is fat's tendency to slow the time it takes food to empty out of your stomach, so that the feeling of fullness is retained longer. Also, because they are fat soluble, the flavor compounds in food are dissolved in the fat, which adds to their contribution to satiety.

Low-fat diets can be problematic when weight control is an issue. Although it is important to reduce fat in a diet to effectively lose weight, some fat consumption is suggested because of fat's satiating effect. Moreover, fat slows

**gastric emptying** (movement of food from the stomach to the small intestine), which blocks the return of the brain's hunger signals to us to consume more food. If you eat a salad without dressing, you are likely to feel hungry soon after finishing. However, if you add ranch dressing, nuts, or grated cheese that contain some fat, then you are not likely to become hungry as quickly. Remember that fat is an essential nutrient, so you shouldn't totally eliminate it from your diet.

## Cell Membrane Structure

Phospholipids are the major component of cell membranes and membranes of organelles within cells. As you may recall, the phosphate group of these lipids allows the membranes to associate with a water environment, while the remainder of the molecule can associate with lipid phases of the cell. These phospholipids allow cells and organelles to have structure and act as barriers to selectively allow only certain compounds to enter and exit.

## Precursor to Steroid Hormones

Cholesterol is the precursor to many hormones. The two sex hormones estrogen and testosterone are made from cholesterol. Another hormone that controls salt balance in your body is aldosterone, also made from cholesterol. Later you will discover that vitamin D is also considered a steroid hormone and is made from cholesterol. We could not exist without cholesterol, because it gives rise to these very powerful hormones that affect our body's metabolism.

**Before you go on . . .**
1. What role does fat play in the absorption of certain vitamins?
2. Why do people feel more full and satisfied after consuming a meal with fat?
3. List at least five functions lipids perform in the body.

## Fat Content of Foods

Fats are found in both animal *and* plant products. Table 4.2 lists the fat and cholesterol content of some commonly consumed foods. Meats, butter, and other dairy products contain significant levels of triglycerides with saturated fatty acids. Polyunsaturated fatty acids are present in larger amounts in fish and poultry than in red meat such as pork, lamb, and beef. Most vegetable oils are high in polyunsaturated fatty acids, but as noted earlier some tropical oils, such as coconut, are high in saturated fatty acids. Olive and canola oils are probably the best dietary sources of monounsaturated fatty acids.

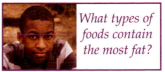

*What types of foods contain the most fat?*

Again, foods of animal origin are the *only* ones that contain cholesterol. Besides meats, foods such as cheese, butter, eggs, and milk all have cholesterol. Because cholesterol is made in the liver, eating cow, chicken, or any other animal's liver *will* give you a high intake of dietary cholesterol (see Table 4.2).

## Table 4.2    Fat and Cholesterol Content of Selected Foods

| | Serving Size | Fat (g) | Cholesterol (mg) |
|---|---|---|---|
| **Foods with Cholesterol** | | | |
| Beef brains, cooked | 3 oz. | 13 | 1,696 |
| Beef kidneys, cooked | 3 oz. | 4 | 609 |
| Liver, pan-fried | 3 oz. | 7 | 410 |
| Cream, 31% fat* | 1 c. | 74 | 265 |
| Shrimp, raw | 1 c. | 3 | 221 |
| Eggs, whole or yolk | 1 large | 5 | 212 |
| Lobster, raw | 1 c. | 1 | 104 |
| Pork chops | 3 oz. | 14 | 78 |
| Ground beef, cooked | 3 oz. | 15 | 76 |
| Chicken breast, cooked | 3 oz. | 7 | 71 |
| Ribeye steak | 3 oz. | 10 | 68 |
| Butter, 81% fat | 1 oz. | 23 | 61 |
| Ice cream, vanilla | 1 c. | 14 | 58 |
| Bacon | 3 oz. | 38 | 58 |
| Noodles, egg | 1 c. | 2 | 53 |
| Beef hot dogs | 2 | 27 | 48 |
| Tuna, water-packed | 1 c. | 1 | 46 |
| Cheese, cheddar | 1 oz. | 9 | 27 |
| Milk, whole, 3.5% fat | 1 c. | 8 | 24 |
| Milk, 2% fat | 1 c. | 5 | 20 |
| Milk, 1% fat | 1 c. | 2 | 12 |
| Mayonnaise, 78% fat | 1 Tbsp. | 5 | 4 |
| **Foods High in Fat That Have No Cholesterol** | | | |
| Coconut | 1/4 c. | 27 | 0 |
| Avocado | 1 | 26 | 0 |
| Peanuts | 1/4 c. | 18 | 0 |
| Almonds | 1/4 c. | 17 | 0 |
| Soybeans | 1/2 c. | 8 | 0 |
| Black olives | 10 | 5 | 0 |

*A "serving size" of cream as an additive to coffee would typically be 1 tsp.

## Label Definitions

Consumers are often confused as to what certain terms regarding fat really indicate when they appear on a food label. We see labels such as "reduced fat" and "fat free" in the supermarket, but do we really know what they mean? As discussed in both Chapters 1 and 2, the Food and Drug Administration (FDA) is responsible for the definitions of these terms and what food manufacturers are allowed to state on a label. Here are some claims and the requirements that must be met to use them on a food label:

- *Fat free*—less than 0.5 g of fat per serving, with no fat or oil added during processing
- *Low fat*—3 g or less of fat per serving
- *Less fat*—25 percent or less fat than the typical comparison food in its category of the same serving size
- *Light (fat)*—50 percent or less fat than in the comparison food (example: 50 percent less fat than the producer's regular product)
- *Saturated fat free*—less than 0.5 g of saturated fat and 0.5 g of trans fatty acids per serving
- *Cholesterol free*—less than 2 mg of cholesterol per serving, and 2 g or less of saturated fat per serving
- *Low cholesterol*—20 mg or less of cholesterol per serving and 2 g or less of saturated fat per serving
- *Lean*—Less than 10 g of fat, 4.5 g of saturated fat, and 95 mg of cholesterol per (100-g) serving of meat, poultry, or seafood
- *Extra lean*—Less than 5 g of fat, 2 g of saturated fat, and 95 mg of cholesterol per (100-g) serving of meat, poultry, or seafood

## Identifying Fats on the Label

As you may recall from the discussions on food labeling in Chapter 2, the grams of total fat per serving size as well as saturated fat, trans fats, and cholesterol are present on food labels. The calories from fat in a serving size plus the percentage of total fat, saturated fat, and cholesterol in meeting the Daily Value (DV) are all listed on a food label (see Figure 4.11).

## Trans-Fatty Acids

Food labels are now required to show the amount of trans fat per serving. Notably, because of their high levels of partially hydrogenated fats, cookies, cakes, crackers, pies, and breads contribute more than 40 percent of the trans fatty acids in our diets.

## Fat Substitutes

Given the increased attention to reducing heart disease in our population and the link between heart disease and the fat we eat, the food industry is producing more fat-free foods. This is especially challenging because fat is one of the main reasons foods taste the way they do. Fat substitutes can be divided into three basic classes:

- Carbohydrate-based fat substitutes
- Protein-based fat substitutes
- Fat-based fat substitutes

*Carbohydrate-based fat substitutes* include compounds such as dextrins, maltodextrins, modified food starches, cellulose, and various gums. They can replace fat's creaminess, bulkiness, and moistness, but not its cooking qualities. While 1 g of fat yields 9 kcal, these carbohydrate-based substitutes yield only 1–4 kcal per gram. Some of these are easily digested, retain more water than fat, and give good mouthfeel. However, fat-free products are not necessarily

---

**APPLICATION TIP**

Learn to cook with and make salad dressings using extra virgin olive oil. It contains monounsaturated fat, which lowers total blood cholesterol, and antioxidants that protect against heart disease and certain types of cancers. However, it does contain the same amount of calories as other oils.

By using extra virgin olive oil in salad dressings and other recipes, you will reduce your cholesterol intake.

---

### Nutrition Facts

Serving Size 1 cup (228g)
Servings Per Container 2

**Amount Per Serving**

Calories 250  Calories from Fat 110

| | % Daily Value* |
|---|---|
| **Total Fat** 12g | **16%** |
| Saturated Fat 3g | **15%** |
| *Trans* Fat 1.5g | |
| **Cholesterol** 30mg | **10%** |
| **Sodium** 470mg | **20%** |
| **Total Carbohydrate** 0.1g | **10%** |
| Dietary Fiber 0g | **0%** |
| Sugars 5g | |
| **Proteins** 5g | |
| Vitamin A | **4%** |
| Vitamin C | **2%** |
| Calcium | **20%** |
| Iron | **4%** |

*Percent Daily Values are based on a 2,000 calories diet. Your Daily Values may be higher or lower depending on your calorie needs.

| | | Calories | 2,000 | 2,500 |
|---|---|---|---|---|
| Total Fat | Less than | | 65g | 80g |
| Sat Fat | Less than | | 20g | 25g |
| Cholesterol | Less than | | 300mg | 300mg |
| Sodium | Less than | | 2,400mg | 2,400mg |
| Total Carbohydrates | | | 300g | 375g |
| Dietary Fiber | | | 25g | 30g |

**Figure 4.11** Nutrition facts label from salad dressing. Note the amounts of fat, saturated fat, and trans fat listed on the label.

low-calorie; many have more carbohydrate added to make up for the difference in taste. In fact, the total calories may be similar. Many people purchase foods with a fat replacer to lose weight, only to learn later that the net calories in the modified product are similar. Some people actually eat more of the food with the fat replacer because of the misconception that it does not have as many calories.

*Protein-based fat substitutes* include modified egg whites and whey from milk. A drawback of this type of substitute is that a high cooking temperature can lead to protein breakdown. An example of such a product is Simplesse® Microparticulated Whey Protein Concentrate, which is made by NutraSweet, the same company that makes the sugar substitute Equal. Because of problems with potential breakdown in cooking, these fat replacers are most often used in frozen desserts. They contain approximately 4 kcal per gram.

Fat substitutes such as Simplesse® Microparticulated Whey Protein Concentrate are proteins that are added to products to give them the mouthfeel and sensory attributes of fat. Are there any disadvantages in cooking with a protein-based fat substitute?

The last class of substitutes is the *fat-based fat* substitutes. Olean, Salatrim, and Caprenin are made from lipids that are nondigestible. Olean (or Olestra) is the most widely used because it does not contain calories and is not digested. It is commonly used in potato chips and other such foods. Salatrim and Caprenin have been chemically altered so that they cannot be digested. They contain half the calories of fat (4–5 kcal per gram). These substitutes give the food product real fat taste and mouthfeel but with less caloric absorption due to the impaired digestion.

Consumer interest groups have raised concerns regarding the possible side effects of Olestra and its interaction with the absorption of other nutrients. As it cannot be digested, Olestra can cause abdominal cramps and diarrhea. Also, Olestra reduces the absorption of fat-soluble vitamins (vitamins A, D, E, and K). In order to continue its use, manufacturers promised the FDA that they would fortify food products with these fat-soluble vitamins. Fortification ensures that what little fat is left in the product is bound to these essential nutrients. The FDA, until recently, required labels to state the following:

> This product contains Olestra. Olestra may cause abdominal cramping and loose stools. Olestra inhibits the absorption of some vitamins and other nutrients. Vitamins A, D, E, and K have been added.

Olestra, a fat-based fat substitute made from nondigestible lipids, can be found in some snack products such as chips. Are products that use fat-based substitutes significantly lower in calories?

The part on abdominal cramping is no longer required by the FDA, but the facts about soluble vitamins are. The FDA restricts the use of Olestra to a handful of snack foods such as chips. Some people have no side effects from Olestra, especially when consumed in limited amounts. Salatrim is mainly used in chocolate chips, and Caprenin is a substitute for the cocoa butter used in candy bars. Despite the limitations of Olestra, Salatrim, and Caprenin, these fat replacers allow consumers to enjoy the sensory attributes of fat without the caloric concerns.

## ■ To Supplement or Not?

*What are fat blockers and do they work?*

There are several types of fat blockers on the market. Some work and some do not. There are different ways in which some of these products work to block fat absorption. One common blocker is marketed over-the-counter as Alli,® sometimes referred to as Xenicol,® which is available through prescription. The chemical name for both is Orlistat. The drug works by inhibiting an enzyme produced by the pancreas that breaks down triglycerides. Studies have shown that if one follows a reduced-calorie diet and takes this drug, a weight loss of almost 7 more pounds over one year can be achieved when compared to following the same reduced-calorie diet without taking the drug. However, it is not without its side-effects. There is a warning on the package of the medication not to wear light clothing when taking this drug as anal seepage of stools is possible. This is due to the fact that the stools contain a lot of undigested fat that make bowel movements loose. The fact that fat is not being digested creates another problem. The fat soluble vitamins A, D, E, and K may not be absorbed as well since they tend to dissolve in the fat that is being passed into the large intestine. More significant is that oral contraceptive agents (e.g., "the pill") are fat soluble and thus may not be absorbed to the full extent if one is taking this drug. Unintended pregnancies can occur with females consuming both oral contraceptive agents and Orlistat.

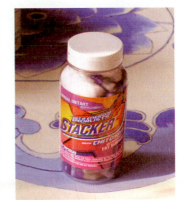

Through the use of a fiber-like compound chitosan, fat blockers are designed to prevent fat absorption. Results as to their effectiveness are mixed. Is there a downside to using these supplements?

There are other types of fat blockers sold on the market that consist of a compound called *chitosan*. These compounds supposedly have the ability to bind fat and cholesterol, thus making them unavailable for absorption. You are supposed to take these products before a meal to get the full benefit. What is chitosan? It is a fiber-like compound that is derived from the shells of crustaceans such as shrimp and crabs. It is thought to lower fat absorption in the small intestine. Is it effective? Some animal studies suggest it is and that it can even raise HDL-cholesterol and lower LDL-cholesterol, which is beneficial in combating heart disease. However, studies with humans have yielded negative results. A study at the University of California-Davis reported there was not a greater excretion of fat in the feces of people taking the chitosan supplements. If fat absorption were being blocked you would have expected to see more fat in the feces. Furthermore, there was no reduction in body weight with the use of these products. For these types of fat blocker the best advice is to save your money and block fat by not eating excessive amounts to begin with! ■

### Before you go on . . .

1. If you want to reduce intake of saturated fatty acids, which foods should you avoid?
2. Define *low-fat food* as used on food labels.
3. Which fat replacer does not contain calories?
4. Define *fat blocker* and describe some possible side effects of using such products.

## Lipids and Health

You have probably heard quite a bit about the link between too much fat in our diet and specific diseases. Government and health agencies have recommended how much and what type of fat we should consume. Also, researchers have studied which diseases may be linked to too much fat intake. Here we consider these factors.

In order for children under two years of age to get adequate fat, it is recommended that they consume whole milk. Why is consumption of milk in which the fat content represents 30 to 35 percent of its total calories important for this age group and not for adults?

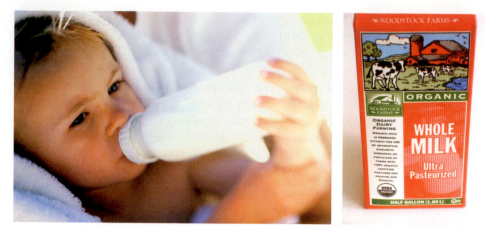

 **Want to know more?**
If you would like more information about the trend of fat consumption in the United States, go to the text website at http://webcom8.grtxle.com/nutrition and click on the Chapters button. Select Chapter 4.

**APPLICATION TIP**

In order to decrease your total fat intake, whenever possible drink skim milk instead of 2% or whole milk.

# Recommendations for Dietary Intake of Fats

The USDA's 2005 *Dietary Guidelines for Americans* provides recommendations for all people over age 2. Intakes of fat representing more than 35 percent of your total calories are discouraged. The report points out that controlling the intake of saturated fat and calories is difficult when the percentage consumed increases above this level. A lower-level target for adults is now 20 percent. Going lower than 20 percent increases the risk of inadequate supply and absorption of important fat-soluble vitamins. It is recommended that children under age 2 consume 30–35 percent of their calories from fat, and not less than 30 percent. The requirements for growth and the nervous system depend on adequate fat intake. Children under age 2 should not limit fat intake, and they should avoid skim and low-fat milk.

Consumers should choose foods that are higher in polyunsaturated and monounsaturated fatty acids. Saturated fat should constitute no more than 10 percent of your total caloric intake. The balance should come from polyunsaturated (10–12 percent) and from monounsaturated (10–12 percent). For someone on a 2,000-calorie diet, this means no more than 20 g of saturated fat per day. Meat, cheese, and whole milk are the chief contributors to saturated fat in the American diet. Trans fat (found in most margarines, shortenings, baked goods, many fast foods, and deep-fried chips) and products that are hydrogenated, including many crackers and snack foods, should be avoided. As an example, Figure 4.12 translates fat recommendations into a 2,000 calorie single day meal plan.

A challenge in reducing fat intake is that much of the fat we consume is invisible. Invisible fat is not readily apparent just by looking at the food item.

Visible and invisible sources of fat. Cookies have a great deal of fat, but it is not readily visible, unlike the fat in butter.

**BREAKFAST**

1 cup cooked oatmeal, sprinkle with 1 tablespoon cinnamon and chopped walnuts; 1 banana; 1 cup skim milk

**LUNCH**

1 cup low-fat (1 percent or lower) cottage cheese with 1 teaspoon ground flaxseed; 1/2 cup peach halves; 5 Melba toast crackers; 1 cup raw broccoli and cauliflower; 2 tablespoons low-fat cream cheese, plain or vegetable flavor
(as a spread for crackers or vegetable dip); Sparkling water

**DINNER**

Grilled turkey burger (4 ounces) with a whole-grain bun; 1/2 cup green beans with toasted almonds; 2 cups mixed salad greens; 2 tablespoons low-fat salad dressing; 1 tablespoon sunflower seeds; 1 cup skim milk; 1 small orange

**SNACK**

1 yogurt; 9 animal crackers

**Figure 4.12** This menu from www.mayoclinic.com is an example of a heart-healthy menu providing approximately 1,600 calories: 23% fat, 20% protein and 60% carbohydrate. It is low in saturated fat (5%), high in fiber (30 g) and low in sodium (1,500 mg).

Examples are mayonnaise and the fat added to crackers and baked products. Visible fat, such as what we can see on meat or poultry, allows us a better way to assess fat intake.

### ■ Make It a Practice
*Cutting fat in your diet*

In order to manage the amount of fat in your diet, you first need to figure out what you are eating that contains fat. You can ask yourself some simple questions in order to identify where to begin to make the cuts.

- How much meat (including hamburger), fish, and poultry do you eat per day?
- How much cheese do you eat per week, including cheese added to sandwiches or cheeseburgers?
- What type of milk do you consume?
- How many eggs do you consume per week?
- How often do you eat lunchmeat, hot dogs, corned beef, spareribs, sausage, bacon, or liver?
- How much and what type of dressing do you put on your salad?
- How many times per week do you eat sweets such as pastries, cookies, doughnuts, ice cream, and chocolate?
- Do you eat snack foods such as potato chips, french fries, and party crackers?
- How much butter do you put on bread? How much butter and sour cream do you put on your baked potato?
- Do you use nonhydrogenated soft tub margarine, regular margarine, or butter?
- Do you consume fried foods?

Now that you have taken an inventory from these questions, here is what you can do:

- Think of meat as a side dish instead of the focus of your meal.
- Eat more poultry and fish than beef, pork, or lamb.
- When you do eat red meats such as beef and pork, choose lean cuts, such as London broil, round steak, or pork tenderloin.
- When you eat poultry, remove the skin.
- Eat foods without adding cheese, or use fat-free or vegetarian cheese products.
- Try main dishes that feature pasta, rice, beans, and/or vegetables. Or create low-meat dishes by mixing pasta, rice, beans, and vegetables with small amounts of lean meat, poultry, or fish. An example is bean soup flavored with a small amount of lean ham, turkey breast, or skinless chicken.
- Choose skim milk.
- Cook with olive or canola oil, which are healthier for you than other oils.
- Use cooking methods that require little or no fat. You can bake, broil, steam, roast, poach, stir-fry, and microwave. You can sautá in very small amounts of oil or use broth, cooking sherry, wine, or even water. You can also use vegetable cooking sprays or nonstick cookware.
- The 5–8 tsp. of fats and oils allowed per day can be used in cooking and baking and/or in salad dressings and spreads.
- Carefully trim off fat from meats *before* cooking. Drain off fat after you brown meat. You can reduce the fat in hamburger by rinsing it under water after browning.
- Chill soups and stews after cooking so that you can skim off the hardened/congealed fat.
- Use soft tub spread or margarine instead of butter. Use trans-fat-free margarines or spreads with olive or canola oils, or Benecol, a soy-based spread, as an alternative.
- Cut down on consumption of lunch meat, bacon, sausage, hot dogs, and baked goods.
- Avoid snacking on high-fat foods such as potato chips.
- Limit the intake of foods prepared with sauces or gravies.
- Limit "battered" or fried foods, or at least do not fry food in saturated fats.
- Ask for salad dressings to be served on the side (use them sparingly).
- Avoid creamy dressings; use fat-free dressings or those made with olive or canola oil.
- Enjoy the roll, but forget the butter, or dip the bread in olive oil.
- Choose steamed vegetables over fried or creamed vegetables.
- Choose sherbet, sorbet, iced milk made from skim milk, and frozen yogurt instead of ice cream or high-fat desserts. ■

## Obesity

Is the obesity epidemic in the United States and other industrialized nations connected with an increased fat intake? Common sense would say yes—fats typically contain twice the number of calories by weight than do carbohydrates and proteins. But in the United States, the *percentage* of calories from fats in our diet has actually *decreased* over the last two decades.

Walter Willett of Harvard University has examined this relationship and found that a small reduction in body weight occurs in individuals who eat diets with a lower percentage of calories from fat. After analyzing data from several short-term studies, he estimated that a decrease of 10 percent of calories from fat would reduce weight by 16 g/day, which would result in a 9-kg (20-lb.) weight loss after 18 months. This was true only when the total amount of calories consumed did not change. However, Willett points out that over longer periods of time, lower levels of fat consumed have not shown a decrease in body weight, suggesting that the body compensates in some way. This viewpoint is certainly controversial. Many nutritionists believe that a high-fat diet has contributed to the increased incidence of obesity.

Several studies indicate that when individuals consume a diet high in fruits, vegetables, and whole grains (low in fat and high in complex carbohydrates), they achieve an effective weight reduction. Lowering the amount of fat in one's diet may not be as difficult as many of us perceive it to be, as indicated in the tips listed previously. There are some concerns over restricting dietary fat too much. Some individuals with very low-fat diets may have an insufficient intake of vitamins A and E, iron, and zinc, because reduced-fat foods are often low in these nutrients. People may overcompensate on a low-fat diet by increasing their intake of carbohydrates with a false sense of security that they may not be getting as many calories. Of course, replacing high-fat foods with pastries and chips made with low-fat substitutes may not constitute a low-calorie diet. These foods often have more sugars and are high in calories, leading to weight gain. In fact, one study revealed that increased carbohydrate intake is associated with a decrease in the more healthy HDL cholesterol in the blood. The bottom line is that caloric intake is much more important than fat or other food components with respect to obesity. How much we consume, portion size, and our expenditure or burning of calories through physical activity all influence the sizes of our waistlines (see Chapter 7 on weight loss).

## Heart Disease

While the number of deaths from heart disease has steadily declined since the 1960s, it is still ranked as the leading cause of death. Although many factors lead to heart disease, including lifestyle and family history, research confirms that diet plays a significant role. An increased intake of fat, particularly saturated fat, has been directly correlated to an increase in heart disease. Moreover, excess consumption of total fat, saturated fat, and trans fat in the diet, and to a lesser extent dietary cholesterol, can raise your blood cholesterol level and increase your likelihood of developing heart disease (see Table 4.3). The main type of heart disease linked with fat intake is **atherosclerosis,** which is characterized by a buildup of fatty deposits and streaks in the arteries. This narrowing of the arteries can reduce and eventually cut off blood flow to the heart and create a condition referred to as **ischemia.** This condition should not be confused with a similar term, arteriosclerosis, which is a loss of elasticity of the major blood vessels. Sometimes this is referred to as hardening of the arteries. This disease is likely to be caused by high blood pressure. However, atherosclerosis is a type of atherosclerosis, where due to the build-up of fatty deposits, there is a loss of elasticity.

A related condition is called *angina pectoris*, or chest pains under the left arm that are normally caused by a partially blocked artery. If the artery becomes completely blocked, it is called a *myocardial infarct* or *heart attack.*

# Real People, Other Voices

**Student:**
### Tricia Ryan,
Gloucester County College

Janine is correct to be concerned about medical interventions, especially since she is in her child-bearing years. Altering the body's chemistry is a slippery slope, and for someone as young as she is, with a relatively modest increase in cholesterol and weight, it makes sense to first consider natural alternatives.

A Mediterranean diet, modified for her culture and dietary preferences, seems ideal. She may wish to abstain from red wine for several reasons, such as religious preference, a genetic predisposition to alcoholism, or a desire not to be slowed down by the effects of alcohol. Some studies show that the primary benefit of red wine is derived from the pyruvic acid and related derivatives found in the grapes rather than from the alcohol, and others have shown benefits from drinking dark grape juices. She may also want to cut back her carbohydrates and simple sugars to avoid the feeling of emptiness, but may actually benefit from using salad dressings that contain fat if doing so causes her to eat more salads. Janine might well benefit from switching to olive oil almost exclusively instead of butter or margarine, and she should consider adding a natural grape juice to her diet instead of red wine.

Finally, she should begin some type of daily, or almost daily, exercise, even if it's just walking. Studies have shown that steady moderate weight loss is the one kind of weight loss that usually persists.

**Instructor:**
### Patricia B. Brevard
James Madison University

Confused by conflicting opinions about what constitutes a healthy diet, Janine must work quickly to lower her serum cholesterol if she wants to avoid taking medications, so she should be highly motivated to make changes. She should find a Registered Dietitian to assist her in developing an individualized eating plan based on her food preferences and current eating patterns. Conducting a comprehensive dietary assessment will identify foods that are contributing to her elevated cholesterol level, such as those high in saturated fatty acids, trans fatty acids, or total fat.

Janine's current physical activity level should also be assessed to determine energy expended compared with energy intake and to determine her caloric needs for gradual weight loss. She should monitor LDL and HDL levels and should adapt her diet/exercise program accordingly. At least 30 minutes of exercise should be implemented daily, such as walking, playing with her children, dancing, rope jumping, or fun exercises that adequately raise her heart rate.

She should identify improvements she can make to her current diet, such as monitoring portion sizes to determine appropriate amounts, eating several small meals daily, or having snacks with her children. She should consume adequate amounts of fruits, vegetables, whole grains, lowfat/nonfat dairy products, lean meats, oils such as olive, canola, or peanut, and a moderate amount of nuts for a healthy balance of foods, while carefully monitoring foods high in sugars and fats. These suggestions should help her lose weight and avoid feeling hungry, and they should lower her total cholesterol and LDL level while raising her HDL.

**Registered Dietitian:**
### Mary Emerson, MS, RD/LD
Gorham, ME

Janine is understandably confused by all the conflicting information that is readily available. The most important thing to keep in mind when evaluating factual nutrition information is what is appropriate for her particular lifestyle and food preferences. Because both of her children are at a formative age in the development of their own food preferences, Janine also has to take their nutritional needs into consideration. For a child under age 2, reducing the amount of fat in the diet (particularly changing to lowfat milk and dairy products) is not recommended because this type of restriction could affect their neurodevelopment.

Janine needs to establish a plan for herself, recognizing that it can be different from that of her children. At the same time, she should combine as many foods as possible for convenience while serving as a positive role model for them with her own dietary choices. For example, snacks are essential to growing children, but adults frequently consume excessive calories in snacks. She could offer the children nutrient-dense, lower calorie snacks such as baked tortilla chips and salsa, selecting a low-calorie beverage for herself and one with higher calories for the children, or yogurt parfaits with particular attention to limiting her own portion size.

It is often helpful to make dietary changes gradually. For example, Janine may be able to increase omega-3 fat sources by incorporating ground flaxseeds in her cooking. Her children's food preferences are just now being formed. The foods she presents to them will shape their eating habits for years to come.

| **Table 4.3** | **Types of Heart Disease** |
|---|---|
| **Disease** | **Definition** |
| Atherosclerosis | A form of heart disease in which deposits of fatty substances, cholesterol, cellular waste products, calcium, and other substances (referred to as plaque) build up in the inner lining of an artery. |
| Ischemia | A restriction in blood supply to the heart, generally due to factors in the blood vessels with resultant damage or dysfunction of tissue. |
| Angina pectoris | Pain in the chest, shoulder, or arm typically caused by insufficient blood flow to the heart. |
| Thrombosis | Formation of a blood clot in a blood vessel. The clot itself is called a thrombus. |
| Myocardial infarct | Destruction of heart tissue resulting from obstruction of the blood supply to the heart muscle (a heart attack). |
| Stroke | An event in which blood supply to the brain is suddenly interrupted by a blood clot, hemorrhage, or other cause. |

If this occurs in the brain it is called a *stroke*. Collectively, these conditions are referred to as *cardiovascular diseases*.

Although no *single* factor leads to heart disease, certain attributes or *risk factors* increase one's likelihood of developing heart disease. Heredity or family history is one such strong risk factor for heart disease. High blood pressure is another, as is an increased level of blood cholesterol.

The form or manner in which cholesterol is present in the blood is very significant in terms of health. We refer to these cholesterol forms as lipoproteins (see Figure 4.13) Lipoproteins are spherical structures that are a combination of lipids and proteins. The lipids found in these structures are triglycerides, cholesterol, and phospholipids; lipoproteins transport these lipids to various tissues. The blood contains four types of lipoproteins:

- Chylomicrons
- Very low-density lipoproteins (VLDLs)
- Low-density lipoproteins (LDLs)
- High-density lipoproteins (HDLs)

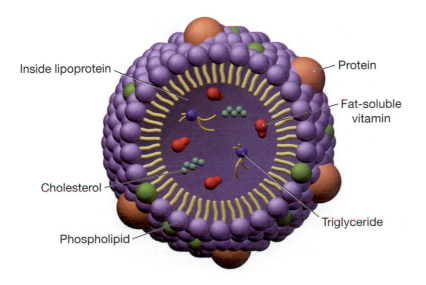

Inside lipoprotein

Protein

Fat-soluble vitamin

Cholesterol

Phospholipid

Triglyceride

**Figure 4.13** Diagram of a lipoprotein. Notice the spherical shape, with phospholipids and protein on the outer shell and triglycerides and cholesterol in the inner portion.

Recall that lipids are not soluble in water. This is a problem for lipid transport in the blood, which is mostly water. To get around this problem, adding a protein to these lipids in a spherical structure allows them to be more soluble in blood so they can be transported throughout the body.

**Chylomicrons** are lipoproteins formed when one consumes a meal and the cells lining the small intestine absorb the fats. They are made in the small intestinal cells and transport dietary lipids to the liver. **Very low-density lipoproteins (VLDLs)** are lipoproteins that are synthesized in the liver and contain both triglycerides and cholesterol. They deliver triglycerides to other tissues. After they do this they become LDLs and are smaller and denser, but now cholesterol rich. **Low-density lipoproteins (LDLs)** are, therefore, remnants of the breakdown of VLDLs and will deliver cholesterol to other tissues, including blood vessels. **High-density lipoproteins (HDLs)** are made mostly in the liver, but in the small intestine as well. HDLs decrease heart disease risk by removing excess cholesterol from cells and blood vessels and returning it to the liver for breakdown and elimination.

High HDL cholesterol levels decrease the risk of heart disease; high levels of LDL cholesterol have the opposite effect. Therefore HDL cholesterol is referred to as the *good* or healthy cholesterol and LDL cholesterol as the *bad* cholesterol. The ratio of these two may be more important. Health researchers believe that HDL takes cholesterol from tissues, including blood vessels and dying cells, and brings it to the liver for breakdown. HDL cholesterol tries to keep the blood vessels from being clogged with fat, which helps prevent heart attacks. LDL does the opposite by bringing cholesterol from the liver and depositing it in other tissues, including the inner lining of blood vessels, leading to the appearance of fatty streaks or deposits in the vessels (see Figure 4.14). Over the years, lipids (fats) build up and the cells become rich in cholesterol. The smooth muscle cells lining the blood vessels then begin to divide, and the cholesterol-laden cells start to become calcified. As this *plaque* develops, the blood vessel becomes narrower and complete blockage can occur, cutting off the flow of blood to the

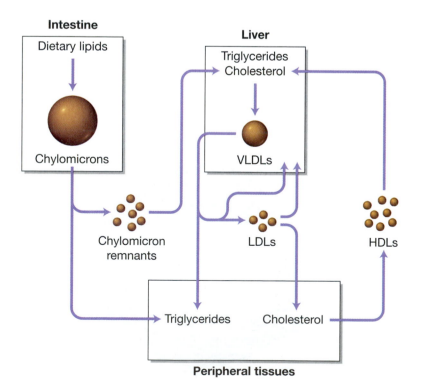

**Figure 4.14** Overview of metabolism of the various lipoproteins present in our bodies with reference to diet, liver, and peripheral tissues.

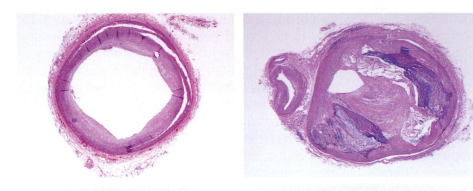

**Figure 4.15** A normal artery (left). Actual sections of an artery showing early and advanced atherosclerosis. (right). Note that the opening for blood flow is almost blocked.

| Table 4.4 | American Heart Association Recommended Blood Cholesterol Levels |
| --- | --- |
| **Type** | **Level** |
| Total cholesterol | Desirable < 200 mg/100 mL |
| | Borderline to high 200–239 mg/100 mL |
| | High >240 mg/100 mL |
| LDL cholesterol | Optimal < 100 mg/100 mL |
| | Near desirable 100–129 mg/100 mL |
| | Borderline high 130–159 mg/100 mL |
| | High 160–189 mg/100 mL |
| | Very High > 190 mg/100 mL |
| HDL cholesterol | Low < 40 mg/100 mL for men |
| | < 50 mg/100 mL for women |
| | High > 60 mg/100 mL |

*Note:* mg/100 mL is the same as mg/dL, which is sometimes found in lab reports or other books.

*Source:* Reprinted with permission. www.americanheart.org. © 2009, American Heart Association, Inc.

heart muscle and resulting in a myocardial infarct (see Figure 4.15). Actually, the terms *bad* and *good* are not really appropriate, because we need both types and they are essential to good health. Table 4.4 provides a guide for the levels of total, LDL, and HDL cholesterol we should maintain for good health as recommended by the American Heart Association. The American Heart Association also recommends a desirable HDL cholesterol to total cholesterol ratio. A person with an HDL cholesterol level of 50 mg per 100 mL and total blood cholesterol of 200 mg per 100 mL has a ratio of 4:1. The American Heart Association recommends an optimal ratio of 3.5 to 1, but no higher than 5 to 1.

**Want to know more?**
You can further explore lipoproteins and LDL receptors by going to the text website at http://webcom8.grtxle.com/nutrition and clicking on the Chapters button. Select Chapter 4.

### ■ What's Hot?

#### Is Coconut Oil Bad for you or not?
Recently there have been a number of claims made about the health benefits of coconut oil. This may seem confusing since it is primarily a saturated fat, and in this chapter we say that a diet high in saturated fat may increase your risk for heart disease. Most of the saturated fats in coconut oil are medium chain fatty acids and are therefore absorbed differently than other saturated fats, most of which are long

chain. Because they are absorbed differently they are used quickly for energy and are less likely to be stored as fat in the body. Additionally, virgin (unhyrogenated) coconut oil made from fresh coconut kernel contains antioxidants. It has been suggested that regular consumption of coconut milk can decrease your risk of heart disease, but well controlled studies have failed to support this claim. If consumed in its unhydrogenated form it has been shown to increase HDL ("good") cholesterol levels. There are also claims that it boosts immune system function and helps the action of anti-HIV drugs, but these claims are not supported by research. There is clearly a need for further research before any recommendations for or against adding coconut oil to the diet can be made. ■

## ■ Nutrition and Disease

*Who's more susceptible to heart disease, men or women?*
Heart disease does not discriminate on the basis of gender. It is the number one cause of death for women, just as it is for men. Historically, many studies on heart disease were done on white males and the treatment was designed for men. We now know that medical treatment for heart attacks is not the same for men and women.

Before menopause, women may have some natural protection against heart disease due to their body's production of estrogen; but after menopause when estrogen levels decline, their risk for heart disease is similar to that of men. Thirty-two percent of women ultimately die from heart disease, which translates into 500,000 women a year. More than 8 million adult women have heart disease, and 13 percent of women over age 45 have had at least one heart attack. Black women are at even greater risk than the general population; they experience a 72 percent higher rate of some form of the disease than do white women in the United States. Black women ages 55–64 are twice as likely as white women to have a heart attack and 35 percent more likely to suffer from coronary artery disease.

Notably, women do not do as well after a heart attack in comparison to men. The National Coalition for Women with Heart Disease lists the following as differences by gender:

- Thirty-eight percent of women and 25 percent of men will die within one year of a first recognized heart attack.
- Among heart attack survivors, 35 percent of women and 18 percent of men will have another heart attack within six years.
- Forty-six percent of women and 22 percent of men who initially survive heart attacks will be disabled with heart failure within six years.
- Women are almost twice as likely as men to die after heart bypass surgery.
- Women are less likely than men to receive heart medication or even aspirin after a heart attack.
- More women than men die of heart disease each year, yet women receive:
    only 33 percent of angioplasties, stint implants, and bypass surgeries
    only 28 percent of implantable defibrillators
    only 36 percent of open-heart surgeries
- Women comprise only 25 percent of participants in all heart-related research studies. ■

## Cancer

Research to date, while not definitive, suggests an increased risk of certain types of cancer for people who consume diets high in fat. As we've noted earlier, research supports recommendations for a low-fat diet and particularly one that limits red meat, high-fat dairy products, and other high-fat foods. The goal is to consume less than 30 percent of our total caloric intake as fat. Interestingly, countries where fat intakes are lower have a lower incidence of a wide variety of cancers, whereas in the United States the greater consumption of saturated fat and red meat is now associated with our higher frequency of cancer of the breast, colon, rectum, and prostate. Research by the National Research Council Committee on Diet and Health found positive correlation between excess fat intake and colorectal cancer. Additionally, data from a comprehensive study of 88,000 nurses showed that those who ate red meat every day were two to three times more likely to develop colon cancer than those who consumed it less than once per month. In this same research, consumption of vegetable fat or dairy foods did not appear to be correlated with a higher incidence of colon cancer.

In general, most health experts suggest that increased consumption of fresh fruits and vegetables and less animal fat lowers our risk of developing cancer. Still, it is difficult to separate out the effects of the different diet components and disease. For instance, people who have diets high in meat may also consume fewer fruits and vegetables. This circumstance leads to the question of whether the increase in fat consumption from meat or a lack of fruits and vegetables in the diet is the primary link to cancer.

### ■ Nutrition and Culture
*Why is the Mediterranean diet so widely recommended?*
Many health professionals recommend the Mediterranean diet. The term *Mediterranean* applies to nations from southern Europe, northern Africa, and the Middle East that border the Mediterranean Sea: Spain, Portugal, France (Provence region), Morocco, Italy, Malta, Greece, Turkey, Lebanon, Israel, Jordan, Egypt, the former Yugoslavia, Libya, and Algeria. Health professionals have studied the diets of individuals living in these nations for many years, because research data has shown that they experience a low incidence of heart disease and certain types of cancers.

The countries that constitute the Mediterranean area are shown in Figure 4.16; the Food Guide Pyramid that has been developed for the Mediterranean diet is depicted in Figure 4.17.

What features does the Mediterranean diet contain? In practical terms, the following eating patterns in these countries are rather common:

- Daily physical activity
- Emphasis on food from plant sources, including fruits and vegetables, potatoes, breads and grains, beans, nuts, and seeds to be consumed daily
- Emphasis on a variety of minimally processed and, wherever possible, seasonally fresh and locally grown foods
- Olive oil (rich in monounsaturates) as the principal fat to be consumed daily; almost no butter, margarine, or other fats
- No trans fats or hydrogenated fats
- Total fat contributing 25–35 percent of calories; saturated fat no more than 8 percent of calories

**Want to know more?**
For more information on the Mediterranean diet, go to the text website at http://webcom8.grtxle .com/nutrition and click on the Chapters button. Select Chapter 4.

- Daily consumption of low to moderate amounts of cheese and yogurt, frequently from goats and sheep—even camels
- Regular (weekly) consumption of small amounts of fish and poultry
- Fresh fruit as the typical daily dessert
- Very small amounts of red meat, eaten occasionally (monthly)
- With the exception of Muslims, moderate consumption of wine with meals—about one to two glasses per day for men and one glass per day for women ■

**Before you go on . . .**

1. List the foods that contribute the most saturated fat to our diets.
2. Is too much fat in our diet a primary cause of obesity? Why?
3. Describe atherosclerosis and its connection to cholesterol.
4. Give the recommended ranges for HDL, LDL, and total cholesterol.
5. What are some problems that could occur if your fat intake is too low?

**Figure 4.16** The Mediterranean countries.

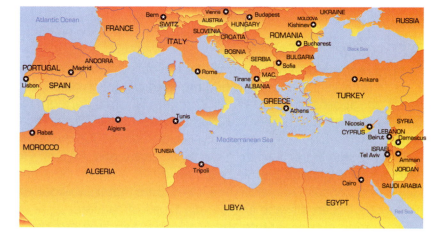

In a typical week, the Celik family of Istanbul, Turkey, spends approximately $150 for food. More than one-third of this amount goes for vegetables, fruits, and nuts. They spend less than $10 on meat and typically eat beef only once or twice a month. Based on the photo, how closely do their food choices reflect the Mediterranean Pyramid?

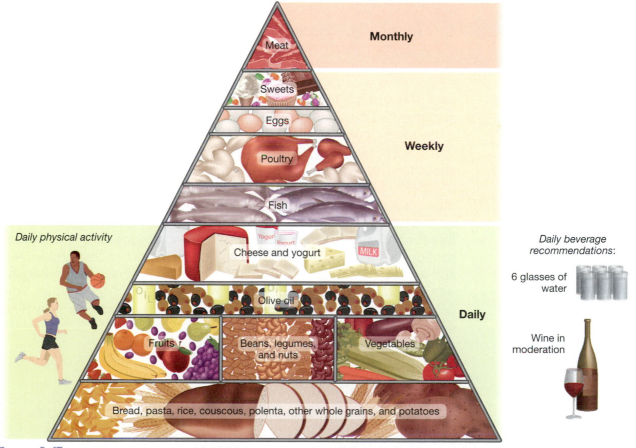

**Figure 4.17** The Mediterranean Diet Food Guide Pyramid. Note the emphasis on whole grains, fruits, and vegetables at the base of the pyramid. Olive oil is an important component of this diet. Fish and poultry are consumed weekly, but beef is eaten only once a month.

## Real People, Real Strategies

Janine decided to visit her local hospital, which offers a wellness program for the general public. There she had an opportunity to talk with a dietitian. Janine explained her concerns, including the report that showed that her total cholesterol is high, around 225 mg/100 mL of blood. The dietitian informed her that the recommended levels are *below* 200 mg/100 mL. The dietitian also confirmed what her doctor had indicated—that although her cholesterol is elevated, it might be premature to look at the lipoprotein levels. The dietitian reviewed the information that Janine had gathered and then made several recommendations to help her try to get her cholesterol into the normal range. She told Janine that if she loses some weight, but not necessarily all of the 30 lbs. she gained after her pregnancies, she may be able to reach her target of less than 200 mg/100 mL. The dietitian stressed that regular walking or some other type of aerobic exercise would also help. Additionally, she discussed the importance of portion control and snacking behavior. People often overlook the impact of these areas in weight management. She then recommended that Janine learn to consume lower-fat items such as skim milk rather than her usual whole milk.

Although these were all reasonable suggestions, and Janine thought they were good advice, she asked the dietitian why she was not recommending a low-cholesterol diet. The dietitian explained that although the American Heart Association suggests consuming no more than 300 mg of cholesterol per day, blood cholesterol and dietary cholesterol do not always correlate. Moreover, she told Janine that having a good source of soluble fiber in her diet would help lower her cholesterol, as would eating more fruits, vegetables, and beans. She emphasized that consuming fibers with oats are known to lower cholesterol, and that the types of fat in her diet are important (see Chapter 3 for information about fiber benefits). She encouraged Janine to use monounsaturated and polyunsaturated vegetable oil, and especially olive oil, in place of other fats in her salad dressing and cooking whenever possible. The dietitian told Janine to try these new recommendations over the next three months and then have her cholesterol rechecked. She expressed confidence that Janine would be able to lower her cholesterol levels if she adhered to these recommendations. As a result, Janine began a walking program and watched her intake of certain food types. After only three months she had lost 15 pounds and her cholesterol level had dropped to 195 mg/100mL.

## Chapter Summary

- Lipids are insoluble in water, but soluble in organic solvents such as ether, acetone, and chloroform. The major types of lipids in food and in our bodies are fatty acids, phospholipids, triglycerides, and cholesterol. Fatty acids are a source of energy; phospholipids are components of cell membranes. Triglycerides are the storage form of fat in our bodies and the major type of fat we consume in food. Cholesterol is found only in foods of animal origin, and it acts as a precursor to hormones.

- Fatty acids are classified based on the number of double bonds in the long carbon chain. If there are no double bonds, then the fatty acid is saturated. Meats and dairy products are sources of saturated fatty acids. Monounsaturated fatty acids have one double bond. Canola and olive oils are monounsaturated fatty acid sources. Polyunsaturated fatty acids have two or more double bonds and are found in most vegetables and vegetable oils such as corn oil.

- Dietary fats provide us with essential fatty acids such as linoleic acid and linolenic acid. These fatty acids are converted to powerful chemicals called eicosanoids that affect our health.

- A major health concern has resulted from the manufacturing process of partial hydrogenation of polyunsaturated fatty acids. This process, used to create products such as margarine, leads to consumption of harmful trans fatty acids and more saturated fats in our diet.

- Several fat substitutes that are much lower in calories have been used in food products. There are three types: carbohydrate-based, protein-based, and fat-based. Items such as dextrins, gums, and cellulose make up the carbohydrate-based fat substitutes and contain less than half of the calories as fat. An example of a protein-based fat substitute is Simplesse® Microparticulated Whey Protein Concentrate. These have 4 kcal per gram. Fat-based fat substitutes are not digested well and include products such as Olean, Salatrim, and Caprenin. Olean has no calories; Salatrim and Caprenin provide 4 kcal per gram.

- Health officials have published recommendations that adults consume not less than 20 percent and no more than 35 percent of their calories in fat. The appropriate range for children and adolescents is between 30 percent and 35 percent, given their increased demands for energy and growth.

- There are four major cholesterol-containing lipoproteins: chylomicrons, VLDL, LDL, and HDL. Greater levels of HDL cholesterol in the blood are associated with reduced risk from heart disease, whereas the opposite is true of LDL cholesterol. High blood cholesterol levels and high LDL cholesterol levels can increase your risk for developing heart disease.

## Key Terms

**atherosclerosis** (ath-er-oh-skler-O-sis) The process in which deposits of fatty substances, cholesterol, cellular waste products, calcium, and other substances (referred to as plaque) build up in the inner lining of an artery. (p. 125)

**chylomicrons** (kye-loh-MY-kronz) Lipoproteins formed in the cells lining the small intestine following absorption of fats. They are made in the small intestinal cells and transport dietary lipids to the liver. (p. 128)

**eicosanoids** (eye-koh-sah-noydz) Metabolically active chemicals synthesized from fatty acids. These chemicals have powerful physiological effects, including relaxing blood vessels and promoting blood clotting. (p. 116)

**essential fatty acids** Fatty acids that cannot be made by the body and can be provided only by the diet. (p. 106)

**gastric emptying** Movement of food from the stomach to the small intestine. (p. 117)

**high-density lipoproteins (HDLs)** Lipoproteins that are made mostly in the liver, but in the small intestine as well; they decrease heart disease risk by removing excess cholesterol from cells and blood vessels and returning it to the liver for breakdown and elimination. (p. 128)

**ischemia** (iss-KEE-mee-ah) A restriction in blood supply to the heart, generally due to factors in the blood vessels with resultant damage or dysfunction of tissue. (p. 125)

**lipoproteins** Molecules in the blood that help transport cholesterol and fatty acids to tissues. (p. 112)

**low-density lipoproteins (LDLs)** Remnants of the breakdown of VLDLs. They deliver cholesterol to other tissues, including blood vessels. (p. 128)

**monounsaturated fatty acid** A fatty acid that contains only one double bond. (p. 105)

**phospholipid** (fos-fo-LIP-id) A lipid that has a three-carbon glycerol backbone; the first two carbons of the glycerol molecule have fatty acids bound to them, and the third carbon has a phosphate group bonded to it. (p. 111)

**polyunsaturated fatty acid** A fatty acid that contains two or more double bonds. (p. 105)

**satiety** (suh-TYE-eh-tee) The feeling of being satisfied after consuming food. (p. 116)

**saturated fatty acid** Fatty acid that contains no double bonds. (p. 105)

**trans fatty acid** An unhealthy fatty acid produced through the addition of hydrogen atoms to double bonds of fatty acids, which causes the molecule to assume an unnatural shape. (p. 109)

**triglyceride** A form of fat found in food and in the body; chemically, it is composed of a three-carbon compound called glycerol in which fatty acids are bonded to each of the carbons. (p. 111)

**very low-density lipoproteins (VLDLs)** Lipoproteins that are synthesized in the liver and contain both triglycerides and cholesterol. They function to deliver triglycerides to other tissues. (p. 128)

# Chapter Quiz

1. If consumed in excess, which of the following fats will contribute to formation of more LDL cholesterol?

   a. polyunsaturated fatty acids

   b. monounsaturated fatty acids

   c. saturated fatty acids

   d. omega-3 fatty acids

2. If consumed, which of the following may reduce heart disease?

   a. trans fatty acids

   b. omega-3 fatty acids

   c. phospholipids

   d. partially hydrogenated fatty acids

3. Lipids normally are not soluble in blood or water. Transporting lipids in the blood requires that

   a. they be absorbed by binding to sugars to make them soluble.

   b. they form a complex with lipoproteins to make them soluble.

   c. they be absorbed along with dietary fiber.

   d. the fatty acids be broken down into smaller molecules before they can be soluble in the blood.

4. Which of the following fat substitutes does not contain any calories?

   a. Olestra

   b. Simplesse® Microparticulated Whey Protein Concentrate

   c. Salatrim

   d. Caprenin

5. An elevated level of which of the following may place you at greater risk for heart disease?

   a. free fatty acids

   b. chylomicrons

   c. LDL cholesterol

   d. HDL cholesterol

6. All of the following foods contain cholesterol except
   a. baked coldwater fish.
   b. barbecued chicken breast.
   c. highly saturated coconut oil.
   d. a baked potato with butter.

7. Pain in the chest, shoulder, or arm, normally caused by insufficient blood to the heart is called
   a. ischemia.
   b. angina pectoris.
   c. atherosclerosis.
   d. thrombosis.

8. A feeling of satisfaction and fullness after consuming a meal or particular food item
   a. depends on the flavor of food.
   b. is called satiety.
   c. occurs more in foods that empty from the stomach more rapidly.
   d. is greater when one consumes more omega-3 fatty acids than omega-6 fatty acids.

9. Which of the following American Heart Association recommendations is the closest to the omega-3 fatty acid recommendation for healthy people without heart disease?
   a. 1 g of EPA+DHA from fatty fish daily
   b. 2–4 g of EPA+DHA from fish oil capsules daily
   c. an equal amount of omega-3 and omega-6 fatty acids
   d. two servings of fatty fish twice per week

10. Which of the following has the most saturated fat?
    a. corn oil
    b. palm oil
    c. safflower oil
    d. olive oil

## < Here's Where You've Been

*The following topics were introduced in preceding chapters and are related to concepts we'll discuss in Chapter 5. Be certain that you're familiar with them before proceeding.*

- The different classes of basic nutrients have important functions in the body. (Chapter 1)
- Healthy eating includes balance, variety, and moderation. (Chapter 2)
- The U.S. government has developed nutrition recommendations described in the Dietary Reference Intake and at MyPyramid.gov. (Chapter 2)
- One of the most important functions of carbohydrates is to spare stored protein from being broken down; they are also used as a source of energy so that muscle mass is maintained. (Chapter 3)

## Here's Where You're Going >

*The following topics and concepts are the ones we'll emphasize in Chapter 5.*

- Proteins are made up of a combination of amino acids linked together. The order of the amino acids in the chain is determined by DNA and makes each protein different.
- Protein is used for body growth, maintenance, and many other important functions. It contributes only a small amount to daily energy needs.
- Many different types of vegetarian diets exist, with many different potential health benefits and health consequences.

## Real People, Real Choices

Richard Zhiming has been working out with weights for about a year but with only modest results. The body shaping he expected developed much more slowly than he anticipated. Consequently, he decided to increase the frequency of his workouts in order to build more muscle mass. After learning of his goal, one of the trainers at the gym told him that he would also have to consume more protein if he really wanted to build muscle. Richard usually eats at least three times a day, and sometimes more often when his schedule allows. Other weight lifters told him that there was no way he could get enough protein from food. They said the secret to rapid muscle growth involves taking a supplemental protein powder. Another friend told him he should consume protein before his workouts; someone else said that eating protein after the workout would be more effective.

In his stepped-up training regimen he now lifts weights four to five days a week, usually at night after work and classes. He also tries to jog or ride the stationary bike whenever he can, but has trouble fitting it in. Richard wants to do everything possible to efficiently meet his goal. What would you suggest? Richard is 5'9" and weighs 160 lbs. How much protein should he eat? Will eating a lot of protein increase Richard's muscle mass? When should he eat—before or after his workouts? Do you think he will have to consume protein supplements to get the total amount of protein he needs?

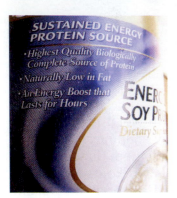

There are many protein supplements and high protein foods that claim to provide "the most complete protein" or "instant gains in muscle mass."

Many of you, like Richard, have probably heard a lot about protein and how it can build muscle or help you lose weight. Protein consumption and its role in weight management have received much attention recently in the media and fad diet books. It has been promoted as the main nutrient required by the body, and has been given a sort of mystical "solve all your health and weight problems instantly" reputation. Some advocates have even suggested that by simply increasing protein intake you can "trick" your metabolism into burning more calories.

Although it is crucial to human health and life, protein alone does not promote optimal health or cure the myriad of weight and health problems some would like you to believe. Protein is, however, an important part of a balanced diet and a vital macronutrient. Like carbohydrates and fats, it is made of carbon, hydrogen, and oxygen, but it differs from carbohydrates and fats because it contains *nitrogen.* Protein is best known for its function in muscle growth. However, it also plays a vital role in the development, maintenance, and repair of all tissues in the body. It is involved in fluid balance, blood clotting, enzyme production, and hormone regulation, and it serves as a carrier for several nutrients. Protein also supplies energy, 4 kcal per gram, but providing energy is not its primary function. Foods high in protein include meats, eggs, dairy products, beans, nuts, soy, and legumes.

# Protein Structure, Function, and Turnover

## Amino Acids

How can protein, one nutrient, have so many functions in the body? In order to answer this question we must discuss some chemistry. Proteins are made up of combinations of **amino acids** linked together. Basically amino acids are the building blocks for protein. All amino acids are made of a central carbon connected to four different groups (see Figure 5.1). One group is called an *amine group* (this is where the nitrogen is), one is an *acid group (carboxyl),* one is *hydrogen,* and the fourth is a *side chain,* or *R group.*

The R groups are unique in each of the different amino acids (see Figure 5.2). This is how you can distinguish one amino acid from the other; the R group dictates the function of each amino acid. The R groups allow the different amino acids and the unique proteins made from them to vary in acidity, shape, size, and electrical charge. This variation allows proteins to serve so many important yet different functions.

Some amino acids are positively charged, some are neutral, and some are negative. The charge plays an important role in the unique qualities of the amino acids and the proteins they make. There are twenty known amino acids, each with a different R group, that the body uses for various functions.

**Essential amino acids** are those that cannot be made in the body, so we must obtain them from the food we eat. If essential amino acids are not consumed in the diet, the body will not be able to make the proteins it needs for growth, maintenance, or any of the other functions mentioned previously without breaking down muscle tissue. **Nonessential amino acids** are also needed in the body, but the body can produce them, so we do not have to obtain them from food. The body can make the nonessential amino acids by reusing the nitrogen groups of essential amino acids and from proteins that have been broken down. This process is called **transamination** because it involves transferring

**Amino acid structure**

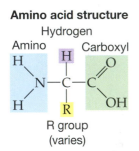

**Figure 5.1** Chemical structure of an amino acid.

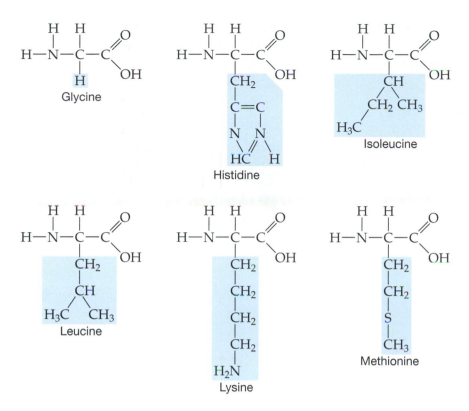

**Figure 5.2** There are 20 different amino acids, each with a different R group that makes the amino acid and the proteins it creates unique.

the amine group (the nitrogen-containing part) from one molecule to another to make an amino acid (see Table 5.1)

In rare circumstances nonessential amino acids cannot be made by the body; they are then called **conditionally essential amino acids.** This can occur because of disease or when the essential amino acid needed to make the nonessential amino acid is limited in the diet. For example, in the inherited disease *phenylketonuria (PKU),* the enzyme that breaks down the amino acid *phenylalanine* is not produced or is deficient. This enzyme typically converts the essential amino acid phenylalanine to the nonessential amino acid *tyrosine.* Without this enzyme, phenylalanine accumulates in the blood and body tissues and can cause brain damage. Because people with PKU can't break down phenylalanine, they must avoided it in their diet. Tyrosine then becomes essential and therefore must be consumed in the diet. People with PKU must follow a strict diet with low protein and avoid consumption of aspartame (brand name NutraSweet) because it contains phenylalanine.

## Protein Structure

Every protein in the body has a different chain of an exact number of amino acids linked together in a specific order by very strong bonds. These are called **peptide bonds** and are formed between the acid group of one amino acid and the amine group of another (see Figure 5.3).

The proteins in the foods we eat and in our bodies are made of many amino acids linked together by strong peptide bonds. As the amino acids are linked into a protein

**Want to know more?**
You can learn more about PKU by going to the text website at http://webcom8.grtxle.com/nutrition and clicking on the Chapters button. Select Chapter 5.

| Table 5.1 | Essential and Nonessential Amino Acids |
| --- | --- |

| Essential Amino Acids | Nonessential Amino Acids |
| --- | --- |
| Histidine | Alanine |
| Isoleucine | Arginine |
| Leucine | Asparagine |
| Lysine | Aspartic acid |
| Methionine | Cysteine |
| Phenylalanine | Glutamic acid |
| Threonine | Glutamine |
| Tryptophan | Glycine |
| Valine | Proline |
|  | Serine |
|  | Tyrosine |

*Note:* Under certain circumstances, nonessential amino acids cannot be made by the body; they are then called *conditionally essential amino acids.*

**Figure 5.3** Amino acids are joined by strong bonds called peptide bonds.

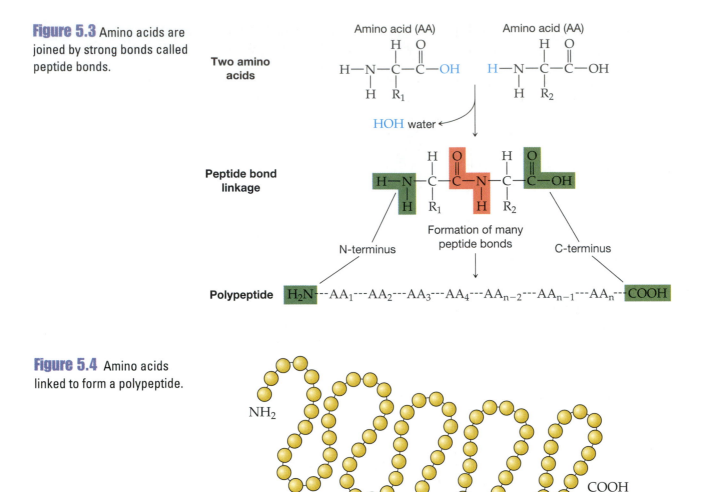

**Two amino acids**

Amino acid (AA)     Amino acid (AA)

HOH water

**Peptide bond linkage**

Formation of many peptide bonds

N-terminus     C-terminus

**Polypeptide**     $H_2N$---$AA_1$---$AA_2$---$AA_3$---$AA_4$---$AA_{n-2}$---$AA_{n-1}$---$AA_n$---COOH

**Figure 5.4** Amino acids linked to form a polypeptide.

$NH_2$

COOH

they develop a three-dimensional shape that is unique for each protein (see Figure 5.4).

## Shape Dictates Function

The specific order of the amino acids is part of what determines a protein's shape, which in turn dictates its function. Why does the order dictate the shape? Recall from our previous discussion that the R groups give the protein its unique and specific qualities. The charge of each amino acid influences how it interacts with the other amino acids in the protein and therefore its shape. For example, if an amino acid's R group is electrically charged, it will be positioned to the outside of the protein so that it can mix in the watery environment of the body. If an amino acid has a neutral charge, it won't mix with water and will move to the middle or core of the protein where it can mix with the other neutral amino acids, causing the chain to curl onto itself into a coil, a globule, or other shape.

If the order of the amino acids is so important, how does the body know the order in which to place them? Our DNA determines the order or sequence in which the amino acids will be linked. We each have a genetic code that we inherit from our biological parents. This code determines the

*What happens if the order of an amino acid gets messed up?*

sequence of amino acids that not only makes each protein unique, but makes people unique from each other and other species. All cells in the body have the DNA in their nucleus to make all proteins. However, different cells make only the proteins needed for their specific function. For instance, only the cells of the *pancreas* will link the amino acids in the specific order to make the protein that is the hormone *insulin* (see Figure 5.5). The cells make their needed proteins not just because the DNA is there, but in response to the ever-changing conditions of the body. The pancreas does not always make insulin just because the DNA for insulin is there. When blood sugar is low, the cells of the pancreas stop producing insulin so that your blood sugar will not keep falling.

If just one amino acid in the link is out of order, or an amino acid is skipped because of genetic error, the shape of the protein is changed and therefore the function is altered. For example, in the inherited disease **sickle-cell anemia** one amino acid is missing in the sequence for the protein **hemoglobin**. Hemoglobin carries oxygen in the blood; it normally has a disc-like shape. This shape is important, as it optimizes the ability to carry oxygen. In sickle-cell anemia the missing amino acid causes the shape of the amino acid link to be more sickle shaped than disc shaped. The sickle-shaped cells do not allow for complete bonding of hemoglobin and oxygen, and can easily stick to one another and block small blood vessels. This causes less blood to reach the part of the body that the blocked vessel supplies. Tissue that does not receive a normal blood flow eventually becomes damaged, which causes the complications of sickle-cell anemia.

Symptoms of sickle-cell anemia include fatigue, delayed growth, bone pain, and yellow eyes and skin. Over time, the condition can lead to permanent damage of the kidneys, lungs, bones, eyes, and central nervous system. Sickle-cell anemia is much more common in some ethnic groups. For example, it affects one out of every 500 African Americans. Frequency of sickle-cell anemia varies significantly around the world. For example, rates are high in areas of Africa and the Middle East because the sickle-cell trait helps protect against malaria. Over time, people who survived in regions with a high incidence of malaria were more likely to have sickle-cell trait and to pass it on to their children. So while this trait has terrible side effects, it protects against another disease. Currently there is no cure for sickle-cell anemia.

## Denaturation

Because a protein's shape determines its function, we can change a protein's function by altering its shape. This occurs when we cook food, when we sterilize items such as bandages or a baby's bottle, or when we break down protein in digestion (see Chapter 6 for more information on digestion). A protein's structure and function can be changed by heat, acid, enzymes, agitation, or alcohol in a process called **denaturation.** Anyone who has ever cooked has a visual example of denaturation.

For example, as you add heat while cooking a liquid egg, you change its shape by making it less liquid and its function by making it less soluble (think of mixing a raw egg in a recipe like cookie dough as compared to mixing a cooked egg to make egg salad). Similarly, when we eat proteins we denature them with stomach acid. Stomach acid unravels the three-dimensional structure just as cooking does.

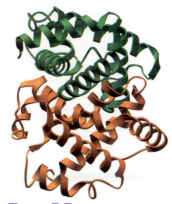

**Figure 5.5** Three-dimensional structure of insulin.

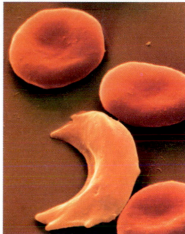

The normal red blood cell is shaped correctly to maintain its function of carrying oxygen throughout the body. In the sickle cell, the shape of the red blood cell is changed and, therefore, it cannot function optimally.

 **Want to know more?** If you would like to explore sickle-cell anemia further, go to the text website at http://webcom8 .grtxle.com/nutrition and click on the Chapters button. Select Chapter 5.

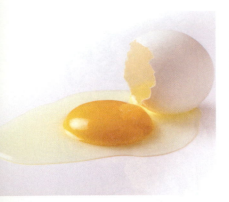

The structure and function of the raw egg is transformed—denatured by heat—in the fried egg.

 **Want to know more?**
To see a video of denaturation occurring, go to the text website at http://webcom8.grtxle .com/nutrition and click on the Chapters button. Select Chapter 5.

Denaturation allows more of the surface area of the protein to interact with digestive enzymes and thus helps with digestion. In addition to breaking down proteins in food, our stomach acid denatures the proteins of many of the bacteria found in foods. This in turn changes their function so that they can no longer harm us. This is an important concept to remember if you are taking medicines that block stomach acid production, such as antacids. In this case you must exercise caution in consuming foods that are uncooked or have a high chance of containing bacteria, such as raw meat and fish. By taking medication to block stomach acid and by not cooking food, you have essentially eliminated two methods of denaturing the protein of potentially harmful bacteria: heat and stomach acid. This can increase your chances of getting a foodborne illness (for more on foodborne illness, see Chapter 13).

## Protein Function

Protein is needed for many functions in the body, and it is part of every physiological system. The following is a summary of some of the most important roles and tasks it performs (see also Figure 5.6).

### Growth, Maintenance, and Repair

Protein is probably best known for its role in body growth, maintenance, and repair. Even adults who have reached their growth potential and who are not working out to increase muscle mass must consistently consume adequate amounts of protein to supply the essential amino acids. The body is in a dynamic state. Proteins are constantly being broken down and synthesized. Many amino acids are reused to make new proteins, but some must be replaced through the diet, particularly the essential ones. These amino acids are used to restore the proteins of the cells that are continually being broken down and renewed. For example, the cells that line your intestine are replaced about every three days, your red blood cells live only for about four months, and your skin cells are constantly sloughing off to be replaced by new skin.

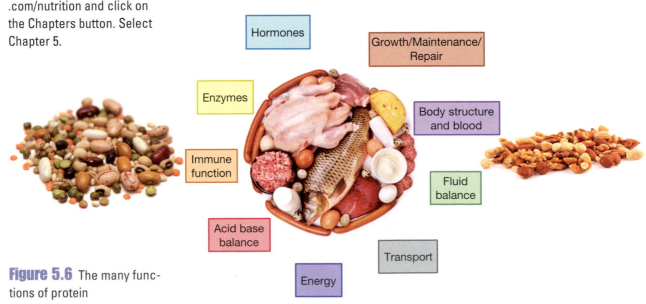

**Figure 5.6** The many functions of protein

### Body Structure and Blood Clotting

As noted earlier, protein is the main building block for muscle. It is also important in blood clotting and as part of connective tissue such as ligaments and tendons. Collagen is part of all the connective tissue in the body including tendons, bones, skin, teeth, and blood vessels; it is made of protein and constitutes the most abundant protein in the entire body. Hair and nails are made of protein and noticeably weaken when protein intake is insufficient.

### Fluid Balance

Protein plays a crucial role in maintaining fluid balance. Proteins in the blood, such as **albumin,** help keep an optimal balance between the fluids inside and outside your cells and blood vessels. When blood is circulating it delivers nutrients across the thin walls of the capillaries to the areas around and inside the cells. A balance of fluids between these spaces and the capillary vessels must be maintained at all times to prevent swelling (*edema*).

### Acid-Base Balance

As a normal part of the body's chemical reactions, acids and bases are constantly being produced. The body strives to maintain its **pH,** or its **acid-base balance,** in a tight range. Proteins help maintain the very narrow range of pH in the body. In other words, they act as buffers, and help neutralize the pH when too many hydrogen ions are present and threaten to make the blood acidic. They also contribute hydrogen ions to make the blood more acidic when it is becoming too alkaline or basic.

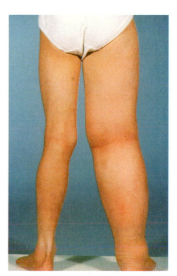

When protein levels are low, fluid balance is not maintained and swelling occurs.

### Immune Function

Many of us tend to take our immune systems for granted. We shouldn't. Even when we don't feel sick, our immune systems are hard at work fighting off foreign substances called *antigens* that constantly threaten the body's health. *Antibodies* are the proteins that the body's immune system produces as a major defense against these antigens. However, many foreign substances never even make it into the body to cause a threat thanks to one of the immune system's first defense mechanisms—the mucus present in the respiratory system and intestine. This mucus is made of amino acids and is constantly being secreted to trap bacteria and keep other foreign substances from invading the body. Without adequate protein, the immune system becomes weakened because it cannot produce enough mucus or enough antibodies to fight off antigens and keep you healthy.

### Enzymes

*Enzymes* are proteins that speed up chemical reactions. They assist in very specific reactions in every cell of the body. Enzymes are made by stringing together between 100 and 1,000 amino acids in a specific and unique order. The chain of amino acids then folds into a unique shape. That shape allows the enzyme to carry out specific chemical reactions. Throughout the body, enzymes play vital roles that keep the body functioning optimally; when they are low, problems or symptoms develop.

   Sometimes a particular enzyme is not created because of a problem in genetic coding. This is referred to as an inborn error of metabolism. Some genetic disorders produce relatively unimportant physical features or skeletal abnormalities. Others produce serious diseases and even death. For example, *hemophilia* is a disease that results in excessive bleeding and bruising from minor injuries. People with this disorder are missing the genetic code for clotting to occur. Normally, when you are cut, your blood clots to prevent excessive bleeding. Hemophiliacs do not have this ability. Therefore, when they are cut they must inject themselves with the clotting factors that are missing. Not all enzyme deficiencies are caused by genetic problems. Sometimes the enzyme is damaged or levels are reduced by medications, illness, or inadequate nutrition. For example, *lactose intolerance* often occurs after abdominal surgery or while taking medications (see Chapter 3 for more information on lactose intolerance).

### Hormones

Hormones are like messengers that help regulate the various systems and functions of the body. Some hormones are made of lipids; some, like insulin, are made from proteins. Insulin has many functions but is perhaps best known for its role in maintaining blood sugar levels (see Chapter 3 for more information on blood glucose regulation).

### Transport

Proteins help transport substances across cell walls by acting as pumps. Transport proteins in the cell membrane, called sodium-potassium pumps, help maintain the balance of sodium and potassium between the outside and inside of the cell. In addition, proteins serve as transporters of nutrients throughout the bloodstream. For example, the protein albumin constitutes 60 percent of the body's *plasma* (the watery part of blood) proteins. Among albumin's many functions, it transports drugs and thyroid hormones and it carries fatty acids from adipose tissue to muscle cells for use as energy. Proteins have water-repelling and water-attracting ends, which allow them to interact with the fat and the water. You may recall from Chapter 4 that proteins are part of the lipoproteins that carry fats from the liver to the body and are part of the chylomicrons that transport long-chain fatty acids after absorption. Without the presence of protein, fat could not mix with the watery environment of the blood.

### Energy

Perhaps the least desirable among the many functions that proteins can perform is energy production. In other words, our bodies really don't want to use protein for energy because it plays such an important role in so many other functions. However, if carbohydrate or calorie intake is too low, protein will be used for energy or to make glucose for energy. This alternate use may compromise its contribution to numerous other functions. This is why protein sparing is often listed among the functions of carbohydrates. Other than the very small amount of amino acids in the blood present as the amino acid pool (discussed later), protein has no storage form in the body as carbohydrates and fats do. Therefore, when the body uses protein as an energy source for any prolonged period, the protein not supplied in the diet will be obtained from body tissue, especially muscle. In a short period of time a significant amount of muscle tissue can be lost. For that reason, it is crucial to consume adequate amounts of carbohydrates, fats, and calories to ensure that protein will be used only minimally for energy, thus conserving most protein for the various vital functions that depend on it.

## Protein Turnover

Proteins are in a constant state of buildup, called **protein synthesis,** and destruction, called **protein breakdown.** This closely connected process of synthesis and breakdown is called **protein turnover.** For example, the cells that make up the lining of your digestive tract are constantly being sloughed off and replaced, much like your skin cells. These cells need protein for regrowth. Protein turnover is influenced by a complex interaction of hormones and nutritional factors, especially amino acid availability. Protein turnover is crucial for the body to meet the ever-changing demands for synthesis of enzymes, immune system function, and growth and repair.

The protein mass and rates of gain or loss within each cell are determined by the balance of synthesis and breakdown. For example, in order to gain muscle mass, synthesis must ultimately be greater than breakdown. Because you synthesize protein in the body from the protein you eat, you must eat an adequate amount of protein every day. (The DRI is 0.8 grams per kilogram of body weight daily). If you do not, then breakdown will be greater than synthesis and you will lose protein from the body. If you eat more protein than you need, more protein synthesis does not occur. If the extra protein is not needed for energy, it is turned into fat and stored.

For protein synthesis to occur, all of the essential amino acids must be present in adequate amounts. If an essential amino acid is not available, either the body will break down its own protein to obtain it or synthesis will not occur. The amino acid that is not available, or the amino acid present in the smallest amount relative to the needs of the body, is called the **limiting amino acid.**

Although carbohydrates have glycogen and fats have triglycerides stored in the body's fat tissue and muscle, protein has no major storage form available for immediate use. Rather, amino acids have short-term storage called the **amino acid pool.** When protein is broken down, the "free amino acids" are dissolved temporarily in body fluids, called the pool. The pool is actually just amino acids that "float" in the blood waiting to be used to make a protein. Although the free amino acids dissolved in the body fluids are only a very small proportion of the body's total amino acids, they are important for maintaining balance in the body's proteins. These amino acids in the pool can be used to make new proteins when essential amino acids are missing from consumed foods. If not used throughout the day, the amine groups will be removed and the rest of the amino acids can be used to make other compounds, synthesized into fat, or eliminated as waste.

## Measuring Protein Turnover

Many of the recommendations for protein intake and information regarding protein turnover have been based on *nitrogen balance techniques*. Nitrogen is excreted when amino acids are broken down; therefore, we can measure the nitrogen contained in the protein we eat and excreted in the urine, feces, skin, hair, and other body fluids. When intake equals the amount of nitrogen excreted, the result is equilibrium, which occurs in most healthy adults. When intake is more than what is excreted, this is referred to as **positive nitrogen balance,** which occurs in periods of growth, recovery from illness, and pregnancy. When more nitrogen is excreted than what is taken in, it is referred to as **negative nitrogen balance.** Such breakdown may be due to illnesses such as AIDS and cancer, starvation, or extremely low-calorie diets. Astronauts also experience negative nitrogen balance due to the stress and the weightlessness of space flight. Most adults, however, remain in equilibrium, which means they are eating enough protein to maintain and repair their bodies. In fact, many in the United States actually consume more protein than needed to stay in balance. Many new techniques are being used to determine protein needs and individual amino acid requirements. Perhaps future recommendations will reflect information obtained from studies using these methods.

**Before you go on . . .**

1. Why does the body need protein?
2. Explain how protein differs chemically from carbohydrates and fats.
3. What determines the shape and function of amino acids?
4. What is the process of denaturation and why is it important?
5. What is protein turnover?

# Food Sources of Protein

## Protein Quality

A **high-quality protein,** also called a **complete protein,** is one that provides all of the essential amino acids in the amount that the body needs and is also easy to digest and absorb. Typically, animal proteins like those found in meats and dairy products and the vegetable protein in soy are considered highly digestible because the human body can absorb almost 90 percent. In contrast, some plant proteins are only 60 percent digestible.

A value is assigned to proteins that accounts for their protein quality (amino acid content) and their digestibility. This value is called the **Protein Digestibility–Corrected Amino Acid Score (PDCAAS).** The PDCAAS is

Food sources of protein.

based on a scale of 0–100, with 100 being the score given to foods that best meet the needs of humans. The score of 100 is given to egg white, meats, dairy, and seafood. Soy is given a score of 94 and beans and legumes a score around 50–60. The utility of this rating system may not be obvious to most consumers, but the Food and Drug Administration (FDA) uses it to determine the percent Daily Value (% DV) used on food labels. For example, if a label states that a serving size of refried beans contains 8 g of protein, and a serving of canned tuna has 8 g of protein, then the % DV (if one is listed) will be higher for the tuna than the beans because the protein quality for the tuna is higher.

You may notice that not all food labels list a % DV for protein. According to the FDA, a % DV is required to be listed only if a claim is made for protein, such as "high in protein." Otherwise, unless the food is meant for use by infants and children under 4 years of age, none is needed." This is because most Americans over age 4 consume more than the recommended amount of protein, and therefore inadequate protein intake is not a public health concern. Furthermore, determining the PDCAAS is very costly. If listed, the % DV for protein is based on 10 percent of calories as protein, which equates to 50 g for a 2,000-calorie diet and 65 g (62.5 rounded up to 65) for a 2,500-calorie diet.

**Want to know more?**
You can review the most common cuts of meat categorized by leaness by visiting the text website at http://webcom8.grtxle.com/nutrition and clicking on the Chapters button. Select Chapter 5.

### ■ Nutrition and Disease

*Are soybeans a miracle food?*

Recent studies have suggested that a variety of health benefits are associated with consuming soy and soy products. For example, soy may protect against a variety of cancers, cardiovascular disease, and bone loss. See Table 5.2 for a list of soy products and suggestions for including them into your daily meals. How many of these are you familiar with, and how often do you consume them?

Soy and soy products provide a complete source of protein with little saturated fat or cholesterol. In fact, 1 c. of soy provides 57 percent of the Daily Value for protein, less than 300 calories, and only 2.2 g of saturated fat. In addition, it contains *isoflavonoids*, which help protect cells against damage. Research has indicated that the isoflavonoids in soy may lower cholesterol, especially when soy products are used as a replacement for higher-fat animal-based foods. Soy may also help prevent prostate and colon cancer. Some isoflavonoids in soy act as *phytoestrogens*, which may help prevent symptoms of menopause and osteoporosis in postmenopausal women. However, there is mixed information regarding soy's effect on the risk of breast cancer. These same phytoestrogens that can be beneficial

| APPLICATION TIP | |
|---|---|
| **Sources of proteins that are low in fat** | |
| *Low-Fat Protein Choices* | |
| Include regularly | Include only occasionally |
| Skim and low-fat dairy products (milk, yogurt, cheese) | Whole milk and dairy products (milk, yogurt, cheese) |
| Broiled, grilled, or baked skinless boneless chicken and turkey breast | Dark-meat chicken and fried chicken |
| Lean cuts of meat such as London broil | High-fat cuts of meat such as prime rib and other cuts with visible marbled fat |
| White-meat pork tenderloin | Bacon, ham, sausage, hot dogs, and fried pork products |
| Broiled, grilled, baked, or sautéed shrimp | Fried shrimp |
| Lean lunchmeats such as chicken and turkey | Highly processed meats |
| Broiled, grilled, baked, and sautéed fish, especially salmon and other coldwater fish | Fried fish |
| Egg whites or egg substitutes | Whole eggs |
| Soy and soy products | Deep-fried tofu |
| Beans, lentils, and legumes | Refried beans cooked with lard |
| Nuts and seeds (small portions) | |

to health may actually increase the risk of breast cancer in some women by raising estrogen levels. Therefore, overconsumption of soy and soy supplements are not recommended. In order to balance the many health benefits associated with soy against the risks of overconsumption, it is recommended that intake should be increased to one or two servings per day. ■

Foods that do not contain all of the essential amino acids in the amount needed by the body are called **incomplete proteins.** Examples of incomplete proteins include beans, legumes, grains, and vegetables. The term *legumes* refers to black beans, kidney beans, garbanzo beans (chickpeas), black-eyed peas, green peas, lima beans, lentils, pinto beans, and other beans.

Because animal products are a traditional source of high-quality protein, many people think that in order to consume adequate protein you must eat meat, seafood, eggs, and dairy products. This is *not* true. You can obtain complete proteins by eating **complementary proteins,** which are foods that when eaten alone may not be complete proteins, but when combined will provide all of the essential amino acids. Anyone who has eaten rice and beans together has consumed complementary proteins. When you eat beans, lysine is the limiting amino acid. Rice is rich in lysine and beans are low. Put them together and they complement each other and provide adequate lysine. For more examples of complementary proteins, see Figure 5.7.

People who consume meats and/or dairy products don't have to worry too much about consciously consuming complementary proteins. However,

Soy is derived from soy beans and comes in many different forms, such as the popular Japanese dish edamame and the many products pictured here. Soybeans are high in protein and low in fat. They contain B vitamins, calcium, potassium, vitamin A, iron, isoflavones, and plant estrogens.

| Table 5.2 | Soy Products and Suggestions for Inclusion in Meals |
|-----------|-----------------------------------------------------|
| **Soy Foods** | **Meal Suggestions** |
| Tofu | Chop extra-firm tofu Into cubes, add to spaghetti sauce, and serve with whole-wheat pasta |
| Tempeh | Place on skewers with vegetables and season (or use barbecue sauce), grill, or broil |
| Soy nuts | Sprinkle over salads or cereal |
| Textured soy (ground meat) | Use in spaghetti, tacos, sloppy joes, chili, etc. |
| Soy dairy products | Soy milk, soy cheese, and soy yogurt can be substituted for cow's milk (i.e. as milk on your cereal) |

**Figure 5.7** Protein Sources

| **Meats** | **Dry Beans and Peas** | **Fish** |
|---|---|---|
| *Lean cuts of:* | Black beans | *Finfish such as:* |
| Beef | Black-eyed peas | Catfish |
| Ham | Chickpeas (garbanzo | Cod |
| Lamb | beans) | Flounder |
| Pork | Falafel | Haddock |
| Veal | Kidney beans | Halibut |
| | Lentils | Herring |
| *Game meats:* | Lima beans (mature) | Mackerel |
| Bison | Navy beans | Pollock |
| Rabbit | Pinto beans | Porgy |
| Venison | Soybeans | Salmon |
| | Split peas | Sea bass |
| *Lean ground meats:* | Tofu (bean curd made | Snapper |
| Beef | from soy beans) | Swordfish |
| Lamb | White beans | Trout |
| Pork | | Tuna |
| | *Bean burgers:* | |
| *Lean luncheon meats* | Garden burgers | *Shellfish such as:* |
| | Veggie burgers | Clams |
| *Organ meats:* | Tempeh | Crab |
| Giblets | Texturized vegetable | Crayfish |
| Liver | protein (TVP) | Lobster |
| **Poultry** | **Nuts and Seeds** | Mussels |
| Chicken | Almonds | Octopus |
| Duck | Cashews | Oysters |
| Goose | Hazelnuts (filberts) | Scallops |
| Turkey | Mixed nuts | Shrimp |
| Ground chicken and | Peanut butter | Squid (calamari) |
| turkey | Peanuts | *Canned fish such as:* |
| **Eggs** | Pecans | Anchovies |
| Chicken eggs | Pistachios | Clams |
| Duck eggs | Pumpkin seeds | Sardines |
| | Sesame seeds | Tuna |
| | Sunflower seeds | |
| | Walnuts | |

vegetarians and those who infrequently consume meat and dairy products do need to pay close attention to complementary proteins to ensure that they are receiving adequate amounts of all of the essential amino acids. It is not necessary to eat the complementary proteins in the same meal, but it is best to consume them in the same day. The amino acids from one food can stay in the pool for the day awaiting the complementing amino acids from other foods in order to combine and synthesize a new protein.

## Supplemental Protein

An additional source of protein for many people, especially vegetarians, highly active people, and those needing to gain weight, is supplemental protein. Most

Protein supplements come in many different forms.

Americans, whether vegetarian or not, consume more dietary protein than they need, and yet protein and amino acid supplements have become very popular. Protein supplements are available as powders, shakes, drinks, bars, pills, puddings, and more. These sources can contribute to meeting daily protein requirements; however, they are not superior to food sources of protein.

In other words, protein supplements do not magically stimulate muscle growth, optimize your immune system, or fulfill any of the other claims marketers may make. In fact, dietary protein may be less expensive and provide a wider variety of vitamins and minerals than some of the costly supplements (see Taking It to the Net on the website).

Many people consume their protein from supplements rather than foods high in protein because they are concerned with the excess fat often found in protein-rich foods. However, many foods are low-fat sources of protein, such as chicken breast with no skin, low-fat or skim milk, and egg whites. See the Application tip on page 00 for some additional suggestions.

As mentioned previously, consuming excess protein does not provide additional health benefits. The protein you eat beyond what your body needs for protein function will be used for energy or stored as fat. In addition, excess protein in the diet can create an imbalance, especially when you are eating protein instead of other healthy foods such as grains, fruits, and dairy products. Intake of too much protein means that the body has to rid itself of the nitrogen groups on the amino acids and excrete them in the urine. This increases the body's water requirements as it attempts to essentially "flush out" the system.

## Recommendations for Protein Intake

The DRI for protein is 0.8 grams per kilogram of body weight of high-quality protein for men and women and is based on the previously discussed nitrogen balance studies. This accounts for about 10 percent of the total calories for the day. So if you weigh 150 lb., divide by 2.2 to get kilograms and then multiply by 0.8. This recommendation is meant for healthy adults. If you are recovering from an injury, ill, stressed, pregnant, or an athlete, then you may need to exceed the DRI for protein.

Endurance athletes, like ultra-runner Dean Karnazes (www.ultramarathonman. com), should consume 1.2 to 1.4 grams of protein per kilogram of body weight daily to help their muscles recover from training.

### ■ Myths and Legends

*More protein = more muscle—do athletes really need more protein?*

No specific DRI addresses protein needs for athletes, but sport nutritionists suggest that they need more protein than nonathletes for tissue and muscle repair and increased protein turnover. This requirement is especially true when you begin a new exercise program.

The two main determinants of whether an athlete needs more protein and how much protein is needed is how hard the athlete is training and the athlete's normal diet. In 2009, a joint position statement by the American College of Sports Medicine, the American Dietetics Association, and Dietitians of Canada stated that protein requirements for athletes are higher than for nonathletes. They recommended that endurance athletes consume 1.2–1.4 grams per kilogram and resistance athletes should consume 1.6–1.7 grams per kilogram.

These recommendations are higher than the DRI of 0.8 grams per kilogram for nonathletes, but not more than most athletes already eat. However, some athletes such as those restricting calories or those consuming vegetarian diets may need to assess their protein intake to make sure they are consuming adequate amounts. Sufficient protein is easy to obtain from a balanced diet that contains an adequate amount of calories. Remember that in order to increase muscle mass you need several things: adequate calorie intake, adequate protein intake, and exercise.

If calorie intake is adequate, research suggests that muscle mass can be maintained within a wide range of protein intakes. Most athletes consume plenty of protein from their normal diets. Many attempt to achieve the extra edge by consuming excessive amounts of protein from supplements. However, there is no magic advantage to consuming protein supplements when compared to consuming protein-rich foods. However, protein supplements are fine to consume when access to whole fresh foods is limited due to time or travel. ■

To promote muscle growth and recovery, strength and power athletes should consume 1.6 to 1.7 grams of protein per kilogram of body weight daily.

**Before you go on . . .**

1. What is the difference between a complete protein and an incomplete protein?
2. What health benefits are associated with consuming soy and soy products?
3. What is a complementary protein?
4. Do athletes need more protein than the DRI?

# Vegetarianism

## Different Types of Vegetarian Diets

There are several types of vegetarians (see Table 5.3), and many people have different ideas about what being a vegetarian really means. One type of vegetarian is a **vegan.** According to the American Dietetic Association, vegans eat only plant foods and do not consume meat, fish, poultry, milk or other dairy products, eggs, or anything else produced from animals. **Lacto-vegetarians** consume milk and dairy products, such as cheese and yogurt, but avoid eggs, seafood, and meat. **Lacto-ovo vegetarians** consume eggs and dairy products, but no meat or seafood. **Macrobiotic vegetarians** consume mostly whole grains, especially brown rice, in their diets along with vegetables, soy, legumes, and fruits.

 **Want to know more?**
If you'd like to calculate your daily protein consumption, go to the text website at http://webcom8 .grtxle.com/nutrition and click on the Chapters button. Select Chapter 5.

**APPLICATION TIP**

Recent research suggests consuming a small amount of protein along with carbohydrates one hour before your workout in order to optimize protein synthesis. Try a glass of milk, a cup of yogurt, or a peanut butter sandwich.

| Table 5.3 | Types of Vegetarians |
| --- | --- |
| **Type of Vegetarian** | **Definition** |
| Vegans | Omit all animal products from their diets, including dairy and eggs |
| Lacto-vegetarians | Include dairy products but no other animal foods |
| Lacto-ovo-vegetarians | Include eggs and dairy products but no meat |
| Macrobiotic vegetarians | Consume mostly whole grains, especially brown rice, in their diets along with vegetables, soy, legumes, fruits, and sometimes whitefish, but avoid meat, poultry, eggs, and dairy |
| Semivegetarians | Occasionally eat meat and seafood, yet predominately practice a vegetarian diet |

They sometimes include whitefish but avoid meat, poultry, eggs, and dairy. People choosing macrobiotic diets are frequently identified as following a vegetarian diet, but they are not vegans because they eat limited amounts of fish. The macrobiotic diet is based largely on grains, legumes, and vegetables. Fruits, nuts, and seeds are eaten to a lesser extent. You may have noted that some people call themselves vegetarians although they eat fish, chicken, or even red meat. These people are sometimes identified as "self-described" vegetarians or **semivegetarians.** Loosely defined, a semivegetarian is someone who occasionally eats meat and seafood, yet predominately practices a vegetarian diet. The more restrictive the vegetarian diet, the more knowledge and planning it takes to obtain all the nutrients.

## Why Do People Choose to Become Vegetarians?

Many people become **vegetarians,** or choose not to eat meat or fish, for a variety of reasons. In some areas of the world not enough meat is available or meat is too expensive, and therefore people may have fewer choices. However, in more affluent countries people usually choose to be vegetarians for more personal reasons, such as:

- **Treatment of animals:** Some people disagree with the way animals are treated in modern meat production facilities. They believe the crowding and slaughtering techniques are inhumane.
- **Hormones and antibiotics:** Some people do not want to expose themselves or animals used for meat production to the hormones that are often given to promote growth or the antibiotics that are used to prevent illness in animals (see Chapter 1 for the information).
- **Health benefits:** Many people choose to be vegetarians because of the associated health benefits discussed in this chapter.
- **Environmental impact:** Many people choose to be vegetarian for environmental reasons: large-scale meat production generates substantial amounts of waste that, as runoff, potentially ends up in local streams and rivers. Raising large numbers of animals requires a considerable quantity of water, and the animals also use valuable land and consume substantial quantities of grain and other types of feed (for more information, see the Sustainable Nutrition feature on page 000).

### Religion and Vegetarianism

Many religions have dietary guidelines as part of their code of conduct. Muslims are not permitted to consume alcohol or animals and birds that are carnivorous (meat-eating). Catholics were traditionally asked to abstain from eating meat on Fridays as a form of penance. Many still abstain during Lent. Vegetarianism is recommended in Hindu scriptures, although Hindus are free to choose their own diet. Of those who eat meat, most abstain from beef and pork.

 **Global Nutrition**
*The body is a temple*
Some members of religious groups that recommend vegetarian diets have been studied to determine whether health benefits result from their dietary practices. For example, Seventh-Day Adventists have practiced predominantly vegetarian diets since the nineteenth century. Principles

The Paktar family of Ujjain, Madhya Pradesh, India, are vegetarians. Their total cost for one week's food, shown here, was $39.27. The major expenditures were $9.70 for dairy; $7.73 for fruits, vegetables, and nuts; $5.35 for grains and other starchy foods; and $4.47 for condiments. Interestingly, in a typical week they spend only about $6.00 in restaurants or for street food.

of healthful living were emphasized in order to keep practitioners healthy in body, mind, and soul. Seventh-Day Adventists saw the body, mind, and soul as organs that needed fresh air and good sanitation and hygienic principles to maintain health.

In order to achieve their goals they encouraged a balance between work and exercise. They adopted practices such as abstaining from tobacco, alcohol, drugs, and some medications. Additionally, they favored the use of natural remedies, increased hygiene, and sanitation, and they placed great emphasis on eating plain and simply prepared foods. The health benefits of these practices have only recently been recognized in Western medicine. This is evident in the 2005 *Dietary Guidelines for Americans*, which recommend greater consumption of whole grains, soybeans, and other legumes for protein and place a greater emphasis on plant-based foods (than previous guidelines). In addition, daily exercise is now recommended as a necessary complement to proper nutrition. The Seventh-Day Adventists Dietetics Association provides "Good Eating Guidelines," which can be found on their website at www.sdada.org/eatingwell.htm. ■

## Health Benefits of a Vegetarian Diet

Although there is still insufficient research to know whether vegetarians live longer than nonvegetarians, they do appear to have a lower risk of heart disease. Some evidence suggests that a vegetarian diet may also help in the prevention of some cancers, but more studies need to be conducted before any definitive conclusions can be made. We do know that vegetarians typically have a lower body mass index (BMI) than nonvegetarians and are therefore much less likely to be obese. It is difficult to determine whether vegetarians are healthier than nonvegetarians as a result of their dietary intake, because most vegetarians also practice other healthy lifestyle behaviors such as abstaining from smoking and engaging in regular exercise.

Although only about 2.5 percent of Americans are vegetarians, and even fewer are vegan, the general population is more aware of the benefits of consuming a plant-based diet. This awareness is partly due to the change of focus in the research of vegetarian diets from one of assessing the nutritional quality of the diet to a recent focus on assessing its health benefits.

Reflective of this change in research focus are the recommendations being made by many leading health organizations. The Unified Dietary Guidelines developed by the American Cancer Society, the American Heart Association, the National Institutes of Health, and the American Academy of Pediatrics recommend a diet based on a variety of plant foods, including grain products, vegetables, and fruits, to reduce the risk of chronic lifestyle diseases. A diet high in plant foods contains less saturated fat and cholesterol and potentially fewer calories. It is also likely to be higher in phytochemicals, antioxidants, vitamins, minerals, and fiber. Therefore, consuming a nutritionally balanced, adequate vegetarian diet may help reduce the risk of many serious diseases such as cancer, high blood pressure, heart disease, and obesity.

## Health Challenges for Vegetarians

Although many health benefits result from consuming a balanced vegetarian diet, some potential health risks are associated with one that is poorly planned and too restrictive. The greatest risk is that of imbalance or nutritional deficiency. The more restrictive the diet, the greater the nutritional risk; therefore, a vegan diet would likely have the greatest possible risks if not planned properly. When beginning a vegetarian diet, ask yourself why you are doing so. Abruptly switching to a vegetarian diet is sometimes an attempt to simply restrict the amount of food consumed and therefore may be a sign of an eating disorder (see Chapter 15 for more information on disordered eating). If not planned adequately, vegetarian diets, especially vegan diets, can lead to anemia due to inadequate intake of iron. In addition, vegan diets can be low in zinc, calcium, protein, vitamin $B_6$, and vitamin $B_{12}$ because these nutrients are most abundant in animal protein. However, with careful planning a vegan diet can provide all of the required nutrients in sufficient amounts. See Chapter 2 for more tips on planning a vegetarian diet.

## Planning a Vegetarian Diet

Following a vegetarian diet requires more than just not eating meat or fish. It includes eating whole grains, legumes, nuts, and dark leafy green vegetables to ensure adequate nutrients. It may take a little bit more effort and thought when planning your meals, eating out, and so forth, especially if your diet is vegan. Vegetarian diets, when well planned, can meet all recommendations and nutrient requirements. It is best to begin by doing a little research so that you plan well-balanced meals that contain adequate nutrients. Many resources are available to help you acquire some background information as well as helpful tips for easy menu planning. See Figures 5.8 and 5.9 for a food guide for North American vegetarians and meal-planning recommendations put forth by the Vegetarian Society.

*Are vegetarians really healthier than people who eat meat, and do they live longer?*

A variety of delicious and healthy vegetarian meals are available from many different cultures. Do your local supermarkets offer a good selection of ethnic foods? Have you noticed an increase in the number of ethnic restaurants in your city or community?

*How do I become a vegetarian?*

### ■ What's Hot

*Protein for Weight Loss*

There is a lot of debate as to what diet is most effective for weight loss. In recent years high-protein diets have taken the limelight. This is mostly a reaction to several studies that showed that high-protein diets resulted in more weight loss over 3-6 months than conventional high-carbohydrate low-fat diets. A smaller group of studies attempted to follow subjects for 12 months or more and found that there was no difference. A Harvard study was conducted with 800 overweight and obese subjects who followed one of four diets for two years. Each diet resulted in a 750 calorie deficit and varied in the amount of protein, carbohydrates, and fats consumed. The diets were equally successful in promoting weight loss and maintaining it over the two years. Furthermore, they had similar effects on decreasing disease risk and improving cholesterol levels. The study emphasized behavioral counseling and support group activities provided equally across the groups. The authors suggest that behavioral factors, rather than the amount of carbohydrates or proteins one consumes, are the main influences on weight loss. Additionally, they suggest that any type of diet, if presented with enthusiasm and persistence, can be effective. This is encouraging news as it makes sense that no one diet will work for everyone. Therefore, health practitioners can utilize a variety of diets to meet the cultural and individual food preferences of each patient they are working with. Perhaps as a society we can stop jumping from one fad to the next and be open to the possibilities to enhance weight loss efforts and help to reverse the obesity epidemic. ■

**Figure 5.8** "The Balance of Good Health" is not difficult to achieve on a vegetarian diet.

*Source:* Courtesy of The Vegetarian Society of the United Kingdom (www.vegsoc.org).

**Figure 5.9** Food Guide for Vegetarians

A "**portion**" is, for example, a slice of bread, an apple, a glass of milk or two tablespoons of baked beans, but remember—it's the balance that matters, so if you have a big appetite, increase the amount you eat in all categories, not just the fatty and sugary foods.

**Fruit and Vegetables 5 portions a day**
Fresh, frozen, juiced, tinned or dried fruit and vegetables are particularly good sources of vitamins, minerals and fiber.

**Bread, other Cereals and Potatoes 5 portions a day**
Base most of your meals on these starchy foods. Use wholemeal or whole-grain versions as much as possible and avoid adding lots of fat. These foods give us carbohydrates for energy, fiber, protein, and some vitamins and minerals.

**High Protein Foods 2–3 portions a day**
Include a variety of beans, lentils, peas and chick peas, nuts, seeds, eggs, Soy or wheat proteins to give you plenty of protein, minerals and vitamins.

**Milk and Dairy Products 2–3 portions a day**
Good sources of calcium, protein and some vitamins. If you are avoiding dairy foods, choose fortified Soy, rice or oat drinks or make sure that you eat other foods that are high in calcium.

**Fatty and Sugary Foods 0–3 portions a day**
Choose foods high in omega-3 fatty acids such as walnuts and flaxseed. Choose olive oil, avocado and other healthy fats. Limit saturated fats. See Chapter 4 for more information on fats.

**Want to know more?**
If you'd like to review guidelines for vegetarians and some vegetarian recipes, go to the text website at http://webcom8.grtxle.com/nutrition and click on the Chapters button. Select Chapter 5.

*Source:* Used courtesy of The Vegetarian Society of the United Kingdom (www.vegsoc.org).

# Real People, Other Voices

**Student:**
## Brian Nolan
Binghamton University

Although it is true that athletes require more protein than non-athletes, Richard does not need to consume protein supplements in order to achieve the total amount of protein his body needs. For Richard, getting the increased amount of protein needed for his activity level does not pose a problem. The real concern comes with the type of protein he is consuming.

Since Richard needs to be consuming more protein, it is my opinion that he needs to make smart choices when deciding on what proteins to eat. There are many low-fat protein choices, such as skinless chicken breasts and pork tenderloins, which Richard can consume in order to reach his protein needs without taking in too many calories or saturated fat. Richard also must remember that a great source of protein is soy products and a combination of grains and vegetables.

In reality, supplements are no better than food sources of protein. It is quite easy to fulfill the requirement for protein through your everyday food sources. By consuming your protein through food, you receive many other nutrients such as phytochemicals, antioxidants, vitamins, and minerals. Plus, protein-rich foods taste better than supplements!

**Instructor:**
## Allison Miner
Prince George's Community College

Although exercise and weight-lifting can help Richard improve or change his body shape and size to his desired image, body-shaping and muscle development are also controlled by genetic influences. If Richard's family is tall and lean, his genetic predisposition will be for a tall and lean stature. Muscle mass is increased when it is stressed, as during weightlifting, and muscles need a recuperative period in order to become stronger and larger. Weightlifting without a period of rest may do more harm than good. In addition, Richard's body will utilize only the dietary protein that it needs, and consuming extra protein will not force the body to make more muscle.

Most Americans consume more than one and one-half times the amount they utilize. This extra protein is simply converted into fat by the liver and stored in fat cells. A byproduct of excess protein intake is nitrogen, which must be excreted through the kidneys, causing water loss that can lead to dehydration and stress the kidneys. Richard should calculate the grams of protein he normally consumes to ensure that he is meeting his *Dietary Reference Intake* before he determines his need.

He should continue his workouts, alternating the body parts that he stresses so that he allows for regeneration of muscle mass. When he snacks, he should concentrate on foods that are higher in protein such as yogurt, nuts, or meat-based foods. Most importantly, Richard should focus on his long-term health rather than his body image. Moderate exercise *and* diet are key ingredients for a long, disease-free life.

**Registered Dietitian:**
## Ben Heinz R.D., L.D.
Bloomington, MN

Richard has a very common dilemma. There is a vast amount of misinformation available regarding nutrition. Simply increasing his protein intake will not solve his problem. The first thing Richard needs to do to achieve his goal is to assess the content of the food he is eating. Writing down his meals for approximately three days will help him understand where he is in terms of diet. Using this food record, Richard should consult with an RD, who will help him make the necessary adjustments and construct a new meal plan to attain his goal.

His first priority is to make sure he is meeting his energy needs. Since he is so active, he will need to consume a large number of calories to reach his goal. After making sure his energy intake is appropriate, he should then make adjustments to assure that his carbohydrate, protein, and fat intake are adequate.

Since Richard is currently doing frequent resistance training, his protein requirement may be equivalent to 1.6 to 1.7g/kg of body weight, or approximately 116 to 123g of protein per day. As long as Richard continues to eat consistent meals and snack throughout the day, he will get the necessary calories and macronutrients from his diet. Protein supplements are not needed! His pre-workout meal should be high in carbohydrate, moderate in protein, and low in fat. His post-workout meal would be similar to his pre-workout meal.

Industrial farming methods typically confine animals in extremely tight spaces and never allow them to go outdoors. They also feed them antibiotics and growth hormones. Do you think these practices are inhumane?

## You Decide
*Is eating meat animal abuse?*

Many individuals and groups do not eat meat because they believe that the processes by which animals are treated to provide that meat are cruel and inhumane. Like many ethical and moral issues, this is a situation in which you simply have to make the decision for yourself. Does eating meat mean supporting an industry that abuses animals? ■

**Want to know more?**
If you'd like to explore both sides of this issue in more detail, go to the text website at http:// webcom8.grtxle.com/nutrition and click on the Chapters button. Select Chapter 5.

**Before you go on . . .**
1. Name and differentiate between the different types of vegetarians.
2. What are the different reasons for choosing to become a vegetarian?
3. What are the health benefits of consuming a vegetarian diet?

## Protein Imbalance

### Too Little Protein

After discussing the important roles of protein in the body, you can imagine how inadequate protein intake might affect overall health. Protein is rarely the only deficient nutrient in a malnourished person, so protein malnutrition is usually not an isolated problem. **Protein energy malnutrition (PEM)** occurs when a person does not consume adequate amounts of protein, calories, or both.

Although PEM is rare in the general population of most other industrialized countries, it does exist in the United States, particularly in those with major illnesses such as cancer, HIV, and anorexia nervosa and in children in low-income areas. In fact, PEM is the most common form of nutritional deficiency diagnosed in hospitalized patients in the United States. It is estimated that half of all patients admitted to the hospital have some degree of malnutrition in the form of PEM. Additionally, several surveys conducted in low-income areas of the United States reported that 22–35 percent of children ages 2–6 had a slower than normal growth rate due to PEM. PEM is an even greater concern internationally. In 2000, the World Health Organization (WHO) estimated that 32 percent of children in developing countries were

Protein energy malnutrition is the most common nutrient deficiency in hospital patients in the United States.

malnourished. In south central Asia and eastern Africa, approximately half of all children have growth retardation as a complication of PEM. This figure is five times the reported rates in Western countries.

According to WHO, PEM is by far the most lethal form of malnutrition. Infants and young children are most susceptible to the devastating medical complications associated with PEM because of their high energy and protein needs and their vulnerability to infection. There are two types of PEM, discussed next.

## Marasmus and Kwashiorkor

People with **marasmus** are characterized by emaciation, or a skeletal appearance due to inadequate intake of protein and calories. Essentially, it is a condition of starvation. Marasmus is most common in infants and children of impoverished regions, but can occur in adults as well. It can occur in industrialized nations, typically as a complication of cancer or HIV, in infants and children because of malabsorption as a result of gastrointestinal disease, or as a result of self-starvation associated with eating disorders such as anorexia nervosa.

The term **kwashiorkor** is taken from the language of Ghana and means "the sickness of the weaning." Kwashiorkor most frequently affects children who are being weaned. Often these children are transitioned from breast milk to a very starchy, low-protein cereal and the kwashiorkor develops quickly. Such children look as if they are developing a "potbelly" as fluid accumulates. Those unfamiliar with malnutrition often mistake this for a child being overnourished. This is not the case. The children may be receiving enough calories, but not enough protein, which is what causes the potbelly appearance. Cases have been observed among minority populations in the United States, but are most common in underdeveloped regions worldwide. Some of the more consequential medical complications include impaired growth, edema, rash, and an impaired immune system.

Whether PEM occurs as a result of poverty, chronic disease, an eating disorder, or poor intake, the rehabilitation is similar. The patient will need a medically supervised nutrition plan to correct the deficiency and to ensure proper fluid and electrolyte balance.

Marasmus *(left)* is a form of PEM common in children of impoverished nations. It is caused by inadequate protein and calorie intake. The child at right, suffering from kwashiorkor, has a "potbelly" appearance due to inadequate protein intake.

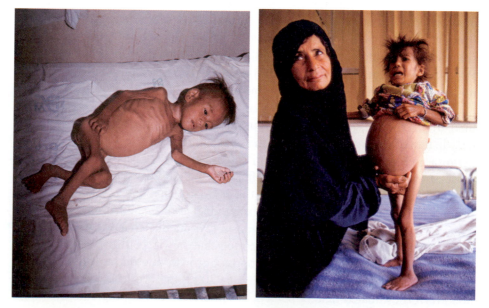

## Too Much Protein

We seem to have a cultural obsession with dietary protein. Many labels and marketing slogans for food products use descriptions such as "high protein" or "good source of protein" as if there were an overall nutritional need to focus on it. Many fad diets and weight-loss programs also stress protein intake.

With all of this attention on protein, one might assume that Americans do not consume enough of it. As we mentioned previously, the opposite is true—the typical American consumes more than the recommended amount. This fact raises the question—are we consuming too much protein? If we do eat too much, what are the consequences? Considerable disagreement exists among scientists and those claiming to be experts as to how much protein is too much, and whether there is even such a thing as eating too much of it. Although several studies have suggested potential health risks associated with a high-protein diet, not enough evidence exists to conclude that consuming more than the recommended amount is harmful. Additionally, there is no agreed upon definition of "high protein." It could mean above the DRI which would cover a wide range of intakes and therefore it would be difficult to make any conclusions on such a broad definition. It is difficult to determine whether protein itself causes many of the associated health problems, or lack of other dietary components commonly associated with a high-protein diet. Therefore, it is important to discuss some of the suggested health concerns of consuming a high-protein diet.

Many popular fad diets claim protein is the secret to successful weight loss. If adequate research hasn't been conducted on these diets, how should you view their claims?

One of the most obvious risks to your health would occur from consuming an unbalanced diet of excess dietary protein. High-protein diets are often low in fruits, vegetables, whole grains, and fiber and may be high in saturated fat. This is not to say that all sources of protein are high in fat. There are many lean sources of protein and many high-quality plant sources of protein such as soy products. However, many high-protein diets are low in fiber, phytochemicals, and many vitamins and minerals. If by eating excess protein one is consuming excess calories, then of course weight gain can occur. In addition, a high-protein diet that consists mainly of animal protein sources is likely to be high in saturated fat.

Several studies have suggested that a high-protein diet, especially one high in animal protein, may increase the risk for certain types of cancer. In particular, colon, prostate, breast, and pancreatic cancers have been linked to a high protein intake. However, researchers have had difficulty in determining whether this risk is associated with the excess protein or the dietary imbalances associated with eating less fiber, fewer fruits and vegetables, and more saturated fat. It has also been suggested that high protein diets may also cause bone loss, which can lead to osteoporosis, especially in those who consume inadequate amounts of calcium. The theory is that this is particularly true if the protein sources in the diet are mostly animal in origin. Compared to plant proteins, animal proteins contain more sulfurous amino acids, which are acidic. Calcium from the body is used to buffer the acid; the calcium used is then excreted from the body in urine. There is little evidence to support that a high protein diet leads to bone loss and it may in fact benefit bone health by helping to offset muscle loss often experienced in the elderly. For some, an additional risk of increased calcium excretion associated with a high-protein diet is an elevated risk for the formation of kidney stones. Drinking plenty of fluids will help offset this potential problem by diluting the contents of the urine.

Some health professionals have suggested that high-protein diets may stress the kidneys and therefore lead to an increased risk of kidney disease. While this may be true for those who are susceptible to developing kidney stones and other kidney problems, such as diabetics, there does not appear to be a concern for the average healthy person. However, it can be a problem for infants and premature infants if there is insufficient water intake and for anyone taking multiple medications and supplements that may be putting stress on the kidneys.

Although experts disagree about the exact amount of protein required and the amount that determines excess, they generally agree that consuming 2 g/day of protein per kilograms (approximately 2.2 lb.) of ideal body weight is safe for most healthy people, although it is higher than the recommended amount. There is no information to suggest any benefits in eating amounts greater than this.

## ■ Sustainable Nutrition
### *Meat production and the environment*

Between 1980 and 2004 global meat production doubled, according to the Food and Agricultural Organization of the United Nations. This increase occurred mostly in developing countries, particularly in Asia. Large industrial farms (or feedlots) were created to raise livestock in concentrated numbers, replacing the more traditional family-run farms where animals were raised in pastures or less confined enclosures. These rapidly increasing industrial farms produce much more pollution than traditional farms and pose a huge threat to the environment. The pollution they generate threatens the soil, water supply, air, atmosphere, ecosystem, and public health. This environmental threat is increased when industrial farms are grouped together and are near major waterways and/or heavily populated areas.

**Figure 5.10** Per-capita meat consumption in the United States. Notice the decline in beef consumption and the steady increase in chicken consumption from 1985 through 2020 predicted consumption.

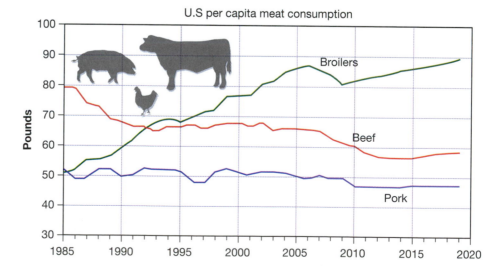

Meat production has rapidly increased in developing countries. Despite that increase, countries such as the United States still consume four times as much meat as people in developing countries. According to the USDA in 2007 Americans ate approximately 66 lbs. of beef per person and 51 lbs. of pork. Figure 5.10 shows the meat consumption of Americans from 1910 to the present. If the world's population today were to match the meat consumption of an average American, the land used for livestock production would have to increase by approximately 67 percent over what it currently is. ■

**Want to know more?**
If you would like to learn more about the impact of meat production on the environment, visit the text website at http://webcom8 .grtxle.com/nutrition and click on the Chapters button. Select Chapter 5.

**Before you go on . . .**

1. What is protein energy malnutrition (PEM)?
2. Describe the primary difference between the diseases kwashiorkor and marasmus.
3. What are the health concerns regarding consumption of too much protein?

## Real People, Real Strategies

The essential questions that Richard needs to answer are how much protein does he need, and how can he best meet his requirement? He weighs 160 lbs. or 72.7 kg, and the DRI is 0.8 grams per kilogram, which would be about 58 g of protein per day for Richard. Because he is weight training, most experts would agree that he needs more protein than the DRI—probably 1.7 grams per kilogram, which would be 124 g of protein per day. Eating more than this will not provide any benefits for him. It is most important for Richard to get adequate calories and protein throughout the day, but it may help to eat a small amount of protein and carbohydrates an hour before his workout and then a small meal afterward. He can use supplements when he is rushed for time and needs a quick meal replacement, but he really should and can get all the protein and calories he needs from food.

Using the diet analysis software he received with his nutrition text, Richard created the following meal plan to meet his adjusted DRI for protein.

**Breakfast—8:00 A.M.**
1 1/2 c. cereal
8 oz. milk
Banana

**Snack—10:00 A.M.**
Yogurt
1 oz. almonds

**Workout—weights from 11:00 A.M.–12:30 P.M.**

**Lunch—1:00 P.M.**
Peanut butter and jelly sandwich:
    2 Tbsp. peanut butter
    1 Tbsp. jelly
    2 slices whole-wheat bread
Tossed salad with tomatoes and baby carrots
1 Tbsp. Italian salad dressing
1 chocolate chip cookie

**Workout—jog 3 miles 5:00 P.M.**

**Dinner—6:00 P.M.**
6-oz. chicken breast
1 1/2 c. wild rice
1 c. steamed broccoli
1 1/2 c. ice cream
1 c. strawberries

**Snack–10:00 P.M.**
3 egg whites
1 multigrain bagel
1 Tbsp. low-fat cream cheese

His analysis shows that by following this eating plan he would consume 147 g of protein and 2,950 calories. In addition, he discovered that this diet would meet or exceed the recommended amounts of all nutrients and of all recommended servings from MyPyramid. Encouraged, Richard decided to try to eat like this while sticking to a regular workout schedule.

# Chapter Summary

- Chemically, proteins (amino acids) are made of carbon, hydrogen, oxygen, and nitrogen.

- Proteins are made up of combinations of amino acids that are linked together by peptide bonds. All amino acids are made of a center carbon connected to four different groups: an amine group (which contains nitrogen); an acid group; hydrogen; and the R group (or side chain).

- The R groups distinguish one amino acid from the other and dictate the functions of the different amino acids. They allow the different amino acids to vary in acidity, shape, size, and electrical charge. This important feature ensures that each protein is unique. So insulin and hemoglobin, although both proteins, have very specific functions.

- There are twenty known amino acids. Essential amino acids cannot be made in the body, so we must obtain them from the foods we consume, such as dairy products, meat, eggs, soy, and vegetables. Nonessential amino acids can be made in the body. However, under certain circumstances, nonessential amino acids that cannot be made by the body in sufficient quantity are called conditionally essential amino acids.

- Our DNA determines the order or sequence in which the amino acids will be linked together. The specific order of amino acids in a protein is part of what determines the shape of the protein, which in turn dictates its function. Proteins form a three-dimensional shape that is unique for each protein.

- A protein's structure and function can be changed by heat, acid, enzymes, agitation, or alcohol in a process called denaturation. For example, stomach acid denatures the protein we eat during digestion.

- Proteins serve many important functions in the body, including growth, maintenance, repair, body structure, blood clotting, fluid balance, acid-base balance, immune function, enzymes, hormones, transport, and energy.

- Proteins are in a constant state of buildup (called protein synthesis) and breakdown (called protein breakdown). This very closely connected process of synthesis and breakdown is called protein turnover; it aids the body in health maintenance as some cells die and need to be replaced.

- All of the essential amino acids must be present in adequate amounts for protein synthesis to occur, or cells will not be replaced as they die off. If you do not consume the foods that supply all of the essential amino acids, a small amount can be taken from the body's short-term storage, called the amino acid pool.

- A high-quality protein, also called a complete protein, is a protein that provides all of the essential amino acids in the amount that the body needs and is easy to digest and absorb. Animal proteins, such as those found in meats and dairy products, and the vegetable protein in soy are examples of foods containing complete protein; they are considered highly digestible because the human body can absorb almost 90 percent of them.

- Foods that do not contain all of the essential amino acids are called incomplete proteins. Examples of incomplete proteins include beans, legumes, grains, and vegetables. These foods, when combined with other incomplete proteins, can make a complete protein.

- Recent studies have suggested that a variety of health benefits are associated with consuming soy and soy products because of the phytoestrogens they contain.
- Most Americans, whether vegetarian or not, consume more protein than they need from foods and therefore supplements are not necessary.
- Although supplements can contribute to meeting daily protein requirements, they are not superior to food sources of protein.
- The DRI for protein is 0.8 grams per kilogram of body weight of high-quality protein for men and women. This accounts for about 10 percent of the total calories for the day. Endurance athletes should consume 1.2–1.4 grams per kilogram, and resistance athletes should consume 1.6–1.7 grams per kilogram. However, most athletes already consume more protein than is recommended and therefore do not have to increase their intake.
- There are several types of vegetarians, and many people have different ideas about what being a vegetarian really means. Being a vegetarian has numerous health benefits. Vegetarians typically have a lower BMI and experience a lower risk of heart disease and cancers than nonvegetarians. Although health benefits result from consuming a balanced vegetarian diet, some potential health risks are associated with one that is poorly planned and too restrictive. The greatest risk is that of imbalance or nutritional deficiency.
- Protein energy malnutrition (PEM) occurs when a person does not consume adequate amounts of protein, calories, or both.
- Although several studies have suggested potential health risks associated with a high-protein diet, not enough evidence exists to conclude that consuming more than the recommended amount is as harmful as was once thought. However, overconsuming protein can lead to nutritional imbalances.

## Key Terms

**acid-base balance** The mechanisms the body uses to keep its fluids close to neutral pH (that is, neither basic nor acidic) so that the body can function normally. (p. 145)

**albumin** A protein that constitutes 60 percent of the body's *plasma* (the watery part of blood) proteins. Among albumin's many functions, it transports drugs and thyroid hormones and carries fatty acids from adipose tissue to the muscle cells for use as energy. (p. 145)

**amino acid pool** Short-term storage of amino acids found in cellular fluids. (p. 147)

**amino acids** The building blocks of protein. They contain nitrogen and link together to form proteins. (p. 140)

**complementary proteins** Two or more foods whose amino acid content, when combined, provides all of the essential amino acids. (p. 150)

**complete protein** A protein that provides all of the essential amino acids in the amount that the body needs and is easy to digest and absorb. Also called a *high-quality protein*. (p. 148)

**conditionally essential amino acids** Essential amino acids that under certain circumstances cannot be made in sufficient quantity by the body and therefore must be consumed in the diet. (p. 141)

**denaturation** (dee-nay-chur-AY-shun) A process in which a protein's structure and function are changed by heat, acid, enzymes, agitation, or alcohol. (p. 143)

**essential amino acids** Amino acids that cannot be made in the body, so we must obtain them from the food we eat. (p. 140)

**hemoglobin** (HEE-moh-gloh-bin) A protein contained in the red blood cells that carries oxygen throughout the body. (p. 143)

**high-quality protein** A protein that provides all of the essential amino acids in the amount that the body needs and is easy to digest and absorb. Also called a *complete protein*. (p. 148)

**incomplete proteins** Foods that do not contain all of the essential amino acids in the amount needed by the body. They include beans, legumes, grains, vegetables. (p. 150)

**kwashiorkor** (kwah-she-OR-kor) A form of protein energy malnutrition (PEM) characterized by a swollen appearance, especially in the abdomen, caused by a lack of protein. (p. 160)

**lacto-ovo vegetarians** People who consume eggs and dairy products, but no meat or seafood. (p. 153)

**lacto-vegetarians** People who consume milk and dairy products, such as cheese and yogurt, but avoid eggs, seafood, and meat. (p. 153)

**limiting amino acid** An essential amino acid that is not present in sufficient amounts through dietary protein. (p. 147)

**macrobiotic vegetarians** People who consume mostly whole grains, especially brown rice, in their diets along with vegetables, soy, legumes, fruits, and sometimes whitefish. (p. 153)

**marasmus** (ma-RAZZ-muss) A form of protein energy malnutrition (PEM) characterized by emaciation, or a skeletal appearance due to inadequate intake of protein and calories. (p. 160)

**negative nitrogen balance** A situation in which the body is breaking down more protein than it is producing, such as during a time of illness or injury. (p. 148)

**nonessential amino acids** Amino acids that can be made in the body by transferring the amine group, or nitrogen, from an essential amino acid to another compound containing a carbon, an acid group, a hydrogen, and an R group. (p. 140)

**peptide bonds** Very strong bonds that link amino acids together to make proteins. The bond is formed between the acid group of one amino acid and the amine group of another. (p. 141)

**pH** A numerical scale that measures and reflects acid-base balance. (p. 145)

**positive nitrogen balance** A situation in which protein intake exceeds what is excreted, such as during periods of growth, recovery from illness, and pregnancy. (p. 147)

**protein breakdown** A process in which proteins in the body are broken down into individual amino acids. (p. 147)

**Protein Digestibility–Corrected Amino Acid Score (PDCAAS)** A value assigned to proteins that accounts for their protein quality (amino acid content) and their digestibility. (p. 148)

**protein energy malnutrition (PEM)** A disorder that occurs when a person does not consume adequate amounts of protein, calories, or both. (p. 159)

**protein synthesis** A process in which amino acids are linked together to make proteins. (p. 147)

**protein turnover** The balance of protein synthesis and protein breakdown. (p. 147)

**semivegetarians** People who occasionally eat meat and seafood, yet predominately practice a vegetarian diet. (p. 154)

**sickle-cell anemia** A form of anemia that occurs when a person inherits two abnormal genes (one from each parent) that cause one amino acid to be missing in the sequence for the protein hemoglobin. The missing amino acid causes the shape of the cell to be more sickle shaped rather than disc shaped. The sickle-shaped cells do not allow for complete bonding of hemoglobin and oxygen and can easily stick together. (p. 143)

**transamination** (tranz-am-in-AY-shun) Transference of the amine group (the nitrogen-containing part) from one molecule to another to make an amino an acid. (p. 140)

**vegan** A person who eats only plant food and does not eat meat, fish, poultry, milk or other dairy products, eggs, or anything else produced from animals. Also referred to as a *strict vegetarian*. (p. 153)

**vegetarians** People who do not consume animal flesh but may eat eggs and dairy products. (p. 154)

# Chapter Quiz

1. Proteins are made of many amino acids linked by what type of bonds?
   a. hydrogen
   b. double
   c. peptide
   d. carbon

2. The element that makes proteins different from fat and carbohydrates is
   a. hydrogen.
   b. carbon.
   c. nitrogen.
   d. oxygen.

3. Which group of amino acids makes it different from the others and therefore dictates its function?
   a. the amine group
   b. the R group
   c. the acid group
   d. the hydrogen group

4. Nonessential amino acids can be made in the body by transferring the nitrogen from an essential amino acid to another compound through a process called
   a. protein degradation.
   b. transamination.
   c. denaturation.
   d. protein breakdown.

5. Why does the order of the amino acids in a protein dictate its shape and therefore its function?
   a. Different amino acids are shaped differently.
   b. Different amino acids contain different DNA.
   c. The charge of each amino acid dictates how it interacts with other amino acids.
   d. Different amino acids are bigger than others.

6. Which of the following statements is true regarding protein turnover?
   a. It determines the protein mass and rates of gain or loss within each cell.
   b. It is influenced by a complex interaction of hormones and nutritional factors, especially amino acid availability.
   c. It represents the constant buildup and breakdown of proteins occurring in the body.
   d. All of the above.

7. Which of the following foods is a complete protein?
   a. rice
   b. peanut butter
   c. egg white
   d. black beans

8. The DRI for protein is
   a. 0.6 g.
   b. 0.8 g.
   c. 1.6 g.
   d. 50 percent of total calories.

9. Which of the following types of vegetarians consume milk but no eggs or meat?
   a. vegans
   b. lacto-ovo vegetarians
   c. lacto-vegetarians
   d. semivegetarians

10. When trying to increase muscle mass, the *most* important thing is
    a. to eat less protein.
    b. to eat more protein than you typically require.
    c. to eat enough carbohydrates.
    d. to eat enough fat.

# CHAPTER 6

# Digestion, Absorption, and Metabolism

## The Link Between Food and Energy

## < Here's Where You've Been

*The following topics were introduced in preceding chapters and are related to concepts we'll discuss in Chapter 6. Be certain that you're familiar with them before proceeding.*

- Dietary fiber has many health benefits and can help prevent some diseases, including colon cancer and heart disease. (Chapter 3)
- Fatty acids are a source of energy, and phospholipids are components of cell membranes. Triglycerides are the storage form of fat in our bodies and the major type of fat we consume in food. (Chapter 4)
- Proteins are made from many amino acids linked together.
- Most Americans get plenty of protein from sources including meats, dairy products, legumes, nuts, and seeds and do not have to take supplements to meet the requirements for growth, maintenance, and repair. (Chapter 5)

## Here's Where You're Going >

*The following topics and concepts are the ones we'll emphasize in Chapter 6.*

- Once food enters our mouth, it must go through a series of steps before we can get energy from it. These steps are digestion, absorption, and metabolism.
- Digestion occurs through a combination of chemical and mechanical processes that begin in the mouth and end when waste is excreted.
- Most absorption takes place in the small intestine.
- Once the macronutrients are absorbed into the blood they must be taken up by the cells, where they can be converted to the usable form of energy called ATP. This is done through a series of steps called metabolism.

## Real People, Real Choices

Cathleen Knierim is a first-semester graduate student. She has just moved to San Francisco from Eugene, Oregon, and is adjusting to her new academic and living environments. She is working for the university as a part-time graduate assistant. Cathleen is also trying very hard to maintain a high GPA while managing a lot of stress caused by these various circumstances. She has no time for exercise and finds herself regularly skipping meals. In fact, on many days she is so busy she forgets to eat, only to come home in the evening with a tremendous appetite. Of course, when she is that hungry she ends up eating a very large meal all at once. The meals she does eat are usually easy to prepare or are from fast-food restaurants. Often after she eats she experiences pain in her stomach and a burning sensation in her chest. Sometimes she even gets this feeling when she just drinks a glass of water. A commercial about heartburn that describes her symptoms gets Cathleen's attention. Although she thinks she is too young to have heartburn, Cathleen decides that she'd better visit her physician to determine exactly what is happening. What advice do you think her physician will give her? What changes would you recommend in her behavior, diet, and eating habits?

Thus far we have discussed food in terms of what we put on our plates and, ultimately, in our mouths. We have not discussed what happens to the food once we can no longer see it. We must keep in mind that eating is only the initial step in generating energy for our body's use. Food that was on our plate needs to be digested into smaller components so that we can absorb its nutrients. After consumption, the next step in the process of converting food to energy is a complex series of chemical reactions and interactions combined with muscular movements that break the food down into smaller compounds. This process is called **digestion.** We must then move the smaller products of digestion across the lining of the intestinal tract, into our bodies, and ultimately into our cells. This is called **absorption.** Once absorbed into our cells, these components have to be converted into **adenosine triphosphate (ATP),** which is a high-energy molecule that can be broken down to a usable form of energy. Multiple organs and several steps are involved in these complex processes. This chapter will give you an overview and understanding of these processes.

## The Organs and the Functions of Digestion

Digestion occurs in the digestive or **gastrointestinal (GI) tract.** The GI tract consists of a series of organs with many complex outer layers of muscles (see Figure 6.1) and an inner mucosal layer of glands and absorptive cells. It starts with the mouth and ends with the anus. When food is in the digestive tract, it is still not "inside" the body. As noted earlier, before it can provide energy it must go through a series of steps that begin in the GI tract (Figure 6.2 and Table 6.1).

The main functions of the GI tract are to take in food, transport it, and secrete substances that help break it into smaller compounds so that they can be absorbed. The period of time it takes food to travel the length of the digestive tract is called **transit time**, and it depends on several factors. See the Myths and Legends feature for more information.

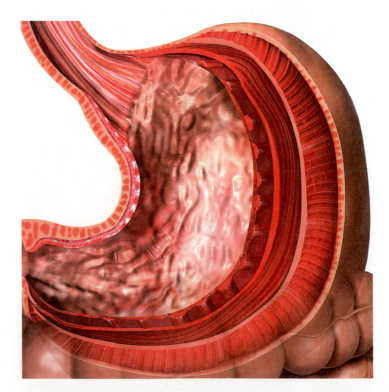

**Figure 6.1** The GI tract has many complex outer layers of muscle and an inner mucosal layer.

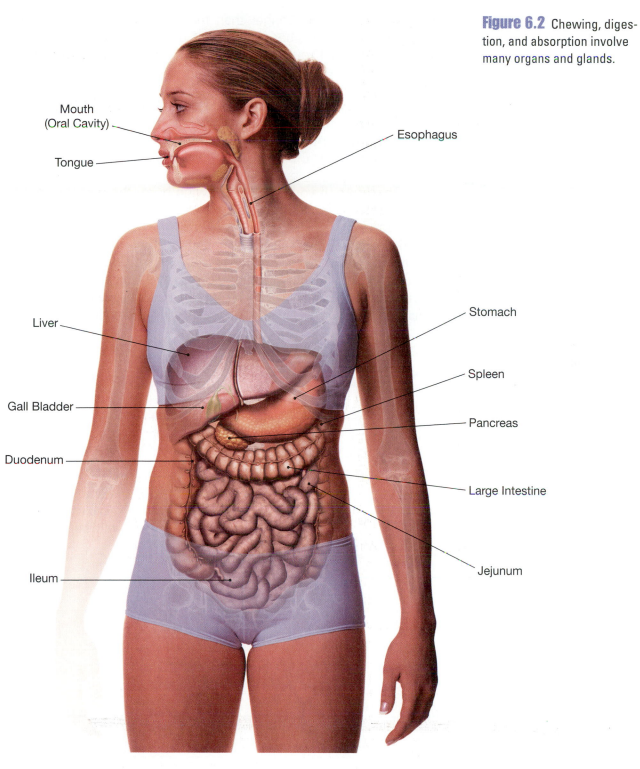

Mouth (Oral Cavity)

Tongue

Esophagus

Liver

Gall Bladder

Duodenum

Ileum

Stomach

Spleen

Pancreas

Large Intestine

Jejunum

 ■ **Myths and Legends**

*If you swallow chewing gum, will it stay in your stomach for seven years?*

How long does food take to get "from one end to the other" of your digestive tract? The time varies widely from person to person and depends a lot on what you eat. For example, diets that are high in fiber cause food to move through faster than those low in fiber. Meals high in fat and/or protein take longer than those higher in carbohydrates, especially those high in fiber. The rate of digestion is also influenced by the amount of fluid you drink. Of course, different health conditions influence transit time. If you have diarrhea, food moves through more quickly. On average, for a healthy adult, it takes anywhere from twelve to forty hours from the time food is eaten until the undigested components and waste materials exit the body as feces. People who have a bowel movement immediately after a meal are not excreting what they just ate. Instead, the food they have just eaten has stimulated **peristalsis**, a muscular movement that propels food through the digestive tract. Therefore, if you swallow chewing gum, the powerful movements of peristalsis move it through the GI tract and it will be excreted in a short time. ■

Digestion occurs through a combination of mechanical and chemical processes. The mechanical process involves chewing, mixing, and peristalsis. The chemical process involves mixing the food with the various secretions and enzymes of the GI tract that help break the larger compounds into smaller forms that can be absorbed. In addition, the digestive tract moves undigested

---

**APPLICATION TIP**

Many people think they are constipated if they do not have a bowel movement every day. However, constipation is defined as fewer than three bowel movements a week. It is not wise to correct the problem by taking laxatives or over-the-counter medicines. The best ways to prevent or correct constipation are to consume a highfiber diet, drink plenty of water, and participate in regular physical activity.

---

**Table 6.1**    **Role of Each Organ in Digestion and Absorption**

| What It is | What It Does |
| --- | --- |
| Mouth | Mechanically digests all food (by chewing and grinding); begins chemical digestion of carbohydrates with amylase. |
| Esophagus | Passes food from the mouth to the stomach. |
| Stomach | Mechanically digests food (by churning and mixing); begins chemical digestion of proteins with pepsin; releases hydrochloric acid (HCl). |
| Small intestine | Releases enzymes; completes chemical digestion of carbohydrates, fats, and proteins; releases bile to emulsify fats; is the primary site of absorption. |
| Large intestine | Absorbs water; prepares indigestible wastes (feces) for defecation. |
| Rectum | Temporarily stores feces. |
| Anus | Eliminates feces from the body. |
| **Accessory Organs** | |
| Tongue | Helps mix food with saliva; assists in swallowing; provides the sense of taste. |
| Salivary glands | Produce saliva, which contains the enzyme amylase that starts digestion of carbohydrates. |
| Liver | Produces bile, which emulsifies fats; receives nutrients after absorption. |
| Gallbladder | Stores bile, then releases it into the small intestine. |
| Pancreas | Produces digestive enzymes released into the small intestine, where they help digest carbohydrates, fats, and protein. |

or unabsorbed substances through its length and, ultimately, to elimination or defecation.

The digestive tract is made up of several organs, including the mouth, esophagus, stomach, small intestine, large intestine, and the rectum, as seen in Figure 6.2. These organs are assisted by other organs such as the liver, the pancreas, and the gallbladder. They are connected by **sphincters**, which are circular muscles located throughout the digestive system that work like one-way doors to control the movement of its contents from one part to another. They relax to allow substances to enter and then close to keep them from leaking or traveling backward. This is very important, as the contents of one organ of the digestive tract may be damaging to another area. For example, when substances from the stomach leak back into the esophagus, a burning sensation in the chest called **heartburn** occurs. Over time this can damage the esophagus, which does not have the thick mucous lining that the stomach has to protect it from its own acid.

Sometimes the sphincters do not push food in a single direction. Under certain circumstances they allow food to travel in the opposite and often undesired direction. So food can "come back up." When this occurs, the lower esophageal sphincter relaxes and the stomach and duodenum contract, allowing the stomach contents to travel backward when the body needs to get rid of what you just ate. This is called vomiting. It can be caused by irritants such as bacteria, alcohol, poisons, and trauma to the abdomen and can even be caused by sights, smells, thoughts, or emotions.

## Absorption

Once the food on your plate has been broken into its smallest units, it is ready to be absorbed, or to cross the lining of the small intestine into the body, into the blood, and finally into the cells, where it can be used for energy or stored (see Figure 6.3). Water, vitamins, minerals, and small molecules such as glucose don't need to be digested or broken into smaller molecules before they are absorbed, but carbohydrates, fats, and proteins do.

## The Sum of the Parts

Now let's look at the different parts of the digestive tract and discuss the role they play in digestion and absorption. We will look at them in order, with the thought of the food on our plate as a mental guide to remember where we started.

### The Nose

Some aspects of the digestive process begin before you even put food in your mouth. The sight, smell, and thought of food can trigger the digestive system to prepare for food. Close your eyes and imagine the smell of freshly baked chocolate chip cookies or of a pizza

Sphincters are circular muscles located throughout the digestive system that work like doors.

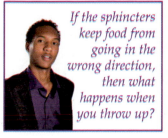

*If the sphincters keep food from going in the wrong direction, then what happens when you throw up?*

**Figure 6.3** Large molecules must be broken into smaller ones before absorption can occur.

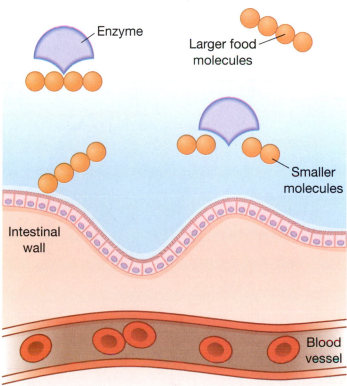

Enzyme

Larger food molecules

Smaller molecules

Intestinal wall

Blood vessel

restaurant as you walk by. Can you almost taste the cookies and the pizza? There is a strong connection between our brain, digestive system, and sense of smell. In fact, digestive secretions and enzymes can be released in response to these smells as a way of preparing for the food that is about to be eaten. Our sense of taste and our ability to identify different flavors are strongly connected to our ability to smell these foods. In fact, taste is 80 percent smell. The rest of the sensation of taste is determined by the appearance, temperature, and texture of the food, and by the taste buds. Five primary tastes are now recognized: *salty, sweet, sour, bitter*, and *umami* (the taste associated with monosodium glutamate, or MSG).

## The Mouth and Esophagus

The digestive process begins in the mouth, where food is chewed. Saliva is added during chewing to help lubricate the food, and enzymes are released to begin the digestive process. This process can start just before food enters the mouth as the release of saliva is increased by just the thought and smell of food. Again, think of the aromas of the cookies and pizza. Saliva does more than just moisten the mouth; it also digests some carbohydrates, helps inhibit bacterial growth, and helps dissolve molecules to enhance taste. Chewing plays an important role in digestion, not only by preparing food for swallowing but by increasing the surface area of the food so that digestive enzymes can reach more of it. Food, now in the form of a *bolus,* is swallowed in a process that involves the coordination of the tongue and twenty-two other muscles. The bolus travels down the esophagus via peristalsis, defined earlier. Because of this action we could swallow food while standing on our heads, or while in space, where gravity does not move food down the digestive tract.

## The Stomach

After traveling down the esophagus, food must pass through the *lower esophageal sphincter* and into the stomach (Figure 6.4). The stomach is a J-shaped sac that mixes and liquefies food into a substance called **chyme.**

The stomach's volume varies depending on the person but on average it holds about a liter after a normal meal. But because it has the capacity to expand, it can hold up to about 4 L when full. Once food enters the stomach, **hydrochloric acid (HCl)** is secreted to begin the breakdown of protein through a process called *denaturation.* As you may recall from Chapter 5, denaturation is the unraveling of proteins from their three-dimensional shape, which changes their function. In addition to breaking down dietary protein, hydrochloric acid also

Note layers of muscle

End of esophagus

Beginning of duodenum

**Figure 6.4** The stomach starts where the esophagus terminates and ends at the beginning of the duodenum. It consists of three parts, and it has several layers of muscles that help generate the churning and mixing motion.

denatures protein in potentially harmful bacteria that are often present in food (see Chapter 13 for more information).

The secretions that contain stomach acid also contain enzymes that help further digest the food that has now become chyme. The stomach contains several layers of muscles running in different directions that allow it to churn and mix the chyme with the secretions while pushing it down toward the small intestine. These secretions, which include mucus, play a very important role in digestion. Mucus protects the stomach from the acid and the digestive enzymes it contains. Without mucus the stomach can be damaged, as when a person acquires a stomach ulcer. The stomach secretions and their roles are listed in Table 6.2.

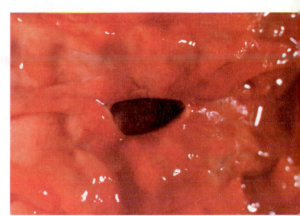

 ### ■ Nutrition and Disease
#### Stomach ulcers

An **ulcer,** also called a peptic ulcer, is an erosion that occurs in the lining of the stomach or the upper part of the small intestine. Stomach ulcers were once thought to be caused by stress and/or eating spicy food. However, we now know that nine out of ten stomach ulcers are caused by a bacterium called **Helicobacter pylori** or **H. pylori** that is resistant to stomach acid. Half of the world's population has *H. pylori* infection, and an estimated 30% of people in North America have it. *H. pylori* invades the protective mucus lining of the stomach and therefore allows the wall of the stomach to become damaged. Most people know they have an ulcer because of frequent and severe stomachaches; others may have no symptoms.

An ulcer is erosion that occurs on the lining of the stomach or the upper part of the small intestine. Ninety percent of stomach ulcers are caused by a bacterium called *Heliobacter pylori,* or *H pylori.*

*H. pylori* is most likely spread from person to person through oral-oral or fecal-oral exposure. Infection may sometimes result from ingestion of food or water contaminated by fecal matter, such as the contaminated water supplies in some developing countries. Fortunately, *H. pylori* is easily treated with antibiotics. While *H. pylori* infection is the most common cause of ulcers, they can also be caused by regular use of aspirin or ibuprofen, excessive consumption of alcohol, and smoking. ■

As the liquid pasty chyme reaches the end of the stomach, it must then pass through the *pyloric sphincter* into the small intestine. The stomach squirts a small amount, about 3 mL, of chyme at a time into the small intestine to allow the highly acidic liquid to be neutralized a little at a time. The contents typically empty completely within four hours of having finished a meal.

The time it takes for a meal to completely empty from the stomach varies based on the contents of the meal. For example, a high-fat meal of steak and french fries can take as long as six hours; and a lower-fat meal like pasta and vegetables with no meat or sauce may only take three or four. Similarly, the consistency of the meal affects the rate of emptying, so that liquids empty more quickly than solid food. Therefore, if you drink a protein shake it may empty more quickly than a protein bar of similar nutrient content. Not much absorption takes place in the stomach. In fact, only aspirin, some fat-soluble drugs, the mineral copper, and a small amount of alcohol are absorbed in the stomach.

*Why do I feel full for so long after I eat a steak, but feel hungry again soon after eating pasta?*

| **Table 6.2** | **The Secretions of the Stomach** | |
| --- | --- | --- |
| **What It Is** | **What It Does** | **Why It Is Important** |
| Mucus | Protects the lining of the stomach from HCl. | Without it, the stomach would be damaged by HCl and pepsin. |
| Hydrochloric acid (HCl) | Denatures proteins; liquefies foods; activates the enzymes pepsin and lingual lipase; helps prepare iron for absorption. | It helps neutralize bacteria and assists in digestion. |
| Intrinsic factor | Is essential to the absorption of vitamin $B_{12}$. | You need vitamin $B_{12}$ to prevent a form of anemia called pernicious anemia. |
| Pepsinogen | Is converted to an active form called pepsin by stomach acid. | It aids in protein digestion by breaking protein into shorter chains. |
| Hormones (twenty different chemical messengers) | Control movement of the stomach and secretion of HCl; communicate with the pancreas, liver, gallbladder, small intestine, and the rest of the body. | Hormones regulate the digestive process and ensure that the right enzyme is released at the right time. |

### The Small Intestine

Most absorption occurs in the small intestine (Figure 6.5). It is about 20 ft. long when stretched and is divided into three sections: the **duodenum**, the **jejunum**, and the **ileum**.

Most of the enzymes and the bile are secreted in the duodenum. Most digestion and absorption occurs in the jejunum. The small intestine is designed to maximize contact with nutrients so that the body can absorb as many of the nutrients as possible; it folds back and forth several times. This unique design of the small intestine results in a huge surface area that is further increased on the inner lining by fingerlike projections called **villi**. Tiny hairlike projections extending from the villi into the inside of the small intestine called **microvilli** further assist absorption and secrete digestive enzymes.

The villi are absorptive cells that are lined with tiny blood vessels called *capillaries*. The capillaries "pick up" nutrients once they are absorbed to carry them to the liver or other parts of the body. The large vessels of the lymph system carry larger fat molecules into the blood. These larger molecules are simply too large for the small capillaries and therefore have to get into the blood by a larger vessel than what is required for the smaller nutrients.

Immediately on entering the top of the small intestine, the acidic chyme from your stomach is neutralized by **alkaline bicarbonate (bicarb)**. Bicarb is released from the pancreas to protect the lining of the small intestine. The pancreas also releases enzymes that help break down carbohydrates, fats, and proteins. The small intestine also contains enzymes that are present in the surface of the microvilli and aid in the digestive process when they come in contact with the chyme. The **gallbladder** releases **bile**. Bile is made in the liver and stored in the gallbladder; it assists in the digestion of fat. Bile contains water, cholesterol, fats, bile salts, proteins, and bilirubin. Bilirubin gives bile and feces

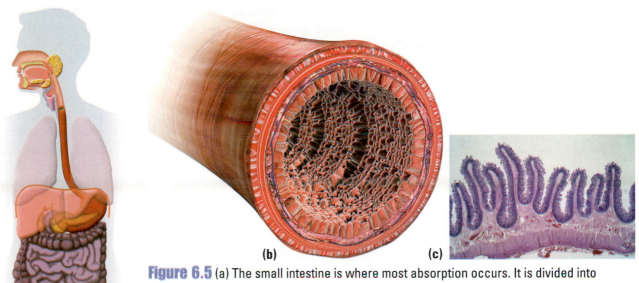

**Figure 6.5** (a) The small intestine is where most absorption occurs. It is divided into three sections: the duodenum, the jejunum, and the ileum. (b) The fingerlike projections of the small intestine, called the villi, enhance its surface area, which maximizes absorption into the capillaries that line it. (c) Close-up views of the microvilli, the villi, and the capillary running on the outside.

a light brown/dark yellow color. If the bile contains too much cholesterol, bile salts, or bilirubin, it can sometimes harden into stones. (See Table 6.3 later in this chapter for more information.)

Almost all of the nutrients consumed, 80 percent of electrolytes such as sodium and potassium, and most of the water we drink are absorbed in the small intestine (see Chapter 8 for more information on electrolytes). By the time digestive contents reach the end of the ileum, they include some water, some indigestible items, plant fibers such as cellulose and pectin, and bacteria.

## The Large Intestine

Once digestive contents reach the large intestine very little breakdown occurs, but the contents may take as long as twelve to twenty-four hours to travel through it. The large intestine is about 5 ft. long, and its main roles in the digestive process are propulsion of contents, absorption of some sodium and water, and preparation of waste for defecation. In addition, the large intestine contains some 800 species of bacteria.

The bacterial flora in your intestine are actually a good thing, and you don't need or want to get rid of them. Therefore, colon cleansing is not a good idea. (We'll discuss this further in the What's Hot feature that follows.) The bacteria metabolize any nutrients that remain in the large intestine. For example, they break down plant fibers such as cellulose and pectin to *short-chain fatty acids* and gases. So, yes, the downside is that they produce gas or *flatus* (it has many other names, but we'll stick with the technical ones). However, short-chain fatty acids are important for the health of the lining of your large intestine and colon.

In addition to breaking down certain plant fibers, the intestinal bacteria also produce vitamin K and some B vitamins. Vitamin K is necessary for our blood to clot properly. Without the bacteria to produce it, we would most likely not get enough vitamin K from the foods we eat. The only absorption that occurs in the large intestine is of the short-chain fatty acids, vitamins produced by the intestinal bacteria, and the sodium and water mentioned earlier.

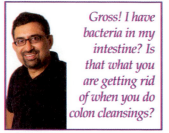

*Gross! I have bacteria in my intestine? Is that what you are getting rid of when you do colon cleansings?*

## ■ What's Hot

### Colon cleansing: beware of parasites

As we've periodically described, misinformation on health and nutrition abounds. Perhaps none is greater than that associated with the process of "colon cleansing." Many products and many ways to supposedly cleanse the colon are available, including seven-day fasts, juice diets and supplementation, toilets that provide enemas, "flushings" . . . you get the idea. Some natural-health practitioners claim that "death begins in the colon" and that "90 percent of all diseases are caused by improperly working bowels." The practices they recommend include fasting, periodic cleansing of the intestines, and colonic irrigation. Fasting is said to "purify" the body. "Cleansing" can be accomplished with a variety of "natural" laxative products.

Colonic irrigation is performed by passing a rubber tube through the rectum. Some pump 20 gal. (320 cups) or more through the tube to "wash" the colon. Just to give you an idea, an enema uses about a quart. Some products contain herbs, coffee, enzymes, wheat or grass extract, or other substances added to the solution. The websites, companies, and "natural health" groups that encourage this cleansing have several things in common (besides a high price for their services). They all suggest that as a modern society we are living with dangerous parasites in our colons as a result of an inadequate, highly refined diet. They go on to say that as a result of these "parasites" our colons have secreted mucus which has developed into pounds and pounds of hard, crusty, clogging black matter lining the walls of our colons. This matter is preventing normal colon function, which results in a long list of supposed health problems from fatigue and acne to cellulite and foot odor. So all you have to do is buy their product and any health ailment imaginable is cured. Sound too good to be true? Well, it is, and more.

Colon cleansing may be extremely harmful to your health, leading to the very problems it supposedly treats. The Mayo Clinic, the National Institutes of Health, and most reputable health professionals strongly recommend against colon cleansing of any type. Doing so, particularly on a regular basis, can lead to fluid and electrolyte loss, a decrease in the ability of the colon to contract and regulate bowel movements, disruption of the bacteria in your colon, heart problems, and, in the case of those already weakened (such as the elderly and those with HIV), death. In addition, many of the more invasive colon cleansing techniques can result in bowel perforation, bacterial infection, and severe illness. If you think you have a parasite, see a doctor. The physician may prescribe medications (herbal or synthetic) or refer you to a Registered Dietitian to alter your diet to encourage the "friendly colon bacteria" that are necessary for optimal health and bowel function. An example of one of the dietary changes you can make is to include food sources of probiotics into your daily food intake. See the feature, To Supplement or Not for more information. ■

### APPLICATION TIP

The average person passes gas six to twenty times per day. If you are passing more gas than that, examine your diet. Although foods that cause gas in some people may not cause it in others, foods that are typically high in carbohydrates and fiber are more likely to cause gas than those high in protein or fat. Common gas-producing foods include beans, vegetables, fruits, wheat, and corn. You can decrease gas production by reducing your intake of uncooked beans, as cooking helps reduce the indigestible carbohydrates in the beans. You can also try eating less wheat and more brown rice, because rice usually causes less gas than wheat.

 ■ **To Supplement or Not**
*Probiotics*

 **Want to know more?**
For more information on probiotics and foods that contain them, go to the text website at http://webcom8.grtxle.com/nutrition and click on the Chapters button. Select Chapter 6.

**Probiotics** are live microbial food products and supplements that improve the health and microbial balance of the intestines. These substances are quickly gaining attention as functional foods (foods that provide health benefits beyond their original nutritional function). Probiotic products have been widely used in other parts of the world for years, but only recently have been recognized in the United States. Although probiotic products contain several different kinds of bacteria, most contain *Lactobacillus* and *Bifidobacterium.* The most common sources of probiotic bacteria are yogurt and other fermented milk products such as kefir. However, they can be found in cheese and some teas as well.

Limited evidence suggests that probiotics may have many beneficial effects on our health, including the following:

- Decreased symptoms associated with many gastrointestinal diseases:
    Irritable bowel syndrome
    Inflammatory bowel disease
    Ulcerative colitis
    Crohn's disease
- Decreased diarrhea, especially in children
- Decreased diarrhea as a result of taking antibiotics
- Decreased growth of the bacterium *H. pylori,* which is responsible for many stomach ulcers and other problems
- Decreased constipation
- Increased intestinal motility
- Enhanced immune response
- Increased absorption of nutrients such as folic acid, niacin, vitamin $B_{12}$, and riboflavin
- Increased ability of people who are lactose intolerant to consume some dairy products

Additionally, preliminary evidence from animal studies and human studies suggests the following benefits:

- Decreased incidence of colon cancer
- Decreased allergies, especially in children
- Decreased incidence of bacterial vaginosis in women
- Decreased total cholesterol and triglycerides
- Improved HDL/LDL ratio
- Decreased blood pressure

Scientists have yet to determine exactly how probiotics produce these benefits, and they are not yet certain exactly how much we need to consume. They recommend that people try to consume food sources as opposed to supplements, because many supplements do not meet suggested minimum criteria and therefore may not survive in the gastrointestinal tract. The benefits

Foods containing probiotics such as the yogurt pictured here may have health benefits, particularly for symptoms associated with gastrointestinal problems.

achieved may be due to a synergistic effect of the probiotics with other compounds in the food. In addition, such foods are also excellent sources of other nutrients such as calcium and vitamin D. Look for the words *live cultures* or *active cultures* on packages of yogurt and other products, as not all of them contain active bacterial culture. *L. bulgaricus, S. thermophilus,* and *L. acidophilus* are the most common cultures added to yogurt. A lot of research still needs to be done before an exact recommendation can be made for consumption of probiotics. In the meantime, including yogurt and other sources of probiotics in a balanced diet is your best bet for experiencing the potential health benefits. ■

---

**Before you go on . . .**

1. Describe how food that is in the digestive tract ultimately gets into the body.
2. Once digested food is absorbed, it travels through the blood to the cells, where it is converted to a usable form of energy; what is this substance that the cells can use as energy called?
3. List the main functions of the GI tract.
4. Where does most food absorption take place?

---

## Digestion and Absorption: From Tongue to Blood

Now that we have had a brief discussion of the major organs and processes involved in digestion and absorption, let's get back to considering the food on our plate. Let's suppose that in an effort to maintain a healthy diet and to meet current dietary recommendations, we have eaten a balanced meal. What happens to that meal once we have chewed and swallowed it? (See Figure 6.9 for a summary of digestion and absorption.)

### Carbohydrates

The breakdown of carbohydrates begins as soon as you put food in your mouth. The enzyme called *salivary amylase* in the saliva breaks carbohydrates into smaller glucose links. To experience amylase at work, chew a piece of bread; you'll notice that it gets sweeter the longer it stays in your mouth. This is because the smaller links of glucose are sweeter than the larger links that make up the bread. Amylase continues to work until it reaches the stomach and the stomach acid inactivates it. Once food is in the stomach, no further carbohydrate breakdown occurs. Therefore, when carbohydrates are consumed alone, particularly those low in fiber, they empty quickly from the stomach. (See Chapter 3 for a review of carbohydrates.)

Once they enter the small intestine, carbohydrates are broken down by an enzyme released from the pancreas called *pancreatic amylase* into smaller chains of glucose. Next, several enzymes from the lining of the small intestine continue the breakdown. An example of one of these enzymes is *lactase*, the enzyme that breaks down the disaccharide lactose found in milk. People who lack this enzyme have *lactose intolerance* and may experience gas, cramps, and diarrhea if they consume too much lactose. An enzyme called *sucrase* breaks down the disaccharide sucrose, and the enzyme *maltase* breaks down the disaccharide maltose. See Table 6.3 for more information on lactose intolerance and other problems associated with the digestive tract.

### Table 6.3   Diseases and Syndromes of the Digestive Tract

| What It Is | What It Does | What Causes It | How To Treat It |
| --- | --- | --- | --- |
| Constipation | Makes having a bowel movement difficult (fewer than three times per week) | Low fiber; not enough exercise; medication; dehydration; ignoring the urge to defecate; disease | Eat at least 25 g of fiber per day; limit processed foods and cheese; drink plenty of fluids; exercise. |
| Diarrhea | Produces loose, watery stools occurring more than three times per day | Bacterial or viral infections from contaminated food or water; food intolerances; medication; disease | Prevent dehydration; avoid dairy, high-fat, and high-sugar foods; take medication (but only if symptoms are prolonged). |
| Heartburn/Gastro-esophageal reflux disease (GERD) | Produces pain in the chest when stomach acid leaks up into the esophagus | Being overweight; pregnancy; hiatal hernia (part of the stomach pushing on the esophagus); diet | Limit any foods that increase symptoms (spicy foods, high-fat foods, alcohol); lose weight; take medication. |
| Lactose intolerance | Prevents the breakdown of lactose (the sugar found in dairy products) because of a lack of the enzyme lactase | Genetic ethnicity (African Americans and Asians are more likely than Caucasians to have this condition); surgery; medication | Limit intake of dairy products; take lactase pills. |
| Irritable bowel syndrome | Affects the large intestine and leads to cramping, diarrhea, and constipation | Overly sensitive muscles and nerves of the large intestine that may react more to stress or certain foods | Increase fiber in the diet; eat small, frequent meals; consume probiotics; avoid foods that aggravate the condition. |
| Ulcerative colitis | Chronically inflames the large intestine (in the manner of an ulceration) | Heredity and an "overactive" immune system | Eat plenty of omega-3 fatty acids such as salmon; during flare-ups, decrease consumption of foods that aggravate the condition, such as grain products, spicy foods, alcohol, and dairy products. |
| Crohn's disease | Inflames the small and/or large intestine | Heredity and an "overactive" immune system | Eat plenty of omega-3 fatty acids such as salmon; during flare-ups, decrease consumption of foods that aggravate the condition, such as grain products, spicy foods, alcohol, and dairy products. |
| Gallstones | Forms stones from bile in the gallbladder that can cause pain, jaundice, and pancreatitis | High cholesterol; obesity; fasting; more frequent in women than men | Surgically remove gallbladder. |

The end product of carbohydrate digestion is single sugars (*monosaccharides*) ready for absorption (see Figure 6.6). The single sugars glucose and galactose are transported across the wall of the small intestine. Fructose is absorbed by a different process but is ultimately made into glucose in the liver. So, eventually, all of the starches and sugars end up as glucose when they reach the blood. What happens after that depends on several factors, mainly the nutritional state of the body—how much has been eaten and whether the glycogen stores (the body's storage form of glucose) in the muscles and liver are full. Depending on these factors, the absorbed glucose can be used to maintain blood glucose, used to replace glycogen stores in the liver and muscle, or made into triglycerides and stored as fat.

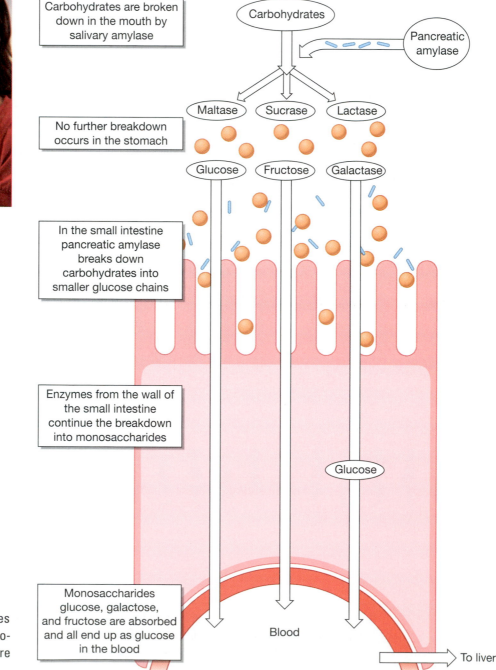

Carbohydrates are broken down in the mouth by salivary amylase

No further breakdown occurs in the stomach

In the small intestine pancreatic amylase breaks down carbohydrates into smaller glucose chains

Enzymes from the wall of the small intestine continue the breakdown into monosaccharides

Monosaccharides glucose, galactose, and fructose are absorbed and all end up as glucose in the blood

Carbohydrates

Pancreatic amylase

Maltase    Sucrase    Lactase

Glucose    Fructose    Galactase

Glucose

Blood

To liver

**Figure 6.6** Carbohydrates are broken down into monosaccharides before they are absorbed.

## Fats

Put simply, fat and water don't easily mix. Therefore, the digestion, absorption, and transport of fats in a predominantly watery environment presents a unique challenge for the body. In the mouth *lipase,* an enzyme that breaks down fats, is released in the saliva. It is not activated, however, until it reaches the acidic environment of the stomach, where it breaks down a small amount, about 10 percent, of fats consumed. Although chewing and combining with watery secretions of the stomach are important to increase the surface area of fats, most digestion and absorption occur in the small intestine.

When chyme enters the duodenum, bile released from the gallbladder acts on large fat molecules in a process called *emulsification* and mixes them in the watery environment of the small intestine. This mixing allows the enzyme *pancreatic lipase* to break the fat molecules down into smaller molecules—fatty acids and glycerol (Figure 6.7). Once inside the cells of the small intestine, the smaller molecules rejoin to make triglycerides. Some free fatty acids enter the capillaries, but the larger triglycerides are too big for the capillaries and therefore must enter the blood through the larger vessels of the lymphatic system. Remember that fat and water don't mix. Therefore, before the larger triglycerides can be transported through the lymph vessels they are formed into special carriers, called *chylomicrons,* that enable the fat to travel in the watery environment of the blood. The triglycerides can then pass into the cells of the body to be broken down and used for energy or stored as fat. After the fat is absorbed, the bile continues through the intestine and is reabsorbed in the ileum or bound by fiber and excreted. (See Chapter 4 for a review of fats.)

## Protein

Protein digestion begins in the stomach when *pepsinogen* is released from the wall of the stomach and converted to its active form, *pepsin,* when exposed to stomach acid. The enzyme pepsin then breaks bonds in proteins into smaller units. Stomach acid also assists in the digestive process by denaturing the proteins, or unraveling their three-dimensional shape. The smaller units then empty into the small intestine, where enzymes secreted by the pancreas break them into still smaller units. Then, enzymes from the wall of the small intestine act on the peptides to break off one amino acid at a time, and the individual amino acids are absorbed (Figure 6.8). The amino acids then travel through the blood to the liver. Once in the liver, their fate depends on several circumstances, such as how many carbohydrates you have consumed. The absorbed amino acids can be used to make proteins, or glucose if you have not consumed enough carbohydrates, and a small amount is kept in the blood for a short time in the amino acid pool. Any amino acids in excess of the body's needs can be made into fat and stored. (See Chapter 5 for a review of proteins.)

## Alcohol

Some alcohol is absorbed right away in the stomach, especially when it is consumed without food, but most is absorbed in the small intestine. It travels to the liver, where it is detoxified. For more information on how alcohol affects the body, see Chapter 12.

**Want to know more?**
To explore digestive diseases more extensively, go to the text website at http://webcom8.grtxle .com/nutrition and click on the Chapters button. Select Chapter 6.

**Figure 6.7** Fats are broken down into fatty acids and glycerol before they are absorbed.

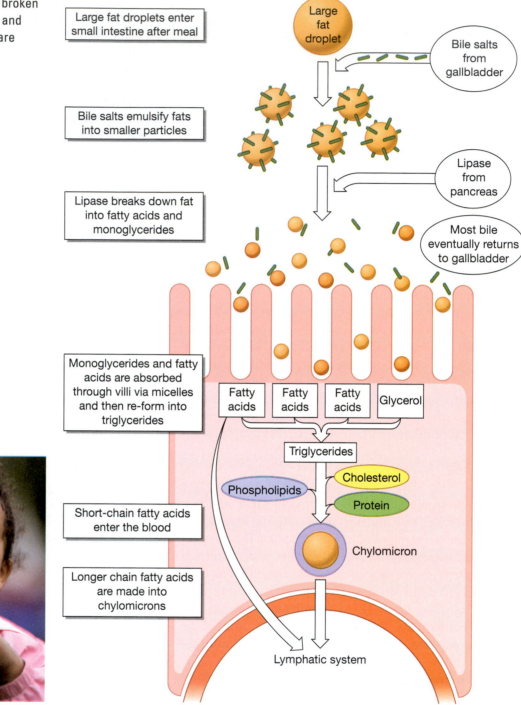

Large fat droplets enter small intestine after meal

Large fat droplet

Bile salts from gallbladder

Bile salts emulsify fats into smaller particles

Lipase breaks down fat into fatty acids and monoglycerides

Lipase from pancreas

Most bile eventually returns to gallbladder

Monoglycerides and fatty acids are absorbed through villi via micelles and then re-form into triglycerides

Fatty acids    Fatty acids    Fatty acids    Glycerol

Triglycerides

Phospholipids

Cholesterol

Protein

Short-chain fatty acids enter the blood

Chylomicron

Longer chain fatty acids are made into chylomicrons

Lymphatic system

## Vitamins and Minerals

Vitamins are absorbed unchanged from the form in which they are found in the food we eat. The fat-soluble vitamins (vitamins A, D, E, and K) are absorbed with fats. Therefore, if you do not consume fat with them, they are not absorbed but are excreted in the feces. The water-soluble vitamins can be absorbed without food. Vitamin $B_{12}$ requires the *intrinsic factor*, which is released in the stomach. Once it binds with this, it is absorbed in the ileum.

Minerals are absorbed all along the small intestine. Sodium is best absorbed with glucose and amino acids, which is why you will often find these nutrients

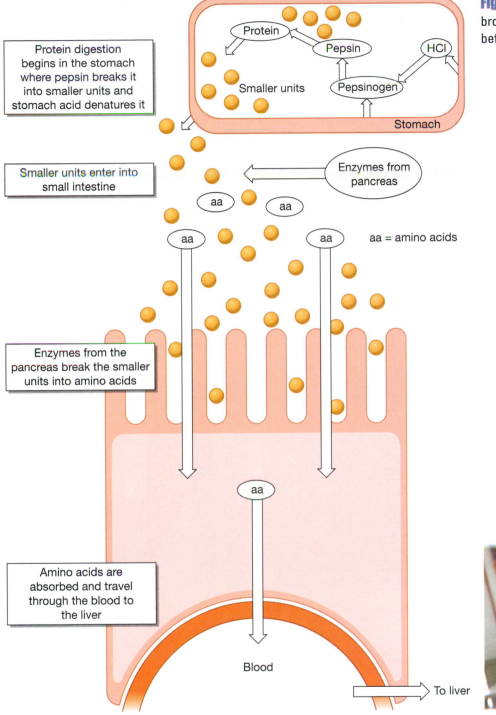

**Figure 6.8** Proteins are broken down into amino acids before they are absorbed.

Protein digestion begins in the stomach where pepsin breaks it into smaller units and stomach acid denatures it

Protein

Pepsin

HCl

Smaller units

Pepsinogen

Stomach

Smaller units enter into small intestine

Enzymes from pancreas

aa

aa

aa

aa

aa = amino acids

Enzymes from the pancreas break the smaller units into amino acids

aa

Amino acids are absorbed and travel through the blood to the liver

Blood

To liver

together in sports drinks. Some nutrients such as iron and calcium are absorbed based on need, so that when your body's stores are low you absorb more from the food you eat. (See Chapters 9 and 10 for a thorough discussion of vitamins and minerals.)

## Water

You may think that the water we are referring to is the water you drink. However, the digestive system contains water from the food we eat, the fluids we drink, our saliva, and all the secretions of digestion. Most is absorbed in the small intestine; a small amount is absorbed in the large intestine, and the rest is excreted in the feces. Water is absorbed by following sodium and other nutrients such as glucose across the wall of the intestine.

### ■ Myths and Legends

*When you mix it up—combining foods*

The popular diet book *Fit for Life* (1986) is based on the notion that when certain foods are eaten together, they "rot," poisoning the system and making the person fat. To avoid this, the authors recommend that fats, carbohydrates, and proteins be eaten at separate meals, emphasizing fruits and vegetables because foods high in water content can "wash the toxic waste from the inside of the body" instead of "clogging" the body. Other books and programs recommend avoiding certain combinations of foods, such as bread and cheese, to increase weight loss. These statements are completely false. In fact, the digestive system is designed to digest and absorb foods in combination. Carbohydrates, fats, and proteins can be broken down and absorbed simultaneously. Certain foods are actually absorbed better in combination. For example, the fat-soluble vitamins A, D, E, and K are absorbed better when fat is present. ■

*Is it true that it is not healthy to mix certain foods because you can't digest them together?*

**Want to know more?**
You can complete an interactive exercise and review additional information about digestion and absorption, by visiting the text website at http://webcom8.grtxle.com/nutrition and clicking on the Chapters button. Select Chapter 6.

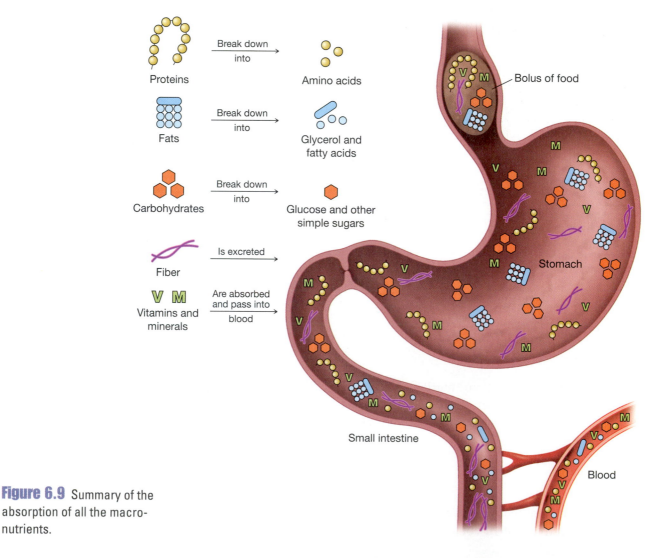

**Figure 6.9** Summary of the absorption of all the macronutrients.

# Real People, Other Voices

**Student:**

### Erika Kugler

Lehigh Carbon Community College

Cathleen's stressful life causes her to make poor food choices that may be the cause of her heartburn. Although it wasn't stated, Cathleen may also be overweight, another factor that could be contributing to her heartburn. A question routinely asked at doctors' offices is, "Any possibility of pregnancy?" But, most likely it is caused by her diet and eating habits. Typically, Cathleen eats one large meal a day, and I am assuming that she does not take her time in eating it. She most likely eats it within two hours of going to sleep, which may also be contributing to her heartburn.

Cathleen's doctor will likely advise her to eat smaller, more frequent meals, and to avoid eating close to bedtime. He or she should also recommend that Cathleen avoid eating spicy foods or foods high in fat. The easy-to-prepare and fast-food meals she's eating are probably high in fat. Cathleen needs to make better meal choices. Eating the one large fatty meal every day may cause an overproduction of stomach acid, and this may continue throughout the day when she drinks water. She should also cut out alcohol, tobacco products, and caffeine, all products that can cause or contribute to heartburn. Cathleen should try keeping a journal of what she eats and when she does not feel well after eating. By doing this she can adjust her diet according to what aggravates her stomach and produces heartburn.

**Instructor:**

### Sharon Antonelli

San Jose City College

Cathleen's physician may want to check her for ulcers and have her take an acid-reducing medication to assist with healing possible gastrointestinal inflammation. In addition, the doctor will probably tell Cathleen to eat at various, regular times throughout the day, and to avoid caffeine, spices, and alcohol.

I would recommend that Cathleen arise earlier in the morning, do some light exercise, and then have breakfast before starting her busy day. She could take some fresh fruits, vegetables, nuts, and cheese with her to eat between classes and work. San Francisco is a mecca for ethnic restaurants, neighborhood grocery stores, and hills to walk for much-needed exercise. On weekends and whenever her schedule permits, Cathleen could take a walk to find places with affordable food other than fast food. She could experience the cultural richness of San Francisco, improve her diet, and get exercise by taking time from her busy schedule daily, if possible. At night, she should limit eating at least two hours before bedtime in order to avoid GERD (gastrointestinal reflux disease), often the consequence of eating late and consuming spicy foods, caffeine, and alcohol.

**Registered Dietitian:**

### Susie Bohanan, RD

Orinda, California

In my experience, even with an official diagnosis of a digestive disorder, many symptoms are directly related to stress. With that in mind, Cathleen may be able to tolerate some of the foods that I suggest she avoid, and vice versa.

Cathleen needs to avoid acid-producing foods and eating habits that may cause the stomach to secrete more acid. She should avoid caffeine, alcohol, and red and black pepper. Other problem foods include peppermint, fried foods, and gas-forming foods such as legumes and cruciferous vegetables (scientific name for a group of vegetables containing antioxidants that research has shown may provide protection against certain cancers). Skipping meals and then eating a large meal causes an overload in the stomach, and more acid is required to digest a large quantity of food. Smaller, more frequent meals and snacks will be better tolerated. I would review her schedule in detail, suggesting times when she could have a snack.

Drinking fluids, especially water, is important, but Cathleen needs to drink liquids between meals, not during meals. A large volume of water with a meal can cause the same problem as a large meal for many people with GERD. She should stop drinking fluids about 30 minutes before a meal and wait about 30 minutes after she finishes before she drinks anything else. She also needs to avoid lying down for at least two hours after eating.

Despite her very busy schedule, I would encourage Cathleen to exercise, primarily for relief of stress.

**Before you go on . . .**

1. Carbohydrates, fats, proteins, vitamins, and minerals must be broken down into what form before they can be absorbed?
2. Identify at least three diseases of the GI tract and describe their causes.
3. What process helps the body mix fat in its watery environment?
4. What nutrients help enhance water absorption?

# Metabolism

All moving things require energy to function. A car must have fuel, a fire must have wood or another substance to burn, and the human body must have a constant supply of energy for movement, maintenance, and basic functions. It may seem that this energy is needed only when the body is moving. However, even as you sleep, your body is using energy to build new cells, to get rid of old ones, to breathe, to pump blood, and so on.

By eating food, you supply your body with this necessary energy. It is stored as **chemical energy**, or energy contained in a molecule that has not yet been released, in carbohydrates, fats, and proteins. Turning chemical energy into a form the body can use requires a series of chemical reactions called metabolism. **Metabolism** is the sum of biochemical reactions that occur in the cells of the body to obtain usable energy in the form of ATP from food. The processes of metabolism do more than just break molecules down for energy, a process called **catabolism**. They can also go in the other direction and build molecules, a process called **anabolism**.

Your body is in a constant state of breakdown and buildup, and if your weight remains relatively stable, then overall these pathways are in balance. An example of an anabolic process is the building of muscle, or *protein synthesis*. An example of a catabolic process is **glycolysis**, which breaks down glucose to a usable form of energy, ATP. We can then use this energy to blink an eye or throw a baseball. We call these processes *metabolic pathways* because they refer to not just one step but a series of chemical steps or reactions that either break down or build up compounds in the body. Metabolic processes occur in every cell of the body. An important part of the cell is the **mitochondria**, where most of the energy-producing pathways occur.

## A Usable Form of Energy

Although the carbohydrates, fats, and proteins we consume contain potential energy in the form of chemical energy, the body cannot use it as is. It must first convert this chemical energy to a usable form, ATP. Vitamins and minerals can't be broken down to give us energy, but they play important roles in the pathways we use to get ATP. So what steps do the molecules stored in carbohydrates, fats, and proteins go through before we can obtain usable energy from them? Well, to begin that discussion, remember the *first law of thermodynamics*: Energy is neither created nor destroyed but transferred from one form to another. This is what is occurring in metabolism. Energy, in the form of *electrons,* is transferred from one form to another by the chemical

The body requires a constant supply of energy from food for exercise, sleep, and basic body functions.

reactions that occur. The ultimate goal of these reactions is to create usable energy for the body. Of course, not all of the potential energy in the food we eat is transferred to ATP; some is given off as heat.

### Pathways to Energy

The pathway by which ATP is produced depends on the availability of oxygen in the cells. If there is enough oxygen, then **aerobic metabolism** takes place and large amounts of ATP are produced. If there is not enough oxygen in the cells (for example, when you are sprinting as hard as you can), **anaerobic metabolism** occurs and smaller amounts of ATP are produced. Anaerobic metabolism can occur only for a short time, until you fatigue.

The pathway used also depends on the source of potential energy. Remember that food on your plate? The carbohydrates that were on the plate are now glucose in our blood and have been delivered to the cells. Similarly, the fats are now triglycerides and the proteins are now amino acids. So let's see what happens to them (for a summary, see Figure 6.10.)

### Carbohydrates and Glucose

Once in the cell, glucose is broken down via glycolysis. Glucose will go through many steps (chemical reactions) in glycolysis to ultimately become a substance called *pyruvate*. Oxygen is not required for these steps to take place. Throughout this pathway, as glucose changes form, ATP is produced. If enough oxygen is available, once the glucose has become pyruvate, it enters the mitochondria for aerobic metabolism and becomes a substance called *acetyl CoA*. Many steps in the metabolic pathways can go in either direction, but once pyruvate becomes acetyl CoA it cannot go back. We will discuss the significance of this point in a moment. Now that the pyruvate has become acetyl CoA, it can join with other substances and start the pathway called the **Krebs cycle or the tricarboxylic acid (TCA) cycle.** The Krebs cycle requires oxygen and produces a lot of ATP.

If not enough oxygen is available, which occurs when we sprint or when we first begin exercise, a substance called *lactate* is created from the pyruvate. This provides some energy, but not as much as the Krebs cycle.

### Fats and Triglycerides

Recall that fats are stored as triglycerides in the body, and therefore the first step in converting fats to ATP is to break down triglycerides into fatty acids and glycerol. The glycerol can be converted to pyruvate or glucose in the liver. The fatty acids are broken down in a pathway called *beta oxidation.* In this pathway, enzymes break the carbon chains that make up fatty acids two carbons at a time and convert them to acetyl CoA, which can join with other substances and begin the Krebs cycle. The substance that acetyl CoA joins with is called *oxaloacetate* or *OAA.*

### Want to know more?

For more information about metabolism and a tutorial using our Interactive Mill of Metabolism, visit the text website at http://webcom8 .grtxle.com/nutrition and click on the Chapters button. Select Chapter 6.

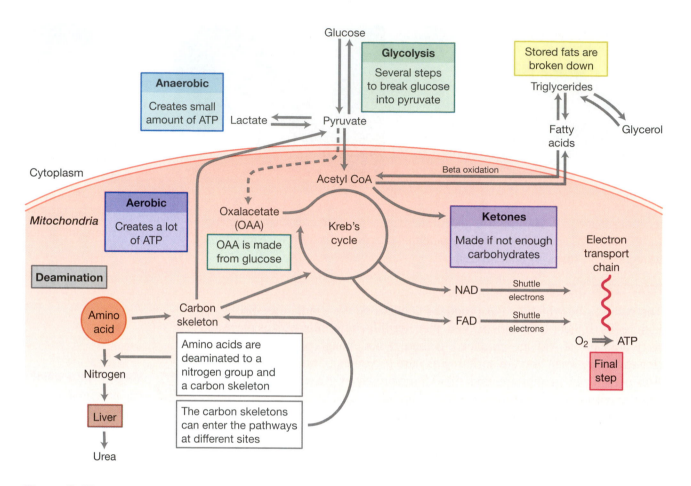

**Figure 6.10** Metabolism: Steps involved in converting carbohydrates, fats, and proteins into a usable form of energy, ATP.

It is made from carbohydrates, so if carbohydrates are low, OAA is also low. To describe this relationship between fat and carbohydrate metabolism, some say that "fat burns in a carbohydrate flame." This means that you need carbohydrates to burn fats. So when carbohydrate supplies are limited, such as during starvation, uncontrolled diabetes, or while eating a very low-carbohydrate diet, fat burning is slowed down because OAA is low, and therefore the Krebs cycle is "slower." When this happens, the body forms *ketone bodies* (see Chapter 4), which can be used as an alternative fuel source for the body, especially for the brain and central nervous system.

## Protein and Amino Acids

Under normal circumstances, protein and amino acids are not used to any large extent for energy. However, during starvation or when carbohydrate supplies are limited, amino acids can be used to make ATP. The first step in the breakdown of amino acids is to remove the nitrogen group. This is called *deamination*. Once the nitrogen is removed, the *carbon skeleton* is what remains of the amino acids. The nitrogen is converted to urea and excreted in the urine. Unlike glucose and fatty acids, carbon skeletons can enter the energy-producing pathways at different spots. Depending on which amino acid the carbon skeleton came from, it can enter at pyruvate, acetyl CoA, or different places in the Krebs cycle.

## The Final Step: Where ATP Is Created

We mentioned previously that metabolism applies the first law of thermodynamics: Energy is neither created nor destroyed but transferred from one form to another. We said that electrons are transferred or shuttled along the various pathways of metabolism to create ATP. In this shuttling, the electrons are picked up by carriers called *NAD* and *FAD*, which take the electrons to the **electron transport chain**. This is the final pathway for the electrons and the primary site in the cell where ATP is made. The electron transport chain is used only for aerobic metabolism because oxygen is the final acceptor of hydrogen in this chain. Remember that when we use anaerobic metabolism, lactate is created as we generate ATP. Consequently, not as much ATP can be created anaerobically as aerobically. Throughout the process, water and $CO_2$ are produced as waste products.

## Building and Storing

Thus far we have focused on the pathways of metabolism that we use to break down molecules to use for energy. Remember, however, that we do not always immediately use the potential energy from the food we eat for energy; we use some of it to build and repair tissue or store it for future use. These pathways, as mentioned previously, are called anabolism.

### Making New Glucose

We create glucose in a pathway called *gluconeogenesis*, which means literally "making new glucose." Your body needs a constant supply of glucose to maintain your blood glucose level and to fuel your brain, central nervous system, and red blood cells. During periods of starvation or when carbohydrate stores are depleted (as on a low-carbohydrate diet or during very long exercise), your body has to get glucose from somewhere. It breaks other substances down to yield glucose. These other substances can be some amino acids, lactate, glycerol, and pyruvate. Fatty acids cannot be made into glucose. If you recall, fatty acids enter the energy-producing pathway at acetyl CoA; once acetyl CoA is created it cannot go back to glucose.

### Storing Glucose

Once we have consumed enough carbohydrates to meet our immediate energy needs, we store the remaining carbohydrates by converting the glucose not being used for energy to **glycogen.** Glycogen is stored in the liver and the muscles. Liver glycogen is used to maintain blood glucose between meals, but muscle glycogen can be used only inside the muscle for energy. Glycogen stores are very limited and can be depleted quickly. For example, after about sixty minutes of intense exercise or ninety minutes of moderate exercise, glycogen stores are depleted and exercise performance decreases. Without replacing carbohydrates, you will most likely experience what many athletes refer to as "hitting the wall." Basically, you will run out of energy and feel bad and have to either stop or slow down. See Chapter 3 on carbohydrates and Chapter 14 on sports nutrition for more information on storing glucose.

### Storing Fat

Fats are stored mostly in the adipose tissue; a small amount is stored in the muscles. Fats are made by a pathway called *lipogenesis*. Because acetyl CoA is the starting point, anything that can form acetyl CoA can be made into fat and stored. This includes fats

**Want to know more?**
Trace a meal from mouth to blood to energy. Visit the text website at http://webcom8.grtxle .com/nutrition and click on the Chapters button. Select Chapter 6 for this interactive video, and watch what your body does to turn the food on your plate into the body's fuel.

themselves, carbohydrates, alcohol, and amino acids (yes, protein in excess can be made into fat). Once the acetyl CoAs are linked, glycerol is added and they are stored as triglycerides.

### Building Protein

As discussed earlier, proteins are made through a process called *protein synthesis*. Unlike fats and carbohydrates, proteins do not have a large storage form in the body. However, a small amount of amino acids, called the amino acid pool, is stored in the blood and cells. To make proteins, the body links amino acids together; it obtains these amino acids from the pool and various other sources. Your body can make nonessential amino acids from the carbon skeletons it gets from pyruvate, essential amino acids, and other compounds. In addition, some amino acids can be used from the breakdown of body tissues. Of course, some amino acids, especially the essentials, must come from your diet.

### Before you go on . . .

1. In order to turn the chemical energy stored in the food we eat into a form the body can use, what must happen?
2. Describe how the steps or pathways of metabolized energy create usable energy for the body.
3. What steps do carbohydrates, fats, and proteins go through to generate ATP?
4. Why can't you get glucose from fatty acids?

## Real People, Real Strategies

After hearing about Cathleen's symptoms and the stress she is under, her physician agreed that she most likely has gastroesophageal reflux disease (GERD), commonly known as heartburn. To make certain nothing else was going on, such as a peptic ulcer or something more serious such as cancer, her physician ordered a test called an endoscopy. During this test a thin, flexible tube with a light and camera (endoscope) was put down her throat. This allowed her doctor to see whether she had an ulcerated or inflamed esophagus or stomach. Samples of the lining of her esophagus were also taken. These samples can determine whether she has *H. pylori* or cancer. After the test results came back her physician assured her that everything was okay. Her esophagus was not damaged and she did not have an ulcer or *H. pylori.* He prescribed Nexium, a proton pump inhibitor that inhibits the release of stomach acid. This will help relieve the burning and stomachaches she is feeling.

In addition, her physician recommended that she see an RD to help her determine what foods to avoid in order to manage her condition. The dietitian first gave Cathleen a few general suggestions. She advised Cathleen to change her schedule so that she can eat meals at regular intervals. She also recommended that Cathleen avoid eating large meals, eating late at night, and going to bed soon after eating. She emphasized the need for daily exercise and weight management as methods for reducing stress. Until Cathleen's symptoms disappear, the dietitian also recommended that Cathleen avoid foods such as alcohol, caffeine, carbonated beverages, chocolate, citrus fruits and juices, tomatoes and tomato sauces, spicy or fatty foods, full-fat dairy products, peppermint, and spearmint. She then suggested that Cathleen keep a food diary to determine what foods were triggering her symptoms. She assured Cathleen that by following these suggestions and the advice of her physician, she would be able to manage her condition and reduce her symptoms. Cathleen was very relieved and resolved to take her medication, make some changes in her diet, exercise, and find a way to better manage her stress.

## Chapter Summary

- When food is in the digestive tract, it is still not "inside" the body. It must go through a series of steps that start in the GI tract, which runs from the mouth to the anus.
- Once digested food is absorbed, it travels through the blood to the cells, where it is converted to a usable form of energy called ATP.
- The main functions of the GI tract are to take in food, transport it, and secrete substances that help break it into smaller compounds so that they can be absorbed.
- On average, for a healthy adult, it takes anywhere from twelve to forty hours from the time food is eaten until the undigested components and waste materials exit the body as feces.
- Digestion begins in the mouth with chewing and the mixing of food with saliva. Saliva lubricates food and contains enzymes.

- Peristalsis is a muscular movement that propels food through the digestive tract and explains why we can swallow and digest without using gravity.
- The stomach churns and mixes food with its secretions, including HCl and many enzymes.
- Mucus is one of the stomach's secretions; it protects the stomach from the acid and digestive enzymes it contains.
- The time it takes for a meal to completely empty from the stomach varies based on the contents and consistency of the meal.
- Most absorption occurs in the small intestine. The small intestine is designed to maximize contact with nutrients so that the body can absorb as many of the nutrients as possible. It folds back and forth several times and contains fingerlike projections called villi.
- The pancreas releases several enzymes and bicarb to help neutralize the acid contents coming from the stomach.
- The gallbladder releases bile to assist with fat digestion.
- The large intestine has important bacteria that produce vitamins. It also absorbs some water, sodium, and short-chain fatty acids.
- Carbohydrates, fats, and proteins are digested into smaller units and then absorbed.
- Turning the chemical energy stored in the food we eat into a form the body can use requires a series of chemical reactions called metabolism. In the steps or pathways of metabolism, energy, in the form of electrons, is transferred from one form to another to eventually create usable energy for the body.
- The processes of metabolism do more than just break molecules down for energy, a process called catabolism. They can also go in the other direction and build molecules, a process called anabolism.
- Carbohydrates, fats, and proteins go through different steps to produce ATP.

## Key Terms

**absorption** The movement of the smaller products of digestion across the lining of the intestinal tract, into our bodies, and ultimately into our cells. (p. 172)

**adenosine triphosphate (ATP)** (uh-DEN-oh-zeen try-FOSS-fate) A high-energy molecule that can be broken down to a usable form of energy. (p. 172)

**aerobic metabolism** (air-OH-bic meh-TAB-oh-lizm) *Aerobic* means "with oxygen"; the term refers to all pathways of metabolism that use oxygen. (p. 191)

**alkaline bicarbonate (bicarb)** A substance released from the pancreas into the small intestine to neutralize the acidic contents from the stomach. (p. 178)

**anabolism** (an-AB-oh-lizm) Any metabolic reaction that builds molecules, such as protein synthesis needed for growth. (p. 190)

**anaerobic metabolism** (AN-air-oh-bic meh-TAB-oh-lizm) *Anaerobic* means "without oxygen"; the term refers to all pathways of metabolism that do not use oxygen. (p. 191)

**bile** A substance made in the liver; it is stored in the gallbladder and released into the small intestine to help with fat digestion. (p. 178)

**catabolism** Any metabolic reaction that breaks down molecules, such as glycolysis, which breaks down glucose. (p. 190)

**chemical energy** Energy contained in a molecule that has not yet been released; it is also called *potential energy*. (p. 190)

**chyme** The substance that results after the stomach mixes and liquefies food. (p. 176)

**digestion** The first step in the process of converting food to energy; it is a complex series of chemical reactions and interactions combined with muscular movements that break the food down into smaller compounds. (p. 172)

**duodenum** (doo-oh-DEE-num) The top part of the small intestine, extending about 25 cm from the pyloric sphincter. (p. 178)

**electron transport chain** The primary site in the cell where ATP is made; it is used only for aerobic metabolism because oxygen is final acceptor of hydrogen in this chain. (p. 193)

**gallbladder** An accessory organ for digestion that releases bile. (p. 178)

**gastrointestinal (GI) tract** A series of organs with many complex outer layers of muscles and an inner mucosal layer of glands and absorptive cells. (p. 172)

**glycogen** The storage form of glucose; it is stored in the liver and the muscles. (p. 193)

**glycolysis** (gly-COLL-ih-sis) The metabolic process that breaks down glucose to a usable form of energy. (p. 190)

**heartburn** A burning sensation that occurs in the chest when substances from the stomach leak back into the esophagus. (p. 175)

**helicobacter pylori or H. pylori** (HEL-ih-coh-bak-ter-pie-LOR-ee) A bacterium that can invade the stomach lining and cause peptic ulcers. (p. 177)

**hydrochloric acid (HCl)** A substance secreted in the stomach to denature protein. (p. 176)

**ileum** (ILL-ee-um) The bottom part of the small intestine. (p. 178)

**jejunum** (jeh-JOO-num) The middle part of the small intestine. (p. 178)

**Krebs cycle or tricarboxylic acid (TCA) cycle** A complex series of reactions following glycolysis that converts carbohydrates, fats, and proteins into ATP. (p. 191)

**metabolism** The sum of biochemical reactions that occur in the cells of the body to obtain usable energy in the from of ATP from food. (p. 190)

**microvilli** (MIKE-roh-vil-ee) Tiny hairlike projections extending from the villi into the inside of the small intestine to assist absorption and secrete digestive enzymes. (p. 178)

**mitochondria** (my-toh-KON-dree-uh) The part of the cell where most of the energy-producing pathways occur. (p. 190)

**peristalsis** (pair-ih-STALL-sis) A muscular movement that propels food through the digestive tract. (p. 174)

**probiotics** Live microbial food products and supplements that improve the health and microbial balance of the intestine; most contain *Lactobacillus* and *Bifidobacterium*. (p. 181)

**sphincters** (SFINK-terz) Circular muscles located throughout the digestive system that work like one-way doors to control the movement of its contents from one part to another. (p. 175)

**transit time** The period of time it takes food to travel the length of the digestive tract. (p. 172)

**ulcer** Also called a peptic ulcer; an erosion that occurs in the lining of the stomach or the upper part of the small intestine. (p. 177)

**villi** Fingerlike projections in the small intestine that increase the surface area to maximize absorption. (p. 178)

# Chapter Quiz

1. Heartburn is caused by
   a. stomach contents emptying too quickly into the small intestine.
   b. poor digestion.
   c. drinking too much milk.
   d. stomach acid leaking up into the esophagus.

2. The series of muscular movements that explains why we can swallow without using gravity is called
   a. chewing.
   b. sphincter function.
   c. peristalsis.
   d. digestion.

3. Most digestion and absorption of nutrients occurs in the
   a. stomach.
   b. small intestine.
   c. large intestine.
   d. pancreas.

4. What is the major role of the villi?
   a. to secrete bile
   b. to increase the absorptive surface area of the intestine
   c. to neutralize the acidic contents of the small intestine
   d. to secrete HCl

5. What is the major role of HCl?
   a. to break down fats
   b. to denature proteins
   c. to liquefy food
   d. to mix food in the stomach

6. What is the primary cause of gas (flatus) formation in the body?
   a. a poor diet
   b. consuming too much fat
   c. genetics
   d. bacteria in the colon

7. What is metabolism?
   a. a step in digestion
   b. something that thin people have
   c. all of the biochemical reactions in the cells of the body
   d. a chemical released in the small intestine

8. What fact related to metabolism explains why the body cannot make glucose from fatty acids?
   a. Fats are not broken down in glycolysis.
   b. Fatty acids enter the pathway at acetyl CoA and can't go back to pyruvate.
   c. Fatty acids enter the pathway at pyruvate and can't go back.
   d. Fatty acids are not part of metabolism.

9. When are ketones formed?
   a. when you want to lose weight
   b. when you consume too many carbohydrates
   c. when you don't consume enough carbohydrates and fat breakdown is slowed
   d. when you consume too much fat

10. What is the final pathway used to make ATP?
   a. the Krebs cycle
   b. beta oxidation
   c. the electron transport chain
   d. glycolysis

# Energy Balance and Obesity

## A Nation Out of Balance

## < Here's Where You've Been

*The following topics were introduced in preceding chapters and are related to concepts we'll discuss in Chapter 7. Be certain that you're familiar with them before proceeding.*

- A healthy diet includes balance, variety, and moderation. (Chapter 2)
- Carbohydrates, fats, and proteins are the macronutrients; they provide calories that the body can use for energy. (Chapters 3, 4, 5)
- After we put food in our mouth, it must go through a series of steps before we can get energy from it: digestion, absorption, and metabolism. (Chapter 6)
- After nutrients are absorbed into the blood they must be taken up by the cells, where they can be converted to the usable form of energy called ATP. This is done through a series of steps called metabolism. (Chapter 6)

## Here's Where You're Going >

*The following topics and concepts are the ones we'll emphasize in Chapter 7.*

- Achieving and/or maintaining a healthy weight really is a balancing act. You must balance calorie intake with calorie expenditure.
- Obesity is a major health concern, as its prevalence has increased dramatically in adults and children in recent years.
- Obesity is associated with an increased risk for many serious diseases such as heart disease, diabetes, high blood pressure, and certain cancers.
- The best way to lose weight is to create a caloric deficit of at least 500 calories per day by eating less and exercising more.

## Real People, Real Choices

Amber Koen, like many Americans, is overweight. After years of dieting and losing weight and then gaining it back again, she is now more than 40 lbs. overweight. She can't figure out why it is so hard for her to lose weight and keep it off. She decides that something must be wrong with her to be such a dieting failure. Maybe she has an abnormal metabolism, or maybe she just doesn't have sufficient willpower. She feels tired most of the time and has very little energy. She is very busy with two kids and has a demanding job as an elementary school teacher. She tries to cook healthy meals for her family but is often too tired and stressed to bother, so she stops to get fast food on her way home. To make matters worse, her 7-year-old son recently came home from school and said the kids were teasing him for being fat.

Amber decides that it is time to make some major changes for the entire family, but she really doesn't know where to start. She hopes that she can help her son by finding a diet that works for him. A further issue that complicates Amber's circumstance is the fact that her husband doesn't have a weight problem, which she must take into account when considering any changes in family meal planning or lifestyle. She decides to do something she's never before thought necessary—she makes an appointment with a Registered Dietitian. What advice and strategies do you think the dietitian will offer Amber?

In the field of nutrition, the topic that has perhaps generated the most misinformation, fueled the most myths, and, unfortunately, been the source of the largest costs both financially and emotionally is the topic of energy balance and weight control. You can hardly turn the television on or open a magazine without seeing an advertisement for a weight-loss plan, food products associated with a diet scheme, or a weight-control pill. It seems as if every newscast has at least one story about the latest study on obesity and dieting. Every aspect of our culture seems to be influenced by the latest dieting trend: coffee break conversations, the newest items on popular restaurant menus, family dinner tables. Although it may seem overwhelming, the attention being given to this topic is somewhat justified. In fact, according to the Centers for Disease Control (CDC), 68 percent of American adults and an alarming number of children are overweight or obese. This is a very serious public health problem that will require a community effort to address. In addition to being a risk factor for approximately thirty potentially deadly and chronic diseases, including heart disease, stroke, Type 2 diabetes, osteoarthritis, and certain cancers, obesity itself is now considered a chronic disease. Whether justified or not, the focus on the topic of weight loss and weight control has left many people feeling confused and misinformed. Furthermore, it has created a social prejudice against overweight and obese people in that they are left feeling ashamed and weak.

In this chapter we will discuss the science behind how the body uses and stores energy and explore why the concept of balance is critical to maintaining a healthy weight. We will also examine popular treatments for weight loss and weight maintenance. We will provide clinical definitions and apply science in an attempt to clarify common misconceptions. In addition, the pros and cons of many weight-loss programs will be discussed.

## Calories In Versus Calories Out

Basically, in order to lose weight you must burn more calories than you consume. In turn, to maintain weight you must burn as many calories as you consume. To gain weight you must consume more than you burn. So, calories in versus calories out is an oversimplified explanation of a complex issue; but this simple statement holds a lot of truth and summarizes the fact that maintaining weight is really an issue of balance.

The concept of getting more for your money has contributed to the increasing portion sizes provided by many restaurants.

# Calories In: The Food We Eat

The "calories in" side of the equation obviously comes from the food we eat. As physical activity has decreased in our society over the last fifty years, the intake side of the weight balance equation has changed as well. We have easy access to a wide variety of food choices. Even pharmacies have food items. Prepackaged foods, fast-food restaurants, and high-calorie beverages are more accessible. The downside of this easily accessible food supply is that many fast and convenient foods are high in fat, sugar, and calories. Choosing these foods on a regular basis can easily contribute to an excessive calorie intake. Foods that are marketed as low-fat or fat-free can be deceiving, because they often contain more calories than the products they are designed to replace. It is important to read food labels for nutritional information and to eat in moderation.

In addition to an increased availability, portion size has increased over time. In the food marketplace, the concept of getting more for your money seems to have eliminated the concept of eating a reasonable portion size. This trend has contributed to the obesity epidemic, because larger portion sizes means consuming more calories as well.

Eating a larger meal away from home on occasion may not be a big problem, but Americans are dining out now more than ever. In fact, food consumed outside the home currently accounts for about 47 percent of the family food budget, whereas in 1970 it accounted for only 34 percent. The increasing portion sizes in restaurant meals and beverages therefore contribute to our excessive caloric intake (Figure 7.1).

## ■ You Decide

*Is the food industry to blame for increasing portion sizes?*
Is the food industry responsible for the increase in obesity rates in the United States? Or do individuals need to take more responsibility for their food choices? Read the article at www.msnbc.msn.com/id/11823972/. What do you think? ■

Of course, one of the reasons people eat away from home more frequently is that there are more and more restaurants. This growth, especially in fast-food establishments, means more competition within the food industry. There is a high density of fast food establishments in low income neighborhoods. It has been suggested, that this is a partial explanation for higher obesity rates in lower income populations. Increasing the portion size of a product is an effective marketing tool. If people think they are getting more for their money, they are more likely to buy the product or patronize the restaurant. Larger portions are often promoted as the best value. The 7-Eleven 16-oz. Gulp (2 c.) costs about 6¢ an ounce, whereas a 32-oz. (4 c. or 1 qt.) Big Gulp goes for 3¢ an ounce. We get more Coke in the Big Gulp for the money, but that is not all we get. The 16-oz. Gulp provides 198 calories and the 32-oz. Big Gulp provides 396 calories. Is the reduced cost per ounce in the larger drink really worth consuming double the calories?

Is getting more for your money really worth the extra calories?

Portion sizes and our idea of what is a reasonable portion size have obviously been distorted. One way to combat this distortion is to educate ourselves as to what constitutes a reasonable portion size. See the Make It a Practice feature on portion sizes for guidelines on judging them.

**Figure 7.1** Increasing Portion Sizes from Year of Product Introduction to Present.

Portion size of packaged foods as well as serving sizes at restaurants have ballooned in the past century, with some of the largest offerings now more than five times their original size, according to a study published in the *Journal of the American Dietetic Association*. Nutritionists believe larger portion sizes have contributed to the nation's obesity epidemic.

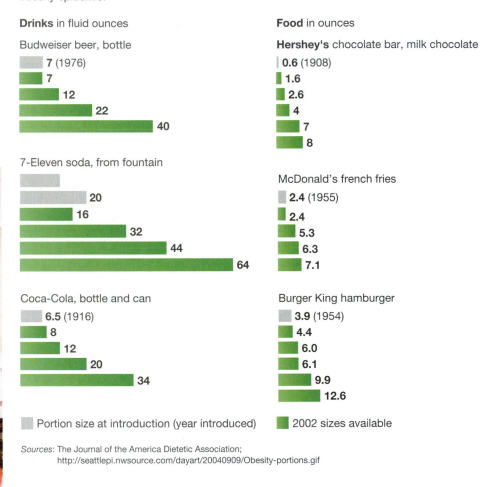

**Drinks** in fluid ounces

Budweiser beer, bottle
- **7** (1976)
- 7
- 12
- 22
- 40

7-Eleven soda, from fountain
- 20
- 16
- 32
- 44
- 64

Coca-Cola, bottle and can
- **6.5** (1916)
- 8
- 12
- 20
- 34

**Food** in ounces

**Hershey's** chocolate bar, milk chocolate
- **0.6** (1908)
- 1.6
- 2.6
- 4
- 7
- 8

McDonald's french fries
- **2.4** (1955)
- 2.4
- 5.3
- 6.3
- 7.1

Burger King hamburger
- **3.9** (1954)
- 4.4
- 6.0
- 6.1
- 9.9
- 12.6

◻ Portion size at introduction (year introduced)     ◻ 2002 sizes available

*Sources*: The Journal of the America Dietetic Association;
http://seattlepi.nwsource.com/dayart/20040909/Obesity-portions.gif

## Make It a Practice

*Achieving a healthy weight starts here: portion sizes*

MyPyramid.gov gives recommendations for how much of each food group should be consumed for each age and gender group. Table 7.1 is taken from that website and describes the recommended daily equivalents of meat for each group.

Estimating an ounce equivalent when you are eating in a restaurant or cafeteria or even just making a quick dinner at home can be confusing. MyPyramid.gov provides some examples of how much of each food group should be consumed. The website says, "In general, 1 ounce of meat, poultry or fish, 1/4 cup cooked dry beans, 1 egg, 1 tablespoon of peanut butter, or 1/2 ounce of nuts or seeds can be considered as 1 ounce equivalent from the meat and beans group." Let's say you are a 19-year-old male. You see on the chart that you should eat the equivalent of about 6.5 oz. of meat. What does that look like in terms of actual food?

Let's say you have a chicken sandwich with a small chicken breast, like the one pictured in Figure 7.2a, for lunch. This is 6 ounce equivalents.

| Table 7.1 | Recommended Daily Equivalents for Meat from MyPyramid.gov | |
|---|---|---|
| | **Age Range** | **Daily Recommendation** |
| **Children** | 2–3 years old | 2 ounce equivalents |
| | 4–8 years old | 3–4 ounce equivalents |
| **Girls** | 9–13 years old | 5 ounce equivalents |
| | 14–18 years old | 5 ounce equivalents |
| **Boys** | 9–13 years old | 5 ounce equivalents |
| | 14–18 years old | 6 ounce equivalents |
| **Women** | 19–30 years old | 5 1/2 ounce equivalents |
| | 31–50 years old | 5 ounce equivalents |
| | 51+ years old | 5 ounce equivalents |
| **Men** | 19–30 years old | 6 1/2 ounce equivalents |
| | 31–50 years old | 6 ounce equivalents |
| | 51+ years old | 5 1/2 ounce equivalents |

For a snack you have an ounce of cashews (13 nuts). This is 2 ounce equivalents (Figure 7.2b). And for dinner, you have black beans with rice. Assuming you had 1/2 c. of black beans, as pictured in Figure 7.2c, this is 2 ounce equivalents. You have consumed 10 ounce equivalents and therefore have met, and exceeded, the recommended 6.5 ounce equivalents for the day. It is easy to see why so many people eat too much from some of the food groups and, therefore, too many calories. If you are not sure how big the serving size on your plate is, you can compare it to real-world objects in several ways to get a better idea (see Table 7.2). ■

## Calories Out: Energy Expenditure

One of the first aspects to examine when discussing body weight is the "calories out" or energy expenditure side of our *balance* equation. Individuals vary widely in the number of calories burned each day. However, everybody expends energy or calories in three ways: resting energy expenditure (REE), physical activity, and the thermic effect of food (TEF). The relative significance of these variables varies somewhat depending on your individual circumstances.

**APPLICATION TIP**

Go to MyPyramid.gov for more examples of what counts as an ounce equivalent, and then see if you can devise your own real-world-object examples to help you judge adequate portion sizes without taking time to weigh and measure foods.

**Figure 7.2** (a) A 6-ounce chicken breast represents 6-oz. equivalents; (b) 1 ounce of cashews represents 2 ounce equivalents; (c) 1/2 cup of black beans represents 2 ounce equivalents.

(a)

(b)

(c)

| Table 7.2 | Some Real-World Objects to Help Judge Portion Sizes | |
|---|---|---|
| **One Serving of . . .** | **Real-World Object** | **MyPyramid Equivalent** |
| Apple | Baseball | 1 c. (1 serving) |
| Bagel | Hockey puck (mini bagel) | 1 oz. equivalent |
| Butter | Thumb (joint to tip) | 2 oz. |
| Cheese | Pair of dice | 1 1/2 oz. (1 serving) |
| Fish, grilled | Checkbook | 4 oz. equivalent |
| Fruit, chopped | Tennis ball | 1 c. (1 serving) |
| Pancake | (4 1/2-in. diameter) | 1 oz. equivalent |
| Potato | Computer mouse | 1 c. (1 serving) |
| Meat: | Matchbox | 1 oz. |
| | Bar of soap | 3 oz. |
| | Thin paperback book | 8 oz. |
| Rice, steamed | Paper cupcake liner | 1/2 c. (1 oz.) equivalent |
| Vegetables, cooked | Palm of hand | 1 c. (1 serving) |

## Resting Energy Expenditure

Did you know that we burn calories even while we are just sitting or sleeping? These calories make up most of the calories we burn in a day and are part of what we call **resting energy expenditure (REE)**, a term that is sometimes used interchangeably with the term **basal metabolism**. **Basal metabolic rate (BMR)**, or the rate at which metabolism occurs, is more precisely defined as the REE measured after waking in the morning, at least twelve hours after the last meal. It is okay to use these terms interchangeably, as there is only a small difference between them. The calories that contribute to REE are used for your heartbeat, breathing, nerve impulse transmission, kidney function, growth and repair, and other basic functions. Although REE varies from one person to another, it generally makes up approximately two-thirds of the total calories expended in a day by the average person. Someone who has a relatively slow or efficient (thrifty) metabolism requires fewer calories than does someone with a faster metabolism and the same lifestyle. The person with a slower metabolism will have a more difficult time keeping excess weight off.

Organs such as the brain and liver and muscle tissue burn most of the calories that make up your daily REE. In comparison, fat tissue does not require very many calories for maintenance. Therefore, how much of your body is muscle and how much is fat influences how many calories you burn in a day. The more muscle you have, the more calories you burn, even when you are just sitting still. In individuals of similar age, sex, height, and weight, differences in muscle mass account for approximately 80 percent of the variance in REE. Differences in muscle mass also account for most of the difference in REE between men and women, and between younger and older adults of similar heights and weights. Although you cannot will your REE to be higher or lower, you can influence it. For example, food restriction, particularly chronic dieting, lowers REE, especially when muscle mass is lost. Building muscle mass, exercising, and eating regular meals are the best ways to increase REE (see Table 7.3).

| Table 7.3 | Factors Affecting Resting Energy Expenditure (REE) |
|---|---|
| **Factors That Increase REE** | **Factors That Decrease REE** |
| Increased muscle mass | Loss of muscle mass |
| Regular or frequent meals (by increasing TEF) | Skipping meals, dieting, meal restriction |
| Exercise (can vary depending on intensity, duration, and type) | Starvation, fasting |
| Exposure to hot or cold temperatures | Aging (especially if accompanied with loss of muscle mass) |
| Fever | Being female (lower muscle mass) |
| Caffeine | Sleep |
| Stress | |
| Pregnancy and breastfeeding | |
| Hormones | |
| Nicotine | |

## Physical Activity

Physical activity refers to energy expenditure through *voluntary* physical effort—in other words, daily activities, exercise, or physical labor. Physical activity is the component of daily caloric expenditure that varies the most from day to day in the same person and from person to person. The more muscles you contract and the more frequently you contract them, the more calories you burn. Body weight, muscle mass, number of muscles used, duration, intensity, the exerciser's fitness, and the type of activity determine how much energy is used. Figure 7.3 lists the amount of time it takes to burn 150 calories while participating in various activities. Note that this varies based on the size of the person. For example, running a mile burns more calories in a 200-lb person than a 150-lb person simply because the heavier person has more weight to carry (see Appendix H).

Table 7.4 lists an estimate of energy expenditure for various activities. Although it may seem discouraging that many moderate activities don't appear to burn a lot of calories, there are more reasons to exercise than just to burn calories. Participation in regular physical activity increases muscle mass, which increases your caloric expenditure by increasing your REE. Exercise has also been shown to decrease the risk of high blood pressure, heart disease, cancer, diabetes, osteoporosis, and obesity. Despite the known health benefits, only 45 percent of adult Americans report that they participate in regular physical activity. Regardless of whether you need to lose weight, gain weight, or just maintain, it is important to your health and well-being to participate in regular physical activity.

## Calories for Digestion

Did you know that you actually burn calories when you eat? Research shows that your body burns about 10 percent of calories consumed, depending on the type and quantity of food eaten (a little higher for protein, a little lower for fat). The process of burning calories as you digest, absorb, transport, store, and metabolize food is called the **thermic effect of food (TEF)**. Dieting lore makes many

**Want to know more?**
For more information, see Appendix H on the text website at http://webcom8.grtxle.com/nutrition and click on the Chapters button. Select Chapter 7.

**Figure 7.3** An estimate of the time required for an adult male weighing 150 lbs (70 kg) to burn 150 calories. A larger person would expend more calories than indicated; a smaller person, less.

*Source:* Centers for Disease Control, www.cdc.gov/nccdphp/dnpa/physical/recommendations/adults.htm

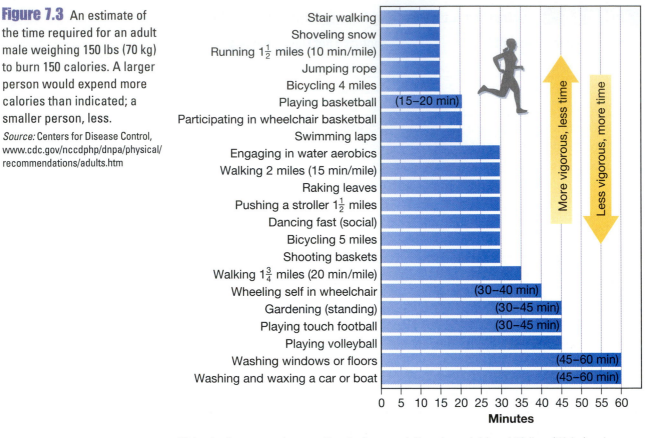

This chart represents an estimate for an adult male weighing 150 lbs. (70 kg); a larger person would expend more calories than indicated, a smaller person less.

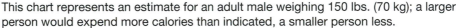

claims about TEF. For example, some diets claim that there are "weight-loss foods," that is, foods that burn more calories than they provide. But no evidence supports the idea that any food makes the body burn more calories than the food provides. Other diets claim that eating a high-protein diet will make one lose weight because of the greater TEF of protein compared to fat or carbohydrates. Recent studies have indicated that if you consume the same amount of calories on a diet that contains 25 percent of total calories from protein as you do on a diet that contains 12 percent of total calories from protein, you will not lose more weight or body fat. However, people who eat a higher-protein diet may eat less because the protein makes them feel fuller longer. As you may recall from Chapter 6, this is because protein empties from your stomach more slowly than carbohydrates do.

### Total Energy Expenditure

**Total energy expenditure (TEE)** is the sum of REE, physical activity, and TEF. Figure 7.4 shows how the differences in energy expenditure among people of the same size and sex can be explained by physical activity.

To measure REE directly requires expensive specialized equipment that is usually found in research facilities. For practical purposes, many different formulas are used to estimate REE, such as the one used in the following Self-Assessment feature. Of course, this would not be a very accurate estimate of the calories you burn in a day if you did not include physical activity. Estimating the calories you burn in physical activity is a bit more difficult because it

## Table 7.4    Energy Costs of Various Physical Activities

| Activity | Intensity | Kilocalories Used per Pound per Hour |
|---|---|---|
| Sitting, quietly watching television | Light | 0.48 |
| Sitting, reading | Light | 0.62 |
| Sitting, studying including reading or writing | Light | 0.86 |
| Cooking or food preparation (standing or sitting) | Light | 0.95 |
| Walking, shopping | Light | 1.09 |
| Walking, 2 mph (slow pace) | Light | 1.2 |
| Cleaning (dusting, straightening up, vacuuming, changing linen, or carrying out trash) | Moderate | 1.2 |
| Stretching—Hatha Yoga | Moderate | 1.2 |
| Weight lifting (free weights, Nautilus, or Universal type) | Light or moderate | 1.42 |
| Bicycling <10 mph | Leisure (work or pleasure) | 1.9 |
| Walking, 4 mph (brisk pace) | Moderate | 2.4 |
| Aerobics | Low impact | 2.4 |
| Weight lifting (free weights, Nautilus, or Universal type) | Vigorous | 2.86 |
| Bicycling 12 to 13.9 mph | Moderate | 3.82 |
| Running, 5 mph (12 minutes per mile) | Moderate | 3.82 |
| Running, 6 mph (10 minutes per mile) | Moderate | 4.77 |
| Running, 8.6 mph (7 minutes per mile) | Vigorous | 6.68 |

*Source:* Ainsworth BE, Haskell WL, MC Whitt, ML Irwin, AM Swartz, SJ Strath, WL O'Brien, Bassett DR Jr., KH Schmitz, PO Emplaincourt, Jacobs DR Jr., AS Leon. (2000) Compendium of physical activities: an update of activity codes and MET intensities. *Med Sci Sports Exerc* 32:S498–S516.

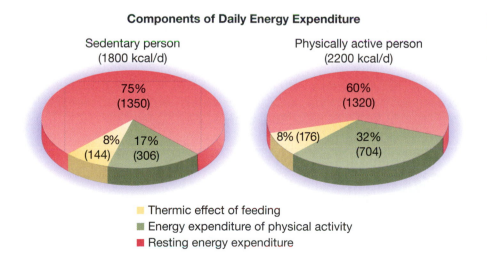

**Components of Daily Energy Expenditure**

Sedentary person (1800 kcal/d)

Physically active person (2200 kcal/d)

- Thermic effect of feeding
- Energy expenditure of physical activity
- Resting energy expenditure

**Figure 7.4** Comparison of the components of daily energy expenditure between an active person and a sedentary person of the same weight.

varies depending on intensity, duration, your fitness level, the environmental temperature, your body size, and the amount of muscle mass you have. One way to account for activity is to make an estimate based on activity factors. This approach is not precise, but it is a quick and useful calculation.

### ■ Self-Assessment
*Estimating your REE*

**Basal Metabolic Rate**

**Step 1:** To change your weight in pounds to kilograms, divide your weight in pounds by 2.2.

**Step 2:** To change your height in inches to centimeters, multiply your height in inches by 2.54.

**Step 3:** To estimate your basal metabolic rate, plug your numbers into formula (a) if you are a woman and formula (b) if you're a man.

     a. Women: BMR = 665.1 + (9.563 × weight in kg) + (1.850 × height in cm) − (4.676 × age) = calories burned

     b. Men: BMR = 66.5 + (13.75 × weight in kg) + (5.003 × height in cm) − (6.775 × age) = calories burned

*So if you are a 19-year-old woman, 5 ft. 2 in., 120 lbs, how many calories do you need to maintain your minimum or basic body functions? In other words, how many calories would you burn just lying in bed all day?*

**Step 1:** 120/2.2 = 54.5 kg

**Step 2:** 62 × 2.54 = 157.5 cm

**Step 3:** 665.1 + (9.563 × 54.5) + (1.850 × 157.5) − (4.676 × 19) = 1,388 calories

*If you are a 19-year-old man, 5 ft. 10 in., 180 lbs, you would calculate your BMR as follows:*

**Step 1:** 180/2.2 = 81.8 kg

**Step 2:** 70 × 2.54 = 177.8 cm

**Step 3:** 66.5 + (13.75 × 81.8) + (5.003 × 177.8) − (6.775 × 19) = 1,885 calories

**Accounting for Physical Activity**

We are not done yet. Although there are days when we would like to just lie in bed all day without moving, that's unrealistic. So we must account for physical activities that require calories to determine how many we need to maintain weight.

**Step 4:** Multiply your BMR by the appropriate activity factor.

*So for the 120-lb woman with a BMR of 1,388, if she is a soccer player and participates in sports six days per week, we multiply her BMR by 1.725 (see Table 7.5) to get* **2,394** *total calories burned per day.*

### Table 7.5   Physical Activity Factors for Calculating Energy Expenditure

| Physical Activity | Activity Factor |
| --- | --- |
| Sedentary (little or no exercise) | 1.2 |
| Lightly active (light exercise/sports 1–3 days/week) | 1.375 |
| Moderately active (moderate exercise/sports 3–5 days/week) | 1.55 |
| Very active (hard exercise/sports 6–7 days a week) | 1.725 |
| Extra active (very hard exercise/sports and physical job or 2 × training) | 1.9 |

For the 180-lb man with a BMR of 1,885, if he is sedentary we multiply his BMR by 1.2 (see Table 7.5) to get **2,262** total calories burned per day. ■

---

**Want to know more?**
You can calculate your calorie needs by checking out the text website at http://webcom8.grtxle.com/nutrition and clicking on the Chapters button. Select Chapter 7.

---

> **Before you go on . . .**
> 1. What is the bottom line to any weight loss?
> 2. List the factors that contribute to daily energy expenditure.
> 3. Which factor contributing to energy expenditure varies the most?
> 4. What factor may help explain why more Americans are overweight now than in the past?

# Out of Balance: Overweight, Obesity, and Underweight

We can measure and define overweight and obesity in a number of ways. The body mass index (BMI) is the simplest calculation; it can be done anywhere with a tape measure and a scale. To be more accurate than BMI alone, we can estimate the actual amount of fat on the body, and, finally, we can examine how that fat is distributed.

## Body Mass Index (BMI)

The **body mass index (BMI)** is a height-weight relationship; it equals (weight in kilograms)/(height in meters squared), or (weight in pounds × 704.5)/(height in inches squared). The National Institutes of Health and the World Health Organization as well as many other major health organizations have proposed the use of BMI as a tool in the diagnosis of overweight and obesity. **Overweight** is characterized by a BMI of 25 or greater, while **obesity** is characterized by a BMI of 30 or greater. Table 7.6 is a convenient tool for looking up your BMI.

### BMI and Disease Risk

Scientists studying the relationship between BMI and health have associated certain disease risks with being overweight or obese (Table 7.7). Being overweight or obese raises the risk for diseases such as cardiovascular disease; hypertension; Type 2 diabetes; chronic inflammation; stroke; gallbladder disease; osteoarthritis; sleep apnea; respiratory problems; and endometrial, breast, prostate, and colon cancers. Obesity is also associated with complications during pregnancy, menstrual irregularities, and psychological disorders such as depression. The classification system used in Table 7.7 is based on research that shows that the risk of disease usually begins to increase at a BMI of 25–29.9, and increases further at a BMI of 30. The death rate increases with BMIs greater than 25; the increase is greatest with a BMI of 30 and greater. For people with a BMI of 30, death rates from all causes, and especially from cardiovascular disease (see Figure 7.5), are increased by 50 to 100 percent above that of people with BMIs of 20–25.

---

**APPLICATION TIP**

Did you know that according to the latest national statistics published by the CDC, the average adult American woman is 63.8 in. tall and weighs 163 lbs. The average man is 69.3 in. tall and weighs 190 lbs. These figures correlate with an average BMI of 28, which puts the average American at an increased risk for many health problems, according to Table 7.7.

## Table 7.6 — Body Mass Index (BMI) Chart

| | 19 | 20 | 21 | 22 | 23 | 24 | 25 | 26 | 27 | 28 | 29 | 30 | 31 | 32 | 33 | 34 | 35 |
|---|---|---|---|---|---|---|---|---|---|---|---|---|---|---|---|---|---|
| **Height (in.)** | | | | | | | | Body Weight (lb.) | | | | | | | | | |
| **58** | 91 | 96 | 100 | 105 | 110 | 115 | 119 | 124 | 129 | 134 | 138 | 143 | 148 | 153 | 158 | 162 | 167 |
| **59** | 94 | 99 | 104 | 109 | 114 | 110 | 124 | 128 | 133 | 138 | 143 | 148 | 153 | 158 | 163 | 168 | 173 |
| **60** | 97 | 102 | 107 | 112 | 118 | 123 | 128 | 133 | 138 | 143 | 148 | 153 | 158 | 163 | 168 | 174 | 179 |
| **61** | 100 | 106 | 111 | 116 | 122 | 127 | 132 | 137 | 143 | 148 | 153 | 158 | 164 | 169 | 174 | 180 | 185 |
| **62** | 104 | 109 | 115 | 120 | 126 | 131 | 136 | 142 | 147 | 153 | 158 | 164 | 169 | 175 | 180 | 186 | 191 |
| **63** | 107 | 113 | 118 | 124 | 130 | 135 | 141 | 146 | 152 | 158 | 163 | 169 | 175 | 180 | 186 | 191 | 197 |
| **64** | 110 | 116 | 122 | 128 | 134 | 140 | 145 | 151 | 157 | 163 | 169 | 174 | 180 | 186 | 192 | 197 | 204 |
| **65** | 114 | 120 | 126 | 132 | 138 | 144 | 150 | 156 | 162 | 168 | 174 | 180 | 186 | 192 | 198 | 204 | 210 |
| **66** | 118 | 124 | 130 | 136 | 142 | 148 | 155 | 161 | 167 | 173 | 179 | 186 | 192 | 198 | 204 | 210 | 216 |
| **67** | 121 | 127 | 134 | 140 | 146 | 153 | 159 | 166 | 172 | 178 | 185 | 191 | 198 | 204 | 211 | 217 | 223 |
| **68** | 125 | 131 | 138 | 144 | 151 | 158 | 164 | 171 | 177 | 184 | 190 | 197 | 203 | 210 | 216 | 223 | 230 |
| **69** | 128 | 135 | 142 | 149 | 155 | 162 | 169 | 176 | 182 | 189 | 196 | 203 | 209 | 216 | 223 | 230 | 236 |
| **70** | 132 | 139 | 146 | 153 | 160 | 167 | 174 | 181 | 188 | 195 | 202 | 209 | 216 | 222 | 229 | 236 | 243 |
| **71** | 136 | 143 | 150 | 157 | 165 | 172 | 179 | 186 | 193 | 200 | 208 | 215 | 222 | 229 | 236 | 243 | 250 |
| **72** | 140 | 147 | 154 | 162 | 169 | 177 | 184 | 191 | 199 | 206 | 213 | 221 | 228 | 235 | 242 | 250 | 258 |
| **73** | 144 | 151 | 159 | 166 | 174 | 182 | 189 | 197 | 204 | 212 | 210 | 227 | 235 | 242 | 250 | 257 | 265 |
| **74** | 148 | 155 | 163 | 171 | 179 | 186 | 194 | 202 | 210 | 218 | 225 | 233 | 241 | 249 | 256 | 264 | 272 |
| **75** | 152 | 160 | 168 | 176 | 184 | 192 | 200 | 208 | 216 | 224 | 232 | 240 | 248 | 256 | 264 | 272 | 279 |
| **76** | 156 | 164 | 172 | 180 | 189 | 197 | 205 | 213 | 221 | 230 | 238 | 246 | 254 | 263 | 271 | 279 | 287 |

## Underweight

Overweight and obesity are not the only potential problems associated with weight. It is also possible to weigh too little. If you are 10 percent below what is considered a healthy weight for your height and build (adult BMI <19), you are considered **underweight**. As you can see in Figure 7.5, the relationship between BMI and prevalence of disease and death is U-shaped. This means that just as risk goes up with an increasing BMI, it increases with a BMI below the recommended level as well. Being underweight is typically associated with inadequate nutritional intake, which can result in decreased overall energy, a weakened immune system, respiratory complications, and delayed wound healing.

Some people are simply born with fewer fat cells and thus are genetically predisposed to being extremely thin. Other factors that can cause underweight include stress, depression, bereavement, smoking, and eating disorders. (See Chapter 15 for information on eating disorders.) Some diseases cause sudden and dramatic weight loss, such as hyperthyroidism, HIV/AIDS, some cancers, and some conditions of the digestive system such as *Crohn's disease.*

Older people who are underweight are especially at risk because they need reserves to fight off illness, heal from injury and surgery, and compensate for the loss of appetite and inadequate absorption of nutrients that sometimes

| Table 7.7 | Body Mass Index (BMI) and Disease Risk |
|---|---|

| Body Mass Index | Disease Risks |
|---|---|
| **25–29.9 (overweight)** | • High blood pressure (hypertension)<br>• High blood cholesterol (dyslipidemia)<br>• Type 2 (non-insulin-dependent) diabetes<br>• Insulin resistance, glucose intolerance<br>• High blood insulin (hyperinsulinemia)<br>• Coronary heart disease<br>• Angina pectoris<br>• Congestive heart failure<br>• Sleep apnea and other breathing problems<br>• Stroke<br>• Gallbladder disease and gallstones<br>• Gout<br>• Osteoarthritis (degeneration of cartilage and bone in joints)<br>• Certain types of cancer (such as endometrial, uterine, breast, prostate, colon, kidney, gallbladder, and esophageal)<br>• Uric acid nephrolithiasis (kidney stones) |
| **30 and greater (obese)** | • All of the risks noted above<br>• Kidney disease<br>• Liver disease<br>• Back problems<br>• Restricted mobility<br>• Complications of pregnancy<br>• Poor female reproductive health (such as menstrual irregularities, infertility, irregular ovulation)<br>• Hirsutism (presence of excess body and facial hair)<br>• Bladder control problems (such as stress incontinence)<br>• Psychological disorders (such as depression, eating disorders, distorted body image, and low self-esteem)<br>• Increased surgical risk<br>• **50–150% greater risk of premature death from any cause** |

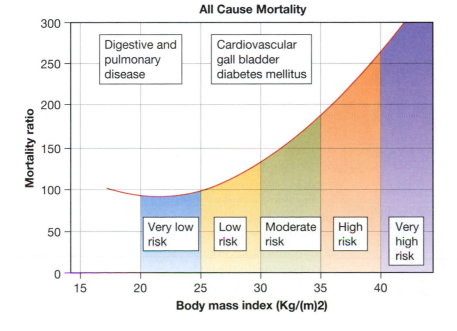

**Figure 7.5** Relationship between BMI and mortality.

**Figure 7.6** A BMI of 32 suggests that this man is obese. However, on further assessment we discover that his body fat is estimated to be very low. BMI is not always an accurate indicator of obesity, especially for very lean and muscular individuals.

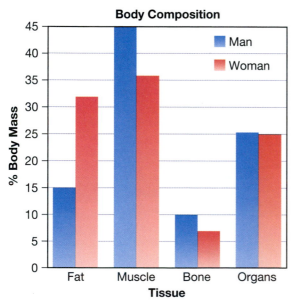

**Figure 7.7** A comparison of the components of body composition between men and women. Note that men have a higher percentage of muscle mass and women have a higher percentage of body fat. Women require more body fat for reproduction.

*Source:* Republished from *Advanced Human Nutrition* by Wildman and Medeiros. © 2000 by CRC Press. Permission conveyed through Copyright Clearance Center.

occurs with age. **Osteoporosis** affects older women in particular and is characterized by a decrease in bone mass and density. This condition leads to an enlargement of bone spaces, which produces porosity and brittleness that can lead to a broken hip. These are also associated with being underweight.

### Limitations of BMI

Although BMI is a simple and convenient tool, it has some limitations in its utility as a method to diagnose overweight and obesity and therefore to determine disease risk. The relationship between BMI and body fat differs according to sex and ethnic group. Women have a higher percentage of body fat than men at the same BMI. Similarly, the need for ethnically specific cutoff points is supported by the evidence of elevated disease risks at low BMI in several populations. For example, Asians tend to have a higher percentage of body fat for any given BMI than Caucasians, meaning they are at a greater risk at any given BMI. Caucasians typically have a higher percentage of body fat for a given BMI than African Americans. This suggests that African Americans may have less disease risk at a given BMI than other ethnic groups. In addition to not being population specific, BMI fails to distinguish between fat and muscle mass. For example, the BMI of the athlete in Figure 7.6 indicates that he is obese; however, he is a lean and muscular individual. Athletes aside, most of the time people with high BMIs are obese. To be certain, we can measure body composition (see Figure 7.7).

### Body Composition

Total body mass is the sum of lean tissue mass and fat mass. The problems associated with obesity stem from the extra body fat. Thus, it is helpful to know what percentage of your body weight is composed of fat. Body-fat norms are associated with age and sex. Body fat usually increases with age, and women should have a higher body fat percentage than men. The desirable ranges of body fat percentage are roughly 10–20 percent for men and 18–25 percent for women.

Body fat is a combination of *essential fat* and *storage fat*. Essential fat is the amount of fat required for normal physiological functioning. It consists of the fat needed for the body's organs, central nervous system, muscles, and bone marrow. In women it also includes sex-specific essential fat, or the amount of fat needed for optimal reproductive function. Storage fat consists mostly of fat from adipose tissue, tissue under the skin, and the fat that "pads" essential organs. Women have more essential body fat than men because of the added sex-specific fat, but they have similar amounts of storage fat. Men with more than 25 percent body fat and women with more than 30 percent body fat are considered obese.

## Techniques to Estimate Body Composition

Although body composition is a much more informative statistic than BMI, it is much more difficult to determine. Several techniques are used to estimate body fat; none are 100 percent accurate, and all are based on equations that

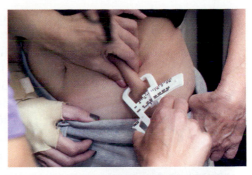

make certain assumptions, which may not be true for every person. Nonetheless, these are the tools currently available to us. **Underwater weighing** is often referred to as the gold standard for estimating body composition. This technique measures the density of the body by comparing weight on land to underwater weight and the volume of water displaced by the body. The person is lowered into a tank of water after exhaling all air from the lungs. He or she is then weighed in the water. Because fat floats and lean tissue sinks, density predicts fatness. Although this test is accurate, it is not convenient and is usually available only in university and research laboratories.

The underwater weighing technique is considered the gold standard for estimating body composition. Although not as accurate as the underwater weighing technique, skin fold calipers are a more convenient technique for estimating body composition.

Although they are not as accurate as underwater weighing, *skinfold calipers* are a more convenient alternative. The calipers are used to measure the thickness of the fat layer under the skin in several locations, such as the triceps, shoulder blade, and abdomen. Plugging these values into an equation yields the percentage of body fat. Although using calipers is much easier and less expensive than underwater weighing, the caliper method requires a trained and skilled operator. It is most accurate with people close to the normal range of body fat and less accurate for the extremely lean and the extremely obese.

Many techniques have been evaluated as alternatives to underwater weighing, but **dual-energy X-ray absorptiometry (DEXA)** has emerged as the most reliable. DEXA uses two X-ray energies to measure body fat, muscle, and bone mineral. During the scan, the person must lie still on his or her back on what looks like an X-ray table. The computer software takes approximately twelve minutes to produce an image of the tissues. DEXA provides several advantages when compared to underwater weighing: it is easier on the person being measured, it is not influenced by fluctuations in body water, and it provides information regarding where fat is stored on the body. It also provides information on bone density, in addition to fat-free mass and fat mass. However, it is expensive and therefore has limited use in a clinical setting.

**Bioelectrical impedance analysis (BIA)**, yet another way to measure body composition, is based on the fact that lean tissue, with high water content, conducts electricity relatively well, while fat tissue, with low water content, conducts electricity poorly. It is often used in scales and hand-held devices. This method is even less accurate than skin folds as it is greatly affected by changes in body water. Using this method, small electrodes are attached to a hand and a foot and a mild electric current is passed through the body.

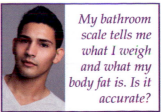

*My bathroom scale tells me what I weigh and what my body fat is. Is it accurate?*

Bathroom scales often use bioelectrical impedance analysis to estimate body fat. It is not a very accurate technique because it is influenced by body water, which can fluctuate significantly.

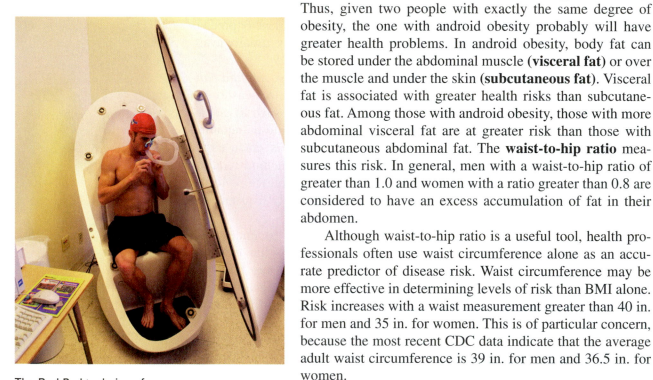

The Bod Pod technique for estimating body composition is very similar to underwater weighing, but it uses air displacement instead of water.

(Subjects do not feel anything.) By measuring the body's impedance, or resistance to current, a technician can determine the amount of lean tissue and the amount of fat.

One of the most recently developed techniques to estimate body composition is the Bod Pod. It uses similar techniques to underwater weighing, except that it uses air displacement instead of water displacement. Of all the alternative techniques to underwater weighing, it is the most accurate.

## Body Fat Distribution

Where on your body you store fat has a significant influence on health and disease risk. Each person carries fat in his or her own pattern of distribution, which is largely genetically determined. In general, there are two kinds of distributions. In the **android** pattern, the so-called apple shape, most body fat is carried in the abdomen. This distribution can occur in either sex but is more common in men. In the **gynoid** pattern, the so-called pear shape, most body fat is carried on the hips and thighs. This pattern can also occur in either sex but is seen more often in women.

In terms of disease risk, android obesity carries a much higher risk for hypertension, Type 2 diabetes, and heart disease than does gynoid obesity. Thus, given two people with exactly the same degree of obesity, the one with android obesity probably will have greater health problems. In android obesity, body fat can be stored under the abdominal muscle (**visceral fat**) or over the muscle and under the skin (**subcutaneous fat**). Visceral fat is associated with greater health risks than subcutaneous fat. Among those with android obesity, those with more abdominal visceral fat are at greater risk than those with subcutaneous abdominal fat. The **waist-to-hip ratio** measures this risk. In general, men with a waist-to-hip ratio of greater than 1.0 and women with a ratio greater than 0.8 are considered to have an excess accumulation of fat in their abdomen.

Although waist-to-hip ratio is a useful tool, health professionals often use waist circumference alone as an accurate predictor of disease risk. Waist circumference may be more effective in determining levels of risk than BMI alone. Risk increases with a waist measurement greater than 40 in. for men and 35 in. for women. This is of particular concern, because the most recent CDC data indicate that the average adult waist circumference is 39 in. for men and 36.5 in. for women.

> **Before you go on . . .**
> 1. How is BMI used to define obesity?
> 2. Why were the recommendations for BMI set where they are?
> 3. What are the recommendations for body fat percentage for men and women, and why are they different?
> 4. How does body fat distribution affect risk of disease?

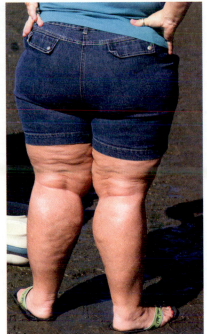

The android pattern of obesity, most common in men, describes those who tend to carry fat in the abdomen. The gynoid pattern of obesity, more common in women, describes those who tend to carry body fat in the hips and thighs. Android obesity is associated with greater health risks than is gynoid obesity.

## APPLICATION TIP

You can determine whether your body fat distribution is putting you at risk by measuring your waist just above the hip bone, with the tape measure snug but not compressed. Women with a waist of 35 in. or greater and men with a waist of 40 in. or greater are at a greater health risk than those with smaller waist measurements.

## Obesity: An Alarming Trend

Years from now, when health historians look back on this time in history they will see a society that grew increasingly obese. In 1995, obesity **prevalence**, or the number of cases in a given population, in each of the fifty states was less than 20 percent. In 2000, only twenty-eight states had obesity prevalence rates of less than 20 percent, and by 2005 there were only four! In 2008 Colorado was the only state to have an obesity prevalence of less than 20 percent. Also in 2008, thirty-two states had obesity prevalence rates equal to or greater than 25 percent, with 6 of those greater than 30 percent (Alabama, Oklahoma, Tennessee, South Carolina, Mississippi, and West Virginia). (See Figure 7.8.)

### Obesity Trends* among U.S. Adults
### BRFSS, 1990, 1999, 2008
(*BMI ≥30, or about 30 lbs. overweight for 5ft. 4in. person)

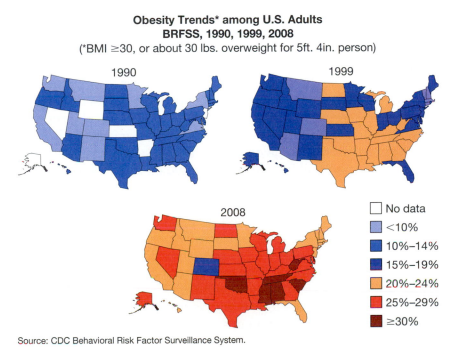

1990          1999

2008

☐ No data
■ <10%
■ 10%–14%
■ 15%–19%
■ 20%–24%
■ 25%–29%
■ ≥30%

Source: CDC Behavioral Risk Factor Surveillance System.

**Figure 7.8** Increasing prevalence of obesity (BMI ≥ 30) in adults in the United States.

**Figure 7.9** Growth in prevalence of overweight and obese adults and children.

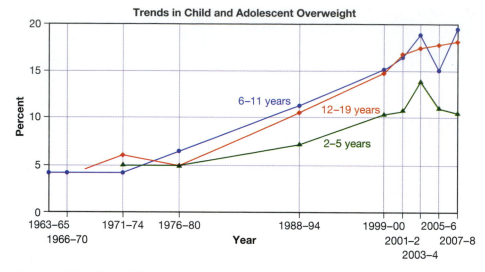

Note: Overweight is defined as BMI ≥ gender- and weight-specific 95th percentile from the 2000 CDC Growth Charts.
Source: National Health Examinations Surveys II (ages 6–11) and III (ages 12–17), National Health and Nutrition Examination Surveys I, II, III and 1999–2004, NCHS, CDC.

---

This trend of rapid growth in the percentages reflects the rate for children as well as adults (see Figure 7.9). According to the National Health and Nutrition Examination Survey (NHANES), 17 percent of children and adolescents age 2–19 (more than 12.5 million) were overweight in 2008. Smaller studies report that 21.6 percent of college students are overweight, and 4.9 percent are obese. The data suggest that more college students are overweight than adolescents, indicating that college may be a time of increased risk of weight gain. See Nutrition and Lifestages for information on "the Freshman Fifteen."

### Nutrition and Lifestages
#### "The Freshman Fifteen"—fact or fiction?

Students entering their first year of college are faced with many stresses and changes, including changes in eating and exercise behavior. A common fear among college students is the reported high risk of gaining 15 lbs. during their freshman year—the dreaded "Freshman Fifteen." Despite the common belief that this is as much a reality of college life as all-night studying and questionable cafeteria food, little documented evidence indicates that a 15-lb. weight gain is common. But don't breathe a sigh of relief yet. Although research has not found that freshmen gain an average of 15 lbs., it does support the perspective that many freshmen add weight. In fact, studies report average weight gains of anywhere from 2 to 9 lbs. Why the weight gain? The stress of handling social life and studies that are new and more challenging; being away from parents for the first time; an environment with unlimited access to food; and a less regular eating, sleeping, and exercising schedule can quickly lead to weight gain. In addition, if you use food to soothe emotional needs that may result from dealing with all of these changes, putting on 15 lbs. is quite possible.

You can do some things to prevent weight gain during college or any other time. You are already using one of the most important prevention techniques—educating yourself about nutrition and health. Here are a few more tips you can use:

- Stay active.
- Stock your dorm fridge with healthy snacks such as yogurt, vegetables, and fruit.
- Don't skip meals.
- Limit your intake of alcohol.
- Limit your intake of high-calorie beverages such as sodas and energy drinks.
- Be aware of what you are eating.
- Have a plan for days when you may be too busy to eat regular meals, such as stocking your backpack with healthy snacks for between classes.
- Watch portion sizes; (this is tough to do when eating every meal in an "all you can eat" cafeteria, but it is a must!)
- Get enough sleep; it helps to go to sleep at the same time every night, regardless of your class and/or work schedule. ■

CDC data from 2008 indicate that 33.8 percent of adults in the United States were obese and 68 percent are either overweight or obese with almost 6 percent being extremely obese. The data also suggest that significant differences in obesity among ethnic groups remain. The prevalence of overweight was highest in Mexican American children compared to black and white children. Among adults, similar differences existed. Approximately 33 percent of white adults were obese, compared to 44 percent of non-Hispanic black adults and 39 percent of Mexican American. Is obesity as a major health concern limited to the United States? The following Global Nutrition feature provides the answer.

###  Global Nutrition
#### *Obesity as a global issue*

Contrary to popular belief, the obesity epidemic is not just an issue for the United States and other industrialized societies. According to the World Health Organization, more than 1 billion adults worldwide are overweight, and at least 300 million of them are clinically obese. Current obesity levels range from less than 5 percent in China, Japan, and certain African nations to more than 75 percent in urban Samoa. But even in relatively low-prevalence countries such as China, rates have risen to almost 20 percent in some cities.

Childhood obesity is already an epidemic in some areas of the world and on the rise in others. An estimated 22 million children under age 5 are estimated to be overweight worldwide. The problem is global and increasingly extends into the developing world; for example, in Thailand the prevalence of obesity in 5-to-12-year-olds rose from 12.2 percent to 15.6 percent in just two years. ■

Obesity and its associated health risks have dramatically increased health care costs in the United States. In 2008, more than 147 billion dollars were spent in the United States for medical costs related to obesity. To these costs can be added time lost from work and spending on weight loss methods. This is

Some colleges are addressing the dreaded weight gain that many college students experience by providing state-of-the-art fitness facilities, by making physical education classes as a requirement for graduation, and by offering healthy menu selections in the cafeterias. Dickinson College of Carlisle, Pennsylvania, was recently named the nation's fittest college by *Men's Fitness* magazine. What is your school doing on the fitness front?

**Want to know more?**
You can review a complete list of statistics related to obesity, by going to the text website at http://webcom8.grtxle .com/nutrition and clicking on the Chapters button. Select Chapter 7.

Escalating obesity rates are a problem not only in the United States. This Australian family spends approximately one-third of their weekly food budget ($118) on meat, fish, and eggs, and almost $30 per week on fast food—the same amount they spend on fruits, vegetables, and nuts.

no longer predominantly an adult concern. The trend toward obesity in younger people is alarming as more and more children and teens are diagnosed with health problems, such as heart disease and Type 2 diabetes, which used to occur much later in life. For more information on children and obesity, see Chapter 17.

**Before you go on . . .**

1. Which diseases are associated with obesity?
2. List the health risks associated with being underweight.
3. What can be said about cultural differences in obesity prevalence around the world?
4. What can be interpreted from the U-shaped curve that represents the relationship between obesity and disease? (See Figure 7.5.)

## Obesity: Choice or Destiny?

While personal food and activity choices have a great deal to do with whether someone becomes overweight, choice is not the only factor. Weight is a complex phenomenon influenced by physiological factors such as hunger, appetite, digestion, satiety, and how and where fat is stored. Psychological factors also play a role; food is often used as a coping mechanism to help people deal with stress, depression, loneliness, and other personal issues. Lifestyle behaviors such as what types of food and how much you eat also play a big role. Social and economic factors also influence weight. Even lack of sleep may contribute to weight gain. Our society has changed dramatically over the past fifty years. The automobile and suburban sprawl, fewer jobs requiring physical labor, lack of physical education in our schools, fewer opportunities for physical activity in our communities, greater opportunity for nonphysical activities such as computer and video games, and a proliferation of inexpensive high-calorie convenience foods have had an impact on weight and health.

# Causes of Obesity

While the increasing numbers of obese and overweight adults and children have raised public awareness of the issue, the causes of obesity are still not completely understood. It is a subject of ongoing scientific research and debate with widely varying views and opinions. Some argue it is strictly genetic, others say it is lifestyle, many argue it is environmental. Modern research reports often offer conflicting information about the issue. The popular media further add to the confusion in their effort to make quick and strongly worded headlines from the already confusing literature. Regardless, one thing is for sure: obesity is a complex multifaceted problem with no easy cause or solution.

## Energetics

As a simple explanation obesity is caused by a positive energy balance, eating more calories than you burn. We discussed the various sides of the "energy equation" in the beginning of the chapter. It makes sense that an unbalanced energy equation is connected to weight gain. Especially when you consider that statistics suggest that the average adult gains about 20 lbs from age 25–55. If you assume that all the weight gain comes from fat tissue with an energy density of 3500 kcal/lb, that equals 70,000 kcal of stored fat over the 30 years period. This is accumulated from an excess of just 97 kcal per day. So if you can increase energy expenditure by just 100 kcal per day perhaps you can offset this excess and prevent the weight gain statistically seen over time.

## Fat Tissue

**Set point theory** says that the body is programmed to gravitate toward a particular weight; the metabolism may adjust upward or downward to ensure that weight is neither lost nor gained. So if a person attempts to drastically reduce caloric intake, his or her metabolism slows down in an attempt to maintain the "set point weight" on fewer calories. Conversely, if a person overeats, metabolism increases perhaps by increasing the thermic effect of food to use the extra calories to prevent weight gain. This may help explain why some people cannot lose weight even when reducing caloric intake. Set point theory appears to have some merit but cannot be entirely true, as some people do change their set point in either direction by consistently eating less (or more) than they burn. So there must be more to how our bodies achieve a certain weight.

## Environment

While the cause of obesity is complex and multidimensional, one thing is for sure, as a society we eat more and exercise less and this has directly paralleled the increase in obesity prevalence over time. A study by Kant et al. used data collected over four consecutive large scale studies of 39,000 U.S. adults to show that increasing intake in the quantity and energy density of foods paralleled the prevalence of obesity of the U.S. population. In addition, similar studies have shown that rising car ownership and increasing television viewing, which are an indirect way to measure level of physical activity, have also closely paralleled trends in obesity. A study by Dietz et al. showed that prevalence of obesity increased by 2 percent for each additional hour of television viewed. There is also evidence that demonstrates the availability and price of food, particularly healthy foods such as fruits and vegetables, significantly impact food intake.

For example in many lower income neighborhoods there are more fast food establishments than there are stores to purchase fresh fruits and vegetables. In addition to being more readily available, the higher fat, higher calorie fast food tends to be less expensive to healthier alternatives. Lack of safe walking and biking routes, the poor quality of local parks and decreased physical activity in schools have also been suggested as contributing factors to the obesity epidemic particularly among those of lower socioeconomic status.

# Genetics

We know that obesity is the product of genetics and environment. Studies that compare identical twins separated at birth and raised in different homes reveal that they are likely to have similar body weights despite their different environments. We know that obesity often runs in families, but many influences other than genes also run in families, including lifestyle practices and attitudes toward food and health. It has been said that one's environment allows the genetics for obesity to "express" itself. In other words, while we cannot do much about our genetics, we have a tremendous degree of freedom in choosing our lifestyle and environment.

## Diet-Induced Thermogenesis

The thermic effect of food (TEF) is known to be different in obese and lean people. In lean people, metabolism speeds up after eating, but in obese people, it does not appear to speed up as much. Although this difference accounts for only a small discrepancy in energy expended, researchers are still investigating the potential ramifications of the phenomenon.

## Fat Tissue

Often overlooked is the fact that fat tissue is an *endocrine organ,* meaning that it secretes hormones. When fat cells contain too much fat, these secretions are disturbed. Fat tissue produces hormones related to hunger and appetite. **Leptin**, for example, is released into the blood to signal the brain that the body has had enough to eat. When body fat increases, it triggers an increase in leptin and the brain is signaled to decrease appetite to bring body fat back to a desired level. In turn, when body fat is low and leptin is low, the brain is signaled to increase appetite. Obese individuals may not produce enough leptin relative to their body fat, or perhaps the brain does not respond to the leptin that is in the blood. Either way, although leptin is important, it explains only the alterations in hunger and appetite that may contribute to obesity and not all of the other factors.

Food Addiction? Obesity may be caused by things other than larger portion sizes and decreasing physical activity. There is some evidence to indicate that, in certain people, obesity may be a direct result of a food addiction. New studies have focused on a chemical in the brain called *dopamine* that is released in association with pleasure and reward. If there is a disturbance in its function, obesity may result. This would explain the behavior of some obese people who are so driven by food and the pleasure that they associate with eating that food comes before pursuit of other rewarding behaviors, similar to the experiences of people with drug and alcohol addictions. Food addiction and its role in the development of obesity remains a topic of controversy due to the fact that hunger, appetite, and body weight are controlled by many systems and chemicals in the body, not just dopamine. Furthermore, many experts contend there is no such thing as food addiction and that the term is simply an overuse of the word *addiction*. Nevertheless, it is now one of many theories regarding causes of obesity.

We still have a lot to learn before we can concretely determine what makes people gain weight. We do know that eating more than you burn causes a positive energy balance and weight gain. We know that it is easier to eat more than you burn if you don't exercise, if you spend a lot of time on the computer or playing video games or watching TV, if you eat highly processed foods high in sugars and fats, if you eat a lot of high-fat foods, and if you genetically burn fewer calories. So with the answers we have available at this time, the best solution is to prevent weight gain or to promote weight loss through a combination of a well-balanced diet of nonprocessed foods and regular exercise.

*So what really makes us gain weight?*

### ■ What's Hot

*Obesity may be contagious!*

A study published in the *New England Journal of Medicine* in July 2007 suggests that an individual's social connections may have a stronger impact on obesity than geographical location or genetics. The study tracked 12,000 people over a 32-year period and found that a person's chances of becoming obese increased 57 percent if a friend was obese, 40 percent if a sibling was, and 37 percent if a spouse

According to David B. Allison, PhD, (director of the University of Alabama at Birmingham Nutrition Obesity Research Center) and his team, in addition to too much food and too little exercise, there are 10 causes of obesity that, while having some small effects when acting alone, have magnified effects when acting together.

#### 10 Causes of Obesity

The Alabama group puts forth these 10 "additional explanations" for obesity:

1. **Sleep debt.** Getting too little sleep can increase body weight. Today's Americans get less shut-eye than ever.

2. **Pollution.** Hormones control body weight. And many of today's pollutants affect our hormones.

3. **Air conditioning.** You have to burn calories if your environment is too hot or too cold for comfort. But more people than ever live and work in temperature-controlled homes and offices.

4. **Decreased smoking.** Smoking reduces weight. Americans smoke much less than they used to.

5. **Medicine.** Many different drugs—including contraceptives, steroid hormones, diabetes drugs, some antidepressants, and blood pressure drugs—can cause weight gain. Use of these drugs is on the upswing.

6. **Population age, ethnicity.** Middle-aged people and Hispanic-Americans tend to be more obese than young European-Americans. Americans are getting older and more Hispanic.

7. **Older moms.** There's some evidence that the older a woman is when she gives birth, the higher her child's risk of obesity. American women are giving birth at older and older ages.

8. **Ancestors' environment.** Some influences may go back two generations. Environmental changes that made a grandparent obese may "through a fetally driven positive feedback loop" visit obesity on the grandchildren.

9. **Obesity linked to fertility.** There's some evidence obese people are more fertile than lean ones. If obesity has a genetic component, the percentage of obese people in the population should increase.

10. **Unions of obese spouses.** Obese women tend to marry obese men. If there are fewer thin people around—and if obesity has a genetic component—there will be still more obese people in the next generation.

**Want to know more?**
Read the complete summary of this interesting and provocative study by visiting the text website at http://webcom8.grtxle .com/nutrition and clicking on the Chapters button. Select Chapter 7.

---

**APPLICATION TIP**

Tips for weight loss

- Create a deficit of about 500 calories per day by:

    increasing exercise.
    decreasing portion sizes.
    avoiding beverages that are high in calories.

- Set a realistic weight loss of 1–2 lbs. per week.
- Eat a balanced diet.
- Eat small regular meals (about every three to four hours).
- Eat breakfast.
- Emphasize the health benefits of weight loss, not the pounds on the scale.
- Remember: this is a lifestyle change, not a short-term fix.

How much does abundance, availability, and choice contribute to the rapid rise of obesity in the United States? What health consequences do you think will result if this trend continues?

was. In the closest friendships, the risk almost tripled. It appears to be more than just people who like similar things hanging out together. The study concluded that, when a person is part of a social network of people who are obese, that individual's idea of what is an acceptable weight increases. This is not to say that if you have overweight friends you should find new ones, but it does suggest that social relationships do have a strong impact on our eating behavior. Therefore, can one assume that this behavior can be influenced in a healthy direction as well? In other words, could you take the initiative to make healthy eating and exercising the socially acceptable norm in your social network? ■

**Before you go on . . .**
1. What does it mean to say that environment allows the genetics of obesity to express themselves?
2. Explain set point theory.
3. Explain the role of leptin in regulating body fat.
4. What is the best solution for the obesity epidemic?

# Weight Management: A Balancing Act

## Hunger, Appetite, and Satiety

Eating behavior is a combination of physiological and psychological factors. When your body needs fuel (food), your stomach and intestines send signals to the brain. The terms *hunger* and *appetite* are often used interchangeably, but they really mean two different things. Put simply, hunger is the need to eat and appetite is the desire to eat.

**Hunger** normally refers to the physiological mechanisms that determine how much and when we eat. This is a complex and not yet entirely understood combination of systems in the body. Low blood sugar levels and low glycogen (carbohydrate stores) levels are believed to increase hunger. However, the interaction of hormones, stomach distension, and nervous system stimuli also make our stomachs rumble. What complicates the clear understanding of the definition of hunger is our "desire" to eat. How many times have you actually felt "hungry," as in your stomach growling, when you ate dessert after a meal?

**Appetite** normally refers to the psychological mechanisms that determine how much we eat and is therefore not the same as hunger. You can have an appetite for a certain food without having any physiological hunger. The sight or smell of food can stimulate your appetite. Talking about food or reading about it can have an effect on appetite, too. A connection between food and an event or memory can increase appetite (such as the desire for pumpkin pie around Thanksgiving or popcorn at the movies). Satiety, discussed in Chapter 4, is the feeling you have when you are no longer hungry or when your appetite has been satisfied.

Satiety signals take a while to reach the brain, so if you eat too quickly, you may overeat—at least in terms of what your body needs to satisfy its hunger. Satiety can also refer to how long you stay satisfied between meals. Many factors influence how long you stay satisfied after a meal. The length of time food stays in your stomach affects how quickly you will be hungry again. Foods that are high in protein have a high satiety value. Foods that are high in fiber also have a high satiety value. Typically, people who eat a lot of vegetables, fruit,

# Real People, Other Voices

### Student:
#### Matt McKellar
University of Nevada-Las Vegas

The first step for Amber should be to realize that the changes she needs to make are permanent lifestyle changes. In order for her to be successful, she must make the time and effort to stick to these changes.

I advise Amber to immediately drop fast-food eating and switch her meals to low-fat foods rich with carbohydrates and proteins. The low-fat aspect will reduce the caloric density of her food, while the carbohydrates will keep her energetic and strong. Furthermore, it is important that a majority of the carbohydrates she consumes be whole grain in the form of breads and pastas, and the rest of the carbs come from fruits and vegetables rich in essential vitamins and minerals. The protein, with exercise, will ensure that Amber's body is promoting the growth and maintenance of lean muscle tissue. Building muscle will increase Amber's basal metabolic rate; thus she will burn more calories at rest than she does now. Part of a close family, Amber has a great tool for motivating herself to exercise. I advise her to begin family exercise routines such as hiking, roller-blading, walks in the park with the dog, or whatever recreational activities exist in her area. Together, clean, wholesome foods and exercise will help create the deficit in calories needed to lose fat while maintaining proper energy and nutrition. Another bonus is that this change in diet will alleviate her son's weight problem and improve her husband's health.

### Instructor:
#### Melanie Tracy Burns
Eastern Illinois University

Although Amber does have several strikes against her—such as work commitments, a busy lifestyle with two children, and tiredness at the end of the day—she does have a strong desire to change. This desire to change is a major factor that can serve as motivation to modify her lifestyle as well as that of her family.

Where to start? Amber needs to think of this, not as a diet—punishable by no weight loss if not followed—but as a healthy lifestyle plan for the entire family. She needs to take the time to clearly identify the barriers to healthy eating and then develop a workable plan that incorporates small behavior changes. These behavior changes can be as minor as switching to a lower fat milk, eating fruits and vegetables as snacks, or not eating after dinner. Including the children in meal preparation can be a great learning experience as well as serving as quality family time.

When the whole family is involved, healthy eating, not the weight loss, is the driving force. Dad, even though he is at a healthy weight, could still benefit from healthy eating and can serve as a very positive role model for the children. For additional tips, Amber can go online at www.kidnetic.com for more information on healthy eating that includes the entire family.

### Registered Dietitian:
#### Rick Weissinger, M.S., R.D.
Middletown, DE

My advice to Amber would be to stop dieting—stop looking for a quick solution to her weight predicament. The problem with diets is that they don't involve making *permanent* reductions in energy intake and increases in energy output. Dieting, as opposed to making permanent changes over time, involves trying to do too many things at once: cut out sugars and excess fats; watch calories; reduce portions; and eliminate snack foods, junk foods, fast foods, all of which leave the dieter feeling overwhelmed.

A better way to lose weight (and keep it off) involves making only one or two important changes in diet and activity at a time. These changes should be decided by Amber, not by a health professional, because evidence suggests that people are more likely to successfully change when they are empowered rather than directed. However, in counseling Amber I would emphasize that some changes (such as replacing sugar-containing drinks with sugar-free varieties and reducing added fats) are fairly easy to accomplish yet can significantly impact weight. Regardless of which changes she makes, I would encourage Amber to continue until she's comfortable with these changes before proceeding to the next ones. However, because working on both diet and exercise is difficult and food is so pleasurable, Amber should reinforce these new eating and activity patterns by using nonfood rewards. Amber can adjust for any decrease in calories in her husband's diet by buying him calorie- and nutrient-dense snacks (e.g., nuts, dried fruit).

and whole grains—all foods rich in fiber—do not get hungry as soon after eating as people who eat highly processed foods. Fats have a high satiety value but have twice as many calories as carbohydrates and protein, so they may not be the best choice when you are trying to lose weight.

## Weight Loss: What Doesn't Work

To date, treatments for obesity have not been very successful. In fact, most people who lose weight gain it back within a short time period. According to a report by the Institute of Medicine, typically two-thirds or more of weight lost by an individual will be regained within one year, and almost all will be regained within five years. Many people lose and regain weight many times in their efforts to battle obesity. As discussed earlier, dieting can lead to a lower resting energy expenditure, which will make it hard to lose weight in the future. Regardless of any negative physical health consequences related to losing and regaining weight, the psychological consequences and negative impact on self-esteem are unquestionable.

### APPLICATION TIP

A key to weight loss is to consume fewer calories than you burn, but when you are hungry this can be difficult. You can use some tricks to help stay fuller longer. Dr. Barbara Rolls from Penn State University has published several books based on her research with different types of food and how they influence hunger and satiety, and thereby influence weight loss. She suggests adding fruits and vegetables to meals and consuming whole-grain foods such as brown rice, whole-wheat pasta, and whole-grain breads. She also suggests consuming water and/or soups with meals to increase fullness.

Which is which? They may look similar, but the pizza on the left is less dense in calories, with more vegetables and less cheese, than the pizza on the right. Overall, the left tray has 22 percent fewer calories for the same apparent volume of food.

Less fat, more filling. The tiny portion of ordinary macaroni and cheese on the left contains 330 calories. So does the huge bowl of this comfort food made using an alternate recipe, at right. The latter was formulated by substituting whole-wheat pasta for regular, nonfat milk for whole, and lowfat cheese for regular. In addition, the lower-calorie recipe uses less butter and cheese and boosts its volume with spinach and tomatoes.

### Want to know more?

If you would like to more thoroughly explore the recommendations of Dr. Barbara Rolls and her Volumetrics eating plan, go the text website at http://webcom8.grtxle.com/nutrition and click on the Chapters button. Select Chapter 7.

### ■ Nutrition and Culture

*Obesity—socially acceptable discrimination?*

One of the most painful problems associated with obesity is social rejection. Just as some people discriminate against those of another race, religion, age, or sexual orientation, others discriminate against people—adults as well as children—who are overweight. In fact, it almost appears socially acceptable to joke about body size or to accept common stereotypes about obese people.

Although being overweight was once a sign of wealth, today obese people are often judged as lazy and lacking willpower. In fact, obesity is a complex medical condition with intricate psychological, physiological, and emotional dimensions. Unfortunately, some people who harbor prejudice against the obese are those to whom the obese look for support and encouragement—doctors, nurses, teachers, coaches, employers, and even friends, parents, siblings, and other relatives. Prejudice against overweight can be a deterrent to weight loss because the overweight person often feels down and helpless after receiving such negativity.

Peer rejection may be an obese child's first encounter with discrimination. Research shows that a bias toward thinness is formed by age 8 and in some cases as early as age 3. In one study 96 percent of overweight adolescent girls reported having negative experiences related to their weight, such as being called names, teased, and mocked throughout elementary, middle, and high school. Among children and adolescents, cruel jokes and teasing can cause permanent scars on the psyche that endure long after any excess weight may disappear. In fact, teasing is one of the risk factors for the later development of an eating disorder. (See Chapter 15 for more on eating disorders.)

Studies show that employers are less likely to hire an overweight person even when his or her credentials are the same as those of a thinner person. Research also reveals that, in general, doctors and nurses—even those who treat and conduct research in obesity—are as prejudiced against the obese as is society at large. Ironically, even obese and overweight people *themselves* report dislike toward overweight people as a group. The pervasiveness of this prejudice shows that despite our growing knowledge about the causes of obesity as a disease, negative feelings toward obese people are deeply ingrained in our culture. Ingrained or not, there is no excuse for making people feel bad about themselves. Next time you hear someone telling "fat jokes" or saying something negative about another person's size, remember that it is just as unacceptable as saying something negative about someone's race—not to mention that there is a person on the other side of that comment whose feelings are being hurt, perhaps for a lifetime. ■

If diets work, then why are there so many? Why does the dieting industry make so much money? If diets did what they said they did, people would go on them, lose weight, and thereafter never need to diet. The dieting industry is based on its failure rate instead of its success. Think about it. If diets were successful, people wouldn't have to keep spending money on new ones, and the industry would not be able to support the never-ending list of diet plans. Experts have estimated that at any given time, approximately 50 percent of women and 25 percent of men are trying to lose weight, with an annual expenditure of billions of dollars on weight-loss treatments. Not surprisingly, the number of new diets has increased in recent years. In fact, if you

The diet industry is a multibillion dollar industry that seems to thrive on the failure of its products. With 95 percent of dieters ultimately failing (eventually regaining their lost weight), why does this industry continue to grow?

search book titles on Amazon.com using the term "weight loss," you will get more than 43,000 matches, including *Weight Loss Surgery for Dummies* and *The Wine Lover's Diet.*

The good news is that dieters may be paying more attention to current recommendations. Data from an independent company that analyzes Internet searches suggest that in comparison to 2004, dieters in 2005 were less focused on fad diets and more interested in a more scientific, balanced approach to dieting and fitness. The shares of Internet searches for "glycemic index," "body mass index," and "weight training" were up 161 percent, 67 percent, and 61 percent, respectively, for the week ending December 31, 2005, compared to the week ending January 1, 2005. In the same time period, searches for "Atkins diet" and "South Beach diet" were down by 12 percent and 36 percent, respectively.

The variety of diets is limitless and includes high-protein, low-carbohydrate, high-carbohydrate, and low-fat diets; diets based on the glycemic index; diets based on blood type; and hundreds of others, most of which limit or eliminate consumption of a particular food group. Of course, they can all work, for a while. In fact, almost any weight-loss plan can work, for as long as you can stick to it. Losing weight is usually not the biggest problem; keeping it off is the real challenge. In the long run, diets do not work. In fact, in studies of many diets and commercially available programs, a long-term success rate of 3 percent is considered good. In addition to their lack of success, most fad diets are unhealthy, disruptive to social and family life, and, ultimately, boring.

## Why Don't Diets Work?

*Most of the diet books and plans don't recommend the same thing as MyPyramid and the other recommendations we've been talking about in class. It's really confusing! How can we know what to believe?*

The advice given in most diet books and plans contrasts sharply with recommendations we have discussed thus far in this book—with good reason. The recommendations in this book are based on scientific information. Such information suggests that the number one reason why diets do not work is that they do not involve permanent lifestyle changes. In order to lose weight and keep it off, you have to make permanent changes in your eating and exercise habits. In addition, most diets do not allow for real-life situations such as holidays, celebrations, and dining out. Many categorize foods as "good" or "bad" and encourage dieters to eliminate certain foods. This, of course, is not realistic for a lifetime. Table 7.8 provides information about some of the problems associated with fad diets.

Many diets instruct dieters to follow extremely low-calorie meal plans, which may lower their metabolism. When this happens, the dieter ends up needing fewer calories for REE (discussed earlier). Because they need fewer calories for basic functions, it becomes more difficult to burn more calories than they take in, which is the bottom line for losing weight. Lowering the metabolism also means that any short-term weight loss will likely be regained.

Loss of body water compounds the situation. Diets that result in an initial rapid weight loss do so from a loss of body water and lean muscle mass. The only way to lose fat is to burn it off, and that takes time. A pound of body fat contains about 3,500 calories. Thus, to lose a pound, you must create a deficit of 3,500 calories. The average person cannot create such a large caloric deficit in a day healthfully. So when you lose more than one or two pounds of weight a week, much of the weight lost is composed of something other than fat—that is, water and muscle.

Although many dieters are encouraged by such a rapid weight loss on the scale, water loss is not permanent or desirable. In addition, losing muscle is not desirable, if only because muscle is metabolically active tissue that uses

| Table 7.8 | Problems with Common Fad Dieting Techniques |
|-----------|---------------------------------------------|

| Technique | Effect |
|-----------|--------|
| Skipping meals | Lowers REE |
| Fasting | Lowers REE |
| Restricting calories with no exercise involved | Loss of lean body mass, which lowers REE |
| Eliminating entire food groups | Likelihood of nutritional inadequacy; poor long-term compliance |
| Restricting variety of foods | Likelihood of nutritional inadequacy; poor long-term compliance |
| Relying on a single food | Certain nutritional inadequacy; poor long-term compliance |
| Liquid diet | Low satiety; nutritional inadequacy; not sustainable over the long term |
| Foods with so-called magical properties (for example, "fat burners") | Not proven to be effective |
| Very low-calorie diet | Lowers REE; poor long-term compliance |
| Unusual food choices or eating patterns | Nutritional inadequacy; poor long-term compliance |

**Want to know more?**
If you would like to learn more about fad diets and review some of the more popular ones, go to the text website at http://webcom8.grtxle.com/nutrition and click on the Chapters button. Select Chapter 7.

calories. Losing muscle lowers metabolism. And to make matters worse, if you lose a large amount of weight from muscle, typically you gain back fat weight before muscle. So even though your weight may go back to being the same as before you started dieting, in terms of body composition you are actually fatter and have a potentially lower metabolism because of lost muscle.

Simply put, most diets fail because they are not lifetime approaches to healthful eating. To be successful, an eating plan must be something you can live with for the rest of your life. Nutrition and health care professionals now recognize that people who are obese have a chronic health condition. Just as a person with Type 1 diabetes must take insulin the rest of his or her life, a person with obesity must treat his or her weight condition over a lifetime.

## Fasting and Skipping Meals

Fasting or meal skipping is not a good idea. The physiological need to eat is one of the strongest drives in the body. Sooner or later, even the most strong-willed among us will not be able to follow an extremely restrictive diet and will eventually have to eat, maybe even to the point of overeating. Have you ever gone all day without eating, or without eating very much, and come home at night ravenous, feeling that you could eat anything and everything? Many dieters consciously choose a one-meal-a-day plan. Other people fast by accident—skipping meals because they are busy, run out of time, or do not plan ahead. In either case, three things usually happen: First, your metabolism drops. As we've seen, a slower metabolism means you need fewer calories to maintain your weight, so it becomes more difficult to lose pounds. Second, your body often reflexively responds to food deprivation with overeating when food becomes available. And when you get that hungry, making wise food choices usually goes out the window. You are too hungry to care what you eat. Third, you train yourself not to eat. You learn to ignore and suppress your hunger, and you get better at it over time. Eventually, you become less in touch with your body's internal hunger and satiety cues and less responsive to them.

### Very Low-Calorie Diets (VLCD)

Diets that are less than about 1,200 calories and often as low as 800 calories per day present the same problems as fasting and meal skipping: lowered metabolism, increased bingeing, and training oneself not to eat. Although this type of diet is sometimes used for extremely obese people with urgent medical problems, it is not recommended, as obtaining adequate nutrients from such a low caloric intake is extremely difficult.

## What Does Work

Once weight loss has been maintained for two to five years, long-term success seems more likely. Studies from the National Weight Control Registry suggest that those who are successful in maintaining weight loss share some commonalities in the way they lost the weight. They ate a low-fat diet (less than 30 percent of calories from fat), they regularly monitored their weight and food intake, they ate breakfast, and they participated in physical activity. As mentioned previously, exercise is the key to maintaining weight loss.

### The Old-Fashioned Way—Eat Less, Burn More

The secret to successful weight loss is simple in principle, but more difficult to actually do. You must burn more than you eat, and you must be patient—weight loss takes a while. If the governing equation of energy balance is that energy intake equals energy expenditure, then it stands to reason that the way to lose weight is to go into *negative* energy balance. You can achieve this most effectively by working both sides of the equation—increasing expenditure and reducing intake just enough, without going to the extreme and starving yourself. Creating a deficit of about 500 calories per day is realistic and appropriate as long as by decreasing calories you do not go below the minimum of about 1,200 calories for women and 1,500 for men. Of course, if you are exercising, these numbers are too low. One of the easiest ways to decrease intake is to decrease portion sizes.

### Physical Activity

The best way to begin a weight-loss program is to increase energy expenditure by incorporating more activity into your daily routine and by setting time aside for exercise. Parking the car farther away and walking, taking the stairs instead of the elevator, and walking instead of driving are simple ways to increase your daily activity. It pays to make these simple lifestyle changes even if you are participating in a full-fledged exercise program.

Remember that you do not need to be continuously active to reap the benefits of exercise. Thirty minutes of activity, no matter how you divide it, burns the same number of calories. A thirty-minute walk is the same as three ten-minute walks in terms of energy expenditure. For optimum cardiovascular benefits, however, you must exercise vigorously enough to increase your heart rate for at least twenty minutes at a time. Although weight lifting often does not burn as many calories as aerobic exercise (running, walking, cycling, and so on), it does have a positive long-term effect on body weight. Recall that metabolism comes largely from muscle. Thus, activities that build muscle contribute to boosting metabolism because muscles burn calories all the time, whether you are using them or not. Even more fundamental than building muscle is simply preserving the muscle mass you already have. As discussed earlier, muscle is often lost when dieting. Therefore, if you include weight training in your exercise program, you will lose less muscle while losing weight. (See Chapter 14 for more on exercise.)

The best approach to exercise for the purpose of weight loss is to engage in a combination of activities—strength training to build muscle and raise metabolism, and aerobic activity to burn calories. And remember, as important as physical activity is for weight loss, it is even more important for the maintenance of that loss.

### Calorie Intake

If you want to lose weight, you must reduce your caloric intake. A balanced diet integrating all food groups is viewed as necessary to promote long-term adherence to a weight management program. There are a few little tricks to doing this, but for the most part you need to look at your current intake and assess where you are overconsuming. As far as the best distribution of fats, carbohydrates and proteins to achieve optimal weight loss, it appears that consistently reduced calorie diets will result in weight loss regardless of which macronutrient is emphasized. The bottom line is that it is best to stick to a macronutrient distribution that you are most likely to stick to. Therefore, if you can't "live without" pasta or steak, etc., don't try to, just limit the portions you consume. Don't forget to look at the calories in the beverages you consume.

Many people do not realize how many calories they drink in a day, so it is often the first place to look at cutting back. The awareness that the calories we drink contribute significantly to weight gain has caused some consumer groups to call for government legislation such as banning vending machines in public schools, BMI scanning in schools, or taxing the sale of sodas. What's your opinion? (See the You Decide feature.)

After assessing how many calories you drink, figure out how many calories you need (see the Self-Assessment feature earlier in the chapter). Then plan a diet incorporating all of the concepts we have discussed so far in this text. Include lots of fruits, vegetables, and whole grains; low-fat dairy choices; protein from lean meats and vegetable sources; and mostly monounsaturated and polyunsaturated fats. MyPyramid.gov is a great place to start when planning your diet (see Chapter 2). Of course, if you are trying to lose weight you will have less room for sweets and desserts, but you can enjoy these foods in moderation as long as you do not exceed your calorie needs.

### Behavior

When you are trying to lose weight it is just as important to examine *why* you eat as *what* you eat. Food intake is governed not only by internal cues of hunger and satiety, but also by social or emotional forces, not to mention just the pleasure of tasting something delicious. If you are like most people, you often eat food your body does not need. This nonphysiological eating may occur in social situations in which food is the medium of social exchange. We talk; we eat; we have fun. For example, holidays, celebrations, and cultural and religious traditions often center on food. Times like these are a big part of enjoying life. One way to control overeating in social situations is to use behavior modification techniques. Eating

Calories in the beverages you consume can add up quickly.

Because of the increase in the number of children who are overweight, many states are now requiring that students be screened for BMI to warn parents when their children are becoming overweight.

**Want to know more?**

You can explore the topic of obesity testing in schools in greater depth by going to the text website at http://webcom8 .grtxle.com/nutrition and clicking on the Chapters button. Select Chapter 7.

habits that can contribute to weight gain, such as snacking at work or eating ice cream before bed, also can be managed with behavior modification techniques. Figure 7.10 offers tips for weight loss.

Some people use food to handle stress, anger, sadness, or loneliness. They look to food as a way to relax, as a reward, or as a way to get the love they feel they are missing. Although food meets nutritional needs, it really cannot fulfill emotional needs. If you use food to cope with emotions and/or stress, seek the assistance of a psychologist or other mental health professional who can help you determine the root of your emotional needs and discover a new and healthy coping mechanism. To find a professional who specializes in this area, go to www.edreferral.com or www.something-fishy.org/treatmentfinder/.

## You Decide

*Is obesity a political issue?*

With an ever-increasing rate of obesity, especially in children, much debate has ensued as to the government's role in the treatment and prevention of this disease. Several states have responded by introducing legislation, such as the following:

1. Vending machine usage—Prohibiting types of foods and beverages sold in school and prohibiting access to vending machines at certain times

2. Body mass index (BMI) measured in school

3. Recess and physical education—State-mandated additional recess and physical education time

4. Obesity programs and education—Programs established as part of the curriculum

5. Obesity research—Legislation directing other institutions or groups to study obesity

6. Obesity treatment in health insurance—Expanding health insurance to cover obesity treatment where applicable

7. Obesity commissions—Commissions established to study obesity

8. Nutrition standards—Controlling the types of foods and beverages offered during school hours

Is it the government's or school's responsibility (or both) to warn parents when their children are overweight and therefore at an increased risk for diseases that may eventually cost taxpayers money? Or is this a case of the government interfering with a personal issue? ∎

## Medications to Treat Obesity

Drug therapy is often used as a component of weight-loss treatment, along with diet, physical activity, and behavior modification. Normally drug therapy is recommended only if the person is extremely obese or has immediately life-threatening health

**Figure 7.10**  Tips for Weight Loss.

Remember that weight loss must be individualized. Try these ideas and see what works for you.

***Have regular meals.*** In addition to keeping your metabolism high, eating small regular meals helps keep your intake low. Research shows that restrained eaters—those who suppress hunger to skip meals and starve themselves—frequently end up bingeing or overeating. This response is a physiological reaction to both hunger and deprivation. Eat three to six meals a day, spaced at fairly regular intervals, about three to four hours apart.

***Eat in a calm, conscious, and relaxed manner.*** As the Japanese dietary guidelines suggest, "Make all activities pertaining to food and eating pleasurable." Chew your food, so you get to taste it. Avoid stress-driven eating by paying more attention to what you are doing—eating—than to what is going on around you. By doing so, you will be more receptive to the internal cues that let you know when you have eaten enough. Make mealtime an oasis of peace and quiet. If time is short, calmly eat what you can.

***Make your life easier with limits.*** At the grocery store, make your food purchases wisely. Bring home only foods that will contribute to a healthy diet. Most people tend to overeat certain foods, usually sweets and salty snacks. You can control how much you eat of these foods by limiting serving size or frequency of consumption. You can limit a food to certain situations, such as having a beer only when out with friends.

***Learn to cook.*** Satisfying food offers a variety of tastes and textures. When its natural flavor has not been killed by overcooking or overprocessing, it does not require as much added fat or sugar to taste good. This food is hard to find in the commercial world. Your best bet is to cook it yourself. The Internet is an excellent resource for quick, easy, and healthy meals. Experiment and be ready for a few failures. The best cooks will tell you that making mistakes here and there is the best way to learn. See Chapter 2 for simple meal preparation tips.

***Make cooking easy.*** Try to cook when you have time, rather than when you are starved and rushed. Learn a repertoire of quick and easy meals. Prepare foods ahead of time as much as possible, and keep a good supply of basic ingredients in the pantry.

***Don't clean your plate.*** There are two ways to waste extra food: throw it out or eat it. If you feel guilty about throwing food out, save it for tomorrow's lunch or compost it. Either alternative is better than consuming unwanted and unneeded calories.

***When you cook, go for it.*** Cook as if you are cooking for several people and then portion the food out before you eat. Put all but the one portion you are eating into freezer-safe containers and refrigerate or freeze. You have just eliminated the excuse that you have no time to cook a healthy meal, as you will have several available throughout the week.

***Don't wait until you are famished to eat.*** You will tend to overeat if you wait until you are so hungry you will eat anything.

***Plan.*** If you know that you tend to get really hungry at 3 P.M. and end up heading for the candy to satisfy your hunger, eat a small healthy snack at 2:30 to prevent that hunger. If you know you are going to come home from work or class at 6 P.M. and be so hungry you will eat anything, keep a snack with you and eat it as you head home.

***Mix your meals.*** Carbohydrates, fats, and proteins together will help keep you fuller longer and will provide a balance of nutrients.

***Don't eat out of a pot or serving dish; fix your plate.*** People are more likely to overeat and not even be aware that they are doing so if they don't fix a set portion size on their plate.

***Don't read or watch TV while eating.*** You will tend to be distracted and may overeat as a result.

***Eat slowly.*** It takes time for the brain to get the signal that you are full. If you eat too fast, by the time you feel full you will end up being stuffed!

***Set realistic Goals.*** Don't attempt to lose a lot of weight in a short period of time just to fit into an outfit or to wear a swim suit for spring break. This sets you up for unhealthy weight loss techniques and for weight gain after the event.

*(Continued)*

**Figure 7.10** (*Conitnued*)

***Pick a plan you can stick with.*** This could be a sensible commercial weight loss program or one you design to fit your own lifestyle.

***Eat smaller portions.*** See Chapter 2.

***Decrease calories.***

***Beware of the calories you drink.***

***Exercise.*** Include regular cardiovascular and strength-training exercise.

***Don't eliminate any one food group.***

complications. Many medications are currently available. These drugs have potentially serious side effects; for example the prescription drug Alli is used to block fat absorption but it may also block absorption of other medications that require fat uptake to be properly absorbed such as birth control pills. Be sure to thoroughly explore all risks and benefits before taking any prescription medications. A physician should supervise anyone taking these medications. None of them are a permanent solution or can be used without changing behaviors.

## Surgery

Surgery is sometimes prescribed for the severely obese—those with a BMI of 40 or greater or a BMI of 35 or greater with other serious health conditions. Surgery as a treatment for obesity is growing in popularity, even with those who are not extremely obese. Surgery should be considered as a last resort for those who have been unable to lose weight through long-term dietary changes and physical activity. There are several types:

- **Vertical Sleeve Gastrectomy** is performed laproscopically. Most of the stomach is removed and a vertical sleeve or tube is fashioned from the remaining stomach. Because the stomach is so much smaller, patients are forced to eat less.
- **Adjustable Gastric Band Procedure** is a type of bariatric surgery that uses an adjustable band that fits around the upper part of the stomach. The band divides the upper portion of the stomach into a pouch and separates it from the lower. This limits food intake. The band can be adjusted to allow more or less food to pass through to individualize weight loss.
- **Roux-en-Y Gastric Bypass** is the most commonly performed bariatric surgery in the United States. In this procedure, stapling creates a small stomach

Many different surgical techniques are available for the treatment of obesity. Vertical sleeve gastrectomy (a), adjustable gastric band procedure (b), and gastric bypass, a more invasive procedure (c) are among the most commonly used techniques.

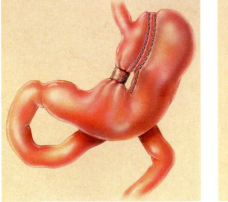
(a)

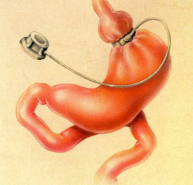
(b)

(c)

pouch. The remainder of the stomach is not removed, but is completely stapled shut and divided from the stomach pouch. The outlet from this newly formed pouch empties directly into the lower portion of the jejunum (part of the small intestine), thus creating some malabsorption as well as limiting intake.

Patients do lose weight as a result of the surgery; about one-third to one-half of those who have surgery lose about 50–60 percent of their initial weight and keep it off. Many do not keep the weight off in the long term because they are unable to eat less or the stomach expands over time. The surgery is associated with tremendous risks, including potential short- and long-term complications. Surgery patients require lifelong medical monitoring. They are at risk for vitamin deficiencies and other health problems.

### ■ Self-Assessment
*What do I need to change to be healthier?*

- Do I skip meals? Do I often go hungry? Why?
- Have I trained myself to ignore hunger?
- How do I feel when I skip meals or ignore my hunger?
- Do I exercise regularly? If yes, do I include both strength training and aerobic activity? If not, what factors are preventing me from exercising? How can I change or eliminate them?
- What is my weight history? Have there been changes during adolescence or adulthood?
- Is my BMI in a healthy range? If not, how much has my risk of disease increased?
- Do I eat a healthful diet?
- Have I succumbed to fad diet claims?
- Do I take steps to lower the energy (calorie) density of my diet and enhance the nutrient density? Do I watch fat and sugar intake? Do I eat vegetables, fruits, legumes, whole grains, and other high-fiber foods?
- Do I eat when I am not hungry? Do I eat in response to emotional needs or social settings? Can I change my eating behaviors to be more in line with my nutritional needs? ■

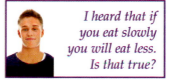

*I heard that if you eat slowly you will eat less. Is that true?*

### Prevention of Obesity

There is a lot we don't know about obesity, but one thing is for sure: it is difficult to treat. Therefore, the best treatment may be prevention. Much can be done both at home and in the community to help prevent obesity.

- Limiting television viewing time among children is an important strategy; a recent study from Stanford University showed that third- and fourth-graders who reduced their television viewing had statistically significant decreases in BMI, regardless of how they spent the reallocated time.
- Results from the Child and Adolescent Trial for Cardiovascular Health (CATCH), which included nutritional interventions at ninety-six elementary schools (fifty-six with interventions and forty control schools) throughout the United States, showed significant reductions in total and saturated fat consumption among students at the schools with the interventions. In response to this and other studies, the Institute of Medicine has issued recommendations as to what schools should offer in vending machines, in à la carte cafeteria lines, and for school fund-raisers.

**Want to know more?**
For an overview of the Institute of Medicine's recommendations for foods in schools, go to the text website at http://webcom8.grtxle.com/nutrition and click on the Chapters button. Select Chapter 7.

**APPLICATION TIP**

How many food advertisements do you see every day? A study by the Kaiser Family Foundation and Indiana University reported that children 8–12 years old watch an average of twenty-one food ads each day. Teenagers see about seventeen food ads per day. This has led Great Britain to ban TV ads for unhealthy foods aimed at child viewers.

- Workplace interventions can have a marked impact on adult dietary habits. The WellWorks Study, a two-year randomized, controlled study of interventions implemented at twenty-four workplaces in Massachusetts, showed significant reductions in the percentage of calories consumed as fat and increased consumption of fruits and vegetables among workers at the intervention sites.
- Public health policy changes have been suggested as potential obesity prevention approaches. Examples include mass media campaigns, increased availability of fitness facilities, taxes on high-fat and high-sugar foods, controlling of junk food advertising during children's television programming, limiting video games and computer time, and restoration of daily physical activity in all schools.

## Seeking Balance

In our 21st-century society, the things that help make you gain unwanted weight are easy to come by; the things that make you fit, however, take some effort. Thus, it is increasingly difficult to strike a healthy balance between "energy in" and "energy out." Much on these pages is an attempt to raise your awareness of the rewards inherent in maintaining this balance and the consequences of ignoring it. The obesity epidemic is a result of many factors coming together; the solution lies in addressing all of these factors on all levels. Changes must occur within the individual, the community, and our culture. The good news is that you can do something about it without going on an extreme diet or starving yourself. So get out there and be healthy, enjoy food, enjoy exercise, and enjoy life.

**Before you go on . . .**

1. Why don't diets typically work for long-term weight loss?
2. What are hunger, appetite, and satiety?
3. What *does* work in terms of weight loss?
4. List some characteristics of a healthy weight-loss plan.

Many U.S. companies are now addressing the rapidly increasing healthcare costs related to obesity by cutting coverage and shifting the premium cost to employees. Other companies are encouraging employees to become healthier by offering educational programs, by providing healthier foods in cafeterias and vending machines, and even by offering incentives for those who successfully make changes.

## Real People, Real Strategies

Have you figured out why it has been so hard for Amber to lose weight and keep it off? Do you think she is a dieting failure? As for many Americans, her mistake appears to have been trying every diet except for the one thing that really does work—permanent lifestyle changes. One important part of these lifestyle changes for Amber is the need to burn more calories than she eats in order to lose the weight. Then she will have to burn as many calories as she eats in order to maintain the weight loss. Her best bet for maintaining the weight loss is to exercise. In addition to these basic changes, she can try several other things to accommodate her busy schedule. She will definitely need to have a plan. This may require cooking healthy meals ahead of time that she can freeze and have readily available during the week. She should also try to teach her family what she learns about proper portion sizes from the RD. Avoiding fast food and high-calorie snacks would also be a good strategy.

As for her husband, he can follow the same lifestyle changes that everyone else in the family does. He just won't have to create a caloric defecit. After all, just because he is not overweight does not mean that he doesn't need to eat healthy and exercise to prevent major diseases and to avoid weight gain in the future. And what about her son? In order to alleviate the effects of the teasing by schoolmates, the best thing Amber can do, in addition to helping him live a healthier lifestyle, is to encourage him to identify and focus on his strengths and attributes outside his physical appearance. She can also help him get involved in activities that he enjoys, which in turn will help him develop positive self-esteem. Eating a healthy diet and exercising daily will help him feel better as he masters his own lifestyle changes.

## Chapter Summary

- Maintaining weight is really an issue of balance. "Calories in" versus "calories out" means that if you want to lose weight you have to burn more calories than you eat.
- In the food marketplace, the concept of getting more for your money seems to have eliminated the concept of eating a reasonable portion size; this trend has contributed to the obesity epidemic.
- Everybody expends energy or calories in three ways: resting energy expenditure (REE), physical activity, and the thermic effect of food (TEF).
- *Resting energy expenditure* (REE) is sometimes used interchangeably with the term *basal metabolism*. Basal metabolic rate (BMR) is more precisely defined as the REE measured after waking in the morning, at least twelve hours after the last meal. The calories that contribute to REE are used for your heartbeat, breathing, nerve impulse transmission, kidney function, growth and repair, and other basic functions.
- Exercise can help you increase your REE by burning calories during the activity and by increasing muscle mass. The more muscle you have, the more calories you burn—even when you are just sitting still.

- We can measure and define overweight and obesity in a number of ways. The body mass index (BMI) is the simplest calculation, it is a height-weight relationship.
- Overweight is characterized by a BMI of 25 or greater; obesity is characterized by a BMI of 30 or greater.
- The risk for diseases such as heart disease, cancers, high blood pressure, and diabetes usually begins to increase at a BMI of 25 to 29.9, and increases further at a BMI of 30.
- Being underweight (adult BMI <19) increases your risk of disease also.
- The desirable ranges of body fat percentage are roughly 10–20 percent for men and 18–25 percent for women. Women should have more essential body fat than men to maintain optimal reproductive function. Men with more than 25 percent body fat and women with more than 30 percent body fat are considered obese.
- Where on your body you store fat has a significant influence on health and disease risk. The storing of fat in the abdomen, called android obesity, carries a much higher risk for hypertension, Type 2 diabetes, and heart disease than the storing of fat on the hips and thighs, which is called gynoid obesity. Those who store abdominal body fat under the abdominal muscle (visceral fat) are at greater risk than those who store abdominal body fat over the muscle and under the skin (subcutaneous fat).
- The waist-to-hip ratio measures the disease risk associated with abdominal body fat. Men with a waist-to-hip ratio of greater than 1.0 and women with a ratio greater than 0.8 are considered to have an excess accumulation of fat in their abdomen. Waist circumference alone is an accurate predictor of disease risk and is often used instead of the waist-to-hip ratio. Risk increases with a waist measurement of greater than 40 in. in men and 35 in. in women.
- Two-thirds of American adults are either overweight or obese. The increase in obesity prevalence is similar in adults and children. There are significant differences in obesity among ethnic groups.
- Weight is a complex phenomenon influenced by genetics, physiological factors, psychological factors, lifestyle behaviors, and social and economic factors.
- Many theories attempt to explain weight gain.
- Losing weight is usually not the biggest problem; keeping it off is the real challenge.
- Diets do not work because they are not lifetime approaches to healthful eating. Fad diets are unhealthy, disruptive to social and family life, and boring. Rapid weight loss usually results from a loss of body water and muscle mass, and the weight is quickly regained. Dieting can lead to a lower REE, which makes it hard to lose weight in the future. Dieting can lead to psychological consequences such as depression, eating disorders, and negative self-esteem.
- In order to lose weight and keep it off you have to make permanent changes in your eating and exercise habits. Exercise is the key to maintaining weight loss.
- When you are trying to lose weight, it is just as important to examine *why* you eat as *what* you eat. You can do several things to modify your behaviors and environment to help manage your weight.
- The best treatment for obesity may be prevention.

## Key Terms

**adjustable gastric band procedure** Performed laproscopically. Most of the stomach is removed and a vertical sleeve or tube is fashioned from the remaining stomach. Because the stomach is so much smaller, patients are forced to eat less. (p. 234)

**android** (An-droyd) A pattern of body fat distribution in which most body fat is carried in the abdomen; the "apple" shape. (p. 216)

**appetite** The psychological mechanisms that determine how much we eat. (p. 224)

**basal metabolic rate (BMR)** The rate at which basal metabolism occurs; it is more precisely defined as the REE measured after waking in the morning, at least twelve hours after the last meal. (p. 206)

**basal metabolism** (BAY-zul meh-TAB-uh-lizm) Body processes involving involuntary activities only, such as heartbeat, breathing, and chemical reactions. (p. 206)

**bioelectrical impedance analysis (BIA)** A method of measuring body composition based on the fact that lean tissue, with high water content, conducts electricity relatively well while fat tissue, with low water content, conducts electricity poorly. When a mild electric current is passed through the body, the body's impedance, or resistance to current, indirectly indicates the amount of lean tissue and the amount of fat. (p. 206)

**body mass index (BMI)** A height-weight relationship used to assess obesity; it equals (weight in kilograms)/(height in meters squared), or (weight in pounds $\times$ 704.5)/(height in inches squared). (p. 211)

**dual-energy X-ray absorptiometry (DEXA)** (Doo-ul EN-er-jee EKS-ray ab-ZORP-tee-om-eh-tree) The most reliable technique in estimating body composition; it uses two X-ray energies to measure body fat, muscle, and bone mineral. (p. 215)

**gynoid** (GUY-noyd) A pattern of body fat distribution in which most body fat is carried on the hips and thighs; the "pear" shape. (p. 216)

**hunger** The physiological mechanisms that determine how much and when we eat. (p. 224)

**leptin** A hormone produced by fat cells that plays a role in body weight regulation. (p. 222)

**obesity** The condition of having a BMI of 30 or greater. (p. 211)

**osteoporosis** (oss-tee-oh-por-OH-sis) A condition that affects older women in particular and is characterized by a decrease in bone mass and density and an enlargement of bone spaces, producing porosity and brittleness. (p. 214)

**overweight** The condition of having a BMI of 25 or greater. (p. 211)

**prevalence** The number or proportion of cases of a condition in a given population. (p. 217)

**resting energy expenditure (REE)** The energy expended by the body for heartbeat, breathing, nerve impulse transmission, kidney function, growth and repair, and other basic functions. (p. 206)

**Roux-en-Y gastric bypass** The most commonly performed bariatric surgery in the United States. In this procedure, stapling creates a small stomach pouch. The remainder of the stomach is not removed, but is completely stapled shut and divided from the stomach pouch. The outlet from this newly formed pouch empties directly into the lower portion of the jejunum (part of the small intestine), thus creating some malabsorption as well as limiting intake. (p. 234)

**set point theory** A theory that states that the body is programmed to gravitate toward a particular weight; the metabolism may adjust upward or downward to ensure that weight is neither lost nor gained. (p. 221)

**subcutaneous fat** (sub-kyoo-TAY-nee-us fat) Body fat stored over the muscle and under the skin. (p. 216)

**thermic effect of food (TEF)** The energy expended by the body in digesting, absorbing, transporting, storing, metabolizing and otherwise processing food; it amounts to about 10 percent of calories consumed. (p. 207)

**total energy expenditure (TEE)** The sum of REE, physical activity, and TEF. (p. 208)

**underwater weighing** A technique for estimating body composition by comparing weight on land to underwater weight and the volume of water displaced by the body. (p. 215)

**underweight** The condition of being 10 percent below what is considered a healthy weight for your height and build, associated with inadequate nutritional intake. (p. 212)

**vertical sleeve gastrectomy** Type of bariatric surgery that uses an adjustable band that fits around the upper part of the stomach. The band divides the upper portion of the stomach into a pouch and separates it from the lower. This limits food intake. The band can be adjusted to allow more or less food to pass through to individualize weight loss. (p. 234)

**visceral fat** Body fat stored under the abdominal muscle. (p. 216)

**waist-to-hip ratio** A measure of the health risks associated with android obesity. (p. 216)

# Chapter Quiz

1. What contributes the most to energy expenditure?
   a. the thermic effect of food
   b. physical activity
   c. resting energy expenditure
   d. voluntary activity

2. Which aspect of energy expenditure varies the most among people?
   a. the thermic effect of food
   b. physical activity
   c. resting energy expenditure
   d. voluntary activity

3. Which of the following factors best explains why people of the same age and gender burn a different amount of calories?
   a. They differ in how much food they eat.
   b. They live in different climates.
   c. They have different amounts of muscle mass.
   d. Different foods can speed up the metabolism.

4. An acceptable BMI for men and women is
   a. 30 or above.
   b. 25–30.
   c. 25 or below.
   d. 19–25.

5. An acceptable percentage of body fat for men and women is
   a. 10–20 percent for men and 18–25 percent for women.
   b. 10–20 percent for men and women.
   c. 10–20 percent for women and 18–25 percent for men.
   d. 18–25 percent for men and women.

6. Among the following people, who do you think would most likely be at the greatest risk for diseases associated with obesity?
   a. a man with a BMI of 28, a waist circumference of 42, and visceral abdominal obesity
   b. a woman with a BMI of 28, a waist circumference of 35, and gynoid obesity
   c. a man with a BMI of 29, a waist circumference of 42, and subcutaneous abdominal obesity
   d. a man with a BMI of 30, a waist circumference of 32, and 5 percent body fat

7. Which of the following diseases are typically not associated with diabetes?
   a. heart disease
   b. certain types of cancer
   c. high blood pressure
   d. osteoporosis

8. Intake of what macronutrient should be decreased the most when trying to lower energy intake?

    a. carbohydrates

    b. fats

    c. proteins

    d. cut just a little from each one

9. Which of the following is not a healthy tip for weight loss?

    a. Create a caloric deficit of about 500 calories per day.

    b. Set a goal of 1–2 lbs of weight loss per week.

    c. Cut caloric intake below 1,200 calories per day.

    d. Do not cut any one food group more than the other.

10. Why is it important to prevent, instead of treat, obesity?

    a. Many obese people are reluctant to seek treatment.

    b. Obese people are sedentary and have a hard time sticking to a diet.

    c. Obesity is a difficult and complex disease to treat.

    d. Obesity is a disease with no cure.

# Water and Electrolytes

## Striking a Balance

## < Here's Where You've Been

*The following topics were introduced in preceding chapters and are related to concepts we'll discuss in Chapter 8. Be certain that you're familiar with them before proceeding.*

- Nutrients are divided into classes, and each has its own basic functions. (Chapter 1)
- Vitamins, minerals, and water are needed to support your metabolism. (Chapter 1)
- Healthy eating includes balance, variety, and moderation. (Chapter 2)
- The process of digestion of food and absorption of nutrients is regulated by many factors. (Chapter 6)
- Weight management and energy balance primarily depend on caloric intake and physical activity. (Chapter 7)

## Here's Where You're Going >

*The following topics and concepts are the ones we'll emphasize in Chapter 8.*

- Among all the nutrients, water is required in the greatest amount and is essential for life.
- Water is the largest component of both intracellular and extracellular fluids in the human body. It serves as a medium in which other nutrients are carried and in which biochemical reactions occur.
- Control of body temperature depends on proper hydration and sweating.
- Sodium, potassium, and chloride concentrations in body fluids are carefully regulated and aligned with hydration.
- Control of sodium and potassium balance in the body may be critical in preventing or managing high blood pressure.

## Real People, Real Choices

Amanda Griffin is in her early thirties and the mother of a 4-year-old. Since her college days she has been interested in nutrition and physical fitness. After running for a couple of years in 5K and 10K runs and performing quite well, she decided to take a major step and run in the Chicago marathon—something she had always dreamed of doing. The training time required a couple of hours a day at least five times a week and represented a major commitment and adjustment in her schedule, but in her mind completing the ultimate race would definitely be worth the sacrifice. She trained for the event for three months.

Amanda got most of her information about how to properly train for a marathon from several fitness and running magazines as well as from the Internet. One thing she learned from her research is that staying well hydrated during a marathon is both crucial and much more challenging than in shorter races. During her training the longest distance she ran was 12 miles, but she did not experience any symptoms of dehydration. Following the advice provided in the literature she began drinking extra fluids, mostly water, the day before the event. To increase her endurance, she consumed a high-carbohydrate diet with items such as rice and whole grains, which are low-sodium foods, several days before the event.

During the event she continued to try to stay hydrated by drinking water every fifteen minutes. She completed the race in about 4 1/2 hours. At the end of the race, she cooled down and again drank about a quart of water. Although she finished the marathon, her time was not what she had hoped and she remembers getting rather tired during the run, which surprised her because she had done well in her training without feeling unusually fatigued. Shortly after the marathon she began to feel dizzy and flushed, and later that evening she was so tired that she lost her appetite and felt apathetic.

What mistakes did Amanda make before, during, and after the run? What nutrition advice would you give her if she decides to continue to run long-distance races?

Water is essential for life. A good, clean, and convenient water supply is taken for granted in many parts of the world. But in others, obtaining water to live is a major part of daily activities. For many people, carrying jugs of water for drinking and cooking each day is a way of life.

Amanda's experience of severe fatigue and light-headedness after the marathon is a result of not appreciating the delicate balance of water and electrolytes and how both interact and affect each other. It is a mistake with respect to hydration to think only about water and ignore other elements such as electrolytes. In this chapter we will explain and discuss the issues that led to Amanda's condition after the marathon.

Although balance among all nutrients is important, water is essential to life and is required in the greatest amount. It is so crucial that signs of *dehydration* (excessive water loss in the body) can begin after just one day without water, and a person generally cannot survive for more than six days without consuming some water.

Fifty-six to 64 percent (by weight) of the adult human body is composed of water, most of which is found in muscle tissues. Because men have more muscle tissue than women do, the male body has a greater percentage of water by weight. In fact, if you compared a man and a woman who both weigh 150 1b., the man's body would contain 10 percent more water. Whether male or female, an adult requires 9–13 c. of water every day to maintain water balance. Water is important for controlling body temperature, maintaining the body's acid-base balance, and regulating blood pressure. Although dehydration is the water-related condition you tend to hear about most, overhydration can occur as well. In diseases in which the kidneys and heart are affected, water retention can be a serious problem.

## Water and Water Balance

Water, like minerals, is an **inorganic** substance, meaning it does not contain carbon. In contrast, fats, protein, carbohydrates, and vitamins are **organic** substances that contain carbon. Water consists of two hydrogen atoms and one oxygen atom bonded together. This bond between the hydrogen and oxygen atoms is different from those found in many other compounds. In water, the bonding causes a shift in charge among the individual atoms. The hydrogen side of the molecules has a slight positive charge and the oxygen side has a slight negative charge (Figure 8.1). This distribution of electrical charge allows water to attract other water molecules. Because water is charged, other substances that are also charged can dissolve in it. A good example is sodium chloride (table salt), which also has positive and negative charges (Figure 8.2).

Within the body, water is found in two major compartments: inside cells as **intracellular** water, and outside cells as **extracellular** water. Sixty percent of the body's total water is intracellular and 40 percent is extracellular. Extracellular compartment water includes the water between tissue cells (*interstitial fluid*) and in the *lymph system*, connective tissues, and joints, as well as plasma, cerebrospinal fluid, mucous secretions, and eyeball fluid (Figure 8.3). (See Table 8.1 for a detailed description of the distribution of water in the body.) Water that is produced during the breakdown of carbohydrate, fats, and proteins is called **metabolic water.** This process produces about 1 1/2 c. of water per day.

### Water Balance

No other nutrient fluctuates within the body as much as water. Water loss depends on many factors. For instance, the temperature of your environment, your age, your activity level, and other factors all influence how much water your body loses daily. Some days people tend to retain more water, but they may eliminate more water a few days later. Athletes typically have a much greater water loss than nonathletes, but this varies with environmental conditions and

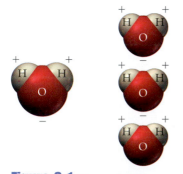

**Figure 8.1** The molecular structure of water. Because of the bonding properties of hydrogen with oxygen, oxygen has a slight negative charge, whereas hydrogen's charge is positive.

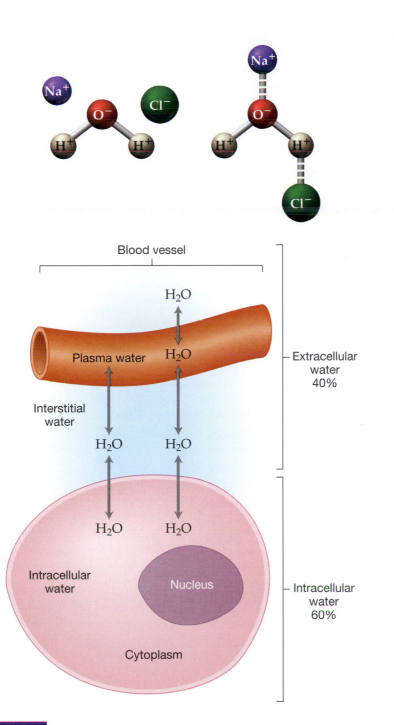

**Figure 8.2** Ever wonder why substances can dissolve in water so easily? The charge distribution of water allows other charged elements to dissolve in water. For example, the positive charge of sodium is attracted to the negative charge of water, as illustrated here.

**Figure 8.3** How is water distributed in the body's compartments? Extracellular water can be found in blood and interstitial spaces, the spaces between cells of tissues. Most water is intracellular.

| Table 8.1 | Distribution of Body Water |
|---|---|
| **Compartment** | **Percentage of Total Body Water** |
| Intracellular (such as muscle cells) | 60% |
| Extracellular | |
| Interstitial fluid and lymph | 20 |
| Connective tissues and joints | 8 |
| Plasma | 7 |
| Eyes, mucous secretions, other | 3 |
| Cerebrospinal fluid | 1 |
| Intestinal secretions | 1 |

the type of activity the athlete performs. Also, athletes tend to be able to adapt and are more efficient at using the body's water. However, they still have higher water requirements than those who do not exercise. Infants tend to lose proportionately more body water than adults and are thus more likely to experience dehydration than adults. Remember, though, that losing weight through water loss is dangerous to your health. To avoid dehydration you must balance water depletion with water ingestion. Unlike other essential nutrients, water has no storage mechanism. When extracellular water is lost, you cannot replenish it from some storage site within your body. In fact, a decreased concentration of extracellular fluid pulls water out of your cells, eventually dehydrating them. Consequently, even a slight inadequacy in your water supply can change the way your body functions. Thus you must consume fluids on a regular basis.

## ■ Myths and Legends
### Is bottled water safer and better for you?

Much of the popularity of bottled water is based on the assumption that it is cleaner and healthier than tap water. Is this assumption always valid? Bottled water, which is sold in a sanitary container, is considered a food and must meet federal and other local regulations. The Food and Drug Administration (FDA) regulates bottled water (if it crosses state lines) at the federal level. Although bottled water contains no calories, added chemicals, sweeteners, or sugar, the FDA has identified different standards of identity for bottled water, such as "spring," "sparkling," and "mineral" water. Water products that contain added ingredients are classified as soft drinks or dietary supplements.

In general, spring water comes from an underground source. Bottled spring water must retain the composition found at its source. Spring water contains less than 250 parts per million (ppm) solids. Mineral water is the same as spring water but contains more than 250 ppm solids. No minerals may be added to mineral water, however; it must be bottled as it exists from its original source. The solids in spring water and mineral water are mostly from minerals such as calcium, magnesium, and trace elements. Sparkling water is similar to spring water, with the additional regulation that it must have the same amount of dissolved carbon dioxide present as at its source.

Bottled water manufacturers are not permitted to make any health claims. No therapeutic benefits from bottled water have been documented. Nevertheless, consumers apparently believe that bottled water tastes better and is healthier for them than tap water. Ironically, however, about 25 percent of the bottled water sold today originates from tap water sources.

So, to answer the question, bottled water is likely to be safe because of the packaging requirements imposed by the FDA. The International Bottled Water Association's safety policies and surveillance are even

Look familiar? Bottled water is a very popular beverage in the food industry today.

stricter than those of the FDA. Although it may not provide any health benefits, bottled water can indeed be safer than tap water in some situations, and mineral water may even offer some protection, albeit small, from chronic diseases such as osteoporosis because of the presence of calcium and magnesium. ■

The most critical role water plays in the body's functioning is temperature regulation. Water is used to cool the body through sweating. The many biochemical reactions that occur within the body generate a lot of heat. Water within the body absorbs heat and carries it away for excretion, primarily to the skin, in order to maintain the body's temperature at 98.6°F (37°C). Excess heat is then released through sweating. Sweating in and of itself doesn't cool you; rather the body is cooled when the sweat evaporates from your skin. The amount of heat lost by the body via sweat equals about 0.58 kcal per gram of sweat water. Sweating 1 L in a day amounts to 580 kcal of lost heat.

## Sources of Water Loss in the Body

Your body loses water every day in a variety of ways. In addition to sweating, you can lose it through urine and feces and through the lungs each time you exhale. Generally, about 900–1,200 mL (3.8–5 c.) of water are lost daily as urine. The amount of urine produced is proportional to the amount of water you drink. Water loss through the lungs is typically 300 mL/day, or less than 1 c, but it is influenced by environmental conditions.

Overall water balance from input to output is summarized in Table 8.2. Because mild daily sweating and the exhalation of air humidified by the lungs generally goes unnoticed, these processes and other minor water loss mechanisms, such as secretions of the eyes, are often referred to as **insensible water loss**. In addition, mild sweating is often separated from activity-induced sweat, which has a higher mineral content and is visually obvious. Sweat can be a significant route of water loss for athletes and for people who live in warm climates. Interestingly, if you change your activity level or environment, your sweat glands adapt to ensure that you stay in balance.

## Hydration: Water Intake and Retention

A region of the brain called the hypothalamus controls the body's perceived need for water, commonly called thirst. Thirst is not always the best indicator of water needs and may lag behind the body's true needs. The brain monitors the body's fluid salt concentration and responds with a signal to take in fluid when

### Table 8.2    Daily Water Balance from Intake and Output

| Water Intake* | | | Water Loss | | |
|---|---|---|---|---|---|
| Source | mL | c. | Source | mL | c. |
| Drinking water (from beverages) | 1,000 | 4.2 | Urine | 900–1,200 | 3.8–5 |
| Water in food | 600–800 | 2.5–3.4 | Insensible: | | |
| Metabolic water (from digestion) | 200–300 | 0.9–1.3 | Mild sweating | 400 | 1.7 |
| Total | 1,800–2,100 | 7.6–8.9 | Lungs | 300 | 1.3 |
| | | | Feces | 200 | 0.9 |
| | | | Total | 1,800–2,100 | 7.7–8.9 |

*These are estimates for adults and can vary widely.

water levels are low or salt concentration is high. In addition to thirst, the body produces two hormones to help maintain hydration. **Antidiuretic hormone** is released by the pituitary gland in the brain to signal the kidneys to retain water. **Aldosterone** is produced by the adrenal glands above the kidneys; it induces the kidneys to retain more sodium and consequently more water.

Although the body has mechanisms to retain and conserve water in some circumstances and to excrete it in others, fluid intake is necessary every day. How much water should we consume? General recommendations for water consumption for adults are 1–1.5 mL/kcal of energy expenditure under average environmental conditions (8–12 c. of water per day total, including beverages and the water contained in food). This guideline has some exceptions. Pregnant women have an increased requirement of about 30 mL/day (an ounce per day more) to accommodate the expanded extracellular fluid, the fluid needs of the fetus, and the amniotic fluid. Breastfeeding mothers need approximately 600–700 mL more water per day (2 1/2–3 c.). They need this water to produce breast milk, which is about 87 percent water; the average milk secretion is 750 mL/day or 3.2 c./day for the first six months.

If you are on a low-carbohydrate or high-protein diet, drinking extra water is advisable. It will help your body remove potentially harmful excess nitrogen and the ketone bodies that these diets produce. In addition to fluids or drinks, several foods are excellent sources of water. For instance, many fruits and vegetables are 85–95 percent water by mass. The water content of some commonly eaten foods is discussed in the Make It a Practice feature.

### ■ Make It a Practice
*Staying hydrated during exercise*

Miguel Rojas is an experienced long-distance runner who knows the importance of staying well hydrated. He consumes extra water both before and during his runs, and he replenishes his lost stores by drinking more water for several hours after running. He is aware that athletes are encouraged to drink 1 1/2–2 1/2 c. of fluids two to three hours before exercise. During exercise, 3/4–1 1/2 c. of fluids every fifteen to twenty minutes is recommended. After exercise, 1–2 percent of body weight in the form of water can be lost, so normally 2–3 c. of fluids should be consumed in the first thirty minutes after exercise. Then 4–4 1/2 c. every one to two hours may be needed until the body returns to the pre-exercise weight.

As part of his daily fluid intake, Miguel also consumes sports drinks. Because he exercises so much and burns a lot of calories, he recognizes that he needs to consume foods in his diet that are rich in both calories *and* water. He begins to research the water content of food and is surprised at how much water some foods contain. At the same time he is aware that he needs to choose foods that contain other electrolytes so that he won't be at risk for **water intoxication**. This is caused by excess water consumption and results in dilution of blood electrolytes, particularly sodium. Here you are replacing the water you have lost but not the electrolytes.

In searching through a food composition table, Miguel discovers that both tomatoes and lettuce get about 95 percent of their weight from water. He is also surprised to learn that even a meat, in this case chicken, is actually 70 percent water. Importantly, the research allows him to identify foods that contain substantial calories but are also sources of potassium, an important electrolyte.

Here are some of the food choices that Miguel discovered he can consume in order to enhance his intake of water:

| Food | Approx. Water Content (% of Total Weight) |
| --- | --- |
| Tomatoes | 95 |
| Lettuce | 95 |
| Zucchini | 95 |
| Cauliflower, cooked | 93 |
| Cabbage | 92 |
| Watermelon | 91 |
| Grapefruit | 91 |
| Cucumber | 91 |
| Broccoli, steamed | 90 |
| Oranges | 87 |
| Apple juice | 87 |
| Milk | 87 |
| Beets, canned | 87 |
| Pineapples | 86 |
| Apples | 84 |
| Seedless grapes | 81 |
| Potatoes | 78 |
| Hard-cooked egg | 76 |
| Bananas | 75 |
| Chicken | 70 |
| Bread, white | 35 |
| Rice | 12 |

Given the importance of electrolyte replacement, he decides to concentrate on foods that are high in both water and potassium. Because he frequently eats out (many restaurant and processed foods have high concentrations of salt), he's quite confident that he's already getting enough sodium in his diet. Further research tells him that some of the items on the list are good sources of potassium, such as bananas, watermelon, and squash. Accordingly, Miguel decides to pay extra attention to these foods and incorporate more of them in his diet. ■

### The Dangers of Dehydration

Even mild or early dehydration can result in significant changes in how your body works. For example, a decrease of 1–2 percent body weight signals thirst and can cause lack of mental concentration and mild fatigue. A loss of water approximating 2 percent of body weight can significantly reduce athletic ability. If dehydration reaches approximately 5 percent of body weight, cramping and heat exhaustion can result. At the 7–10 percent level, hallucinations and heatstroke are common. Shock and coma may soon follow. In extreme situations, failure to consume water with electrolytes or obtain it intravenously can result in death within several days (see Table 8.3 for signs of dehydration).

**APPLICATION TIP**

In order to stay hydrated during exercise, you should consume 3/4–1 1/2 c. of fluids for every fifteen to twenty minutes of activity.

| Table 8.3 | Signs of Dehydration |
|---|---|
| **Mild Dehydration** | **Moderate to Severe Dehydration** |
| Dry and sticky mouth | Extreme thirst |
| Feeling of tiredness and sleepiness | Lack of sweating |
| Thirst | Very dry mouth and skin |
| Decreased urine | Little or no urine; dark-colored urine |
| Lack of tears when crying | Sunken eyes |
| Muscle weakness | Shriveled skin and lack of elasticity |
| Headache | Low blood pressure |
| Dizziness | Rapid heartbeat |
| Cramping in arms and legs | Rapid deep breathing |
| | Fever |
| | Unconsciousness and convulsions |

Dehydration can occur from excessive loss through sweating without adequate fluid replacement. In athletes who exercise in hot environments, dehydration continues with continued sweating. Dehydration also occurs in temperate environments, but stabilizes more easily. Dehydration can also occur as a result of vomiting and diarrhea. Initially, dehydration is characterized by a shift in fluid from intracellular and interstitial areas to the blood. As dehydration becomes more severe, blood volume is reduced. This means less blood is returned from the body to the heart and the heart pumps less blood, which decreases blood pressure. When the flow of blood to tissues and organs (including the brain) is reduced, they starve for oxygen and nutrients. Mild dehydration can reduce one's metabolism as much as 3 percent. In addition, dehydration reduces your ability to remove excessive heat through sweat, leaving you vulnerable to **hyperthermia** (increased body temperature) and heatstroke because your body does not have enough water to cool itself.

### ■ Nutrition and Lifestages
#### *Dehydration in infancy*
The smaller an animal, including humans, the greater the tendency to lose water. This is due to an increase in the body's surface-area-to-volume ratio. Infants are at risk for dehydration for two primary reasons. First, they have a higher water requirement in relation to their body weight. Second, they have a greater metabolic rate and therefore burn more calories at rest than older children or adults. These factors become more of a problem when infants are ill and have vomiting or diarrhea. In fact, these conditions are typically the major cause of dehydration in infants. Infants cry for various reasons, including thirst. Keeping them well hydrated is critical. Infants require 2 oz. of fluids per day per pound of body weight. Normally this is not a problem for breast-fed or formula-fed infants. However, in hot weather, infants may need more formula or breast milk. If the infant is already dehydrated, it is common to supplement with water or, preferably, oral rehydration solutions. Oral rehydration solutions contain electrolytes and often save the lives of infants and children in areas where death from diarrhea and dehydration is common. If you suspect that an infant is dehydrated, consult a physician immediately.

Dehydration in infants leads to poor kidney function. Remember, however, that it is also easy to overhydrate an infant. This can lead to low blood sodium levels. No more than 4 oz. of fluids per day from sources other than breast milk or formula is needed. Because infants cannot tell us when they are dehydrated, caregivers should look for the following signs of dehydration:

- Dry mouth and tongue
- No tears when crying
- Irritability
- No wet diapers for three hours or more (five to six wet diapers per day is normal)
- Sunken eyes and cheeks
- Inactivity or sleepiness
- Most significantly, a sunken fontanel (the soft spot on the infant's head)

Remember to monitor these signs if you believe that an infant is not feeling well or if the child is vomiting or has diarrhea, because dehydration can occur rapidly. ■

### The Role of the Kidneys and Urine in Water Balance

Urine is the major source of water loss and is also the primary path for excretion of metabolic waste and the regulation of extracellular fluid composition. The kidneys control the composition of urine and blood through microscopic structures called **nephrons**. Each kidney is composed of about 1 million nephrons (Figure 8.4), which collectively generate approximately 1–2 L (4–8 c.) of urine daily. Urine has several components, the most significant being water, electrolytes, urea, and creatinine. Urea and creatinine are by-products of protein and muscle metabolism, respectively, and are the major nitrogen waste products.

When you are at rest, your kidney receives about 1 L of blood per minute via the pumping action of your heart. In the nephrons, blood is filtered under high pressure. As this fluid flows through, water and electrolytes are reabsorbed into the body. The body tightly controls how much is reabsorbed based on need and hydration levels. Whatever is not absorbed constitutes the 1–2 L or 4–8 c. of urine you excrete each day.

### Before you go on . . .

1. Why is water considered an inorganic nutrient?
2. Explain the importance of the electrical charge in water molecules.
3. What is the most critical role of water in the body?
4. What part of the brain controls thirst?
5. Describe some of the effects of dehydration on the body.

# Electrolytes: Sodium, Potassium, and Chloride

Electrolytes are minerals that, when placed in water, become charged particles. Minerals that are positively charged are **cations;** minerals that are negatively charged are **anions.** Sodium and potassium are positively charged and chloride is negatively charged.

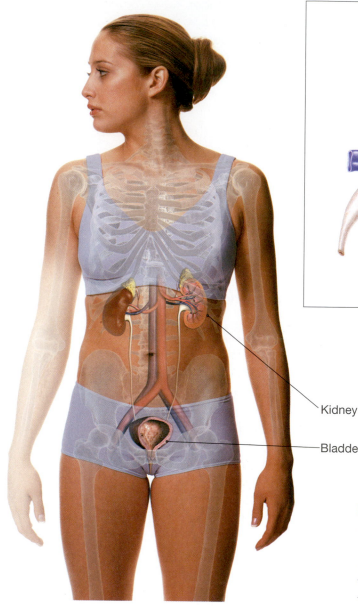

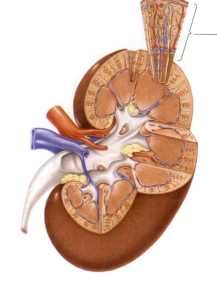

Magnified nephron unit that produces urine

Kidney

Bladder

**Figure 8.4** The kidney and the microscopic nephron structures are the components that regulate water and salt in our bodies. Blood is filtered through the glomerulus of the nephron and the materials we want to keep are reabsorbed from the nephron back into the blood supply.

*Should someone who does not exercise be concerned about electrolytes?*

Sodium, potassium, and chloride are some of the most recognized electrolytes important to humans. They are often discussed together and are commonly called electrolytes because their metabolic and biochemical functions are interrelated. Sodium ($Na+$) is the primary cation found in the extracellular fluid; potassium ($K+$) is the primary intracellular cation (Figure 8.5). Chloride ($Cl-$), an anion, is usually associated with sodium and therefore is more concentrated in the extracellular fluid. These elements, particularly sodium and potassium, are heavily involved in the proper maintenance of water balance.

The DRI for sodium for adolescents and adults up to age 50 is 1,500 mg/day. It is 200–300 mg lower for older adults. Table salt is 40 percent sodium. By consuming 10–15 g/day of salt (which equals 4–6 g of sodium), the average American takes in close to eight to twelve times the estimated daily requirement. So someone who does not exercise does not need to worry about sodium intake, because we get more than enough in our diets. However, this is not the case for potassium. Although the DRI for potassium is 5,700 mg/day for

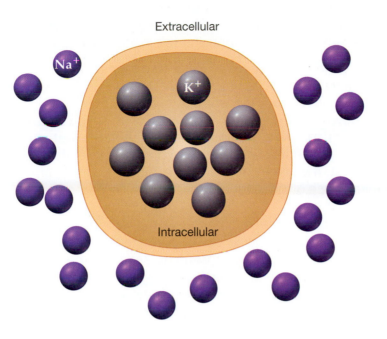

Extracellular

Na⁺

K⁺

Intracellular

**Figure 8.5** Cells are high in potassium. The extracellular, or outside, area surrounding the cell is high in sodium. The cell pumps sodium out and potassium in to maintain this distribution. What would happen to this distribution if the cell died?

teenagers and all adults, 4,700 mg is considered an adequate intake for adults. Many people, especially those not consuming five servings of fresh fruits and vegetables per day, do not meet the *adequate* daily intake requirement. One banana contains 450 mg of potassium.

Chloride has a DRI of 2,300 mg/day for teenagers and adults up to age 50; it declines by 300–500 mg/day for older adults. Table salt, or sodium chloride, is a major contributor of chloride to our diets. Accordingly, we typically get enough chloride from our diets.

## Dietary Sodium

Most people who are trying to reduce sodium intake cut back on the salt they add to their food. However, most of the sodium we consume comes from processed foods rather than table salt. As much as 50–75 percent of sodium in the American diet is added to foods by manufacturers for taste or as a preservative. Individuals add another 15 percent during cooking and by salting food at the table. The sodium occurring naturally in foods such as eggs, milk, meats, and vegetables may supply only about 10–15 percent of your total sodium intake. Drinking water may also contribute to our sodium consumption, as do certain medicines, mouthwash, and toothpaste. Foods with the highest sodium content include luncheon meats (ham, turkey, salami, pepperoni), snack chips, french fries, hot dogs, cheeses, soups, and gravies. Table 8.4 and Figure 8.6 illustrate some common foods and their sodium content.

Although Table 8.4 gives you the level of sodium in select serving sizes for particular foods, following the tips listed in Figure 8.6 may be more practical if you are trying to reduce your sodium intake.

### ■ Make It a Practice
*Minimizing salt in your diet*

Health professionals universally advise moderating our salt intake. Many of us have acquired a taste for salt, which makes adhering to a low-salt diet challenging. Next time you go out to eat with family or friends,

observe how many people salt their food before they even taste it. Here are some simple steps for reducing salt in your diet:

- Avoid consuming too many processed foods. Canned foods such as vegetables and soups typically contain much more salt than fresh or frozen foods. Check the labels.
- Cut down on the use of salt when cooking. Even when cooking pasta or rice, there is no need to add salt to the water.
- Try to avoid adding salt to your food at the table. At least taste your food first. If you think it needs salt, add only a small amount.
- Learn to use other flavor enhancers such as lemon juice and salt-free herb mixtures.
- When cooking, use sodium-free herbs, spices, and flavorings such as allspice, garlic, garlic powder, mustard powder, onion powder, paprika, parsley, pepper, rosemary, sage, thyme, and vinegar. Try using other flavor enhancers. However, be cautious when using dried celery or parsley, as they may have added sodium. The best option is to use fresh herbs whenever possible.

Following a low-salt diet will likely be difficult at first, so give yourself at least two months for your taste buds to adapt. They will. ■

**Table 8.4** **Sodium Content of Selected Foods**

| Food | Sodium (mg) | Food | Sodium (mg) |
|---|---|---|---|
| **Meat and Alternatives** | | **Other** | |
| Corned beef (3 oz.) | 808 | Salt (1 tsp.) | 2132 |
| Ham (3 oz.) | 800 | Pickle, dill | 1930 |
| Fish, canned (3 oz.) | 735 | Broth, chicken (1 c.) | 1571 |
| Sausage (3 oz.) | 483 | Ravioli, canned (1 c.) | 1065 |
| Hot dog | 477 | Broth, beef (1 c.) | 782 |
| Bologna (1 oz.) | 370 | Gravy (3 c.) | 720 |
| **Milk and Milk Products** | | Italian dressing (2 Tbsp.) | 720 |
| Cream soup (1 c.) | 1070 | Pretzels, thin (5) | 500 |
| Cottage cheese (1/2 c.) | 114 | Olives, green (5) | 465 |
| Cheese, American (1 oz.) | 405 | Pizza, cheese (1 slice) | 455 |
| Cheese, Parmesan (1 oz.) | 247 | Soy sauce (1 tsp.) | 444 |
| Milk, skim (1 c.) | 125 | Bacon (3 slices) | 303 |
| Milk, whole (1 c.) | 120 | French dressing (2 Tbsp.) | 220 |
| **Grains** | | Potato chips (10) | 200 |
| Bran flakes (1 c.) | 363 | Ketchup (1 Tbsp.) | 155 |
| Corn flakes (1 c.) | 325 | **Fast Foods** | |
| Bagel | 260 | McDonald's cheeseburger | 739 |
| English muffin | 203 | Big Mac | 1062 |
| Bread, white (1 slice) | 130 | Pizza Hut Meat Lover's pizza (1 slice) | 750 |
| Bread, whole-wheat (1 slice) | 130 | | |
| Crackers, saltine (4) | 125 | Taco Bell taco | 350 |

**Figure 8.6** High-Sodium Foods to Limit or Avoid.

1. Cured, processed, or smoked meats and fish such as ham, bacon, corned beef, cold cuts, hot dogs, chipped beef, pickled herring, sardines, tuna, and anchovies

2. Meat sauces, bouillon cubes, and meat extracts

3. Salted snacks such as potato chips, corn chips, pretzels, salted popcorn, nuts, and crackers

4. Salad dressings, relishes, Worcestershire sauce, barbecue sauce, soy sauce, salsa, ketchup

5. Packaged frozen foods such as frozen lima beans; packaged sauce mixes, gravies, and casseroles; packaged noodle, rice, and potato dishes

6. Canned soup

7. Cheese, including processed cheese and cheese spreads

## Dietary Chloride

As with sodium, the natural chloride content of most foods is low. However, sodium chloride, or table salt, is approximately 60 percent chloride. As discussed, it is frequently added to foods in substantial amounts as a flavor enhancer or preservative. A food containing 1 g of sodium chloride includes approximately 600 mg of chloride. Because we typically consume 10–15 grams of salt per day, it's easy to see how we are exceeding the DRI of 2,300 mg for chloride.

## Dietary Potassium

Unlike sodium and chloride, potassium is not routinely added to foods. Rich sources of potassium are typically fresh, unprocessed foods. Fresh fruits and vegetables are ranked among the best potassium sources. Tomatoes, carrots, potatoes, beans, peaches, pears, squash, oranges, and bananas are all notable for their high potassium content (Table 8.5). Milk, meats, whole grains, coffee, and tea are also among the most significant contributors to our daily consumption of potassium.

Sodium is hidden in many food items. To reduce your sodium intake, try to avoid adding salt to your food and limit consumption of salty snacks and processed foods. Do you consume many of the foods shown here?

## Hypertension and Sodium

Medical research suggests that for certain individuals, a diet high in sodium may increase the risk of developing high blood pressure or **hypertension.** Therefore, the U.S. government requires food manufacturers to list the per-serving sodium content on food labels. Moreover, any manufacturer claims regarding sodium content must follow the labeling criteria shown in Table 8.6. Terms such as *sodium-free, low sodium,* and *unsalted* must adhere to a strict definition.

Roughly a quarter of Americans have high blood pressure, a confirmed risk factor for coronary heart disease and stroke. Millions of Americans have these diseases. The cause behind 85 percent of hypertension cases is unknown; high blood pressure that is due to an unknown cause is called **essential hypertension.** The remaining 15 percent of cases have known causes, such as kidney disease. Fortunately, most hypertension is treatable with lifestyle modifications

| APPLICATION TIP |
|---|

The simplest ways to reduce your sodium intake are to avoid adding salt at the table and, when cooking, to limit the intake of foods listed in Table 8.5. In many instances, doing just these two things can reduce your sodium intake by half.

## Table 8.5   Potassium Content of Selected Foods

| Food | Potassium (mg) | Food | Potassium (mg) |
|---|---|---|---|
| **Vegetables** | | **Meats** | |
| Potato | 780 | Fish (3 oz.) | 500 |
| Squash, winter (2 c.) | 327 | Ground beef (3 oz.) | 480 |
| Tomato | 300 | Lamb (3 oz.) | 382 |
| Celery (1 stalk) | 270 | Pork (3 oz.) | 335 |
| Carrot | 245 | Chicken (3 oz.) | 208 |
| Broccoli (2 c.) | 205 | **Grains** | |
| **Fruit** | | Bran buds (1 c.) | 1080 |
| Avocado (2) | 680 | Bran flakes (1 c.) | 248 |
| Orange juice (1 c.) | 469 | Raisin bran (1 c.) | 242 |
| Banana | 440 | Wheat flakes (1 c.) | 96 |
| Raisins (3 c.) | 370 | | |
| Prunes (4) | 300 | | |
| Watermelon (1 c.) | 158 | | |
| **Milk and Milk Products** | | | |
| Yogurt (1 c.) | 531 | | |
| Milk, skim (1 c.) | 40 | | |

## Table 8.6   Sodium Labeling

| Label Claim | Sodium Content |
|---|---|
| Sodium free | Must contain < 5 mg sodium/serving |
| Very low sodium | Must contain ≤ 35 mg sodium/serving |
| Low sodium | Must contain ≤ 145 mg sodium/serving |
| Reduced sodium | 25% reduction in sodium content |
| Unsalted | No salt added to recipe |
| No added salt | No salt added to recipe |

Do you have your blood pressure checked on a regular basis? This is done quickly and easily and is a painless process.

(diet and exercise) and/or medication. Everyone should have his or her blood pressure checked annually.

Much debate among health professionals has centered on what constitutes high blood pressure. Because blood pressure increases with age, what may be normal for an adult may be considered high for a child or teenager. Blood pressure readings consist of two components. When the heart contracts and forces blood to move because of an increase in pressure from the pumping action, the peak pressure generated is called the **systolic blood pressure.** When the heart relaxes and blood pressure falls, the lowest blood pressure reading during cardiac relaxation is called **diastolic blood pressure.** Normally, a person with a systolic reading of 140 mm Hg or greater, or a diastolic reading of 90 mm Hg or greater, or both, is considered hypertensive. Table 8.7 outlines normal and high blood pressure readings for adults age 18 or older. People in Stages 1 and 2 are at increased risk for a heart attack or kidney disease. Normalizing blood

| Table 8.7 | Normal and High Blood Pressure Measurements for Adults Age 18 or Older |

| | Blood Pressure, mm Hg | | |
|---|---|---|---|
| **Category** | **Systolic** | | **Diastolic** |
| Normal | <120 | and | <80 |
| Prehypertension | 120–139 | or | 80–89 |
| High | | | |
| Stage 1 | 140–159 | | 90–99 |
| Stage 2 | 160 or higher | or | 100 or higher |

*Source:* Reprinted with permission from the American Heart Association.

pressure, through either lifestyle change, medication, or a combination, is an important step in reducing the risk of these diseases.

Regardless of the classification scheme, the role of diet in the control of hypertension has been studied and debated for years. Hypertension is often associated with obesity, and losing weight can result in a significant drop in blood pressure. Sodium has long been linked with an increased incidence of hypertension. For many years, health professionals advocated reducing salt intake to decrease the incidence of hypertension. But continued research has shown that not all individuals with a high sodium intake develop hypertension. Some studies have shown that individuals who have a difficult time excreting the sodium they consume experience higher blood pressure. Other studies suggest that the greater the reduction of sodium in the diet, the greater the reduction in blood pressure. People whose blood pressure responds well to a low-sodium diet (declines) are called *salt sensitive*. However, many other factors are involved with high blood pressure, such as the food choices we make and our level of physical activity.

Potassium appears to exert an antihypertensive effect by relaxing blood vessels. Maintaining the proper balance of sodium and potassium is therefore very important. However, the typical American diet is high in sodium and low in potassium. Nutrition experts often identify the sodium-potassium consumption ratio as a critical determinant of hypertension.

Other minerals may also play a role in determining a person's blood pressure. Studies suggest that a high intake of dietary calcium and magnesium may be as important in controlling hypertension as limiting sodium. A diet high in calcium from dairy products or calcium supplements has been shown to lower blood pressure significantly in people with hypertension. Hardness in drinking water may also play a role. *Hard water* contains elevated levels of calcium and magnesium. Populations living in hard-water areas reportedly experience a lower incidence of coronary heart disease compared to those living in soft-water areas. Home water softeners remove calcium and magnesium, replacing them with sodium. Given that calcium and magnesium seem to protect people from heart disease, and that

**Classification of Blood Pressure According to the U.S. Dept. of Health & Human Services (JNC7—May 2003)**

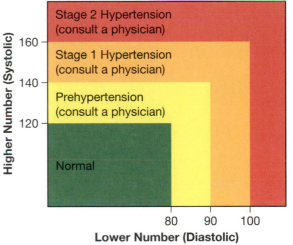

The classification of blood pressure reading among Americans as defined by the American Heart Association.

**Want to know more?**
You can learn more about other factors related to hypertension by visiting the text website at http://webcom8.grtxle .com/nutrition and clicking on the Chapters button. Select Chapter 8.

high levels of sodium intake may increase blood pressure and the risk for heart disease, this use of water softeners is likely dubious from a health perspective.

One of the most effective campaigns against hypertension is called the **Dietary Approaches to Stop Hypertension (DASH)** eating plan, which is rich in fruits, vegetables, and low-fat dairy products, and is low in fat and saturated fat. When used in combination with moderate salt intake, the DASH plan (Table 8.8) lowers blood pressure significantly. The DASH plan also calls for consuming foods high in calcium and potassium, which can help reduce blood pressure. Given these findings and those outlined earlier, a diet that conforms to DASH would seem to go a long way in reducing high blood pressure.

## ■ Culture and Ethnic Foods

*Salt intake and high blood pressure around the world*

The amount of salt consumed in different parts of the world varies. Of course, cultural distinctions among populations account for many of the differences in foods consumed, including salt. A strong factor in predicting the amount of salt consumed in a particular country may be its level of Westernization. Cultural differences aside, within a country's population a direct link appears to exist between the level of salt intake and the incidence of high blood pressure. For example, some Asian countries are high salt consumers and others are not. Residents of northern Japan, for instance, have a high incidence of hypertension; they consume about 20–30 grams of salt per day, more than twice what Americans consume. They also have a large number of deaths from stroke and stomach cancer. Monosodium glutamate is another source of sodium that is frequently used in Asia, although its effect on high blood pressure is not as direct as that of table salt or sodium chloride. Pickled and smoked foods are also popular in these cultures, and they are high in salt as well.

Cultures with less Western influence on their diets and who live under primitive conditions have minimal or no incidence of high blood pressure. Cultures in Africa, the South Pacific, the highlands of Malaysia, and the Amazon basin of South America are good examples. Studies on populations within these areas demonstrated that when salt was introduced into their diets, blood pressure increased. One study evaluated two Polynesian tribes that were similar in ethnicity but culturally different. Sodium intake in one tribe was 7 1/2 g/day, and high blood pressure was common. The other group had a much lower sodium intake, and high blood pressure was rare. On the Solomon Islands, six tribes were studied. Those with low salt intake had little high blood pressure; the opposite was true of those who added salt to their diets. High blood pressure is virtually absent in populations that consume less than 0.1 g/ day, which is 1/100 of what most Americans consume. ■

**Before you go on . . .**

1. Distinguish between cations and anions.
2. How much sodium per day is recommended for an adult, and how much sodium do we typically consume per day in the United States?
3. What is the difference between a reduced-sodium and a low-sodium product?
4. Where does most of the sodium in our diets come from and why?

| Table 8.8 | The DASH Eating Plan |

| Food Group | Daily Servings | Serving Sizes | Examples and Notes | Significance of Each Food Group to the DASH Eating Pattern |
|---|---|---|---|---|
| Grains | 6–8 | 1 slice bread<br>1 oz. dry cereal<br>1/2 cup cooked rice, pasta, or cereal | Whole wheat bread and rolls, whole wheat pasta, English muffin, pita bread, bagel, cereals, grits, oatmeal, brown rice, unsalted pretzels and popcorn | Major sources of energy and fiber |
| Vegetables | 4–5 | 1 cup raw leafy vegetable<br>1/2 cup cut-up raw or cooked vegetable<br>1/2 cup vegetable juice | Broccoli, carrots, collards, green beans, green peas, kale, lima beans, potatoes, spinach, squash, sweet potatoes, tomatoes | Rich sources of potassium, magnesium, and fiber |
| Fruits | 4–5 | 1 medium fruit<br>1/4 cup dried fruit<br>1/2 cup fresh, frozen, or canned fruit<br>1/2 cup fruit juice | Apples, apricots, bananas, dates, grapes, oranges, grapefruit, grapefruit juice, mangoes, melons, peaches, pineapples, raisins, strawberries, tangerines | Important sources of potassium, magnesium, and fiber |
| Fat-free or low-fat milk and milk products | 2–3 | 1 cup milk or yogurt<br>1-1/2 oz. cheese | Fat-free (skim) or low-fat (1%) milk or buttermilk, fat-free, low-fat, or reduced-fat cheese, fat-free or low-fat regular or frozen yogurt | Major sources of calcium and protein |
| Lean meats, poultry, and fish | 6 or less | 1 oz. cooked meats, poultry, or fish<br>1 egg | Select only lean; trim away visible fats; broil, roast, or poach; remove skin from poultry | Rich sources of protein and magnesium |
| Nuts, seeds, and legumes | 4–5 per week | 1/3 cup or 1-1/2 oz. nuts<br>2 Tbsp. peanut butter<br>2 Tbsp. or 1/2 oz. seeds<br>1/2 cup cooked legumes (dry beans and peas) | Almonds, hazelnuts, mixed nuts, peanuts, walnuts, sunflower seeds, peanut butter, kidney beans, lentils, split peas | Rich sources of energy, magnesium, protein, and fiber |
| Fats and oils | 2–3 | 1 tsp. soft margarine<br>1 tsp. vegetable oil<br>1 Tbsp. mayonnaise<br>2 Tbsp. salad dressing | Soft margarine, vegetable oil (such as canola, corn, olive, or safflower), low-fat mayonnaise, light salad dressing | The DASH study had 27 percent of calories as fat, including fat in or added to foods |
| Sweets and added sugars | 5 or less per week | 1 Tbsp. sugar<br>1 Tbsp. jelly or jam<br>1/2 cup sorbet, gelatin<br>1 cup lemonade | Fruit-flavored gelatin, fruit punch, hard candy, jelly, maple syrup, sorbet and ices, sugar | Sweets should be low in fat |

*Source:* National Heart, Lung, and Blood Institute, www.nhlbi.nih.gov/health/public/heart/hbp/dash/how_make_dash.html.

# Real People, Other Voices

**Student:**

## Robie Mills

James Madison University

Amanda's problems during the run were caused by overhydrating without replacing the electrolytes needed to maintain fluid balance. Low sodium intake on the days preceding her run caused lower than normal blood sodium levels, and running 26 miles in four or more hours caused tremendous fluid and electrolyte losses. Drinking too much water without replacing electrolytes can cause hyponatremia or low blood sodium levels, resulting in sodium being diluted and water flowing into the body's cells. Symptoms are loss of appetite, weakness, uncontrolled muscle twitching, and brain swelling, which can cause death.

Amanda was correct in being concerned about dehydration because it also has serious consequences. She should weigh before and after a long training run to determine actual fluid losses, and she should consume 2 1/2 to 3 cups of fluid for every pound of weight lost. She should drink enough fluids and liberally salt her food to replace sodium losses. A sports drink may be helpful, and increasing fruit and vegetable intake will optimize potassium levels. General recommendations are difficult to make for the period of time during exercise and should be customized to the athlete and conditions. Recommendations by a *sports dietitian* who is experienced in marathons would be best; advice obtained from fitness magazines and websites is not individualized.

Water intoxication is rare when intake of calories and electrolytes are sufficient. Drinking too little or too much fluid can be dangerous. The key is to balance fluid and electrolyte intake with sweat losses to avoid both dehydration and hyponatremia.

**Instructor:**

## Carol W. Turner Phd, RD

New Mexico State University

Amanda suffered from one of the most common conditions affecting marathon runners who have been instructed to over-hydrate: hyponatremia (low sodium), which can be a potentially dangerous condition.

USA Track & Field (USATF), the national governing body for track and field, long-distance running and race walking in the United States, recommends that for exercise lasting four hours or longer athletes consume 100 percent of fluids lost due to sweat while racing. This means that for every liter of fluid lost one liter of fluid should be replaced, equaling a 1:1 ratio. Runners lose not only water, but significant amounts of sodium and other minerals while sweating during the course of a marathon.

While Amanda was running the marathon she consumed water every 15 minutes. This contributed to an increase in her body's water content but caused a drop in her overall sodium levels. To prevent this from happening in the future, Amanda should begin the race well hydrated and drink during the race when she feels thirsty. She may also want to consider using sports drinks, which would replace not only the fluid but electrolyte losses.

**Registered Dietitian:**

## Peachy Seiden, MS, RD

Cincinnati, OH

Not everyone is fond of sports drinks, and it is understandable that Amanda prefers to drink water before, during, and after exercise. She does, however, need to consume adequate amounts of sodium-, potassium-, and chloride-containing foods *before* a marathon.

Electrolytes are readily accessible and are present in a wide array of foods, and obtaining the needed amounts is quite simple. Amanda needs to understand that the amount of electrolytes lost during vigorous exercise is tremendous, and a conscious effort must be made to replenish the reserves and replace the losses.

While carbohydrate loading several days before the event, Amanda should include foods that will add substantial amounts of electrolytes to her intake. Amanda likes rice and whole grains, which can be excellent sources of electrolytes when combined with other ingredients. For example, scrambled eggs, scallions, vegetables, and soy added to rice make a delicious Asian fried rice. Serving grains with seafood and poultry is another way to increase her electrolyte intake. Cooking whole grains with leafy greens and seasonings makes them both tasty and loaded with potassium.

Eating fresh salads with small amounts of cheese and condiments like capers or olives will ensure the presence of sodium and chloride in her diet. Snacking on fresh fruits will add the much-needed potassium.

I do not recommend additional salt on the table because by eating a wide variety of fruits, vegetables, poultry, seafood, and low-fat dairy, Amanda can easily obtain the appropriate amounts of electrolytes she needs for water balance and regulation.

# Absorption and Functions of Electrolytes

Absorption of electrolytes in the body is high, and their function affects our water balance. In addition to their role in water balance, electrolytes perform other important physiological functions. Because electrolyte deficiencies can be life-threatening, it is not sufficient to discuss water balance without considering the full role electrolytes play in maintaining good health.

## Absorption

The total amount of sodium, potassium, and chloride our bodies absorb is greater than that of other minerals. Once consumed, more than 90–95 percent of these minerals are absorbed. For other minerals, it is not surprising to experience less than 50 percent absorption. Because the body absorbs most of the electrolytes consumed, the kidneys must maintain balance. They can either rid the body of excess electrolytes or save them when the diet supplies inadequate amounts.

Sodium is absorbed by the small intestine and colon. It is required for the absorption of other important nutrients such as amino acids, glucose, and some B vitamins. Potassium absorption occurs along the length of the intestines, especially in the colon. Potassium is necessary for the absorption of sodium by the small intestine and colon. Chloride is absorbed along the length of the small intestine; its absorption is associated with sodium absorption.

## Physiological Functions

The movement of water and electrolytes across the cells of your body is extremely important for basic bodily functions. Water and electrolytes are moved across cells through two processes, diffusion and osmosis. **Diffusion** is the movement of electrolytes from an area of greater concentration to an area of lesser concentration. **Osmosis** is the movement of water across a membrane from an area where there are fewer particles to an area where there are more particles in order to equalize the concentration (Figure 8.7). Physiologically, this means that if sodium builds up outside the cells of a tissue, water moves from the inside to the outside of the cells to equalize the concentration of sodium. In practical terms, this means that excess salt intake can lead to edema, which is swelling in the extracellular tissues due to excess fluid retention.

Because sodium and potassium have charges when they dissolve in water, they can carry electrical currents. Sodium and potassium play a critical role in the function of what are known as excitable cells, such as those in nerves (neurons). When nerves transmit or send signals, sodium moves into the cell while potassium moves out (Figure 8.8). The cell quickly returns to equilibrium (rebalances) after the impulse has occurred.

As a component of hydrochloric acid (HCl), chloride establishes and maintains the acidic nature of the stomach. Cells within the stomach wall secrete HCl. This is especially important to help with the digestion of protein. Electrolytes play a critical role in buffering fluids in the body to maintain acid-base balance (pH). A very minor change in pH can have a dramatic negative effect on cell metabolism and overall health.

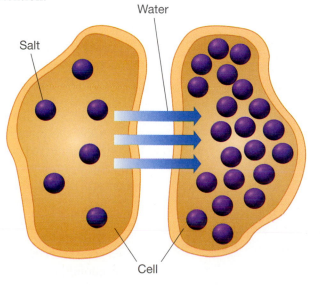

**Figure 8.7** Osmosis is a fundamental principle of biology whereby water is distributed among organs, tissues, cells, and the blood. Water moves to the area of greater salt concentration to equalize the concentration in both cells. The membrane is permeable to the water but not to the sodium in this example.

Water

Salt

Cell

**Figure 8.8** Involvement of sodium and potassium in a nerve impulse transmission.

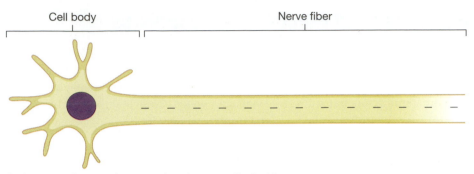

A. A nerve cell at rest has negative charge on the inside.

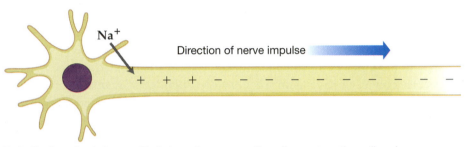

B. As the impulse is transmitted along the nerve cell, sodium enters the cell and causes a slight positive charge inside the cell.

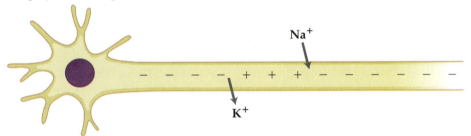

C. As the impulse travels along the nerve cell, potassium leaves the nerve cell and sodium continues to enter the cell. After the impulse is transmitted along the nerve cell, sodium is pumped out of the cell and potassium is pumped in to reestablish the resting state.

*Is it possible to not have enough sodium or potassium in our diets?*

## Deficiencies

A sodium deficiency rarely occurs, but it does happen. Loss of sodium is often accompanied by loss of body water or dehydration, which in extreme cases can lead to shocklike symptoms as blood volume falls and veins collapse. Loss of sodium through sweat, followed by replacement of water *without* adequate sodium, can lead to water intoxication. This occurs because the sodium concentration in the extracellular fluids is diluted. This condition is called **hyponatremia** or low blood sodium. Another way of stating this is that the blood becomes too dilute. Drinking several gallons of water in a few hours can lead to this. Common symptoms include loss of appetite, weakness, mental apathy, uncontrolled muscle twitching, and brain swelling. Death can result if the condition is severe. Water intoxication, or *overhydration* has been reported in marathon runners and other endurance athletes. They often consume plenty of water without electrolytes, and the water consumption dilutes the electrolyte content in their body fluids.

Although your potassium intake may be adequate, some situations can result in a potassium deficiency. For example, persistent use of laxatives can decrease the amount of potassium absorbed in your digestive tract. Chronic use of certain diuretics intended to control blood pressure may also result in increased urinary loss of potassium. Diuretics are substances that increase urine volume; water and electrolytes can be eliminated through the use of diuretics. Kidney disease and diabetes also may result in the excess excretion of potassium because of increased urination. In addition, frequent vomiting after eating, either involuntarily or voluntarily, ultimately reduces the absorption of potassium in the digestive tract. Diarrhea and vomiting over a period of a few days can lead to a potassium loss that results in muscle weakness, complete paralysis and failure of the digestive tract muscle, tachycardia (rapid heartbeat), and hypotension (low blood pressure). Extreme weight loss can lead to loss of muscle and potassium deficiency. In most cases, when you see your physician for an annual checkup, he or she will order blood tests that will include an assessment of your blood levels of sodium, potassium, and chloride.

## ■ What's Hot

### Should you use sports drinks when you exercise?

The issue of consuming sports drinks to improve performance when exercising or competing has been and continues to be a subject of much debate. Proper hydration is always critical for athletic performance because temperature regulation is highly dependent on hydration and the capacity to sweat. The amount of water lost during many events is tremendous, and it may take several days to replace what is lost. For instance, in endurance activities such as running, 2 qt. of fluid can be lost per hour. If you are involved in an event that lasts less than an hour in a mild climate, plain water will do fine. However, if you are participating in a longer event or one in which the intensity of exercise or performance is high or excess sweating is likely, then a sports drink may help. Not only do these beverages have electrolytes to replace those lost during sweating, some are composed of compounds (such as glucose) that help with water absorption in the small intestine. Even the presence of sodium in the beverage increases the body's absorption of water. In some cases, athletes may want to consume these beverages a day or two ahead of such vigorous events and afterward as well to ensure replenishment. However, a word of caution is in order. When these beverages are consumed during an event, gastrointestinal cramping may occur if their glucose content is too high. Some people dilute these drinks with water, but this is warranted only if the carbohydrate concentration is much greater than 6 percent. Carbohydrate concentrations in most sports drinks are less than or equal to 6 percent. Weighing before and after a strenuous physical activity can help determine how much fluid replacement is needed. In general, 2 1/2 c. of fluid are needed to replace 1 lb. of weight lost due to water depletion.

When you choose a sports drink, the carbohydrate concentration should be 6 percent (from a combination of sucrose, fructose, and glucose) for optimal water absorption. Fructose-only drinks should be avoided because they can decrease water absorption and cause abdominal cramping. The drink should contain sodium (which will give it a somewhat salty taste) in order to increase the desire to take in fluids. It is not advisable to use beverages that contain caffeine, as the caffeine can lead to mild dehydration. Although, the impact of caffeine on dehydration in athletes may be overstated, there has been a call from some experts for the Food and Drug Administration to regulate

**Want to know more?**

You can explore the topic of fluid and electrolyte intake during exercise more completely, by visiting the text website at http://webcom8.grtxle .com/nutrition and clicking on the Chapters button. Select Chapter 8.

highly caffeinated beverages and place a warning sign on them. In general, sports drinks may be preferable to consuming large amounts of plain water to help prevent water intoxication or dangerously low blood sodium levels. Water intoxication rarely occurs in people who consume adequate calories and electrolytes. ■

### Before you go on . . .

1. How do sodium and potassium play a role in the work of muscle and nerve cells?
2. What is the difference between diffusion and osmosis?
3. What is the relationship between dietary sodium, potassium, and calcium intake and blood pressure?
4. When can you be at risk for potassium deficiency?
5. Describe a potential benefit and potential problem of consuming a sports drink in connection with exercise.

## Real People, Real Strategies

Amanda discussed her postmarathon reaction with a friend who informed her about the danger of becoming overhydrated and developing hyponatremia while running, especially longer distances, and suggested that the fact that she drank plain water without replacing lost electrolytes could have been her problem. Amanda's friend suggested that a sports drink that contains 6 percent glucose, or other simple sugar, plus sodium and potassium for electrolyte replacement, might be her best bet. She went to a sports medicine physician who told her she might be experiencing water intoxication. Based on his recommendations, Amanda addressed the problem by adding a little extra salt to her meals in the following days and by consuming fruit juices containing potassium. Although most Western diets have sufficient salt, in this case a little extra salt was warranted. The doctor warned her not to take salt pills before a marathon or other athletic event, as this would strain her heart and kidneys during the actual event. Amanda's symptoms went away, and she learned a good lesson about staying properly hydrated during exercise. The next time she runs a marathon she will know more precisely what to do both before and after the event. Moreover, she learned a valuable lesson in how to interpret information on hydration from the various magazines and websites she consults.

## Chapter Summary

- Fifty-six to 64 percent (by weight) of the adult human body is composed of water. Women have less water than men because of their higher body fat percentage.
- Water consists of two hydrogen atoms and one oxygen atom bonded together. Hydrogen has a slight positive charge, whereas oxygen has a slight negative charge. This difference in charges makes water an ideal medium for dissolving elements that have charges.
- Water is the largest component of both intracellular fluids (inside cells) and extracellular fluids (outside cells). It serves as a medium in which other nutrients are carried and in which biochemical reactions occur. These biochemical reactions generate body heat, which water absorbs to maintain the body's temperature at 98.6° F or (37°C).
- Water loss occurs in several ways: urine, mild to severe sweating, feces, and lungs (breathing). Losses should be balanced with intake of water in food, beverages, and metabolic water.
- The hypothalamus within the brain controls our sensation of thirst and monitors the body's fluid salt concentration. If the salt concentration is high, antidiuretic hormone is released by the pituitary gland to signal the kidneys to retain water. Aldosterone is produced by the adrenal glands; it induces the kidneys to retain more sodium and consequently more water.
- Dehydration is dangerous. During exercise, dehydration can occur rapidly along with electrolyte loss. Dehydration may also occur through vomiting and diarrhea. It can lead to cramping, heat exhaustion, stroke, and death. Drinking fluids with electrolytes is the best way to compensate for dehydration.

- Urine is the chief excretory route for body water and metabolic waste. The kidneys control the composition of urine and blood through microscopic structures called *nephrons.*
- Electrolytes are minerals that when placed in water become charged particles. Some minerals are positively charged (cations); others are negatively charged (anions).
- Sodium is the primary cation found outside cells, while potassium is the primary cation found inside cells. Chloride, an anion, is usually associated with sodium and therefore is more concentrated outside cells. These elements are heavily involved in the proper maintenance of water balance. If sodium builds up outside cells, water moves from inside the cells and blood compartment to outside the cells via osmosis.
- The adult dietary requirement for sodium may be as low as 100–500 mg/day. Americans tend to consume about 10–15 g/day of salt, or 4–6 g of sodium—about eight to twelve times the estimated requirement. The sodium occurring naturally in foods such as eggs, milk, meats, and vegetables may supply only about 10–15 percent of sodium intake. The remainder comes from salt added to food in processing, in cooking, and at the table.
- Populations that consume a high level of salt normally experience a greater incidence of hypertension. For many years, health professionals have advocated reducing salt intake to decrease the incidence of hypertension. The DASH diet is frequently recommended to people who need to lower their sodium intake.

## Key Terms

**aldosterone** Hormone produced by the adrenal glands above the kidneys. It induces the kidneys to retain more sodium and, consequently, more water. (p. 248)

**anion** (AN-eye-on) A mineral that is negatively charged. (p. 251)

**antidiuretic hormone** Hormone released by the pituitary gland in the brain to signal the kidneys to retain water. (p. 248)

**cation** (CAT-eye-on) A mineral that is positively charged. (p. 251)

**diastolic blood pressure** When the heart relaxes and blood pressure falls; the lowest blood pressure reading during cardiac relaxation. (p. 256)

**Dietary Approaches to Stop Hypertension (DASH)** A diet advocated to reduce the incidence of high blood pressure. (p. 258)

**diffusion** The movement of electrolytes from an area of greater concentration to an area of lesser concentration. (p. 261)

**essential hypertension** High blood pressure that is due to an unknown cause. (p. 255)

**extracellular** Outside a cell. (p. 244)

**hypertension** High blood pressure. (p. 255)

**hyperthermia** Increased body temperature. (p. 250)

**hyponatremia** (high-poh-na-TREE-mee-uh) Low blood sodium. (p. 262)

**inorganic** Describes a substance that does not contain carbon. (p. 244)

**insensible water loss** Water lost through daily sweating, exhalation of air, and other mechanisms. (p. 247)

**intracellular** Inside a cell. (p. 244)

**metabolic water** Water that is produced during the breakdown of carbohydrate, fats, and protein. (p. 244)

**nephrons** Microscopic structures in the kidneys that control the composition of urine and blood. (p. 251)

**organic** Descrbes a substance that contains carbon. (p. 244)

**osmosis** The movement of water across a membrane from an area where there are fewer particles to an area where there are more particles in order to equalize the concentration. (p. 261)

**systolic blood pressure** The peak pressure generated when the heart contracts and forces blood to move because of an increase in pressure from the pumping action. (p. 256)

**water intoxication** A condition caused by excess water consumption that results in dilution of blood electrolytes, particularly sodium. (p. 248)

# Chapter Quiz

1. Insensible water loss is all of the following *except:*
   a. occurs via mild sweating.
   b. occurs through exhalation of air through the lungs.
   c. occurs through fecal loss.
   d. urine.

2. Water produced in the body is
   a. oxidative water.
   b. edema.
   c. metabolic water.
   d. sweat.

3. Extracellular water is found in
   a. the blood.
   b. the lymph system.
   c. secretions of the eyes.
   d. all of the above

4. All of the following are high sources of sodium except
   a. baked ham.
   b. hot dogs.
   c. canned tomatoes.
   d. watermelon.

5. Including the water in foods, how many total cups of water per day should an adult consume under average environmental conditions?
   a. 1–2 c.
   b. 4–6 c.
   c. 8–12 c.
   d. 16–24 c.

6. Excess water consumption can lead to
   a. hyponatremia.
   b. hyperkalemia.
   c. hypernatremia.
   d. hyperthermia.

7. Which of the following electrolytes is found primarily inside a cell?
   a. sodium
   b. chloride
   c. water
   d. potassium

8. The microscopic structure that is involved with water and electrolyte balance and the disposal of waste from your body is
   a. the urine.
   b. the adrenal glands.
   c. the nephron.
   d. DASH.

9. A food item with a 75 percent reduction in sodium content can be described on the label as
   a. sodium free.
   b. no salt added.
   c. unsalted.
   d. reduced sodium.

10. Which of the following statements about water is false?
    a. It can absorb a lot of body heat.
    b. It lubricates the joints.
    c. It has a neutral charge.
    d. It makes up more than half of your body weight.

1. d; 2. c; 3. d; 4. d; 5. c; 6. a; 7. d; 8. c; 9. d; 10. c

Chapter Quiz Answer Key

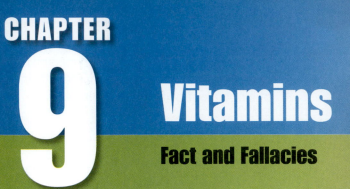

# CHAPTER 9

# Vitamins

## Fact and Fallacies

## < Here's Where You've Been

*The following topics were introduced in preceding chapters and are related to concepts we'll discuss in Chapter 9. Be certain that you're familiar with them before proceeding.*

- Vitamins are organic because they contain carbon. (Chapter 1)
- Carbohydrate, fats, and proteins are energy-yielding nutrients. (Chapters 3, 4, and 5)
- Vitamins are involved with energy metabolism. (Chapter 6)
- Sodium, potassium, and chloride are micronutrients and electrolytes. (Chapter 8)

## Here's Where You're Going >

*The following topics and concepts are the ones we'll emphasize in Chapter 9.*

- There are two classes of vitamins: fat soluble and water soluble.
- Vitamins do not provide energy, but many help the body obtain energy from the breakdown of carbohydrates, fats, and even proteins.
- Several vitamins work together to maintain physiological functions.
- Deficiencies of vitamins lead to specific physical symptoms.
- Some vitamins can produce toxic effects when consumed in excess.

## Real People, Real Choices

Anthony Pulz is a student at the University of Southern California. As an elective, he is taking an introductory nutrition class. Anthony works out regularly, plans his meals ahead of time, and is careful not to skip them. Although he believes he already knows quite a bit about nutrition and has good eating habits, he is interested in learning more about the relationship between health and nutrition. In addition to trying to eat a healthy diet, Anthony has been taking several vitamin supplements as part of a program promoted by his gym. Of the various vitamins he is taking, many provide 500 percent or more of the DRI. Anthony believes that these are a bonus, that the excess actually gives him an extra boost of energy when he works out. He has also been drinking protein shakes for breakfast and eating energy bars for snacks. He is eager to see the extra protein end up on his legs and arms as muscle mass. During a lecture in his nutrition class, Anthony's professor cautioned that taking supplements may not be wise, and he emphasized that a good diet should provide sufficient nutrients. During another class the possibility of toxicity resulting from an excess intake of vitamins was discussed. Moreover, Anthony's nutrition text reinforced his instructor's perspective.

Based on this new information Anthony becomes concerned that he may be overdoing his vitamin intake, but he also doubts that the fitness experts at the gym would promote a potentially harmful practice. What should Anthony do to resolve this conflict and still achieve his goal? Do you think he may be overdoing his vitamin intake? Do you think it is dangerous if he is?

Anthony's concerns about vitamin supplements and whether he should be taking them are very common. Many people take vitamin supplements, but wonder if they are choosing the right ones and how much they should take. Many consumers believe that more of a good thing is better for your health. But is it? In this chapter we will discuss the health benefits of vitamins and consider the question of how much is too much (see Chapter 11 for more on supplements).

During the twentieth century, the list of essential nutrients exploded. Thirteen organic substances, which came to be known as vitamins, took their place among nutrition's elite ranks as the essential nutrients. Although certain foods had long been associated with disease prevention and health promotion, technology and the capabilities of laboratory scientists took some time to catch up with speculation. Once scientists isolated vitamins from food, they could determine their functions and optimal levels, leading to the Dietary Reference Intakes (DRI) for vitamins (see Chapter 2 for more information).

Vitamins continue to fascinate nutritionists, medical professionals, and the general public. Today, vitamins and minerals are among the most popular dietary supplements, accounting for approximately $16 billion in sales in 2004. Although our current knowledge and understanding of vitamins may seem complete to the general public, we still have a lot to learn. As a result, DRI levels for vitamins continue to evolve.

Vitamins perform numerous roles in your body. They often work together to support common structural or functional goals. Many of the vitamins optimize health and can prevent disease. Fruit and vegetables contain many of these vitamins, and an increased intake of these foods can prevent chronic diseases such as cancer. In this chapter we will discuss which vitamins are found in what types of foods, and we'll explore what can happen if you get too much or too little of these nutrients.

## Vitamins: A Little Goes a Long Way

As we discussed in Chapter 1, the macronutrients (carbohydrates, proteins, and fats) are found in your body by the *pound* and are required in your diet in *gram* amounts. In contrast, micronutrients such as vitamins are found in your body in much lower levels and are required in your diet only in milligram and microgram amounts. One reason for this difference is that carbohydrates, proteins, and fats serve major structural roles in the body and provide the fuel that powers your cells. Vitamins, however, are involved with biochemical reactions or metabolism and therefore are needed in much smaller amounts. This does not mean that they are less important than macronutrients; in fact, macronutrients need vitamins to function properly. For example, the B vitamins are needed in the pathways used to break down macronutrients into a usable form of energy—ATP (see Chapter 6).

Although several vitamins are involved in regulating energy metabolism, they are not a fuel source and do not provide energy. Carbohydrates, fats, and proteins are stored in the body and serve as readily available fuel resources. An adult male can store about a pound of carbohydrate as glycogen and, depending on diet and activity, can store 10, 50, or 100 or more pounds of fat. In contrast, although vitamin $B_1$, which is known as thiamin, is critical for proper energy metabolism, your body contains less than a teaspoon of this nutrient. Figure 9.1 compares recommended intakes for both vitamins and minerals and the recommended intake levels of carbohydrate, fat, and protein.

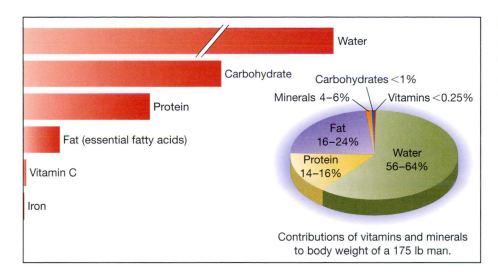

**Figure 9.1** Recommended intakes (bar graph) and contribution to body weight (pie chart) of macronutrients and micronutrients.

# *Vitamin* Refers to "Vitality"

Originally the term *vitamine* was developed in reference to the essential or vital *(vita)* and the presence of nitrogen *(amine)*. As more "vitamines" were identified, scientists learned that not all of them contain nitrogen. Thus, the term *vitamine* was shortened to the more familiar term *vitamin*.

As they were discovered, vitamins were assigned a letter (A, B, C, D, E, and K). This system became complicated, however, when researchers realized that vitamin B wasn't a single vitamin, but rather several different ones involved in similar functions in the body. Each vitamin was therefore assigned a subscript. Thus, thiamin is also known as vitamin $B_1$, riboflavin as $B_2$, niacin as $B_3$, pyridoxine as $B_6$, and cobalamin as $B_{12}$. Pantothenic acid, biotin, and folate are also B vitamins.

In addition to being assigned a letter and a subscript, vitamins are also categorized into two groups based on solubility (see Table 9.1). Thiamin, riboflavin, niacin, folate, biotin, pantothenic acid, and vitamins C, $B_6$, and $B_{12}$ are classified as water soluble. Vitamins A, D, E, and K do not dissolve well in water and are classified as fat soluble. There are also some vitamins called **provitamins** or precursors; these substances need to be converted in order to have vitamin-like activity in the body. Examples include **beta-carotene**, which is converted to vitamin A, and *tryptophan* (an essential amino acid), which is converted to niacin. Beta-carotene, an orange pigment with antioxidant properties, is produced in fruits and vegetables such as cantaloupe and sweet potatoes.

| **Table 9.1** | **Water-Soluble and Fat-Soluble Vitamins** |
|---|---|
| **Vitamins** | |

| **Water Soluble** | **Fat Soluble** |
|---|---|
| Vitamin C (ascorbic acid) | Vitamin A |
| Thiamin ($B_1$) | Vitamin D |
| Riboflavin ($B_2$) | Vitamin E |
| Niacin ($B_3$) | Vitamin K |
| Pyridoxine (vitamin $B_6$) | |
| Cobalamine (vitamin $B_{12}$) | |
| Biotin | |
| Pantothenic acid | |
| Folate | |

**Before you go on . . .**

1. List the water-soluble vitamins.
2. Why are vitamins A, D, E, and K called fat-soluble vitamins?
3. What is the origin of the term *vitamin*?
4. What is a provitamin?

# Fat-Soluble Vitamins

As mentioned previously, the four fat-soluble vitamins are A, D, E, and K. Fat-soluble vitamins are more likely to be toxic than water-soluble vitamins because they are stored for longer periods of time and in larger amounts. Because of this you do not need to consume fat-soluble vitamins daily. Fat-soluble vitamins are stored in the liver and the body's fat cells, which are not renewed as quickly as the body's water. Although these vitamins are stored longer and in larger amounts than the water-soluble vitamins, people can develop deficiency signs for them if they do not consume adequate amounts. It just usually takes longer for the deficiency to occur.

## Vitamin A

Vitamin A occurs in nature in three different chemical forms: retinol, retinal, and retinoic acid. These three forms are found in animal tissues. Retinol is the most active form of vitamin A and is stored in the liver. It can go to other tissues, and specific cells convert it to one of the other two forms. Beta-carotene, as noted previously, is an antioxidant found in plants. This plant pigment is converted into vitamin A if needed in the small intestine, and thus it is referred to as a precursor to vitamin A. The units in which beta-carotene and other precursors such as carotenoids are measured are called **retinol activity equivalents** or **RAE**. About 12 mcg of beta-carotene will produce 1 mcg of retinol; thus, you need twelve times as much beta-carotene to get the same benefit as retinol.

Vitamin A has many functions. It is involved in normal vision, gene regulation, immune function, bone growth, reproduction, cell membrane stability, integrity of epithelial cells (cells that make up the skin and lining of the digestive tract), synthesis of the hormone cortisol by the adrenal glands, maintenance of the lining that insulates nerves, production of red blood cells, and production of thyroid hormone. Let's consider some of these functions of vitamin A in more detail.

### Vitamin A and Eyesight

Vitamin A is so crucial to normal vision that a deficiency results in blindness. In fact, vitamin A deficiency is the leading cause of nonaccidental blindness throughout the world. An early sign of a vitamin A deficiency is night blindness or poor vision in dim lighting (see Figure 9.2). Night blindness is often coupled with poor flash recovery, such as when the lights are turned on in a dark room and you must adjust your eyes to seeing in the bright light. A person with a marginal vitamin A deficiency takes longer to recover from the flash and to reestablish vision. In fact, the eyes are so sensitive to vitamin A status that an injection of vitamin A can alleviate night blindness within minutes. Because carrots are an excellent source of beta-carotene, they are known for being "good" for your eyesight.

Vitamin A is also involved in the maintenance of healthy *cornea* tissue (the outer layer of the eye). When vitamin A is deficient, the cornea is transformed from moist and healthy to dry and hardened. Normal cells, which secrete mucus to help keep the cornea moist, become keratin-forming cells that dry out the eye covering. *Keratin* is a type of protein that is hard and tough, somewhat like fingernails. Not only is vision impaired as a result, but the change also makes the cornea more prone to infections and scarring. Irreversible damage to the eye caused by vitamin A deficiency is referred to as **xerophthalmia** and can lead to

*My grandmother always told me that eating carrots was good for my eyesight. Is that true?*

**(a)**

**(b)**

**(c)**

**Figure 9.2** Role of vitamin A in night vision. Note that after a flash of light (b), the eyes have difficulty adjusting and the room appears darker (c) compared to (a) before the light flash.

permanent loss of vision. Vitamin A deficiency can also lead to small grayish, foamy, triangular deposits on the eye called *bitot spots* (see Figure 9.3).

One of the most common age-related eye disorders is **macular degenerative disease**. It is actually a group of disorders characterized by the breakdown of the *macula*, the center portion of the retina that makes basic visual acuity possible. Several micronutrients are thought to be helpful in slowing this progressive disorder, including vitamin A. The carotenoids *lutein* and *zeothanthin* may also be protective because they have vitamin A–like activity. Carotenoids have vitamin A–like activity with a structure similar to beta-carotene. However, they are not as potent as beta-carotene; 24 mcg of carotenoids are equal to 1 mcg of retinol.

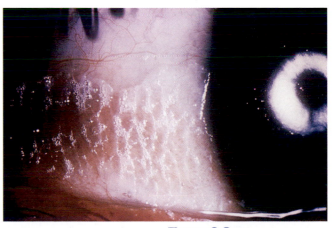

**Figure 9.3** Bitot spots on the cornea of the eye caused by vitamin A deficiency.

## Vitamin A and Immunity

Vitamin A plays an important role in immunity, particularly for children. It is important in the production of white blood cells, which destroy harmful bacteria and viruses. A vitamin A–deficient child has a weakened immune system and is more likely to become ill from a bacterial infection than a child who has ample stores of vitamin A. If the child who has low vitamin A stores becomes infected, any stores he or she does have can be further depleted. This creates a vicious cycle, and ultimately general malnutrition may result.

### Gene Regulation and Vitamin A

Vitamin A influences many functions of the body through its role in gene regulation. For example, many proteins that are produced by genes are enzymes that regulate metabolism. Vitamin A plays a role in whether these genes are turned on or off and therefore plays an indirect role in the regulation of metabolism through its influence on gene regulation. The form of vitamin A that has the greatest influence on gene regulation is retinoic acid.

### Bone Development and Growth

The role of vitamin A in the development of bone cannot be underestimated. Bone undergoes a process known as remodeling. This means that for bone to grow, it must be constantly broken down and rebuilt. Your body does not simply add more bone material on top of existing bone; the inner part of the bone is broken down and new bone is laid on the top and ends of the bone to make them wider and longer. Vitamin A stimulates the bone cells that break down the inner part of bone. Therefore, children who are deficient in vitamin A will most likely fail to grow.

### Skin Integrity, Lung Function, and Gastrointestinal Issues

*Epithelial* cells are found in the skin and lungs, and they also line the gastrointestinal tract. Vitamin A is very important in the maintenance of this type of cell and the tissues they compose. In vitamin A deficiency, epithelial tissue is often compromised. **Cell differentiation** is the process by which specialized cells develop that are capable of performing specific functions. These cells become specialized as they mature. This process depends on vitamin A. Also, special mucus-producing cells rely on vitamin A for development, and when vitamin A deficiency occurs, these cells die and the tissue becomes dry. Skin becomes flaky, hardened, and rough because of the production of keratin, as discussed earlier. These hard, rough cells compromise the integrity of the epithelial tissue barrier, which allows pathogens to more easily enter the body, increasing the risk of infection.

### Vitamin A Toxicity

Vitamin A has toxic effects because it is stored in the fat tissue and in the liver and therefore can be stored in the body for a long time and potentially accumulate to high levels. Eskimos are a primary example of people who have experienced the results of such accumulated levels. Historically, they consumed a lot of polar bear liver, which contains high levels of vitamin A. As a result they experienced *hypervitaminosis* or vitamin A toxicity. The tissues and cells affected by excess vitamin A are often the same ones affected by vitamin A deficiency. Symptoms of vitamin A toxicity include headache, abdominal pain, skin rashes, liver damage, diarrhea, nausea, hair loss, joint pain, and bone and muscle soreness. Itching skin, blurred vision, growth failure in children, and increased bone fractures are also common.

Pregnant women should be particularly concerned about consuming excessive amounts of vitamin A, because toxicity can cause fetal malformations. In fact, three to four times the DRI for vitamin A can lead to birth defects in newborn babies. Vitamin A toxicity can come from sources other than food. For example, Accutane, a drug used to

treat acne, is a vitamin A derivative. Women who are pregnant or planning to become pregnant should *not* take this medication because of the high risks of vitamin A toxicity.

### Recommended Intakes for Vitamin A

The DRI for vitamin A is 900 mcg per day for men and 700 mcg per day for women. Children have lower requirements. Women who are breast-feeding will need more vitamin A, ranging from 1,200 to 1,300 mcg per day depending on age. These amounts can easily be met through a balanced diet. Most healthy people do not require a vitamin A supplement. As mentioned previously, care should be taken not to exceed the Tolerable Upper Intake Level of 3,000 mcg per day, as there is a risk of toxicity.

Older tables and charts may list vitamin A recommendations in **International Units (IU)** instead of micrograms. That is because in previous years, the standard measurement of vitamin A requirements was in IUs. For example, one IU of retinol is equivalent to 0.3 mcg of retinol. However, the use of IUs has been abandoned, except on supplement labels, and the recommendations are now expressed in micrograms.

### Food Sources of Vitamin A

Vitamin A can be found in animal foods and products such as fortified milk, cheese, cream, butter, eggs, liver, and margarine with vitamin A added. Plant sources of provitamin A include spinach, dark green leafy vegetables, and broccoli. Vitamin A is abundant in orange and red foods such as apricots, cantaloupe, and certain vegetables such as winter squash, carrots, sweet potatoes, and pumpkins.

### ■ You Decide

*Should I take beta-carotene as a supplement?*

Although vitamin A is toxic if taken in large doses, beta-carotene is not. When you have enough vitamin A stores, your body is not as efficient at converting beta-carotene to vitamin A, and thus a toxicity problem is not likely. This is not to say that overconsuming beta-carotene has no side effects. Taking large doses of beta-carotene can turn your skin orange, especially the palms of your hands and soles of your feet. In fact, health food stores once sold "suntanning" pills that turned out to contain high levels of beta-carotene.

Because vitamin A is needed for health, yet can be toxic, it seems logical that beta-carotene supplementation may be safer than consuming large amounts of vitamin A. Furthermore, research has suggested that beta-carotene may help prevent heart disease and cancer. According to one significant study, a higher intake of certain green and yellow vegetables, which are rich sources of beta-carotene, may decrease the risk of lung cancer. Many bright red and orange fruits and vegetables are also good sources of beta-carotene.

It appears, however, that taking beta-carotene supplements does not prevent disease and may lead to some adverse effects. For example, one study that evaluated both vitamin E and beta-carotene supplementation in 30,000 men who smoked cigarettes reported that those who took just the beta-carotene supplement had an 18 percent increase in the incidence of lung cancer over a five-to-eight-year trial period compared to those who took no supplement, a vitamin E supplement, or a combination of beta-carotene and vitamin E supplement.

A second study called the Carotene and Retinol Efficiency Trial (CARET) gave either vitamin A supplements or beta-carotene supplements to adults to determine whether they could prevent lung cancer. The study had to be stopped because those who received the beta-carotene supplement had an *increased* incidence of lung cancer! In fact, those who took the beta-carotene supplement had a 46 percent higher chance of dying from lung cancer than those who did not receive the supplement.

Largely because of these studies, health professionals do not recommend beta-carotene supplementation for the general public. Again, getting too little or too much of a vitamin has associated risks. Based on this information, how would you propose to get enough vitamin A? ∎

## Vitamin D

### A Vitamin with Many Roles

Another name for vitamin D is *cholecalciferol*. In addition to being classified as a vitamin, vitamin D is classified as a hormone and a steroid. Its precursor is cholesterol, as mentioned in Chapter 4.

In recent years, scientists have discovered many new roles of vitamin D. Traditionally, it was known for its important role in bone development and maintenance. The main effect of vitamin D on bone is its ability to control metabolism of both calcium and phosphorus, two important minerals involved in bone integrity (see Chapter 10).

Vitamin D plays a crucial role in the regulation of calcium metabolism. It stimulates the cells of the small intestine to produce a calcium-binding protein called *calbindin*, which increases calcium absorption. When blood calcium levels begin to decline, vitamin D stimulates calbindin production, and more calcium is absorbed from food. In addition, when blood levels of calcium begin to drop, vitamin D stimulates the kidneys to conserve calcium by decreasing urinary excretion. Vitamin D also causes the bones to release calcium to help maintain blood levels.

Vitamin D has many important functions besides bone health. We have already mentioned the role of vitamin A in cell differentiation; vitamin D also plays a role in cell differentiation by activating or repressing certain genes.

### Vitamin D Deficiency and Bone Effects

Vitamin D deficiency in children results in a disease called **rickets** (see Figure 9.4). Rickets is a softening and deformity of long bones. This results in a "bowlegged" appearance because of the inability to deposit calcium in newly formed bone. Essentially, the bone is unable to support the body weight, and it "bows" outward. Vitamin D deficiency can also cause the skull, the rib cage, and the ends of long bones to be malformed. Brain development, tooth spacing, and normal respiration can be affected as the result of these malformations. Years ago, it was

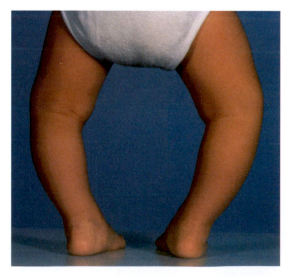

**Figure 9.4** A child with rickets. Note the classical bowlegged appearance.

discovered that the consumption of cod liver oil could prevent this because of its high vitamin D content. Children who do not get sufficient sunlight can also have the same deficiency signs.

In adults, a lack of vitamin D leads to softening of bone called **osteomalacia** caused by decalcification. Because adult bones are already developed, the bowlegged appearance is not present. Older adults, particularly older women, are often at high risk when they do not get enough vitamin D in their diets or adequate exposure to sunlight.

### Making Your Own Vitamin D

Although vitamin D is a nutrient, some contend that it is not essential. The human body can make vitamin D as long as it has adequate exposure to sunlight. Cholesterol in the liver combines with ultraviolet rays (from sunlight or tanning lamps) and is converted into a precursor of vitamin D. Through a series of steps it is ultimately converted to the active form of vitamin D (see Figure 9.5). Despite the ability to obtain vitamin D from sunlight, you should also consume vitamin D–rich foods, because many people do not get enough sunlight.

Those who live in areas of the world with limited daylight during winter months may be at risk for vitamin D deficiency. The farther you live from the equator, the longer the exposure time needed to get enough vitamin D. Cloud cover, smog, clothing, and sunscreen all interfere with or block UV rays. A sunscreen with SPF 8 can block the body's ability to produce vitamin D by 95 percent. In addition, those with darker complexions require longer periods under UV rays to convert cholesterol to the vitamin D precursor. People with light skin may require only ten to fifteen minutes of sunlight per day to get several days' worth of vitamin D, whereas people with darker skin may need

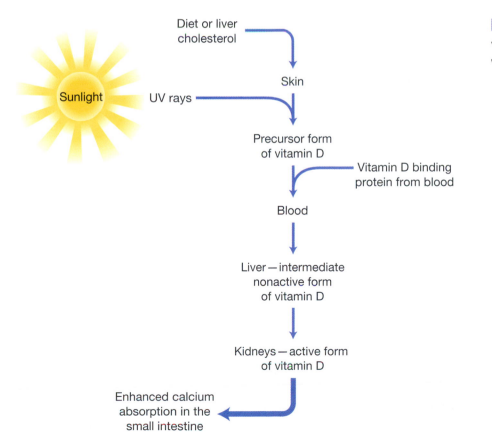

**Figure 9.5** Production of vitamin D in the body, starting with exposure to sunlight.

several hours of sun exposure to get the same amount. Without adequate dietary intake, those who live in northern areas with long winters may be at risk for vitamin D deficiency. In order to receive the benefits of exposure to sunlight, 20 percent of the skin should be exposed. Getting sunlight through windows does not work, as UV light cannot penetrate glass. Tanning beds have UV light and contribute to the formation of vitamin D. However, prolonged UV exposure is not recommended because of its link to skin cancer.

## Vitamin D Toxicity

As with vitamin A, vitamin D can lead to toxicity because it can be stored in fat and is not readily excreted from the body. Symptoms of vitamin D toxicity include nausea, vomiting, and diarrhea. It may also lead to the calcification of soft tissues. For instance, the heart, blood vessels, brain, and kidneys may be targeted for calcium deposition with excess vitamin D intake. The ability to fortify foods with vitamin D is strictly regulated because of the potential high risk of toxicity. Additionally, one must be careful not to oversupplement with vitamin D.

## Recommended Intakes for Vitamin D

The DRI for vitamin D was 5 mcg per day for adults until recently. In November 2010, the DRI was increased to 15 mcg per day for infants, children, adolescents, and adults up to 70 years of age. For adults older than 70, the DRI increases to 20 mcg per day because of their decreased ability to convert vitamin D to its active form and decreased likelihood of adequate exposure to sunlight. The Tolerable Upper Intake Level for vitamin D has been increased to 100 mcg per day.

There has been controversy over whether the recommended levels of dietary vitamin D are sufficient to promote health. Much of this arises from the corresponding blood vitamin D concentrations thought to be optimal. A level of the active form of vitamin D in the serum of 15 ng/ml of serum is recommended to optimize health. Some advocate even 30 ng/ml or greater. However, many individuals, particularly children, do not achieve this level. This issue is compounded even more by race, because individuals with darker skin have more pigmentation, which decreases the synthesis of active vitamin D. Therefore the American Academy of Pediatrics in 2008 recommended that the intake of vitamin D for children be increased from 5 mcg per day to 10 mcg per day. This lead to the most current recommendation of a DRI of 10 mcg per day for all age groups.

## Food Sources of Vitamin D

In addition to sunlight, food sources that contain good quantities of vitamin D include vitamin D–fortified milk or margarine, liver, sardines, salmon, and shrimp. Cheeses and yogurts are not often fortified with vitamin D. There are two types of vitamin D. Vitamin D2 is found in milk, cereal and fortified juices, and vitamin D3 is found in oily fish and also obtained from skin production. For teens, 3 c. of milk per day will provide 50 percent of the DRI for vitamin D. Remember that a combination of sunlight and food sources will *best* meet the daily requirement for vitamin D.

### ■ To Supplement or Not

Recently there has been an increased interest in vitamin D. Much of this growing interest is powered by new data being extracted from the National Health and Nutrition Examination Survey (NHANES). The newest statistics demonstrate that more than 90% of people of

---

**APPLICATION TIP**

Exposure of a person in a bathing suit to a minimal dose of sunlight, no more than 15–20 minutes at noon time, is the equivalent to taking 20,000 IU of vitamin D orally.

ethnicities that have darker skin in the United States (Blacks, Hispanics, and Asians) now suffer from vitamin D insufficiency (25-hydroxyvitamin D <30 ng/ml), and that nearly three fourths of the white population in this country is also vitamin D insufficient. This represents a near doubling of the prevalence of vitamin D insufficiency over levels seen just 10 years ago in the same populations. We have known for some time that vitamin D insufficiency is linked to bone diseases such as osteoporosis. In addition, recent evidence has suggested a link between vitamin D insufficiency and heart disease, respiratory infections, diabetes, hypertension, and obesity. Some experts are recommending that all obese patients and those at risk for the associated diseases be screened for vitamin D insufficiency by measuring levels of 25-dihydroxyvitamin D. If levels are below normal, large doses are given over several weeks and monitored by a clinician. Because natural sunlight is our primary source of vitamin D and many people are limiting their exposure to sunlight, many experts are recommending that individuals either increase exposure to sunlight to 15 minutes a day, or take a daily vitamin D supplement that contains at least the DRI. There is evidence to suggest that adults over 65 may require as much as 20 mcg to prevent falls. ■

# Vitamin E

## A Vitamin That Fights Against Free Radicals

Vitamin E is not just one compound, but a group of compounds called **tocopherols**. There are four different types of tocopherols; the Greek letters *alpha, beta, gamma,* and *delta* are used to identify them. They all have different degrees of vitamin E activity, with alpha-tocopherol having the greatest vitamin E activity.

Besides being essential for reproduction, vitamin E fights against **free radicals** and is thus an *antioxidant nutrient*. Remember that free radicals are unstable compounds with an unpaired electron that attack other molecules and break them down, damaging cell membranes, proteins, enzymes, molecules, and even the genetic material DNA. Free radicals can increase the risk of cancer, heart disease, and accelerated aging. Vitamin E acts as a "shock absorber" by donating one of its unpaired electrons to the free radical to neutralize it. If left unpaired, free radicals cause a chain reaction in which one free radical sets off other compounds to becoming free radicals, leading to rapid destruction (see Figure 9.6).

Because vitamin E is fat soluble, it affords greater protection to lipid membranes or other fat-soluble compounds in a cell as opposed to free radicals found in the watery parts of cells and tissues. In fact, vitamin E in cells is located in the fat portion of membranes. Tissues that have high exposure to oxygen, such as the lungs and red blood cells, are much more susceptible to free radical damage that can be lessened by the presence of vitamin E. In addition to its potent role as an antioxidant, vitamin E also enhances the immune system and is needed for nerve cell development.

In the past, some health professionals recommended the use of vitamin E supplements to protect against cancer and cardiovascular disease. It would appear that adhering to a healthy diet, moderating the intake of alcohol, and enhancing physical activity all provide much more benefit than taking large doses of vitamin E. Government reports suggest that a claim that vitamin E supplements can reduce the incidence of cancer and cardiovascular disease lacks sufficient evidence at this time.

**Figure 9.6** Free radicals can damage cells in the body. Notice the various sources that can cause free radical damage.

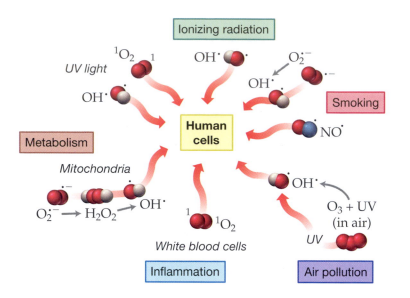

### Vitamin E Deficiency

Vitamin E deficiency has been reported in laboratory animals but rarely occurs in humans. This is because vitamin E is abundant in the food supply, the human body has large stores of it, and the body recycles what it does have. Deficiency is most likely to occur in premature infants because they have not had sufficient time to build up vitamin E stores, which normally begins during the last weeks of pregnancy. Red blood cells in an infant are fragile and tend to rupture in vitamin E deficiency, which leads to **anemia** (below-normal levels of red blood cells, hemoglobin, or both). In adults, deficiency is most likely to appear in those who have malabsorption of the fat-soluble vitamins due to medications or disease. In addition, those on an extremely low-fat diet or taking large amounts of fat blockers for prolonged periods can experience deficiency. Signs of vitamin E deficiency include loss of muscle coordination and reflexes, muscle weakness, reproductive failure, and impaired vision. All of these are reversible with vitamin E supplementation.

### Vitamin E Toxicity

Vitamin E can be toxic. Years ago popular literature advocated the benefits of vitamin E for its ability to enhance sexual pleasure and as an anti-aging nutrient. At that time many people taking vitamin E supplements began to show signs of toxicity. These included headache and nausea, blurred vision, reduced sexual function in men, accelerated signs of aging, inflammation of the mouth, chapped lips, fatigue, gastrointestinal disturbances, muscle weakness, and increased bleeding. Research shows that extra vitamin E does not enhance sexual performance or slow the aging process.

### Recommended Intakes for Vitamin E

The DRI for vitamin E is 15 mg per day for adults. The requirement increases among those who have a diet high in polyunsaturated fatty acids, which increases the likelihood of free radical formation. The Tolerable Upper Intake Level for vitamin E is 1,000 mg per day. It may be lower for some people, such as those who smoke, because some research suggests an increased incidence of brain hemorrhage among smokers who take vitamin E supplements.

### Food Sources of Vitamin E

Foods that are good sources of vitamin E include vegetable oils and products made with them, such as margarine and salad dressings. Wheat germ, nuts, seeds, and green leafy vegetables are also good sources of vitamin E.

## Vitamin K

### Roles in Blood Clotting and Bone Development

Vitamin K is best known for its role in blood clotting (see Figure 9.7). Vitamin K is indirectly involved with the production of the protein **fibrin**, which forms blood clots. Those without sufficient vitamin K stores may have trouble clotting when they bleed.

Blood clotting is a complex process in which several biochemical reactions occur before fibrin is formed. Vitamin K is needed to activate several proteins in these biochemical reactions. One of the steps is the conversion of *prothrombin* to *thrombin,* which requires vitamin K. Thrombin can then form the clot by converting *fibrinogen* to fibrin.

Of more recent interest has been the role of vitamin K in bone development, because it is needed for the synthesis of some key bone proteins. Without the presence of these proteins, minerals such as calcium cannot bind to the bone. Thus bone becomes soft, as in vitamin D deficiency.

### Vitamin K Deficiency and Toxicity

Despite the risk in newborns, vitamin K deficiency is rare in adults. Those who take antibiotics for a prolonged period of time may have difficulty because the antibiotics kill the bacteria in the large intestine, which in turn can decrease vitamin K stores. Overall, though, the chance of a vitamin K deficiency is rare. The DRI for vitamin K is 120 mcg per day for men and 90 mcg per day for women.

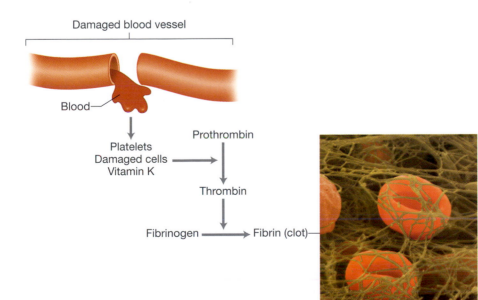

**Figure 9.7** Role of vitamin K in the blood clotting process.

There is no Tolerable Upper Intake Level. However, this does not mean that excess consumption has no negative effects, because large amounts have been shown to cause red blood cells to break apart. Cases of jaundice in infants have also been reported with vitamin K excess.

### Food and Other Sources of Vitamin K

Good sources of vitamin K include green leafy vegetables such as spinach and collard greens, and vegetables from the cabbage family such as broccoli and brussels sprouts. Soybeans and vegetable oils also contain vitamin K. The most significant source of vitamin K is not food—it is your body. The bacteria in the large intestine can synthesize vitamin K. In fact, newborns are given a shot of vitamin K at birth because they do not have an adequate amount of bacteria, and breast milk is a poor source of vitamin K.

## ■ What's Hot?

### Soda for breakfast?

Fortified cereals and orange juice with added calcium were the highest-selling functional foods in 2006. Because of their growing popularity, there is increased competition in the functional foods market as producers of sodas and other beverages join the battle for the consumer's dollar. With the increase in new beverages claiming to provide 100 percent of the DRI for vitamins and minerals, many children will no doubt attempt to argue that soda is the best choice for a beverage at mealtime. After all, if you believe the marketing hype, these drinks appear to offer all the vitamins and minerals, not just the calcium of milk or the vitamin C of orange juice. The hype of these new products is in direct contrast to the recent campaigns by the Dairy Council and other groups to try to get kids to stop drinking soda. The contrasting messages have left many consumers a bit confused.

The surge in availability and variety of nutrient-enriched drinks has occurred as a direct response to consumers' desire for healthier beverage alternatives to soda. According to the Beverage Marketing Corporation, nutrient-infused beverages tripled in sales in the United States between 2001 and 2006. By comparison, the U.S. beverage industry overall experienced only a 5 percent annual rate of growth.

With so many beverages to choose from, companies are making questionable and even outlandish claims. For example, Vitaminwater's peach-and-mango "endurance" flavor says it contains as much vitamin E as two apples and that it can "enhance physical endurance." The Food and Drug Administration, which regulates the claims food and drink makers can put on their labels, does not require companies to seek approval for these declarations before the drinks reach store shelves. Specific health claims of links between a product and disease or about how a nutrient affects functions of the body (such as energy and endurance) are supposed to be backed by scientific evidence. However, the FDA cannot get involved until after the product is available to consumers and questionable claims have been made.

Many experts agree that, unlike regular soda, these beverages do contain some added nutrients. However, the nutrients that they most often contain are the ones we need the least. The B vitamins and vitamin C are what are most often added because they are water soluble and can be added without significantly changing the taste. These vitamins are therefore added to a lot of foods and are abundant in the food supply. So it's overkill. Some companies have tried to address the overkill by adding nutrients that are often lacking in the U.S. diet, such as fiber. Dasani Plus has 1 g of fiber, but this is only 4 percent of the daily value.

In addition to making suspect claims and adding potentially unnecessary nutrients, these beverages also contain calories. Although most do not contain as much as a regular sugared soda, it is still more than water. The other concern is that because they are marketed as health-oriented products, many consumers may overlook the extra calories, which in the long run can add up to weight gain. Of course, there is also the high cost. Many of these drinks cost twice as much as bottled water or regular soda.

The bottom line: although these drinks may be healthier than the sugared versions of regular soda in that they typically have a few less calories and more nutrients, they are not a wise or useful substitute for nutrient-dense foods, particularly fruits and vegetables, which have many healthy phytochemicals and health benefits. If you really want to drink your vitamins and minerals, make fruit smoothies by blending fresh or frozen fruits with water, juice, or milk and crushed ice, and you can even add honey, yogurt, or peanut butter and make it into a meal.

Reprinted by permission of Wall Street Journal, Copyright © 2007 Dow Jones & Company, Inc. All Rights Reserved Worldwide. License number 2498951037707. ■

**Before you go on . . .**

1. List the food sources of vitamin A.
2. How does vitamin A deficiency influence the eye and vision?
3. What are some good sources of vitamin D?
4. What is the major role of vitamin E?
5. What is the primary role of vitamin K, and why is deficiency rare?

## Water-Soluble Vitamins

As indicated previously, water-soluble vitamins are not as toxic as fat-soluble vitamins because they are rapidly excreted with the urine. Therefore, it is difficult to get toxic levels of these vitamins from food sources. However, some water-soluble vitamins can be toxic if taken in large enough quantities, such as those that may occur with extreme supplement use. People often take large doses of vitamins to prevent or treat various conditions. For example, vitamin C is often taken in large doses to prevent or treat the common cold.

## Vitamin C

Another name for vitamin C is **ascorbic acid**. Its use goes back several centuries to when British sailors on long voyages came down with **scurvy**, a disease noted for bleeding gums that eventually leads to death. Scurvy is caused by a vitamin C deficiency. Consumption of limes was found to prevent and treat it, which is how British sailors got the nickname "limeys." It was later discovered that other fruits could also prevent this disease, and sailors began to take ample supplies of fruit on long voyages.

### Role of Vitamin C

Vitamin C plays several roles. Like vitamin E, vitamin C is an antioxidant. However, because it is water soluble, it protects cell constituents in the watery part of the cell. For example, immune system cells have a lot of vitamin C in order to protect themselves against free radicals. This is important, because a lot of free radical production occurs when the white blood cells of the immune system attack and kill bacteria and other foreign substances that cause illness.

Another important function of vitamin C is the production of the protein **collagen**. Collagen forms connective tissues such as tendons, bone, teeth, and skin. Vitamin C helps with the enzyme functions that are involved with the synthesis of collagen. Without vitamin C, the collagen that is made is abnormal. Vitamin C plays a critical role in healing wounds and maintaining the structure of blood vessels.

### Vitamin C Deficiency

Scurvy is the result of severe vitamin C deficiency. Most of its symptoms are due to the improper formation of collagen. Bleeding gums, a classic sign, is caused by a lack of collagen in the structure of the blood vessels of the gums. Other signs of deficiency include loss of appetite, impaired growth, weakness, swollen wrists and ankles, and tiny hemorrhages on the skin surface that look like red spots. Anemia can also occur, because vitamin C helps enhance iron absorption from nonmeat sources in the small intestine, and without it iron may not be adequately absorbed. In infants, a sign of vitamin C deficiency is a *scorbutic rosary*, an abnormal formation on the rib cage where the ribs appear "beaded."

### Vitamin C Toxicity

Although the Tolerable Upper Intake Level is 2,000 mg per day, there is controversy as to whether vitamin C is actually toxic. Many individuals supplement far in excess of the DRI and show no signs of vitamin C toxicity. For some individuals, however, supplementing at greater than 1,000 mg per day may lead to diarrhea and bloating.

Vitamin C contributes to a healthy immune system, but does consuming an amount beyond the DRI provide any benefit? Studies examining this issue have found that people who supplement their intake of vitamin C are just as likely to get a cold as those who do not. In addition, in very large doses it can cause adverse symptoms. Despite some individuals' ability to tolerate excessive intake without serious symptoms, there is concern that excess vitamin C may lead to kidney stones; those with compromised kidney function should refrain from supplementing and should consume less than 200 mg per day. Vitamin C excess can also affect certain diagnostic tests. For instance, people who consume excess vitamin C may not have any evidence of blood in their stools, but may have internal bleeding. Physicians usually ask patients to refrain from high levels of vitamin C during such tests.

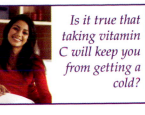

*Is it true that taking vitamin C will keep you from getting a cold?*

### Recommended Intakes for Vitamin C

The DRI for vitamin C is 90 mg per day for men and 75 mg per day for women. This is much higher than the ten to fifteen mg needed to prevent scurvy.

One population is at risk for low vitamin C stores: people who smoke. Studies have demonstrated that smokers consistently have lower blood levels of vitamin C because their bodies use the vitamin C to help protect against the damaging compounds introduced by the tobacco. Therefore, male smokers should consume 125 mg of vitamin C per day and female smokers 110 mg per day.

### Food Sources of Vitamin C

The best sources of vitamin C are fruits and vegetables. Orange juice is perhaps the best-known source. Foods such as peppers, brussels sprouts, broccoli, citrus fruits, strawberries, and sweet potatoes are also excellent sources of vitamin C. However, cooking can affect the level of vitamin C in these foods, because heat and exposure to air can destroy or diminish it. The health benefits associated with the various methods for preparing and cooking vegetables are discussed in the following Make It a Practice feature.

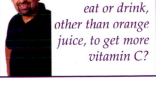

*Is there anything that I can eat or drink, other than orange juice, to get more vitamin C?*

### ■ Make It a Practice

#### How to cook your vegetables

There's more than one way to cook a vegetable, and all methods do not yield the same nutritional results. For example, boiling vegetables can result in loss of vitamins (especially water-soluble vitamins) and minerals into the cooking water. Microwaving, stir-frying, and steaming are more nutritious alternatives. Some experts maintain that steaming is superior to microwaving because it helps retain health-promoting flavonoids. On the other hand, microwaving's reduced cooking time can mean greater retention of vitamins that are sensitive to heat, such as vitamin C. When cooking vegetables, it is best to keep them as whole as possible; this results in less surface area being exposed, and thus fewer nutrients are lost. Regardless of cooking style, eating some vegetables every day is better than having no vegetables at all! ■

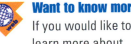

**Want to know more?**
If you would like to learn more about the role of vitamin C in the prevention of disease, go to the text website at http://webcom8.grtxle.com/nutrition and click on the Chapters button. Select Chapter 9.

## B Vitamins

The B vitamins play multiple roles in energy metabolism. For example, thiamin, riboflavin, niacin, pantothenic acid, and biotin participate in the release of energy from carbohydrate, protein, and fat (Figure 9.8). Vitamins $B_6$ and $B_{12}$ are key nutrients in the processing and release of energy from amino acids. Vitamin $B_{12}$ is also involved in the breakdown of glycogen stores to provide fuel during fasting and exercise.

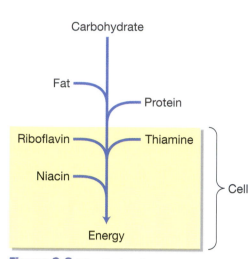

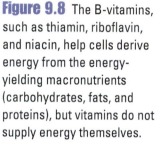

**Figure 9.8** The B-vitamins, such as thiamin, riboflavin, and niacin, help cells derive energy from the energy-yielding macronutrients (carbohydrates, fats, and proteins), but vitamins do not supply energy themselves.

The B vitamins function in energy metabolism as **coenzymes** or *cofactors* (see Figure 9.9). Coenzymes combine with an enzyme to increase its activity. Cofactors are molecules that are absolutely necessary for enzymes to work. As coenzymes and cofactors, the B vitamins are "energy helpers," although they don't provide energy directly.

Because of their role as "energy helpers," B vitamins are often added to energy drinks and other supplements marketed as energy boosters. Little scientific evidence suggests that B vitamins in excess of the DRI provide any extra "energy." Furthermore, without adequate calories, macronutrients, and other nutrients, B vitamins alone will not increase energy.

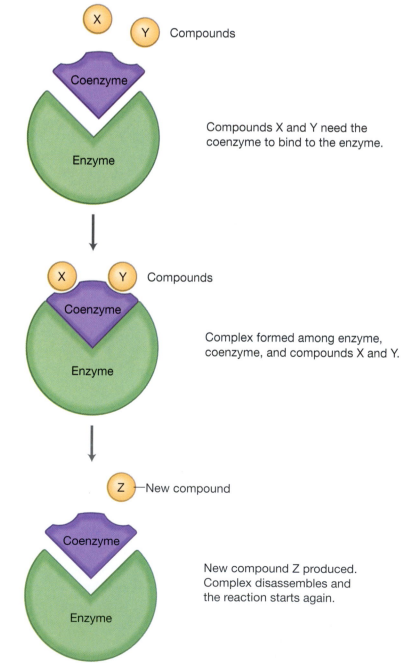

**Figure 9.9** Some vitamins take part in biochemical reactions by acting as coenzymes. This scheme illustrates how a coenzyme helps an enzyme bind to a compound to create a biochemical reaction, which usually means that less energy is needed for the reaction to occur.

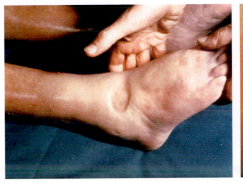

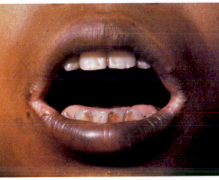

**(a)**                                        **(b)**

**Figure 9.10** (a) Thiamin deficiency causes the disease beriberi. Here we see one sign of the disease, swelling of tissue under the skin at the ankle. (b) A riboflavin deficiency can affect the mouth. In this individual, we see cracks at the corners of the mouth and a glossy tongue, both of which are symptoms of an inadequate intake.

## Thiamin, Riboflavin, and Niacin

Thiamin, riboflavin, and niacin, as they are more commonly known, are also referred to as vitamins $B_1$, $B_2$, and $B_3$, respectively. They are all involved in the processes used to obtain usable energy, or ATP, from carbohydrates, fats, and proteins (see Chapter 6). Despite their similar functions, deficiencies in each can produce different physical signs in humans.

### Functions and Deficiencies

Thiamin's major role is to help release the energy from carbohydrates. It also plays a role in nerve function because thiamin can be found within the cell membranes of a nerve cell. **Beriberi**, the result of thiamin deficiency, is a condition in which the heart becomes enlarged, fluid under the skin can accumulate, and the muscles become weak and may atrophy. Riboflavin also plays a major role in the release of energy from carbohydrates and is also a cofactor for enzymes involved in the breakdown of fatty acids for energy. Riboflavin deficiency often occurs along with thiamin deficiency. The signs of riboflavin deficiency include cracks at the corners of the mouth, inflammation of the tongue, hypersensitivity to light, and skin rashes (see Figure 9.10).

Niacin can be found in two chemical forms: nicotinic acid and nicotinamide. Like thiamin and riboflavin, niacin is used to release energy from the macronutrients, and it is also involved in fatty acid synthesis. Almost every metabolic pathway in the body has an enzyme that depends on niacin as a cofactor. Thus, when you have a niacin deficiency, the symptoms appear to result in more changes. Niacin deficiency leads to a condition called **pellagra**. The symptoms of pellagra are often referred to as "the four Ds": diarrhea, dermatitis, dementia, and death (Figure 9.11). Pellagra was a major problem in the southeastern part of the United States in the early 1900s through the 1930s. Many impoverished Southerners at that time had three basic items in their diets: fatback (the layer of fat along the back of a pig), grits (white corn), and molasses. All three of these food items are devoid of niacin.

Niacin can also be synthesized in the body from an essential amino acid known as tryptophan. People who consume sufficient levels of protein, as do most

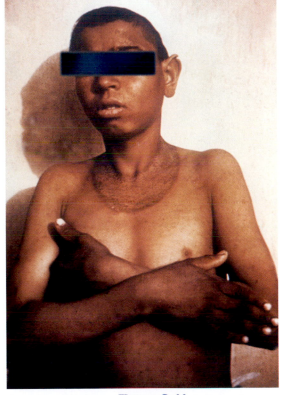

**Figure 9.11** Pellagra is a disease caused by niacin deficiency. One of the most prominent signs is illustrated here: scaly skin and darkened pigmentation. This disease was more common in the United States in the early part of the 20th century than it is today.

people in the United States, are not likely to develop pellagra because the level of tryptophan in protein-rich foods is sufficient to make the needed amount of niacin. For every 60 mg of tryptophan in the diet, we can produce 1 mg of niacin.

### Recommended Intakes

The DRI for thiamin is 1.2 mg per day for men and 1.1 mg per day women; for riboflavin, 1.3 mg per day for men and 1.1 mg per day for women; for niacin, 16 mg per day for men and 14 mg per day for women. In most cases, attaining these levels is not difficult. Furthermore, food composition tables often do not consider the tryptophan contribution to the niacin pool. Toxicity for thiamin and riboflavin has not been reported; however, there are reported cases of niacin toxicity, perhaps because nicotinic acid has been prescribed in high doses as a medication for lowering blood lipid levels. The side effects of using such large doses (two to three times the DRI), include risk for liver injury, stomach ulcers, vision loss, and flushes and rashes of the skin. The Tolerable Upper Intake Level for niacin is 35 mg per day.

### Food Sources

For thiamin the main food sources include pork, whole grains, breakfast cereals, enriched grains and pasta, green beans, milk, orange juice, organ meats, peanuts, dried beans, and seeds. Good sources for riboflavin are milk, enriched breads, cereals, and pasta. Niacin sources include milk, eggs, meat, poultry, fish, whole-grain and enriched breads and cereals, and nuts. Red meat, dairy products, nuts, seeds, bananas, tuna, shellfish, turkey, soybeans, and soy products are good sources of tryptophan, which can be converted to niacin.

## Vitamin B$_6$

Vitamin B$_6$ has three active forms. The most common and most active of these is called *pyridoxine*. Vitamin B$_6$ participates in many biochemical reactions. One of the most important is the conversion of one type of amino acid into another type. This involves the non-essential amino acids we discussed in Chapter 5. It also helps convert tryptophan to niacin, as we just discussed. It is important in the production of a neurotransmitter called *serotonin* from the amino acid tryptophan, as well as in hemoglobin synthesis. Therefore, a vitamin B$_6$ deficiency can lead to anemia. Other important roles for this vitamin include aiding immune function by helping in the synthesis of white blood cells, assisting in the release of glucose from glycogen, and development of the fetal brain. Because this vitamin is used in so many reactions, deficiency signs are diverse and include depression, vomiting, dermatitis, convulsions, and decreased immune response.

Sources of vitamin B$_6$ include beef liver, meats and poultry, baked potatoes, bananas, broccoli, spinach, watermelons, salmon, and navy beans. The DRI for vitamin B$_6$ is 1.3 mg per day for adults. The Tolerable Upper Intake Level is 100 mg per day. Levels above 100 mg per day can be toxic. Numb feet, loss of sensation in the hands, depression, fatigue, headache, nerve damage that progresses to the inability to walk, and convulsions have been reported in women taking 2 g per day. Many of these symptoms are not reversible. Women sometimes supplement with vitamin B$_6$ above 100 mg per day to help alleviate *premenstrual syndrome* (PMS), only to achieve these toxic effects. However, lower doses are sometimes used for PMS. Physicians sometimes advise taking 50 to 100 mg per day to treat PMS and morning sickness. Pregnant women should never take a supplement or medication without checking with their health care provider first.

The use of vitamin B$_6$ to treat *carpal tunnel syndrome*, a nerve disorder of the wrist, is another application that has had mixed results. Some people with carpal tunnel syndrome have been helped by supplements, but overall the data supporting this is mixed, thereby making any recommendation for using vitamin B$_6$ supplements to treat it controversial.

### ■ Nutrition and Lifestages
*Food for thought for all ages*

The statement "you are what you eat" has recently taken on a whole new meaning, signifying a new awareness of the effect that the quality of the diet has on brain and nervous system function. For instance, to produce energy, the use of glucose by nervous tissue requires vitamin B$_1$, which helps with cognitive performance, especially in the elderly. Vitamin B$_6$ is likely to benefit in treating premenstrual depression. Vitamins B$_6$ and B$_{12}$, among others, are directly involved in the synthesis of some neurotransmitters. Vitamin B$_{12}$ delays the onset of signs of dementia, provided it is administered before the onset of the first symptoms. Supplementation with cobalamin has been shown to enhance some brain functions in the elderly. Adolescents who have a borderline low level of vitamin B$_{12}$ develop signs of cognitive changes.

In the brain, the nerve endings contain the highest concentrations of vitamin C in the human body (after the suprarenal glands). Vitamin D deficiency is being investigated in the development of certain neurological diseases. Among the various vitamin E components (tocopherols and tocotrienols), only alpha-tocopherol is actively uptaken by the brain and is directly involved in nervous membranes protection. Even vitamin K has been involved in nervous tissue biochemistry. Iron is necessary to ensure oxygenation and to produce energy in parts of the brain, and for the synthesis of neurotransmitters and myelin. Iron deficiency is found in children with attention-deficit/hyperactivity disorder. Iron concentrations in the umbilical artery are critical during the development of the fetus. Infantile anemia is linked to inadequate development of cognitive functions.

Iron deficiency anemia is common, particularly in women, and is associated, for instance, with apathy, depression and rapid fatigue when exercising. Magnesium plays important roles in metabolism. Zinc participates, among others, in the perception of taste. Low copper levels (due to dietary deficiency) could be linked to Alzheimer disease. The iodine provided by the thyroid hormone ensures the energy metabolism of the brain cells; the dietary reduction of iodine during pregnancy induces severe cerebral dysfunction, and can lead to stunted mental and physical growth. Manganese, copper, and zinc participate in mechanisms that protect against free radicals.

More specifically, the full genetic potential of the child for physical growth and mental development may be compromised due to deficiency (even subclinical) of micronutrients. Children and adolescents with poor nutritional status are exposed to alterations of mental and behavioral functions that can be corrected by dietary measures, but

**Want to know more?**
To learn more about the effectiveness of vitamin B$_6$ in controlling the symptoms of PMS, go to the text website at http://webcom8 .grtxle.com/nutrition and click on the Chapters button. Select Chapter 9.

Some manufacturers are not at all hesitant to make unproven claims.

only to a certain extent. Indeed, nutrient composition and meal pattern can exert either immediate or long-term effects, beneficial or adverse. Brain diseases during aging can also be due to dietary deficiencies, for instance in anti-oxidants and nutrients (trace elements, vitamins, non essential micronutrients related with protection against free radicals).

So the bottom line: eat a nutrient-dense diet that contains a variety of foods to ensure that you are getting all of your vitamins and minerals throughout your life to develop and maintain not just a healthy body but a healthy mind. ■

## Folate and Vitamin B₁₂

Folate and vitamin B$_{12}$ are presented together because they have a close relationship. The deficiency symptoms of each are similar. If a person has a folate deficiency but is misdiagnosed with a vitamin B$_{12}$ deficiency, supplementation with vitamin B$_{12}$ will not correct the problem and folate deficiency will still be present. The reverse situation can also occur, in which a person with a vitamin B$_{12}$ deficiency may be mistakenly misdiagnosed with a folate deficiency.

Folate and vitamin B$_{12}$ work together in producing red blood cells, and a deficiency of either one results in anemia. In addition to their shared role in red blood cell formation, both vitamins are important to the function of the nervous system. However, their exact roles vary slightly and we will consider each one separately.

### Folate

Folate is crucial to the maintenance of numerous tissues in the body, in particular hair, skin, and linings of the digestive and urinary tracts. Folate is important in cell division, because DNA needs folate to make copies of itself during cell division. In folate deficiency, **macrocytic anemia** occurs when the red blood cells cannot mature or form properly because of the inability to synthesize DNA. These immature cells become larger rather than dividing; they are fewer in number than normal cells. Other signs of folate deficiency are heartburn, diarrhea, frequent infection, inflammation of the tongue, depression, fatigue, irritability, and headache.

Folate is so important to the developing central nervous system that deficiencies during pregnancy can result in severe abnormalities of the spine. **Spina bifida**, the most frequently occurring and permanently disabling birth defect, affects approximately one out of every 1,000 newborns in this country. Spina bifida results from the failure of the spine to close properly during the first month of pregnancy. As shown in Figure 9.12, the spinal cord can protrude through the back. Surgery is needed within twenty-four hours after birth to minimize the risk of infection and to preserve existing function in the spinal cord.

### Recommended Intakes for Folate

The DRI for folate is 400 mcg per day for adults. Women who are pregnant or are planning to become pregnant should have 600 mcg of folate per day. Some health professionals recommend that *all* women of childbearing age consume 600 mcg of folate per day because adequate folate is most critical in the very beginning of pregnancy, before most women realize they are pregnant.

A distinction is made between dietary folate and the synthetic form of folate called **folic acid** used in supplements and enriched foods. Folic acid is more potent than folate because more of it is absorbed in the small intestine.

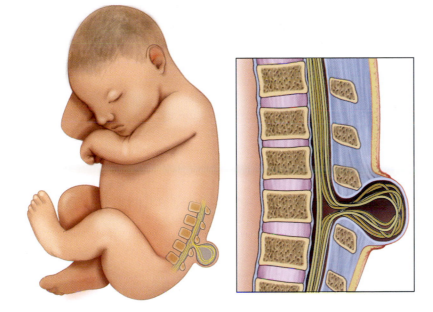

**Figure 9.12** Neural tube defects can be caused by a lack of folate in pregnant mothers. The diagram shows how spina bifida results when the canal that houses the spinal cord fails to close, exposing the spinal cord to the external environment.

Therefore, there is a greater chance of toxicity caused by consuming large amounts of the synthetic form compared to the naturally occurring form found in food. For this reason the DRI is based on folic acid and not folate. A **dietary folate equivalent** is a unit of measure used to represent the conversion of folic acid to folate. For example, if you take a 200-mcg supplement of folic acid and obtain 150 mcg of naturally occurring folate from foods such as vegetables, the dietary folate equivalent is calculated as follows: 200 mcg of folic acid in the supplement $\times$ 1.7 = 340 mcg folate activity. Add to this the 150 mcg of dietary folate for a total of 490 mcg of dietary folate equivalents.

The Tolerable Upper Intake Level of folate is 1,000 mcg (1 mg) from the synthetic source, folic acid. One reason for this limit is that higher doses may mask a vitamin $B_{12}$ deficiency. Too much folic acid can cause convulsions in people with epilepsy.

### Food Sources of Folate

Orange juice and green leafy vegetables are excellent sources of folate. Other good sources are organ meats, sprouts, beans, and vegetables. Breakfast cereals and bread are also good sources. A drawback is that folate is unstable and can be easily destroyed by heat, so much of it is destroyed through food processing. Preparation methods for vegetables that minimize the destruction of folate include microwaving, steaming, and stir-frying. Boiling vegetables in water too long destroys most of the folate in them.

### Vitamin $B_{12}$

Vitamin $B_{12}$ is unique in several ways. First, it contains the mineral cobalt as part of its structure. Second, it is synthesized by bacteria and other microorganisms. Third, it is found only in foods of animal origin and not in plant foods.

One of the most important roles of vitamin $B_{12}$ is to convert folate coenzymes to active forms. In other words, vitamin $B_{12}$ is essential in converting folate into forms that the cell can use. Thus, a vitamin $B_{12}$ deficiency can result in a folate deficiency. However, vitamin $B_{12}$ has a separate function; it maintains the insulating lining that covers nerve fibers known as the **myelin sheath**. People with a vitamin $B_{12}$ deficiency have a breakdown in

the myelin sheath that disrupts nerve conduction, which can lead to paralysis and even death.

Vitamin $B_{12}$ deficiency can occur because of factors other than insufficient diet levels. To utilize vitamin $B_{12}$, the stomach secretes a protein called **intrinsic factor** that binds to vitamin $B_{12}$ and protects it from degradation until it can be absorbed. Some individuals have a genetic condition that causes an inability to produce intrinsic factor. As a result, vitamin $B_{12}$ is destroyed by digestive enzymes without protection from its intrinsic factor, and very little is absorbed. This genetic defect becomes apparent in early adulthood. Many people lose the ability to produce intrinsic factor because of aging. Sometimes illness, medications, and surgeries can cause a decrease in production of intrinsic factor as well. For example, those who have had their stomachs removed for cancer surgery or even weight-loss surgery (gastric bypass surgery) have decreased levels of intrinsic factor. Another factor is stomach acidity, or the presence of hydrochloric acid. Acid is needed to liberate vitamin $B_{12}$ from dietary protein and bind it to the intrinsic factor protein. Older adults have decreased hydrochloric acid production, which decreases the amount of vitamin $B_{12}$ liberated from dietary protein. Thus the combination of decreased acidity and intrinsic factor in older adults can dramatically lower vitamin $B_{12}$ absorption.

People who are affected by vitamin $B_{12}$ deficiency because of the lack of intrinsic factor develop an anemia known as **pernicious anemia**. The red blood cells look the same as those found in folate deficiency. The cells are immature, larger in size, but fewer in number; these cells are termed **megaloblasts**. Other symptoms of pernicious anemia include weakness, sore tongue, back pain, apathy, and tingling and numbness in the hands and feet. To overcome this problem, injections of vitamin $B_{12}$ are given to patients lacking intrinsic factor. However, in many cases, nerve damage has already occurred and is irreversible. Pernicious anemia results in death if not treated.

### Food Sources of Vitamin B₁₂

As mentioned earlier, foods of animal origin provide vitamin $B_{12}$. Milk, cheese, meat (especially organ meats), poultry, and seafood are excellent sources. However, cereals and soy products are often fortified with vitamin $B_{12}$ and they are also a good source. Vegans can use breakfast cereals to get vitamin $B_{12}$, and fortified soy milk is another option. Vegans and particularly those who are pregnant or lactating must make an extra effort to consume sufficient vitamin $B_{12}$, as a fetus without enough of it from the mother can suffer irreversible nerve damage. People older than 50 are encouraged to take a vitamin $B_{12}$ supplement because of decreased intrinsic factor synthesis. The DRI for vitamin $B_{12}$ is 2.4 mcg per day. Toxicity from vitamin $B_{12}$ has not been reported.

**Want to know more?**
To discover more about the role of vitamin $B_{12}$ in mental development and Alzheimer's disease, go to the text website at http://webcom8.grtxle .com/nutrition and click on the Chapters button. Select Chapter 9.

### ■ Nutrition and Disease

*The impact of folic acid and vitamin $B_{12}$ on blood homocysteine levels and heart disease*

*Homocysteine* is an amino acid that is found in our cells and blood. Accumulated evidence from many studies indicates that elevated blood homocysteine levels can lead to heart disease. Homocysteine is thought to injure blood vessels and may accelerate the deposition of fat on the lining of blood vessels. The injury to blood vessels also increases the risk of forming blood clots.

Why are folate and vitamin $B_{12}$ important in the regulation of blood homocysteine levels? Both of these vitamins help control the blood levels of homocysteine through their role in converting homocysteine to *methionine,* another amino acid used in protein synthesis. In other words, adequate levels of these vitamins enhance the conversion, thus lowering homocysteine levels in the blood. Because of this lowering effect, some scientists have advocated the use of folic acid supplements to control blood homocysteine levels. One study suggests that 400 mcg of folic acid per day reduces blood homocysteine levels. However, the American Heart Association does not believe there is sufficient evidence to warrant the recommendation of taking folic acid supplements to prevent heart disease. Although the AHA admits that these supplements lower blood homocysteine levels, there is not sufficient evidence that taking the supplements reduces heart disease for most people. Despite this lack of evidence, the American Heart Association advises people at risk for heart disease to meet the DRI for folate and vitamin $B_{12}$ through diet by consuming foods such as green leafy vegetables for folate and animal products for vitamin $B_{12}$. ■

## Biotin and Pantothenic Acid

The B vitamins biotin and pantothenic acid are very important for obtaining energy from carbohydrates, fats, and proteins. In many ways they function like thiamin, riboflavin, and niacin. Biotin is a cofactor for enzymes in the metabolism of the energy-yielding macronutrients; it is also important in gluconeogenesis, fatty acid synthesis, and the breakdown of fatty acids and amino acids. Pantothenic acid is a part of a much larger molecule that is critical for harnessing energy, but it is not a cofactor. It is involved in the synthesis of lipids, steroid hormones, neurotransmitters, and hemoglobin. Deficiencies are not known to occur. Raw eggs have a protein that can bind up biotin and make it nonabsorbable by the small intestine, but one would need to consume twenty-four to thirty raw eggs per day to have any visible effects.

See Table 9.2 at the end of the chapter for a summary of the functions, deficiency and toxicity symptoms, and food sources of the vitamins discussed in this chapter.

> **Before you go on . . .**
> 1. What are pellagra and beriberi?
> 2. In general, what foods are good sources of vitamin $B_{12}$ and why?
> 3. What is spina bifida, and what nutrient deficiency causes it?
> 4. List two functions of vitamin $B_6$.
> 5. Which vitamin plays a significant role in cell division because of its impact on DNA?

## Enrichment, Fortification, and Supplementation

We have discussed the various vitamins and the foods that contain them. It is important to remember that supplemental forms of vitamins also contribute to our daily intake.

**APPLICATION TIP**

To ensure that you consume sufficient folate in your diet, drink orange juice, add sunflower seeds to your salad, include beans in a meal, or eat strawberries for dessert.

**APPLICATION TIP**

If you have a hard time getting enough fruits and vegetables into your diet because you just don't like them, try adding them in with other foods or "hiding them." Frozen fruits can be used to make nutrient-dense smoothies and shakes by blending them with milk and/or yogurt. It is easy to create different flavors and textures. Vegetables can be chopped into small pieces and easily added to spaghetti sauces, soups, and stews, or baked into casseroles, lasagnas, omelets, and pizzas.

**Want to know more?**
You can test your IQ regarding the consumption of fruits and vegetables to maximize your vitamin intake, by going to the text website at http://webcom8.grtxle.com/nutrition and clicking on the Chapters button. Select Chapter 9.

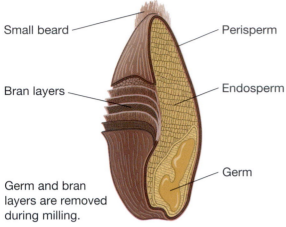

Small beard

Bran layers

Germ and bran
layers are removed
during milling.

Perisperm

Endosperm

Germ

**Figure 9.13**  Nutrients are lost during the grain milling process. Germ and bran layers, rich in nutrients, are also lost during the milling process. The lost nutrients are often added back (enrichment).

## Enrichment

Food manufacturers enhance the vitamin and mineral content of many of their products by enrichment and fortification. **Enrichment** is the restoration of micronutrients that were originally present in the food but were lost during processing. Enrichment is mandatory when a manufacturer uses grain-based ingredients that have been milled, refined, or polished. These processes strip away the bran and germ, leaving only the starchy center region of the grain, which is referred to as the endosperm (see Figure 9.13). Flour made with the endosperm only is fluffier than whole-grain flour and easier to use in food manufacturing and home baking.

From a nutritional perspective, however, the endosperm contains few vitamins. Most of the vitamins are found in the germ and the bran. For example, white rice is more refined than brown rice, which has more natural nutrients. In white rice, enrichment is needed to replace what has been lost through the refinement process. Not all of the nutrients that were lost are actually replaced, which means that brown rice is more nutrient dense than white rice. During the nineteenth and early twentieth centuries, the widespread use of milled grains lead to serious nutritional deficiencies such as pellagra and beriberi, discussed earlier.

The Enrichment Act of 1942 states that U.S. food manufacturers must add thiamin, riboflavin, niacin, and iron to refined grain products. Although enrichment has eradicated many B vitamin deficiencies in countries such as the United States, they are still found in several underdeveloped countries.

## Fortification

Some food manufacturers add vitamins and minerals to foods that are not naturally present in those foods. This process is called **fortification**. Breakfast cereals are an excellent example. The calcium added to orange juice is another example. Law mandates some fortification, such as vitamins A and D in milk and folic acid in enriched cereal and grain products. Fortification makes a significant contribution to the daily intake of vitamins. In addition to enrichment and fortification, many people supplement their diet with pills that contain individual vitamins or combinations of vitamins.

### ■ To Supplement or Not

*Vitamin supplements—who needs them?*

Just a few decades ago, vitamin supplements were available almost exclusively in a "multi" format. Although multivitamins continue to be a mainstay in the supplement industry, many vitamins are now marketed individually or in functional complexes. Vitamins E and C are among the leading single-vitamin supplements. Vitamins C and E are also combined into antioxidant supplements, and the B vitamins are marketed as energy boosters.

Until recently, the general consensus among nutritionists was that a balanced diet contained all the vitamins needed to prevent deficiencies. Because of trends in eating and the emphasis on preventing diseases such as heart disease and cancer, many nutritionists have rethought this position. What is the bottom line? Do you need to take vitamin supplements?

## Real People, Other Voices

**Student:**

### Kathy Bourque

West Valley Mission Community College

By planning his meals ahead of time and choosing healthy options, Anthony is most likely getting his recommended amount of daily vitamins from his food. To help retain the vitamins in his food, he could lightly cook or steam his vegetables. He can meet his protein requirements by following a nutritionally balanced diet. He can find suggestions for protein-rich foods and serving sizes that match his criteria by consulting the Food Guide Pyramid.

Anthony may be doubling his recommended daily allowance for protein and vitamins with the addition of protein shakes and energy bars to his diet. Also, he is taking vitamin supplements that contain more than 500 percent of the recommended daily value of vitamins. This could pose health risks because some vitamins can be toxic when ingested in amounts above the daily upper limit.

In my opinion, he should eliminate the protein shakes, energy bars, and vitamin supplements. He would avoid potential toxic effects of exceeding upper limits of vitamins and save money in doing so. Anthony should also research the credentials of his fitness trainer because the trainer may not be certified to give nutritional advice, and may be required by the gym to sell certain supplements to clients.

Because Anthony is confused by the information on vitamin supplements, he should speak to a physician or a Registered Dietitian who could help him with his specific dietary needs.

**Instructor:**

### Norman R. Trezek, MS

Pima Community College

Anthony's dilemma poses an interesting question; namely, who can you trust to provide accurate nutritional information? Although many well-meaning individuals are willing to offer all sorts of nutrition advice, only nutrition professionals are qualified to evaluate the myriad of sometimes contradictory research reports and make meaningful dietary recommendations to optimize health and well-being. These professionals include nutritionists with a science degree from an accredited university, Registered Dietitians.

So what should Anthony do? Taking megadoses of nutrients over time can be toxic and can pose a serious health risk. Anthony would do well to follow the recommendation of the Committee on Diet and Health and not take supplements in excess of 100 percent of the DRI. Anthony should also address the basic question of whether he even needs a supplement. He can do this by consulting a Registered Dietitian and having his current diet evaluated for nutrient content. He could also use a diet analysis computer program and evaluate his diet over time. These options will give him the insight he needs to make an informed decision about the need for supplements.

Concerning the need for supplements, Anthony must remember a fundamental truth—even though small amounts of vitamins and minerals are vital components of good health, excess levels can be harmful. In other words, more is not necessarily better. This also applies to the extra protein Anthony has been consuming. When protein is consumed beyond the body's need for growth and repair, the extra amount will simply be used for energy or stored as body fat. So once again, more is not necessarily better.

**Registered Dietitian:**

### David Rowell, RD, LN

Garrison, MT

Anthony is doing well to plan his meals with attention to the details of his daily diet.

Weight lifters are keenly aware that muscle is constructed primarily of protein. However, the average American eats close to the amount of protein daily that a bodybuilder needs to consume. Simply eating a diet that is appropriately balanced to personal calorie needs with approximately 50 to 55 percent of calories from carbohydrate, 15 to 20 percent from protein and 30 to 35 percent from fat would provide plenty of protein as well as the other necessary energy nutrients.

Athletes also correctly understand that many individual vitamins, minerals, and other nutrients are needed to make the body strong and energetic. People who are in the business of selling supplements marketed to athletes take advantage of that concern when they promote these products.

If Anthony includes naturally healthy snacks from protein foods, fruits, and complex carbohydrate-rich whole grains, he will have no need for expensive drinks and energy bars. His carefully planned diet would also eliminate any need for excessive vitamin and mineral supplementation.

It would be safe for Anthony to take a multivitamin that provides 100 percent of the DRI, but further supplementation would not provide added benefit and may indeed result in toxicity. Many gyms not only promote expensive supplements and protein drinks, but also make them available for sale at a high profit. Understanding this fact may help Anthony see why his professor and the staff at the gym are not singing the same tune.

The safest answer: maybe. It depends on your current nutritional status and your diet. One of the best ways to get a definitive answer is to make an appointment with a Registered Dietitian (RD) for a nutritional assessment. You'll find out exactly how well your diet stacks up to recommended nutrient intakes and whether you are achieving your nutritional goals.

Keep in mind that enrichment and fortification of various foods help you consume more vitamins even if your diet is not well balanced or includes restrictions. For example, vegans may not get enough vitamin $B_{12}$ from plant-based foods alone. Fortified breakfast cereals and other foods can help fill the void. It is recommended that women of childbearing age should also obtain folic acid from supplements or fortified foods. Although ideal, simply eating folate-rich foods may not always be practical or sufficient.

Some vitamins are used therapeutically to treat medical conditions. For example, a form of vitamin A called Accutane (or the chemical name isotretinoin) is used to treat severe acne. Vitamins $B_6$ and $B_{12}$ as well as folic acid are involved in controlling homocysteine, a substance thought to increase the risk of heart disease. Niacin in large doses can be used to help reduce elevated blood cholesterol.

If you decide to take a nutritional supplement of any kind, make sure you do your homework first. Supplements are not as strictly regulated as drugs and can have misleading label claims that suggest you absolutely must have that particular product in order to achieve your health goals. See Chapter 11 for more information on supplements. In addition, tell your doctor about any vitamins you are taking, especially if you are also taking any prescription medications or planning to have surgery. Remember that having more of something in your diet is not necessarily better for your health. Supplements are druglike substances, and, as with drugs, you can consume too much. ■

### Before you go on . . .

1. What vitamins and minerals must food manufacturers add to refined grain products and why?
2. Define the differences between enrichment and fortification.
3. When is enrichment mandatory?
4. List some examples of fortified foods.

## Real People, Real Strategies

Anthony decided to consult a Registered Dietitian (RD). Once the RD thoroughly understood his dilemma and goal, she asked him to begin by recording everything he ate for a few days and to keep track of all the supplements and shakes he consumed. She also asked him to bring in the supplements he had been taking. When she examined the labels, the dietitian was surprised to learn that Anthony was consuming more than 500 percent of the DRI for several potentially toxic vitamins such as vitamin A and vitamin D. She pointed out that he is getting most of what he needs to accomplish his goal from the food he is eating, once again confirming what his nutrition instructor had emphasized in lecture. She also informed him that several of the supplements overlap. For example, the protein shakes and energy bars are fortified with several of the same vitamins. The dietitian told him that if he chooses to take a supplement, then he needs to select one that does not exceed the DRI for each nutrient. Moreover, she encouraged him to consider the supplements together, not separately. In other words, if a protein shake contains 100 percent of the DRI for vitamin A and his multivitamin also contains 100 percent, then this is 200 percent in addition to what he is consuming in his diet. Her recommendation was for Anthony to try a simple multivitamin to compensate for any potential deficiencies resulting from his diet.

Anthony ultimately concluded that the risks of toxicity from supplements, not to mention their costs, far outweighed any benefits he might have received.

## Chapter Summary

- Vitamins are found in our bodies in much lower levels than the macronutrients and are required in our diets in only milligrams and micrograms. DRIs have been determined for all of the vitamins, although information continues to evolve as new discoveries are made.
- Vitamins interact so that several of them may affect a similar bodily function. Many are directly involved in metabolic pathways; others are cofactors or coenzymes for biochemical reactions.
- Vitamins can be toxic if consumed in large enough amounts. Fat-soluble vitamins and minerals can be more toxic when taken in large amounts, because they can be stored in the body. Water-soluble vitamins are not as toxic because they are better able to be excreted.
- Vitamins do not provide your body with energy, but may facilitate the body's breakdown and release of energy from carbohydrates, fats, and proteins. The B vitamins are all involved in chemical pathways that aid in energy metabolism.
- Vitamins A and D are tightly connected to protein synthesis and can turn genes on and off. Bone strength and development depend to a large extent on vitamins A, C, D, and K.
- Vitamins can play a role as antioxidants. Vitamins C and E and beta-carotene are all antioxidants that protect us from harmful free radicals.
- Reproduction, growth, development and even repair are heavily dependent on vitamins A, D, and C. Folate is involved because it promotes cell division.

- Deficiences of thiamin, riboflavin, and niacin were once much more widespread in the United States than they are today.
- Thiamin deficiency leads to a disease called beriberi, and niacin deficiency leads to a disease called pellagra.
- The signs of folate and vitamin $B_{12}$ deficiencies are similar. Folate deficiency during pregnancy can lead to spina bifida in infants. A lack of intrinsic factor can prevent absorption of vitamin $B_{12}$ and lead to pernicious anemia in some people.
- An elevated level of the amino acid homocysteine is a risk factor for heart disease. An increased level may be related to a lack of folate and vitamin $B_{12}$ in the diet. Folic acid supplements lower blood homocysteine levels. However, there is not sufficient evidence to recommend that all people supplement with folic acid to prevent heart disease.
- Food processing, prolonged storage, or prolonged cooking can result in a loss of vitamins.
- Enrichment is the restoration of micro-nutrients that were originally present in a food but were lost during processing. Fortification is the addition of a nutrient to a food that did not originally contain it.

## Key Terms

**anemia** (uh-NEE-mee-uh) A condition characterized by below-normal levels of red blood cells, hemoglobin, or both. (p. 280)

**ascorbic acid** (uh-SCOR-bick AS-id) Another name for vitamin C. (p. 284)

**beriberi** The result of thiamin deficiency. (p. 287)

**beta-carotene** A precursor of vitamin A found in plants. (p. 271)

**cell differentiation** The process by which specialized cells develop that are capable of performing specific functions. (p. 274)

**coenzymes** Molecules that combine with an enzyme to increase its activity. (p. 286)

**collagen** (COLL-uh-jen) A protein that forms connective tissues such as tendons, bone, teeth, and skin. (p. 284)

**dietary folate equivalent** A unit of measure used to represent the conversion of folic acid to folate. (p. 291)

**enrichment** The restoration of micronutrients that were originally present in the food but were lost during processing. (p. 294)

**fibrin** A protein that forms blood clots. (p. 281)

**folic acid** The synthetic form of folate that is used in dietary supplements and enriched foods. (p. 290)

**fortification** The addition of vitamins and minerals to foods that are not naturally present in those foods. (p. 294)

**free radicals** Unstable compounds with an unpaired electron that attack other molecules and break them down. (p. 279)

**International Units (IU)** A standard measurement that was once used for several vitamins. (p. 275)

**intrinsic factor** A protein produced by stomach cells that binds to vitamin $B_{12}$ and protects it from degradation until it can be absorbed. (p. 292)

**macrocytic anemia** Anemia characterized by enlarged, immature red blood cells that are fewer in number than normal cells. (p. 290)

**macular degenerative disease** A group of eye disorders characterized by the breakdown of the macula, the center portion of the retina that makes basic visual acuity possible. (p. 273)

**megaloblasts** (MEG-uh-low-blasts) Immature, enlarged red blood cells. (p. 292)

**myelin sheath** (My-uh-lin) An insulating sheath for nerve fibers that enhances conduction. (p. 291)

**osteomalacia** (os-tee-oh-ma-LAY-she-uh) A softening of the bones in adults that results from vitamin D deficiency. (p. 277)

**pellagra** (puh-LAG-ruh) A disease caused by a niacin deficiency. (p. 287)

**pernicious anemia** (per-NISH-us uh-NEE-mee-uh) Anemia that results from a vitamin $B_{12}$ deficiency because of a lack of intrinsic factor. (p. 292)

**provitamins** Substances that need to be converted in order to have vitamin-like activity in the body. (p. 271)

**retinol activity equivalents** or **RAE** The units in which carotenoids are measured. (p. 272)

**rickets** A softening and deformity of long bones that results from vitamin D deficiency in children. (p. 276)

**scurvy** A disease caused by vitamin C deficiency. (p. 284)

**spina bifida** (SPY-nuh BIF-ih-duh) A birth defect that results from the failure of the spine to close properly during the first month of pregnancy. (p. 290)

**tocopherols** (toe-COFF-er-alls) A group of compounds with vitamin E activity. (p. 279)

**xerophthalmia** (zeer-off-THAL-mee-uh) Irreversible damage to the eye caused by vitamin A deficiency. (p. 272)

## Table 9.2    Summary Table of Vitamins

| Vitamin | What It Does and Why It Is Important | Deficiency: What Happens If You Get Too Little |
|---|---|---|
| Vitamin A | Essential for proper development and maintenance of eyes and vision; needed to maintain the integrity of skin, digestive tract, and other tissues; needed for proper function of the immune system; cell differentiation | Night blindness, reduced hair growth in children, loss of appetite, dry/rough skin, lowered resistance to infection, dry eyes, xerophthalmia |
| Beta carotene (provitamin A) | Antioxidant; like other provitamin A carotenoids (alpha-carotene and beta-cryptoxanthin), can be converted to vitamin A in the body | No direct effects; may cause symptoms associated with vitamin A deficiency |
| Vitamin D | Helps maintain adequate calcium in the blood by increasing calcium absorption from digestive tract; decreases calcium loss in urine | Rickets in children; bone softening and osteomalacia in adults |
| Vitamin E | Antioxidant; helps protect red blood cells, muscles, and other tissues from free radical damage | Rare; seen primarily in premature or low-birth weight babies or children who do not absorb fat properly; causes nerve abnormalities |
| Vitamin K | Needed for normal blood clotting; bone strength | Defective blood coagulation |

| Toxicity: What Happens If You Get Too Much | Food Sources[1] | | |
|---|---|---|---|
| **Headaches, blurred vision, fatigue, diarrhea, irregular periods, joint and bone pain, dry/cracked skin, rashes, loss of hair, vomiting, liver damage** | **Food Item** | **Serving Size** | **Amount** |
| | Beef liver | 3 oz. | 6852 µg |
| | Vitamin A fortified milk | 1 c. | 137 µg |
| | Margarine | 1 Tbsp. | 115 µg |
| | Butter | 1 Tbsp. | 103 µg |
| | Egg, hard-boiled | 1 | 85 µg |
| | Cheddar cheese | 1 oz. | 74 µg |
| No known toxic effects; may cause yellowish discoloration of skin; may increase lung cancer in smokers | **Food Item** | **Serving Size** | **Amount** |
| | 1 REA equals (1 mcg retinal) | | |
| | Sweet potatoes | 1 baked | 961 RAE |
| | Pumpkin, canned | 1/2 c. | 953 RAE |
| | Squash, butternut | 1/2 c. | 572 RAE |
| | Kale | 1/2 c. | 478 RAE |
| | Collards | 1/2 c. | 386 RAE |
| | Carrots, raw | 1/2 c. | 367 RAE |
| | Cantaloupe | 1/2 c. | 136 RAE |
| | Apricots | 4 | 134 RAE |
| | Broccoli | 1/2 c. | 52 RAE |
| Calcium deposits in organs, fragile bones, renal and cardiovascular damage | **Food Item** | **Serving Size** | **Amount** |
| | Cod liver oil | 1 tbsp. | 34 µg |
| | Pacific oysters | 3.5 oz. | 16 µg |
| | Salmon | 3 oz. | 8.0 µg |
| | Sardines | 1-3/4 oz. | 6.25 µg |
| | Vitamin D fortified milk, 2% | 1 c. | 2.45 µg |
| | Shrimp | 3 oz. | 2.25 µg |
| | Egg, cooked | 1 | 0.65 µg |
| | Beef | 3.5 oz. | 0.18 µg |
| | Yogurt | 1 c. | 0.10 µg |
| | Cheddar cheese | 1 oz. | 0.09 µg |
| | Margarine | 1 oz. | 1.68 µg |
| | Liver | 3.5 oz. | 0.38 µg |
| Unknown | **Food Item** | **Serving Size** | **Amount** |
| | Corn oil | 1 Tbsp. | 2.87 mg |
| | Salad dressing, French | 2 Tbsp. | 2.63 mg |
| | Wheat germ | 2 Tbsp. | 2.04 mg |
| | Margarine | 1 Tbsp. | 1.80 mg |
| | Peanuts, roasted | 1/4 c. | 2.27 mg |
| | Spinach | 1/2 c. | 1.42 mg |
| | Pistachio nuts | 1/4 c. | 1.36 mg |
| | Collards | 1/2 c. | 0.84 mg |
| | Pumpkin seeds | 1/4 c. | 0.57 mg |
| Jaundice in infants | **Food Item** | **Serving Size** | **Amount** |
| | Collards | 1/2 c. | 530 µg |
| | Spinach | 1/2 c. | 514 µg |
| | Brussels sprouts | 1/2 c. | 150 µg |
| | Broccoli | 1/2 c. | 110 µg |
| | Cabbage | 1/2 c. | 82 µg |
| | Asparagus | 1/2 c. | 72 µg |

(*Continued*)

## Table 9.2    Summary Table of Vitamins (*Continued*)

| Vitamin | What It Does and Why It Is Important | Deficiency: What Happens If You Get Too Little |
|---|---|---|
| Vitamin C (ascorbic acid) | Antioxidant; involved in collagen formation; aids in iron absorption | Muscle weakness, bleeding gums, easy bruising, scurvy (in extreme cases) |
| Thiamin (Vitamin $B_1$) | Coenzyme for several reactions in energy metabolism; necessary for muscle coordination and proper development and maintenance of the central nervous system | Anxiety, hysteria, depression, muscle cramps, loss of appetite, beriberi (mostly in alcoholics) |
| Riboflavin (vitamin $B_2$) | Coenzyme for several reactions in energy metabolism | Cracks/sores around mouth and nose, visual problems |
| Niacin (Vitamin $B_3$) | Coenzyme for several reactions in energy metabolism; in very large doses, lowers cholesterol (*Note: Large doses should be taken under the care of a physician.*) | In extreme cases, pellagra (a disease characterized by dermatitis, diarrhea, mouth sores) |
| Vitamin $B_6$ (pyridoxine) | Coenzyme for reactions involving the processing of amino acids; involved in the breakdown of carbohydrate stores (glycogen) in muscles and liver | Anemia, irritability, patches of itchy/scaling skin, convulsions |

**Toxicity: What Happens If You Get Too Much** | **Food Sources[1]**

| Toxicity: What Happens If You Get Too Much | Food Item | Serving Size | Amount |
|---|---|---|---|
| Largely unknown; some concerns over kidney stones | Orange juice | 1/2 c. | 62 mg |
| | Green peppers | 1/2 c. | 60 mg |
| | Broccoli, cooked | 1/2 c. | 51 mg |
| | Strawberries | 1/2 c. | 50 mg |
| | Brussels sprouts | 1/2 c. | 48 mg |
| | Grapefruit | 1/2 c. | 36 mg |
| | Sweet potato, baked | 1 | 20 mg |

| Toxicity: What Happens If You Get Too Much | Food Item | Serving Size | Amount |
|---|---|---|---|
| Unknown (*Note: Excess of one B vitamin may cause deficiency of others.*) | Cereal (Special K) | 1 c. | 1.13 mg |
| | Pork chop | 3 oz. | 0.53 mg |
| | Beef liver | 3 oz. | 0.15 mg |
| | Peanuts, roasted | 1/4 c. | 0.15 mg |
| | Great northern beans, boiled | 1/2 c. | 0.14 mg |
| | Spaghetti | 1/2 c. | 0.12 mg |
| | Orange juice | 1/2 c. | 0.11 mg |
| | White bread | 1 slice | 0.11 mg |
| | Brown rice (long grain) | 1/2 c. | 0.09 mg |
| | Milk, 2% | 1 c. | 0.09 mg |
| | Lima beans, cooked | 1/2 c. | 0.06 mg |
| | Pumpkin seeds | 1 Tbsp. | 0.05 mg |

| Toxicity: What Happens If You Get Too Much | Food Item | Serving Size | Amount |
|---|---|---|---|
| Unknown | Cereals (Special K) | 1 c. | 1.28 mg |
| | Milk, 2% | 1 c. | 0.45 mg |
| | Spaghetti | 1/2 c. | 0.12 mg |
| | White bread | 1 slice | 0.08 mg |

| Toxicity: What Happens If You Get Too Much | Food Item | Serving Size | Amount |
|---|---|---|---|
| Hot flashes, ulcers, liver disorders, high blood sugar and uric acid, cardiac arrhythmia | Peanuts, roasted | 1/4 c. | 4.94 mg |
| | Rib steak | 3 oz. | 4.08 mg |
| | Whole-wheat flour | 1/2 c. | 3.82 mg |
| | Cereal (Special K) | 1 c. | 1.50 mg |
| | Brown rice (long grain) | 1/2 c. | 1.49 mg |
| | Codfish, baked | 3 oz. | 1.11 mg |
| | White bread | 1 slice | 1.10 mg |
| | Egg, hard-boiled | 1 | 0.26 mg |
| | Milk, 2% | 1 c. | 0.22 mg |

| Toxicity: What Happens If You Get Too Much | Food Item | Serving Size | Amount |
|---|---|---|---|
| Nerve damage | Beef liver | 3 oz. | 0.87 mg |
| | Spinach, cooked | 1/2 c. | 0.86 mg |
| | Potato, Baked | 1 | 0.70 mg |
| | Chicken, white meat, roasted | 3 oz. | 0.46 mg |
| | Banana | 1 | 0.43 mg |
| | Rib steak | 3 oz. | 0.34 mg |
| | Salmon, broiled | 3 oz. | 0.19 mg |
| | Broccoli | 1/2 c. | 0.16 mg |
| | Navy beans | 1/2 c. | 0.15 mg |
| | Watermelon | 1/2 c. | 0.03 mg |

*(Continued)*

## Table 9.2    Summary Table of Vitamins (*Continued*)

| Vitamin | What It Does and Why It Is Important | Deficiency: What Happens If You Get Too Little |
| --- | --- | --- |
| Folic acid (folacin) | Essential for manufacture of genetic material; helps form red blood cells; cell division | Impaired cell division, anemia, diarrhea, gastrointestinal upsets |
| Vitamin $B_{12}$ (cobalamin) | Essential for building blocks of DNA; helps form red blood cells; maintains myelin sheath or insulation of nerves | Pernicious anemia, nerve damage (*Note: Deficiency is rare except in strict vegetarians, the elderly, or people with malabsorption disorders.*) |
| Pantothenic acid | Coenzyme for several reactions in energy metabolism | Fatigue and vomiting, abdominal cramps |
| Biotin | Involved in energy metabolism | Seborrhea (greasy scales) in infants; anorexia, nausea, vomiting, dry/scaly skin in adults (*Note: Can be induced in adults by consuming large amounts of egg whites*) |

| Toxicity: What Happens If You Get Too Much | Food Sources[1] | | |
|---|---|---|---|
| | **Food Item** | **Serving Size** | **Amount** |
| Convulsions in people with epilepsy; may mask pernicious anemia | Cereal (Special K) | 1 c. | 300 µg |
| | Beef liver | 3 oz. | 221 µg |
| | Navy beans, cooked | 1/2 c. | 127 µg |
| | Collards, cooked | 1/2 c. | 88 µg |
| | Brussels sprouts | 1/2 c. | 78 µg |
| | Orange juice | 1/2 c. | 62 µg |
| | Spinach, raw | 1 c. | 58 µg |
| | Lettuce, iceberg | 1 c. | 31 µg |
| | White bread | 1 slice | 28 µg |
| | Kale, cooked | 1/2 c. | 9 µg |
| Skin problems | **Food Item** | **Serving Size** | **Amount** |
| | Clams | 3 oz. | 84 µg |
| | Beef liver | 3 oz. | 71 µg |
| | Oysters | 3 oz. | 15 µg |
| | Cereal (Special K) | 1 c. | 6 µg |
| | Rib steak | 3 oz. | 3 µg |
| | Tuna, canned | 2 oz. | 2 µg |
| | Milk, 2% | 1 c. | 1 µg |
| | Cheddar cheese | 1 oz. | <1 µg |
| | Chicken, white meat, roasted | 3 oz. | <1 µg |
| Sensitivity of teeth | Abundant in many foods | | |
| Unknown | Abundant in many foods | | |

[1] *Source:* USDA National Nutrient Database for Standard Reference, Release 19.

# Chapter Quiz

1. A lack of which of the following nutrients during pregnancy can lead to a birth defect involving the spine?

   a. vitamin $B_{12}$

   b. folate

   c. thiamin

   d. vitamin E

2. Which of the following nutrients are most involved with liberating energy from carbohydrates, fats, and proteins?

   a. vitamin C

   b. vitamins A, D, and E

   c. thiamin, riboflavin, and niacin

   d. folate and vitamin $B_{12}$

3. The condition xerophthalmia is best described as

   a. the result of vitamin D deficiency that affects bone structure.

   b. due to a lack of vitamin K that leads to fragile bones.

   c. due to a lack of vitamin $B_1$ or thiamin.

   d. caused by a deficiency of vitamin A that leads to irreversible eye damage.

4. Which of the following nutrients is important in red blood cell formation and the prevention of anemia?

   a. vitamin $B_6$

   b. folate

   c. vitamin $B_{12}$

   d. all of the above

5. The addition of vitamins and minerals to foods that normally do not contain them is called

   a. adulteration

   b. enrichment

   c. fortification

   d. enhancement

6. All of the following are good sources of vitamin $B_{12}$ *except*

   a. meat.

   b. eggs.

   c. fish.

   d. green leafy vegetables.

7. Which of the following nutrients is most likely related to improved blood clotting?

   a. vitamin K

   b. vitamin C

   c. vitamin $B_{12}$

   d. vitamin $B_6$

8. A deficiency of which of the following vitamins leads to pellagra?

   a. beta-carotene

   b. vitamin D

   c. pantothenic acid

   d. niacin

9. All of the following are considered fat soluble vitamins *except*

   a. vitamin A.

   b. vitamin C.

   c. vitamin D.

   d. vitamin E.

10. Which of the following nutrients is the most critical to cell division?

    a. niacin

    b. vitamin E

    c. vitamin K

    d. folate

Chapter Quiz Answer Key
1. b; 2. c; 3. d; 4. d; 5. c; 6. d; 7. a; 8. d; 9. b; 10. d

## < Here's Where You've Been

*The following topics were introduced in preceding chapters and are related to concepts we'll discuss in Chapter 10. Be certain that you're familiar with them before proceeding.*

- Sodium, potassium, and chloride are classified as macrominerals, and each has unique functions in addition to water balance. (Chapter 8)
- Vitamins function mostly in biochemical reactions of cells. (Chapter 9)
- Vitamins are classified based on their solubility in water. (Chapter 9)
- Many vitamins come from fruits and vegetables. (Chapter 9)
- People who consume too little or too much of a vitamin can experience serious adverse effects. (Chapter 9)

## Here's Where You're Going >

*The following topics and concepts are the ones we'll emphasize in Chapter 10.*

- Minerals can be separated into two categories: macrominerals (major minerals) and microminerals (trace minerals).
- The macrominerals that will be discussed in this chapter are calcium, phosphorus, and magnesium; the microminerals that will be discussed are iron, zinc, copper, selenium, iodine, fluoride, and chromium.
- Minerals provide structure to the body or help enzymes carry out metabolism.
- A lack of minerals in the diet leads to specific deficiency signs for each.
- Minerals, like many vitamins, can be toxic when consumed in excess.

## Real People, Real Choices

Shereen Ward is a young mother of three children. She has a 6-month-old boy, a 3-year-old girl, and a 5-year-old girl who is starting kindergarten. She breast-fed all of her children and has recently weaned her son from breast milk onto solid foods. Austin, her husband, is a mechanic at a Honda dealership in Miami. His income provides the basics for the family, but they live on a very tight budget with almost no money available for discretionary spending.

Shereen spends most of her time at home doing housework and caring for her children. Typically, she also spends two to three hours a day preparing breakfast and dinner for the family. She feels run-down a lot of the time, a condition she began to notice before her last pregnancy. She saw her doctor sporadically while she was pregnant and took a prenatal supplement. Her 3- and 5-year-olds both seem tired as well, and Shereen finds this odd because they are not that physically active. In fact, she knows she should get more exercise herself and, in order to do so, she's started taking her children to the park at least two or three times a week. One day while shopping at the local mall, she notices a health fair that promotes free screening for anemia. Shereen has her finger pricked to get her blood tested and is very surprised to learn that she is anemic. After further evaluation and discussion with the health fair workers, she is referred to the Women, Infants, and Children's (WIC) clinic, where she and her children can get help with their health issues, such as anemia. This clinic provides free treatment and is sponsored by the federal government.

What advice regarding treatment for her anemia do you think the staff at the clinic will give Shereen? Do you think they will refer her to an RD?

Shereen's situation is very common in the United States. Although many of us do not think of the United States as a place where people consume insufficient nutrients, iron deficiency anemia is our second-largest public health nutrition problem, after obesity. Worldwide, about 1.5 billion people have iron deficiency anemia. Pregnant mothers, women of childbearing years, and children are the most often affected.

In the latter part of the twentieth century our knowledge about mineral nutrition increased dramatically. Scientists had discovered that calcium is needed not only for rapidly growing children, but throughout life to maintain bone health. Scientific research has also established that magnesium is important in maintaining a healthy heart. As technology improved, the ability to measure minerals that are found only in small amounts in our food and bodies was developed. Furthermore, research has shown that even in small amounts certain minerals are critical to normal health and functioning. Other minerals, such as iron, zinc, copper, selenium, and iodine are required on a daily basis in order to maintain good health. As with vitamins, the Dietary Reference Intakes (DRI) for many minerals have now been determined, and as research and knowledge continues to evolve, some DRIs are likely to change. In some instances, sufficient information on which to base a specific DRI recommendation is lacking, and therefore only a range is given. As in the previous chapter on vitamins, we will discuss the function of each of these minerals, what occurs when consumption is too high or too low, and the primary food sources of each.

## *Mineral* Refers to Mining

Minerals are elements from the periodic table of elements that are essential components in the diet (Table 10.1). This class of essential nutrients was so named because minerals can be acquired by mining the Earth's crust.

The list of minerals has grown over the years and includes nutrients that are recognizable, such as calcium, iron, and potassium, as well as more obscure nutrients such as copper, selenium, and chromium. Researchers continue to study how and why minerals are essential to the body. They also are trying to determine whether more minerals should be added to the list—some, such as gold, are found in the body in very small amounts, but an essential function has yet to be established for them.

Minerals are classified based on their content in the body and recommended level of dietary intake. The macrominerals—calcium, phosphorus, sodium, potassium, chloride, and magnesium—are found in greater amounts in the body, and each contributes a total mass of about 5 g (about a teaspoon). Their dietary recommendation is at least 100 mg per day. The microminerals (or trace minerals) include copper, iron, fluoride, selenium, iodine, zinc, and chromium. Each contributes less than 5 g to your body weight. Recommended intake for each micromineral is less than 100 mg per day. Figure 10.1 displays the contributions made by the individual minerals to our body. See Table 10.4 at the end of the chapter for a summary of all minerals and their food sources and functions.

| **Table 10.1** | **Essential Minerals Needed to Sustain Optimal Health** |
|---|---|
| **Macrominerals (require 100 mg or more per day)** | **Microminerals (require less than 100 mg per day)** |
| Calcium | Iron |
| Phosphorus | Zinc |
| Sodium | Copper |
| Potassium | Selenium |
| Chloride | Iodine |
| Magnesium | Fluoride |
| | Chromium |
| | Manganese |
| | Boron |
| | Molybdenum |
| | Cobalt |
| | Vanadium |

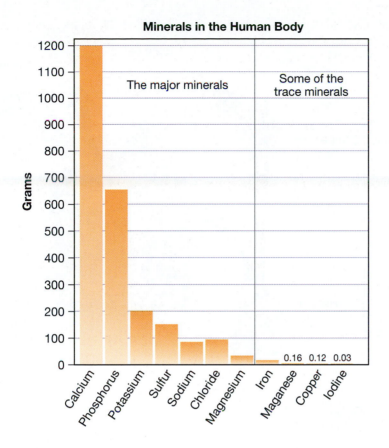

**Minerals in the Human Body**

**Figure 10.1** The amount of minerals in the average human body. The differences in levels do not mean that one is more important than another.

# The Macrominerals

In Chapter 8 we introduced three macrominerals: sodium, potassium, and chloride. In this chapter we will cover and discuss three additional macrominerals: calcium, phosphorus, and magnesium.

## Calcium

Calcium is the most abundant mineral in the body. It represents 40 percent of all the minerals in the body and contributes 1.5 percent of total body weight, which is remarkable for a mineral. More than 99 percent of the calcium is found in the skeleton and teeth. Bone calcium acts as a storage pool for calcium to be used for other purposes, such as muscle contraction and metabolism. Calcium in the bone is constantly being released to the blood and vice versa.

### Calcium in Bone

A critical role for calcium is in the building and maintenance of bone. Bone is a combination of two types of building materials: minerals—primarily calcium and phosphorus—and the connective tissue protein collagen that was discussed in Chapter 9. Nutrients and information are delivered to bone via blood vessels and nerves in a complex network of canals (Figure 10.2).

Bone exists in a constant state of remodeling or turnover, meaning that bone is always being simultaneously broken down and rebuilt. This process allows bone to adapt to physical stress, injury, growth, and nutritional changes. Bone turnover can be thought of as a simple mathematical equation, with the result being bone loss, gain, or maintenance (Figure 10.3).

**Figure 10.2** Bone anatomy is complex. Bones are composed of a series of networks and cells. Most bone is made up of collagen. The key role calcium plays in bone is the formation of calcium crystals, called *hydroxyapatite,* which gives bone its strength.

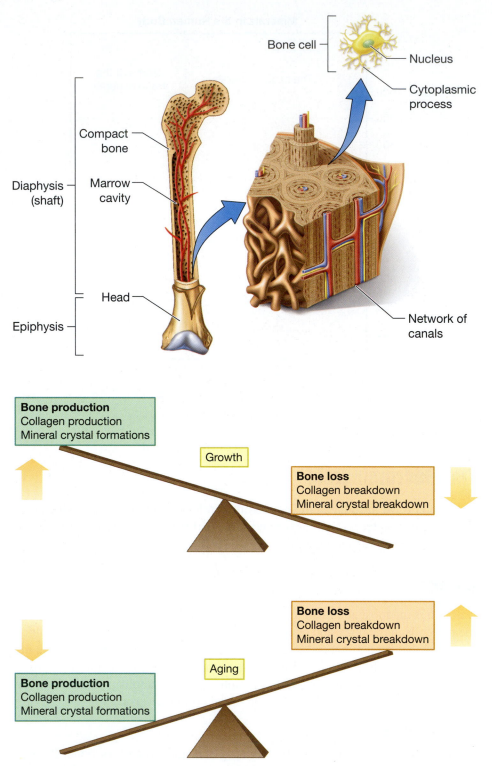

**Figure 10.3** Bone "remodeling" illustrated. There are times when, under normal conditions, bone is being broken down and built up at the same time. During growth, more bone is made than lost. As we age, the opposite occurs.

Collagen provides the major structural framework for bone and can be thought of as the frame of a house. Once the frame of a house is in place, drywall can be attached. In a similar manner, once the collagen framework is established, mineral complexes can be added to bone. Calcium makes up a crystal in bone called **hydroxyapatite**. This bone crystal is large and complex and gives bone its strength. When calcium is absent, bone becomes weak because of lack of these crystals. Magnesium, sodium, phosphorus, and fluoride are also part of this crystal.

Fluoride plays a role in making teeth and bones harder; its hardening effect on tooth enamel is one of the reasons its use is recommended in preventing decay.

### Calcium in Muscle and Nerve Cells

While less than 1 percent of calcium is found in muscle and nerve cells, its role there is not to be underestimated. Calcium plays a fundamental role in muscle contraction. When we want a muscle to contract, calcium enters the cells to initiate the contraction. In nerve cells, calcium is critical in allowing the release of neurotransmitters for conduction of nerve impulses. Calcium also regulates the levels of sodium and potassium ions across the nerve membrane, both of which are necessary for nerve conduction. Adequate calcium intake is essential in the prevention of several diseases, including osteoporosis.

### ■ Nutrition and Disease

#### Calcium and vitamin D in bone health

One of the most common bone diseases in Western countries is osteoporosis. Osteoporosis is a disease in which the bones lose their mass, become fragile, and are more likely to break. According to the National Institutes of Health (NIH), this disease affects 44 million Americans, 68 percent of whom are postmenopausal women. Although it is more prevalent in people over age 50, osteoporosis can occur at any age, even as early as the twenties. This disease develops gradually over a lifetime, and there are no obvious symptoms until the bone becomes so weak that frequent fractures occur. Although there have been significant advances in medications to help slow the rate of bone loss in individuals who've been diagnosed, there is no cure. Figure 10.4 shows a comparison between a normal spine and an osteoporotic spine.

To prevent osteoporosis, both men and women should acquire as much bone mass as possible during youth and adolescence. The young teen years are the most important, because at age 18 for women and age 20 for men, you will have achieved 90 percent of your peak bone mass. You will continue to add a small amount in your twenties, reaching your peak at about age 30. After age 30 you gradually begin to lose bone mass. Whether you develop osteoporosis will depend on how much bone mass you accumulated as a teen.

When you are a teenager, calcium intake and sufficient vitamin D are critical in making sure you gain as much bone mass as possible. Women are at greater risk for this bone disease than men because they are less likely to eat foods that include calcium and vitamin D and also have lower bone mass to begin with. Many women, especially young ones, are likely to

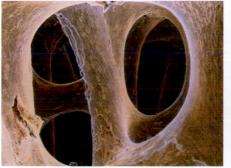

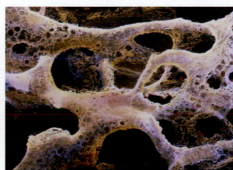

**Figure 10.4** Osteoporosis illustrated. The diagrams demonstrate what appears to be loss of total bone. However, in the microscopic structure, osteoporotic bone develops (right) a honeycomb appearance, with reduced bone density compared to normal bone (left).

**Want to know more?**
You can explore more information on superfoods by going to the text website at http://webcom8.grtxle.com/nutrition and clicking on the Chapters button. Select Chapter 10.

diet and often avoid foods rich in calcium and vitamin D, such as milk, in an effort to cut calories. Females may also lose calcium during frequent pregnancies. Also, men have greater muscle mass and tend to do more weight-bearing exercise, which helps build bones and slows the rate of breakdown.

As you age, it is important that you take as many actions as possible to slow your rate of bone loss. What does this mean? You should consume sufficient quantities of calcium and vitamin D and exercise regularly, engaging specifically in weight-bearing exercise. Estrogen also has a positive effect on bone. After menopause, estrogen levels drop, which can lead to accelerated bone loss in older women. ■

Osteoporosis is a much more serious disease than many people think. Older people who fall often break a bone. What many do not realize is that those who have this condition who break a hip often die within a year because of complications resulting from the injury. In the case of bone health, lifelong prevention is the key.

Calcium is present in many foods. Table 10.2 lists the calcium content of some high-calcium foods and drinks.

Many food manufacturers have begun to address a lack of calcium in our diet by adding calcium to beverages. The most well-known practice is the addition of calcium to orange juice. The practice of adding a nutrient to a food or beverage has led to the development of a new area of nutrition known as **functional foods**. Simply defined, functional foods are foods and beverages that have been developed or altered in some way in order to optimize health.

### ■ What's Hot

#### Superfoods

If you have been searching for the latest information on eating a healthy diet, you have probably heard the term "Superfoods." It has become a buzzword in recent popular nutrition information. This term was introduced by Steven G. Pratt, a medical doctor. He introduced the term and the concept in a popular book he authored called *Superfoods Rx*. According to his website (http://www.superfoodsrx.com/superfoods/), superfoods are referred to as being high in critical nutrients and low in calories. He makes the argument that these nutrients can prevent or even reverse age-related chronic diseases such as heart-disease, type 2 diabetes, high blood pressure, and certain cancers.

Nutritionists would call these foods nutrient dense. A list of these superfoods follows:

| | | | |
|---|---|---|---|
| Apples | Dark Chocolate | Oats | Spinach |
| Avocados | Dried fruits | Onions | Tea |
| Beans | Garlic | Oranges | Tomatoes |
| Blueberries | Honey | Pomegranates | Turkey |
| Broccoli | Kiwi | Pumpkin | Walnuts |
| Cinnamon | Low Fat Yogurt | Soy | Wild Salmon |

Most nutritionists would concur that these foods are loaded with nutrients, with the possible exception of honey. However, all would agree that vitamins and minerals are crucial nutrients in optimizing health and preventing disease. Therefore, before using supplements to get your vitamins and minerals, you may want to check out these foods and add them to your diet. ■

## Table 10.2    Calcium-Rich Foods

| Food | Serving Size | Calcium (mg) | Fat (g) | Calories |
|------|------|------|------|------|
| **Milk** | | | | |
| Skim* | 8 oz. | 301 | 0.4 | 86 |
| 1%* | 8 oz. | 300 | 2.6 | 102 |
| 2%* | 8 oz. | 298 | 4.7 | 121 |
| Whole* | 8 oz. | 290 | 8.2 | 149 |
| **Yogurt** | | | | |
| Plain, fat-free* | 8 oz. | 488 | 0.4 | 137 |
| Plain, low-fat* | 8 oz. | 448 | 3.8 | 154 |
| Fruit, low-fat* | 8 oz. | 338 | 2.8 | 243 |
| Frozen, vanilla, soft-serve | 1/2 c. | 103 | 4.0 | 114 |
| **Cheese** | | | | |
| American | 1 oz. | 163 | 6.9 | 93 |
| Cheddar* | 1 oz. | 204 | 9.4 | 114 |
| Cottage, 2% | 1 c. | 156 | 4.4 | 203 |
| Mozzarella, part-skim | 1 oz. | 183 | 4.5 | 72 |
| Muenster* | 1 oz. | 203 | 8.5 | 104 |
| Parmesan | 1 Tbsp. | 69 | 1.5 | 23 |
| Ricotta, part skim* | 1/2 c. | 337 | 9.8 | 171 |
| Ricotta, whole milk* | 1/2 c. | 257 | 16.1 | 216 |
| **Ice Cream, Vanilla** | | | | |
| Low-fat | 1/2 c. | 92 | 2.8 | 92 |
| High-fat | 1/2 c. | 87 | 12 | 178 |
| **Fish and Shellfish** | | | | |
| Sardines, canned in oil, drained, including bones* | 3.75 oz. | 351 | 10.5 | 191 |
| Salmon, pink, canned, including bones | 3 oz. | 181 | 5.1 | 118 |
| Shrimp, canned, drained | 3 oz. | 50 | 1.7 | 102 |
| **Vegetables** | | | | |
| Bok choy, raw (Chinese cabbage) | 1 c. | 74 | 0 | 9 |
| Broccoli, cooked, drained, from raw | 1 c. | 74 | 0.6 | 44 |
| Broccoli, cooked, drained, from frozen | 1 c. | 94 | 0.2 | 50 |
| Soybeans, mature, boiled | 1 c. | 175 | 15 | 298 |
| Collards, cooked, drained, from raw* | 1 c. | 226 | 0.7 | 49 |
| Turnip greens, cooked, drained, from raw, leaves and stems | 1 c. | 197 | 0.3 | 29 |
| **Others** | | | | |
| Tofu, raw, regular, prepared with calcium* | 1/2 c. | 434 | 5.9 | 94 |
| Orange (navel) | 1 whole | 56 | 0.1 | 65 |
| Tortilla, corn | 1 med. | 46 | 0.7 | 58 |
| Tortilla, flour | 1 med. | 40 | 2.3 | 104 |
| Almonds (dry-roasted) | 1 oz. | 75 | 15 | 169 |
| Sesame seeds, kernels, toasted | 1 oz. | 37 | 13.6 | 161 |
| Dried figs, uncooked* | 1 c. | 287 | 2.3 | 507 |

*Source*: USDA Nutrient Data Laboratory, 2002.

Note: You also can increase the calcium in foods by following these suggestions:
1. Add nonfat powdered milk to all soups, casseroles, and drinks.
2. Buy juices, cereals, breads, and rice that are fortified with calcium.
3. Replace whole milk and cream with skim and low-fat milk in recipes.
4. Replace sour cream with yogurt in recipes.
5. Some bottled waters contain calcium, so check the labels for more information.

*Indicates a high calcium source

## Calcium's Role in Metabolism

Calcium plays a very important role in hormone regulation. The impact of a hormone on a cell can be mediated or diminished through the hormone's effect on cell calcium levels, a process referred to as a *second messenger* role. Also, calcium can enter a cell and bind to a calcium-binding protein that activates enzymes in cells.

**APPLICATION TIP**

To get the most out of calcium-rich foods and increase your overall absorption, spread your consumption of them throughout the day. So, rather than a glass of milk and a yogurt for breakfast, have the milk for breakfast and the yogurt for lunch.

## Calcium's Role in Blood Clotting

In Chapter 9 we discussed the importance of vitamin K in blood clotting. Calcium also is central to blood clotting. Like vitamin K, calcium is needed to convert the protein prothrombin to thrombin. Thrombin is an enzyme that converts fibrinogen to fibrin. Both vitamin K and calcium play roles in the blood-clotting process by making fibrin (see Figure 9.7 for review).

## Calcium and Blood Pressure

Calcium can have a protective effect against hypertension. Years ago, it was discovered that some women suffered from a serious blood disorder during pregnancy called toxemia of pregnancy or **pre-eclampsia** (see Chapter 16 for more information). It is characterized by headache, fatigue, protein in the urine, and high blood pressure. Women who are overweight and teenagers who are pregnant are especially prone to this condition. Scientists reported that mothers who had a lower chance of pre-eclampsia had higher dietary calcium intake, primarily from dairy products. When women with pre-eclampsia increased their calcium intake from dairy products or supplements, the result was a dramatic lowering of blood pressure. Further studies were conducted to determine whether calcium could be used to lower blood pressure in other groups of people with hypertension, and the results were the same. Hypertensive subjects who consumed greater levels (more than 800 mg per day) of calcium, as either dairy products or supplements, had significantly lower blood pressure.

### ■ What's Hot

*Can calcium decrease body weight or prevent obesity?*
In addition to its role in the prevention of osteoporosis and hypertension, calcium may help prevent other diseases as well. Recently there has been increased interest in the role that calcium may play in obesity. Obese African Americans were studied over a one-year period to determine whether their blood pressure could be reduced. They were given yogurt daily, which raised calcium consumption from 400 mg per day to 1,000 mg per day. This resulted in an average weight loss of almost 11 lb. Studies such as the Nationwide Food Consumption Survey suggest that those who had the lowest calcium intakes also had greater weight and were more likely to be obese. According to surveys conducted in the United States, African Americans have the lowest level of calcium intake and the highest incidence of obesity.

Animal and human studies both support the idea that a diet high in calcium may moderate body weight. Dairy products tend to be more effective than calcium supplements at demonstrating this phenomenon. Research has been ongoing to determine why calcium may have this antiobesity impact. It is believed to be related to how much calcium is inside a cell. How does this work? Researchers believe that the real culprit is vitamin D. When calcium levels are high in the diet, we do not make as much vitamin D. When calcium is low, we make more vitamin D. One of the roles of vitamin D is to increase calcium levels in the cell. When this happens, the cells produce more fat.

First, let's look at the evidence. In a human study on thirty-two obese subjects, a University of Tennessee group studied both calcium supplements and extra calcium from dairy products. These subjects were divided into three groups for a twenty-four-week trial:

1. Control group: 400 to 500 mg of calcium per day were fed to subjects through their diet, and a placebo pill was also given.

2. Calcium-supplemented group: subjects consumed 800 mg per day from a calcium carbonate pill each day, and they were fed a diet that provided a *total* of 1,200 to 1,300 mg of calcium per day.

3. High-dairy group: Subjects were given three servings of dairy products per day, plus a placebo supplement.

The researchers observed that subjects on all three diets lost weight. The control group lost about 6.4 percent of their initial body weight. Those in the second group, who were given a calcium supplement but also absorbed some calcium from their diet, lost 8.1 percent of their body weight. The third group, which consumed calcium from only dietary sources (mostly dairy), lost 10.9 percent of their initial body weight. Furthermore, the loss of body fat followed the same pattern. An interesting finding was that those in the second and third groups with extra calcium lost the weight from the abdominal area. Although this study demonstrated that consuming dairy calcium resulted in weight and fat loss, not all studies have yielded such results. However, consuming the recommended intake of calcium from foods is certainly a good idea for the prevention of other diseases, as we discussed, whether or not it prevents obesity. ■

## Calcium Absorption and Blood Levels

Blood levels of calcium are tightly regulated within a narrow range by various hormones and mechanisms. **Parathyroid hormone** is a hormone produced by the parathyroid glands located next to the thyroid gland in the neck; it is released if blood calcium levels decrease. Parathyroid hormone causes more active vitamin D to be made, as well as causing the bone to release calcium into the bloodstream. The vitamin D produced causes the kidneys to retain calcium and stimulates absorption of calcium from the small intestine. Vitamin D then enters the cells of the small intestine, where it stimulates the production of a calcium-binding protein to absorb more calcium. Thus the net effect of parathyroid hormone is to increase calcium levels if they begin to decrease in the blood.

Dietary factors can decrease the absorption of calcium and many other minerals in the diet. Some plant-based foods contain a compound called

**Want to know more?**
You can learn more about the relationship between calcium intake and weight control by visiting the text website at http://webcom8.grtxle.com/nutrition and clicking on the Chapters button. Select Chapter 10.

**APPLICATION TIP**

Pizza is a great way to get calcium, but it can be loaded with saturated fat. To keep the fat content down, make it yourself. You can use a tortilla as the crust, add spaghetti sauce and cheese (low-fat, soy, or rice cheese), and top it with vegetables. If you order out, buy from a place that does not grease the pan, avoid the high-fat meat topping, and ask them to go light on the cheese.

**Figure 10.5** Phytate and oxalate can decrease the absorption of several minerals. This illustration shows how the negative charge of phytate and oxalate can attract and bind up the positive-charged minerals.

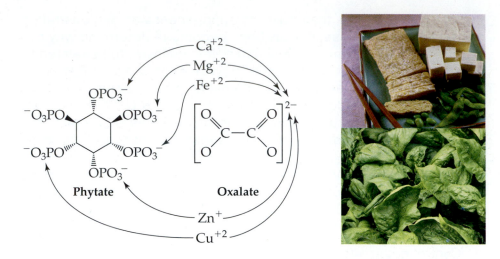

**phytate**. This substance looks like a sugar molecule and is found in soy products and the husk of whole grains and cereals. Phytate binds certain minerals—calcium and zinc in particular—making them unavailable to cells. **Oxalate** is another compound with negative charges that binds calcium and other minerals that have positive charges. Spinach is a good source of calcium, but it is also high in oxalates, making this food's role as a calcium source questionable (Figure 10.5).

Other factors increase calcium absorption. Spreading your calcium more evenly throughout the day results in more calcium being absorbed. Also, for some unknown reason, the presence of milk sugar or lactose in the gut at the same time as calcium results in greater absorption. The increased physiological need for calcium, such as during growth, pregnancy, and lactation, results in better absorption.

### Requirements and Food Sources

In setting recommendations for calcium, the level needed to achieve peak bone mass during the late teen to early adult years is a primary factor. Therefore, much of the recommendation for intake is focused upon this. In November 2010, the DRI for calcium changed. The DRI recommendation for calcium is 1,000 mg per day for adults, and for those females older than 50 the DRI is 1,200 mg per day. For adolescents, the recommendation is 1,300 mg per day; this is the age group that most often does not meet the recommended levels.

Table 10.2 has already given you an idea of some good sources of calcium. Dairy products are the best calcium sources, but other sources include such varied foods as canned sardines and salmon if the bones are eaten, cheddar cheese, turnip greens, spinach, and broccoli. However, plant sources of calcium may not be as absorbable. Calcium may bond to other substances, as mentioned earlier, which does not allow for it to be absorbed by the small intestine. A number of calcium supplements are on the market; the amount absorbed varies. About 50 percent of the calcium in milk is absorbed. Less than that is absorbed from calcium supplements, as indicated in Table 10.3.

## Phosphorus

Phosphorus ranks second after calcium in terms of abundance in our bodies. Approximately 85 percent of the phosphorus is in our bones, with the remainder

| Table 10.3 | Percentage of Absorption of Calcium from Several Supplement Sources | |
|---|---|---|
| **Calcium Form** | | **Percentage of Absorption** |
| Calcium citrate malate | | 45–50% |
| Calcium carbonate | | 36–42% |
| Calcium acetate | | 24–36% |
| Calcium citrate | | 24–36% |
| Calcium gluconates, phosphates, lactates, oyster shells | | 24–36% |

*Are some calcium supplements better than others?*

in soft tissues such as muscle. Phosphorus is not normally found by itself but is complexed with four oxygen atoms. The resulting structure is referred to as phosphate (see Figure 10.6).

### Roles of Phosphorus

Phosphorus plays many roles in our bodies. It is part of bone and teeth. It is also a part of the molecule ATP, the "usable" form of energy (see Chapter 6) (Figure 10.7). Without phosphorus, our bodies would be unable to deliver energy or store it. Phosphorus is also very important in allowing some enzymes to function and at the same time turning off the function of other enzymes.

Phosphorus is a part of DNA and RNA; it links the basic components together (Figure 10.8). It is also a part of cell membranes and lipoproteins. Earlier we discussed the role of phosphorus in helping cell membranes associate with water in the body. Phosphorus is a critical part of lipoproteins, whose role it is to transport lipids in our blood to tissues.

The acid-base balance or pH of the blood depends on several compounds of salts. Phosphorus ions act as a buffer so our blood does not become too acidic or too basic. A slight shift in the acid-base balance in the blood could make the difference between life and death.

### Requirements and Food Sources

The DRI for phosphorus is 700 mg per day. Getting sufficient phosphorus from our diets is no problem because it is so abundant in our food supply and phosphorus deficiency is rarely reported. Good sources include meat, fish, poultry, eggs, milk and milk products, cereals, legumes, and grains. Other sources include tea, coffee, chocolate, and soft drinks. Soda products typically contain considerable amounts of phosphorus. There have been reports that excess phosphorus intake can decrease blood levels of calcium and contribute to osteoporosis. However, this is controversial. Some scientists do not agree that the phosphorus content in soda, or the amount consumed, will lower blood calcium. The issue may not be the actual amount of soda consumed, but that those who drink soda are not consuming enough calcium-rich dairy products.

## Magnesium

Of all of the macrominerals, magnesium is the one found in the smallest amount in the body. The average adult human has 24 to 28 mg of magnesium in his or her body. About half of the magnesium is located in bone;

**Figure 10.6** The chemical structure of phosphate, showing negative charges. The negative charge allows the phosphate groups to bond to other positively charged atoms to form larger compounds.

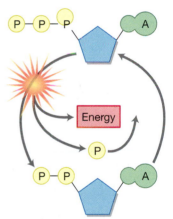

**Figure 10.7** Role of phosphorus in a cell's energy metabolism. Most of the energy produced in a cell ends up in the form of ATP. When a phosphate group is liberated from ATP to produce ADP, a great deal of energy is released to drive biochemical processes.

**DNA Molecule: Two Views**

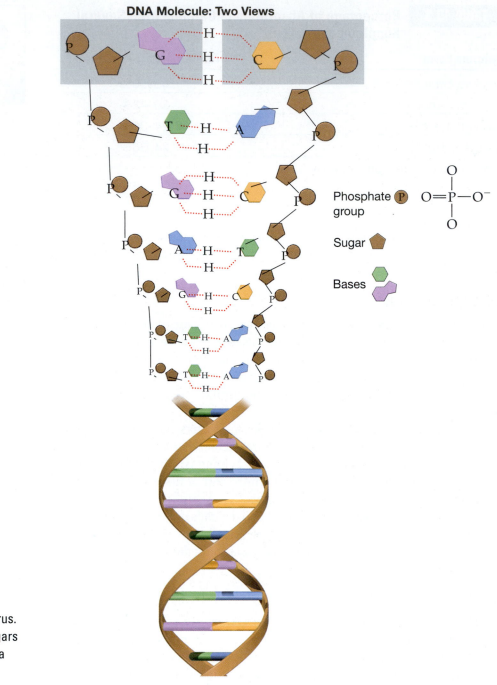

Phosphate P
group

$$O=P-O^-$$
with O above and O below

Sugar

Bases

**Figure 10.8** The backbone of DNA is phosphorus. Phosphorus links the sugars of DNA together to form a strand.

the remainder is in soft tissues, such as skeletal muscle, heart, and liver, and about 1 percent is found in the blood and fluids. In soft tissue, most magnesium is found within the cell, similar to potassium, as discussed in Chapter 8.

## Roles of Magnesium

Magnesium is part of the bone crystals that give our skeleton strength and serve as a store for magnesium if other areas, such as the blood, need it. Magnesium is important in maintaining the integrity of DNA and RNA by working with phosphorus in maintaining the genetic material. It is also very important in stabilizing ATP.

Magnesium plays the opposite role to calcium in muscle contraction. Whereas calcium is involved in contraction, magnesium is involved in relaxation. Some health experts advocate consuming more dietary magnesium because of its effect on relaxing muscles, including the muscles of the heart.

In the cell, magnesium acts as a cofactor for almost 300 different enzymes. One of the enzymes is responsible for pumping sodium out of the cell and potassium into the cell. If magnesium deficiency occurs, the ability to keep these two electrolytes balanced is limited and can lead to decreased nerve conduction. People with low magnesium may experience heart arrhythmia.

Magnesium deficiency, although rare, can occur in cases of severe diarrhea, vomiting, or heavy sweating, all of which result in excess fluid loss. Some alcoholics may also become magnesium deficient because alcohol is a diuretic and causes nutrient loss through the kidneys. In some instances, people on medications for controlling blood pressure may lose magnesium and can become deficient. They should have their blood levels checked periodically.

### Requirements and Food Sources

About half of the magnesium we eat can be absorbed by the small intestine. The DRI for magnesium is 400 mg per day for men and 320 mg per day for women, but 75 percent of Americans are below these levels. One reason is that the increased consumption of refined foods has caused a decrease of magnesium in the food supply. There are a variety of sources of magnesium, one of the best being green leafy vegetables (spinach, collards, and turnip greens). Magnesium is part of the plant pigment chlorophyll, making green plants high in magnesium. Other sources of magnesium are unpolished grains, nuts, and legumes. Whole-grain cereals and breads are good sources of magnesium, but the refined products are not. Finally, chocolate is a source of magnesium, which is good news for chocolate lovers.

### ■ Nutrition and Disease

*Does hard water protect against heart disease?*

Many people have often complained about the hardness of their water. Those who have hard water can attest to the discoloration it leaves on clothes and the rings it leaves in bathtubs. Many people have installed home water softeners to rectify these issues. Water softeners remove calcium and magnesium in exchange for sodium. However, is this a good thing to do? The distinguishing factor between hard and soft water is that hard water has much higher levels of calcium and magnesium.

Many research studies have reported that populations living in hard-water areas have lower rates of high blood pressure and mortality from heart disease. Studies of people in several British towns that increased their water hardness between 1900 and 1955 by 50 parts per million or more, revealed that they experienced a lower incidence of cardiovascular disease. In contrast, towns that decreased water hardness did not show such a favorable trend. Another British study obtained blood pressure, plasma cholesterol, and heart rate measurements from

Cambridge, England, is located in the eastern part of the country, where many municipalities have deliberately maintained higher levels of magnesium and calcium in their water supply.

middle-aged male residents in six hard-water and six soft-water towns. Results showed higher blood pressure, plasma cholesterol levels, and heart disease rates for those who lived in soft-water towns than those in hard-water towns. In the United States, research has also shown that water hardness is associated with lower rates of heart disease and hypertension. On the other hand, a study conducted in the Netherlands failed to show any connection between tap water hardness, calcium, and magnesium with heart disease.

Calcium can lower blood pressure in hypertensive subjects. Magnesium also has a health benefit on the heart. A study in Taiwan suggested that magnesium has a greater protective effect than calcium levels in hard water. Many other survey studies throughout the world suggest that the magnesium content of hard water is a very important factor in reducing heart disease. Given these facts, it is probably best to drink hard water. If water softeners are used, they should be added to the water used in washing clothes or even bathing, if possible, but not to the water used for drinking. Remember that when you use water softeners for drinking water, you are removing healthy minerals such as magnesium and calcium, and increasing sodium, which has been linked to high blood pressure. ■

### Before you go on . . .

1. How does calcium give strength and structure to bone?
2. Which mineral has been shown to lower blood pressure in hypertensive people?
3. What minerals are involved in maintaining the integrity of DNA and RNA?
4. Which foods would you choose to get enough magnesium?
5. What are five major roles that phosphorus plays in our body?

## The Microminerals

As mentioned previously, much has been learned during the last part of the twentieth century of the role minerals play in body functions and health. This is particularly true of the microminerals, which are sometimes referred to as *trace minerals*. Breakthroughs in analytical techniques have allowed scientists to detect smaller quantities of minerals and are the primary reason for the explosion of new knowledge about microminerals. Even though we need less than 100 mg of each of these minerals per day, a lack of these nutrients can be just as problematic as with any of the other nutrients discussed so far. A number of diseases and conditions have been linked to a lack of these microminerals in our diets.

# Iron

We have only a total of 2 to 4 grams of iron in our body, but it is one of the most important of the microminerals and also one that is the most lacking worldwide as well as in the United States. Its role in preventing anemia is well known and forms the basis of much of our discussion. However, you will learn that iron has roles beyond that of simply preventing anemia.

## Roles of Iron

One of the most important roles of iron is to help deliver oxygen to the tissues and cells of our bodies. Oxygen is bound to hemoglobin and is circulated in the blood via red blood cells (RBCs). Every second of every day, your body produces 2.5 million RBCs, which matches the number of RBCs destroyed in your liver, spleen, and lymph nodes. A typical RBC might circulate for only 120 days before being replaced. This balance maintains a level of circulating RBCs that approximates 25 trillion.

Red blood cells have been described as "bags of hemoglobin" because the protein hemoglobin accounts for as much as a third of cell weight. Hemoglobin is the iron-containing protein that carries oxygen to the tissues and cells throughout your body. It contains four heme units. At the core of each heme unit is iron, which binds oxygen to be delivered to tissues and cells.

In order for iron to be used to make heme, it must be transported to the bone marrow aboard a protein called **transferrin**, which is the major means by which iron is transported in the blood to organs. Iron bound to transferrin is delivered to the liver for storage. Iron stored in the liver is bound to the protein **ferritin**. Blood ferritin levels are therefore good indicators of how much iron you consume.

Because hemoglobin is vital to effective oxygen circulation and delivery to all parts of the body, your physician will measure its level as part of a routine checkup. Normally, the level of circulating hemoglobin is between 13.8 and 17.2 g/100 mL of blood for men and 12.1 to 15.1 for women. As we discussed in Chapter 9, anemia refers to a clinical condition in which the level of hemoglobin is too low. It can be caused by poor hemoglobin production, decreased RBC formation, or increased blood loss (as in hemorrhage). Another measure of anemia is the **hematocrit**, which is the percentage of blood that is composed of red blood cells. Normal values are 40 to 48. A level below 37, although not unusual, is a sign that anemia may be setting in. Although iron deficiency can lead to anemia, this condition has other causes. A deficiency of vitamin $B_6$, vitamin $B_{12}$, or folate can lead to anemia, as can an acute or chronic disease.

Iron-deficiency anemia in pregnant women can lead to premature delivery. Decreased immune response, fatigue, inability to regulate body temperature, decreased thyroid gland metabolism, and decreased ability to synthesize neurotransmitters are all signs of iron deficiency. In pregnancy, intake of iron is important so that the newborn baby will have at least six months of iron stores in the liver, because breast milk is a poor source of iron. Often this does not happen, even in the United States, and infants are often depleted of their iron stores by three months of age. When introducing solid foods to an infant, it is important that the food be enriched with iron (see Chapter 16 for more information).

## Iron Absorption

Compared to other minerals and even vitamins that we have discussed so far, the amount of iron absorbed in a typical diet is very low. To complicate matters,

## APPLICATION TIP

To enhance absorption of non-heme iron such as that found in iron-fortified breakfast cereal or an iron supplement, drink a glass of orange juice with them.

the form of the iron is important in determining the amount of iron absorbed by the small intestine. There are two major forms of iron in our diets. One is **heme iron**, an organic form of iron that is still part of the complex ring structure that makes up hemoglobin (Figure 10.9). Twenty-five to 35 percent of this form of iron is absorbed. The second form is **nonheme iron**, or the elemental form of iron that is not a part of hemoglobin. The amount of nonheme iron absorbed is less than heme iron and ranges from 2 to 20 percent.

The heme form of iron is found only in meats, fish, and poultry. Of the iron found in these foods, 60 percent is in the heme form and the rest in the elemental form. The heme form can cross the cells of the small intestine much more easily than the elemental form. However, elemental forms in the diet from both plant sources and animal sources vary by other factors. Two factors that enhance the absorption of elemental iron are the presence of vitamin C and the presence of meat, fish, and poultry in the diet. Vitamin C increases the solubility of elemental iron and allows it to be better absorbed. In practical terms, this means that having orange juice along with your cereal in the morning will result in more iron absorbed. When meat, fish, and poultry are consumed, the absorption of elemental iron is enhanced. This phenomenon has been referred to as the **meat, fish, and poultry factor (MFP)**.

The presence of about 3 oz. of meat, fish, or poultry in the diet, or the same amount of vitamin C (equivalent to a cup of orange juice) can increase the amount of elemental iron absorbed from 2 to 3 percent to 7 to 8 percent. To some extent, the small intestine can regulate the amount of iron absorbed based on need. If you go to a high altitude where there is less oxygen, your body responds by making more red blood cells, which means more iron is required. The small intestine absorbs more iron as a result. A diet too high in fiber (more than 30 g per day) and phytate content of grains can impair nonheme iron absorption. Also, too much dietary calcium decreases iron absorption.

### Toxicity

Iron can be toxic if too much enters the body. In some individuals, the levels of iron absorbed cannot be regulated, and iron builds up to dangerous levels.

**Figure 10.9** Structure of the heme molecule. Note that iron (Fe) is at the center of this complex compound. The entire molecule is easily absorbed by the small intestine.

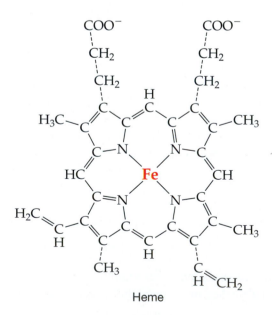

Heme

Cases of iron toxicity were first noted in a tribe in Africa that learned to make beer in iron pots. The brew contained much iron, and over a long period of time they consumed enough excess to cause iron toxicity. Iron toxicity often occurs as a result of a genetic disorder called *hemochromatosis*. An individual who has two copies of a certain defective gene is at risk for hemochromatosis. Many people may have this genetic disorder; up to 10 percent of those of northern European descent may have one copy of the gene, meaning they are carriers, and 1 out of 250 have both copies, which is rather high for a genetic disorder. Symptoms of iron overload include abdominal pain, fatigue, and mental depression in the early stages, and advance to liver damage in the later stages due to iron accumulation. Infections, joint pain, skin pigmentation due to iron deposits, diabetes, blood in the stools, and shock are symptoms of iron toxicity. High iron in tissues or even in the diet may be a risk factor for heart disease. Those with hereditary hemochromatosis need to be careful about iron intake, especially when many foods are either enriched or fortified with iron; these individuals should not take iron supplements. This is a challenge because many people do not know they have the disorder, and signs may not occur until midlife because it may take that long to build up iron stores sufficient to cause negative health effects. Asking your physician to test for it when you are a young adult may be prudent for lifelong health, and many health professionals advocate better screening of this disorder. The tests used to evaluate hemoglobin and hematocrit for iron status are also used to screen for hemochromatosis. If these indicators suggest high iron stores, you can be tested to determine whether you carry the gene for hereditary hemochromatosis.

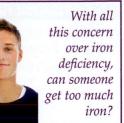

*With all this concern over iron deficiency, can someone get too much iron?*

## Requirements and Food Sources

How much iron should we consume? The recommended amounts have changed over the years. Generally speaking, the recommended amounts are higher for women than men. Monthly blood loss through the menstrual cycle accounts for some of the higher requirements. In addition to the monthly blood loss, women of childbearing age tend to have lower iron intakes, which compounds the problem of iron-deficiency anemia. Men have a DRI of 8 mg per day. Women over age 50 also have a DRI of 8 mg per day, but women of childbearing age (ages 19 to 50) have a DRI of 18 mg per day. It is often difficult to attain this level in typical diet patterns. During pregnancy the DRI goes up to 27 mg per day. There is much debate as to whether women should supplement with iron because of the difficulty of getting the DRI amounts from the diet alone. For pregnant women, physicians often prescribe prenatal vitamins, which contain the DRI for iron. Many dietitians have advocated an iron supplement for women of childbearing age. Of course, whenever possible everyone should try to obtain iron from food. Men consuming a 2,500-calorie diet should not have any problems reaching the DRI for iron.

Women who are vegetarians need to be extra careful because they lack heme iron in their diets. It has been suggested that they multiply their DRI by a factor of 1.8 to compensate for the lack of heme iron in their diets. For a woman of childbearing age, this would mean 18 mg per day × 1.8 = 32 mg per day, which would require a supplement. Vegetarian men would need 14 mg per day, which they should be able to get from their diets.

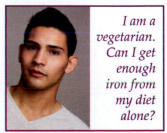

*I am a vegetarian. Can I get enough iron from my diet alone?*

**APPLICATION TIP**

To best absorb the iron in your food, avoid drinking coffee, tea, or milk with your meal.

Good iron sources include not only meat, fish, and poultry but also shellfish (especially oysters), beans, enriched cereal, green leafy vegetables, eggs, and even dried fruit. Coffee and tea should be avoided or limited when consuming these foods because they contain substances that bind up iron and make them unavailable for absorption.

# Zinc

Zinc has been the subject of a great amount of research investigation in the last thirty years. Deficiencies of zinc have been known to occur worldwide. Zinc is important for the function of nearly 200 different enzymes. It was also one of the first nutrients known to exert its effects at the genetic level.

## Roles of Zinc

Microminerals function as cofactors for many enzymes, and zinc exerts much of its physiological effects through enzyme activities. It is involved in enzymes that break down alcohol in the liver, is a cofactor for an antioxidant enzyme that fights against free radicals, helps enzymes involved with protein digestion, works with enzymes that replicate DNA, and is a cofactor for enzymes involved with blood pressure regulation. Many of the enzymes in which zinc plays a role are involved with protein synthesis, and when there is a lack of dietary zinc, protein synthesis and growth are markedly retarded. Zinc plays a critical role in wound healing. Zinc supplements are often given to patients recovering from burns and decubitus ulcers (bed sores). Zinc is a component of proteins that turn genes on and off. When we make hemoglobin, there is an enzyme that is zinc dependent. Insulin depends on zinc for storage and function. It is also a very important nutrient in supporting the immune system. Sexual development and the growth of bones are zinc dependent.

The functions of zinc are as follows:

- Alcohol metabolism
- Hemoglobin synthesis
- Protein digestion
- Antioxidant enzyme function
- Blood pressure regulation
- DNA replication
- Protein synthesis, growth, and development
- Immune function
- Development of sexual organs and bone growth
- Insulin release and function
- Gene regulation

## Zinc Deficiency Signs

Zinc deficiency was originally seen among adolescent males in the Middle East in such places as Egypt and Iran. It has been also been found among the Hispanic population of Denver, Colorado—again, primarily among adolescent males. The most notable deficiency signs were dwarfism and delayed sexual development (see the Nutrition and Lifestages feature that follows). Zinc deficiency was reported among hospitalized patients who were maintained through *total parenteral nutrition*. Total parenteral nutrition, or TPN, is a technique used to inject calories and nutrients through a central vein (as opposed to being given through a vein in the arm via an IV solution). In these cases, zinc was not added to the intravenous fluid. Some people have a genetic defect in the ability to absorb zinc, and alcoholics may also have a mild zinc deficiency.

Worldwide, zinc deficiency remains a large concern, especially among children. Children with zinc deficiency have mental disabilities and an inability to withstand infection, which only increases the requirement for additional zinc. Many international aid programs have focused on supplementing foods with micronutrients such as zinc to prevent some of these problems from occurring.

Signs of zinc deficiency include the following:

- Dwarfism in young teens, particularly males
- Poor sexual development (underdeveloped testes in males)
- Deformed bones
- Poor healing of wounds
- Abnormal hair and nails; loss of hair
- Hypogeusia, or the inability to taste food
- Gastrointestinal disturbances, impaired lipid absorption
- Central nervous system defects
- Impaired folate and vitamin A absorption

### ■ Nutrition and Lifestages

#### Zinc in teenage males

Trace minerals exist in your diet in small amounts. What could possibly happen if you didn't have enough of the metal zinc in your diet? Well, plenty can happen if you are a young adolescent boy. Years ago, nutritionists discovered that some boys around age 11 to 12 living in certain areas of the world were short compared to others in the same country. They could not blame this entirely on the culture because some boys were normal height and others were dwarfed. Areas that were affected included Middle Eastern countries such as Iran and Egypt. However, a young group of Hispanic males living in Denver, Colorado, showed similar signs. Besides being short for their age, they appeared to be sexually underdeveloped (Figure 10.10).

It was later learned that the boys had a zinc deficiency. This puzzled some, because it looked as if they had enough zinc in their diets. However, in the Middle East and in some Hispanic cultures, it is common to consume unleavened, or flat, breads. These breads contain phytate. The phytate in the flat bread or tortillas in the young boys' diets was binding up the zinc and making it unavailable for absorption by the intestine. Fortunately, this was not permanent. When the nutritionists gave these boys zinc supplements, they grew about six to eight inches in six months! It was clear that zinc is needed to support growth and sexual development. However, you should be aware that taking a zinc supplement will not make you grow taller or improve sexual performance if you are not deficient, and too much could be toxic. ■

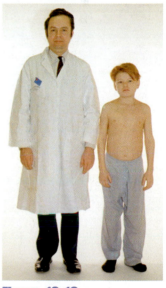

**Figure 10.10** Dwarfism in a teenage boy suffering from zinc deficiency. Such problems were once common among young adolescent males in the Middle East and even in Denver, Colorado.

### Zinc Absorption

The absorption of zinc is regulated by the small intestine. About 40 percent of dietary zinc can be absorbed. When there is a sufficient store of zinc, the small intestine makes a protein to bind up the zinc and prevent it from being absorbed. The cells that line the gastrointestinal tract are sloughed off every twenty-four to forty-eight hours. The zinc is lost this way when it binds to the proteins in the cells. When you need more zinc, the protein is not made and zinc is absorbed into the bloodstream. As with iron, the presence of meat, fish, and poultry in the diet improves the amount of zinc absorbed.

### Requirements and Food Sources

Men have a higher DRI for zinc than women because of the greater muscle mass of men and thus their greater dependence on increased protein synthesis to maintain that muscle mass. Remember that zinc is needed for protein synthesis. The DRI for zinc is 11 mg per day for men and 8 mg per day for women. The Tolerable Upper Intake Level for zinc is 40 mg per day; consuming more than this amount can lead to decreased copper absorption. A decrease in HDL cholesterol has been reported in men receiving 50 mg of zinc per day over a three-month period. Vomiting, diarrhea, and cramps can occur at dosages greater than 100 mg per day.

Meats, poultry (turkey in particular), oysters, herring, eggs, legumes, and whole-grain cereals are good sources of zinc. Fruits are very poor zinc sources. The refinement of grains can result in significant zinc losses, and zinc needs to be added back into cereals; therefore, reading food labels is important to help prevent a zinc deficiency.

## Copper

### Roles of Copper

Copper, like zinc, exerts its physiological effects as a cofactor for enzymes, but not for as many enzymes as zinc does. Fewer than twenty enzymes have been reported as being dependent on copper. Copper has several well-known functions. First, it is needed for absorption, storage, and metabolism of iron. Here again, we can see how one nutrient depends on the function of another. In copper deficiency, animals and humans can become anemic, and it appears to be iron-deficiency anemia. In a sense, it is. Without copper, iron cannot be incorporated into hemoglobin and red blood cells. Another important role for copper is that of strengthening connective tissue. Recall from Chapter 9, that the protein collagen depends on vitamin C to make it stronger. Here again, another nutrient strengthens collagen. Collagen depends on a copper-containing enzyme to enhance its strength by promoting cross-linking among the various collagen proteins. In copper deficiency, connective tissue is weakened. Another important function of copper is that it is needed for enzymes involved in the production of neurotransmitters, for an enzyme involved in the production of ATP, and as an enzyme that fights against free radicals in the body.

The functions of copper are as follows:

- Iron use and incorporation into hemoglobin and red blood cells
- Antioxidant defense against free radicals
- Strengthening collagen and therefore connective tissue
- Immune defense
- Synthesis of neurotransmitters
- Energy production via ATP synthesis

## Copper Absorption

Copper is absorbed to a certain extent by the stomach, but most is absorbed by the small intestine. The same protein that regulates zinc uptake regulates how much copper is absorbed, and too much zinc can interfere with copper absorption. Generally speaking, more than half of dietary copper is absorbed.

## Requirements and Food Sources

The DRI for copper is 900 mcg per day for adults. Few cases of copper deficiency have been reported. Premature infants and hospitalized patients on TPN without copper added to the solution have had deficiency symptoms. Some genetic diseases preclude copper absorption. One such disease is a genetic form of copper deficiency in which the small intestine cannot produce the correct protein that absorbs copper. This is a fatal disease, and children with it rarely live past three years. Many children experience neurological and cardiovascular disorders because of the lack of copper.

The Tolerable Upper Intake Level of copper is 10 mg per day. Vomiting and liver damage can occur at this or higher levels.

Good food sources of copper include organ meats, shellfish, mushrooms, chocolate, nuts, legumes, and the germ and bran portions of cereals. Drinking water, especially where water runs through copper pipes, is a good source of dietary copper.

## ■ You Decide

### Can a lack of dietary copper lead to heart disease?

For a number of years, nutritionists have expressed concern that Americans may not be obtaining adequate levels of copper in their diets. Only recently has there been sufficient evidence to make a recommendation on how much copper we should consume. Before the issuing of the DRI for copper, this mineral did not have a recommended intake, but rather a range of 1.5 to 3 mg per day was suggested. Using the latter as a basis, quite a few survey studies suggested that many Americans would not come close to meeting this level. With the new DRI of 0.9 mg (900 mcg) per day, many more people can meet this requirement, but there are still concerns that a significant part of the public does not.

It is difficult to determine whether people are getting enough copper per day. First, we have only recently discovered more foods that contain copper. Second, water is a good source of copper, and this is not often considered in intake studies. Third, there is no sensitive biochemical test to determine whether you are mildly deficient in copper.

Animals fed a copper-deficient diet rapidly develop heart disease that is characterized by heart enlargement (Figure 10.11). The animals have abnormal electrocardiograms (a measure of heart electrical activity) and elevated blood cholesterol, triglycerides, and glucose. The deficiency sets in rapidly (within four to five weeks), and almost all animals die of heart-related causes. Can this be the case in humans? To date, no convincing studies have linked copper deficiency to heart disease. Some evidence suggests that individuals with a genetic inability to handle copper have heart disease, but these types are rare. This does not mean that those who have some copper in the diet but are still below the DRI may not eventually have heart problems. We can show cause and effect in the laboratory, but in the real world a definite link has not been made. Given this information, would you be concerned about how much copper is in your diet? ■

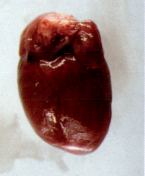

**Figure 10.11** Hearts from rats fed copper-adequate and copper-deficient diets. Note, in the bottom photo, the enlarged heart caused by copper deficiency.

## Selenium

Selenium has received a lot of attention in the last thirty years, as we have learned more about it. Many agricultural communities have naturally occurring high levels of selenium in the soil that can get into plants. In some parts of the country, cattle that forage on plants grown in high-selenium-soil areas develop selenium toxicity, which is deadly. For this reason, and for many years, selenium was thought to be a toxic metal only. Today we know that selenium is essential for good health and can prevent several diseases.

### Roles of Selenium

The most important role that selenium plays is in the antioxidant defense system against free radical damage to cells and tissues. Selenium is part of an antioxidant enzyme called *glutathione peroxidase*. The activity of this enzyme depends on how much selenium is present. Glutathione peroxidase works with vitamin E in protecting against free radical damage. In fact, many selenium deficiency symptoms resemble those of vitamin E deficiency, such as in muscle effects. In China, areas of selenium deficiency were discovered to be correlated with a type of heart disease characterized by weak muscle. Today this disease has disappeared because either selenium supplements can be given to avoid the disease or foods from various parts of the world have enough selenium. In earlier years, the level of selenium in foods depended on the amount of selenium in the soil. In China, for instance, some areas were low in selenium, and consequently the locally grown food people depended on was low in selenium.

Selenium also plays an important role in the production of active thyroid hormone. Selenium deficiency can mimic thyroid dysfunction to some extent. Because selenium is a cofactor for glutathione peroxidase, many studies have been conducted to evaluate the impact of selenium on cancer prevention. Survey studies and studies on animals and on cells suggest that selenium, acting as an antioxidant, can lessen the likelihood of cancer. Even stronger evidence suggests that selenium may protect against developing prostate cancer in men. This does not mean we should megadose with selenium—it is a metal and, like most metals, can be toxic when consumed in excess.

Selenium may mediate HIV and AIDS progression. Children and adult men and women who are infected with the HIV virus are reported to have a high death rate when selenium deficient. This is not surprising given that selenium helps to maintain the integrity of the immune system.

**Want to know more?**
To further investigate the role selenium may have in protecting against cancer, go to the text website at http://webcom8.grtxle .com/nutrition and click on the Chapters button. Select Chapter 10.

### Requirements and Food Sources

The DRI for selenium is 55 mcg per day for adults. The Tolerable Upper Intake Level is 400 mcg per day. Seafood is an excellent source of selenium. Fish (especially tuna), meats, organ meat, and eggs are also good selenium food sources. Wheat-based cereals and sunflower seeds are good sources, but only if these plants are grown in areas where there is adequate selenium in the soil.

### Iodine

The most important role of iodine involves the thyroid gland and the production of a hormone with powerful effects, **thyroid hormone** or **thyroxine**. Thyroxine is a hormone that controls the basal metabolic rate and heat production in our bodies. Although we need only very small quantities of iodine, the amount is critical for the activity of this powerful chemical. Thyroxine is made from an amino acid, tyrosine, and iodine in the thyroid gland found in our neck.

## Real People, Other Voices

**Student:**

### Becky Kramer

Southeast Community College

Shereen needs to focus her meal planning on increasing the amount of iron-rich foods she offers her family throughout the week. Family-friendly recipes incorporating beans and eggs are not only affordable but also quick to prepare. Enriched cereals are another simple meal idea that could entice her children to increase their iron intake. Watching for sales at the local grocery store can stretch the budget for meat, poultry, and fish. Dark green leafy vegetables can be an interesting side or main dish. The variety in menu planning abounds, even on a tight budget. Using several sources of iron-rich foods is a challenge but may keep Shereen interested in trying new recipes and meal combinations. A varied diet is pleasing not only to the eye but also to the palate. Shereen's children may become more open to trying different foods throughout their lifetime. Educating Shereen empowers her to care for herself and her family.

For beverages, I would encourage Shereen to keep orange juice in the refrigerator. She may want to continue taking an iron supplement with a glass of orange juice every day. This will aid in iron absorption. Reducing the amount of coffee and tea Shereen intakes, especially around mealtime, may also help, as these beverages limit iron absorption.

**Instructor:**

### Rebecca Pobocik

Bowling Green State University

Shereen's family meals should routinely include foods that are good sources of iron, and at least a little meat, fish, or poultry along with foods containing vitamin C such as peppers, broccoli, and fruits. Examples of less-expensive meals she could serve include casseroles, stir-fries, spaghetti, salads, tacos, sandwiches, and soups. To economize, Shereen can make legumes frequently and use frozen or canned vegetables and fruit. If she drinks her coffee or tea between rather than with meals, she will absorb more iron.

I'd show Shereen how to interpret the iron and vitamin C portion of the Nutrition Facts Panel and encourage her to teach her children this skill so they can learn about the nutrients in food and make informed choices.

She should continue to have the family's iron status checked at the clinic. If iron supplements are recommended, she should be careful to store them safely, as accidental poisoning is a hazard for children. If a multivitamin/mineral supplement is also recommended, the iron should be taken at a different time and between meals so they won't compete for absorption.

If Shereen wants to have another child, she should verify that her iron stores are normal before becoming pregnant. Regular prenatal care is imperative.

It is very important to take iron nutrition seriously, as deficiency affects not only energy levels but also children's brain development, making it harder for them to learn. For children under age 2 this is critical, as the negative effects of inadequate iron in early life are harder to correct and can be permanent.

**Registered Dietitian:**

### Nicole Kerneen-Fasules, RD, CD

Milwaukee, WI

Based on Shereen's symptoms and her children's symptoms, they may all be experiencing a slight case of anemia.

Living on a single income and providing for a family of five can make affording quality nutrition a challenge. Typical foods that are high sources of iron can be more expensive. However, by becoming involved with the WIC program, Shereen will be able to meet the iron requirements for the entire family. Using the foods that WIC provides, Shereen can create an affordable, iron-rich menu.

For example, breakfast could be as simple as a bowl of iron-enriched cereal and a glass of vitamin C-packed orange juice to increase the absorption of the nonheme iron in the cereal. As an alternative, breakfast could include a scrambled egg, whole-wheat toast, and a glass of orange juice. By combining the heme iron food source of eggs as well as the high-vitamin-C juice, she will increase her absorption rate of iron.

For lunch, her family could enjoy heme iron–packed tuna fish sandwiches, served with spinach and a bowl of strawberries (both sources of nonheme iron). Dinner could be a casserole containing rice and beans (both high in nonheme iron), chopped chicken (a great source of heme iron), and tomato (a source of vitamin C). And for dessert, they could have a wedge or two of watermelon, which is a high source of vitamin C.

With a day like this, Shereen and her family have a greater chance of absorbing the proper amount of iron.

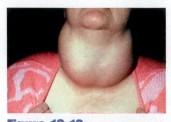

**Figure 10.12** Iodine deficiency leads to enlarged thyroid glands. Here we see the results of iodine deficiency, called *goiter*.

When iodine is lacking in our diets, the cells of the thyroid gland become enlarged in an attempt to absorb more iodine from the blood. Over time this results in an enlarged thyroid gland, called **goiter** (Figure 10.12). People with goiter tire easily and may gain weight because of decreased basal metabolism. People are more likely to develop goiter in areas where the soil has low levels of iodine. The level of iodine in food depends, like selenium, on the mineral level in the soil. Coastal areas and the sea are rich in iodine. Mountainous areas and the central parts of the United States are very low in iodine. Consequently, people who live in the mountains or away from the seacoast are more likely to have goiter.

Mothers who are iodine deficient in pregnancy have offspring who are mentally and physically retarded. This is called **cretinism**, and it is not normally reversible.

Most table salt has iodine added to it in order to combat iodine deficiency. This means that many processed foods are made with iodized salt. Given this and the fact that much of the food consumed in this country comes from a variety of geographic settings, iodine deficiency is rare in the United States. However, it is still a major problem in some parts of the world. Health relief organizations are trying to add iodine to foods to help relieve iodine deficiency. Mental retardation from iodine deficiency still remains a large worldwide problem, and micronutrient fortification costs much less than caring for these individuals. Iodine supplements given to pregnant women living in iodine-deficient areas of China have revealed that IQ levels of their children can be significantly increased. Similar results have been reported in the country of Albania, where visual problem solving, fine motor skills, and information processing were increased by iodine supplementation of children 10 to 12 years old.

If you are not consuming many processed foods, you are most likely not over-consuming sodium; the minimal difference between table salt and sea salt will not significantly impact your overall sodium intake. The bottom line: consume whichever one you like better, and decrease intake of processed foods, to limit your daily sodium intake to the recommended 1500 milligrams.

### What's Hot...
#### *Is Sea Salt Healthier for You?*
Sea salt is sold in most grocery and specialty stores around the world and is often touted as the healthiest form of salt. Sea salt comes from the evaporation of seawater. The process usually involves little or no processing which helps to retain many trace

Sea salt comes from the evaporation of sea water.

minerals that are removed in the processing that table salt undergoes. Table salt is mined from underground salt deposits and then processed. Then Iodine is usually added. This was first started in Michigan in 1924 and in that same year, Morton Salt Company started to distribute iodized salt on a national level. Despite minimal differences between the two, sea salt is often marketed as the healthier lower sodium choice. However, when measured by weight, sea salt and table salt usually contain about the same amount of sodium by chloride. If you are not consuming many processed foods you are most likely not over consuming sodium, the minimal difference between these products will not significantly impact your overall sodium intake. The bottom line: consume whichever one you like better and decrease intake of processed foods to limit your daily sodium intake to the recommended 1,500 milligrams. ■

### Requirements and Food Sources

The DRI for iodine is 150 mcg per day. The Tolerable Upper Intake Level is 1,000 mcg per day. Iodine can be toxic in large amounts. Excess intake of iodine can lead to enlargement of the thyroid gland just as iodine deficiency does. Food sources are seafood and iodized salt. Plants grown in areas with sufficient iodine in the soil are also good sources of iodine.

## Fluoride

Fluoride is a mineral that is associated with healthy teeth. Recall that bone and teeth are composed of crystals. These crystals are composed primarily of calcium and phosphorus. However, fluoride can be incorporated into the crystal at certain places, which makes the crystal harder and more stable. Thus the overall effect of fluoride incorporation into teeth is a hardening of the enamel, which makes the teeth more resistant to tooth decay. Tooth decay is caused when bacteria and a sticky sugar substance adhere to teeth and acid is produced. Normally the acid causes the enamel to erode, but fluoride makes tooth enamel more resistant to acid. People living in areas with greater fluoride levels in the water have a much lower incidence of tooth decay.

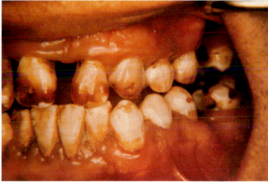

Intake of excess fluoride can lead to a condition called *fluorosis*, the effects of which are shown here.

Too much fluoride can result in **fluorosis**, which causes discoloration and mottling (abnormal ridges) of the teeth. It occurs only when teeth are being developed and cannot be reversed. Fluoridated water is the best diet source of fluoride. However, most toothpastes and mouthwashes also contain small amounts. More foods may contain fluoride if they have been processed or canned with fluoridated water. The DRI for fluoride is 4 mg per day for men and 3 mg per day for women. The Tolerable Upper Intake Level for those older than age 8 is 10 mg per day.

In the United States, water is routinely fluoridated. The evidence suggests that this is both effective and inexpensive in preventing tooth decay. However, the practice of water fluoridation was and still remains controversial. Communities allowed to vote on this issue often vote against it. When fluoridation has occurred, it has been through elected officials via legislative action. Individual rights versus the public good are often the central questions in such issues.

 **Want to know more?**
You can discover more about the role of fluoride in preventing tooth decay by going to the text website at http://webcom8 .grtxle.com/nutrition and clicking on the Chapters button. Select Chapter 10.

## Chromium

The major function of chromium is facilitating glucose uptake by improving the function of the hormone insulin, which transports glucose across cell membranes. Studies have reported that insulin function is impaired when chromium is lacking, and thus it is thought to be helpful to some people with diabetes. Elevated blood cholesterol and triglycerides have also been reported in hospitalized patients with TPN without any chromium added to the solution.

The DRI for chromium is 35 mcg per day for men and 25 mcg per day for women. No Tolerable Upper Intake Level has been established for chromium because toxicity has not been reported. Foods that are good sources of chromium include brewer's yeast, liver, nuts, whole grains, and cheese.

### ■ Myths and Legends

*Can chromium picolinate supplements increase lean tissue in your body?*

Chromium picolinate has been advocated as a supplement to increase lean body mass while decreasing fat mass. In particular, the use of this supplement is advocated to add to the benefit of strength training. Does it really work? Human studies have been performed to answer this question. One small study on older men (ages 56 to 69) had them take chromium picolinate while going through resistance training. Over a twelve-week period, while undergoing a twice-per-week intensive resistance training program, one group of nine men took the supplement and another group of nine men were given a placebo. The researchers concluded that chromium picolinate did not improve muscle size, strength, power, or lean tissue. Another study with football players did show that those taking a chromium picolinate supplement developed more lean body mass and experienced a decrease in body fat. However, a similar study on another group of football players produced different results. Players did not see a change in body composition as a result of supplementation. Overall, there are more studies showing no effect on body composition than those with positive results.

Studies on animals in the livestock industry have produced different results. In particular, many changes in body composition among pigs supplemented with chromium picolinate have been reported. Pigs given this supplement have shown enhanced lean tissue and decreased fat. A review of many other similar studies supports these results. Apparently, the results reported for livestock are not translatable to humans. One major difference, though, is that in the livestock industry, these supplements are given to rapidly growing animals in which the time from infancy to adulthood is a matter of months. The human studies have been conducted mainly on adolescents and adults, but not over the length of a human growth period. ■

### Before you go on . . .

1. Which micromineral is most likely to be lacking in our diets?
2. What are some good food sources of copper?
3. How do zinc and copper exert their physiological effects?
4. What minerals are likely to be involved with protection against free radicals as antioxidants?
5. Which micromineral is important for the utilization of iron?

## Real People, Real Strategies

Shereen decided to visit the Women, Infants, and Children's (WIC) clinic and discovered that under government guidelines she is eligible for the program. She met with a Registered Dietitian to learn more about the program, and the RD suggested further testing. They tested her blood again for anemia and found that her hematocrit was 25, which is below the norm of 40 to 48. Also, the test revealed that her hemoglobin level was 8 g per 100 mL of blood—again below the norm. It was confirmed that she has anemia, which could explain her tiredness and lack of energy. Shereen requested that her two youngest children also be tested; they also showed signs of anemia, with hematocrit levels around 32. Shereen was concerned about these results and asked the dietitian how something like this could happen. The dietitian informed her that although this is a serious issue, it is not all that uncommon.

After the dietitian learned of Shereen's history and conducted a diet evaluation with her, the reasons for the anemia become more apparent. Even though Shereen did visit a physician during her pregnancies, she took her prenatal supplement sporadically. The dietitian explained to Shereen that iron requirements are high during pregnancy and that she must also consume enough dietary iron to enable her babies to have enough iron stores for their first six months of life. After Shereen had her first child, her iron stores were most likely low, and she failed to build up sufficient levels for the next two pregnancies. A study of her diet revealed that she eats meat infrequently because of its expense. The dietitian told Shereen that she is eligible to receive certain foods that have been approved by WIC as being nutritious, and she gave her vouchers to obtain cereals with added iron and other similar foods. Given Shereen's anemia, the dietitian referred her to the physician at the local public health clinic. The doctor prescribed three months of therapeutic doses of iron for Shereen. For the children, the physician recommended eating high-iron foods and taking daily iron supplements that contain the necessary DRI. A year later, after improving the family diet and taking the recommended supplements, Shereen and her children are much more energetic and eager to play and exercise during their frequent visits to the park.

## Chapter Summary

- Our knowledge of minerals, especially microminerals, continues to evolve, with most of the information obtained in the latter part of the twentieth century. New analytical methods for detecting small quantities of minerals were a primary force behind these new findings.
- Minerals can act as structural parts of the body or as cofactors for enzymes. Some minerals exert their influence at the gene level. The amount of many minerals absorbed depends on storage level. More minerals are absorbed when stores are decreased.
- Calcium is the most abundant mineral in the body. It is well known for its role in bone development. It also plays important roles in the physiology of cells, muscle contraction, and nerve impulse transmission.

- A lack of calcium over a period of time, particularly during adolescence, can lead to osteoporosis later in life. New research suggests that calcium, especially from dairy products, may lower body weight in obese individuals.

- Phosphorus is present in the body and in foods as phosphate. In this form, phosphorus stabilizes DNA, RNA, and ATP. It is a component of cell membranes and lipoproteins. It plays a central role in blood pH balance.

- Most Americans do not attain the DRI for magnesium. However, severe magnesium deficiency is observed only in cases of extended vomiting, diarrhea, or excessive sweating. Magnesium is a cofactor for about 300 different enzymes. It plays a role in muscle contraction that leads to relaxation of the muscle, and it is part of a pump that moves sodium out of a cell and potassium into the cell.

- Iron-deficiency anemia is the number two public health nutrition problem in the United States and the number one problem worldwide. Women of childbearing years, infants, and children are especially vulnerable to iron-deficiency anemia.

- Iron toxicity is more common than previously thought. Consuming high quantities of iron can cause liver and red blood cell damage called hemochromatosis. However, a significant cause is genetic and involves the inability to regulate the amount of iron absorbed by the small intestine.

- Zinc was one of the first nutrients known to function at the genetic level. Zinc exerts its function as a cofactor for about 200 enzymes. Zinc deficiency has been documented in young boys showing symptoms of poor growth, poor sexual development, lack of taste and appetite, impaired wound healing, and compromised immunity.

- Copper is essential as a cofactor for fewer than 20 enzymes. It is involved in enzymes that improve the utilization of iron, increase the strength of connective tissue, and increase synthesis of neurotransmitters. Copper is part of an enzyme that protects against free radical damage, and is involved with ATP production.

- Selenium is a critical part of the body's antioxidant system. Deficiencies of selenium have been reported to lead to weakening of heart muscle. Selenium is thought to decrease the risk of certain cancers, such as prostate cancer.

- Iodine's main function is to produce thyroid hormone, which regulates basal metabolism. Iodine deficiency results in goiter or enlarged thyroid. Infants born to mothers with low iodine develop cretinism, in which irreversible mental and physical retardations occur.

- The drop in tooth decay in this country has largely been a result of water fluoridation. However, too much fluoride during tooth development can harm teeth and leave them discolored.

- Chromium is an essential mineral that is believed to help insulin transport glucose across cell membranes and consequently is thought to be helpful to some people with diabetes. Reported signs of deficiency are elevated blood cholesterol and triglyceride levels.

# Key Terms

**cretinism** (CREE-tin-izm) The mental and physical retardation of children whose mothers were iodine deficient during pregnancy. (p. 332)

**ferritin** (FAIR-uh-tin) A protein that binds iron for storage and is a good indicator of iron status. (p. 323)

**fluorosis** (flor-OH-sis) Fluoride toxicity that causes discoloration and mottling of the teeth. (p. 333)

**functional foods** Foods and beverages that have been developed or altered in some way in order to optimize health. (p. 314)

**goiter** An enlarged thyroid gland due to an iodine deficiency. (p. 332)

**hematocrit** The percentage of blood that is composed of red blood cells. (p. 323)

**heme iron** (HEEM EYE-rn) An organic form of iron that is still part of the complex ring structure that makes up hemoglobin. (p. 324)

**hydroxyapatite** (hi-DROX-ee-ap-uh-tite) The large and complex crystal in bone that contains calcium and gives bone its strength. (p. 312)

**meat, fish, and poultry factor (MFP)** A factor in these foods that enhances the absorption of elemental iron. (p. 324)

**nonheme iron** The elemental form of iron that is not a part of hemoglobin. (p. 324)

**oxalate** (ox-uh-late) A compound with negative charges that binds calcium and other minerals that have positive charges. (p. 318)

**parathyroid hormone** A hormone produced by the parathyroid glands located next to the thyroid glands in the neck; it is released if blood calcium levels decrease. (p. 317)

**phytate** (FYE-tate) A substance that looks like a sugar molecule and is found inside the husk of whole grains and cereals; it binds certain minerals—calcium and zinc in particular—making them unavailable to cells. (p. 318)

**pre-eclampsia** (pre-ee-CLAMP-see-uh) A serious blood disorder in pregnancy characterized by headache, fatigue, protein in the urine, and high blood pressure. (p. 316)

**thyroid hormone or thyroxine** A hormone that controls the basal metabolic rate and heat production in our bodies. (p. 330)

**transferrin** A blood protein that carries iron to organs. (p. 323)

## Table 10.4    Summary Table for Minerals

| Mineral | What It Does and Why It Is Important | Deficiency: What Happens If You Get Too Little |
|---|---|---|
| Calcium | Component of mineral crystals in bone and teeth; involved in muscle contraction, initiation of heartbeat, blood clotting, and release and function of several hormones and neurotransmitters | Rickets in children; bone softening and osteoporosis in adults |
| Phosphorus | As phosphate, a component of mineral crystals in bone and teeth; part of high-energy molecules (ATP and CP) in cells; part of cell membrane molecules | Weakness, bone pain, anorexia (rare) |
| Magnesium | Involved in energy metabolism; component of enzymes involved in numerous bodily operations | Nausea, irritability, muscle weakness, twitching, cramps, cardiac arrhythmia |
| Iron | Component of heme structures found in hemoglobin, myoglobin, and cytochromes, which transport oxygen in the blood or store and handle oxygen in cells; found in molecules that are involved in collagen production, antioxidation, and energy metabolism | Skin pallor, weakness; fatigue, headaches, shortness of breath (all signs of iron-deficiency anemia), occurs during lead poisoning |
| Zinc | Component of numerous enzymes | Slow healing of wounds, loss of taste, retarded growth and delayed sexual development in children |

| **Toxicity: What Happens If You Get Too Much** | **Food Sources[1]** | | |
|---|---|---|---|
| Constipation, kidney stones, calcium deposits in body tissues; hinders absorption of iron and other minerals | **Food Item** | **Serving Size** | **Amount** |
| | Yogurt, plain | 1 c. | 488 mg |
| | Milk, 2% | 1 c. | 271 mg |
| | Cheddar cheese | 1 oz. | 192 mg |
| | Sardines, canned | 2 | 108 mg |
| | Turnip greens, boiled | 1/2 c. | 99 mg |
| | Spinach, raw | 1 c. | 30 mg |
| | Broccoli, raw | 1/2 c. | 21 mg |
| Hinders absorption of calcium (rare) | **Food Item** | **Serving Size** | **Amount** |
| | Lentils, cooked | 1/2 c. | 356 mg |
| | Milk, skim | 1 c. | 247 mg |
| | Chicken breast | 3 oz. | 155 mg |
| | Almonds | 1 oz. | 139 mg |
| | Mozzarella cheese | 1 oz. | 131 mg |
| | Egg, boiled | 1 large | 104 mg |
| Nausea, vomiting, low blood pressure, nervous system disorders (*Warning: Overdose can be fatal to people with kidney disease.*) | **Food Item** | **Serving Size** | **Amount** |
| | Cashews | 1/4 c. | 89 mg |
| | Whole-wheat bread | 1 slice | 37 mg |
| | Tofu | 3 oz. | 33 mg |
| | Spinach, raw | 1 c. | 24 mg |
| | Rib steak | 3 oz. | 22 mg |
| | Collard greens, boiled | 1/2 c. | 19 mg |
| | Turnip greens, boiled | 1/2 c. | 16 mg |
| | Cereal (Special K) | 1 c. | 16 mg |
| Toxic buildup in liver and (in rare instances) heart | **Food Item** | **Serving Size** | **Amount** |
| | Cereal (Special K) | 1 c. | 8.70 mg |
| | Beef liver | 3 oz. | 5.24 mg* |
| | Chuck roast | 3 oz. | 3.12 mg |
| | Rib steak | 3 oz. | 2.18 mg |
| | Great northern beans | 1/2 c. | 1.89 mg |
| | Red kidney beans, boiled | 1/2 c. | 1.61 mg |
| | Whole-wheat bread | 1 slice | 1.43 mg |
| | Raisins | 1/4 c. | 1.07 mg |
| | Chicken, white meat, roasted | 3 oz. | 0.92 mg |
| Nausea, vomiting, diarrhea, abdominal pain, gastric bleeding | **Food Item** | **Serving Size** | **Amount** |
| | Total Whole Bran cereal | 1 c. | 19.95 mg |
| | Oysters, raw | 3 oz. | 14.14 mg |
| | Rib steak | 3 oz. | 5.94 mg |
| | Beef liver | 3 oz. | 4.45 mg |
| | Turkey, dark meat | 3 oz. | 3.79 mg |
| | Blue crab, canned | 2 oz. | 2.28 mg |
| | Shrimp, cooked | 3 oz. | 1.33 mg |
| | Peanuts, roasted | 1/4 c. | 1.20 mg |
| | Cereal (Special K) | 1 c | 0.90 mg |
| | Great northern beans | 1/2 c. | 0.78 mg |
| | Whole-wheat bread | 1 slice | 0.64 mg |

*(Continued)*

| Table 10.4 | Summary Table for Minerals (*Continued*) | |
|---|---|---|
| **Mineral** | **What It Does and Why It Is Important** | **Deficiency: What Happens If You Get Too Little** |
| Copper | Component of several enzymes involved in energy metabolism, antioxidant activity, collagen production, and hormone and neurotransmitter production | Rare in adults; in infants, rare type of anemia marked by abnormal development of bones, nerve tissue, and lungs |
| Selenium | Component of antioxidant enzyme; involved in thyroid hormone function | Weakened heart |
| Iodine | Component of thyroid hormone | Goiter (enlargement of thyroid gland) |
| Fluoride | Involved in strengthening teeth and bones | Dental caries |
| Chromium | Involved in glucose metabolism | Elevated blood glucose, cholesterol, and triglycerides |

| **Toxicity: What Happens If You Get Too Much** | **Food Sources[1]** | | |
|---|---|---|---|
| Liver disease, vomiting, diarrhea | **Food Item** | **Serving Size** | **Amount** |
| | Beef liver | 3 oz. | 12.4 mg |
| | Oyster | 1 medium | 0.67 mg |
| | Clams, cooked | 3 oz. | 0.59 mg |
| | Sunflower seeds | 1/4 c. | 0.57 mg |
| | Great northern beans, boiled | 1 c. | 0.43 mg |
| | Pecans | 1 oz. | 0.34 mg |
| | Shrimp, canned | 3 oz. | 0.23 mg |
| | Mushrooms, raw | 1 c. | 0.22 mg |
| | Peanuts, roasted | 1 oz. | 0.19 mg |
| | Cereal (Special K) | 1 c. | 0.06 mg |
| Fingernail changes, hair loss | **Food Item** | **Serving Size** | **Amount** |
| | Tuna, canned, packed in water | 2 oz. | 46 µg |
| | Rice, brown (medium grain) | 1/2 c. | 38 µg |
| | Beef liver | 3 oz. | 28 µg |
| | Sunflower seeds | 1/4 c. | 21 µg |
| | Whole-wheat bread | 1 slice | 18 µg |
| | Crab, boiled | 3 oz. | 17 µg |
| | Cereal (Special K) | 1 c. | 7 µg |
| | Rice, white (long grain) | 1/2 c. | 6 µg |
| Results from overdose of medications or supplements; burning in mouth, throat and stomach and/or abdominal pain, nausea, vomiting, diarrhea, weak pulse, coma | **Food Item** | **Serving Size** | **Amount** |
| | Codfish | 3 oz. | 99 µg |
| | Iodized salt | 1 g | 77 µg |
| | Shrimp | 3 oz. | 35 µg |
| | Potato, baked, with skin | 1 | 62 µg |
| | Egg, hard-boiled | 1 large | 29 µg |
| | Tuna, canned, packed in water | 3 oz. | 17 µg |
| Mottling of teeth | **Food Item** | **Serving Size** | **Amount** |
| | Shrimp, canned | 3 oz. | 169 µg |
| | Fluoridated water | 1 c. | 159 µg[1] |
| | Carrots, cooked | 1/2 c. | 53 µg |
| | Spinach, cooked | 1/2 c. | 43 µg |
| | Potatoes, boiled | 3 oz. | 42 µg |
| | Cheese | 1 oz. | 9.8 µg |
| | Milk, 2% fat | 1 c. | 6.8 µg |
| | Tomatoes, canned | 1/2 c. | 6.7 µg |
| | Broccoli, boiled | 1/2 c. | 4.5 µg |
| | Egg, hard-boiled | 1 large | 2.5 µg |
| | Cabbage, boiled | 1/2 c. | 1.1 µg |
| | Toothpaste | | 500–1500 µg/g |
| Unknown | **Food Item** | **Serving Size** | **Amount** |
| | Broccoli | 1/2 c. | 11 µg |
| | Grape juice | 1 c. | 7.5 µg |
| | Potatoes, mashed | 1 c. | 2.7 µg |
| | Rib steak | 3 oz. | 2.0 µg |
| | Green beans | 1/2 c. | 1.1 µg |
| | Banana | 1 medium | 1.0 µg |

[1]*Source:* USDA National Nutrient Database for Standard Reference, Release 19.

# Chapter Quiz

1. All of the following are considered micro-minerals except
   a. magnesium.
   b. iron.
   c. zinc.
   d. copper.

2. All of the following minerals can be found in the bone crystal hydroxyapatite except
   a. calcium.
   b. phosphorus.
   c. fluoride.
   d. copper.

3. Which of the following minerals may lower blood pressure in people with high blood pressure?
   a. calcium
   b. copper
   c. selenium
   d. iron

4. Decreased ability to taste and a decrease in sexual development in young boys may be due to a lack of dietary
   a. copper.
   b. iodine.
   c. zinc.
   d. chromium.

5. A major role for the micromineral chromium is
   a. transport of iron to other tissues.
   b. helping the hormone insulin lower blood glucose levels.
   c. regulating basal metabolism.
   d. strengthening bone and tooth enamel.

6. A storage protein for iron that is a good indicator of iron stores is
   a. parathyroid hormone.
   b. transferrin.
   c. ferritin.
   d. heme.

7. A lack of which mineral may result in free radical damage?
   a. phosphorus
   b. magnesium
   c. selenium
   d. iron

8. A genetic disease that can lead to iron toxicity is
   a. hemochromatosis.
   b. cretinism.
   c. fluorosis.
   d. osteoporosis.

9. A deficiency of which of the following minerals during pregnancy can lead to mental and physical retardation in the offspring?
   a. copper
   b. zinc
   c. iodine
   d. selenium

10. Which of the following will enhance the absorption of elemental iron?
    a. a high-fiber diet
    b. unleavened bread
    c. orange juice
    d. phytate

# CHAPTER 11

# Supplements

## A Little Bit of Science Goes a Long Way

## < Here's Where You've Been

*The following topics were introduced in preceding chapters and are related to concepts we'll discuss in Chapter 11. Be certain that you're familiar with them before proceeding.*

- The most successful and safest way to lose weight and keep it off is to create a deficit of 500 calories per day, which leads to a gradual weight loss of 1–2 lb. per week. (Chapter 7)
- Vitamins can be toxic if consumed in large enough amounts. Fat-soluble vitamins and minerals can be more toxic when taken in large amounts, because they can be stored. Water-soluble vitamins are not as toxic because they are better able to be excreted. (Chapter 9)
- Vitamins can play a role as antioxidants. Vitamins C and E and beta-carotene are all antioxidants that protect us from harmful free radicals. (Chapter 9)
- The amount of most minerals the human body absorbs depends on the storage level. More minerals are absorbed when stores are decreased. (Chapter 10)

## Here's Where You're Going >

*The following topics and concepts are the ones we'll emphasize in Chapter 11.*

- Supplements are regulated under the Dietary Supplement Health and Education Act of 1994 (DSHEA), which gives the Food and Drug Administration (FDA) no control over them before release in the marketplace.
- Because supplements are not regulated by the FDA before they are sold, consumers need to be knowledgeable about what they are taking.
- We will review the claims and science behind several of the many different types of supplements.
- Herbs and botanicals are becoming more popular, and many people believe they are safe because they are "natural." This is not always true; consumers need to be informed.

## Real People, Real Choices

Marissa Hruby is an 18-year-old freshman at the University of Illinois. She has gained a few pounds since beginning college, and she wants to lose the weight for spring break. She has just returned for the spring semester and realizes she has only about two months before the break. This short time frame causes her to feel a sense of desperation, and she is therefore willing to try anything in order to look good in her bathing suit. She sees an advertisement on TV for a weight-loss pill, which says it is guaranteed to help you lose 10 lb. in two weeks or your money back. The refund part of the advertisement appeals to Marissa for two reasons: she is on a restricted budget, and she believes that the manufacturer is unlikely to make a full-refund guarantee if the product doesn't work. She figures she can use the small amount of money left over from her financial aid to get the pills. The advertisement claims that clinical studies have proven that the pills are effective. She assumes this means they are safe.

Marissa tells her roommate Ashley about the supplement, and Ashley expresses concern. She is skeptical about the claims and tells Marissa to make sure she is not wasting her money—or worse—harming herself. How do you think Marissa should go about determining whether these pills really work and whether they are safe? What advice would you give her?

Dietary supplements are a multi-billion dollar industry.

Want to gain muscle? Improve athletic performance? Improve sexual performance? Lose weight? Grow stronger fingernails and hair? Obtain more energy? Increase concentration? Relieve depression? If you believe the advertising, whatever you desire to change about your health or appearance, you can seemingly achieve it by taking a supplement. We have all seen promotions for supplements on television, on the Internet, and in newspapers and magazines. With so many claims and promises, is it any wonder that millions of us fall prey to their marketing hype? In fact, marketing data shows a dramatic increase in the sales of supplements in the United States since 1997. Estimates indicate this will become a 20 billion dollar industry (Figure 11.1). As another indication of how successful these companies are, a recent study of 1,280 teenagers ages 14–19 reported that 46 percent admitted to having taken a dietary supplement.

Not all supplements provide false claims; several have been shown to provide health benefits when taken correctly. The difficult part is telling the beneficial ones from those that are harmful and those that simply fail to do what they claim. In this chapter we will review some tips on deciding whether to take a supplement, and we will review research on some of the more common ones on the market. As this industry continues to grow, the scientific research into the validity of its claims grows as well. Therefore, you need to keep up-to-date on the latest information.

**Want to know more?** To keep up to date with the latest scientific information regarding supplements, go to the text website at http://webcom8.grtxle.com/nutrition and click on the Chapters button. Select Chapter 11.

# Defining a Dietary Supplement

The economic implosion of 2009 didn't offer many silver linings for businesses, but one positive effect for the U.S. nutrition industry was the spike in consumer interest in dietary supplements. Some predicted that consumers' falling disposable income would hamper dietary supplement sales, but in fact the opposite

**Figure 11.1** Growth in dietary supplement sales since passage of DSHEA Act of 1994.

*Source:* Nutrition Business Journal *estimates ($mill., consumer sale)*

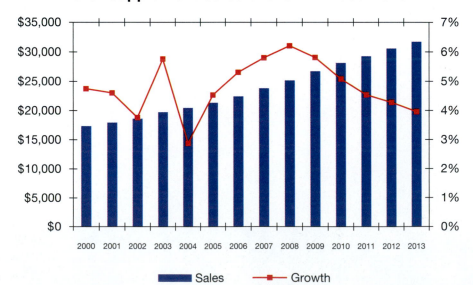

**U.S. Supplement Sales & Growth: 2000-2013**

actually occurred: As more people lost their jobs and ability to pay for healthcare, many turned to supplements to remain healthy and ward off expensive doctor visits and pharmaceutical drugs. From an overall growth perspective, U.S. consumer sales of dietary supplements lagged behind those of other nutrition industry categories. Yet, of all the categories, supplements was the only one to actually grow more in 2008 than in 2007—which is saying a lot for a relatively mature business in a tough economy. Nutrition Business Journal estimates showed that total U.S. consumer sales of dietary supplements expanded 6.2% to $25.2 billion in 2009.

Dietary supplements are not new. In fact, the personal effects of the mummified prehistoric "Ice Man" found in the Italian Alps in 1991 included medicinal herbs. By the Middle Ages, thousands of botanical products had been inventoried for their medicinal effects. Many of these form the basis of modern drugs. Before the Nutrition Labeling and Education Act of 1990, supplements consisted only of vitamins, minerals, and other essential nutrients. In 1990 "herbs or similar nutritional substances" were added to the official definition of a "dietary supplement." The expanded meaning then included such substances as ginseng, garlic, fish oils, psyllium, enzymes, glandulars, and mixtures of these. At that time, dietary supplements were still regulated by the Food and Drug Administration (FDA) and subject to reviews similar to those for medicines. In the early 1990s, Congress debated various bills to revise the laws governing dietary supplements. The supplement industry took action and lobbied to ensure that the FDA did not acquire any more regulatory control. The supplement industry's efforts resulted in the **Dietary Supplement Health and Education Act of 1994 (DSHEA)**. In addition to drastically changing the role the FDA plays in supplement regulation, the DSHEA further expanded the formal definition of *dietary supplement*. According to the DSHEA, a supplement is:

- A product (other than tobacco) intended to supplement the diet that contains one or more of the following dietary ingredients: a vitamin; a mineral; an herb or other botanical; an amino acid; a dietary substance used to supplement the diet by increasing the total dietary intake; or a concentrate, metabolite, constituent, extract, or combination of these ingredients.
- Intended for ingestion in pill, capsule, tablet, or liquid form.
- Not represented for use as a conventional food or as the sole item of a meal or diet.
- Labeled as a dietary supplement.

**Want to know more?**
You can explore the history of dietary supplements by visiting the text website at http://webcom8.grtxle.com/nutrition and clicking on the Chapters button. Select Chapter 11.

## Supplement Regulation

Since the passing of the 1994 bill, the FDA regulates dietary supplements under a different set of regulations from those covering "conventional" foods and drugs (prescription and over-the-counter).

Under the DSHEA, the supplement manufacturer must ensure that a dietary supplement is safe before it is marketed. According to the FDA,

"Unlike drug products that must be proven safe and effective for their intended use before marketing, there are no provisions in the law for the FDA to 'approve' dietary supplements for safety or effectiveness before they reach the consumer. Also, unlike drug products, manufacturers and distributors of dietary supplements are not currently required by law to record, investigate or forward to the FDA any reports they receive of injuries or illnesses that may be related to the use of their products. Under DSHEA,

*So who is responsible for making sure the supplements that we buy are actually safe?*

**Want to know more?**
To review the FDA's latest supplement safety alerts, go to the text website at http://webcom8 .grtxle.com/nutrition and click on the Chapters button. Select Chapter 11.

**Want to know more?**
To learn more about a supplement before taking it and to see whether any warnings have been issued against the supplement, go to the text website at http://webcom8 .grtxle.com/nutrition and click on the Chapters button. Select Chapter 11.

once the product is marketed, the FDA has the responsibility for showing that a dietary supplement is '*unsafe*,' before it can take action to restrict the product's use or removal from the marketplace."

## ■ Make It a Practice

*Buyer beware*
### Examples of Supplements That Have Carried FDA Cautions About Safety

- Androstenedione
- Aristolochic acid
- Certain products marketed for sexual enhancement that claimed to be "natural" versions of the drug Viagra, and were found to contain an unlabeled drug (sildenafil or tadalafil)
- Comfrey
- Ephedra

- GHB (gamma hydroxy-butyric acid), GBL (gamma butyrolactone), and BD (1, 4-butanediol)
- Kava
- L-tryptophan
- PC SPES and SPES
- St. John's wort
- Some "dieter's teas"
- Red yeast rice ■

The important thing to remember is that the FDA does not get involved until *after* the product has been on the market. In other words, the FDA does *postmarketing surveillance* of supplements, but does not ensure their safety or effectiveness. The agency may restrict a substance only if it poses a "significant and unreasonable risk" after it is being sold and used. The FDA handles consumer complaints of unsafe products, improper or illegal labeling claims and package inserts.

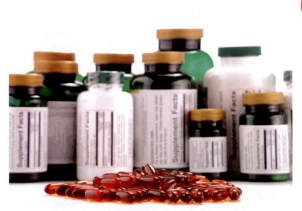

The FDA does not get involved in determining the safety of dietary supplements until after they are marketed. Nor does the FDA restrict any substance unless it poses a "significant and unreasonable risk".

## ■ Myths and Legends

*Ephedra—a matter of life and death for some!*

One example of the FDA's postmarketing surveillance is the supplement **ephedra**. Also called *ma huang*, ephedra is an herbal stimulant used for respiratory illnesses such as asthma because it helps open the airways. It has also been marketed for weight loss and performance enhancement. Side effects include high blood pressure, heart irregularities, and nausea. Numerous studies have indicated the negative side effects of ephedra on the heart; it was also connected to several deaths, including that of Baltimore Orioles pitcher Steve Bechler in 2003. It was banned in the United States (by the FDA) shortly thereafter, but marketers subsequently challenged the ban in court. Ultimately, a federal appeals court upheld the FDA's ban, and the FDA issued the following statement on August 17, 2006: "The FDA informed consumers and healthcare professionals that all dietary supplements containing ephedrine alkaloids are illegal to market in the United States. Dietary supplements containing ephedrine alkaloids, regardless of the dosage, are considered adulterated and pose an unreasonable risk of illness or injury to users, especially those suffering from heart disease and high blood pressure." ■

The **Federal Trade Commission** is responsible for monitoring the accuracy of the advertising and labeling of supplements. Although manufacturers are not required to register their products with the FDA or the FTC or get FDA approval before producing or selling supplements, they do have to make sure that product label information is truthful and not misleading. This would seem to be an adequate way to prevent false claims. Unfortunately, it does not protect the consumer as much as many think. The federal government does not oversee the *quality* of supplements from manufacturer to manufacturer, or even between different batches of a product from the same manufacturer.

**Want to know more?**
If you would like to know more about the FDA's decision to ban ephedra, go to the text website at http://webcom8.grtxle .com/nutrition and click on the Chapters button. Select Chapter 11.

### ■ To Supplement or Not

*What's in the bottle does not always match what's on the label*

When considering whether to take a supplement, keep in mind that what's on the label does not always match what is in the bottle. Here are a few tips from the National Center for Complementary and Alternative Medicine (NCCAM):

- Supplements may not contain the correct ingredient (plant species). For example, one study that analyzed fifty-nine preparations of echinacea found that about half did not contain the species listed on the label.
- Supplements may contain higher or lower amounts of the active ingredient. For example, a study of ginseng products funded by the NCCAM found that most contained less than half the amount of ginseng listed on their labels.
- Supplements can damage your health—in some cases severely.
- Supplements may be contaminated—with other unlabeled herbs, pesticides, heavy metals, or prescription drugs.
- Supplements can interact dangerously with prescription drugs, for example:
  - St. John's wort can increase the effects of prescription drugs used to treat depression. It can also interfere with drugs used to treat HIV infection, to treat cancer, or for birth control.
  - Ginseng can increase the stimulant effects of caffeine (as in coffee, tea, and cola). It can also lower blood sugar levels, creating the possibility of problems when used with diabetes drugs.
  - Ginkgo, taken with anticlotting drugs, can increase the risk of bleeding. ■

**APPLICATION TIP**

Don't be fooled by "fake science"! Manufacturers often say, "Studies show that . . . ," but they never provide a reference. Or it was only one study underwritten by the company, conducted by company employees in their facility. Therefore, before purchasing and taking these products, always go to an outside source and search independent scientific journals for information about such claims.

## Partially True Claims

Although it is important to be aware that the contents of the bottle may not match the label, it is also important to understand that manufacturers' health-related claims for many supplements are only partially true. Frequently, the claims are "sort of true." A perfect example is the claim made for **carnitine**. The claim is that carnitine will increase fat burning. In truth, carnitine does carry long-chain fatty acids from one part of the cell to another part where it can be used in metabolism. However, carnitine is needed in very small amounts, which are provided easily in food and made in the body. There is no evidence that supplemental use of carnitine enhances fat metabolism in any way. However, in theory the claim on the bottle is not false.

Claims made about supplements are often "sort of true"—as in the case of carnitine. It is always important to research and evaluate the scientific evidence regarding the claim's validity.

**Claims for Carnitine:**
Energizing nutrient
Promotes healthier weight
Enhanced recovery
Maintains heart health

**SCIENCE**

DHEA is a supplement that has gained popularity in our youth-obsessed society.

Another example of a claim that is based on the function of the components but lacks evidence that the supplement is effective is **dehydroepiandrosterone (DHEA)**, discussed in the Nutrition and Lifestages feature.

### ■ Nutrition and Lifestages

*The fountain of youth in a bottle?*

We are a nation obsessed with youth and its maintenance, almost without regard to the cost of doing so. Everywhere you look there are advertisements for wrinkle creams and other products to make you look younger. Plastic surgery is more popular than ever. The supplements market has definitely made note of and cashed in on our youth-obsessed society. An ever-increasing number of products promise to help you retain or recapture your youthful appearance. One of the best known of these is DHEA. DHEA is a steroid hormone that is synthesized and secreted by the adrenal glands. DHEA is ultimately converted into estrogen (the female sex hormone) and androgen (the male sex hormone). It has been marketed as a virtual fountain of youth, with miraculous claims that it can slow aging, melt away fat, enhance memory, prevent osteoporosis, and increase libido. The level of circulating DHEA usually peaks during the twenties and thirties, and then declines steadily therafter.

Interest in DHEA as a supplement has been reviewed in the last decade or so as several investigators have reported that increased DHEA levels are associated with a decreased incidence of heart disease, various cancers, and several other age-related diseases. However, the scientific evidence regarding its effectiveness is unclear at this time. Furthermore, DHEA can produce serious side effects. Therefore, you should not take DHEA until your physician does a blood test to determine whether you have low levels. This hormone can have potentially dangerous and undesirable side effects, including male sex characteristics (such as facial hair in women) and cancer. More clinical investigations are warranted before general dose recommendations can be made. ■

**Before you go on . . .**

1. To what extent are supplements regulated and by whom?

2. What is the formal definition of a dietary supplement, and what federal legislation established it?

3. List the potential hazards of relying on the accuracy of supplement labels.

4. Since the DSHEA was passed, what role does the FDA play in ensuring that supplements are safe?

# Who Takes Supplements and Why

## Who's Buying Them?

According to the National Health and Nutrition Examination Survey (NHANES), 53.7 percent of adults surveyed (47.4 percent of men, 59.6 percent of women) had taken a dietary supplement in the previous month. The most commonly consumed supplements were standard or senior formula multivitamin/multiminerals and vitamins E and C.

Use of supplements may be even more prevalent in certain populations. It is highest in women, people age 60 or older, whites, those who have more than a high school education, and those who exercise. In addition, it appears that the higher an individual's BMI, the less likely he or she is to use supplements. This is interesting because many supplements are marketed for weight loss.

Athletes are often looking for an extra edge in competition and training and are therefore a vulnerable target of supplements marketers. In fact, in one study of 513 athletes, 88.4 percent of those surveyed reported using at least one type of supplement. Sports drinks, multivitamin/multimineral supplements, and energy bars were the most common dietary supplements reported.

Supplement use is so prevalent among athletes that the National College Athletic Association (NCAA), the International Olympic Committee, and governing bodies for many sports have had to establish rules and guidelines about their use. In addition to identifying banned drugs, they have issued regulations regarding what supplements may be provided to athletes by coaches and trainers.

 **Want to know more?** You can review the complete list of the NCAA's permitted and banned substances by visiting the text website at http://webcom8.grtxle.com/nutrition and clicking on the Chapters button. Select Chapter 11.

**Banned**

- Amino acids
- Androstenedione
- Caffeine (guarana)
- Chondroitin
- Chrysin
- Conjugated linoleic acid
- Creatine and creatine-containing compounds
- Garcinia cambogia (hydroxycitric acid)
- Ginkgo biloba
- Ginseng
- Glucosamine (unless prescribed by a doctor)
- Glutathione
- Glycerol
- Green tea

Use of banned substances is prevalent among athletes at all levels, prompting the governing bodies of most sports to conduct strict testing for all banned substances. Floyd Landis of the United States won the 2006 Tour de France, the world's most prestigious cycling race. However, shortly after he was awarded the trophy, he was accused of a violation due to the presence of elevated levels of testosterone found in his urinalysis. He lost an appeal in 2007 of the French lab's analysis and was stripped of the title. He has since implicated other cyclists as using similar substances.

- HMB (beta-hydroxy beta-methylbutyrate)
- Melatonin
- MSM (methylsulfonyl methane)
- Protein powders that contain more than 30 percent of calories from protein
- St. John's wort
- Tribulus
- Weight Gainers
- Yohimbine

## Supplement Use by College Students

Few studies have been done to determine the prevalence of supplement use by college students in general. However, this limited research suggests that use may be similar or higher in college students compared to their same-age peers who are not attending college and the older adult population. One study surveyed 272 students, of which 48.5 percent reported that they took a non–vitamin and mineral supplement during the past twelve months. The most frequently used products were echinacea, ginseng, and St. John's wort. Ten percent of the students took supplements to promote weight loss. Interestingly, most of those taking weight-loss supplements had BMIs in the recommended range and therefore did not need to lose weight. Eleven of the nineteen participants who reported an adverse reaction to a supplement continued to take the products despite negative effects. Users and nonusers of supplements did not differ significantly by ethnicity, gender, or exercise habits, or in how balanced they thought their diets were. More research needs to be conducted on college students, as they are often the target of supplement marketing claims such as those made for the many popular "energy drinks" discussed in the What's Hot feature.

### ■ What's Hot?

*Energy drinks—do they give you wings or leave you hangin'?*

Energy drinks such as Red Bull, Venom, Adrenaline Rush, 180, ISO Sprint, and WhoopAss are intentionally marketed to people under age 30, especially to college students, and are widely available both on and off campus. They seem to have replaced coffee as the study companion for the average college student's all-nighter. Indeed, they are very popular, and as a verification of this consider that worldwide revenues for Red Bull exceeded $1 billion in 2006. Since bringing the product to the United States in 1997, Red Bull's maker claims that its revenue has doubled each year.

Most energy drinks contain large doses of caffeine and other stimulants such as ephedrine, guarana, and ginseng. Some may provide more than the 80 mg of caffeine in a cup of coffee. Compared to the 37 mg of caffeine in a Mountain Dew or the 23 mg in a Coca-Cola Classic, that's one wide-eyed jolt. Caffeine may seem benign, but it is a drug—albeit a legal one—and can be associated with negative responses. The response will not be the same for everyone, and will be stronger for those who do not regularly consume caffeine. These responses can include a rapid heart rate, increased blood pressure, dizziness, inability to concentrate, and insomnia. In addition to the stimulants, most drinks contain sugar and quite a few empty calories. Depending on the brand, many also contain taurine (an amino acid said to act as an "energy booster"), guarana (a caffeine derivative), and B vitamins (said to boost energy). Despite their resemblance to sodas, the name and the marketing campaigns make energy drinks seem somehow healthier than sodas and coffee. When one considers the caffeine and calorie content, as listed in Table 11.1, the energy drinks hardly appear healthier.

Many energy drinks are even sold as sports drinks. In fact, it is not unusual to see a Red Bull van or tent handing out free product to participants at local sporting events. This is of particular concern because the high caffeine content along with the high sugar concentration could lead to cramping and impairment in fluid absorption. Energy drinks have also become popular on the club and party scene. They are promoted as a healthier mix for vodka than sodas or juices. It is never a good idea to mix the two because alcohol is a depressant and the drinks are stimulants. Therefore, they tend to mask the intoxicating effects of alcohol, and people are more likely to overdrink and think that they are sober when in fact they are not. Also, like caffeine, alcohol is a diuretic. When the two are combined they can increase the risk of overdrinking and significantly enhance the misery of your hangover the next day.

The bottom line is: beware of popular energy drinks that "give you wings." Although the associated evidence is inconclusive, some of these products have been blamed for several deaths in Europe and are now banned in France, Denmark, Canada, and Iceland. ■

These are just a *few* of the energy drinks on the market! What do the number of choices shown here say about the popularity of these beverages?

## Why Are They Buying Them?

Whether young, old, athletes, or college students, people take supplements for many reasons. Most do so in order to be healthier or to make up for nutrients they believe they are lacking. Interestingly, results from large-scale nutrition surveys indicate that those most inclined to take supplements also show an increased likelihood of obtaining more vitamins and minerals in their diet than those who don't. Perhaps people who take supplements are just more concerned with their health in general. A study published in the *Journal of the American*

**Table 11.1**  **Caffeine and Calorie Content of Selected Drinks**

| Soda (12 oz.) | Caffeine (mg) | Calories | Sugar (g) |
|---|---|---|---|
| Dr Pepper | 39 | 150 | 39 |
| Coca-Cola Classic | 34 | 144 | 30 |
| Diet Coke | 45 | 0 | 0 |
| Pepsi | 38 | 150 | 37 |
| Diet Pepsi | 36 | 0 | 0 |
| Mountain Dew | 55 | 165 | 46 |
| Diet Mountain Dew | 55 | 0 | 0 |
| **Energy Drink (12 oz.)** | **Caffeine (mg)** | **Calories** | **Sugar (g)** |
| Amp | 112 | 171 | 42 |
| Monster Assault | 120 | 150 | 39 |
| Red Bull | 115.5 | 165 | 40 |
| Red Bull Sugar Free | 115.5 | 15 | 0 |
| Rockstar | 120 | 180 | 45 |
| SoBe Adrenaline Rush | 114.2 | 180 | 47 |
| Hype | 115 | 171 | 38 |
| Jolt Energy | 150 | 100 | 40 |
| Full Throttle | 100 | 0 | 0 |
| **Coffee** | **Caffeine (mg)** | | |
| Percolated (7 oz.) | 140 | | |
| Drip (7 oz.) | 115–175 | | |
| Espresso (1.5–2 oz.) | 100 | | |
| Brewed (7 oz.) | 80–135 | | |
| Instant (7 oz.) | 65–100 | | |
| Decaf, brewed (6 oz.) | 5 | | |
| Decaf, instant (6 oz.) | 3 | | |
| **Tea** | **Caffeine (mg)** | | |
| Iced (12 oz.) | 70 | | |
| Black (6 oz.) | 70 | | |
| Green (6 oz.) | 35 | | |
| Instant (7 oz.) | 30 | | |
| Yerba maté (3 g teabag) | 10–24 | | |
| Yerba maté (10 g dried, loose) | 30 | | |

**APPLICATION TIP**

The best course of action before taking any supplement is to make sure you are making that decision based on facts, following a consultation with your physician, and without your emotions.

*Medical Association* in 2002 surveyed more than 2,500 Americans regarding their use of supplements (given the two categories of vitamins/minerals and herbal products/natural supplements) and for what reasons. Their responses are summarized in Table 11.2. As the table indicates, most took vitamin and herbal supplements because they believed such supplements were healthy or good for them. However, many people take supplements hoping for a quick fix or magical cure. Many marketing campaigns pick up on these reasons and the emotions that can be tied to them, with slogans such as "Lose weight in one week" and

## Table 11.2    Reasons People Take Supplements

| Vitamins/Minerals | % of Responses | Herbals/Supplements | % of Responses |
|---|---|---|---|
| Health/good for you | 35 | Health/good for you | 16 |
| Dietary supplement | 11 | Arthritis | 7 |
| Vitamin/mineral supplement | 8 | Memory improvement | 6 |
| Prevent osteoporosis | 6 | Energy | 5 |
| Physician recommended | 6 | Immune booster | 5 |
| Prevent colds/influenza | 3 | Joint | 4 |
| Don't know/no reason specified | 3 | Supplement diet | 4 |
| Immune system booster | 2 | Sleep aid | 3 |
| Recommended by friend/family/media | 2 | Prostate | 3 |
| Energy | 2 | Don't know/no reason specified | 2 |
| All others | 22 | All others | 45 |

*Source:* Adapted from Kaufman DW, Kelly JP, Rosenberg L, Anderson TE, Mitchell AA (2002). Recent patterns of medication use in the ambulatory adult population of the United States: the Slone survey. 287(3):337–344.

"Find the new you." They play on the hopelessness and desperation many dieters feel after repeated attempts to lose weight. Perhaps even more disturbing are the many supplements marketed to those who have potentially life-threatening diseases such as cancer and HIV. These people often fall victim to expensive supplements that promise to alleviate symptoms, prolong life, or even cure the disease.

As noted, and as Table 11.2 shows, the reasons why people use supplements are varied. Marketers are aware of these rationales as well, and they rely on them in developing their marketing strategies.

## ■ Vegetarianism

### Do vegetarian kids need extra vitamin supplements?

Studies suggest that the diets of most children who are vegan or vegetarian meet or exceed recommendations for most nutrients. In addition, vegan children typically consume more fiber and have lower intakes of total fat, saturated fat, and cholesterol than children who eat meat. However, some studies indicate that children who eat a vegan diet may have a calcium deficiency. In addition, the absorption of some nutrients such as zinc and iron is lower when consumed from plant sources than from meat sources. Nutritionists suggest that parents be sure to provide a diet that enhances absorption of these minerals. For example, providing a source of vitamin C with a plant source of iron enhances absorption of the iron. The American Dietetic Association reports that protein needs are slightly higher for vegan children but can be easily met with a varied vegan diet that provides adequate calories. Good sources of the omega-3 fatty acid linolenic acid (see Chapter 4) such as flaxseed should be provided to enhance synthesis of the long-chain fatty acids needed for growth and development. Parents should also be sure that their vegan children are consuming adequate amounts of vitamin B-12, riboflavin, and, if sun exposure is not adequate, vitamin D. Nutrient needs can be met by consuming fortified vegan foods, many

Chicken nuggets and other foods that children typically like are offered in a vegan version and are fortified with nutrients that may otherwise be missing in a vegan diet.

of which are marketed specifically to children. Therefore, with education and appropriate food choices, vegan children can meet all their nutrient needs without vitamin supplements (see vegan pyramid). Of course, parents should always discuss with their pediatrician whether or not their child needs a supplement. ■

### ■ Make It a Practice
*Always do your homework!*

Not all supplements have negative side effects, and some can be helpful if taken correctly. However, no strict regulations protect consumers from potentially harmful supplements. So that leaves it up to you, the consumer, to beware. The first step in deciding whether to take a supplement, or in deciding whether a claim made by a certain product has any value, is to do your homework. Here are some things to look into before taking anything.

- *Think about your total diet.* The concept of "too much of a good thing" certainly applies when it comes to supplements. Before you decide to take a vitamin, mineral, or other supplement, consider *everything* in your diet. This is important, because it all adds up. For example, if you eat foods that are fortified, such as cereal, you are getting added vitamins and minerals. Then, in addition to that fortified

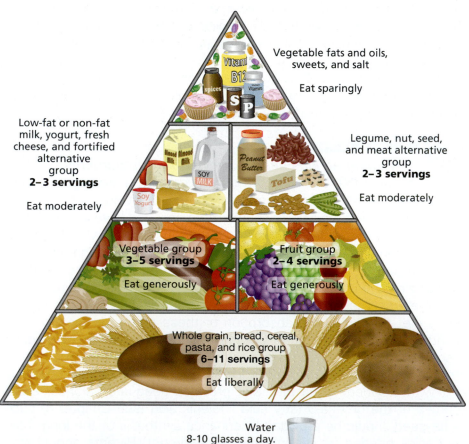

By following a carefully planned diet that includes fortified foods, vegetarian children can meet all of their nutrient needs without supplements.

cereal, suppose you have a smoothie made with a supplement that contains added vitamins. You might take a daily multivitamin and then, of course, you eat food with nutrients in it. As you can see, you can easily consume an excessive amount of vitamins and minerals without even realizing it.

- *Check with your health care practitioner.* Many supplements that are safe under normal conditions may not be advisable for children; teenagers; or those who are ill, pregnant, having surgery, or taking certain medications. Therefore, always check with your health care practitioner before taking a new supplement. Furthermore, be sure to tell your practitioner what you are taking before any medications are prescribed, as some supplements interfere with the action of some medications. Also be careful about who you are defining as a "health care practitioner." Many who call themselves health care experts have a vested interest in whether you take a supplement because they are selling them and, therefore, receive a financial gain from your purchase. So, before you even consult a practitioner, find out what his or her credentials are and whether he or she sells supplements. A reputable practitioner does not profit from your taking a medicine or supplement.

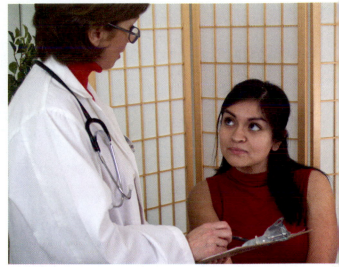

Always check with your healthcare practitioner before taking a supplement.

- *Ask yourself, does it sound too good to be true?* If it seems too good to be true, it probably is. Therefore, be cautious of any claims that promise quick and easy solutions in a pill. Always question the source of the information regarding a product.

- *Learn to recognize a fraudulent claim.* The FDA and FTC provide the following guidelines to help consumers recognize fraudulent claims by supplements manufacturers and retailers.

    1. Statements that the product is a quick and effective "cure-all" or diagnostic tool for a wide variety of ailments—for example, "Extremely beneficial in the treatment of rheumatism, arthritis, infections, prostate problems, ulcers, cancer, heart trouble, hardening of the arteries, and more." What exactly does "extremely beneficial" mean anyway? If it meant that symptoms were alleviated or a disease was cured, wouldn't they say that instead of using such a vague statement? Furthermore, drugs that are effective are rarely effective for such a wide variety of conditions; they are usually very specific. So the fact that a supplement says it is effective for so many different conditions should be a warning sign.

    2. Statements that suggest the product can treat or cure diseases—for example, "Shrinks tumors" or "Cures impotence."

    3. Promotions that use words such as "scientific breakthrough," "miraculous cure," "exclusive product," "secret ingredient," or "ancient remedy"—for example, "A revolutionary innovation formulated by using proven principles of natural health-based medical science."

    4. Advertising that uses impressive-sounding terms, such as these for a weight-loss product: "hunger stimulation point" and "thermogenesis."

**Want to know more?**
For information on how to tell whether a website is reputable, go to the text website at http://webcom8.grtxle.com/nutrition and click on the Chapters button. Select Chapter 11.

**APPLICATION TIP**

If you think you have experienced any adverse health effects from taking any supplement, you, your health care provider, or anyone else can and should report the adverse event or illness directly to the FDA by calling 1-800-FDA-1088, by faxing 1-800-FDA-0178, or online.

5. Undocumented case histories or personal testimonials by consumers or doctors claiming amazing results—for example, "My husband has Alzheimer's disease. He began taking a teaspoonful of this product each day. And now, in just twenty-two days, he is mowing the grass, cleaning out the garage, weeding the flower beds, and taking his morning walk again."

6. Limited availability and advance-payment requirements—for example, "Hurry. This offer will not last. Send us a check now to reserve your supply."

7. Promises of no-risk "money-back guarantees"—for example, "If after thirty days you have not lost at least 4 lb. each week, your uncashed check will be returned to you."

- *Be skeptical.* Research any health claims about the benefits of a product; don't just take the word of a friend, co-worker, or personal trainer at the gym. Ask yourself, what is his training? Is she just telling me this because she thinks it worked for her? Then do some research of your own. Search for scientific studies done on the product and reported in reputable peer-reviewed scientific journals. You can do this by consulting a trained and licensed health professional or by searching PubMed or Google Scholar. ■

**Before you go on . . .**

1. What is the NCAA's guideline for coaches and trainers in supplying supplements to their athletes?
2. Why should consumers be cautious about consuming so-called energy drinks such as Red Bull?
3. Who is taking supplements?
4. What are three signs of a fraudulent claim by a supplement manufacturer?

## Types of Supplements

### Vitamins and Minerals

As mentioned previously, vitamin and mineral supplements that provide at least 100 percent of the Daily Value are by far the most popular type of supplement. To compensate for perceived dietary deficiencies or promote optimal health, many Americans (52 percent of adults) take at least one dietary supplement.

As a general rule, scientific evidence suggests that if you consume a varied and balanced diet, you should not need to take a supplement. However, exceptions exist, such as those for iron and calcium as discussed in Chapter 10. These are most often recommended for women, as large studies looking at the nutritional intake of various populations indicate that women often do not consume adequate amounts of these nutrients.

It is always best to try to obtain your nutrients from foods by eating a balanced diet, as discussed in Chapter 2 and stressed throughout this book. However, many Americans believe they cannot do so every day, or at all. Therefore, multivitamins seem like a good replacement. But a vitamin and mineral

*Since I don't eat a lot of fruits and vegetables, should I take a multivitamin?*

supplement, by definition of the word *supplement,* means "in addition to," not "instead of." Often, when deciding whether to take vitamin supplements, many people believe that if vitamins are good for you, then getting more of them is even better. As we discussed in Chapters 9 and 10, this approach can be harmful, especially for supplements that contain potentially toxic fat-soluble vitamins. Furthermore, if you take supplements instead of eating food, you will not be getting the fiber and other beneficial compounds such as phytochemicals that are found in the food.

As for whether taking vitamins and minerals in amounts greater than the DRI decreases your risk of developing diseases such as cancer and heart disease, most researchers agree that there is not enough evidence to show that supplements are effective in preventing chronic diseases. However, as long as the multivitamin does not contain more than 100 percent of the DRI, no major health agencies discourage its use.

## Individual Supplements

In addition to multivitamin/multimineral supplements that contain many vitamins and minerals in one dose, most vitamins and minerals are also sold individually. In Chapters 9 and 10 we discussed several of these, such as vitamin C and iron. There are many more. The following are a few of the more common ones.

### Boron

**Boron** is a trace element found in foods such as avocados, peanut butter, peanuts, prune and grape juice, chocolate powder, wine, pecans, and raisin bran cereals. Research suggests that it influences calcium and magnesium metabolism. However, a definitive function for boron in the human body has not been found. Therefore, no recommendations for minimal intake have been established. Some people believe that boron provides benefits for memory, menopausal symptoms, osteoarthritis, and more. However, there is no strong evidence that it is effective for any of these. Supplemental boron is most widely marketed for its supposed ability to increase testosterone release. This claim is based on one study of postmenopausal women taking 3 mg of boron per day that demonstrated elevations in serum estrogen and testosterone. However, boron supplementation for seven weeks in nonsteroid-using male bodybuilders failed to increase lean body mass, strength, or circulating testosterone levels. Other investigations failed to demonstrate changes in circulating hormone levels as well. Therefore, boron supplementation is unlikely to provide any benefit.

### Carotenoids

The **carotenoids** are the recognizable form of coloring pigment in plants such as carrots and sweet potatoes. The carotenoid family includes molecules such as alpha-, beta-, and gamma-carotene; lutein; zeaxanthin; lycopene; cryptoxanthin; vioaxanthin; and bixin. As many as 450 different carotenoids may exist.

An increased intake of carotenoids has been associated with a decreased risk of heart disease and certain cancers. Some of the protection may be related to its antioxidant activity. Beta-carotene is the predominant carotenoid in the human diet; it is commonly used in supplements. However, several investigations have failed to demonstrate that beta-carotene supplementation helps prevent or treat heart disease and cancer. In fact, as mentioned in Chapter 9, beta-carotene

Half of Americans take at least one supplement every day.

 **Want to know more?**
You can review the full evidence-based report on multivitamin use from the Agency for Healthcare Research and Quality by going to the text website at http://webcom8.grtxle .com/nutrition and clicking on the Chapters button. Select Chapter 11.

**APPLICATION TIP**
Before spending money on a supplement, try to get the recommended amount of the nutrient from your diet. You will most likely save money, and you will be getting other important nutrients from the food you eat.

supplementation actually increased the incidence of lung cancer in cigarette smokers. Oversupplementation can also lead to an orange discoloration of the skin, especially in the palms of the hands and the soles of the feet. Researchers believe that fruits and vegetables may contain other factors that are necessary in combination with, or supportive of, the health benefits of beta-carotene. Therefore, isolating it as a supplement does not provide the same benefit. It appears that carotenoids are best obtained from a diet rich in fruits and vegetables rather than from supplements.

### Chromium

**Chromium** is a trace mineral that is widely distributed in the food supply, though most foods provide only small amounts (less than 2 micrograms [mcg] per serving). Meat and whole-grain products, as well as some fruits, vegetables, and spices, are relatively good sources. Chromium is a widely used supplement. Estimated sales to consumers were $85 million in 2002, representing 5.6 percent of the total mineral-supplement market. Chromium is sold as a single-ingredient supplement as well as in combination formulas, particularly those marketed for weight loss, to enhance athletic performance, and to regulate blood sugar. Chromium is marketed mostly as chromium picolinate, but other forms such as chromium nicotinate and chromium chloride are also available. The picolinate form has been found to be more absorbable.

Research has indicated that chromium, in any form, is ineffective as a supplement to increase lean body mass, significantly alter body composition, or improve strength in both trained and untrained individuals. Even if supplementation did provide the benefits it claims, most people don't need extra chromium because it is easy to get from any healthy diet. Although there is limited information pertaining to the safety of chromium, a recent case study reveals that supplemental chromium picolinate may become toxic when ingested at six to twelve times the recommended dosage over the course of many months. Such ingestion caused kidney problems and required dialysis to restore kidney function. At this time, supplemental chromium is considered safe when consumed in recommended quantities (50–200 mcg/day), but its lack of effectiveness doesn't warrant usage.

### Vanadium

**Vanadium** is a trace mineral found in mushrooms, shellfish, black pepper, parsley, dill seed, and some processed foods. Although no functional role in the human body has been clearly established for vanadium, several roles have been suggested. For example, vanadium may mimic insulin and therefore help lower fasting blood glucose in those with Type 2 diabetes mellitus. Studies in animals with diabetes indicate that vanadium can help improve blood sugar levels. Studies using human subjects have produced encouraging results, but more research needs to be done before any concrete conclusions can be made. Human studies were conducted in small numbers of people for short periods of time and involved relatively high dosages. Because vanadium "mimics" insulin, it has been marketed to athletes and bodybuilders for its potential role in increasing amino acid uptake in the muscle, leading to greater growth of skeletal muscle. However, research indicates that it does not appear to be effective for this purpose. As is the case with vanadium, many supplements are marketed to athletes by promising increased performance and enhanced muscle growth. Amino acid supplements are among those almost exclusively marketed to athletes.

# Protein and Amino Acid Supplements

Most people, athletes included, get plenty of protein, and therefore amino acids, in their diet. Of course, if you listen to the marketing put forth by the supplements manufacturers, you might believe that amino acids are the answer to all of our health problems. Amino acid supplements are particularly marketed toward athletes. The advertisements claim that amino acid supplements will provide the cutting edge in performance, increase muscle mass, and enhance recovery. Many of these claims are just plain hype or are exaggerated from the findings of small studies. Research indicates that the type and timing of amino acids consumed may provide a small benefit to athletes by enhancing protein synthesis in the presence of exercise and adequate calories. It appears that only the essential amino acids are required to achieve any benefit; in addition, timing of the amino acid ingestion is important too. In fact, in one study a mixture of 6 g of essential amino acids and 35 g of glucose, given one hour before exercise, resulted in a greater stimulation of protein synthesis over time than when the same mixture was given either immediately or one hour after exercise.

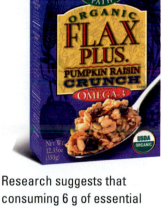

Research suggests that consuming 6 g of essential amino acids and 35 g of glucose before exercise leads to greater protein synthesis than consuming the same mix after exercising.

## Whey Proteins

Whey proteins are often marketed to athletes and those wishing to increase muscle mass. They are often described as superior to other forms of protein in building muscle mass. However, no credible evidence shows that they build muscle faster than other protein sources. Although whey proteins are a good source of protein, they are not superior to other forms. Whey proteins and casein constitute the two major protein groups of cow's milk. Milk protein is 80 percent casein and 20 percent whey proteins.

**Whey** is derived as a by-product of cheese making. In its raw form whey consists of fat, lactose, and other substances. The raw form is further processed to produce whey protein concentrates (WPC) and whey protein isolates (WPI). A few different types of whey proteins are marketed. Whey protein concentrates are rich in whey proteins and also contain fat and lactose. Whey protein isolates are low in fat and lactose. Whey proteins may have antimicrobial functions, act as antioxidants, and aid the immune system. They may also be useful in the nutrition of infants and others, and some very preliminary evidence shows that they may have some immune-modulating and anticancer effects. Whey proteins have been used as the sole proteins in some infant formulas, and this has reportedly resulted in fewer allergies in infants who consume them. Use of whey proteins by healthy adults has not generated any reports of adverse effects. However, anyone with milk allergies or sensitivities should not supplement with whey protein. The bottom line: it is okay to add some whey protein to your smoothie if you like, but don't expect it to be superior to milk, meat, soy, or other proteins in helping you build muscle. Furthermore, as we discussed in Chapter 5, most Americans already consume more than enough protein in their diet and don't need protein supplements.

Whey protein is a complete source of protein but is not superior to other sources.

## Arginine

**Arginine** is a conditionally essential amino acid (see Chapter 5). A typical American diet contains about 3–6 g of arginine per day, mostly from seafood, watermelon, nuts, seeds, algae, meats, rice protein and soy protein. Normally, the body can synthesize sufficient amounts to meet its needs. However, under certain conditions, such as in rare genetic disorders, during surgery, or recovering from burns, the body cannot make enough to meet the increased demand and it becomes essential. Arginine is involved in protein synthesis and the formation of several compounds in the body such as urea, nitric oxide, creatine, glutamate, and proline. Evidence shows that Arginine plays an important role in reproduction, fetal and postnatal development, wound healing, immune function, and tissue integrity, as well as prevention and treatment of blood vessel dysfunction. Additionally, it may provide effective therapies for obesity, diabetes, and the metabolic syndrome.

Supplemental arginine is being investigated for its role in the treatment of several conditions, including kidney disease, reduced sperm count, and erectile dysfunction. Current research indicates that arginine is most beneficial to people who are going through a period of rapid growth, are recovering from trauma, or have a compromised immune function. It does not appear to be effective for enhancing lean body mass in healthy individuals; however, more research needs to be done before a definitive statement on this can be made. Appropriate use of Arginine is safe for animals and humans in dietary supplementation and clinical therapy.

Nitric Oxide (NO) is a free radical and a powerful blood vessel dilator. It is created from the amino acid arginine and oxygen. In addition to its properties as a blood vessel dilator, it has been shown to help prevent heart disease and to have anti-inflammatory effects. Many supplements advertise that they contain NO. However, if you look closely on the label they don't contain NO; rather they contain its building block L-arginine. As we discussed previously, there appears to be no performance benefits to supplementing with arginine in healthy individuals.

## Aspartic Acid

**Aspartic acid** or **aspartate** is a non-essential amino acid used to make urea, proteins, glycogen, and energy. Its role in glycogen and energy production were the rationale for the claim that supplemental aspartate has an antifatigue effect on skeletal muscle. This claim was never supported by research. There may be some benefit to high doses taken during disease states when the body's ability to make nonessential amino acids is compromised.

## Branched-Chain Amino Acids

The **branched-chain amino acids (BCAAs)**—leucine, isoleucine, and valine—are essential. They are different from the other amino acids because they can be used for energy directly in the muscle, without having to go to the liver to be broken down during exercise. It has been suggested that ingesting them before and/or during long-duration activity may help delay fatigue, but studies have not strongly supported this theory. However, the BCAAs may play a critical role in recovery from exercise by preventing muscle breakdown. In one study, ingestion of 5 g of BCAAs before exercise reduced muscle soreness and muscle fatigue for several days after exercise. Other studies have shown that BCAA supplementation improves immune system function after exercise to exhaustion. Supplementation may also be beneficial for people with chronic diseases that often lead to rapid muscle breakdown, such as HIV, AIDS, and cancer. It may also benefit those at risk of muscle loss due to age, immobility, or prolonged bed rest, including trauma, orthopedic, or neurological patients. Research is ongoing to determine the extent of any benefits, the amount needed to achieve a benefit, maximum dosage, and potential side effects.

### Glutamine

**Glutamine** can be obtained from food but is made in the body and was initially considered a non-essential amino acid. Because of the body's need for an increase in glutamine beyond what it can produce under certain conditions, such as illness and stress, it has been reclassified as a "conditionally essential amino acid" (see Chapter 5). It is often marketed as an immune system, brain function, and digestion enhancer. When the body experiences injuries, surgery, infections, and prolonged stress, glutamine needs may increase, and therefore levels can become depleted. Studies have reported enhanced immune function and shortened recovery times in trauma and cancer patients at doses of 20–30 g/day. Glutamine also decreases after long-duration exercise and after daily training, which may impair immune system function and make an athlete more likely to get sick. In such cases, glutamine supplementation may be helpful, but clear evidence of its benefits after exercise is still inconclusive.

The bottom line is, unless you are participating in intense or exhaustive exercise or recovering from a burn, surgery, or other major physical stress, you most likely do not need to take a glutamine supplement. Moreover, if you are recovering from intense exercise or from the conditions described previously, you can increase your dietary intake of glutamine. A 3-oz. serving of meat contains 3–4 g of glutamine; many other foods contain glutamine, including milk, cheese, yogurt, peanuts, lentils, tofu, beans, and eggs.

---

**Before you go on . . .**

1. Name two supplements frequently recommended by professionals, and explain why they are advocated.
2. What do most researchers say about the role of multivitamins in promoting health and preventing disease?
3. What are the health benefits of whey in comparison to other protein sources such as milk, meat, and soy?
4. Glutamine and arginine are conditionally essential amino acids. Who might benefit from their use as a dietary supplement? Why?

---

# Supplements for Performance

## Glucosamine Chondroitin

**Glucosamine chondroitin** has been widely promoted as a treatment for arthritis. Glucosamine is thought to stimulate the production and repair of cartilage. Chondroitin is a cartilage component that is thought to promote water retention and elasticity and to inhibit the enzymes that break down cartilage. Both compounds are produced in the body. Some research suggests that glucosamine may stimulate the production of cartilage-building proteins. Other studies suggest that chondroitin may inhibit production of cartilage-destroying enzymes and fight inflammation. A 2-year study of over 662 patients with osteoarthritis showed no differences in pain between groups taking glucosamine and those

# Real People, Other Voices

### Student:
### Onome Owereh
Prairie View A & M University

It is Marissa's responsibility to be aware of the statement made by the advertiser because, if it sounds too good to be true, it probably is. The advertiser's promises will only hinder her planning strategies for weight management. It will be difficult for her to determine if the pill is beneficial, safe, and effective when considering her own diet because dietary supplements do not need to present specific evidence of safety and effectiveness to the FDA before the product is marketed. Most of the time, they contain large or small amounts of added nutrients that can damage her health or produce negative side effects.

Marissa needs to set a realistic goal and establish a proper diet and physical activity to aid weight loss. She needs to avoid food deprivation and plan and eat regular balanced meals. Marissa should eat smaller, more frequent meals. This will help to increase the body's metabolism and burn more calories. High-fiber foods such as fresh fruits and vegetables; low-fat foods such as yogurt, fat-free milk, and milk products; and complex carbohydrates should replace high-fat, sugary foods and drinks in her diet. She should strive to eat breakfast daily to reduce food intake throughout the day.

Engaging in physical activities of low to moderate intensity will also help Marissa lose weight. Activities may include brisk walking, taking the stairs instead of the elevator, and jogging. She also needs to spend less time watching television or using the computer. Weight loss supplements offer no special benefits and may be harmful. They are also useless unless accompanied by regular physical activity and proper diet.

### Instructor:
### Erin Caudill, MS, RD, LMNT
Southeast Community College

Marissa finds herself in a very common college situation: Many freshman students gain weight after they arrive at college. My first suggestion to Marissa is to analyze her current eating habits to determine how much she eats and to identify other factors that have impacted her weight gain. Other factors may include the amounts of food she consumes, the times of day she eats, whether she eats alone or with someone, her state of mind when eating, and her level and frequency of physical activity. Once these factors are considered, we can determine what changes she needs to make to achieve her weight goal.

It is also important that she understand how many calories make up one pound of body weight so she will realize why weight loss products/pills are not effective. Based on the two months she has to lose the weight, an appropriate calorie level and exercise plan can be set up for her.

In addition, Marissa needs to understand the motivation behind the advertisements and realize that the manufacturers of supplements are appealing to people's desire for a "quick fix." Ads for supplements don't mention that weight loss on the scale may only be temporary and is made up mostly of water weight. Also, there are always other potential health risks that are not explained in the ads. Only lifestyle changes—decreasing caloric intake and increasing physical activity—will have a long-term impact on Marissa's weight. Without lifestyle changes, any possible weight loss will quickly be reversed. The old saying that "If it sounds to good to be true, it probably is" holds true in this situation.

### Registered dietitian:
### Ryan D. Andrews, MS, MA, RD, LDN, CSCS, CISSN
Lutherville, MD

This situation is a great case for "nutrition triage." Marissa needs to take a step back and assess the big picture. The reason she gained a few pounds at school is most likely poor daily nutrition and exercise habits, not lack of dietary supplements. Trying to mask the symptom (recent weight gain) with a supplement will not be effective and may even work against her in the long run.

Slow and steady is the name of the game when it comes to body fat loss. Trying to drop a large amount of body weight in a short time leads to muscle loss and rebound cravings with weight gain. Dietary supplements will not be effective for weight management unless a solid nutrition and exercise foundation are in place.

I stress, in my counseling of clients for weight management, that most of the dietary supplements that influence body fat come with risks. If the claims made by the supplements manufacturer sound too good to be true, they probably are. Typical weight loss supplements act as *thermogenic* agents; that is, they raise body temperature and increase heart rate, blood pressure, and rate of breathing.

Marissa should focus on developing healthy nutrition and exercise habits. With good habits in place, the body weight will fall off.

taking prescription medication or placebos. The best news is that no study so far has found any serious side effects from either glucosamine or chondroitin.

Experts suggest that anyone choosing to take this supplement should be advised to take glucosamine sulfate rather than glucosamine hydrochloride, and to do so for three months. If positive results are not experienced after this length of time, then it probably isn't going to work. As always, anyone thinking about taking this or other supplements should consult with a physician, as it could interfere with medications or other methods of treatment.

## Coenzyme Q$_{10}$

**Coenzyme Q$_{10}$**, also called **ubiquinone**, is a key component of aerobic metabolism discussed in Chapter 6. It is an antioxidant and a coenzyme for several of the key enzymatic steps of energy production within the cell. It is present in small amounts in a variety of foods, particularly beef, soy oil, sardines, mackerel, liver, and peanuts. In healthy individuals, normal levels are maintained by intake and by the amount made in the body. Many claims have been made for coenzyme Q$_{10}$, many of which have not been supported by well-controlled studies. It is currently being tested for its ability to slow the progress of Parkinson's disease, boost stamina in people with AIDS, stabilize blood sugar levels in people with diabetes, enhance athletic performance, decrease allergies, and prevent the retinal deterioration that occurs with macular degeneration. Taking coenzyme Q$_{10}$ in pill form may not provide any potential benefits, as it can lose its structure in digestion. Evidence indicates that coenzyme Q$_{10}$ supports the heart, especially in congestive heart failure and angina (chest pain), at 100–200 mg/day. However, other studies show that it is *not* effective. Because of inconclusive evidence, and the fact that long-term studies have not been conducted as to its safety and effectiveness, the American Heart Association does not recommend that heart disease patients take coenzyme Q$_{10}$.

Studies supporting the efficacy of coenzyme Q$_{10}$ appear most promising for neurodegenerative disorders such as Parkinson's disease. Several investigations have found improvements in athletic performance and antioxidant potential. In fact, coenzyme Q$_{10}$ supplementation (90 mg/day) was reported to improve aspects of physical performance in Finnish top-level cross-country skiers. Despite some promising results, experts are hesitant to recommend use until further studies are completed.

## Caffeine

Caffeine is one of the most widely used drugs in the world. In some supplements it is listed as guarana or kola nut. It can be found in coffee, tea, chocolate, soft drinks, some pain relievers such as Excedrin, some cold medicines, and many weight-loss pills. It is sometimes used as a nervous system stimulant to offset fatigue, and in the 1990s it was thought to benefit the endurance of athletes by helping release fat stores into the bloodstream. Unfortunately, more fat in the blood does not translate into more fat utilization by muscle.

Studies have shown that caffeine alone or combined with ephedra increases performance by delaying fatigue or increasing the time it takes to reach exhaustion in endurance exercise. Increases in endurance performance have been shown after consuming doses of 3–9 mg/kg of body weight. People who consume it on a daily basis can become adapted and may have to use more caffeine to get the same effect. Caffeine has some side effects. People who do not regularly

Caffeine may help to offset fatigue in prolonged endurance exercise. However, people who consume it regularly may not get the same benefit as those who do not.

 **Want to know more?**
Can you spot false weight-loss supplement claims? To find out how, go to the text website at http://webcom8.grtxle.com/nutrition and click on the Chapters button. Select Chapter 11.

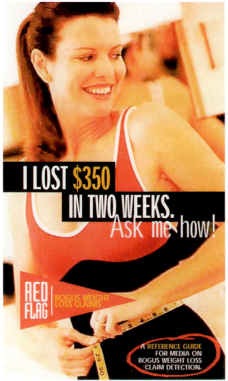

**I LOST $350 IN TWO WEEKS. Ask me how!**

**RED FLAG** | BOGUS WEIGHT LOSS CLAIMS

A REFERENCE GUIDE FOR MEDIA ON BOGUS WEIGHT LOSS CLAIM DETECTION.

Beware of supplements with false weight loss claims. If claims appear too good to be true, they probably are.

consume it can experience gastrointestinal distress, nervousness, rapid heart rate, headaches, and increased blood pressure. Caffeine can also have a diuretic effect, but this is usually most pronounced during rest and does not appear to have as large an effect during exercise.

## Carnitine

Carnitine transports long-chain fatty acids into the mitochondria for metabolism, so the thinking is more carnitine, more transport, and therefore more fat burned. The flaw in this thinking is that you already have all the carnitine you need, and more is not better. It's available in foods, and you readily synthesize it from amino acids. Carnitine supplements provide no performance advantage.

### ■ Myths and Legends

*Weight-loss supplements—trading on the hopes and desperation of an overweight nation*

We have all seen the advertisements in pop-ups on the Internet, in magazines, on television. They all say something like, "Lose 30 lbs. in thirty days and eat all you want," "Lose 5 inches off your waist by drinking this," or "The fat will melt away while you sleep." These advertisements may seem outrageous, but they appear to be working. Consumers spend about $38 billion annually on weight-loss products. People desperate to lose weight are especially vulnerable to advertisements claiming easy, quick results. Several consumer groups have sought to protect and warn consumers about such false claims and about new tactics used to appeal to the vulnerable. They warn consumers to beware of supplements that claim the following:

- You can eat all you want and not gain weight.
- You can lose more than 2 lbs. per week.
- You don't need to exercise.
- One miracle food or drug is all you need.
- The pill blocks nutrient absorption.
- If you rub this cream on your skin, it will melt the fat away. ■

**APPLICATION TIP**

When consuming any food or supplement before or after a competition, try it during practice to prevent any "game-ending" side effects during the event.

## Creatine

**Creatine** is made in the body and can be consumed in the diet, mostly from meat and fish. It is part of creatine phosphate, the key component of the immediate energy system used primarily during sporting events lasting thirty seconds or less (such as track sprints). Higher intakes of creatine seem to result in higher levels of creatine phosphate in the muscle cells, thus making more energy available for very high-intensity activity such as strength training. The more you consume or take as supplements, the less is made in the body.

Much has been written and said in recent years about creatine and its influence on performance. Studies show that creatine supplementation results in somewhat greater gains in strength when combined with appropriate training. However, not everyone responds to creatine supplementation. Response depends on the frequency and type of training and on the levels produced and present in the body when supplementation begins. Vegetarians and others who don't consume much creatine appear to achieve a greater response. Absolutely no result exists without training, and creatine does not benefit aerobic conditioning. Many people who have taken it complain of side effects, including headaches, abdominal cramps, and muscle cramps. Long-term creatine use may lead to kidney and/or liver damage, and an increased risk of muscle tears and pulls; however, no research evidence currently supports a connection between creatine and these problems. On the other hand, creatine supplementation in common dosages results in urinary concentrations ninety times greater than normal, which suggests that it could damage the kidneys if used long-term.

## Glycerol

**Glycerol** is part of triacylglycerols (triglycerides or fats) and phospholipids. It is also used as a sweetener in syrups, liquors, and some foods. Glycerol combined with water intake has been suggested to help prevent dehydration in endurance athletes who exercise in hot, humid environments. The theory is that glycerol causes the body to hold more water so that you can sweat more before you become dehydrated. Research regarding glycerol's effect is mixed, with one study showing that pre-exercise intake of glycerol significantly improved cycling endurance time and lowered the average heart rate. However, in another study of triathletes, pre-exercise consumption of glycerol failed to enhance their performance. The study results may differ because participants used different amounts of glycerol and water. If an athlete is going to try to hyperhydrate with

Florida State shotputter Garrett Johnson competing in the NCAA track and field championships. Athletes participating in events that last 30 seconds or less are most likely to benefit from creatine supplementation.

glycerol, studies indicate they should ingest glycerol 1.2 g/kg body weight (BW) in 26 mL/kg BW of fluid over a period of 60 minutes, ending 30 minutes prior to exercise. During exercise they should ingest glycerol 0.125 g/kg BW in a volume equal to 5 mL/kg BW during exercise. Adding glycerol 1.0 g/kg BW to each 1.5 L of fluid consumed following exercise will accelerate the replacement of fluids. Always experiment during training to make sure that this protocol does not cause adverse effects. The side effects include abdominal cramps, bloating, and nausea.

## HMB (Beta-Hydroxy Beta-Methylbutyrate)

**HMB (beta-hydroxy beta-methylbutyrate)** is a product of the breakdown of the essential amino acid leucine. It is synthesized naturally in humans and is also available in some foods (such as citrus fruits and catfish). Whether HMB has a necessary physiological function or is merely a product of leucine breakdown remains unclear. HMB is marketed to prevent muscle breakdown associated with resistance training, to enhance strength, and to decrease body fat. Because of its supposed uses, HMB has become a popular nutritional supplement among bodybuilders and strength trainers and is often recommended along with creatine supplementation. As is typical with many supplements sold for muscle building, the marketing hype exceeds the supporting evidence from research. Supplementation with HMB during resistance training results in small overall and leg strength gains in previously untrained men, but effects in trained lifters are trivial. The HMB effect on body composition is negligible. Although no adverse side effects have been reported, too few well-controlled studies have been conducted to conclude that it is safe.

### Before you go on . . .

1. What does the research regarding the possible benefits of glucosamine and chondroitin suggest?
2. How conclusive is the research about the effect of coenzyme $Q_{10}$ in the treatment of heart disease?
3. Why has ephedra been banned as a supplement in the United States?
4. What types of sports would benefit most from creatine supplementation?

## Herbs and Botanicals

### Are Natural Supplements More Effective?

A study conducted in 2000 indicated that up to 40 percent of the adult population in the United States uses at least one herbal supplement. Many different herbal and botanical supplements are on the market. They range from lesser-known ground herbs such as the kava kava root to well-known and widely used supplements such as ginseng and garlic. **Herbs** and **botanicals** are supplements that contain extracts or active ingredients from the roots, berries, seeds, stems, leaves, buds, or flowers of plants. It is a common misconception that supplements made from plants are safe because they are "natural" or "organic." An example of a dangerous plant extract that we have already mentioned is ephedra, also known as ma huang, epitonin, or ephedrine. Nonetheless, many herbs and botanicals provide a benefit when taken correctly and in the right dosage. For example, cranberries seem to help prevent urinary problems. We will discuss some of the more commonly used herbs and botanicals.

### Black Cohosh

**Black cohosh** is a member of the buttercup family that is also called black snakeroot, macrotys, bugbane, bugwort, rattleroot, and rattleweed. It has a history of use for rheumatism (arthritis and muscle pain), but it has been used more recently to treat postmenopausal symptoms such as hot flashes, night sweats, and vaginal dryness. Additionally, it has been used to ease the effects of menstrual irregularities and premenstrual syndrome and to induce labor. As with so many other supplements, no scientific evidence supports its effectiveness or indicates whether it is safe. However, Great Britain and Australia now require any supplement that contains black cohosh to carry a warning label, as it has been associated with liver damage in several cases. Similarly, in August 2006 Health Canada issued a consumer health advisory after three cases of liver damage associated with its use were reported. Health Canada has indicated that negative health reports are rare, but consumers should still take the supplement with caution and should consult a health care practitioner before doing so. The FDA in the United States has not yet issued any warnings.

It is a common misconception that supplements made from plants are safe because they are natural or organic.

### Cranberries

Historically, cranberry fruits and leaves were used for a variety of problems, such as treating wounds, urinary disorders, diarrhea, diabetes, stomach ailments, and liver problems. More recently, cranberry products have been used to prevent or treat urinary tract infections, *Helicobacter pylori* infections that can lead to stomach ulcers, and dental plaque. Cranberries have also been reported to have antioxidant and anticancer properties. Although preliminary results are not conclusive, they suggest promise for the use of cranberry products to prevent and treat urinary problems. Side effects are minimal and include diarrhea and minor stomach upset.

### Echinacea

**Echinacea** is one of the most widely used herbs worldwide, primarily because it is believed to strengthen the immune system. Echinacea is a plant with tall

Cranberries contain antioxidants, may help relieve urinary problems, and may have "anticancer properties."

Echinacea is one of the most widely used herbs because of its reputation for helping to prevent and treat colds.

stems, single pink or purple flowers, and a central cone that is usually purplish-brown in color. Of the nine echinacea species, only three are used for medicinal purposes (*Echinacea angustifolia, Echinacea pallida,* and *Echinacea purpurea*).

Its proponents believe that it can prevent colds as well as reduce their symptoms and duration. However, determining whether echinacea really works as suggested and marketed is difficult because preparations available on the market vary significantly. Different types (species) and parts (herb, root, or both) of the plant and different manufacturing methods are used, and sometimes other herbs are added. Studies investigating whether taking echinacea preparations for eight to twelve weeks prevents colds have been conducted, but the results show no clear effect. Other research has focused on whether taking echinacea preparations after the onset of cold symptoms shortens their duration or decreases their severity. Some preparations, based on the herb *Echinacea purpurea,* may be effective for this purpose in adults, though the evidence remains unclear regarding the effectiveness of other preparations or whether children may benefit.

Research suggests that echinacea is nontoxic, but use for more than eight weeks is not recommended because of a loss of effectiveness. Although echinacea currently seems safe as a supplement, allergic reactions can occur, especially in people who are allergic to related plants in the daisy family, such as ragweed, chrysanthemums, and marigolds.

## Garlic

Along with its more common use in food preparation, garlic—in both fresh and processed form—has become a popular nutritional supplement. It has grown in popularity because of associated decreases in cholesterol and its ability to help control blood pressure. It has also been shown to have potential anti-cancer effects. Used as a food item all over the world, garlic belongs to the *allium* vegetable family, along with onions, ginger, scallion, leeks, and chives. Thus, these food items have many of the same beneficial compounds as garlic.

Garlic is popular for its flavor as well as the associated benefits of preventing cancer and decreasing cholesterol.

Supplementation of garlic may cause bad breath and body odor, which has led many manufacturers to develop odorless garlic supplements. It is unclear whether these have the same benefits as natural garlic. The most dangerous side effect associated with garlic supplementation is the risk of bleeding. Therefore, supplementation should be discontinued before any surgical procedure and is not advisable for people who take anticoagulants or blood thinners.

## Ginger

The pungent, spicy *rhizome* (rootlike) ginger has been gaining considerable attention for use in the relief of nausea, vomiting, and motion sickness. It has also been reported to have anti-inflammatory properties, and although the evidence is still inconclusive, ginger may be effective in relieving morning sickness during pregnancy. However, pregnant women should not take ginger, or any supplement, until consulting their physician.

## Ginkgo Biloba

Extracts of the leaves of the maidenhair tree, **ginkgo biloba**, have long been used in China to treat many diseases and conditions. A standardized extract is widely prescribed in Germany and France to treat various conditions including memory and concentration problems, confusion, depression, anxiety, dizziness, ringing in the ears, and headache. Ginkgo biloba is thought to increase blood flow by dilating blood vessels and decreasing blood thickness, as well as improving neurotransmitter systems and decreasing oxygen free radicals. Preliminary studies strongly support the use of ginkgo biloba for mental functioning. More studies need to be conducted, but no severe side effects appear at doses of less than 200 mg/day.

## Ginseng

The root of the Asian plant **ginseng** contains active chemicals that are thought to have medicinal properties. The root is dried and used to make tablets or capsules, extracts, and teas, as well as creams or other preparations for external use. It is often added to iced teas, energy bars, and drinks. A lot of claims have been made about ginseng, but it is most commonly sold to improve overall health and boost the immune system.

Research conducted to date is still inconclusive with respect to proving any of the health claims made about ginseng. Only a few large clinical trials have been conducted; most studies have been small or have had flaws in design and reporting. The National Center for Complementary and Alternative Medicine (NCCAM) is supporting research studies to better understand its use and potential uses. NCCAM is studying how ginseng interacts with other herbs and drugs and its potential to treat chronic lung infection, impaired glucose tolerance, and Alzheimer's disease. Other studies are exploring whether ginseng may lower blood sugar levels, which may support its use by people with diabetes. However, people with diabetes should use extra caution when taking ginseng, especially if they are using medicines or taking other herbs to lower blood sugar. Side effects are rare but have been reported; they include headache, gastrointestinal upset, breast tenderness, menstrual irregularities, and high blood pressure. The difficulty in identifying side effects is that ginseng is often added to other products, such as teas and energy drinks, making it difficult to determine whether the side effect is from the ginseng or from other ingredients in the product.

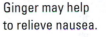

Ginger may help to relieve nausea.

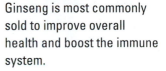

Ginseng is most commonly sold to improve overall health and boost the immune system.

Ginkgo is best known for its publicized role in enhancing mental function.

## Spirulina

**Spirulina** is a blue-green algae available in a whole food, tablet, flake or powder form. It contains a high amount of protein and is considered a complete protein, but with lower amounts of some amino acids when compared to animal sources of protein such as meat, eggs and milk. It is high in many nutrients including potassium, calcium, iron, zinc, etc. It has been promoted as having strong antioxidant and lipid-lowering properties. Most of the research done in animal models does support its cholesterol-lowering benefits. However, most of the human studies have had a small number of subjects and poor design. Spirulina is generally considered safe for humans but regular supplementation cannot be recommended at this time.

## Resveratrol

**Resveratrol** is a natural compound found in grapes, red wine, mulberries, and peanuts. It is the component responsible for the beneficial effects of red wine. It is promoted as having anticancer, anti-inflammatory, and antioxidant effects. In addition, it is said to help in preventing clotting and in promoting dilation of blood vessels by enhancing the production of nitric oxide (a powerful blood vessel dilator). Recent studies have suggested it may have beneficial effects against aging and lifestyle diseases. Most of the studies to date have been done on rats, and the benefits for humans are less conclusive. Therefore, most experts recommend consuming grapes and berries for their antioxidant benefits rather than supplementing with resveratrol.

## St. John's Wort

**St. John's wort** comes from a plant with yellow flowers called *Hypericum perforatum* and has been used for centuries to treat mental disorders as well as nerve pain. Today, St. John's wort is used to treat mild to moderate depression, anxiety, and sleep disorders. The major benefit of St. John's wort is that it costs less than prescription medications for depression, and it does not typically produce the undesirable side effects of prescription antidepressive drugs.

Results from several studies have supported the effectiveness of certain St. John's wort extracts for depression. An overview of twenty-three clinical studies found that the herb may be useful in cases of mild to moderate depression. Other recent studies have found no benefit from the use of St. John's wort for certain types of depression. The most common side effects of taking St. John's wort include dry mouth, dizziness, diarrhea, nausea, increased sensitivity to sunlight, and fatigue. As with any supplement, taking St. John's wort may interfere with the action of other drugs, so be sure to consult your physician before you begin taking it.

## Valerian

**Valerian** is a plant native to Europe and Asia that has been grown in North America. The use of valerian dates back to the Greek and Roman physicians and was mentioned by Hippocrates. In the second century valerian was prescribed for insomnia; in the sixteenth century it was used to treat nervousness, trembling, headaches, and heart palpitations. Currently, it is used as a mild sedative and sleeping agent. Studies conducted on the effectiveness of valerian for insomnia have been poorly controlled and therefore are inconclusive. Until more well-controlled studies can be done, experts are not certain whether valerian works. To date, no adverse side effects have been reported in humans. However, not enough studies have been done to conclude that it is harmless.

### Yohimbine

**Yohimbine** comes from the bark of the West African tree *Pausinystalia yohimbe*. It has been used to treat sexual side effects caused by some antidepressants, to increase female sex drive, and to treat very low blood pressure and dry mouth. It is probably best known, however, for its reputation as an aphrodisiac. This regard is based primarily on testimonials, as its true effect on the sex drive of humans has not been properly demonstrated. However, for more than seventy years, yohimbine has been used to treat male sexual difficulties.

The use of yohimbine is based on evidence from studies using the prescription drug yohimbine hydrochloride, which appears to effectively treat male impotence. The supplemental form is made from the bark, and although yohimbine is present in yohimbe bark extract, levels are variable and often very low. Yohimbe bark extract has not been shown to share the effects of yohimbine hydrochloride. Therefore, although yohimbe bark has been used traditionally to reduce male erectile dysfunction, not enough scientific evidence exists to form a conclusion. Safety has not been evaluated scientifically, but many adverse side effects have been reported, such as excessive sweating, facial flushing, increased heart rate and blood pressure, restlessness, irritability, shakes, and increased anxiety.

**Want to know more?**
To learn more about the herbs mentioned in this chapter—and many others—go to the text website at http://webcom8 .grtxle.com/nutrition and click on the Chapters button. Select Chapter 11.

### Before you go on . . .
1. Name and define three examples of herbal supplements.
2. Cranberries may be beneficial in treating what conditions?
3. For what condition is garlic recommended, and what are its potential negative side effects?
4. What do the early studies of ginkgo suggest as one of its uses?

## Real People, Real Strategies

Marrissa's roommate was wise to tell her to be skeptical of the claims made about the weight-loss product she was planning to try. Marissa first went to the FDA's website to see whether any adverse events had been reported about the supplement or any of its listed ingredients. She was shocked to discover that supplements did not have to undergo strict research and investigation before appearing on the shelf. She wondered how and whether the public could be protected, given that the responsibility for ensuring that dietary supplements are safe is left to the manufacturers. She erroneously assumed that supplements were treated like other medicines she saw on shelves at the pharmacy. She decided that Ashley was right and that before taking any supplement she needed to be fully informed of its potential effects, good and bad. She found helpful information on the web, where tips on how to evaluate a supplement are provided. These tips warned her against chasing the latest "quick fix" and pointed out that when the claim for a supplement sounds too good to be true, it probably is. Marissa ultimately and wisely concluded that the best and safest way to shed the weight she needed to lose was through diet and daily exercise (see Chapter 7).

## Chapter Summary

- Supplements are regulated under the Dietary Supplement Health and Education Act of 1994 (DSHEA).
- Since the passing of the DSHEA, dietary supplements are defined as a product (other than tobacco) intended to supplement the diet that contains one or more of the following dietary ingredients: a vitamin; a mineral; an herb or other botanical; an amino acid; a dietary substance used to supplement the diet by increasing the total dietary intake; or a concentrate, metabolite, constituent, extract, or combination of these ingredients.
- The FDA does not approve supplements before they are marketed. It gets involved only in postmarketing surveillance and, therefore, handles claims of adverse effects only after a supplement is made available to consumers.
- The Federal Trade Commission monitors the advertising and labeling of supplements.
- Manufacturers of supplements have to make sure that product label information is truthful and not misleading. However, the term *truthful* is not clearly defined.
- Because no strict regulations protect consumers from potentially harmful supplements, it is up to you, the consumer, to beware.
- Beware of popular "energy drinks," as they are marketed to look like health or sports drinks but often contain amounts of caffeine higher than most sodas. In addition, they contain other stimulants that may lead to negative side effects such as rapid heart rate, elevated blood pressure, and dehydration.
- Before taking a supplement, check with your health care practitioner, look at your entire dietary intake, and remember that if something seems too good to be true, it probably is.

- Many false and fraudulent claims are made about the effectiveness of supplements. Be wary of any statements asserting that the product is a quick and effective "cure-all" or diagnostic tool for a wide variety of ailments. Other tips that the claim you are reading may be false include undocumented case histories or personal testimonials by consumers or doctors claiming amazing results; "limited availability" and advance-payment requirements; and promises of no-risk "money-back guarantees."
- When researching information about supplements on the Internet, be sure the sites you check are reputable.
- Vitamin and mineral supplements are the most popular type of supplement. Limited evidence suggests that people who are healthy will achieve additional protection against disease by supplementing above the DRI.
- Limited evidence suggests that taking a multivitamin and mineral supplement at or below 100 percent of the DRI does not have harmful side effects. However, few studies have assessed the long-term effects in healthy people.
- Although most people get plenty of protein and amino acids from their diet, consuming essential amino acids immediately after exercise may provide a small benefit.
- Herbs and botanicals are becoming more and more popular. They are supplements that contain extracts or active ingredients from the roots, berries, seeds, stems, leaves, buds, or flowers of plants.
- It is a common misconception that supplements made from plants are safe because they are "natural" or "organic."
- Consult your health care practitioner before taking any supplement, vitamin, herb, and so on, just as you would before taking any medication.

## Key Terms

**arginine** (AR-jin-een) A conditionally essential amino acid. Supplementation appears most beneficial for people who have heart disease, are recovering from trauma, or have a compromised immune function. (p. 362)

**aspartic acid** or **aspartate** (uh-SPAR-tick AS-id; AS-par-tate) A non-essential amino acid used to make urea, proteins, glycogen, and energy. (p. 362)

**black cohosh** A member of the buttercup family that is also called black snakeroot, macrotys, bugbane, bugwort, rattleroot, and rattleweed. It has a history of use for rheumatism (arthritis and muscle pain), but it has been used more recently to treat postmenopausal symptoms. (p. 369)

**boron** A trace element found in foods such as avocados, peanut butter, peanuts, prune and grape juice, chocolate powder, wine, pecans, and raisin bran cereals. (p. 359)

**branched-chain amino acids (BCAAs)** The essential amino acids—leucine, isoleucine, and valine—that are different from other amino acids because they can be used for energy directly in the muscle, without having to go to the liver to be broken down during exercise. (p. 362)

**carnitine** (CAR-nih-teen) The substance that transports long-chain fatty acids into the mitochondria for metabolism. Carnitine supplementation is said to enhance fat burning, but it appears to be ineffective. (p. 349)

**carotenoids** (kuh-ROT-en-oyds) The recognizable form of coloring pigment in plants such as carrots and sweet potatoes. The carotenoid family includes molecules such as alpha-, beta-, and gamma-carotene; lutein; zeaxanthin; lycopene; cryptoxanthin; vioaxanthin; and bixin. As many as 450 different carotenoids may exist. (p. 359)

**chromium**  A trace mineral that is widely distributed in the food supply, though most foods provide only small amounts (less than 2 micrograms per serving). Meat and whole-grain products, as well as some fruits, vegetables, and spices, are relatively good sources. (p. 360)

**coenzyme $Q_{10}$ (ubiquinone)**  A fat-soluble vitamin-like substance made in the body. It is an antioxidant and a coenzyme for several of the key enzymatic steps in the production of energy within the cell. (p. 365)

**creatine**  (KREE-uh-teen) Part of creatine phosphate, the key component of the immediate energy system used primarily during sporting events lasting thirty seconds or less. It is made in the body and can be consumed in the diet, mostly from meat and fish. (p. 367)

**dehydroepiandrosterone (DHEA)**  (dee-hy-droh-ep-ee-ann-DRAHS-ter-own) A steroid hormone that is synthesized and secreted by the adrenal glands. (p. 350)

**Dietary Supplement Health and Education Act of 1994 (DSHEA)**  A federal law that significantly changed the role the FDA plays in supplement regulation and further expanded the formal definition of "dietary supplement." (p. 347)

**echinacea**  (ek-ih-NAYSH-uh) A plant with tall stems, single pink or purple flowers, and a central cone that is usually purplish-brown in color. It is believed to reduce the symptoms and duration of a cold. (p. 369)

**ephedra**  (ef-ED-ruh) An herbal stimulant used for respiratory illnesses such as asthma because it helps open the airways. It has also been marketed for weight loss and performance enhancement. Side effects include high blood pressure, heart irregularities, and nausea. (p. 348)

**Federal Trade Commission**  The federal agency that has the responsibility for monitoring the accuracy of the advertising and labeling of supplements. (p. 349)

**ginkgo biloba**  (GINK-go bye-LOBE-uh) An extract of the leaves of the maidenhair tree that has long been used in China to treat many diseases and conditions. Ginkgo is thought to increase blood flow by dilating blood vessels and decreasing blood thickness, as well as modifying neurotransmitter systems and decreasing oxygen free radicals. (p. 371)

**ginseng**  The root of the Asian ginseng plant; it is said to improve overall health and well-being. (p. 371)

**glucosamine chondroitin**  (gloo-KOSE-uh-meen kon-DROIT-in) Glucosamine is thought to stimulate the production and repair of cartilage; chondroitin is a cartilage component that is thought to promote water retention and elasticity and to inhibit the enzymes that break down cartilage. The combination is marketed to help with symptoms of osteoarthritis. (p. 363)

**glutamine**  (GLOO-tuh-meen) A nonessential amino acid that is abundant in the body. Supplementation may enhance immune system function and recovery after exhaustive exercise, surgery, or trauma. (p. 363)

**glycerol**  An organic compound that is part of triacylglycerols (triglycerides or fats) and phospholipids. It is also used as a sweetener in syrups, liquors, and some foods. Glycerol combined with water intake has been suggested to help prevent dehydration in endurance athletes who exercise in hot, humid environments. (p. 367)

**herbs and botanicals**  Supplements that contain extracts or active ingredients from the roots, berries, seeds, stems, leaves, buds, or flowers of plants. (p. 368)

**HMB (beta-hydroxy beta-methylbutyrate)**  A product of the breakdown of the essential amino acid leucine. It is synthesized naturally in humans and is also available in some foods (such as citrus fruits and catfish). It is marketed to prevent muscle breakdown associated with resistance training, to enhance strength, and to decrease body fat. (p. 368)

**St. John's wort**  The extract of a plant with yellow flowers called *Hypericum perforatum;*

it has been used for centuries to treat mental disorders such as depression as well as nerve pain. (p. 372)

**valerian** A plant native to Europe and Asia that has been grown in North America; it has been used as a treatment for insomnia. (p. 372)

**vanadium** (vuh-NAY-dee-um) A trace mineral found in mushrooms, shellfish, black pepper, parsley, dill seed, and some processed foods. (p. 360)

**whey** A by-product of cheese making that is used as a source of protein in many protein supplements. (p. 361)

**yohimbine** (yoh-HIM-been) An extract of the bark of the West African tree *Pausinystalia yohimbe* that is best known as an aphrodisiac. It has also been used to treat sexual side effects caused by some antidepressants, to increase female sex drive, and to treat very low blood pressure and dry mouth. (p. 373)

# Chapter Quiz

1. Who is responsible for the safety of supplements that are sold to the public?

   a. the FDA

   b. the Federal Trade Commission

   c. the manufacturer

   d. the National Institutes of Health

2. What role does the FDA play in ensuring that supplements are safe for consumers?

   a. It requires that all supplements be tested prior to selling.

   b. It requires manufacturers to register their supplements with the FDA.

   c. It is not involved at all.

   d. It handles claims against a supplement after it is on the market.

3. The first step in deciding whether a claim made about a certain supplement has any value is

   a. taking the supplement and stopping use if you experience any side effects.

   b. checking the FDA's website to see if it has approved the supplement.

   c. doing some research to determine its safety and effectiveness.

   d. asking a friend who took the same supplement whether it was effective.

4. How can you tell if a claim made about a supplement is fraudulent?

   a. Read the claim carefully and look for words such as "cure-all" and "miraculous."

   b. See if any studies have been reported in reputable journals to support the claim.

   c. Check with your doctor.

   d. all of the above

5. Why isn't it a good idea to drink Red Bull mixed with vodka?

   a. The combination will make you more dehydrated than drinking one or the other alone.

   b. The combination produces an unpleasant taste.

   c. Drinking a stimulant (Red Bull) with a depressant (vodka) may mask the effects of alcohol, making you feel more sober than you really are.

   d. both a and c

6. Which of the following is true about vitamin and mineral supplements?

   a. You should try to get the vitamins and minerals you need from your diet.

   b. It is okay to take supplements instead of eating a balanced diet.

   c. Everybody should take a vitamin and mineral supplement.

   d. Vitamin and mineral supplements help prevent disease in healthy people.

7. When considering amino acid supplementation, one should consider that

   a. most Americans already consume plenty of amino acids and protein.

   b. everybody can benefit from extra protein.

c. the more amino acids, the better.

d. amino acids make you bigger, so if you don't want to get bigger, don't take them.

8. Which of the following statements regarding herbs and botanicals is false?

a. Just because they are natural does not mean they are safe, so you should investigate their safety just as you should for all supplements.

b. There is a need for further research on many of the most widely used herbs and botanicals.

c. They are natural, so therefore they are safe.

d. They can interact with other medications, so you should check with your doctor before taking them.

9. What is whey protein?

a. a superior form of protein used for building muscle mass

b. part of what is left over when you make cheese

c. an herb

d. an amino acid

10. For what condition are cranberries said to be beneficial?

a. sexual dysfunction

b. Parkinson's disease

c. urinary tract infections

d. postmenopausal symptoms

## < Here's Where You've Been

*The following topics were introduced in preceding chapters and are related to concepts we'll discuss in Chapter 12. Be certain that you're familiar with them before proceeding.*

- Carbohydrates and proteins provide 4 kcal per gram; fats provide 9 kcal per gram. (Chapters 1, 3, 4, and 5)
- Water and electrolyte balance are tightly regulated by the body, and several hormones are responsible for this regulation. (Chapter 8)
- Water-soluble vitamins are excreted in the urine rapidly, whereas fat-soluble vitamins are stored. (Chapter 9)
- A lack of vitamins and minerals results in deficiency signs that are unique for that nutrient. (Chapters 9 and 10)
- Zinc is essential for the metabolism of alcohol. (Chapter 10)

## Here's Where You're Going >

*The following topics and concepts are the ones we'll emphasize in Chapter 12.*

- Alcohol is not an essential nutrient, but it does provide calories.
- Alcohol abuse and its negative health effects are a major societal problem.
- Alcohol is broken down by the body but can damage organs in the process and lead to cardiovascular disease and cancer.
- The quality of life is significantly decreased among those who abuse alcohol.
- Some evidence indicates that moderate intake of wine may have health benefits that are due to nonalcohol components.

## Real People, Real Choices

Mark Filmyer is a 22-year-old math major who attends a major state university in Ohio. Although he is concerned about his health and weight, that concern goes only so far. His only exercise is walking from his apartment to and from classes and around campus. He belongs to a campus fraternity and has always enjoyed the active and varied social life a large university offers. When Thursday night rolls around, Mark and some of his friends like to start celebrating the weekend a bit early. The group usually begins the party by visiting one of their favorite nighttime establishments where alcohol is served. Mark and his friends drink beer much of the evening, starting around 8 P.M. and typically ending around midnight.

Recently, Mark had a late appointment (on a Thursday) with one of his professors, which resulted in his skipping dinner. He did have a big lunch that day, so he didn't feel very hungry when the party group gathered to go out. During the evening he experienced a little light-headedness, but he was able to stay out until the group had had enough. He finally woke up Friday morning around 10 A.M. and realized that he was going to miss his first class. Although he had slept for ten hours, his head was throbbing with a headache, his mouth was dry, and he felt both dizzy and shaky. Mark really didn't understand why he felt so awful just because he had five or six beers. He did remember passing out when he returned to his apartment. He also recalled that he'd skipped dinner, but because he really hadn't been hungry the night before, he didn't associate his severe hangover with the missed meal. Should he have? What risks do Mark's weekly drinking sessions pose to his health, and what advice in terms of nutrition, exercise, and alcohol consumption would you give him?

Do you know someone with a similar experience to Mark's? Every college population includes students who like to socialize and frequently overdo the use of alcohol. Usually, the next day is a similar story to Mark's, and the questions are the same. Did I drink that much? Why do I feel so bad? Not only did Mark feel awful, he ended up missing class. In this chapter, we will explore why Mark felt so bad and discuss the warning signs for excessive alcohol consumption.

Do you think alcohol is a nutrient? Most nutritionists insist that it is *not*, because it does not promote growth or maintenance, nor does it have any critical function in the body. As you may remember, nutrients promote growth and maintenance of your body and organs. Although it does not promote growth or maintenance, it does provide calories, thus we discuss alcohol in this text. Alcohol provides approximately 7 kcal per gram—less than the 9 kcal per gram for fat, but greater than the 4 kcal per gram for carbohydrate or protein.

Consuming alcohol as an energy source is *not* recommended. It is clearly not an essential nutrient, because calories can be obtained from carbohydrates, protein, and fats. Overconsumption often leads to many health problems and social and mental debilitation. Chronic drinkers have many nutritional problems, as alcohol intake can depress the appetite, interfere with absorption, and increase excretion of several vitamins and minerals. Once alcohol is absorbed by the body, it can also interfere with the ability of tissues and cells to fully utilize nutrients.

Alcohol is also a **diuretic**. A diuretic is a compound that causes you to urinate more and can lead to dehydration. Alcohol can also cause an increased loss of nutrients through the urine, particularly the water-soluble vitamins. Liver damage is a well-recognized result of excess alcohol consumption, and even moderate alcohol consumption can lead to health problems. On the other hand, research studies have suggested that modest wine consumption (no more than two 3-oz. glasses per day for men, or one glass for women) may provide certain health benefits. Thus, a major challenge for nutritionists is to determine how much alcohol is excessive to human health and whether its intake via beverages such as wine should be recommended to promote good health.

## Alcohol Production

### How Alcoholic Beverages Are Made

There are three main classes of alcoholic beverages: beer, wine, and distilled spirits or hard liquor. The process in making each class of beverage is quite different. Beer is made from grain, malt, hops, yeast, and water. Fermentation of grains with yeast produces alcohol. Fermentation is the process by which yeast and a simple carbohydrate such as glucose react with one another. Fermentation is normally the breakdown of glucose into smaller molecules by enzymes in the yeast organism. The alcohol content of beer in the United States is generally between 3 and 6 percent, although some can be as high as 14 percent. Grain drinks with a higher level of alcohol are called malt, lager, or ale.

Wine making has a long history. A number of fruits are used to make wine, including over a

Beverages containing alcohol have been around almost since the beginning of civilization. The alcohol content varies depending on the type of beverage and the raw ingredients and processes used in making each of them.

Commercial wines are typically made and fermented in large stainless steel tanks or oak barrels of various sizes.

hundred varieties of grapes, numerous other berries, and fruits such as apples and peaches. The fruits are crushed, and yeast may or may not be added. When yeast is added, fermentation occurs to produce alcohol from the fruit sugars. Darker-colored wines are normally produced through longer contact of the juice with the fruit's skins. As a result, these wines may also contain more of the plant's healthy chemicals. Most wines made in the United States typically contain about 8–15 percent alcohol. Fortified wines commonly, but not always, have an alcohol content higher than 14 percent. A fortified wine, such as sherry, contains added alcohol or brandy to increase the total alcohol content to approximately 20 percent. Lighter wines such as those made from the white Riesling grape typically contain 8–9 percent alcohol, whereas a Merlot (wine made from a red grape of the same name) generally has 12–15 percent alcohol, and more robust wines such as Syrah and Zinfandel may have approximately 15–17 percent alcohol.

Distilled spirits go through an added step beyond the fermentation process. The conversion of fruit sugars to alcohol of most wines typically stops when the alcohol content reaches 14 percent. However, distillation leads to a different type of beverage with a higher alcohol content. Distillation involves heating the substance of choice and capturing the steam released. The steam contains less water and more alcohol when it is cooled. A number of different grains and other plant-derived products are used for distilled spirits, including corn (bourbon), potatoes (vodka), sugar cane (rum), and malts/grains (scotch). In the case of brandy, wine is used as the base and is distilled into a more concentrated alcohol product.

## Proof and Percentage of Alcohol

When labeling distilled spirits, the word *proof* is often used to indicate the relative alcohol content. Proof is related to the percentage of alcohol the beverage contains. If a beverage contains 40 percent alcohol, it is 80 proof. If it is 50 percent alcohol, it is 100 proof. Thus, to determine the percentage of alcohol, simply divide the proof by 2. Typically, the alcohol content in wines is stated as a percentage rather than using the term *proof*.

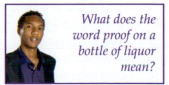

*What does the word proof on a bottle of liquor mean?*

Some consumers measure the quality of a beverage by the proof.

Never consume alcohol on an empty stomach. A full stomach significantly slows absorption of alcohol into the blood.

 **Want to know more?**
To learn more about blood alcohol concentration and the legal limit in other countries, go to the text website at http://webcom8.grtxle.com/nutrition and click on the Chapters button. Select Chapter 12.

All states have cracked down on both underage drinking and drinking and driving under the influence of alcohol. Sobriety tests such as this one are common.

How did the word *proof* come about? The term dates back several centuries. Alcohol is less dense than water, so the more alcohol, the less dense the beverage. Beverages with a lot of alcohol were highly prized (and still are). To determine the relative quality of a beverage in terms of alcohol content, one would try to ignite it with gunpowder. Some of the liquid was poured onto black gunpowder and an attempt to ignite it was made. If the mixture ignited, this was said to be "proof" that the beverage had a high enough alcohol content to be of good quality. However, this also means that there is more alcohol that can affect your mental abilities and decrease your health. A higher proof does not mean it is better for you.

## Alcohol Consumption and Its Influence on Blood Alcohol Concentration (BAC)

**Blood alcohol concentration (BAC)**, sometimes referred to as *blood alcohol level (BAL)*, is simply the percentage of alcohol present in your blood. A blood alcohol level of 0.1 percent means that there is one part alcohol for 1,000 parts blood in the body (one divided by 1,000 = 0.001 or 0.1 percent). The higher the level, the more negative physiological effects on the body. How much a single drink will raise your blood alcohol level depends on several factors, such as whether you are male or female, how much you weigh, whether you have eaten or have consumed the alcohol on an empty stomach, and your physical condition. The U.S. Department of Health and Human Services defines "one drink" as 1.5 oz. of 80-proof liquor, 12 oz. of regular beer, or 5 oz. of table wine. Each drink contains roughly the same amount of alcohol (about 0.5 oz.). That is why there is such a difference in serving sizes for these various drinks. Table 12.1 provides a guide to how the number of drinks per hour can affect your BAC, based on your sex and body weight. The legal driving limit for blood alcohol concentration in all fifty states and the District of Columbia is now

| Table 12.1 | Blood Alcohol Concentration Levels (Percent) | | | | | | | |
| --- | --- | --- | --- | --- | --- | --- | --- | --- |
| | **Weight in Pounds** | | | | | | | |
| **No. of Drinks in 1 Hour** | **100** | **120** | **140** | **160** | **180** | **200** | **220** | **240** |
| **Women** | | | | | | | | |
| 1 | 0.05 | 0.04 | 0.04 | 0.03 | 0.03 | 0.03 | 0.02 | 0.02 |
| 2 | 0.10 | 0.08 | 0.07 | 0.06 | 0.06 | 0.05 | 0.05 | 0.04 |
| 3 | 0.15 | 0.13 | 0.11 | 0.10 | 0.08 | 0.08 | 0.07 | 0.06 |
| 4 | 0.20 | 0.17 | 0.15 | 0.13 | 0.11 | 0.10 | 0.09 | 0.09 |
| 5 | 0.25 | 0.21 | 0.18 | 0.16 | 0.14 | 0.13 | 0.12 | 0.11 |
| 6 | 0.30 | 0.26 | 0.22 | 0.19 | 0.17 | 0.15 | 0.14 | 0.13 |
| 7 | 0.36 | 0.30 | 0.26 | 0.22 | 0.20 | 0.18 | 0.16 | 0.15 |
| 8 | 0.41 | 0.33 | 0.29 | 0.26 | 0.23 | 0.20 | 0.19 | 0.17 |
| 9 | 0.46 | 0.38 | 0.33 | 0.29 | 0.26 | 0.23 | 0.21 | 0.19 |
| 10 | 0.51 | 0.42 | 0.36 | 0.32 | 0.28 | 0.25 | 0.23 | 0.21 |
| 11 | 0.56 | 0.46 | 0.40 | 0.35 | 0.31 | 0.27 | 0.25 | 0.23 |
| 12 | 0.61 | 0.50 | 0.43 | 0.37 | 0.33 | 0.30 | 0.28 | 0.25 |
| 13 | 0.66 | 0.55 | 0.47 | 0.40 | 0.36 | 0.32 | 0.30 | 0.27 |
| 14 | 0.71 | 0.59 | 0.51 | 0.43 | 0.39 | 0.35 | 0.32 | 0.29 |
| 15 | 0.76 | 0.63 | 0.55 | 0.46 | 0.42 | 0.37 | 0.35 | 0.32 |
| **Men** | | | | | | | | |
| 1 | 0.04 | 0.04 | 0.03 | 0.03 | 0.02 | 0.02 | 0.02 | 0.02 |
| 2 | 0.09 | 0.07 | 0.06 | 0.05 | 0.05 | 0.04 | 0.04 | 0.04 |
| 3 | 0.13 | 0.11 | 0.09 | 0.08 | 0.07 | 0.07 | 0.06 | 0.05 |
| 4 | 0.17 | 0.15 | 0.13 | 0.11 | 0.10 | 0.09 | 0.08 | 0.07 |
| 5 | 0.22 | 0.18 | 0.16 | 0.14 | 0.12 | 0.11 | 0.10 | 0.09 |
| 6 | 0.26 | 0.22 | 0.19 | 0.16 | 0.15 | 0.13 | 0.12 | 0.11 |
| 7 | 0.30 | 0.25 | 0.22 | 0.19 | 0.17 | 0.15 | 0.14 | 0.13 |
| 8 | 0.35 | 0.29 | 0.25 | 0.22 | 0.19 | 0.17 | 0.16 | 0.14 |
| 9 | 0.37 | 0.32 | 0.26 | 0.24 | 0.20 | 0.19 | 0.17 | 0.15 |
| 10 | 0.39 | 0.35 | 0.28 | 0.25 | 0.22 | 0.20 | 0.18 | 0.16 |
| 11 | 0.48 | 0.40 | 0.34 | 0.30 | 0.26 | 0.24 | 0.22 | 0.20 |
| 12 | 0.53 | 0.43 | 0.37 | 0.32 | 0.29 | 0.26 | 0.24 | 0.21 |
| 13 | 0.57 | 0.47 | 0.40 | 0.35 | 0.31 | 0.29 | 0.26 | 0.23 |
| 14 | 0.62 | 0.50 | 0.43 | 0.37 | 0.34 | 0.31 | 0.28 | 0.25 |
| 15 | 0.66 | 0.54 | 0.47 | 0.40 | 0.36 | 0.34 | 0.30 | 0.27 |

*Source:* http://www.ou.edu/oupd/bac.htm

0.08 percent. A woman who weighs 100 lbs. could be over the legal limit with just two drinks in one hour.

The question of different effects that varying levels of blood alcohol concentration (BAC) may have on you may arise. Table 12.2 lists some effects that can occur at certain levels of BAC.

| **Table 12.2** | **Blood Alcohol Level and Behavioral Effects** |
|---|---|
| **BAC%** | **Behavioral Effect(s)** |
| 0.02–0.03 | Alcohol starts to relax the drinker. |
| 0.04 | Often drinkers at this stage are relaxed, happier, chatty. |
| 0.05 | Skills begin to diminish, as far as judgment, attention, and control. Decision-making ability (such as whether to drive) is impaired, as are sensory-motor skills. |
| 0.08 | All states recognize this as the legal point of intoxication. Driving skills and coordination are impaired. |
| 0.10–0.125 | Several effects are likely at this point, such as balance, vision, speech, and control problems. Reaction time increases. |
| 0.12–0.15 | Peripheral vision is diminished, so less detail is visible. Balance and coordination are problematic. A sense of tiredness, displays of unstable emotions, diminished perception, memory, and comprehension are seen at this level. A person may vomit if not accustomed to drinking or if this BAC level has been reached too quickly. |
| 0.18–0.25 | Often the drinker is in a state of apathy and lethargy, and is less likely to feel pain. Vision is certainly diminished in the areas of color, form, motion and dimensions. Drinkers are intense with emotions, confused, dizzy, and disoriented. Walking is often difficult or impossible as muscle coordination is diminished and speech is slurred. |
| 0.25–0.30 | Drinkers may lose consciousness during this stage. They have almost completely lost motor functions, have little response to stimuli, can't stand or walk, and experience vomiting and incontinence. |
| 0.30–0.50 | Once the BAC reaches 0.45 percent, alcohol poisoning is almost always fatal, and death may occur at a level of 0.37 percent. Unconsciousness, diminished or absent reflexes, lower than normal body temperature, circulatory and respiratory problems and incontinence commonly occur. |

Do you think a cup of black coffee will sober you up? Think again!

### Alcohol Poisoning—The Ultimate Danger

Numerous deaths have resulted from excessive alcohol intake among college students. A recent well-known case involved a 19-year-old Colorado State University student, Samantha Spady, who died of alcohol poisoning, with a BAC of 0.436 percent. Investigation by the coroner's office suggested that she had consumed alcohol over an eleven-hour period and ended the day at a fraternity house, where she consumed significant additional amounts of alcohol. Drinking games were also being played at the fraternity house. She had consumed an amount of alcohol equivalent to thirty to forty 12-oz. beers.

### ■ Myths and Legends

*Will drinking coffee make you sober?*

Many people think that you can "sober up" someone who is under the influence of alcohol by having him or her consume coffee, particularly black coffee. Many drinking establishments and other places where alcohol is served keep coffee on hand for this purpose. The active ingredient in coffee, caffeine, does stimulate the central nervous system. But does giving black coffee to an intoxicated person really help? According to the National Safety Council, neither coffee nor caffeine is helpful in sobering an individual who is under the influence of alcohol. In fact, the council reports that consuming coffee when inebriated may actually increase alcohol's adverse effects. Only time will help, as most alcohol is broken down gradually in the liver or expelled from the body through respiration (breathing) or urine. The bottom line on consuming coffee when intoxicated is that you will be a wide-awake drunk! ■

## Levels of Consumption

In establishing relative alcohol consumption, the Centers for Disease Control (CDC) uses the following definitions for light, moderate, and binge drinking:

- Light use is up to three drinks per week.
- Moderate use is four to fourteen drinks a week for men and four to seven drinks a week for women.
- Heavy use is more than fourteen drinks a week for men and more than seven drinks a week for women.
- Binge drinking usually corresponds to more than four drinks on a single occasion for men or more than three drinks on a single occasion for women, generally within about two hours.

Based on these definitions, of those who do drink, 7 percent are heavy drinkers, 22 percent are moderate drinkers, and 71 percent are light drinkers.

### What Is "Moderate"?

Despite the CDC's definitions, health experts do not agree on what constitutes *moderate* alcohol consumption. The term *moderate* can mean different things to different people. For example, some say it is no more than one drink per day, whereas others interpret it as four or fewer drinks per day. Other factors include age, gender, alcohol content, and the type of beverage consumed: beer, wine, or distilled spirits. The USDA *Dietary Guidelines* state that moderate intake consists of one serving per day for women and two for men. Generally speaking, this is the standard normally used when using the term *moderate* in regard to alcohol consumption.

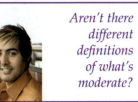

*Aren't there different definitions of what's moderate?*

A national epidemic? Concerns over an increase in the number of college students who consume alcohol several times a week have recently received considerable attention in the media and from college administrators. Does this scene look familiar to you? What would you suggest is the best way to address this problem?

### ■ To Supplement or Not

*Will supplements prevent or cure a hangover?*

This topic has two parts. First, does taking supplements prevent or lessen a hangover? Second, should you take supplements before or even after excess drinking? The latter question is much easier to answer. In general it is not a bad idea to take a supplement, particularly the B vitamins and vitamin C, because they are water soluble and excess loss can occur because of increased urination with alcohol intake. As noted earlier, alcohol is a diuretic, which causes the body

A chaser supplement to cure a hangover. Advice: save your money!

to excrete more fluid. More water-soluble vitamins are lost with alcohol intake, and taking a supplement with B vitamins or vitamin C can replace this loss. However, many products are being marketed as "chaser" supplements designed to prevent hangovers. The bottom line, though, is that these products are not likely to prevent or diminish the physical symptoms of a hangover. Moreover, it is really not clear what causes a hangover—possibly alcohol itself, dehydration, the breakdown products, the body's process of removing the ethanol, or a combination of these factors. ■

**Before you go on . . .**

1. In the United States, what is the typical range of alcohol content in beer, expressed as a percentage?
2. What is the relationship between percentage of alcohol and the term *proof*?
3. What does BAC stand for, and what do the numbers mean?
4. Give the CDC's definitions of light, moderate, heavy, and binge drinking.

## Digestion and Metabolism

### Alcohol, Absorption, and the Liver

Alcohol is absorbed by the gastrointestinal tract, primarily the stomach, and then enters the bloodstream. In fact, the body absorbs alcohol more rapidly than other nutrients. Moreover, when consumed on an empty stomach, alcohol enters the bloodstream faster than when the stomach is full.

The only organ in the body capable of metabolizing alcohol is the liver. Ninety percent of blood alcohol is metabolized in the liver (Figure 12.1). The remaining 10 percent is eliminated through the lungs and urine. Once alcohol is absorbed, it can enter the body's liver cells and be converted to **acetaldehyde**, which is a toxic compound. The catalyst for this conversion is an enzyme, **alcohol dehydrogenase**. Alcohol dehydrogenase requires zinc in order to function properly. The acetaldehyde produced is then "detoxified" through another enzymatic reaction. The enzyme **aldehyde dehydrogenase 2** converts ethanol to *acetic acid*. Acetic acid is not toxic and can be metabolized by the body for energy or used to make fat. A fatty liver can result from these reactions (see the Nutrition and Disease feature). However, some individuals lack this enzyme and therefore cannot metabolize ethanol. As a result, they cannot consume alcohol without major mental impairment and damage to their organs. Asians, Native Americans, and other groups tend to have a higher percentage of individuals without the aldehyde dehydrogenase 2 enzyme.

The direct harmful effects of alcohol consumption are produced by acetaldehyde. This compound is thought to damage the liver mitochondria and lead to **hepatitis** (inflammation of the liver). It may also cause hardening and scarring of the liver which we call **cirrhosis**. Advanced cirrhosis is irreversible. In the brain, alcohol is thought to interfere with enzymes involved with neurotransmitter synthesis so that slightly different compounds are produced, which then react with acetaldehyde to produce morphinelike compounds. This may help explain why alcohol becomes so addictive. The following Nutrition and Disease feature more thoroughly examines alcohol's effects on the liver.

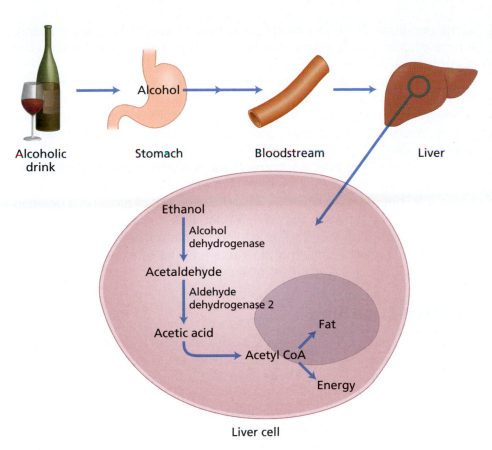

**Figure 12.1** Alcohol is absorbed in the stomach. From the stomach the alcohol enters the bloodstream and then travels through the bloodstream into the liver, where liver cells break it down. When alcohol is broken down by the liver, it is either used as a source of energy or, more likely, converted to fat.

## ◾ Nutrition and Disease
### *Alcohol and liver disease*

Alcohol can affect many organs. As we have already observed, the central nervous system is impaired by alcohol intake. However, of the many potential health consequences of alcoholism, the most well known is its impact on the liver. Remember that alcohol goes to the liver, where it is processed, and its metabolites are toxic to cells. Three types of liver conditions/diseases may result from alcohol abuse:

1. Fatty liver
2. Hepatitis
3. Cirrhosis

Fatty liver is simply the accumulation of fat within liver cells. For reasons other than alcohol consumption, obese people can experience the

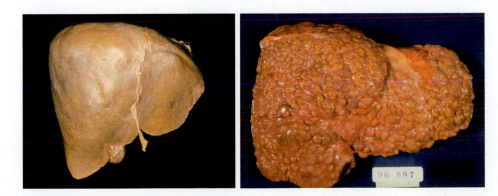

The effects of long-term alcohol consumption on the liver. Cirrhosis of the liver (right) may be irreversible if the damage is severe. A healthy liver is shown on the left.

same condition. The good thing here is that if the person stops drinking, it is reversible. This condition can lead to inflammation of the liver in the short term.

Hepatitis is an inflammation of the liver that can cause fluid accumulation in the abdomen, jaundice (yellowing of the skin), and neurological problems when the condition advances and results in liver failure. Hepatitis is reversible if the person abstains from alcohol and consumes an adequate diet.

In cirrhosis, the liver becomes hardened and scarred. Cirrhosis is a serious, often fatal liver condition. The early stage of liver cirrhosis is reversible, but not the late stage. Ten to 15 percent of alcoholics develop liver cirrhosis by the time they die. In fact, liver cirrhosis resulting from alcohol abuse is one of the ten leading causes of death in the United States. Women who consume the same amount of alcohol as men are even more likely to develop liver disease. ■

## Alcohol and the Brain

Alcohol has a profound impact on the brain's ability to function that results in behavior changes. One of the prime effects of alcohol is that the brain's inhibiting processes are decreased. People often appear more relaxed and say things they normally would not without alcohol. The frontal lobe, the area of the brain that handles reasoning and judgment, is compromised. As more alcohol is consumed, other parts of the brain that control speech, vision, and muscle movement are impaired. Intoxicated people may be unable to walk and thus stagger; they slur their speech; and their eyes may not be able to focus. With higher alcohol levels in the blood and consequently in the brain, the parts of the brain that control respiration and heart contractions are impaired, and the person becomes unconscious. If too much alcohol has been consumed before unconsciousness, the impact could be fatal. In essence, alcohol is a poison.

### ■ What's Hot
#### *Binge drinking on college campuses*
Binge drinking has steadily increased among adolescents and young adults. As noted earlier, binge drinking usually corresponds to more than 5 drinks on a single occasion for men or more than three drinks on a single occasion for women, generally within about two hours. Today, research indicates that binge drinking may begin as early as age 12. It is higher in males than females, but that is not to say that females do not do their share of binge drinking. The 21-to-25 age group has the highest percentage of binge drinkers, about 46 percent overall. Among college students, one recent study reported that half admitted having four to five drinks in one sitting within a two-week period. Those living in fraternity or sorority houses had the largest incidence, with 86 percent and 80 percent, respectively, admitting to having engaged in an episode of binge drinking. The behavior is highest among whites and lowest among African Americans.

Many college students who binge drink do not realize that they are in fact "binge drinking." Many actually consider themselves light to moderate drinkers. Studies also show that college students who binge drink have more difficulties in their studies and experience depression and anxiety more frequently. Binge drinkers may become abusive to

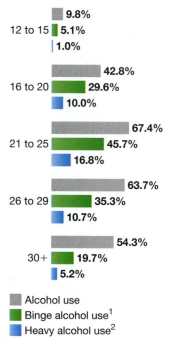

Binge drinking and heavy drinking are most prevalent among those in their 20s. Percent of those 12 or older who reported using alcohol, engaging in binge drinking or heavy drinking in the past month, by age group:

| | |
|---|---|
| 12 to 15 | 9.8% |
| | 5.1% |
| | 1.0% |
| 16 to 20 | 42.8% |
| | 29.6% |
| | 10.0% |
| 21 to 25 | 67.4% |
| | 45.7% |
| | 16.8% |
| 26 to 29 | 63.7% |
| | 35.3% |
| | 10.7% |
| 30+ | 54.3% |
| | 19.7% |
| | 5.2% |

■ Alcohol use
■ Binge alcohol use[1]
■ Heavy alcohol use[2]

1 – Five or more drinks on one occasion at least once in the past month
2 – Five or more drinks on one occasion at least five times in the past month
Note: Sample size around 68,500; age range is 12 or over.

*Source:* From Marcy E. Mullins, 8/15/2007. USA Today, August 15, 2007. Reprinted with permission.

others, and many sexual assaults on college campuses have been linked to this behavior. According to another study, about 1,400 deaths per year among college students can be attributed to binge drinking and the resulting behavior.

Although the effects of a hangover are not totally understood, some possibilities exist. A hangover could be partly due to the dehydration effects of alcohol. As alcohol is consumed, the brain blocks a hormone that promotes water retention by the kidneys (see Chapter 8). The hangover effect of a dry mouth and a headache is due to this dehydrating effect. Excess fluid loss via frequent urination results in a loss of potassium, magnesium, and other salts. The electrolyte imbalance can lead to further fluid imbalance and muscle soreness, which are common with hangovers. Rehydration will help in recovering from some of the hangover effects. One glass of water for each alcoholic beverage serving consumed is a good rule of thumb. Even better may be fluids to replace lost electrolytes, such as Gatorade. Also, impurities in alcoholic beverages that are really toxins can contribute to hangovers. Beer and red wines contain some of these toxins, which can lead to a headache. These toxins are termed *congeners*, which are by-products of the fermentation process. ■

---

**Before you go on . . .**

1. What is acetaldehyde, and what effects can it have on the liver?
2. Name and distinguish between three diseases of the liver that can result from alcohol abuse.
3. What is the liver disease that can be caused by chronic alcohol intake and may be irreversible?
4. What are some possible causes of a hangover?

---

# Health and Alcohol Consumption

A curse and a cure? We've already discussed some of the serious consequences of excess alcohol intake. Conversely, are there health benefits to *moderate* alcohol consumption? Is it the *type* of alcoholic beverage consumed that determines whether it is a curse or a cure, or the alcohol itself? As we further explore potential health risks and benefits of alcohol consumption, keep in mind that these questions are all difficult to answer with absolute certainty.

## Health Risks

The negative health outcomes of excess alcohol intake definitely outweigh the benefits simply because many Americans are not moderate but heavy drinkers. For heavy drinkers the quality of life, which we will discuss later, is compromised. Alcohol intake also has physiological consequences.

### Disease Risk

Excess alcohol intake can lead to high blood pressure and weakening of the heart muscle *(cardiomyopathy)*. A number of cancers have also been linked to alcohol abuse, particularly cancers of the esophagus, mouth, throat, colon, and breast. Women who consume more than two drinks per day have a 25 percent increased

**Want to know more?**
If you would like to explore the potential connection between alcohol and cancer development more thoroughly, go to the text website at http://webcom8.grtxle.com/nutrition and click on the Chapters button. Select Chapter 12.

risk of developing cancer. As discussed earlier, the biggest health issue is to the liver, where alcohol abuse can cause inflammation (hepatitis), degeneration, and hardening or scarring (cirrhosis). An even more serious issue is the combination of alcohol consumption and cigarette smoking. This combination can increase the risk of cancer even more.

### Interactions with Medications

Another negative and dangerous aspect of alcohol intake is its potential interaction with medications. Medications prescribed for depression or anxiety, painkillers, or sedatives can have an enhanced and even deadly interaction. Alcohol and many medications may make you sleepy, and the combination of both only intensifies this effect. Combinations of drugs and alcohol are a prescription for accidents involving motor vehicles and machinery. People are more likely to fall or lose the ability to concentrate even on simple tasks. Alcohol can influence the potency of some medications and render others ineffective. Also, some drugs become toxic when alcohol is metabolized first, allowing the drugs to accumulate in the blood and tissues to dangerous levels. See http://pubs.niaaa.nih.gov/publications/Medicine/medicine.htm to look up specific medications and the effects alcohol may have.

**Figure 12.2** Fetal Alcohol Syndrome (FAS) has long been known to occur in pregnant mothers who consume alcohol. The effects of FAS on the facial features are not reversible, and often the child is mentally retarded.

### ■ Nutrition and Lifestages
*Alcohol and pregnancy*

*All* alcohol intake should be avoided during pregnancy and several months before you plan to become pregnant. Alcohol intake during pregnancy can lead to birth *anomalies* (deviations from the norm) in the infant. Infants who are born to mothers who consumed alcohol regularly during pregnancy may exhibit slow growth; smaller heads; irregular facial features, defective hearts and organs; mental impairment; and malformed arms, legs, and genital organs. Later in life these children tend to be hyperactive, have limited attention spans, have difficulty in reasoning, and be unable to view cause-and-effect relationships. These symptoms are collectively known as **fetal alcohol syndrome** or FAS (see Figure 12.2). These conditions are not reversible, as the alcohol affects the developing fetus directly. This issue is more of a danger because the impact of alcohol intake on the fetus is much more problematic during the first trimester of pregnancy, and mothers are often unaware they are pregnant when they consume alcohol. Additionally, it may not be the amount of alcohol, but the presence of any alcohol at the wrong time, that matters. This means that only one drink consumed at a certain time during pregnancy can result in FAS. For some organs the period of critical development may be only a few hours long, and alcohol intake during these few hours could cause lifelong defects in the body. Thus, FAS is the primary reason the medical community now recommends complete abstinence from alcohol during pregnancy. ■

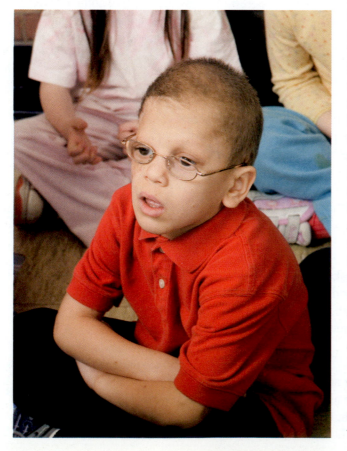

## Nutritional Implications

People who consume alcohol in excess may develop nutritional problems. First, because alcohol contains a significant amount of calories, the energy intake without proper caloric expenditure leads to weight gain. On the other hand, many drinkers satisfy their caloric intake needs at the expense of not consuming energy-yielding macronutrients: fat, carbohydrates, and proteins. This can lead to displacement of calories from these foods by alcohol. Alcohol has few other nutrients, and not consuming other foods with vitamins and minerals may lead to inadequate intake. Alcoholics frequently experience vitamin and mineral deficiencies because of decreased consumption of nutrient-dense foods and liver malfunction as a result of fatty liver and/or cirrhosis.

As we have discussed, alcohol is a diuretic. Water-soluble vitamins may be excreted at a greater rate through the urine, because these vitamins are not stored in the body to any significant extent. Thus, B-complex vitamins (thiamine and folate in particular) and vitamin C status may be compromised in those with heavy alcohol intakes. The group of symptoms that result from the loss of these water-soluble vitamins, particularly thiamine, is called **Wernicke-Korsakoff syndrome**; these symptoms include eye muscle paralysis, loss of memory, and damaged nerves. Another vitamin that is lost with alcohol, especially in the liver, is folate. Because one of the enzymes (alcohol dehydrogenase) used to metabolize alcohol contains zinc, decreased zinc stores are common among heavy alcohol users. Potassium, magnesium, and phosphates are other nutrients lost through alcohol abuse.

### ■ You Decide

*Alcohol intake and advertisement in youth: Should alcohol advertisement be banned?*

Is there a connection between alcohol advertisement and consumption of alcohol by youth? Apparently so, according to a number of studies on the topic. One in particular focused on 15- to 26-year-old teens and young adults living in major U.S. media markets. Data on alcohol related advertisements such as radio, television, billboards, and newspapers were collected from these locations. Self-reported alcohol intake was collected from subjects in these markets. The study revealed that alcohol intake was greater in those areas where alcohol advertisement expenditures were greater. For every advertisement viewed, alcohol intake increased by 1%.

Studies on middle school students in Los Angeles, California revealed that students exposed to alcohol television advertisements in the seventh grade were more likely to drink in the eighth grade. Other similar studies support similar findings. One study in South Dakota reported that exposure of alcohol advertisements in beer displays in stores during seventh grade could predict intake in ninth grade. There are many other similar studies that have the same conclusion. Do you think that advertisement of alcohol containing beverages should be outlawed based on these studies? ■

## Quality of Life

Excess consumption of alcohol negatively affects your quality of life. Students are all too familiar with the "hangover" effect of excess alcohol intake: headaches,

Do the fun and excitement of excessive alcohol intake really outweigh the effects of a hangover? Many people lose days at work or school and make errors in their performance as a result of alcohol consumption.

nausea, and even vomiting. Individuals who abuse alcohol are typically fatigued without even exerting themselves. Moreover, judgment is impaired. Alcohol-related car deaths are a major national problem. In 2006, there were more than 16,000 alcohol-related car fatalities. In fact, four out of ten fatal car accidents are alcohol related. Most victims are drivers, but passengers, innocent bystanders, and occupants of other cars are not spared either. A BAC of 0.17 percent is the average alcohol level of the driver in fatal alcohol-related car accidents, and in almost half of the fatal accidents the driver had a BAC of 0.20 percent or higher. Driving under the influence of alcohol is now a felony in many states, and even a first conviction may cost thousands of dollars in fines and possible jail time.

Acts of violence represent another behavior frequently associated with alcohol intake. Sexual assaults, homicides, battery, and domestic violence have a significantly greater incidence among alcohol abusers than nonabusers. Suicide incidence is greater among drinkers. People who drink are twice as likely as nondrinkers to commit suicide, and those whose drinking results in work-related problems are six times as likely. Many alcohol abusers have trouble getting to work on time, have a troubled home life, and experience a greater rate of divorce. Child abuse also occurs more frequently when parents and guardians abuse alcohol. The major cause of these behaviors is the alcohol-induced impairment of the part of the brain that controls reasoning and inhibition.

## Dependency and Abuse

Professional criteria are used to determine whether someone is alcohol dependent. Alcohol abuse in general terms is often defined as a destructive pattern of alcohol use that leads to damaging social, occupational, or medical consequences. Scores of diagnostic criteria have been published over the years. The *Diagnostic and Statistical Manual of Mental Disorders* has had several definitions of dependency as editions evolved. The *International Classification of Diseases* has its own criteria. Of the following characteristics, you must have at least three of the following to be diagnosed as alcohol dependent:

1. *Alcohol tolerant:* Either a need for markedly increased amounts of alcohol to achieve intoxication, or a markedly diminished effect with continued use of the same amount of alcohol
2. *Alcohol withdrawal symptoms:* Either **a** or **b:**
   a. Two of more of the following:
   - Sweating or rapid pulse
   - Increased hand tremor
   - Insomnia
   - Nausea or vomiting
   - Physical agitation
   - Anxiety
   - Transient visual, tactile, or auditory hallucinations or illusions
   - Grand mal seizures
   b. Alcohol is taken to relieve or avoid withdrawal symptoms
3. Alcohol is often taken in larger amounts or over a longer period than intended
4. Persistent desire or unsuccessful efforts to cut down or control alcohol use

5. Great deal of time spent using alcohol or recovering from hangovers
6. Important social, occupational, or recreational activities given up or reduced because of alcohol use
7. Alcohol use continues despite knowledge of having a persistent or recurrent physical or psychological problem that is likely to have been worsened by alcohol (e.g., continued drinking despite knowing that an ulcer was made worse by drinking alcohol)

People do not develop alcohol dependency quickly; rather, it evolves over time. Many people try to moderate their intake but find that things get worse despite their attempts to control it. The individual often feels a sense of guilt or shame and is remorseful. Attempts to stop can result in some or all of the withdrawal symptoms identified earlier. Individuals often plan to have "just a couple of drinks" only to end up drunk. The drinking problem worsens, and the individual often becomes depressed. In some cases the depression can lead to suicide. Recent evidence suggests some genetic predisposition, but an "alcoholism gene" has yet to be identified. Alcohol dependency can be overcome, but doing so typically requires professional help, and the strong support of families and friends is critical. Some individuals join organizations such as Alcoholics Anonymous as an essential part of their therapy. Medications can help stop alcohol consumption. Some drugs make the person severely ill when taken in combination with alcohol. Specialty clinics also exist where individuals can go and receive help to get through the difficult withdrawal phase. However, long-term abstinence is an ongoing challenge, and efforts to prevent relapses must be continuous.

The social costs of excessive alcohol consumption are high. The social stigma of being arrested and convicted of driving under the influence of alcohol can have a permanent effect on relationships, your career, and your status in the community.

### ■ Self-Assessment

*Do you have a problem with alcohol?*

Various screening tools can be used to determine whether you have a problem with drinking, are an alcoholic, or are in the stages of developing the disorder. Figure 12.3 is the Alcohol Use Disorder Identification Test, one of many screening tests used by professionals in counseling.

1. How often do you have a drink containing alcohol?
   - ☐ Never
   - ☐ Monthly
   - ☐ 2 to 4 times a month
   - ☐ 2 to 3 times a week
   - ☐ 4 or more times a week

2. How many drinks containing alcohol do you have on a typical day when you are drinking?
   - ☐ 1 or 2
   - ☐ 3 or 4
   - ☐ 5 or 6
   - ☐ 7 to 9
   - ☐ 10 or more

3. How often do you have 6 or more drinks on one occasion? (4 or more for women)
   - ☐ Never
   - ☐ Less than monthly
   - ☐ Monthly
   - ☐ Weekly
   - ☐ Daily or almost daily

**Figure 12.3** Alcohol Use Disorder Identification Test (AUDIT)

*(Continued)*

4. How often during the past year have you found that you were not able to stop drinking once you started?

☐ Never ☐ Weekly

☐ Less than monthly ☐ Daily or almost daily

☐ Monthly

5. How often during the past year have you failed to do what was normally expected from you because of drinking?

☐ Never ☐ Weekly

☐ Less than monthly ☐ Daily or almost daily

☐ Monthly

6. How often during the past year have you needed a first drink in the morning to get yourself going after a heavy drinking session?

☐ Never ☐ Weekly

☐ Less than monthly ☐ Daily or almost daily

☐ Monthly

7. How often during the past year have you had a feeling of guilt or remorse after drinking?

☐ Never ☐ Weekly

☐ Less than monthly ☐ Daily or almost daily

☐ Monthly

8. How often during the past year have you been unable to remember what happened the night before because you had been drinking?

☐ Never ☐ Weekly

☐ Less than monthly ☐ Daily or almost daily

☐ Monthly

9. Have you or someone else been injured as a result of your drinking?

☐ No ☐ Yes, during the past year

☐ Yes, but not in the past year

10. Has a relative, friend, a doctor or other health worker been concerned about your drinking or suggested you cut down?

☐ No ☐ Yes, during the past year

☐ Yes, but not in the past year

**Procedure for scoring:**
Questions 1–8 are scored 0, 1, 2, 3, or 4. Questions 9 and 10 are scored 0, 2, or 4. The maximum possible score is 40. A score of 8 or more is suggestive of problem drinking. For women, a score of 4 or more is suggestive.

*Source:* Reprinted courtesy of the World Health Organization, www.who.int. ■

## Health Benefits

*Are there any health benefits from alcohol consumption?*

Researchers have discovered some possible health benefits associated with moderate alcohol consumption (one drink per day for women and two drinks per day for men). The most consistently identified benefit of alcohol intake on human health has been associated with the heart and circulatory system. More than 100 studies have indicated that *moderate* consumption of alcohol can reduce the risk of heart attack, stroke, and peripheral vascular disease. Depending on the study, a 25–40 percent reduction in risk can be achieved, which is

# Real People, Other Voices

### Student:
### Julie Schlosky

University at Buffalo

Mark's lifestyle poses several risks to his health. First, although finding the time for a healthy, nutritionally dense meal can be difficult for a college student, it is definitely possible. A large campus offers many types of nutritious meals that are readily available. Also, if Mark knows that he has a busy day ahead of him, he could grab some snacks of fresh fruits and vegetables or a sandwich of whole grain bread with roasted lean turkey. It is very important to Mark's health that he have a nutritionally balanced diet and eat regularly, because skipping meals can cause nutrient deficiencies.

Second, Mark does not get enough exercise, which can cause problems later in life such as overweight, type two diabetes, and cardiovascular problems. Exercise is extremely important to maintaining a healthy heart and sustaining a healthy body weight. Mark should make time to run, use the cardio machines at his campus gym, or perhaps join a club or intramural sport for exercise.

Finally, Mark binge drinks, a cause of major health problems and a lifestyle that is harmful to his body and overall nutrition. Binge drinking can cause liver problems and can make exercise and eating nutrient-dense foods difficult. Mark's night of drinking caused him to become dehydrated, miss a class, and miss his breakfast. It also kept him from eating his dinner the night before. He should consider the risks he is posing to his health by missing meals, not exercising, and binge drinking. If Mark plans to drink alcohol when he goes out on Thursday nights, he should try to eat dinner and limit himself to two drinks, which is a moderate amount for a male his age.

### Instructor:
### Heather Rothenberg

West Valley Mission Community College

Skipping dinner significantly contributed to Mark's hangover. Drinking on an empty stomach leads to alcohol being rapidly absorbed into the bloodstream. Mark's liver could not metabolize the alcohol quickly enough, which led to a higher blood alcohol level. His lightheadedness was caused by intoxication.

Because alcohol is a diuretic, it is not surprising that Mark felt terrible the next day. A headache, dry mouth, fatigue, and dizziness are all signs of dehydration. He may also be feeling the effects of the congeners in the beer.

Consuming five or six drinks on a single occasion is categorized as binge drinking. A more reasonable amount of alcohol would be three drinks in the four hours that Mark was out partying, although even that number of drinks is somewhat excessive. Mark should cut down on the alcohol he consumes to a more moderate amount of four to fourteen drinks per week.

Recommendations for Mark include *never* skipping a meal before a night out. Even if he is not hungry, he should try to eat something. To combat the effects of dehydration, he should consume one glass of water for every alcoholic beverage consumed.

Mark should always be sure to take care of himself by eating well balanced meals and exercising at a moderate intensity three to five days per week. Because he leads an active social life, he should get involved in a team sport to help him stay motivated.

### Registered dietitian:
### Lalita Kaul, RD

Rockville, MD

On their own, alcoholic beverages provide calories but essentially no nutrients, so they don't nourish the body. In fact, calories from heavy drinking make it difficult to get sufficient nutrients without excessive calories, which can result in a weight problem. When calories from alcohol replace those from nutritious food and beverages, the risk for poor nutrition increases, especially for heavy drinkers.

Mark's drinking begins on Thursday and likely continues through the weekend. A friend, professor, or parent needs to talk to him and refer him to health professionals. Mark should see a college counselor and a registered dietitian, and should do so soon, before things deteriorate further. The dietitian can explain to him the risks of heavy drinking and going without food for a long period of time, as well as the importance of balanced nutrition and daily physical activity. Based on this advice, Mark should work with an RD to plan a diet that includes breakfast, lunch, dinner, and snacks. The plan needs to take into account weekends and should be based on his likes and dislikes. Besides the diet plan, Mark needs to develop an exercise program.

The bottom line for Mark is the need to make changes that will ensure good health and allow him to enjoy life at the same time.

quite significant. This reduction applies to both men and women. Factors that lead to blood clotting are typically reduced by moderate alcohol intake, and the protective type of cholesterol we mentioned in Chapter 4, HDL cholesterol, is increased. We do not see this relationship or benefit in heavy drinkers; therefore, more alcohol intake is not a plus.

A large study conducted with nurses as the research subjects suggested that moderate alcohol consumption provides health benefits beyond a reduced risk of cardiovascular disease. According to this significant study, women who consume moderate amounts of alcohol are less at risk for developing gallstones, and curiously, Type II (adult-onset) diabetes. It is not yet clear from research exactly why these benefits occur, but researchers are aware that some alcohol intake generates a more relaxed state and a brief vacation from stress.

## Red Wine and Phytochemicals

Since the 1970s there has been an increased interest in the potential health-promoting benefits of wine. Research has focused on the compounds in grapes and wine that may produce these benefits. These compounds are termed *phytochemicals* (*phyto* means "plant"), as discussed in Chapter 1. It appears that red wines have more of these phytochemicals than white wines, and research suggests that, accordingly, dark-colored wines may provide somewhat greater health benefits than their white counterparts. The primary reason for this is that red wines are made with longer contact between the juice and grape skins during fermentation. The healthy compounds are found in the grape skins and seeds, and so with extended contact with the grape juice, more of them are extracted in red wine.

The specific phytochemicals involved in health promotion are called *polyphenol*. This class of plant chemicals protects cells against free radical damage. There are two polyphenols: **catechin** and **resveratrol**. Resveratrol is probably the most healthful component of grapes from which wine is made. It is found in grapes, raspberries, and peanuts. Catechins are not found in wine, but they are present in green tea.

These compounds protect the cell's DNA from becoming damaged. Cell membranes and important proteins are protected by polyphenolic compounds. Animal studies suggest that consuming polyphenols reduces the risk of certain types of cancers, such as leukemia, breast, prostate, and skin cancer. These health benefits are *not* due to alcohol, but to the polyphenolic compounds present. Besides acting as antioxidants, polyphenols also decrease inflammation. Resveratrol has also been shown to reduce the chances of clots forming in the blood and thus may help prevent strokes and other diseases affecting the cardiovascular system.

The French, who normally consume a diet rich in fat, cholesterol, and saturated fat, have low risks for developing cardiovascular disease. This circumstance has been labeled the **French paradox**. This low incidence of heart disease among the French, in tandem with a dietary pattern that U.S. health officials advocate *against*, has puzzled scientists. However, two factors may explain this phenomenon. The more typical or common French diet shares many similarities

Wine *may* offer some beneficial health effects—not necessarily from the alcohol, but due to various antioxidant chemicals found in grapes and wines.

with the Mediterranean diet (discussed in Chapter 4). Surveys have shown that the French have a high per-capita consumption of red wine, which may impart the observed health benefits. Wine drinkers have higher levels of HDL, the "good" type of cholesterol, which can protect against heart disease. Another aspect of red wine consumption has to do with LDL cholesterol. If LDL cholesterol becomes oxidized, it is likely to form more plaque in blood vessels. Studies have demonstrated that the polyphenolic compounds in red wine decrease the oxidized form of LDL cholesterol, making it less likely to contribute to atherosclerosis. This latter property may be the most important in explaining the French paradox.

Some scientists believe that other aspects of French culture, unrelated to wine consumption, may also contribute to their good cardiovascular health. On average, the French eat smaller portions, eat more slowly, and walk more than we do. They tend to take more vacations (five weeks on average) and lead less stressful lives. Although these factors represent generalizations, some researchers caution against ignoring them when attempting to explain the French paradox. Regardless, there is a fine line between the benefits of consuming small amounts of wine on a daily basis and the risks of too much alcohol.

### Grape Juice and Health

Drinking grape juice can provide benefits similar to those associated with drinking moderate amounts of wine. Grape juice contains flavenoids, as do red wines. In one study, patients with signs of cardiovascular disease were asked to consume one glass of grape juice per day. Another group was asked to drink one glass of wine per day. LDL oxidation, a risk factor for heart disease, was reduced in both groups. The artery walls were improved in both groups. Grape

**Want to know more?**
If you would like to learn more about the prevalence of alcohol consumption around the world, go to the text website at http://webcom8.grtxle .com/nutrition and click on the Chapters button. Select Chapter 12.

*Can I get the same benefit by drinking grape juice instead of wine?*

**APPLICATION TIP**

Drinking grape juice provides many of the health benefits of wine.

The French paradox. The French are noted for consuming foods and sauces that are high in fat, yet they experience a significantly lower death rate from heart disease than the populations of most other Western nations, including the United States. On a per capita basis their consumption of wine is very high, and some argue that the antioxidant properties of wine, along with a less stressful lifestyle, may help to explain this low incidence of heart disease.

juice lowered the risk of developing blood clots. Wine can accomplish the same thing, but it would require consumption in an amount that causes intoxication. Also, alcohol can generate free radicals, whereas grape juice will not (because it does not have free radicals). Thus, if grape juice is your beverage of choice, you do not have to drink wine in order to obtain its benefits.

### ■ Nutrition and Culture
*Alcohol intake in the United States*

In the United States, there are differences in alcohol consumption by race. Caucasians have a higher per-capita intake of alcohol than Hispanics. African Americans have the lowest. The percentages of heavy drinkers (people consuming more than five drinks per sitting) in these three groups were 6.6 percent for Caucasians, 4.7 percent for Hispanics, and 4.5 percent for African Americans. The percentage of heavy drinkers has decreased over recent years for Caucasians, but remained stable for the other two groups. These percentages were similar for both males and females in all groups. Among Caucasian men, increased intake of alcohol was associated with lower educational attainment, as well as with those who are single. Caucasian men older than age 50 for whom religion is important in their lives often abstain from using alcohol. Among Hispanic men, unemployment status was the only risk factor for increased intake. No risk factors were identified for African American men. Among Caucasian women, never being married was a risk factor for increased alcohol consumption, whereas being older than age 50 appeared to be a protective factor. Unemployment and low income were risk factors for African American women. For Hispanic women, being unemployed was a risk factor, but older age, retirement, and a greater importance of religion in their lives was associated with decreased alcohol usage. ■

### Before you go on . . .

1. Which vitamins will be deficient because of excess alcohol intake, and why?
2. Name four withdrawal symptoms associated with alcohol abuse.
3. List three quality-of-life issues most often associated with excess alcohol intake.
4. Define the *French paradox*.
5. Explain why researchers think moderate wine consumption may provide cardiovascular health benefits.

## Real People, Real Strategies

Mark's severe hangover is due primarily to alcohol-induced dehydration. Moreover, because he skipped dinner and the intake of fluids before beginning his evening out, he was underhydrated at the outset. He probably feels shaky because of low blood glucose, which could also make him tired. Although he had ten hours of sleep, it wasn't quality sleep—with so much alcohol in his system he did not reach the needed dream sleep (sometimes called the REM stage of sleep). If he had eaten dinner, it would have slowed the absorption of alcohol into his body and helped create a slower rise in his BAC.

The best way for Mark to alleviate his symptoms is to rehydrate, replace electrolytes, eat bland food, and take antacids to settle his stomach. He should begin his recovery by drinking a sports drink such as Gatorade, eating a bowl of cereal, and taking a multivitamin and then an aspirin coated with antacids to protect his stomach. He should not take acetaminophen, because alcohol may increase the chance of toxicity to his liver. After eating he should go back to sleep and let time do the rest. Most important, Mark needs to stop drinking in excess and recognize that the college experience doesn't exempt him from the need to live a healthy lifestyle.

## Chapter Summary

- Alcohol is not considered a nutrient because it does not promote growth or maintenance or have any critical function in the body. However, it does contain substantial calories, contributing 7 kcal per gram.
- The various methods used to make alcoholic beverages influence their alcohol content. Distilled alcohol beverages have much more alcohol than beer and wines that are fermented.
- The health consequences of alcohol consumption vastly outweigh any potential benefits. Excess alcohol intake can cause serious liver diseases such as fatty liver, hepatitis, and cirrhosis.
- Alcohol consumption during pregnancy is not recommended. A common result of alcohol intake during pregnancy is a condition called fetal alcohol syndrome (FAS), in which the baby has facial, leg, and arm abnormalities and lower-than-normal intelligence.
- A set of defined criteria has been established to identify those who are alcohol dependent. Binge drinking is a type of alcohol abuse that appears to be most common on college campuses.
- Researchers increasingly think that moderate consumption of wine, especially red wine, has some potential health benefits, but these are due to chemical components other than the alcohol. It is also believed that the French paradox may be related to wine consumption in that the French often have a high-fat diet, but a low incidence of heart disease.
- Alcohol abuse can vary by race and ethnicity, with Caucasians having the greatest abuse rate and African Americans the lowest. The quality of life decreases among heavy alcohol consumers. Alcohol abusers are involved in more violent crimes, car accidents, sexual assaults, and family disruptions than are nonabusers.

# Key Terms

**acetaldehyde** (a-she-tal-de-hide) A toxic compound resulting from the conversion of ethanol in the liver. (p. 388)

**alcohol dehydrogenase** A liver enzyme that converts ethanol to the toxic acetaldehyde. (p. 388)

**aldehyde dehydrogenase 2** (AL-de-hide dee-hi-DRAH-jen-ase) A liver enzyme that converts toxic acetaldehyde to nontoxic acetic acid in the breakdown of ethanol. (p. 388)

**blood alcohol concentration (BAC)** The percentage of alcohol present in the blood. It is used to measure the amount of intake and to predict correlations with physiological effects. (p. 384)

**catechin** (KA-teh-kin) A polyphenol found in grapes and other plants that protects against free radical damage. (p. 398)

**cirrhosis** (sir-ROH-sis) A disease resulting in the hardening and scarring of the liver. (p. 388)

**diuretic** A compound that, when consumed, causes you to urinate more and can lead to dehydration. (p. 382)

**fetal alcohol syndrome (FAS)** A set of birth abnormalities in babies born to mothers who consume alcohol during pregnancy, characterized by abnormal facial features, abnormal arms and legs, and lower-than-normal intelligence. (p. 392)

**French paradox** The low incidence of heart disease among the French despite their consumption of a diet relatively high in fat and cholesterol. (p. 398)

**hepatitis** Inflammation of the liver. (p. 388)

**resveratrol** (rez-VIR-uh-trol) A polyphenol found in grapes and other plants that protects against free radical damage. (p. 398)

**Wernicke-Korsakoff syndrome** The symptoms that result from the loss of water soluble vitamins, particularly thiamine, from excess alcohol consumption over time. (p. 393)

# Chapter Quiz

1. Which of the following would you consider *moderate* alcohol consumption?

   a. one can of beer a day

   b. two to three shots of vodka per day

   c. four 5 oz. glasses of wine each evening

   d. one drink per week containing 1–2 oz. of distilled alcohol

2. What is the name for toxins that result from the fermentation process of wine and beer?

   a. acetaldehyde

   b. cirrhosis

   c. congeners

   d. a diuretic

3. The effect of too much alcohol consumption that results in what we refer to as a "hangover"

   a. can be corrected by the consumption of hot black coffee.

   b. is likely due to dehydration.

   c. is only a result of wine intake and not beer intake.

   d. is due to a loss of vitamin C.

4. Which of the following blood alcohol levels comes closest to the legal limit at which driving may be impaired?

   a. 0.40 percent

   b. 0.20 percent

   c. 0.08 percent

   d. 0.01 percent

5. A condition that causes liver inflammation through excess alcohol consumption and is reversible if the person stops alcohol intake and consumes a healthy diet is

   a. liver failure.

   b. late-stage cirrhosis.

   c. hepatitis.

   d. liver scarring.

6. If you buy whiskey that is 90 proof, what is the percentage of alcohol content?

    a. 45 percent

    b. 40 percent

    c. 65 percent

    d. 90 percent

7. An individual who continues to consume a high level of alcohol but does not become as intoxicated as he or she once did

    a. is legally intoxicated.

    b. has diminished capacity to break down alcohol.

    c. has a failing liver.

    d. is becoming alcohol tolerant.

8. Alcohol consumption may

    a. increase HDL or good cholesterol.

    b. lower LDL or bad cholesterol.

    c. lower blood triglycerides.

    d. raise blood glucose levels.

9. How would you classify someone who normally drinks infrequently and then consumes five mixed drinks on a single occasion?

    a. light drinker

    b. moderate drinker

    c. heavy drinker

    d. binge drinker

10. Which of the following groups has the highest rate of alcohol abuse?

    a. African American men

    b. Hispanic men

    c. Asian men

    d. Caucasian men

## < Here's Where You've Been

*The following topics were introduced in preceding chapters and are related to concepts we'll discuss in Chapter 13. Be sure that you're familiar with them before proceeding.*

- Organic food is grown without the use of pesticides, herbicides, or other synthetic products. (Chapter 1)
- Food additives are used to improve the quality and nutritional content of food. (Chapter 2)
- The rapid increase in the number of industrial farms, especially in developing countries, produces much more pollution than traditional farms and poses a significant threat to the environment. The pollution they generate threatens the soil, water supply, air, atmosphere, and public health. (Chapter 5)
- Meat production puts a significant strain on the environment. (Chapter 5)
- Vitamins and minerals can be lost if you overcook vegetables. (Chapters 9 and 10)

## Here's Where You're Going >

*The following topics and concepts are the ones we'll emphasize in Chapter 13.*

- Food safety is the responsibility of everyone throughout the entire food system, from growers to consumers.
- Food-borne illness is caused by bacteria, viruses, and parasites that enter the food supply.
- Consumers can do a lot to prevent food-borne illness.
- Hand washing, avoiding cross-contamination, cooking food to proper temperatures, and keeping food out of the temperature range in which contamination is likely are important steps in maintaining food safety.

## Real People, Real Choices

It was finals week and Kevin Shapiro, a sophomore at Trinity University, and some students from his biology class were meeting in his room to study. It was already 11 P.M, and most of them had missed dinner while preparing for the exam that was sure to be the "grade breaker" for all. They ordered a few pizzas and continued to study. When they were done, they closed the pizza box and forgot about it. The next morning Kevin woke up after only a few hours of sleep to review his notes one last time before the exam. He grabbed a slice of the leftover pizza on his way to the library. About six hours later, halfway through his exam, he started to feel terrible. He was nauseated, had stomach cramps, and broke out in a cold sweat. He barely made it through the exam. He continued to vomit and have diarrhea for several hours before his roommate took him to the emergency room. After running several tests and hooking Kevin to an IV, the doctors told him he had food poisoning. He was shocked. He figured that with no sleep and the stress of finals week, he had picked up the flu. How could he have gotten food poisoning? What could he have done to prevent it? Food-borne illness is common in college students, especially those who live on campus. Why do you think that is? What can be done to prevent food-borne illness?

Although the United States has one of the safest food supplies in the world, public concern regarding **food-borne illnesses** remains substantial. According to the World Health Organization, "Food-borne illnesses are defined as diseases, usually either infectious or toxic in nature, caused by agents that enter the body through the ingestion of food." More than 250 different food-borne diseases have been identified. Most of these diseases are infections caused by a variety of **pathogens** or infectious agents such as bacteria, viruses, fungi, mold, and **parasites** that can be transmitted in food. Although significant advances have been made in food safety, food-borne illness is still a reality. An estimated 76 million cases of food-borne illness occur each year in the United States. Most of the reported cases are mild and cause symptoms for only a few days; many people don't even realize they have a food-borne illness and consider their symptoms part of a "twenty-four-hour flu." Some cases are more serious, and the Centers for Disease Control (CDC) estimates that 325,000 hospitalizations and 5,000 deaths are related to food-borne diseases each year. Symptoms vary, but most food-borne illnesses are associated with nausea, vomiting, and diarrhea.

One needs only to listen to or read any news report to recognize that food safety issues have never been more important than now, especially considering the recent outbreaks of *Escherichia coli (E. coli)* contamination, antibiotic-resistant microbes, and mad cow disease in the United States. From planting to consumption, microbes, chemicals, and other harmful agents have many opportunities to enter the food supply. Contamination can occur at the farm or ranch, at the processing plant, in a retail food establishment, or in your own kitchen. The mere presence of pathogens does not always cause problems; it is when they are in the right place, in the right amount, and under the right conditions that they can multiply to the point of causing illness. So prevention is very

Food safety from farm, to processing plant, to grocery store, to the consumer.

important, and care goes a long way. Prevention includes washing your hands, paying attention to dates on food, cooking food to the correct temperature, and discarding old leftovers. Food safety is the responsibility of everyone throughout the entire food system, including the consumer.

### ■ Myths and Legends
*The "five-second rule"*

Have you ever applied the "five-second rule"? You may have dropped food on the floor and justified picking it up and eating it by the five-second rule—meaning that it can't pick up anything harmful from the floor as long as it stays there for five seconds or less. Well, the five-second rule is a myth. A high school student in Illinois conducted a research project that demonstrated that food can pick up harmful substances from the floor almost immediately, particularly if harmful bacteria such as *E. coli* are on the floor. So the next time you drop your favorite piece of candy on the floor, think again before picking it up and popping it into your mouth. ■

**Want to know more?**
You can explore the complete story regarding the five-second rule, by going to the text website at http://webcom8.grtxle.com/nutrition and clicking on the Chapters button. Select Chapter 13.

## The Food Supply Chain

We have already mentioned that food safety is at risk throughout the supply chain—from farm, to processing plant, to grocery store, to consumer. For example, meat and poultry carcasses can become contaminated during slaughter by contact with small amounts of feces from the intestines of the animals and birds. Oysters and other shellfish sometimes contain concentrated amounts of bacteria and viruses that are naturally present in seawater, or that are present in human sewage dumped into the sea. Fresh fruits and vegetables can be contaminated if they are washed or irrigated with water that is tainted with animal manure or human sewage. Produce can also be contaminated by pesticides applied to protect crops, and from damage caused by insects, rodents, and other pests.

Later in the food-processing chain, bacteria and viruses can be introduced via the unwashed hands of food handlers. The food handler can be a restaurant employee or you in your own kitchen. In food-processing plants and retail food establishments, microbes can be transferred from one food to another when handlers use the same equipment or utensils to prepare different foods without cleaning and sanitizing the equipment or utensils in between; this is called **cross-contamination**. Even fully cooked food can become recontaminated if it touches raw foods or drippings from raw foods that contain pathogens. Regardless of the source, the final recipient of the product, the consumer, can become very ill from ingesting the contaminated food. Therefore, food safety requires an awareness of food-borne hazards and a system to identify and eliminate or control them throughout the flow of food from production to consumption.

### ■ What's Hot
*The "American food supply": a return to a local approach*

What exactly does "the American food supply" mean, and why does that term keep coming up in news reports about food safety and

## VOTE for Small Farms & Local Food

Join Slow Food U.S.A.

SLOW FOOD USA supports sustainable farms and producers at farmers markets across the country

*For more information visit www.slowfoodusa.org*

**Eating is an agricultural act**
Wendell Berry

Nonprofit organizations, such as Slow Food USA, have been created to promote public awareness regarding the value of supporting small, local farms and farmers' markets.

*Source:* Reprinted with permission of Slow Food USA. For more information, go to www.slowfoodusa.org

**Want to know more?**
If you would like to learn more about this issue and how to buy locally grown foods, see the text website at http://webcom8 .grtxle.com/nutrition and click on the Chapters button. Select Chapter 13.

food-borne illness? After all, haven't we always had a food supply in the United States? The American food supply describes the entire food system that grows, harvests, manufactures, and sells the food we consume. When food-borne illness outbreaks occur, the Centers for Disease Control and Prevention (CDC) and other government agencies must do some detective work to determine the source of the disease. In other words, they have to trace the food items consumed back through the system to determine where the contamination may have occurred.

The term "American food supply" would have made very little sense just 100 years ago because the food supply meant only what you or your neighbors could grow, raise, or hunt. There was no industrial food production that distributed foods nationally and worldwide. Back then "outbreaks" of *E. coli* or other food-borne illnesses occurred, but they were more isolated and the news media of the time rarely focused on them. Most people became sick from food they grew on their own farms or bought from local farmers. Therefore, fewer people were affected by a given instance. Our awareness today, combined with an uncertainty in the general public about safe handling practices on large commercial farms, has led many consumers, including restaurants, to attempt to return to a more local approach to food by growing their own produce and purchasing from local farmers. People who support "the local foods market" claim several advantages to consuming locally grown foods: supporting the local economy; fresher foods that require fewer preservatives; fewer steps in the production process and therefore fewer people handling foods; and food production methods that result in less environmental impact. Think of how many gallons of gasoline and environmental toxins are produced just to bring one truckload of lettuce from California to New York. Did you know that the average American food product travels an estimated 1,500 miles before being consumed? ■

## Causes of Food-Borne Illness

Most food-borne diseases are infections caused by a variety of bacteria, viruses, and parasites. Other agents that can cause illness are less common or perhaps less reported. For example, naturally occurring toxins such as marine biotoxins (or toxic algae), molds, and fungi such as those occurring in poisonous mushrooms sometimes cause severe illness. Unconventional agents, such as the agent that causes *bovine spongiform encephalopathy (BSE, or "mad cow disease")*, are associated with a deadly brain disease in humans. Humans are most likely infected after consumption of infected cows or cow products that contain brain tissue. *Persistent organic pollutants (POPs)* are compounds that accumulate in the environment and the human body. Known examples are *dioxins* and *PCBs (polychlorinated biphenyls). Dioxins* are by-products of industrial processes and waste burning. Exposure to POPs can lead to a wide variety of adverse effects in humans. Metals such as lead and mercury cause neurological damage in infants and children. Exposure to cadmium can also cause kidney damage, usually seen in the elderly. These metals (and POPs) may contaminate food through pollution of air, water, and soil.

Pathogens or infectious agents can also be acquired through drinking water, from contact with animals or their environment, or from person-to-person contact. Fresh produce can also be a source of infection. In addition, some pathogens are spread by infected people who contaminate food while preparing it. Several risk factors contribute to food-borne illness; we will discuss them in more detail later. Following are the factors the Florida Department of Agriculture believes are the most important:

- Improper cooling of foods
- Time between preparing and serving
- Infected people touching food
- Not cooking food properly
- Not keeping hot foods hot
- Improper reheating of foods
- Contaminated raw foods
- Cross-contaminating raw and cooked foods

### Bacteria

Many different types of bacteria can contaminate our food. Most are harmless; some are eliminated through cooking methods, and some are fine in small amounts. However, others can cause food-borne illness. See Table 13.1 for a thorough list of the causes, symptoms, and prevention of many of these.

Rinsing produce under running water won't get rid of all *E. coli* if it is present, but it does make a difference. To be absolutely sure that you have killed the bacteria, you would have to thoroughly cook the produce. Of course, this would mean never eating raw vegetables, and, as we've discussed, eating raw vegetables provides numerous health benefits. Therefore, it is best to wash raw produce under running water, even items you peel such as carrots and potatoes. If you thoroughly rinse the food, you can remove dirt and reduce the amount of bacteria that may be sticking to the produce. Therefore, plain water is fine; soap or commercial cleaners are not necessary. Rinsing prewashed and bagged

*I have read that just washing produce in water is not enough and that you need to buy special produce cleaner—is that true?*

Fruit market in Madeira, Portugal. Different cultures and different governments can and do function with remarkably varying standards when it comes to food safety.

**Table 13.1     Common Bacterial Causes of Food-Borne Illness**

| Bacteria | Source | Symptom | Prevention |
|---|---|---|---|
| *Campylobacter* | Raw poultry, meat, and milk (most common cause of diarrhea in the world) | Diarrhea and abdominal cramps | Cook meat; consume pasteurized dairy products |
| *Campylobacter jejuni*, *E. coli* O157:H7, *L. monocytogenes*, *Salmonella* | Raw and undercooked meat and poultry | Abdominal pain, diarrhea, nausea, and vomiting | Avoid poultry that is pink in the center; use a thermometer to be sure proper cooking temperatures are reached; avoid cross-contamination |
| *L. monocytogenes*, *Salmonella*, *Shigella*, *Staphylococcus aureus*, *C. jejuni* | Raw (unpasteurized) milk and dairy products, such as soft cheeses | Nausea and vomiting, fever, abdominal cramps, and diarrhea | Don't consume unpasteurized dairy products |
| *Salmonella enteriditis* | Raw or undercooked eggs | Nausea and vomiting, fever, abdominal cramps, and diarrhea | Do not consume raw eggs or foods that contain raw eggs, such as homemade hollandaise sauce, fresh Caesar salad dressings, tiramisu, ice cream, mayonnaise, cookie dough, and frostings |
| *Vibrio vulnificus*, *Vibrio parahaemolyticus* | Raw or undercooked shellfish | Chills, fever, and collapse | Be cautious with raw oysters; note that shellfish in sushi establishments is okay as it is typically cooked |
| *C. botulinum* | Improperly canned goods, smoked or salted fish | Double vision, inability to swallow, difficulty speaking, and inability to breathe (seek medical help right away!) | Avoid buying dented or bulging cans; follow proper canning technique when canning at home |
| *E. coli* O157:H7, *L. monocytogenes*, *Salmonella*, *Shigella*, *Yersinia enterocolitica*, viruses, and parasites | Fresh/raw produce | Diarrhea, nausea, and vomiting | Wash produce; avoid cross-contamination with raw meats |
| *Staphylococcus aureus* | Contact with food workers or consumers who have soiled or infected hands and fingers or who are coughing or sneezing; repeated use of tasting spoons | Nausea, vomiting, abdominal cramping; in more severe cases, headache, muscle cramping, changes in blood pressure and pulse rate | Avoid touching foods with bare hands; wash hands before and during food-handling activities; keep foods cold to slow the rate of bacterial growth |

| C. perfringens | Meats, meat products, and gravy and other foods not kept at proper temperatures before serving | Intense abdominal cramps and diarrhea, which begin 8–22 hours after consumption of foods containing large numbers of C. perfringens | Keep food at proper temperature; store leftovers within 2 hours |
|---|---|---|---|
| Shigella | Fecal-oral contamination likely to occur among toddlers who are not fully toilet-trained, among day care workers who change diapers, or among infected food handlers who don't wash their hands; vegetables can become contaminated with Shigella if they are harvested from a field contaminated with sewage. Flies that breed in infected feces and then land on crops can also contaminate food | Diarrhea, fever, and stomach cramps | Wash hands |

*Source*: Adapted from http://digestive.niddk.nih.gov/ddiseases/pubs/bacteria/index.htm.

produce is also a good idea. Drying foods with a clean towel or paper towel can help too. To avoid contaminating other foods and kitchen surfaces, wash your hands, utensils, and kitchen surfaces with hot, soapy water before and after handling fresh produce.

## Viruses

A virus is a small particle that infects cells and can reproduce only by invading and taking over other cells. The *hepatitis A* virus causes a liver disease known as infectious hepatitis. Victims of infectious hepatitis do not always have symptoms, but when symptoms are present, they may include fever, fatigue, loss of appetite, nausea, abdominal discomfort, dark urine, and **jaundice**, in which the liver is inflamed and the skin may appear yellow.

Hepatitis A is usually transmitted through fecal matter. Raw and lightly cooked shellfish harvested from polluted waters, vegetables irrigated or washed with polluted water, and foods contaminated by infected food handlers pose the greatest threats for the transmission of the hepatitis A virus.

*Noroviruses* are members of a group of viruses previously known as "Norwalk-like viruses." Infection with norovirus affects the stomach and intestines, causing an illness called *gastroenteritis* (inflammation and irritation of the stomach lining). The symptoms of gastroenteritis are nausea,

The Freedom of the Seas docked in Southampton, UK. More than 380 passengers and crew aboard the world's largest cruise ship were sickened by a virus during a seven-day Caribbean cruise in February of 2006.

**Want to know more?** Planning to travel abroad? To see recommendations for preventing food-borne illnesses while traveling, go to the text website at http://webcom8 .grtxle.com/nutrition and click on the Chapters button. Select Chapter 13.

vomiting, and/or diarrhea accompanied by abdominal cramps. Norovirus is thought of as a "cruise ship virus" because of reports of several outbreaks on cruise ships in 2006. Norovirus is not specific to cruise ships. It is believed that noroviruses spread primarily from one infected person to another. Therefore, they can spread quickly anywhere there are a lot of people in a confined area, including nursing homes, restaurants, hotels, dormitories, and cruise ships. They can also be spread by contaminated food and water. Infected food handlers can also contaminate food as they prepare or harvest it.

## Parasites

Parasites are organisms that derive nourishment and protection from other living organisms known as *hosts*. They may be present in food or in water and can cause disease. According to the USDA Food Safety and Inspection Service, parasites are more and more frequently being identified as causes of food-borne illness in the United States. The problems they can cause range from mild discomfort to debilitating illness and possibly death. They may be transmitted from animals to humans and from humans to humans. These organisms live and reproduce within the tissues and organs of infected human and animal hosts and are often excreted in feces. Several parasites have emerged as significant causes of food-borne and water-borne disease. These include *Giardia duodenalis, Cryptosporidium parvum, Cyclospora cayetanensis, Toxoplasma gondii, Trichinella spiralis, Taenia saginata* (beef tapeworm), and *Taenia solium* (pork tapeworm). The best way to prevent becoming a host is to wash your hands frequently and be sure to drink only treated water. If you are camping or traveling and have no access to bottled or treated water, boil water for one to two minutes before drinking.

### ■ Sustainable Nutrition
#### *Safe levels of fish consumption*

Some species of fish can contain high levels of a form of mercury called *methylmercury* that enters waterways from industrial pollution. Smaller organisms consume it, and then it works its way up the food chain (Figure 13.1). Thus larger fish, such as swordfish, tuna, shark, and mackerel, contain very high levels. Humans consume these fish and can accumulate levels of mercury that can be harmful to anyone, but they are especially harmful to an unborn baby or a young child's developing nervous system. In adults, mercury poisoning can adversely affect fertility and blood pressure regulation; may cause memory loss, tremors, vision loss, and numbness of the fingers and toes; and may lead to heart disease.

The risks from mercury in fish and shellfish depend on the amount of fish and shellfish eaten and the levels of mercury they contain. The FDA recommends averaging no more than 7 oz. per week of the fish most likely to contain mercury, such as those mentioned previously. For a list of mercury content of fish caught in your area, contact your local Environmental Protection Agency (EPA) office. Food and Drug Administration (FDA) and EPA guidelines suggest that women who may be or are attempting to become pregnant, pregnant women, nursing mothers, and young children follow these recommendations:

1. Do not eat shark, swordfish, king mackerel, or tilefish. They contain high levels of mercury.

**Want to know more?** You can see a general list of the mercury content of fish caught in your area by going to the text website at http://webcom8 .grtxle.com/nutrition and clicking on the Chapters button. Select Chapter 13.

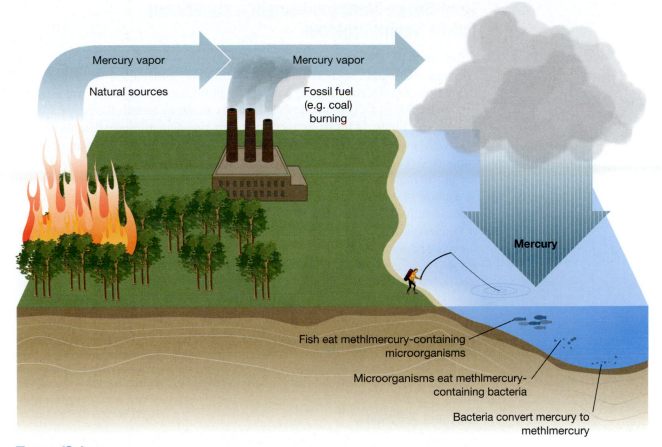

**Figure 13.1** Mercury is released into the environment from natural sources but is released primarily from industrial pollution. It then enters the waterways, where bacteria convert it to methylmercury. Microorganisms then eat the bacteria, fish eat the microorganisms, humans eat the fish, and the mercury works its way up the food chain.

2. Feel free to eat up to 12 oz. per week of fish and shellfish that are lower in mercury, such as shrimp, canned light tuna, salmon, pollock, and catfish.

3. Check local advisories about the safety of fish caught by family and friends in your local lakes, rivers, and coastal areas. If no advice is available, feel free to eat up to 6 oz. per week of fish caught from local waters, but don't consume any other fish during that week. ■

### Ciguatoxin

*Ciguatoxin poisoning* is an illness caused by eating certain types of contaminated tropical reef fish. The toxin originates in algae that live within certain coral reefs. When this toxic algae is eaten by small fish, it is stored in their flesh, skin, and organs. The small fish, in turn, are eaten by larger fish such as grouper, snapper, mackerel, and barracuda, and the toxin then becomes concentrated in the flesh and skin of the larger fish. Although the contaminated fish are not themselves affected by this toxin, humans are. Preventing ciguatoxin poisoning can be very difficult because the toxin is not destroyed by cooking or freezing and doesn't affect the smell or taste of the fish. The best way to prevent this type of intoxication is to decrease consumption of large fish (fish over 6 lbs.) and to avoid eating the parts of any fish where the toxin may be heavily concentrated, such as the liver, head, intestines, and roe (eggs).

**Want to know more?**
To explore and learn useful guidelines on how to buy, store, and prepare seafood safely, go to the text website at http://webcom8.grtxle.com/nutrition and click on the Chapters button. Select Chapter 13.

# Food-Borne Illnesses Remain a Significant Public Health Problem

Substantial progress in preventing particular food-borne illnesses that were common years ago, such as typhoid and cholera, perhaps has led to a certain degree of complacency among the public, politicians, and health and medical professionals. In fact, as the news media has made us aware, the battle against food-borne illness is far from over. Although significant improvements in food safety such as pasteurization of milk, safe canning, and disinfection of water supplies have conquered many diseases, other food-borne infections exist and are problematic today. For example, in 1996, the parasite *Cyclospora* appeared as a cause of diarrhea related to raspberries imported from Guatemala. In 1998, a new strain of the bacterium *Vibrio parahemolyticus* contaminated oyster beds in Galveston Bay in Texas and caused an epidemic of diarrhea in people who ate the oysters raw. Newly recognized microbes emerged as public health problems for several reasons: microbes can easily spread around the world, new microbes can evolve, the environment and ecology are changing, food production practices and consumption habits change, and better laboratory tests can now identify microbes that were previously unrecognized. Food scientists have identified some factors they believe will make food-borne illnesses even more of a public health problem in the years to come, such as new pathogens, changing eating habits, an increase in mass food production and transport, a global food supply, and a growing number of highly susceptible people.

## Emerging Pathogens

Microorganisms continue to adapt and evolve, sometimes strengthening their ability to cause illness. Microorganisms previously not recognized as human pathogens, or those unexpectedly found in particular foods, have been identified as causes of food-borne disease outbreaks. An example of such an **emerging pathogen** is *Listeria monocytogenes*, a bacterium that has been found in raw foods, such as uncooked meats and vegetables. It has also been found in processed foods that become contaminated after processing but before packaging or consumption, such as soft cheeses, hot dogs, and lunch meats. Unpasteurized (raw) milk or foods made from unpasteurized milk may contain the bacterium.

## Changing Eating Habits

We no longer expect to eat foods seasonally or when they are available locally. Americans demand a constant supply of fruits, vegetables, meat, poultry, fish, shellfish, and produce throughout the year. In addition, we have accepted the foods and dishes common to many cultures around the world. This translates to an increase in the importation of foods from all over the country and all over the world, as well as more time and more opportunity for food to become exposed to harmful pathogens.

Although any food can become contaminated if not handled safely, most food-borne illnesses are caused by eating foods that support the rapid growth of disease-causing microorganisms. These foods are commonly referred to as **potentially hazardous foods**. Some common examples of potentially hazardous foods are raw animal products such as red meat, poultry, shellfish, eggs, and unpasteurized milk.

It is okay to consume sushi as long as you consume it from a reputable establishment. Look for the words *sushi grade* or *sashimi grade* and eat products prepared for immediate consumption rather than those that are prepared and packaged.

**Want to know more?** If you would like to more thoroughly investigate the topic of sushi and how to avoid food-borne illnesses when eating raw seafood, go to the text website at http://webcom8.grtxle.com/nutrition and click on the Chapters button. Select Chapter 13.

*I love eating sushi. Does this mean I should not eat it, or if I do will I get sick?*

Potentially hazardous foods, such as Steak Tartare, sushi, and prepackaged fruits and vegetables are OK to consume if you are healthy. Just be aware that consuming these foods increases your risk of contracting a food-borne illness.

Other examples of easily contaminated foods are prewashed and presliced fruits and vegetables and premade ready-to-cook meals that are widely sold in grocery stores. Simply stated, the more times an item is handled, the greater the chance for exposure. This is not to say that you should avoid eating these foods. You just need to be aware that the risk exists and avoid taking unnecessary risks.

Although consuming raw fruits and vegetables is healthy, doing so may increase the risk of obtaining a food-borne illness. However, as we noted earlier, you can significantly reduce this risk by washing your hands, washing fruits and vegetables, discarding any expired products and making sure not to prepare vegetables and meats on the same surface.

*Okay, now I am confused. I thought it was healthy to eat raw fruits and vegetables.*

Industrial food production increases the chances of food-borne illness because, if one animal being processed is infected with a pathogen, chances are that all the other animals being processed at the same time will be also.

## Mass Food Production and Transport

We don't often realize it, but many of the foods we eat are made from the parts of many different animals. For instance, a single hamburger may contain meat from hundreds of different cows. A carton of milk may contain milk from hundreds of cows. A broiler chicken carcass can be exposed to the drippings and juices of thousands of other birds that went through the same cold-water wash tank after slaughter. This of course was not the case prior to the mass industrial food production we rely on today. Mass food production increases the chances of food-borne illness because if one animal is infected, there is an increased chance that all being produced at the same time will be too.

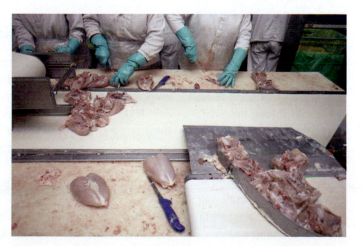

## The Global Food Supply

To accommodate the changing eating habits of Americans, an ever-increasing proportion of our food is imported, especially from developing parts of the world. In fact, the average American eats about 260 lbs. of imported food per year, or about 13 percent of the annual diet. As a result, we are being exposed to more pathogens not historically found in the United States. New products, processing methods, and packaging have the potential to trigger nationwide illness outbreaks of unprecedented scale. Mass production and wide commercial distribution of food items means that outbreaks can affect many people simultaneously over a large geographic area. The FDA and USDA inspect imported foods but with a slightly different approach. The FDA operates under a "risk-based" approach to inspection. This means that it inspects only foods from sources and producers thought to pose the greatest risk. The USDA requires inspection of all imported meats and poultry, which it regulates. Critics blame the FDA's limited resources for its risk-based approach, which, in effect, puts the consumer at greater risk. Many consumers are now calling for stricter regulations, especially after the 2007 contamination of the pet food supply imported from China.

## Highly Susceptible Populations

A growing number of people in **highly susceptible populations** are more likely than others in the general population to develop food-borne illness. Young children, pregnant and nursing women, the elderly, and those with low-functioning immune systems experience the most serious food-borne illnesses. They also tend to become ill from smaller doses of organisms and may be more likely than other people to die of food-borne disease. Young children tend to have higher rates of food-borne infections. Other high-risk populations include residents in nursing homes, cancer and organ transplant patients, individuals with HIV/AIDS or liver disease, and people with reduced stomach acid due to antacid medications.

**Want to know more?**
You can learn more about the regulations for imported foods by going to the text website at http://webcom8.grtxle.com/nutrition and clicking on the Chapters button. Select Chapter 13.

**Want to know more?**
You can tap into more sources of information on food safety and review the role each government agency plays in establishing regulations by going to the text website at http://webcom8.grtxle.com/nutrition and clicking on the Chapters button. Select Chapter 13.

**Want to know more?**
To access the most current information on national food safety programs and related news, go to the text website at http://webcom8.grtxle.com/nutrition and click on the Chapters button. Select Chapter 13.

> **Before you go on . . .**
> 1. How is food-borne illness defined?
> 2. What is meant by the statement, "Food safety is a concern from farm to table"?
> 3. Name the primary causes of food-borne illness.
> 4. What are the key factors most likely to contribute to making food-borne illnesses even more of a public health problem in the years to come?

# Food Processing and Safety: From Farm to Table

As previously discussed, food-borne diseases are largely preventable, but it takes effort in every step along the way, from farm to table. Food safety is a responsibility shared by every level of the food industry, including food producers, food processors, retailers, food-service workers, and even consumers in their homes. To oversee all these steps, the U.S. government has created several programs through a collaboration of the FDA, USDA, EPA, and CDC.

## The Hazard Analysis Critical Control Point System

Perhaps the program that has established the foundation for others is the **Hazard Analysis Critical Control Point (HACCP) system**, which has set

**Figure 13.2** The Seven Principles of HACCP

1. Conduct a hazard analysis to identify potential hazards that could occur in the food production process.

2. Identify the **critical control points (CCPs)**—the points in the process where the potential hazards could occur and can be prevented and/or controlled.

3. Establish critical limits for preventive measures associated with each CCP. A critical limit is a criterion that must be met for each CCP. (Where appropriate, critical limits may reflect relevant current regulations.)

4. Establish CCP monitoring requirements to ensure that each CCP stays within its limit. Monitoring may require materials or devices (such as thermometers) to measure or otherwise evaluate the process at CCPs.

5. Establish corrective actions if monitoring determines that a CCP is not within the established limits.

6. Establish effective record-keeping procedures that document that the HACCP system is working properly.

7. Establish procedures such as inspections for verifying that the HACCP system is working properly.

forth the seven principles listed in Figure 13.2. HACCP establishes guidelines to promote food safety at every step of food production: the farm, storage, retail stores, restaurants, and consumers. It provides a detailed manual of educational materials and training workshops for organizations and individuals to follow. It covers detailed operating procedures for tasks such as the design and layout of food-processing plants and restaurants and training employees on proper personal hygiene.

## Food Safety at the Farm

Food production, which starts at the farm, has a huge impact on our diets, the environment, and ultimately our health. You may recall that we explained the benefits of organic farming, the development of genetically engineered foods, and the use of hormones and antibiotics in the production of meat and dairy products in Chapter 1. In Chapter 2 we covered food additives and defined several terms used by food producers—for example, the meaning of *cage-free* versus *free-range*. In Chapter 3 we considered the environmental impact of sugarcane plantations. Meat production and the environment was a key topic in Chapter 5. Regardless of the techniques or processes used or the specific industry involved, all farms, large and small, must follow basic food safety guidelines.

Farmers and ranchers are expected to use *good agricultural practices* (GAPs) and *good handling practices* (GHPs) to control soil and water management, crop and animal production, storage, processing, and waste disposal, and ultimately to ensure the safety of their product. GAPs usually deal with preharvest practices in the field; GHPs cover postharvest practices, including packing and shipping. Although contamination can occur anywhere on the farm or ranch, specific practices such as manure management, water use, farm worker health and hygiene, sanitation of food production facilities, and transportation are of particular concern.

**Want to know more?**
You can survey more examples of HACCP regulations by visiting the text website at http://webcom8 .grtxle.com/nutrition and clicking on the Chapters button. Select Chapter 13.

## ■ You Decide

*Agribusiness—feeding a growing nation, or corporate bad guy?*

What is **agribusiness?** The term has two meanings, depending on whom you ask. Within the agricultural industry it is used to refer to any business involved in food production: farming, supply, production, and so on. To critics of industrialized (large-scale) food production, the term carries a negative connotation and is typically used in contrast to "family farming." For them, agribusiness means big corporations that are governed more by profit maximization than food safety or animal welfare. Critics such as the Organic Consumers Association contend that industrial farms and their increased use of high-nitrogen pesticides and fertilizers for plant crops, and use of hormones and antibiotics in raising livestock, have led to a loss of nutrients in food. However, the USDA and companies that use these industrial farming methods claim that they are just as safe as those used in organic farming and that there is no difference in the nutrient content of the foods they produce. The large-scale farming industry claims that its methods save consumers money and provide the volume of food needed by a growing population. What do you think? Is large-scale industrial farming necessary? Are its methods improving or harming the quality of our food and environment? ■

**Want to know more?**
To explore in detail both sides of the agribusiness debate, go to the text website at http://webcom8.grtxle.com/nutrition and click on the Chapters button. Select Chapter 13.

## Food Safety and Common Food-Processing Techniques

Drying, freezing, pasteurization, irradiation, canning, and aseptic packaging are some of the most commonly used food preservation techniques. Each of these processes helps make the food supply in the United States one of the safest in the world.

### Pasteurization

The process of **pasteurization** was named after Louis Pasteur, the French scientist who discovered that organisms causing spoilage in wine could be inactivated by applying heat at temperatures below wine's boiling point. The process was later applied to milk and remains one of the most important processing techniques for dairy and other products from farm to table. The process of pasteurization is similar to boiling something to sterilize it. The difference is that in pasteurization the item is not boiled but is brought to a temperature just below its boiling point. The reason for stopping short of boiling is to maintain taste while

Small, family farms typically require more human labor per acre and therefore generate less pollution.

still killing most of the harmful substances. This process makes products safer and extends their shelf life. Before pasteurization, many diseases were transmitted through raw milk to children and adults alike, and significant risk remains today in consuming unpasteurized dairy products. Pasteurization does not affect the flavor of the milk and has no significant effect on its nutritional value.

**Ultrapasteurization (UP)** is similar to traditional pasteurization, but it uses slightly different equipment, higher temperatures, and longer processing times. A product that has been ultrapasteurized still needs to be refrigerated, but it will last longer than a product that is pasteurized by normal methods. Another method, **ultra high temperature (UHT)** sterilization, raises the temperature of milk even higher, and the milk is then rapidly cooled and aseptically packaged. This is the milk you find in a box that doesn't require refrigeration.

### ■ Myths and Legends
*Is raw milk better for children?*

There is a growing and alarming trend among many nutrition "enthusiasts" to give children raw unpasteurized milk. Supporters claim it fights everything from allergies to asthma, digestive problems to learning disabilities. They say it eases arthritis pain and improves cholesterol, boosts immunity and clears cataracts. Many who suggest it is a healthier alternative to pasteurized milk are in opposition to government health agencies regulating food production on any level. They claim that they support local farmers and the local food movement. However, even those who are credited with founding the local food movement, such as author Michael Pollan, claim that these people are going to an extreme and ignoring basic food safety concerns. In fact, according to the Center for Science in the Public Interest, along with the growth in popularity of raw milk has come a rise in dairy related food-borne illness outbreaks. Because of such a high risk of food-borne illness, the FDA banned interstate sale of raw milk in 1987 and now only 7 states allow its retail sale. According to the FDA, raw milk can carry dangerous bacteria such as Salmonella, E. coli, and Listeria.

### Raw Milk & Pasteurization Debunking Milk Myths

While pasteurization has helped provide safe, nutrient-rich milk and cheese for over 120 years, some people continue to believe that pasteurization harms milk and that raw milk is a safe and healthier alternative.

Here are some common myths and proven facts about milk and pasteurization:

- Pasteurizing milk *DOES NOT* cause lactose intolerance and allergic reactions. Both raw milk and pasteurized milk can cause allergic reactions in people sensitive to milk proteins.
- Raw milk *DOES NOT* kill dangerous pathogens by itself.
- Pasteurization *DOES NOT* reduce milk's nutritional value.
- Pasteurization *DOES NOT* mean that it is safe to leave milk out of the refrigerator for an extended time, particularly after it has been opened.
- Pasteurization *DOES* kill harmful bacteria.
- Pasteurization *DOES* save lives.

*Source:* http://www.fda.gov/Food/ResourcesForYou/Consumers/ucm079516.htm ■

**Figure 13.3** The radura symbol, which must be placed on irradiated foods.

## Irradiation

While not yet widely used, **food irradiation** (exposure to low levels of radiation) is a food safety technology that prolongs shelf life and eliminates pathogens. It reduces spoilage, and in certain fruits and vegetables it inhibits sprouting and delays the ripening process. Its use is somewhat controversial because of public concern regarding cancer risks with the use of irradiation and the belief that the process leads to a product with a lower nutrient value.

The FDA has evaluated the safety of irradiated foods for forty years and concluded that the process is safe and effective. In addition, the FDA claims that any loss of nutrients is minimal. To date, irradiation has been approved for red meat, poultry, spices, fruits, vegetables, fresh eggs, juices, and shellfish. The FDA requires that irradiated foods be labeled with either "treated with radiation" or "treated by irradiation" and the international symbol for irradiation (pictured in Figure 13.3), called the *radura 1*. Have you noticed either of these phrases on foods you have purchased or seen in the supermarket?

## Canning

Canning is a widely used method for preserving food. The canning process involves placing food in a glass jar or metal can and then heating the container to a temperature that destroys microorganisms that cause food spoilage. While the food is being heated, air is removed from the container. The container is then cooled and vacuum sealed. The canning process can be done at home and preserves food for long periods of time. Once the cans or jars are sealed and heat processed, the food maintains its quality for more than two years and is safe to eat as long as the container is not damaged in any way.

## Aseptic Packaging

**Aseptic packaging** is a system for storing beverage and liquid foods without refrigeration for periods of six months or more. A sterilized package is filled with a sterile food product in a sterile environment. Aseptically packaged products include milk, juices, tomatoes, soups, broths, tofu, soy beverages, wines, liquid eggs, whipping cream, and teas. Aseptic techniques require less time and lower temperatures than traditional canning techniques. Using lower temperatures means that products packaged aseptically retain more nutritional value and have more natural texture, color, and taste than canned products.

**Nitrates and nitrites** are salts used in the curing and smoking process that have been used for centuries to preserve meats. It is part of what gives foods such as ham, hot dogs, and lunch meats their pinkish color. These salts are converted into *nitrosamines* when they are exposed to heat during processing. Nitrosamines have been found to cause cancer in animals, but it is not yet clear whether they have the same cancer-causing effect in humans. Nonetheless, the FDA requires manufacturers to add antioxidants to any foods high in nitrites to help offset the potential cancer-forming effects.

## The Role of the Restaurant Industry

More than 3,000 state and local agencies share the responsibility of regulating the retail food and food-service industries in the United States. They inspect and oversee restaurants and grocery stores as well as vending machines, cafeterias, and other outlets in health care facilities, schools, and correctional facilities. To minimize the incidence of food-borne illness, the FDA assists these agencies and the industries they regulate by providing a model *Food Code*. It helps agencies and food establishments follow the code by providing training, evaluation, and assistance. Restaurants and food-service organizations must follow certain guidelines in order to pass health inspections. You have probably noticed an example of these guidelines in the signs posted in restaurant restrooms indicating that employees must wash their hands after using the facilities. Many retail establishments go above and beyond the basic guidelines to prevent food-borne illness by influencing or taking responsibility for how food is grown and how the animals used for food production are treated (see What's Hot below).

## What's Hot

### Humane treatment of animals tastes better

As part of a growing concern regarding animal cruelty in food production, celebrity chef Wolfgang Puck, who heads one of the largest restaurant groups in the United States, announced in 2007 that he will no longer serve foie gras, the fatty liver produced by force-feeding ducks and geese. In addition, all of his establishments will use only eggs from cage-free chickens; veal from pasture-raised calves; and lobsters that have not been kept in crowded holding tanks. Chef Puck indicated that he was not responding to pressure by animal welfare organizations, but that he and the managers within his organization, after conducting considerable research, are operating under the belief that humanely treated, less-stressed animals actually produce better-tasting dishes. Many cities and some states have enacted or are now considering a ban on foie gras and other such foods obtained through inhumane treatment of animals.

Celebrity chef Wolfgang Puck has taken a stand against many of the practices of agribusiness by eliminating the use in his restaurants of products and prepared food products, such as foie gras, obtained by inhumane treatment of animals.

Puck has taken it a step further and has created a partnership with the Humane Society of the United States (HSUS). They have developed a 9-point program aimed at stopping the worst practices associated with factory farming. Pucks aims to position all of his companies to be in full compliance with the 9 points, which are as follows:

1. Only use and serve eggs from cage-free hens not confined to battery cages.

2. Only serve all-natural or organic crate-free pork. Crates prevent pigs from turning around.

3. Only serve all-natural or organic crate-free veal. Crates prevent calves from turning or walking.

4. Only serve certified sustainable seafood.

5. Eliminate foie gras from their menus. Force feeding swells ducks' livers up to 10 times their normal size.

6. Only serve all-natural or organic chicken and turkey meat from farms that are compliant with progressive animal welfare standards.

7. Continue to feature and expand certified organic selections on all menus.

8. Continue to offer and expand vegetarian selections on all menus.

9. Send a letter to suppliers regarding methods of poultry slaughter that involve less suffering. ■

## The Future of Food Safety

**Want to know more?**
To learn more about food safety regulations for retail establishments, go to the text website at http://webcom8.grtxle.com/nutrition and click on the Chapters button. Select Chapter 13.

Food safety and the concerns surrounding it are a huge issue. Policy makers, consumers, manufacturers, and scientists are trying to develop ways to improve the safety of our food supply now and in the future. The increased research and use of genetically engineered foods, discussed in Chapter 1, is a direct effect of attempts to address this issue. In addition, new pesticides, new farming techniques, new ways to house and breed livestock, and new food preservation techniques, many of which are controversial, are being developed as you read this. One of the most widely discussed and controversial techniques available is cloning, discussed in the You Decide feature that follows.

### ■ You Decide

*Animal cloning—cruel and unsafe or agricultural advancement?*

In December 2006, the FDA released a statement regarding the safety of food derived from cloned animals. Cloning involves genetically copying an animal in the laboratory so that the cloned animal is essentially an identical twin to the original animal. It differs from genetic engineering in that the animal's DNA is not altered or changed in any way. The statement says, "meat and milk from clones of adult cattle, pigs and goats, and their offspring, are as safe to eat as food from conventionally bred animals." The statement was issued by the FDA following a review of existing scientific information by a group of independent scientific experts in cloning and animal health. The statement is similar to that of the National Academy of Sciences released in a 2002 report. Cloning is used in livestock breeding to enhance the passing on of positive genetic traits such as disease resistance. Although the technique has been available for twenty years, the FDA has attempted to limit commercial availability until more research could be done.

**Want to know more?**
You can read the full report regarding public opinion of using cloned animals for food by going to the text website at http://webcom8.grtxle.com/nutrition and clicking on the Chapters button. Select Chapter 13.

Despite the FDA's position, you probably won't see meat from cloned animals on your grocery store shelf anytime soon. At present, producing one cloned animal costs approximately $20,000. Because of the significant expense, most cloned animals will be used primarily for livestock breeding. Their offspring are more likely to be used for food and dairy production. For now, the FDA has concluded that there is no value in requiring food producers to indicate on their labels when products come from cloned animals or their offspring.

Whether the FDA considers cloning safe or not, many consumers are not comfortable with consuming anything using cloned animals. The Pew Initiative, an independent nonprofit organization, conducted a 2006 poll to determine public opinion about using cloned animals for food production. It reported that 64% of Americans polled say that they are uncomfortable with animal cloning (46% are "strongly uncomfortable"), compared to just 22% who said they would find it acceptable. The reasons for the discomfort varied. Most said that they are concerned with the impact this will have on themselves and their families. A mistrust of the information, ethical concerns, and religious beliefs were also indicated as factors that influenced whether consumers were comfortable with cloning.

Fueling public concern, some groups refute the FDA's statements supporting cloning. In fact, in October 2006, the Center for Food Safety, along with reproductive rights, animal welfare, and consumer protection organizations, filed a legal petition with the FDA calling for a delay in the introduction of food products from cloned animals. They report that there are not enough well-controlled studies to indicate that food from cloned animals is safe. They have voiced several other concerns, including whether a lack of diversity in livestock increases the likelihood of some diseases, whether increased stress in cloned animals may raise the likelihood that they will spread bacteria, and that the procedure used to conduct cloning is cruel to animals, as many of the offspring are sick and deformed at birth.

The scientific evidence to date indicates no apparent difference in the nutritional quality of milk and meat produced from cloned compared to noncloned livestock. Moreover, there appears to be little difference in the incidence of disease, at least in the early stages of the animal's life. Related information regarding both food safety and animal cruelty is still limited. What's your perspective? In your opinion, do concerns regarding food safety justify the practice? What limits, if any, should government impose on this type of research? ■

Federal scientists have concluded that there is no difference between food from cloned animals and food from conventional livestock.

**Want to know more?**
Your can review and analyze both sides of the cloning issue by going to the text website at http://webcom8.grtxle.com/nutrition and clicking on the Chapters button. Select Chapter 13.

---

**Before you go on . . .**

1. What major agencies of the federal government are involved in food safety?
2. Define *HACCP* and describe the significant role it has played in food safety.
3. Identify four common techniques used in food manufacturing to preserve food.
4. Define *food irradiation* and explain the FDA's position on its use.
5. Why is animal cloning for food production controversial?

---

## Consumers: The Last Line of Defense

### Food Safety Practices You Can Use

#### At Home

As we've previously noted, major outbreaks of food-borne illnesses typically receive considerable media coverage and attention. After hearing stories of people getting sick from eating contaminated food, many people understandably decide to avoid the particular restaurant or establishment where the reported illness occurred. Some consumers even avoid dining out at all, at least for a while. This decision naturally results in eating more meals at home. However, the

## Real People, Other Voices

**Student:**
### Emily Grooms
Bowling Green State University

Kevin's food poisoning was related to improper food handling. First, Kevin failed to promptly place the leftover pizza in sealed containers for storage in the refrigerator and instead let it sit out at room temperature overnight. Bacteria grow rapidly at room temperature; therefore, any leftovers that have been unrefrigerated for longer than two hours should be discarded. The next morning, Kevin consumed the pizza that had remained in the temperature danger zone (40°F–140°F) for several hours. If he had stored the pizza properly, it would have been safe to eat for three or four days.

In addition to the food not being stored and cooled properly, the pizza was not reheated correctly. It is recommended that leftovers be reheated to 165°F to kill any bacteria that may have grown while in storage. Kevin could have avoided the food poisoning and the emergency room if he had promptly refrigerated the leftovers and had reheated the pizza to a safe temperature.

Food-borne illness is common among college students because many are unaware of the dangers related to improper food handling—unless they have received this information in a course. To reduce the occurrence of food-borne illness among college students, colleges should consider providing a food safety course for all incoming freshmen. The information could be transmitted in a simple hour-long program during orientation and registration.

**Instructor:**
### Jo Taylor
Southeast Community College

It appears obvious that Kevin should not have eaten the pizza, or that it should have been refrigerated. However, in his dormitory setting, there may not have been a refrigerator—or at least none big enough for the pizza. Because food should not be held between 40°F–140°F for longer than two hours, the leftover pizza should have been sent home with someone who has a refrigerator, or it should have been thrown away.

Food-borne illness is common among college students, who are at a time in their lives at which they feel invincible and make decisions without thinking of the consequences. Their living arrangements are often not suitable for the proper care of leftover food, and they think about the money they are wasting if they throw food away.

Education about food handling and food-borne illnesses, occurring in the dorms and schools in a variety of ways and on a continuous basis, would be helpful. This process could begin during college orientation and could be supported with posters in the elevators, hallways, and bathrooms as reminders. Attention could be drawn to the posters by changing them frequently, at which time additional information could be added to them.

**Registered dietitian:**
### Cindy Brison, MS, RD, LMNT
Omaha, NE

Kevin probably contracted food poisoning from the pizza. The pizza contained ingredients that are potentially hazardous, and he left it out in the temperature danger zone (40–140°F) for more than two hours. These factors set up the perfect conditions for bacterial growth. Kevin also failed to reheat the pizza to 165°F, which might have killed some of the bacteria.

Food-borne illness is common among college students because they may not have adequate refrigeration to store leftovers, and they may not be aware of the causes. In the future, Kevin should immediately refrigerate his leftover pizza and he should eat it the next day. He should handle all leftovers quickly and should reheat them to 165°F. He should also avoid cross-contamination with other foods in his refrigerator. His leftovers should be discarded after four days. Finally, Kevin should practice good handwashing techniques before eating.

assumption that these consumers make—that by eating at home they are safe from food-borne illness—is not correct. In fact, food-borne illnesses in the home are quite common and mostly occur as a result of cross-contamination during preparation.

Cross-contamination, as discussed earlier, is the transfer of a substance that can cause illness from one food to another, usually on a cooking utensil or a surface such as a cutting board or plate. Food-borne illness can be prevented during processing, as we discussed earlier, but it can also be prevented at home by following a few simple guidelines.

As we've emphasized, food-borne illnesses are a national concern. In fact, one of the goals of Healthy People 2020 (see Chapter 2) is to reduce the amount of food-borne illness. In order to reach this goal, programs are being developed to increase the number of consumers who follow very important food safety guidelines. These guidelines are based on the Fight BAC! messages. The Fight BAC! campaign (www.fightbac.org) is an educational program developed by the food industry, food regulatory agencies, and consumer groups to teach consumers that home food safety is a serious issue and to create awareness of the dangers posed by pathogens that cause food-borne illness. The campaign's primary message is that even though you can't see, smell, or taste bacteria, they are commonly found in and on food and food-contact surfaces. Figure 13.4 illustrates the Fight BAC! messages, which are also described in detail in Figure 13.5.

Efforts to improve consumer knowledge have increased because of information indicating that many consumers are not informed of safe food-handling practices. In fact, a study reported in the September 2003 issue of the *Journal of the American Dietetic Association* surveyed more than 1,000 people to assess how well they were following the food safety guidelines. Only 9 percent of

Food-borne illness can occur at home and is usually due to cross-contamination.

 **Want to know more?**
Many people think they are following food safety guidelines when in fact they are not. Are you? To take a quiz and find out how savvy you are about food safety, go to the text website at http://webcom8.grtxle.com/nutrition and click on the Chapters button. Select Chapter 13.

## FIGHT BAC!

CLEAN:
Wash hands and surfaces often

SEPARATE:
Don't cross-contaminate

CHILL:
Refrigerate properly

COOK:
Cook to proper temperatures

Keep Food Safe from Bacteria

**Figure 13.4** Fight BAC! Messages.

*Source:* Reprinted with permission from the Partnership for Food Safety Education.

**Figure 13.5** Avoiding Food-Borne Illnesses

The CDC offers some helpful suggestions on how consumers can avoid food-borne illnesses. These are consistent with the Fight BAC! messages.

**Cook:** Meat, poultry, and eggs must be cooked thoroughly. Using a thermometer to measure the internal temperature of meat is a good way to be sure that it is cooked sufficiently to kill bacteria. For example, ground beef should be cooked to an internal temperature of 160° F. Eggs should be cooked until the yolk is firm.

**Separate:** Avoid cross-contamination of one food with another. Wash hands, utensils, and cutting boards after they have been in contact with raw meat or poultry and before they touch another food. Put cooked meat on a clean platter, rather than back on one that held the raw meat.

**Chill:** Refrigerate leftovers promptly. Bacteria can grow quickly at room temperature, so refrigerate leftover foods if they are not going to be eaten within two hours. Large volumes of food will cool more quickly if they are divided into several shallow containers for refrigeration.

**Clean:** Wash produce. Rinse fresh fruits and vegetables in running tap water to remove visible dirt and grime. Remove and discard the outermost leaves of a head of lettuce or cabbage. Be careful not to contaminate these foods while slicing them up on the cutting board, and avoid leaving cut produce at room temperature for many hours. Wash your hands with soap and water before preparing food. Avoid preparing food for others if you yourself have an illness. Changing a baby's diaper while preparing food is a bad idea, as you can easily spread illness. If you have to change a diaper, wash your hands thoroughly before touching anything.

**Report:** Report suspected food-borne illnesses to your local health department. Calls from concerned citizens are often how outbreaks are first detected. Should a public health official contact you to find out more about a food-borne illness you experienced, your cooperation is extremely important.

**Dining Out:** As a consumer you can go a long way in protecting yourself from food-borne illness by being selective about the food retailers you patronize. As mentioned earlier, restaurants, supermarkets, convenience stores, and other food establishments are inspected by food regulatory agencies to ensure that they are clean, have adequate food production facilities, and follow proper food-handling practices. If you have any doubts about the cleanliness of a restaurant or food store, ask how the operation scored on its most recent inspection and use that score to help guide your choices. In many jurisdictions, the latest inspection report and score must be posted. Some jurisdictions and food establishments also require food managers to be certified in retail food safety.

people surveyed knew the proper cooking temperatures for meat, 70 percent did not think there was a big chance for food-borne illness to occur from foods prepared at home, and many thought that leftovers should be cooled to room temperature before refrigeration. See Figure 13.5 for specific recommendations.

In addition to taking these precautions, when dining out, avoid raw or undercooked animal foods. Hamburgers, for example, should be cooked to an internal temperature of 160° F. If your hamburger is still pink in the middle, send it back. Before ordering an egg dish such as scrambled eggs, omelets, or French toast, ask your server if the item is made with pasteurized eggs. If not, think about choosing something else from the menu. Also, keep an eye on the media for consumer advisories warning against consumption of certain foods, and avoid eating high-risk foods such as raw or lightly cooked oysters and Caesar salad made with raw eggs.

### ■ Sustainable Nutrition

*Is seafood caught in the Gulf of Mexico safe to eat?*

The recent *Deepwater Horizon* oil spill disaster has left many in shock from the unfathomable and far-reaching effects this tragedy will have on the environment and subsequently on the people living in it. Perhaps the worst aspects of this lasting impact are the unanswered questions, such as: How bad and how long? Can we ever safely consume seafood from the Gulf waters? Perhaps most perplexing, who can adequately answer these questions? Scientists from Louisiana state laboratories and the National Oceanic and Atmospheric Administration's (NOAA) Northwest Fisheries Science Center in Seattle are using advanced techniques to examine thousands of samples of shrimp, crab, and fish taken from the Gulf of Mexico. However, these techniques only measure the level of contaminants in the fish. Determining whether or not the food is safe is less clear cut. This is especially problematic when one considers the implications of ruling Gulf seafood "unsafe". Consumers and public health advocates want to know whether the food is safe, fisherman and processors want to maintain business as long as they can, and BP wants to limit its liability. So, who decides? The decision will most likely require a collaborative effort between the FDA, EPA and NOAA. Among other issues, they will need to determine the level of contaminants that can safely be consumed without increasing an individual's risk of cancer. These decisions may be based on a 2002 NOAA report entitled "Managing Seafood Safety after an Oil Spill," which was issued after the *Exxon Valdez* oil spill in 1989. The bottom line is, consumer beware. Know where your seafood is coming from and keep up-to-date on safety warnings issued by the FDA and EPA.

*Sources:* http://www.fda.gov/Food/FoodSafety/Product-SpecificInformation/Seafood/ucm210970.htm http://www.aolnews.com/gulf-oil-spill/article/gulf-seafood-after-the-oil-spill-who-decides-how-safe-is-safe/19534995 ∎

The consumer's role in food safety begins at the store.

## Tips for Grocery Shopping

Believe it or not, the consumer's role in safe food handling and food-borne illness prevention begins at the store. A few simple things can make a big difference. For example, always check cans and packages before purchasing to ensure that they are in good condition. As noted earlier, never purchase packages or cans that are damaged or appear to have been opened or tampered with. See the following list for more tips:

- Select frozen foods, meats, and other perishables as the last step in your shopping sequence.
- Don't buy cold foods that don't feel cold.
- Have meats placed in separate bags at checkout.
- Don't buy *any* items (not just canned goods) that are dented, bulging, leaking, etc.
- Avoid anything that looks or smells strange.
- Examine fruits and vegetables closely; avoid any that are brown, slimy, or bruised.

*When buying food in the grocery store, should you avoid buying items that are past the "sell by" or "use by" dates on the package?*

**APPLICATION TIP**

Many consumers think that goods that do not have dates, such as canned goods, will last forever. This is not true. You should discard any canned goods that have been in your pantry for twelve months or more.

Most fresh fruits and vegetables are best when consumed in peak season.

• Check expiration dates on labels and packaging closely.
• If you have a long drive home, make the grocery store your last stop. In addition, consider bringing a cooler for cold items.

When determining how long to keep food many consumers go by the **"sell by," "use by,"** and **"best before"** dates listed on food labels. There is a lot of confusion as to the interpretation of these dates among consumers. Here are some brief definitions provided by the USDA:

• *"Sell by"* dates tell the store how long to display a food product. It is best to buy the item before the "sell by" date, but this date does not necessarily refer to the safety of the product. In fact, some products such as eggs are considered safe to eat for four to five weeks beyond the sell-by date *as long as they have been maintained at proper temperatures*. However, this does not mean that the eggs will maintain quality for this longer time period. Using eggs that are long past their sell-by date may ruin the texture of a souffle or baked good.
• *"Use by"* is placed on a package voluntarily by the manufacturer and suggests when the product will start to lose peak quality. It is mostly used as a guideline for stores so that they know when to remove items from the shelves.
• *"Best before"* refers to the relationship between the shelf life and quality, of the product. It suggests that for ideal quality, the product should be consumed prior to the date indicated. It does not refer to food safety. Therefore, it is okay to eat food after the "best before" date, but it has probably deteriorated either in flavor, texture, appearance, or nutrition.

It is a good idea to check these dates, avoid buying products that are past the "sell-by" date, and avoid consuming foods beyond the "use by" date. However, these may not be the best guideline for how long foods are safe. Although some states have laws governing dating on labels, there are no federal regulations (except for baby formula). It is best to also go by the cold-storage recommendations listed in Table 13.2.

### Buying Fresh Fruits and Vegetables

When you are purchasing fresh fruits and vegetables, several concerns emerge. Consumers are often unsure how to choose the freshest fruits and vegetables, and many are concerned that these items will spoil before they can be used, resulting in their being thrown away. See the following tips on what to look for when buying fresh fruits and vegetables:

• Know the peak season for the most common fruits and vegetables.
• Buy them in season (they are best at the peak of their season).
• Don't overpurchase, because fresh fruits and vegetables have a short life.
• Most fresh vegetables can be stored for two to five days, except for root vegetables, which can be stored from one to several weeks.
• Buy vegetables that are mature, look fresh, and are free from bruises, skin punctures, and decay.
• The USDA has established voluntary grade standards for most fresh vegetables. If a package carries an official grade, the packer is legally obligated to ensure that its contents measure up to the grade shown. Grade designations are most often used on packages of potatoes and onions, but may be seen on other produce items as well.

**Table 13.2**    **Cold Storage Times**

| Product | Refrigerator (40° F) | Freezer (0° F) |
| --- | --- | --- |
| Eggs, fresh | 3–5 weeks | Do not freeze |
| Eggs, hard-cooked | 1 week | Does not freeze well |
| Eggs, liquid, opened | 3 days | Does not freeze well |
| Eggs, liquid, unopened | 10 days | 1 year |
| Mayonnaise (refrigerate after opening) | 2 months | Do not freeze |
| Frozen dinners & entrees (keep frozen until ready to heat) | — | 3–4 months |
| Egg, chicken, ham, tuna, and macaroni salads | 3 to 5 days | Does not freeze well |
| Hot dogs, opened | 1 week | 1–2 months |
| Hot dogs, unopened | 2 weeks | 1–2 months |
| Lunch meat, opened | 3 to 5 days | 1–2 months |
| Lunch meat, unopened | 2 weeks | 1–2 months |
| Bacon | 7 days | 1 month |
| Smoked breakfast links/patties | 7 days | 1–2 months |
| Hard sausage—pepperoni, jerky sticks | 2–3 weeks | 1–2 months |
| Hamburger and stew meat | 1–2 days | 3–4 months |
| Ground turkey, veal, pork, and lamb | 1–2 days | 3–4 months |
| Steaks | 3–5 days | 6–12 months |
| Chops | 3–5 days | 4–6 months |
| Roasts | 3–5 days | 4–12 months |
| Chicken or turkey | 1–2 days | 1 year |
| Fried chicken | 3–4 days | 4 months |
| Chicken pieces, plain | 3–4 days | 4 months |
| Chicken nuggets/patties | 1–2 days | 1–3 months |
| Pizza, cooked | 3–4 days | 1–2 months |

**Want to know more?**
Check out a list of the USDA's voluntary grade standards for fresh vegetables by going to the text website at http://webcom8.grtxle.com/nutrition and clicking on the Chapters button. Select Chapter 13.

### Buying Meat

Look for the USDA stamp indicating that the meat has been inspected for "wholesomeness." All meats that display quality standards have also passed wholesomeness inspection. Each grade of USDA beef is a measure of a distinct level of quality. The eight grades (in decreasing order of quality) are USDA Prime, Choice, Select, Standard, Commercial, Utility, Cutter, and Canner. Standard and Commercial grade beef frequently are sold as ungraded or as "brand name" meat. The three lowest grades—USDA Utility, Cutter, and Canner—are seldom, if ever, sold at retail but are used instead to make ground beef and manufactured meat products such as hot dogs.

**Want to know more?**
You can review the definitions for all USDA beef grades by going to the text website at http://webcom8.grtxle.com/nutrition and clicking on the Chapters button. Select Chapter 13.

**Want to know more?**
To review a list of suggested storage times for pantry items, go to the text website at http://webcom8.grtxle.com/nutrition and click on the Chapters button. Select Chapter 13.

---

**APPLICATION TIP**

You might think that focusing on hand washing is not necessary, that most people do it anyway. The question is, do you wash your hands correctly? The CDC recommends that you wash your hands with warm water and soap for at least twenty seconds before and after handling food and after using the bathroom, changing diapers, and handling pets.

---

**APPLICATION TIP**

When preparing food, you can use a helpful technique called *mise en place* (pronounced "MEEZ ahn plahs"). Translated literally, it means "to put in place"; it involves planning ahead and having all of your ingredients selected, assembled and ready to go *before* you start cooking. This way you'll know if you are missing an ingredient in a recipe or a favorite must-have item for a simple meal. After all, it can be very frustrating to be making a great salad only to realize you are out of a necessary ingredient for the salad dressing.

## Storing Food

Having returned from the grocery store, you now must find an appropriate place in the kitchen or pantry for all your food purchases. Storing food is not only important to maintaining counter space in your kitchen but is also a crucial step to ensure food safety.

### Refrigerator

The ideal temperature for your refrigerator is no higher than 40° F. It is a good idea to buy a small thermometer if your refrigerator does not have one so that you can keep track of the temperature. In addition to maintaining the temperature of your refrigerator, you should store items properly. Do not overstock your refrigerator; allow some air to flow around items. Use the method of **first in, first out (FIFO)**, a practice followed by many restaurants and retail establishments, in which older items are placed in front of newer items and therefore used first. Label and date leftovers so that you know when you put them in the refrigerator and therefore how long they are safe to consume.

### General Storage Guidelines

If you do not intend to freeze purchased meat, put it in the bottom of the refrigerator or meat keeper, if one exists. This serves two purposes: (1) usually, this is the coldest spot in the refrigerator, and (2) it keeps liquid from the meats from dripping down onto other food. Store eggs, dairy products, lunch meats, leftovers, and any product marked "Refrigerate when opened" on either the middle or top shelves. Do not place eggs or milk in the door of the refrigerator. This is the warmest spot in the refrigerator and should contain only food and condiments that won't spoil easily, such as drinks and non-cream-based condiments. Put fruits and vegetables at the bottom in the drawers designed for their storage. It is a bit warmer within these drawers, and therefore they protect vegetables that tend to be damaged by temperatures that are too low. Some fruits and vegetables can be left out at room temperature, such as exotic fruits, tomatoes, green beans, cucumbers, and zucchini. Fruits and vegetables that need to ripen should also be kept at room temperature. See Table 13.2 for a list of proper storage temperatures and times for a wide variety of foodstuffs.

### Storing Meat

Have you ever dug in the back of your refrigerator's freezer compartment and discovered a food you didn't know was there? Many people assume that freezing food is the equivalent of permanent preservation. As with canned goods, this is not the case. Even frozen food, if kept too long, can cause food-borne illnesses and certainly will lose quality over time. However, properly wrapped cuts of meat, frozen at 0° F or lower, will maintain their quality for several months. Exactly how many months varies with the kind of meat. Table 13.3 shows a range within which you can store meats with a reasonable expectation that they will remain safe and retain quality.

## Preparing Food

When it is time to prepare food, *always* begin by thoroughly washing your hands.

Yes, hand sanitizers do work, and they appear to be just as effective as soap and water. However, the same cannot be said for antibacterial soaps. New

| Table 13.3 | Suggested Storage Times for Raw Meat | |
|---|---|---|
| **Product** | **Refrigerator (40° F)** | **Freezer (0° F)** |
| Beef, roasts and steaks | 3–5 days | 6–12 months |
| Lamb, roasts and chops | 3–5 days | 6–9 months |
| Pork, roasts and chops | 3–5 days | 4–6 months |
| Beef and lamb, ground | 1–2 days | 3–4 months |
| Pork, sausage | 1–2 days | 1–2 months |

information suggests that they may not be the best type of soap to use. They do not appear to be more effective than traditional soap and may actually do more harm than good. It appears that some bacteria can become resistant to the antibacterial compounds used in these soaps, making regular use actually less effective than soap and water. Moreover, there is evidence that these compounds are accumulating in the environment and contaminating the food supply. Bottom line—wash your hands thoroughly with either traditional soap and water or a water-free hand sanitizer.

Next, make certain your utensils and food preparation surfaces are clean. Never place fruits and vegetables on the same preparation surface used for raw meat or eggs. Always use a clean knife or spoon with each different food product or dish.

*My friend is always rubbing waterless hand sanitizer on her hands. Does that stuff work?*

### Temperature and Bacteria

The temperature range at which microbial growth is most likely to occur is between 40° F and 140° F; this is referred to as the **danger zone**. Therefore, a primary goal of food preparation is to keep cold food at 40° F or below and hot food at 140° F or above.

### Defrosting

The USDA offers several guidelines for defrosting food: thawing in the refrigerator, using cold water, and using the microwave. In following the defrosting guidelines, the most important thing to remember is that you should never leave frozen food in a room-temperature environment. Even if the food still feels

**Want to know more?**
To review and evaluate the most recent information about why antibacterial soaps may be doing more harm than good, go to the text website at http://webcom8.grtxle.com/nutrition and click on the Chapters button. Select Chapter 13.

The first and most important step in food safety: Washing your hands.

This person is washing her hands with Purell.

**Want to know more?** You can access the details regarding the USDA's recommended thawing methods by going to the text website at http://webcom8.grtxle.com/nutrition and clicking on the Chapters button. Select Chapter 13.

frozen in the middle, the outer portions may be above 40° F and therefore at an ideal temperature for bacterial growth.

## Cooking Food

One of the most important steps in guaranteeing food safety, and perhaps the one most frequently ignored, is the need to achieve proper temperatures in cooked food. When cooking meats and many other foods, some people rely on color and appearance to indicate that the item is "done." Appearance and/or changes in texture are not reliable methods when judging doneness. Instead, food should be cooked to the specified temperatures. There are some exceptions regarding texture. You *can* judge whether certain foods such as vegetables and pastas are properly cooked by their texture. For example, if you like crunchy vegetables, just steam or boil them for a few minutes. If you like them mushy, cook them longer, but be aware that the longer you cook them, the more nutrients you are losing. For meat and most other cooked foods, you should go by temperature. In fact, the USDA advises, "The color of cooked meat can be quite variable. At 160° F, a safely cooked beef patty may look brown, pink, or some variation of brown or pink." Achieving proper temperature is even more important for meat in order to prevent the spread of food-borne illnesses such as *E. coli*. As noted earlier, the goal is to keep food out of the danger zone. This is pictured in Figure 13.6. To ensure that food has reached a safe temperature throughout, use a food thermometer. These can be purchased at a reasonable cost at any grocery or cooking store. When a patty is cooked to 160° F throughout, it should be safe and can still be juicy, regardless of color. See Table 13.4 for recommended cooking temperatures.

To communicate the importance of cooking food to its proper temperature and of using a thermometer, the Food Safety and Inspection Service (FSIS) of the USDA developed the Thermy campaign. The program is based on the Fight BAC! message of "cook" and uses a character called Thermy (see Figure 13.7).

## Serving Food

We have now discussed food safety from the time of purchase through the cooking process. It may seem as if we have exhausted our discussion on food safety at home, but we are not done yet. The next step is actually putting the food on your plate and eating it. Proper food handling does not end at the table. Leftover foods must be stored quickly and dishes and silverware must be washed properly. See Figure 13.8 for the USDA's guidelines on these important topics.

## Cleaning Up

For most of us, this is the dreaded last step after preparing and eating a meal. Most important, put all leftovers away in tightly sealed containers within two hours. Make sure your dishwasher is functioning properly; if you don't have one, use hot water and plenty of dish soap. Wipe down all preparation and cooking surfaces with bleach or another antibacterial agent. How often do you

Avoid cross-contamination by keeping raw produce and meats separate.

A meat thermometer is one of the most important tools for preventing food-borne illness. You can purchase one at a grocery store or any store that sells kitchen utensils.

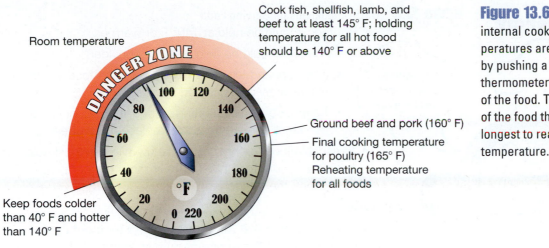

Cook fish, shellfish, lamb, and beef to at least 145° F; holding temperature for all hot food should be 140° F or above

Room temperature

Ground beef and pork (160° F)

Final cooking temperature for poultry (165° F)
Reheating temperature for all foods

Keep foods colder than 40° F and hotter than 140° F

**Figure 13.6** Minimum internal cooking temperatures are measured by pushing a probe-stem thermometer into the middle of the food. This is the part of the food that takes the longest to reach the required temperature.

## Table 13.4    USDA Cooking Temperature Rules

| Food | Temperature (°F) |
| --- | --- |
| **Ground Meat and Meat Mixtures** | |
| Beef, pork, veal, lamb | 160 |
| Turkey, chicken | 165 |
| **Fresh Beef, Veal, Lamb** | |
| Medium rare | 145 |
| Medium | 160 |
| Well done | 170 |
| **Poultry** | |
| Chicken and turkey, whole | 180 |
| Poultry breasts, roast | 170 |
| Poultry thighs, wings, legs | 180 |
| Duck and goose | 180 |
| Stuffing (cooked alone or in bird) | 165 |
| **Fresh Pork** | |
| Medium | 160 |
| Well done | 170 |
| **Ham** | |
| Fresh (raw) | 160 |
| Precooked (to reheat) | 140 |
| **Eggs and Egg Dishes** | |
| Eggs | Cook until yolk and white are firm |
| Egg dishes | 160 |
| **Leftovers and Casseroles** | **165** |

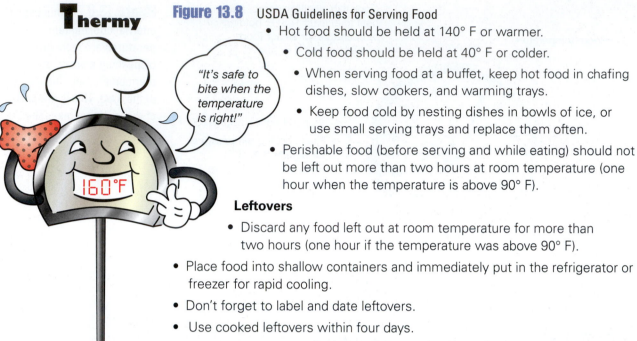

**Thermy**

*"It's safe to bite when the temperature is right!"*

160°F

**Figure 13.8** USDA Guidelines for Serving Food

- Hot food should be held at 140° F or warmer.
  - Cold food should be held at 40° F or colder.
    - When serving food at a buffet, keep hot food in chafing dishes, slow cookers, and warming trays.
    - Keep food cold by nesting dishes in bowls of ice, or use small serving trays and replace them often.
  - Perishable food (before serving and while eating) should not be left out more than two hours at room temperature (one hour when the temperature is above 90° F).

**Leftovers**

- Discard any food left out at room temperature for more than two hours (one hour if the temperature was above 90° F).
- Place food into shallow containers and immediately put in the refrigerator or freezer for rapid cooling.
- Don't forget to label and date leftovers.
- Use cooked leftovers within four days.
- Heat leftovers to proper temperatures.

**Figure 13.7** Thermy.

*Source:* Food Safety Inspection Service, USDA.

replace your sponge and dish towel? Would you be able to grow something in the science lab if you took a sample? Use a clean sponge and dish towel every day. Be sure to wash the sponge in the dishwasher or disinfect it regularly and use a clean dish towel.

## Putting It All Together

To achieve food safety, all precautions must be taken at every step of food production—in the use of chemicals and fertilizers in the growing of produce, care and feeding of livestock, food processing, preparation, and disposal. Washing your hands, avoiding cross-contamination, cooking food to proper temperatures, and keeping food out of the danger zone are perhaps the most important "take-home" messages to ensure food safety.

**Before you go on . . .**

1. What is cross-contamination and how should it be prevented?
2. Define the USDA terms "sell by," "use by," and "best before."
3. What are the "Fight BAC!" messages?
4. Define the *danger zone* and explain its significance to food safety.
5. Within what time period after cooking should all leftovers be refrigerated or frozen?

# Real People, Real Strategies

Many college students are at risk for food-borne illness simply because they are unaware of proper food-handling techniques. Kevin's first mistake was not putting the leftover pizza in the refrigerator as soon as the group was done eating. Even if he had placed it in the refrigerator, it would have been a good idea before eating it the next day to reheat it to the proper temperature of 165° F. As an aside, it's worth noting that dorm room refrigerators may not be kept at the proper temperature of 40° F and other appliances, even if permitted by school policy, may not be in proper working order.

Students eating meals in the school cafeteria may also be at risk by consuming foods that are left out on buffet lines for extended periods of time. Always make certain that hot foods are hot and cold foods cold before purchasing and consuming them. Inform the food-service director if you observe foods not being kept at their proper temperatures. Also, don't hesitate to inform management if you observe food handlers not using proper techniques such as hand washing or wearing gloves. College students are also likely to consume foods in social situations such as fraternity or sorority events, barbecues, and tailgate parties. Again, when eating in these situations make sure that foods are kept at the proper temperatures (hot food hot and cold food cold). Avoid eating foods such as wings and pasta salad that have been left out at room temperature for more than two hours.

> **Want to know more?**
> The USDA offers some food safety tips specific to college students. See the text website at http://webcom8.grtxle.com/nutrition and click on the Chapters button. Select Chapter 13. Remember, you represent your own last line of defense in avoiding a food-borne illness.

# Chapter Summary

- Food-borne illnesses remain a public health concern, and food safety is the responsibility of everyone throughout the entire food system.
- Food-borne illnesses are defined as diseases, usually either infectious or toxic in nature, caused by agents that enter the body through the ingestion of food.
- Most food-borne illnesses are caused by a variety of pathogens or infectious agents such as bacteria, viruses, fungi, mold, and parasites that can be transmitted in food.
- Pathogens can be acquired through food and drinking water, from contact with animals or their environment, or from person-to-person contact. Fresh produce can also be a source of infection if it is contaminated by bacteria and viruses in the field or after harvest. In addition, some pathogens are spread by infected people who contaminate food while preparing it.
- New pathogens, changing eating habits, an increase in mass food production, a global food supply, longer transport, and a growing number of highly susceptible people are the primary reasons for food safety concerns.
- To oversee safety in food production, the U.S. government has created several programs through a collaboration of the FDA, USDA, EPA, and CDC.
- Drying, freezing, pasteurization, irradiation, canning, and aseptic packaging are some of the processes used to enhance preservation in food manufacturing.

- More controversial techniques, such as cloning and genetically engineered foods, that are said to enhance food safety are emerging as techniques of the future.
- Many food-borne illnesses occur as a result of cross-contamination during home preparation of food.
- Cook, separate, chill, and clean are the Fight BAC! campaign's messages to promote food safety at home.
- The consumer's primary role in food safety begins at the grocery store.
- You can and should do several things at home to prevent food-borne illnesses. Among them are to wash your hands, cook food to the proper temperature, avoid cross-contamination, keep food out of the danger zone, store food properly in the refrigerator and freezer, and reheat leftovers thoroughly.

# Key Terms

**agribusiness** Farming and related food processing operated as a large-scale industry. (p. 418)

**aseptic packaging** (ay-SEP-tic) A method in which food is sterilized and then placed in previously sterilized containers, which are then sealed in a sterile environment; used for liquid foods such as concentrated milk and soups. (p. 420)

**"best before"** A date that appears on food labels and refers to the relationship between the shelf life and the quality of the product. (p. 428)

**critical control points (CCPs)** Points in the food production process where the potential hazards could occur and can be prevented and/or controlled. (p. 417)

**cross-contamination** The transfer of a substance that can cause illness from one food to another, usually on a utensil or a surface such as a cutting board or plate. (p. 407)

**danger zone** The temperature range (40° F to 140° F) at which microbial growth is most likely to occur. (p. 431)

**emerging pathogen** Microorganisms previously not recognized as human pathogens, or those unexpectedly found in particular foods. (p. 414)

**first in, first out (FIFO)** A practice followed by many restaurants and retail establishments in which older items are placed in front of newer items and therefore used first. (p. 430).

**food-borne illness** Diseases, usually either infectious or toxic in nature, caused by agents that enter the body through the ingestion of food. (p. 406)

**food irradiation** (food ir-ray-dee-AY-shun) Exposure of food to low-level radiation to prolong shelf life and eliminate pathogens. (p. 420)

**Hazard Analysis Critical Control Point (HACCP) system** Guidelines established to promote food safety at every step of food production; the farm, storage, retail stores, restaurants and consumers. It provides a detailed manual of educational materials and training workshops for organizations and individuals to follow. (p. 416)

**highly susceptible population** People who are more likely than other people in the general population to develop food-borne illness. (p. 416)

**jaundice** A condition in which the liver is inflamed and the skin may appear yellow. (p. 411)

**nitrates and nitrites** Salts used in the curing and smoking process that have been used for centuries to preserve meats. (p. 420)

**parasite** An organism that derives nourishment and protection from another living organism known as the *host*. (p. 406)

**pasteurization** (pass-chur-ih-ZAY-shun) The process of heating food to temperatures below the boiling point to kill harmful organisms while still maintaining its quality. The process is usually associated with milk and was named after its inventor, the French scientist Louis Pasteur. (p. 418)

**pathogens** Microorganisms or infectious agents such as bacteria, viruses, fungi, mold, and parasites that can be transmitted in food and cause illness. (p. 406)

**potentially hazardous foods** Foods that support the rapid growth of disease-causing microorganisms—usually proteins or carbohydrates with high moisture content and low acidity. (p. 414)

**"sell by"** A date that appears on food labels and tells the store how long to display a food product. (p. 428)

**ultra high temperature (UHT)** A sterilization process that raises the temperature of milk even higher than in ultrapasteurization, and the milk is then rapidly cooled and aseptically packaged so it can remain on the shelf without refrigeration. (p. 419)

**ultrapasteurization (UP)** A process similar to traditional pasteurization that uses slightly different equipment, higher temperatures, and longer processing times. (p. 419)

**"use by"** A date that is placed on a food package voluntarily by the manufacturer and suggests when the product will start to lose peak quality. (p. 428)

# Chapter Quiz

1. What causes food-borne illness?
   a. bacteria
   b. viruses
   c. parasites
   d. all of the above

2. What is the recommendation for cleaning raw produce before eating it?
   a. Wash in soap and water.
   b. Rinse well with water.
   c. Wash with a commercial produce cleaner.
   d. Soak it in water.

3. What is HACCP?
   a. a group of government agencies established to ensure food safety
   b. a set of guidelines to ensure food safety for everyone from farmers to consumers
   c. a set of regulations the food industry must follow to ensure food safety
   d. a set of strict regulations for farmers

4. What is the best way to determine whether something has been in your refrigerator too long?
   a. Look at the "sell by" date on the label.
   b. Determine how long it has been in there and go by the cold storage times.

   c. Smell the food.
   d. Look to see if the container or package is open.

5. What is the ideal temperature for your refrigerator?
   a. 32° F
   b. 45° F
   c. 40° F
   d. 0° F

6. What is the ideal temperature for your freezer?
   a. 32° F
   b. 45° F
   c. 40° F
   d. 0° F

7. What is the danger zone or the temperatures at which bacteria are most likely to grow?
   a. between 60° F and 90° F
   b. below 0° F and above 40° F
   c. below 40° F and above 140° F
   d. between 40° F and 140° F

8. In terms of food safety, what is the best way to determine whether you have properly cooked a hamburger patty?
   a. Check to see if it has reached an internal temperature of 150° F.

b. Check to see if it has reached an internal temperature of 160° F.

c. Make certain that it is not juicy inside.

d. Cook it just until the inside is pink.

9. How many hours can cooked food be left out before it must be refrigerated or frozen?

a. four

b. five

c. two

d. one

10. What is cross-contamination?

a. when contaminated foods come in contact with each other

b. when you use a cutting board to cut raw meat and then to cut fruits or vegetables

c. when you use the same fork in cooked chicken as you did in the same chicken when it was raw

d. all of the above

# CHAPTER 14

# Sports Nutrition

## Fine-Tuning a Good Thing

## < Here's Where You've Been

*The following topics were introduced in preceding chapters and are related to concepts we'll discuss in Chapter 14. Be certain that you're familiar with them before proceeding.*

- Although athletes may need more protein than inactive people, most already consume adequate amounts of protein. (Chapter 5)
- A decrease of 1–2 percent body weight due to dehydration can negatively influence exercise performance. (Chapter 8)
- Replacing fluid loss during exercise in the heat without replacing sodium loss can lead to hyponatremia. (Chapter 8)
- Supplements should be used in addition to a healthy diet, not instead of one. (Chapter 11)

## Here's Where You're Going: >

*The following topics and concepts are the ones we'll emphasize in Chapter 14.*

- Nutritional requirements for an athlete are not that different from those we have discussed for non-athletes in previous chapters. They typically only need some "fine-tuning."
- Sports nutrition is about energy production, and energy comes from fuels such as carbohydrates and fats.
- Intensity and duration of an activity should determine your choice of fuels.
- An optimal sports nutrition diet requires that you consume adequate nutrients before, during, and after training and competition.

## Real People, Real Choices

Ryan and Philip are roommates and sophomores at the University of South Florida. Both were athletes in high school and have always been active. The fall semester is about to start and they want to get serious about their training and nutrition.

Ryan is attending school on a soccer scholarship and has coaches and trainers dictating his training, but he is less clear about the nutritional aspect of his sport. He knows he needs to eat the right things to support the intense practices and games that he is participating in daily and sometimes twice daily.

Philip is trying to stay fit in order to play in weekly intramural flag football games. He is training and eating on his own and is not always as consistent as he would like to be, but when he can find the time he does lift weights and runs three to five miles three or four days per week. When both Ryan and Philip recognized from their conversations that neither really had reliable information regarding an optimal sports nutrition plan, they decided they should pursue this goal together. They eat most of their meals on campus in the cafeteria and not always at normal times. How should they start? Do you think their plans should be the same or different, and why?

Nutritional requirements for an athlete are not that different from those for non-athletes that have been discussed throughout this text. In fact, we have specifically mentioned nutrition recommendations that apply to athletes as well as non-athletes, such as the *Dietary Guidelines*, MyPyramid, and DRIs. In the discussions of carbohydrates, fat, proteins, vitamins, and minerals in Chapters 3, 4, 5, 9, and 10 respectively, we frequently related the information to non-athletes and athletes alike. Moreover, in Chapter 5 we addressed the protein needs for athletes. In Chapter 8 we reviewed ways of staying hydrated while you exercise and whether you should use sports drinks while doing so. Finally, in Chapter 11 on supplements, we discussed numerous topics and issues that are pertinent to athletes.

Basically, an athlete needs to eat a balanced diet just like anyone else, only more of it and with plenty of carbohydrates, electrolytes, and water before, during, and after exercise. This should be the foundation of any physically active person's diet, whether he or she is a competitive athlete or not. Of course, you can "fine-tune" a healthy diet by looking at the specific demands of the activity in which you are participating. In other words, you need to determine how long, how often, and how hard you are exercising. Typically sports nutrition recommendations are aimed at athletes and highly active people who exercise more than one hour a day.

In Chapter 6 we discussed how the body uses various biochemical pathways to get usable energy in the form of ATP from carbohydrates, fat, and protein (see Figure 14.1). Which pathway your body uses during exercise is determined mostly by the intensity and the duration of the exercise.

The intensity of the exercise—that is, how fast you are running, biking, skiing, and so on—dictates the rate at which energy must be produced. So the faster you go, the higher the intensity, and therefore the faster the rate at which energy must be produced. When your energy demands are low or moderate, sufficient oxygen can be delivered to meet your needs. Thus, you are using

Immediate energy system (ATP-PC)—uses stored ATP

■ 8–10 seconds (100 m)
Sprinter

Glycolysis (anaerobic)—uses carbohydrates, mostly from glycogen

■ to approx. 2 minutes (400 m)
Swimmer

**Figure 14.1** The three primary systems or biochemical pathways by which usable energy in the form of ATP is obtained from carbohydrates, fat, and protein.

Aerobic—uses carbohydrates and fats and a small amount of protein

■ Unlimited time
Marathon runner

oxygen-requiring pathways and *aerobic* conditions exist (see Chapter 6 for more on aerobic metabolism). You can use both fat and carbohydrates in aerobic conditions. You can also use protein if you have to, but your body prefers to reserve it for maintenance and repair; it is used for energy only if carbohydrates are low.

When your need for energy exceeds the amount that can be produced using oxygen, your body falls back on systems that don't require oxygen to release energy. In this case, *anaerobic* conditions exist (see Chapter 6). You can, if necessary, produce energy from carbohydrates without oxygen. This is called anaerobic metabolism. When you rely on anaerobic metabolism you produce **lactic acid**. When it accumulates in the cells, it eventually causes changes in your muscles, leading to fatigue and a desire to stop exercising. Have you ever experienced a burning sensation in your muscles after sprinting as fast as you could, after which you had to stop or slow down? That sensation resulted from the formation of lactic acid.

So, in a nutshell, sports nutrition is geared toward athletes and highly active people, it is about energy production, and energy comes mostly from fuels such as carbohydrates and fats. The intensity and duration of the activity should determine your choice of fuels. The higher the intensity, the more your body relies on carbohydrates—so in an all-out effort like a sprint, you rely solely on carbohydrates. The lower the intensity, the more you rely on fat for energy. The longer the duration of the exercise, the more likely that you will run out of carbohydrates and will have to rely more on fats. It is therefore important to consume carbohydrates during exercise that lasts longer than sixty to ninety minutes.

**Want to know more?**
For more information on lactic acid and its role in exercise performance, go to the text website at http://webcom8.grtxle.com/nutrition and click on the Chapters button. Select Chapter 14.

# Exercise Basics

## The Benefits of Exercise

Nutritionists and other health professionals have a number of reasons for promoting exercise. Some of the benefits of exercise from a nutritional standpoint are as follows:

- Increases HDL (the good cholesterol)
- Lowers resting heart rate
- Lowers blood pressure
- Helps prevent:
    Heart disease
    Stroke
    Type 2 diabetes
    Cancer
    Osteoporosis
- Helps manage stress
- Improves quality of sleep
- Helps decrease mild depression and anxiety
- Enhances self-esteem
- Helps manage weight
- Helps maintain muscle mass
- Improves overall feeling of well-being

Exercise is an important factor in chronic disease prevention. It raises HDL cholesterol (the "good" cholesterol), lowers resting heart rate and blood pressure, and essentially makes the heart much more efficient so that it works less. Exercise helps prevent other chronic diseases as well, including Type 2 diabetes and a number of cancers, particularly of the breast and colon. Weight-bearing exercise strengthens bone, thus delaying the onset of *osteoporosis*, a disease in which bones become fragile and more likely to break. In addition, exercise has several psychological benefits. It can reduce stress and may help alleviate symptoms of mild depression and anxiety. For some, it may even improve their self esteem. An improved sense of well-being generated by exercise frequently motivates individuals to improve their diet, thus increasing the likelihood that they are meeting their nutrient requirements.

### ■ Self-Assessment

#### *How do you choose the right exercise?*

An ideal exercise program includes some aerobic exercise such as walking, jogging, cycling, or swimming as well as stretching and strength training. The most important factor in choosing an exercise is finding one that suits you. What do you need to balance your life? Only through experimentation can you discover what will meet your needs and, perhaps, what those needs even are. Think about the changes exercise can offer, and think about what appeals to you. The next thing to keep in mind is to be realistic. If you have only one hour to exercise, don't join a gym that's thirty minutes away. Avoid signing up for an activity you know or think you will hate, because doing so will make failure more likely. Figure out how much time you have, and avoid rationalizing that you don't have enough. We all have some time—so plan and then go do something you enjoy.

It is important to find a form of exercise that you enjoy. Sometimes exercising with a friend or enjoying a peaceful environment help to make it a positive experience.

Exercise can offer good opportunities to connect with the environment. Hiking a trail or canoeing down a river can be very intimate, just you and the outdoors. Even walking a city street lets you experience the weather, and a sunny day or a snowstorm puts a new face on a familiar landscape.

Exercise can also offer quiet and solitude, balancing a loud and intrusive work or school environment. It can be your quiet time, providing needed relaxation and stress relief. At other times, your workout can be social, offering shared conversation with friends. Shared physical activities, particularly if they are challenging or rewarding, can create a great way to meet people with similar interests.

There's also the nature of the activity itself to consider. Some people prefer the mental and physical state they experience by performing a technically challenging activity such as skiing or rollerblading. Some prefer games of strategy and teamwork, such as soccer, basketball, or bike racing. Other people choose activities that are more of a solo endeavor, such as running or walking. Many like a broad range of activities and would rather do something different each day.

Finding a match between exercise and your everyday life is a matter of meeting your needs in a way that creates balance. If the exercise helps establish that balance, you are likely to keep at it. It's also a matter of having an adventurous spirit, trying new experiences at every opportunity.

Make your vacations a time of discovery. Use exciting locations to try an activity you wouldn't normally participate in, such as golf, mountain biking, hiking, or backcountry skiing. Think of exercise as play and as a time for yourself, a reward as opposed to drudgery. The following questions are meant to help you get started or to try a new activity.

**Self-Assessment Questions**

- Have I found an exercise I really enjoy, that meets my needs on physical, social, and even emotional levels? If not, what other activities could I try to achieve these goals?
- Do I get at least twenty to thirty minutes of aerobic exercise at least three to five times per week?
- Do I make certain not to go into exercise sessions when hungry?
- Do I always replace losses of carbohydrates, water, and electrolytes during prolonged exercise?
- Do I take in adequate carbohydrates, water, and electrolytes to recover from exercise?
- Do I eat a balanced diet? ■

## The Role of Exercise in Weight Management and Strength Training

### Weight Management

As discussed in Chapter 7, many people exercise because they want to lose weight or keep from gaining weight. Exercise may also help control weight by regulating appetite. Some evidence shows that formerly sedentary people who begin exercising often decrease their energy intake. Although exercise is essential in weight control, it should not be the only reason for participating in physical activity. Exercise provides many health benefits, as listed earlier, and it helps maintain weight by increasing the number of calories burned each day; that is your *metabolic rate*. This increase in daily metabolism results not just from the activity itself, which sometimes can actually burn a minimal number of calories, but from building or maintaining muscle mass. Muscle mass burns more calories than fat, even while you are just sitting in class, and therefore it keeps your metabolism increased. Maintaining muscle mass becomes very important as you age because it keeps your metabolism from decreasing too much, thus preventing the weight gain often thought to be a normal part of aging. More important, exercise helps older adults maintain the strength needed to maintain daily activities and to recover when injury and illness do occur.

### ■ Nutrition and Lifestages

*It's never too late—exercise and sports nutrition for the older adult*

Are your grandparents in good physical shape? Do they exercise on a daily basis? Do they watch what they eat? Sports nutrition guidelines can be of great benefit to older adults. The associated increase in nutrition quality may be particularly helpful, as the elderly are at risk for inadequate intake. In addition, the elderly can benefit from the improved strength that often occurs with exercise. More than anything else, lack

At age 73, Ed Whitlock ran a 2:54 in the 2004 Toronto Waterfront Marathon.

To determine whether you are exercising within the heart rate target zone, take your pulse at your neck, wrist, or chest; the CDC recommends the wrist. You can feel the radial pulse on the artery of the wrist in line with the thumb, as shown in the photo. Place the tips of your index and middle fingers over your artery and press lightly; do not use your thumb. Take a full 60-second count of your heartbeats, or count your heartbeats for 30 seconds and multiply by 2. Start the count on a beat, which is counted as zero.

*Which is better for you, high-intensity or low-intensity exercise?*

of strength limits their ability for self-care. Getting out of bathtubs, opening jars, lifting pots of water, and even getting out of a chair often require more strength than some older adults have, which is often why they have to live in assisted-living facilities and nursing homes. Exercise and adequate nutrition have been proven to be very beneficial in helping older adults stay healthy and enhancing their recovery when they are injured or sick. ◼

## Recommendations: How Much Exercise Is Enough?

Before we discuss recommendations for how much exercise is enough, it is important to define fitness. Fitness is more than being able to do push-ups or run a certain distance without being out of breath. The American College of Sports Medicine (ACSM), one of the leading professional organizations in the health and fitness field, defines **fitness** as "the ability to perform moderate-to-vigorous levels of physical activity without undue fatigue and the capability of maintaining this capacity throughout life."

Many people think of fitness as being able to exercise for a certain period of time. However, there are actually several components to fitness:

Cardiorespiratory endurance
Muscular strength
Muscular endurance
Flexibility

How long you exercise and the level of intensity achieved should depend on your goals and whether you are training for a specific sport or event or just trying to achieve or maintain the basic health benefits of exercise. The ACSM recommends that in order to achieve a cardiovascular benefit you should exercise three to five days a week at a **moderate intensity**, which is about 55–70 percent of your **age-predicted maximum heart rate**. This means that when exercising you need to keep your heart rate up within the specified range (described shortly) for twenty to sixty minutes during continuous or intermittent (minimum of two to six ten-minute sessions throughout the day) aerobic activity. *How long you should exercise depends on your level of intensity.* If you are exercising at a **low intensity** (below 55 percent of your age-predicted maximum heart rate), such as a fast walk, you will need to go for thirty minutes or more. If you are exercising at **high intensity**—for example, running fast (more than 70 percent of your age-predicted maximum heart rate)—you will need to continue for twenty minutes or longer.

As you probably know or suspect, there are many myths and recommendations about exercise. Although it's very difficult to keep up with all of them, we address three of the more common ones in the Myths and Legends feature that follows.

### ■ Myths and Legends
*What not to believe!*

*"In order to lose weight and burn more fat, it is better to exercise in the morning on an empty stomach."* This statement is false. Engaging in extended training on an empty stomach first thing in the morning means training on a less-than-full tank, which means lower-intensity training, lower fitness, and lower performance. Liver glycogen reserves have been used to maintain blood sugar in the eight to twelve hours since the previous night's meal and by morning may be largely depleted. Eating a morning meal high in carbohydrates will allow you to have a higher-quality training session and avoid muscle breakdown. However, if you really can't handle eating a full breakfast, try eating something light such as a banana or an energy bar, or try drinking a beverage high in carbohydrates. Something is better than nothing.

*"To burn more fat, exercise at a lower intensity."* This is also not true. This myth is related to the previous one, and, despite solid scientific evidence to prove otherwise, it is advice still given in gyms and some fitness magazines. Fat is the predominant fuel used in low-intensity exercise, while high-intensity exercise burns carbohydrates. Because this is true, it is often suggested that in order to lose weight, you should work out at a lower intensity. An associated myth is that high-intensity exercise burns only carbohydrates and therefore does not contribute to weight loss.

Two physiological facts explain why this is not so. The first involves energy balance. What matters is energy expenditure versus energy intake. If your intake is less than your expenditure, you will lose weight. It doesn't matter which form of calories you burn. Higher-intensity exercise burns more calories per hour. Walking, you might expend 300 calories per hour, while you might burn 600 calories or more running for the same amount of time. An hour of high-intensity exercise contributes more to weight loss than the same time spent doing low-intensity exercise. If time is limited, increase your intensity. In addition, high-intensity exercise burns more calories after exercise, as it keeps your metabolism elevated.

Second, if you burn 300 calories walking and 60 percent of those calories come from fat and 40 percent from carbohydrates, that is 180 calories from fat and 120 from carbohydrates. Meanwhile, if you burn 600 calories running and 30 percent of those calories are from fat and 70 percent from carbohydrates, that is 180 fat calories and 420 carbohydrate calories. So although the percentage of calories burned from fat is lower, the total amount of calories from fat is not different.

*The best athletes are the ones with the lowest body fat.* Not true. Every person has an ideal percentage of body fat (which allows them to perform at their best), and many athletes have compromised their performance by trying to lower their body fat to achieve unrealistic ideals. Assuming an athlete is not obese, no evidence suggests a direct link between percentage of body fat and performance. ■

### APPLICATION TIP

To estimate your age-predicted maximum heart rate, simply subtract your age from 220. In order to exercise at a moderate intensity, take 55–70 percent of that by multiplying that number separately by 0.55 and then by 0.70. This will give you the *heart rate range* you should maintain while exercising in order to achieve an optimal cardiovascular benefit. In order to exercise at a high intensity, subtract your age from 220 and multiply by 70–85 percent (0.70 to 0.85). So if you are 20 years old, this would mean that your age-predicted maximum heart rate is 200 and that your heart rate during moderate exercise should be between 110 and 140 beats per minute. During vigorous activity it should be 140 to 170 beats per minute.

## Strength Training

**Want to know more?**
You can explore other sports nutrition myths (and then test your friends) by going to the text website at http://webcom8.grtxle.com/nutrition and clicking on the Chapters button. Select Chapter 14.

If you have ever done strength training, you're probably aware that there is no shortage of sources for advice. Predictably, many supposed experts and manufacturers claim that their way of training and/or use of their equipment is the best or only way to gain optimal strength. The truth is that there are many different and effective ways to train for strength. According to the ACSM, to achieve the maximum benefits from strength training, you should perform one to three sets of eight to ten exercises (conditioning all major muscle groups), each with eight to twelve or ten to fifteen repetitions, two to three days per week.

Benefits of strength training include the following:

- Build muscle mass
- Increase metabolism (due to increased muscle mass)
- Control weight (due to increased metabolism)
- Build and maintain bone mass
- Enhance psychological well-being
- Prevent injury
- Improve daily functioning, especially in the elderly
- Enhance sport performance
- Prevent chronic diseases:
    Diabetes
    Heart disease
    Cancer
    High blood pressure

In order to maintain range of motion and to prevent injury and soreness, the ACSM recommends that you incorporate stretching into all workouts. Before stretching, warm up with five to ten minutes of light cycling, walking, rowing, and so on. Each stretch should be held for fifteen to thirty seconds and repeated two to four times, alternating sides. Do not force stretches. Figure 14.2 represents the basic recommendations to achieve fitness.

**Before you go on . . .**

1. How do the nutritional requirements of athletes differ from non-athletes?
2. List at least eight health benefits of exercise.
3. What is the ACSM and what are its recommendations for exercise?
4. Define *fitness*.
5. Explain why the statement "To burn more fat, exercise at lower intensity" is false.

## Converting Food to Energy for Exercise

You know that when you exercise, you burn more calories than when you are just sitting on the couch. What you may not know is how your body burns those extra calories to meet the demands of exercise. There are three systems or pathways for converting carbohydrates, fats, and protein into useful energy: (1) the **immediate energy system**, (2) *anaerobic metabolism,* and

# Physical Activity Pyramid

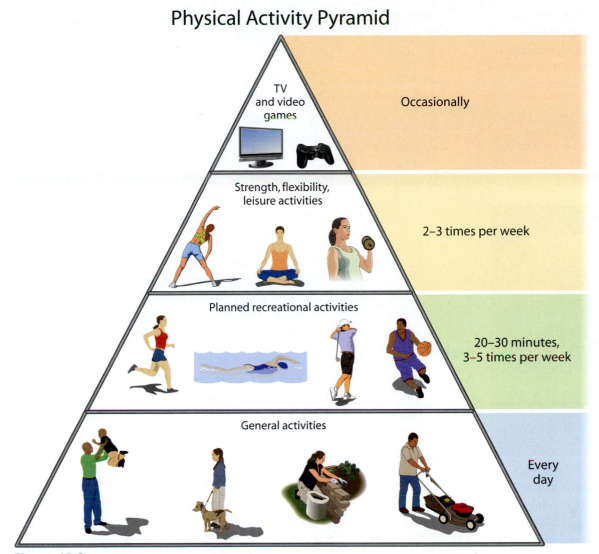

**Figure 14.2** Physical activity pyramid.

(3) *aerobic metabolism.* We will discuss them separately, and although it may seem as if one turns on when another turns off, they actually overlap. In other words, you are always using all three energy pathways even when one predominates. Figure 14.3 shows you how these energy systems overlap.

## The Immediate Energy System

The immediate energy system, also called *the ATP-PC system,* is what you use in the first ten seconds or so of any exercise. It is what you rely on for very short-duration maximal efforts such as power lifting, kicking a soccer ball, or short sprints. This system uses the very small amount of stored ATP kept in your body. It also does not require oxygen, which makes it very useful for extremely high-intensity exercise or when you need a lot of energy quickly for a quick burst. You don't have much of it, so to go beyond that quick burst you will have to burn some additional fuel.

**Figure 14.3** Percent contribution of each pathway relative to exercise duration, assuming intensity remains constant. Note how they overlap.

*Source:* McArdle, Katch, and Katch, *Exercise, Physiology, Energy, Nutrition, and Human Performance,* 5th ed., Fig 11.2, p. 223. Reprinted with permission.

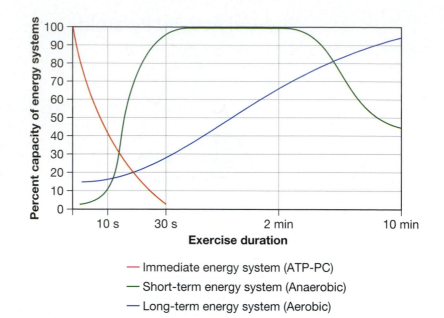

— Immediate energy system (ATP-PC)
— Short-term energy system (Anaerobic)
— Long-term energy system (Aerobic)

For quick bursts of energy and power, we rely primarily on ATP-PC. An example of this is an athlete throwing a shotput or javelin.

We can break glucose down anaerobically as the primary source of energy in exercise that lasts up to 2 or 3 minutes, such as a round of boxing.

## Glycolysis

As exercise continues beyond the first ten seconds, up until about two to three minutes, you will break down glucose anaerobically, mostly from muscle glycogen, in glycolysis. In other words, you will get ATP from glucose, but the process does not require oxygen.

### Anaerobic Metabolism

Anaerobic metabolism can produce energy very rapidly, but not for long periods of time. Therefore, it is used in high-intensity activities, in the first two to three minutes of exercise, or during a sprint to the finish line at the end of a race. You cannot rely primarily on this energy system for very long because when you break down glucose without oxygen you produce lactic acid, discussed earlier. As lactic acid begins to accumulate in the blood, it makes the blood more acidic. This increase in acidity impairs muscle contraction, which eventually contributes to a burning sensation in your working muscles and ultimately to muscle fatigue.

### Aerobic Metabolism

Let's say you begin running. At first the run may feel difficult, but after about two to three minutes it begins to feel easier, your breathing feels even, and you feel as if you have reached a comfortable pace. You have reached aerobic metabolism. You are using oxygen to help you provide energy. It takes a few minutes to have enough oxygen available to do this because blood flow must increase to the working muscle to deliver the extra oxygen you need. Once the blood flow has increased, oxygen will begin arriving to the exercising muscle. Once sufficient oxygen is available to your cells, glucose can be broken down through aerobic metabolism to provide energy. In addition, fat can be used to create energy so you won't have to rely so much on your limited carbohydrate stores. Protein will be used to a small extent. Much more energy (ATP) can be created aerobically compared to the other energy systems discussed, but it is done at a much slower rate. Aerobic metabolism is a major energy pathway in events lasting anywhere from two minutes to several hours.

## Continual Use of Energy Pathways

It's important to remember that all energy systems are in use at any given time. For instance, in a very high-intensity activity lasting ten to fifteen seconds, such as a 100-meter dash, even though the body derives most of its energy from the immediate energy system and from anaerobic glycolysis, it still uses the aerobic energy system to some extent. The body takes all the oxygen it can get and makes as much energy with it as it can, even if that is a very small part of the total. Likewise, even a slow walk leads to some small production of lactate from anaerobic glycolysis, though most of the energy needed will come from fat. You are always using all of your energy pathways even when one predominates. Table 14.1 illustrates where energy comes from in a variety of activities.

Aerobic metabolism uses carbohydrates and fats. It is what we rely on for endurance activities.

**Before you go on . . .**

1. Identify and differentiate between the three main energy systems used for exercise.
2. What are some examples of sports or physical activities that rely primarily on each system?
3. What does it mean to say that these energy systems overlap?

**Table 14.1**   **Percent Contribution of Energy Systems for Various Activities**

| Sport | Energy Systems Immediate | Glycolysis Anaerobic | Aerobic |
|---|---|---|---|
| Basketball | 60 | 20 | 20 |
| Fencing | 90 | 10 | 0 |
| Field Events | 90 | 10 | 0 |
| Golf swing | 95 | 5 | 0 |
| Gymnastics | 80 | 15 | 5 |
| Hockey | 50 | 20 | 30 |
| Rowing | 20 | 30 | 50 |
| Running (distance) | 10 | 20 | 70 |
| Skiing | 33 | 33 | 33 |
| Soccer | 50 | 20 | 30 |
| Swimming (distance) | 10 | 20 | 70 |
| Swimming (50m freestyle)* | 40 | 55 | 5 |
| Tennis | 70 | 20 | 10 |
| Volleyball | 80 | 5 | 15 |

Foss ML and Keteyian S. (1998) *The Physiological Basis for Exercise & Sport: 6th Edition.* Copyright 1998 McGraw-Hill. Reprinted by permission of the author.

*Stager JM and Tannger DA. (2005) *Swimming: 2nd Edition.*

# Fuel for Exercise

## Calorie Needs

Having enough calories to fuel the body during exercise is probably the most important nutritional requirement for athletes. When you exercise intensely, your calorie needs can easily be double that of a person who does not exercise at all. This, of course, does not mean that as an athlete or physically active person you can meet those increased calorie needs by eating a lot of sweets and junk food. Athletes and those who exercise regularly need to consume a lot of nutrient-dense foods such as whole-grain carbohydrates, fruits, vegetables, lean sources of proteins, and fats—basically, a healthy diet similar to that recommended for a sedentary person, just more of it. The good news is that you will have a little more room for some sweets here and there if you desire. Sweets should not be the cornerstone of your diet, or your performance will suffer along with your overall health. In order to more successfully meet their energy needs, athletes and those who are physically active should consume smaller meals about every three to four hours throughout the day to maintain adequate energy levels for exercise.

Some athletes participating in sports in which weight or appearance is judged, such as wrestling, gymnastics, and figure skating, may attempt to cut calories to achieve a weight category or a very lean physique. This can be very dangerous for health and performance. By cutting calories too low, athletes put themselves at risk for low bone density, injury, illness, eating disorders, menstrual dysfunction, fatigue, and impaired performance. Similarly, many athletes go to great lengths to gain weight and to achieve a more muscular physique. Many even risk taking illegal drugs such as anabolic steroids to gain muscle mass. Taking these drugs can lead to physical consequences just as devastating as those caused by severely restricting calories. This topic will be discussed more thoroughly in Chapter 15.

### ■ Make It a Practice
*Gaining weight the healthy way*

Many athletes, whether recreational or professional, want to gain weight. You may think this is as easy as just eating more. However, just as weight loss requires planning and time, so does weight gain. The goal should be to gain muscle mass, not fat. You must establish a realistic goal for your body type and your activity level. Consider a 20-year-old college football player who is 5'11" and weighs 175 lbs. He, his coach, and his Registered Dietitian (RD) who specializes in sports nutrition agree that he should attempt to gain 10 lbs. during the four months of his off-season. This would result in a gain of about 1/2 lb. per week. To gain this weight he will have to do two things: lift weights and eat a little bit more than he typically does. His RD determines that to maintain his current weight he needs about 3,000 calories. To gain weight they increase his daily consumption to 3,600 calories, or 120 percent of his current intake. They advise him to consume 60 percent of his calories from carbohydrates, 20 percent from protein, and 20 percent from fat. To add these extra calories he will need to consume healthy foods that are calorie dense, such as granola, nuts, and raisins. In addition he should eat frequently throughout the day. And last, he will need to monitor his body fat and calorie intake periodically to assess his progress.

The following is a representative menu from his 3,600-calorie-per-day weight gain plan.

**Breakfast**

1 c. granola

1 oz. walnuts

1 oz. raisins

16 oz. skim milk

**Snack**

1 fruit yogurt

1 banana

Total (cereal) (1/2 cup)

**Lunch**

2 slices whole-wheat bread

6.5-oz. portion of tuna

1 Tbsp. light mayo

1 c. raw carrots

1 oat bran muffin

8 oz. apple juice

**Snack**

1/2 c. trail mix

1 oz. pretzels

16-oz. sports drink

**Dinner**

1.5 c. whole-wheat spaghetti with tomato sauce

4 oz. ground beef

1 c. broccoli

Dinner roll

1 pat butter

12 oz. iced tea with 1 Tbsp. sugar

**Snack**

Protein bar

8 oz. skim milk

*\*Note:* This daily meal plan provides greater than 100 percent of the DRI for every nutrient without the use of any vitamin/mineral supplements.
Adapted from Wildman, R. and Miller, B. (2004). *Sports and Fitness Nutrition.* Belmont, CA: Thomson Wadsworth, p. 105. ■

## Carbohydrates as a Fuel

As exercise begins, working muscles primarily use their store of carbohydrates, muscle glycogen. As exercise continues and aerobic metabolism takes over, the use of stored glycogen is much less. How much less depends on how hard you are exercising. The higher the intensity, the more you will use muscle glycogen. If you begin the exercise activity with a full store of glycogen but do not eat or

**Want to know more?**
If you would like to explore more menu ideas for athletes, go to the text website at http://webcom8.grtxle.com/nutrition and click on the Chapters button. Select Chapter 14.

**APPLICATION TIP**

Be aware of the contents of the beverages you drink during exercise. Beverages that purposely have higher carbohydrate content, such as Hammer Nutrition's Recoverite, can slow the rate at which fluids empty from your stomach and may cause stomach upset. These drinks are best used after exercise to promote glycogen replacement.

Hammer Nutrition's Recoverite is an example of a beverage with a high carbohydrate content: ideal for recovery but not intended to be consumed during exercise.

*How can I avoid "hitting the wall"?*

drink any carbohydrates during the exercise, your stored glycogen will last from sixty to ninety minutes. As your glycogen stores get low, you will experience what many athletes refer to as **"hitting the wall" or "bonking."** You will feel tired, weak, possibly confused and nauseated, and unable to continue.

You can prevent "hitting the wall" and improve your performance in endurance events lasting longer than one hour by consuming foods high in carbohydrates (see Chapter 3) or beverages with carbohydrates in them such as most popular sports drinks. Carbohydrate-containing sports drinks such as Gatorade and Powerade can improve performance during endurance events and intermittent higher-intensity sports such as soccer and ice hockey. These drinks typically contain 6–8 percent carbohydrates in the form of easily absorbable glucose, sucrose, and/or fructose. (See Figure 14.4 for insight into reading a sports drink level). The rest of the drink contains water, sodium, and potassium. The sodium and glucose help enhance absorption of fluids (see Chapter 8 for more on water and electrolytes).

This will benefit performance by helping maintain blood glucose and glycogen levels and replacing fluids and electrolytes lost through sweating. By having enough carbohydrates available, you will be able to exercise faster and longer. Of course, these drinks also contain about 50 calories per 8-oz. serving. So if you are not exercising in the heat or for longer than sixty to ninety minutes, you may not want the extra calories. Just consuming carbohydrates during exercise is not enough; it is important that you consume adequate carbohydrates before and after exercise as well in order to optimize performance and recovery.

Your daily carbohydrate needs depend on the frequency, level, and duration of exercise.

**Figure 14.4** How to read a sports drink label.

Reprinted by permission of Iowa State University.

- You need at least 4–5 g of carbohydrate per kilogram of body weight per day, or more if you do cardio longer than 1 hour (if you weigh 135 lb., about 305 g).
- You may need as much as 7–8 g of carbohydrate per kilogram of body weight per day for endurance activity (if you weigh 135 lbs., about 427 g).

**How to read a sports drink label—**

A sodium level of about 50 to 170 milligrams per 8 ounces enhances the taste, facilitates absorption, and maintains body fluids. Higher amounts can lead to stomach upset and dehydration because the body sends water to the stomach to dilute the mixture.

Research shows that 8% or less concentration of carbohydrate (0 to 19 grams per 8 ounces) promotes rapid fluid replacement.

| Nutrition Facts | | |
|---|---|---|
| Serving Size 8 fl oz. (240ml) | | |
| Servings Per Container 2 | | |
| **Amount Per Serving** | | |
| Calories 50 | | |
| | | % Daily Value* |
| Total Fat 0g | | 0% |
| Sodium 110mg | | 5% |
| Potassium 30mg | | 1% |
| Total Carbohydrate 14g | | 5% |
| Sugars 14g | | |
| Proteins 0g | | |

Not a significant source of Calories from Fat, Saturated Fat, Cholesterol, Dietary Fiber, Vitamin A, Vitamin C, Calcium, Iron.

*Percent Daily Values are based on a 2,000 calorie diet.

**Fluid replacement drink**

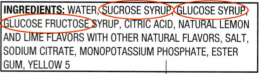

INGREDIENTS: WATER, SUCROSE SYRUP, GLUCOSE SYRUP, GLUCOSE FRUCTOSE SYRUP, CITRIC ACID, NATURAL LEMON AND LIME FLAVORS WITH OTHER NATURAL FLAVORS, SALT, SODIUM CITRATE, MONOPOTASSIUM PHOSPHATE, ESTER GUM, YELLOW 5

The type of carbohydrate (as well as the percent) affects sweetness and can reduce fluid intake if too sweet. High fructose levels can cause gastrointestinal distress by slowing absorption. (Ingredients are listed from greatest amount to least amount.)

The level of potassium also replaces body losses in proportion to what is lost in sweat. A potassium level of 30 to 50 milligrams is recommended.

**Carbohydrate concentration is NOT the same as % Daily Value.**
To calculate the carbohydrate concentration of any beverage as a percentage, divide the amount of carbohydrate in one serving (in grams) by the amount of fluid in one serving (8 ounces equals 240 milliliters), and then multiply by 100.

$$\frac{14 \text{ grams carbohydrate}}{240 \text{ milliliters}} \times 100 = 5.83 \text{ or } 6\% \text{ carbohydrate concentration}$$

- If you participate in intense daily training you may even need as much as 8–10 g of carbohydrate per kilogram of body weight per day, or 65–80 percent of total calories (if you weigh 135 lb., about 488–610 g).

## The Importance of Maintaining Carbohydrate Reserves

A high-carbohydrate diet prevents the chronic fatigue that gradually builds when glycogen stores are not maintained between workouts. It also promotes faster rebuilding of glycogen stores after they are depleted by prolonged exercise. If, after a long training session, you eat a high-fat diet and you don't consume sufficient carbohydrates to rebuild your glycogen stores, then you will go into the next day's training with fewer reserves. Most likely, you will not be able to train as hard and will feel sluggish. Do this again, and you have even fewer reserves the third day. Eventually, if you don't consume adequate carbohydrates, you'll be training completely devoid of glycogen reserves. This circumstance will force your body to rely entirely on fat as muscle fuel, which means higher-intensity exercise will be impossible. In addition, you will feel tired and maybe even a bit cranky. High carbohydrate intake means better recovery from exercise, which allows more consistent training and results in greater fitness and therefore better performance.

It is important to replace fluids while exercising. If you are going to be out for an hour or more, you should consider a sports drink to enhance fluid and electrolyte replacement and to provide glucose.

## Fat as a Fuel

Fat can be relied on as a primary fuel source only at rest and during aerobic activities at lower intensities. Fat cannot be used as a fuel for anaerobic metabolism. The higher the intensity of exercise, the less you rely on fats and the more you rely on carbohydrates for energy (see Figure 14.5a). The longer the duration of activity, the more you will rely on fat.

Fat has one advantage over carbohydrate as an energy source—it does not run out. The skinniest person has probably twenty times as many fat calories as carbohydrate. That's why the body burns fat when it can, because it wants to spare its small carbohydrate reserves by using its abundant fat stores. Therefore, fat is used as the dominant fuel for extended, lower-intensity exercise (see Figure 14.5b). Some experts advocate high-fat diets for athletes. This is not a good idea, especially for endurance athletes or any athlete exercising at high intensity. As discussed in previous chapters, a diet high in fat, particularly saturated fat, can increase your risk of heart disease. Similarly, a diet too low in fat (below 15 percent of total calories) can impair health and performance. Optimal fat intakes haven't been firmly established yet, but it appears that 15–35 percent of calories from fat is adequate for most active people.

| APPLICATION TIP |
|---|

If you find that sports drinks taste too "strong" or that you can't tolerate them during exercise, try cutting them in half with water.

 **Want to know more?**
You can determine the carbohydrate content of numerous foods by going to the text website at http://webcom8.grtxle .com/nutrition and clicking on the Chapters button. Select Chapter 14.

## Protein as a Fuel

Protein has many important functions in exercise, especially in muscle recovery and as a part of the enzymes that regulate energy metabolism. Therefore, your body does not want to use it for energy to a great extent. Although not a

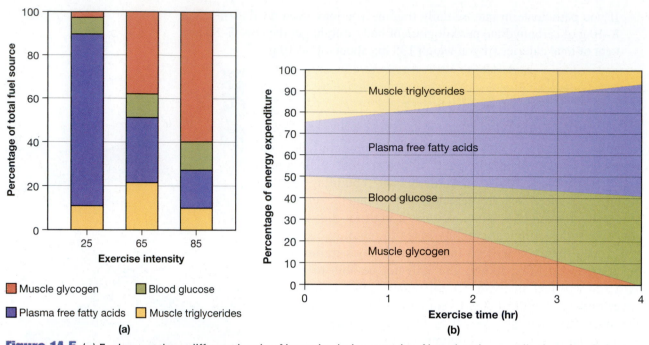

**Figure 14.5** (a) Fuel use at three different levels of intensity during exercise. Note that the contribution of carbohydrates (glucose, glycogen) increases as intensity increases. (b) Relationship between exercise duration and fuel use. Note that the contribution of fats increases as duration increases.

preferred fuel source for exercise, protein can be used to produce energy when carbohydrate availability is low.

### Protein's Contribution to Energy Needs

Protein rarely provides more than about 5–10 percent of our energy needs. This is a good thing because we want to use protein for muscle growth and repair. Exactly how much energy protein provides during exercise is determined largely by how much carbohydrate is available. If you do not consume adequate carbohydrates and your glycogen becomes depleted during exercise lasting longer than sixty to ninety minutes, you will use more protein to make the glucose needed to maintain blood glucose levels. If you start out exercising with very low glycogen stores, you may begin to use protein for energy even earlier than sixty to ninety minutes. This is very important because your brain needs adequate blood glucose to function, and the protein can be used to help maintain glucose for the brain.

### Protein and Muscle Building

Muscle is mostly protein. Because of this, protein will always be linked to strength and power. And, certainly, building muscle takes protein. As we discussed in Chapter 5, just eating protein doesn't stimulate muscle growth. You have to eat enough calories overall and you have to exercise. The muscle growth caused by exercise, however, requires protein to happen. Adequate protein intake is essential to support exercise-induced muscle gain. Because of this, exercise increases the protein requirement.

### Protein Requirement

Both strength and endurance athletes have higher protein needs than a sedentary person, though for different reasons. The strength athlete needs more protein for muscle repair and growth. The endurance athlete needs the extra protein for muscle repair, muscle growth, and possibly for energy needs. Both strength and endurance athletes may need as much as 1.2–1.7 g of protein per kilogram of body weight per day compared to the RDA of 0.8, or as much as double the requirement of the average person. Providing 15–20 percent of calories as protein will help rebuild muscle after exercise. However, most Americans get that much from their typical diet, so supplementation may not be needed.

### ■ Vegetarianism

*Does being a vegetarian impair performance?*

A carefully planned vegetarian diet that supplies all the necessary nutrients will neither benefit nor hinder athletic performance. Many vegetarians, because of the absence of meat in their diets, end up consuming lots of empty calories, which then results in an inadequate diet. This can lead to inadequate nutrient balance and impaired performance. However, vegetarians can consume adequate protein from plant-based sources as long as they eat a variety of food and achieve adequate calorie intake (see Chapters 2 and 5 for more information on this topic). To ensure adequate protein intake, plant proteins can be combined to make complete proteins. Some examples of food combinations that constitute complete proteins include rice and beans, tortillas and beans, and corn bread and vegetarian chili.

Vegetarian athletes are at increased risk for inadequate intake of some vitamins and minerals. In particular, they are at risk for iron-deficiency anemia or marginal deficiency that can impair performance. Even if they consume adequate iron from plant sources, it may not be absorbed as efficiently as iron from meat. Consuming adequate vitamin C helps enhance absorption of iron from plant-based sources. Other nutrients of concern for vegetarian athletes include zinc, vitamin B$_{12}$ (cyanocobalamin), vitamin D (cholecalciferol), and calcium. The main sources of these nutrients are animal products; however, they are found in many vegetarian food sources as well, including fortified soy milk and soy products (such as tofu) and whole-grain cereals. Vegetarians may actually enjoy an advantage over their meat-eating peers in that they typically consume higher levels of antioxidants by eating foods rich in vitamin C (ascorbic acid), vitamin E (tocopherol), and beta-carotene, which may help in exercise recovery. The bottom line is that eating a vegetarian diet that provides adequate nutrients, calories, and protein does not impair performance and provides the same health benefits experienced by non-athletes who follow a vegetarian diet. ■

## Vitamin and Mineral Needs for Exercise

Vitamins and minerals play important roles in the energy pathways used to supply energy. They also contribute to the physical changes that your body goes through when

Scott Jurek won the 2006 Badwater 135-mile ultramarathon and set the course record. He is a vegan. In 2010 Scott ran to a silver medal and set a new US record of 165.7 miles for the Road 24-Hour event. It is also a USATF all-surface record. No American has run further in 24 hours.

**Want to know more?** To explore the topic of vegetarian diets for athletes more thoroughly, go to the text website at http://webcom8.grtxle.com/nutrition and click on the Chapters button. Select Chapter 14.

### APPLICATION TIP

It is best to try small pre-exercise meals at first. Over time you can train yourself to tolerate bigger meals before exercise, but this takes practice—and the first time should not coincide with a competition. Instead, stick with smaller meals and/or liquids. In addition, be aware that many people cannot tolerate high-fiber foods before exercise; they can lead to unplanned bathroom stops and general gastrointestinal discomfort. If you discover during training that you are one of these people, it may be best to lower the fiber content in your diet for a day or two before competition.

you become fit and the recovery your body goes through after you exercise. Therefore, it seems reasonable to assume that athletes need more vitamins and minerals than sedentary people and that they need to get these extra nutrients from supplements. Well, this is partially true. Although athletes may have increased requirements for some vitamins and minerals, they can meet these needs through their diet. As mentioned earlier in this chapter, athletes should meet their increased calorie and nutrient needs by consuming nutrient-dense foods and thus consuming more vitamins and minerals. Athletes who cannot do this, for whatever reason, may need to take a supplement. They should, however, consult a physician or RD for a complete dietary analysis before doing so.

## Ergogenic Aids

Most highly competitive athletes seek to "fine-tune" their training and nutrition any way they can. Many turn to supplements or *ergogenic aids* to give them the enhanced performance they seek. Many producers of ergogenic aids make outlandish claims that appeal directly to an athlete's desire to be the best. Unfortunately, few can support their marketing claims with sound science. Remember, even if a supplement does what it claims, there is no substitute for an effective training program and consuming a balanced diet based on the sports nutrition you have learned in this chapter. (Chapter 11 contains a detailed discussion of supplement laws and a review of many of the most popular ergogenic aids.)

## Pre-Exercise Meals

If you are just going out to jog for thirty minutes or for a slow walk, you probably don't need to worry about a pre-exercise meal. However, if you are going out to train for longer than an hour, consider eating a pre-exercise meal. It should be high in carbohydrates, as they are an immediate source of energy and easy to digest. You can try bread, oatmeal, rice, pasta, potatoes, bananas, cereal, energy bars, and so on.

In an effort to maximize glycogen stores, many athletes begin their pre-exercise meals several days before competition. This strategy is called **carbohydrate loading** (or commonly, *carb loading*). Carbohydrate loading is intended for events lasting ninety minutes or longer and for events requiring high-intensity efforts such as soccer, ice hockey, or lacrosse. Research has shown that it increases time to exhaustion by 20 percent and can enhance performance by 2–3 percent. There are different methods for carb loading. We'll explore one example in the following Make It a Practice feature.

 **■ Make It a Practice**
*Carb loading*

There are many different protocols for carb loading. The following schedule begins seven days before an event. Maintain your training intensity at 70–75 percent for six days prior to the event, but decrease the duration of your sessions each day. While doing this, increase your carbohydrate intake from 50 percent of total calories to 70 percent or 4–10 g per kilogram of body weight. It is important to experiment with this or any other protocol before applying it to an actual competition, and remember to consume adequate fluids throughout.

| Days before Event | Duration of Training (min.) | Intensity of Training (%) | Carbohydrates (% of calories) | Carbohydrates (g/kg) |
|---|---|---|---|---|
| 6 | 90 | 70–75 | 50 | 4–5 |
| 5 | 40 | 70–75 | 50 | 4–5 |
| 4 | 40 | 70–75 | 50 | 4–5 |
| 3 | 20 | 70–75 | 70 | 10 |
| 2 | 20 | 70–75 | 70 | 10 |
| 1 | Rest | 0 | 70 | 10 |
| EVENT DAY | COMPETE | | | Eat high-carb meal 4 hours before event, 15–30 min. before, and during |

*Source:* Adapted from Wildman R, Miller B. (2004). *Sports and Fitness Nutrition.* Belmont, CA: Thomson Wadsworth, p. 105. ■

When should you eat a pre-exercise meal, and what foods are optimal? Table 14.2 provides samples of a pre-exercise meal. The timing of pre-exercise meals and the food consumed are very individual. The goals are to "top off" glycogen stores, to prevent hunger during competition, and to minimize gastrointestinal upset. A pre-exercise meal should be eaten about four hours before beginning exercise. It should be high in carbohydrates (about 140–330 g) and low in fat and proteins. See the table for specific recommendations.

 **Want to know more?**
You can review examples of some carb-loading meals, by going to the text website at http://webcom8.grtxle.com/nutrition and clicking on the Chapters button. Select Chapter 14.

## Table 14.2   A Sample Pre-Exercise Meal for a Morning Event

| | | Carbohydrate | Calories |
|---|---|---|---|
| Dinner (day before): | 2 c. spaghetti | 60 g | 320 |
| | 1 c. pasta sauce | 30 g | 125 |
| | 1 dinner roll, plain | 15 g | 80 |
| | 1 c. mixed greens | 5 g | 25 |
| | 1/2 c. cooked broccoli | 5 g | 25 |
| | Total | 115 g | 575 |
| Bedtime snack: | 1 c. orange juice | 30 g | 120 |
| | 1 banana (small) | 15 g | 60 |
| | 1 granola bar | 15 g | 60 |
| | Total | 60 g | 240 |
| Light breakfast: | 1 1/2 c. Cheerios | 45 g | 180 |
| | 1 c. skim milk | 12 g | 80 |
| | 1 banana | 15 g | 60 |
| | Total | 72 g | 320 |

*Source:* Reprinted by permission of Iowa State University, www.extension.iastate.edu/nutrition/sport/diet.html#pre

# Real People, Other Voices

### Student:
### Sara Sabata
Southeast Community College

Because Ryan and Philip are starting to train for athletic events, it is particularly important that they plan and follow balanced diets, including all the food groups: grains, vegetables, fruits, dairy, meat, and fat. They need to eat more from each food group, especially carbohydrates and protein, and drink plenty of water.

The events of both Ryan and Philip are endurance events, so they will need to eat and train for a higher intensity workout, obtaining enough energy from foods to last the entire workout. Energy comes from carbohydrates, and increasing their intake will make it possible for both of them to sustain longer and harder workouts. Good sources of carbohydrates include whole-grain breads, oatmeal, pasta, fruits, cereals, and starchy vegetables. They should both eat carbohydrates before, during, and after those workouts. Adequate protein intake will also be required to rebuild muscle tissue, and it should come from foods such as red meat, fish, poultry, milk, cheese, eggs, peas, and beans.

I would suggest they eat smaller, more frequent meals throughout the day in order to sustain adequate energy levels. Keeping themselves hydrated is also very important. While exercising, they will lose those fluids through sweat. As a result, they need to drink water or sports drinks.

### Instructor:
### Tawni Holmes,
University of Central Oklahoma

Ryan and Philip can benefit from working together. Because they are both active, they will need to make sure they are getting adequate calories. One way to do this is to eat smaller meals and snacks throughout the day. By timing their eating every 3 to 4 hours and choosing nutrient-dense foods such as lean meat, low-fat cheese sticks or yogurt, and baby carrots, they will be able to maintain their energy level when they are active and avoid hunger, which leads to unhealthy eating.

In addition to eating a balanced diet, consumption of carbohydrates will be important pre-workout, and a mixture of carbohydrate and protein will be important post-exercise to restore and build muscle tissue.

Ryan will likely need more calories since his training schedule is more intense and of longer duration. Because they are both active, staying adequately hydrated is important. Drinking water before, during, and after activities is recommended. For Ryan, during days when he is working out for longer periods of time or several times a day, 6- to 8-percent carbohydrate sports beverages may be beneficial.

When they eat in the cafeteria, I suggest they focus on whole grains, lean meats, low-fat dairy options, and fruits and vegetables, staying away from junk food, which adds extra calories with no real benefit. Finally, I would recommend that Ryan and Philip check with their student health center or wellness center on campus to see if there is a Registered Dietitian who can help them with personalized recommendations.

### Registered Dietitian:
### John Snyder, DTR, RD
Harrisburg, PA

Ryan, as a soccer player, is training as an endurance athlete, able to run or jog almost continuously during a game that lasts for 90 minutes with a 15-minute break between halves. Philip's training shares some similarities in that he is also a runner.

Ryan and Philip should follow similar nutritional programs: both should consume diets that are 65 to 70 percent carbohydrate (CHO), 10 to 15 percent protein (PRO), and 20 percent fat. Runners typically experience stomach upset due to the constant impacts associated with that exercise, so both will need to experiment with foods and fluids to determine what their body tolerates well before, during, and after exercise.

Because of the longer duration of Ryan's high-intensity sprint/walk-type training, he will need to consume more total calories and focus on more CHO than Philip. He should focus on hydration levels during training and competition to prevent dehydration, as well as post-exercise meals to promote recovery. Ryan may also need to consider liquid meal replacements during twice-daily training to meet his daily caloric requirements without feeling overfull.

Philip should focus on a basic balanced diet that encourages increased performance without the potential for overeating and weight gain. Because his exercise sessions are shorter, he can focus less on eating prior to and during exercise, but should focus on hydration during and after exercise, as well as an adequate recovery meal for glycogen replacement.

On the other hand, food consumed immediately before exercise (fifteen to thirty minutes) is better if it has a higher glycemic index, resulting in a spike in blood sugar *after* the exercise has started. Insulin response during exercise is decreased, so the fall in blood sugar is less likely to occur.

Consumption of fried or fatty foods should be avoided before exercise. Fat, particularly fried fat, slows stomach emptying and may cause a heavy feeling, which could lead to nausea and vomiting. Finally, no pre-event meal, no matter how perfect, compensates for a poor diet at other times. Your training diet is every bit as important as your pre-competition meal.

## Nutrition during Exercise

During an exercise period longer than an hour, you need to replace water, carbohydrates, and possibly electrolytes. Intensity and environmental conditions are the primary factors.

For relatively high-intensity exercise such as running, basketball, and cycling, you should take in around 25–30 g of carbohydrates (or 100–120 calories), along with fluid every twenty to forty minutes while engaged in the activity. Carbohydrate-replacement drinks containing around 6 percent carbohydrates (such as any of the popular sports drinks) will accomplish this. Most contain about 50 calories and 14 g of carbohydrate per 8 fl. oz. For less intense exercise, say, easy hiking or cycling, carbohydrate replacement can be a little less frequent because you are burning them more slowly.

During exercise, the carbohydrates you consume should have a fairly high glycemic index. These foods will empty out of your stomach rapidly and will quickly be available for energy. The amount of needed fluid intake depends on your sweat rate, but somewhere around 5–12 oz. every fifteen to twenty minutes is ideal under normal conditions. Too much at a time can cause nausea or heaviness, but you can train yourself to tolerate more fluid. The goal should be to replace at least half of sweat losses.

If exercise is prolonged much more than a couple of hours and it's hot, you also need to replace electrolytes. Fluids containing 500–700 mg of sodium per liter are absorbed well. Most commercial sports drinks provide roughly these amounts of carbohydrates and electrolytes.

### ■ Make It a Practice
*Eating and drinking when you're literally "on the run"*
You now know that your body needs food to replenish energy during prolonged exercise, even if it means juggling a Snickers bar while you're pedaling down the road. But there are easier ways to accomplish the task.

If it's hot and electrolyte replacement is a concern, you know that sports drinks are hard to beat. But if their taste tends to give you palate fatigue or is unpleasant, there are alternatives. If you are drinking plain water and need electrolytes, either add a pinch or two of salt to the beverage or eat some salty food. Trail mixes, crackers, and pretzels can help too. You can also take electrolytes in capsule form, or you can find them in chews such as Clif Bloks and Sharkies.

Getting the fluid, whatever it is, to where you need it can sometimes be a problem if you haven't planned in advance. If you are playing a field sport like soccer or lacrosse, you should prepare as big a water supply as you think you'll need and have it readily accessible. If it's hot, be certain the container is insulated.

**Want to know more?**
To review what some experts suggest for pre-exercise meals, go to the text website at http://webcom8.grtxle.com/nutrition and click on the Chapters button. Select Chapter 14.

Plan ahead so you can replace electrolytes lost during exercise.

On the move, replenishing energy and fluids is a little more difficult. To facilitate fluid intake you can mount water bottles on your bike or get a backpack with a water bladder and a drink tube, such as a Camelback. These are great for trail running and mountain biking. Bottle fanny packs made for running work well, though typically these don't hold up as well as the backpacks. In cold weather, run any drink tubes inside your clothes and keep water bottles in inside pockets. You can also stash water on your running or cycling course, insulated if necessary, or plan your route around water sources.

If you're not using a sports drink, bring other carbohydrates. Carbohydrate gels work well, but they must be taken with water. They contain approximately 110–120 calories of carbohydrates, making them just about the right dose. They are very palatable and quick, though some people find their texture unpleasant. Getting rid of the packages is a problem, but you shouldn't drop them on the road or trail. Stash them in a pocket or just down your shirt.

Sports bars are for the most part nutritionally appropriate, but they are much slower to eat than gels and can be difficult to eat during certain types of competition. Also, cold weather tends to turn them into bricks, hot weather into a paste. Actually, any carbohydrate that your digestive system tolerates and is either easy to carry or available en route works fine. Some people have their own bizarre personal favorites, such as the person who drinks hot gelatin while backcountry skiing, or the distance runner who drinks warm Ensure. Again, as long as it doesn't cause digestive problems, it'll probably work. As always, experiment during training, *before* you're in a competition or engaged in a physically demanding exercise of long duration. ■

## Post-Exercise Recovery

If your exercise session lasts longer than an hour, you need to think about enhancing your recovery. A well-thought-out and well-implemented recovery plan will ensure that you maximize muscle training benefits and minimize stress on the body. Not eating after a long workout can even enhance your susceptibility to infection.

To optimize recovery, consume a fairly high-glycemic-index carbohydrate within about fifteen to twenty minutes of finishing. Simple-carbohydrate beverages have the highest of all GIs and typically work best for this purpose. These include sports drinks, fruit juice, and lemonade. Try to consume about 1 g of carbohydrate per kilogram of body weight. This translates into about 50 g for a 100-lb. person, or about 70 g for a 150-lb. person. Drinks are the quickest way to get carbohydrates into your system, and they work especially well if you can't eat solid food right after you've finished. Drink fluids until you have regained the weight lost during the exercise and until your urine is light in color.

Try to have a meal within a half hour after exercise if you can, but certainly within about two hours. This is the window within which the enzymes needed to replace your carbohydrate stores (glycogen) are the highest. Glycogen stores are best replenished right away, and you'll feel recovered faster if you do. Consuming adequate protein will also help enhance recovery. Therefore, a balanced meal is what you want, with carbohydrates of fairly low glycemic index—perhaps whole-wheat spaghetti and meatballs (made with lean ground beef, turkey breast, or soy) with marinara sauce and a salad with Italian dressing.

## ■ What's Hot?

*Energy bars—do you really need them?*

Energy bars, such as Power, Clif, and Balance, have, over time, crossed from sports foods to the mainstream. It seems they are being sold everywhere. People eat them for meals and snacks, and generally because they taste good. But the nutritional question is, do you need to eat them in order to replace the nutrients you've burned during exercise? The answer is no. This is not to say that there is anything wrong with eating energy bars. In fact, they make an easy and packable snack. However, they are not the only answer, and you should really try to get all the nutrients you need from the food in your daily diet. And keep in mind that even though the bars are usually fortified with vitamins and minerals, they tend to cost a bit more than regular food. In summary, energy bars can play a part, but are *not* the key to an ideal sports nutrition diet. The following chart shows the calorie and nutrient content of some of the more popular bars. Note that there are significant differences in calories as well as the other categories. ■

**Want to know more?**
To review the nutritional contents of a more comprehensive list of energy bars, carbohydrate gels, and sports drinks, go to the text website at http://webcom8.grtxle.com/nutrition and click on the Chapters button. Select Chapter 14.

| Bar | Calories | Weight (g) | Protein (g) | Fat (g) | Fiber (g) | Sugars (g) | Carbs (g) |
|---|---|---|---|---|---|---|---|
| Tiger's Milk | 140 | 35 | 7 | 5 | 2 | 14 | 18 |
| Kashi Go Lean Crunch (Chocolate Caramel) | 150 | 45 | 8 | 3 | 6 | 14 | 28 |
| Detour (small) (S'mores) | 160 | 43 | 15 | 4 | 1 | 16 | 17 |
| Genisoy Low-Carb (Chocolate Chip) | 160 | 45 | 15 | 6 | 3 | 0 | 18 |
| Luna Bar (S'mores) | 180 | 48 | 10 | 5 | 3 | 9 | 26 |
| Balance Original (Cookies & Cream) | 200 | 50 | 15 | 6 | 0 | 18 | 22 |
| Zone Perfect (Strawberry Yogurt) | 210 | 50 | 15 | 7 | 1 | 14 | 21 |
| Lara Bar (Banana Cookies) | 210 | 51 | 6 | 10 | 5 | 19 | 24 |

*(Continued)*

| Bar | Calories | Weight (g) | Protein (g) | Fat (g) | Fiber (g) | Sugars (g) | Carbs (g) |
|---|---|---|---|---|---|---|---|
| Perfect 10 Bliss (Apricot Bliss) | 215 | 50 | 5 | 9 | 5 | 24 | 29 |
| Atkins Advantage (S'mores) | 220 | 60 | 17 | 9 | 11 | 5 | 27 |
| Powerbar Triple Threat (Choc. Caramel Fusion) | 230 | 55 | 10 | 8 | 4 | 15 | 30 |
| PureFit (Chocolate Brownie) | 230 | 58 | 18 | 6 | 2 | 17 | 27 |
| Greens+ (Original) | 240 | 59 | 10 | 8 | 5 | 23 | 32 |
| Odwalla (Chocolate Chip Peanut) | 250 | 62 | 8 | 7 | 4 | 14 | 38 |
| Clif Bar (Chocolate Chip Peanut) | 250 | 68 | 11 | 6 | 5 | 20 | 43 |
| Promax Bar (Cookies & Cream) | 290 | 75 | 20 | 6 | 1 | 29 | 38 |
| Kashi Go Lean Original (Malt Chocolate Chip) | 290 | 78 | 13 | 6 | 6 | 35 | 49 |
| PowerBar Protein+ (Chocolate Crisp) | 290 | 78 | 23 | 6 | 2 | 18 | 37 |
| PN Odyssey (Caramel Nut) | 300 | 80 | 30 | 9 | 1 | 29 | 30 |
| Met-Rx Big 100 (Chocolate Graham Cracker) | 360 | 100 | 24 | 4 | 2 | 26 | 55 |

## Before you go on . . .

1. What is the most important sports nutrition goal for any athlete?
2. How can you prevent "hitting the wall"?
3. What types of carbohydrate are best to consume just before, during, and immediately after exercise? Why?
4. What fuel will provide most of the energy during an intense soccer game that lasts for ninety minutes or more?

A superior choice: insulated water bottles keep beverages colder longer.

## Maintaining Fluid Balance during Exercise

During exercise the body produces a large amount of heat, which must be released in order to keep body temperatures in an acceptable range. The body's primary method of doing this is sweating. As sweat evaporates, it draws off heat and cools the body. In hot-weather exercise, you can sweat as much as 1–3 L of water per hour. How much you sweat is determined by the type of clothing you are wearing, the intensity of your training, your sex (men usually sweat more than women), and the weather. If the weather is hot and humid, sweat doesn't evaporate as quickly, making it more difficult to adequately cool our bodies. In dry climates, by contrast, sweat evaporates very quickly to cool us—sometimes so quickly that we may not realize how much fluid we are losing and may become dehydrated. The symptoms of advanced dehydration include headaches, dizziness, cramps, nausea, and vomiting—unpleasant and dangerous conditions.

Dehydration can affect performance and threaten health and ultimately, even life. A loss of 2–3 percent of body weight as water (3–4.5 lb. for a 150-lb. person) can both decrease exercise capacity and increase the risk of death. If dehydration reaches 5 percent of body weight, cramping and heat exhaustion can result. (See Table 8.3 in Chapter 8 for the signs of dehydration). Dehydration, which affects the body's ability to cool itself with sweat and leads to overheating, is often compounded with a severe loss of electrolytes and can result in heatstroke. Confusion typically results from dehydration and heatstroke, causing victims to make poor decisions and further worsen their condition. Acute kidney failure is also a possible outcome of dehydration.

## Drink Early, Drink Often

The classic advice when exercising has been, "Drink early, drink often." If it's hot and you'll be exercising for a while, don't wait until you are thirsty before drinking, as it may be too late. To stay ahead of your losses, begin taking in fluid before your workout begins and then continue periodically throughout. You might even set a timer on your watch as a reminder. In addition, if your ultimate goal is participation in a competitive event, you should carefully integrate fluid replenishment into your training sessions.

*Will drinking coffee before training or competition help my performance?*

Studies suggest that caffeine taken an hour before exercise may enhance performance because of its ability to spare glycogen use by increasing fat breakdown. It may also make the exercise feel easier. Intake of 1.5–3 mg of caffeine per pound of body weight (225–450 mg of caffeine for a 150-lb. person; the equivalent of 10–20 oz. of coffee) is the amount recommended in order to experience these benefits. Response to the effects of caffeine is very individual, so experiment during training sessions. Also, if you regularly consume caffeine you are likely to have less of a response than a person who does not.

At this point you may think that *more* would be *better* when it comes to drinking water during exercise. This is not entirely true. Overzealous endurance athletes, trying to prevent dehydration, have consumed so much water that they have actually overhydrated, diluting electrolytes, particularly sodium, to dangerously low levels. This condition, called *hyponatremia,* can cause fatal heart arrhythmias in severe cases. The best approach may be to drink an electrolyte replacement drink rather than plain water so that if you accidentally overhydrate, you are at least replenishing electrolytes.

**APPLICATION TIP**

Consume cold beverages whenever possible during exercise. Cold water empties more quickly from your stomach. You can use an insulated bottle to help keep beverages colder longer.

## Adjustments in Cold Weather

When exercising in cold weather, athletes and non-athletes both often overlook the amount of water their bodies are losing. You can easily become dehydrated in these conditions even when you don't seem to be heavily sweating. Cold air is very dry, and significant amounts of water can be lost through respiration. This circumstance is compounded in subfreezing temperatures by the problem of keeping water from freezing and by the difficulty many people have in drinking really cold water. Being aware of this possibility and planning for it are the first steps in avoiding cold-weather dehydration.

## Monitoring Hydration Status

Another important and objective way to check hydration status, and the easiest next to thirst, is urine color and volume. If your urine is light in color when the volume and frequency are near normal, you are probably getting enough water. If not, you need to drink more. Be aware, though, that some vitamins color urine if taken in large supplemental doses. Another effective method to monitor fluid loss is to weigh yourself before and after exercise. For every 1 kg or 2.2 lb. of weight you lose, you should drink 1 L or about 34 oz. of fluids. For athletes, you can monitor water loss through sweat and determine how much fluid you will need during competition by weighing yourself before and after training sessions.

## Electrolytes

As discussed in Chapter 8, our bodies need and use electrolytes both for their electrical properties and to control fluid balance between various systems of the body. Because electrolytes are lost in sweat, dehydration and heatstroke are frequently made even worse by electrolyte imbalance. Sodium and potassium are the most important electrolytes depleted in sweat. They must be replaced when significant amounts are lost or the condition of hyponatremia (low sodium) and/ or *hypokalemia* (low potassium) may result.

Electrolyte replacement is most important in prolonged physical activity, and severe depletion is unlikely to occur in workouts or exercise of less than two hours' duration—unless you begin in a dehydrated or depleted state. Temperature and humidity will affect loss rates. In athletes who train in the heat and eventually are conditioned to it, electrolyte concentrations in sweat are reduced, and sodium and potassium conserved, so they are at less risk of electrolyte depletion. Without extremes of heat, prolonged exercise, or high-intensity workouts, salt losses are usually replaced by normal post-exercise dietary intake. Moreover, most Americans eat plenty of salt and therefore are less susceptible to electrolyte depletion from normal exercise. Not until you spend a few hours working out in the sun do you experience hyponatremia and/or hypokalemia, conditions usually restricted to endurance athletes and those who spend a lot of time working outdoors.

## Wrapping It All Up

Figure 14.6 summarizes the guidelines discussed in this chapter and can be used as a reference for both planning and getting the maximum benefits from exercise.

**Figure 14.6** Summary of Basic Sports Nutrition Recommendations
**Before Competition:**

1. One to 4 hours before an event, eat a "meal" (this is an individual choice).
   - If within 15 minutes to 1 hour before an event, it is best to consume a meal that has a high glycemic index of carbohydrates and is low in fat, protein, and fiber.
   - Foods/meals do not have to be solid; they can be in the form of a sports drink or a meal replacement product.
2. Sixty minutes before exercise, consume 1–2 g/kg of body weight as carbohydrates (if you weigh 150 lb. = 68 kg: 136 g of carbohydrates); note that a 16-oz. sports drink (28 g) and an energy bar (42 g) combined provide 70 g of carbohydrate).
3. Immediately before exercise, consume 50–60 g of carbohydrates.

**Fluid before Exercise:**

1. Consume 14–20 oz. (1.75–2.5 c.) of fluid 2 hours before exercise (additional 16 oz. if urine is dark yellow).
   - Consume water or sports drinks rather than soda or juice.
   - Fluid absorption is accelerated with a 6 percent carbohydrate drink (any popular sports drink).
   - Cold water or fluid is more rapidly absorbed.

**During Exercise:**

1. In high-intensity workouts lasting 60 minutes or more, or in longer-duration training, it is most important to consume carbohydrates.
2. Start eating and drinking early in exercise, within the first 15–30 minutes.
   - Consume 15–20 g of carbohydrates (0.2–03 g/kg) every 15–30 minutes.
   - Carbohydrates consumed can be liquid or solid (liquid may be better tolerated if running; e.g., an 8-oz. sports drink = 14–18 g of carbohydrates)
   - May consider including small amount of protein.
3. Watch fluid intake.
   - Drink 4–8 oz. (0.5 to 1.0 c.) every 15–20 minutes, or 500–1,000 mL of fluid every hour.
   - If the weather is very hot, more fluid may be required.
   - Drink 6–8 percent glucose drinks (e.g., Gatorade, Powerade).
   - Sodas, teas, and juices are not ideal and may have the reverse of the desired effect, especially if they contain caffeine.
   - Drinking plain water without electrolytes can also be a problem.
   - If you dislike sports drinks or other alternatives, take electrolyte pills with the water and/or eat food.

**After Competition:**

1. The first 2 hours is the optimal time for replacement of glycogen (i.e., glucose stores); consume 100–150 g (1.5 g/kg body weight) of carbohydrates in the first hour after exercise, combined with some protein, to help in recovery.
2. High glycemic intake (plain bagel, rice cakes, toasted oat cereals, carrots, muffins, sports drinks, potatoes, some cereals, rice) may be best after exercise and between same-day competitions or training.
3. Glycogen replacement should be highest in the first 2 hours following exercise.
4. If another event occurs within 4 hours, consume 1 g/kg of carbohydrate immediately following the first session and then 2 hours before the second.
5. It is best to combine carbohydrates and protein, because protein is important for recovery.

**Recovery:**

1. Consume 6–8 g of carbohydrate per kg of body weight for women and 8–10 g of carbohydrate per kg of body weight for men during a 24-hour period.
2. Choose mostly complex carbohydrates.
3. Protein is important, too.

**Protein:**

1. Protein is not an important source of energy during exercise if you have sufficient carbohydrates.
2. Protein plays an important role in recovery and may help in prolonged endurance and in multiple training sessions occurring within a 24-hour period.
3. Protein may play a small role in glycogen replacement.
4. Athletes probably need more than RDA (0.8 g/kg), for example, 1.2–1.8 g/kg.

*(Continued)*

**Figure 14.6** Summary of Basic Sports Nutrition Recommendations (*Continued*)

5. Choose mostly low-fat meats and dairy and vegetable proteins.

6. There's nothing magic about protein in terms of its contribution to postcompetition recovery.

7. Protein empties from the stomach more slowly than carbohydrates (and thus stays with you longer).

**Fats:**

1. Your body uses more fat for energy in low-intensity exercise (compared to high-intensity exercise).

2. Fat empties from the stomach more slowly than carbohydrates.

3. You should eat about 25 percent of total daily calories from fat (no less than 15 percent and no more than 35 percent).

4. Avoid eating fat during shorter races (other than to feel satisfied).

5. It's important to consume enough fat daily for health, hair, skin, brain function, and so on.

6. The type of fat consumed is very important.

   a. Limit consumption of saturated fats and trans fatty acids (partially hydrogenated).

   b. Eat mostly polyunsaturated (omega-3) and monounsaturated fats.

---

**Before you go on . . .**

1. What advantage, if any, do sports drinks have over plain water for replacing fluids lost during exercise?
2. Define *hyponatremia* and *hypokalemia* and explain how they can be avoided.
3. Describe two ways to monitor hydration status.

## Real People, Real Strategies

Despite some differences in the intensity and frequency of their exercise, Ryan and Philip can start off on similar nutrition plans. They can both follow the guidelines discussed in Chapter 2 to help them plan a healthy, balanced diet. Because both are about the same size, Ryan will need to consume more calories than Philip in order to compensate for his more intense training. Philip will burn some calories with the running and weight lifting he is doing, but he will have to be careful not to eat as much as Ryan or he may gain weight.

Ryan will need to make sure that most of the extra calories he consumes are from nutrient-dense sources such as lean proteins, whole grains, fruits, and vegetables. If he consumes too many empty calories, such as those found in candy and junk food, he may compromise his performance by failing to consume adequate nutrients. Ryan will also have to consume sufficient fluids and electrolytes to replace those he loses during training in the hot and humid environment of Florida. Additionally, he will also need to consume adequate carbohydrates before, during, and after exercise in order to maintain optimal glycogen stores. And last, Ryan needs to build in protein consumption, especially after exercise, to optimize muscle recovery and help with glycogen replacement. On days that he has two practices or matches, he will have to be extra diligent to consume fluids and carbohydrates in between sessions. Ryan decides to consult the athletic department's RD, who specializes in sports nutrition, to help him create his plan. The RD reinforces Ryan's inclination about the importance of developing and following a proper sports nutrition plan for optimal training and performance.

Philip knows that he needs to eat a balanced diet and avoid junk food to support his activities. Ryan shared some of the RD's advice with Philip, especially the importance of staying hydrated. Although their tastes differ somewhat and Philip's exercise is less frequent than Ryan's, the types of foods he plans to consume are similar. Both agreed to help each other monitor and stay true to their plans, not the easiest thing to accomplish on a college campus.

## Chapter Summary

- An athlete needs to eat a balanced diet, similar to non-athletes, only more of it and with plenty of carbohydrates, electrolytes, and water before, during, and after exercise.
- Exercise plays a big role in chronic disease prevention.
- Physical fitness incorporates muscular strength, endurance, flexibility, and body composition.
- The American College of Sports Medicine (ACSM) recommends that you participate in physical activity at 60–90 percent of your age-predicted maximum heart rate for twenty to sixty minutes three to five days per week.
- According to the ACSM, to achieve maximum benefit from strength training, you should perform one to three sets of eight to ten exercises (conditioning all major muscle groups), each with eight to twelve or ten to fifteen repetitions, two or three days per week.

- To maintain a flexible range of motion and prevent injury and soreness, you should incorporate stretching into your workouts at least two or three days per week.
- The intensity of the exercise—that is, how fast you are running, biking, skiing, and so on—dictates the rate at which energy must be produced.
- Your immediate source of energy is stored ATP-PC.
- You use ATP-PC in the very beginning of exercise and in events lasting ten seconds or less.
- The aerobic energy system can be used in lower intensities when enough oxygen is available to provide energy.
- Fats, carbohydrates, and a small amount of protein can be used for fuel during aerobic exercise.
- When your need for energy exceeds the amount that your body can produce using oxygen, you use glycolysis. Glycolysis is anaerobic and therefore requires no oxygen; it produces lactic acid.
- Glycolysis can use only carbohydrates for fuel.
- You rely on glycolysis for the first two to three minutes of exercise or in high-intensity events that last only two to three minutes.
- The higher the intensity of the exercise, the more you rely on carbohydrates.
- The longer the duration of exercise, the more your body burns fat to provide energy.
- If you do not replace carbohydrates during exercise, you will deplete glycogen stores following sixty to ninety minutes of physical activity. You will have to slow down or stop.

## Key Terms

**age-predicted maximum heart rate** The maximum heart rate you can achieve while exercising; it is calculated by subtracting your age from 220. (p. 446)

**carbohydrate loading** A method of manipulating training and diet for several days before an event in order to maximize glycogen stores. (p. 458)

**fitness** The ability to perform moderate-to-vigorous levels of physical activity without undue fatigue, and the capability of maintaining this capacity throughout life. (p. 446)

**high intensity** A level of activity in which you exceed 70 percent of your age-predicted maximum heart rate. To reach this level requires intense exercise for twenty minutes or longer. (p. 446)

**"hitting the wall" or "bonking"** Slang terms used by endurance athletes to describe a condition in which glycogen stores in the liver and muscles are depleted, resulting in a major performance drop. (p. 454)

**immediate energy system** Also called the ATP-PC system; the body uses this system in the first ten seconds or so of any exercise. We also rely on it for very short-duration maximal efforts, such as power lifting, kicking a soccer ball, or short sprints. (p. 448)

**lactic acid** A three-carbon molecule formed from pyruvate in glycolysis during anaerobic exercise; also called *lactate*. (p. 443)

**low intensity** A level of activity in which you stay below 55 percent of your age-predicted maximum heart rate. (p. 446)

**moderate intensity** A level of activity that increases your heart rate to 55–70 percent of your age-predicted maximum heart rate. (p. 446)

# Chapter Quiz

1. What is the most important benefit of exercise for the elderly?

   a. It helps them lose weight.

   b. It helps them feel better.

   c. It helps them maintain their activities of daily living.

   d. none of the above

2. How does exercise help prevent heart disease?

   a. It increases LDL cholesterol.

   b. It increases HDL cholesterol.

   c. It increases triglycerides.

   d. It increases total cholesterol.

3. During low-intensity exercise, you are most likely to rely on which energy system?

   a. ATP-PC

   b. anaerobic

   c. aerobic

   d. carbohydrates

4. What fuel do you use the most during anaerobic exercise?

   a. carbohydrates

   b. fat

   c. protein

   d. vitamins and minerals

5. Which of the following activities primarily uses the ATP-PC energy system?

   a. running a 5K (3.2-mile) race

   b. hitting a baseball

   c. cross-country skiing

   d. playing a game of tennis

6. Why is it so important to consume carbohydrates during exercise?

   a. because they are the only fuel you use during exercise

   b. because performance will decrease if you don't

   c. because you can't store them at all

   d. because they are available in convenient forms

7. As the *duration* of exercise increases, you rely more on what fuel?

   a. carbohydrates

   b. fats

   c. protein

   d. all fuels equally

8. As the *intensity* of exercise increases, you rely more on what fuel?

   a. carbohydrates

   b. fats

   c. protein

   d. all fuels equally

9. For optimal exercise performance, when is it most important to consume carbohydrates?

   a. before exercise

   b. during exercise

   c. after exercise

   d. before, during, and after exercise

10. A general guideline for staying hydrated during exercise would be

    a. to drink when you are thirsty.

    b. to drink early and drink often.

    c. to drink when you sweat.

    d. to drink as much water as you can.

# CHAPTER 15 Eating Disorders

## Do Not Discriminate

## < Here's Where You've Been

*The following topics were introduced in preceding chapters and are related to concepts we'll discuss in Chapter 15. Be certain that you're familiar with them before proceeding.*

- Diets do not work and they can be detrimental to your physical and psychological health. Balancing energy intake with energy expenditure is the key to successful weight loss. (Chapter 7)
- Because supplements are not regulated by the FDA before they are sold, consumers need to be knowledgeable about what they are taking. (Chapter 11)
- In order to gain muscle it is important to work out, to eat every three or four hours, and to add extra calories from foods that are calorie-dense such as granola, nuts, and raisins. (Chapter 14)
- Nutritional requirements for an athlete are not that different from those for non-athletes. They typically need only some "fine-tuning." This sometimes includes eating more calories in the form of nutrient-dense foods than a person who is not active. (Chapter 14)

## Here's Where You're Going >

*The following topics and concepts are the ones we'll emphasize in Chapter 15.*

- Eating disorders are complex and multidimensional. They are caused by many different factors, which can vary from person to person.
- Men and women of all ages and ethnicities are affected by eating disorders.
- Eating disorders exist on a continuum that ranges from the more familiar, diagnosable disorders such as anorexia nervosa and bulimia nervosa to occasional dieting.
- We can all help prevent eating disorders.

## Real People, Real Choices

Todd left nutrition class concerned but hopeful. They had just finished a discussion on eating disorders that was very enlightening. He had been worried about his girlfriend, Jennifer. She had been very moody and distant lately. He'd also noticed that she had lost a lot of weight, and she had mentioned to him that she had been exercising twice a day. She almost never ate meals with him anymore and rarely wanted to go out with their friends. When she did go out, she ordered very little food and ate only a few bites. At first he thought it was great that she wanted to get in shape and lose the few pounds she had gained during their freshman year. But when he realized how much she was changing, he was not so sure. One of her friends told him she was worried that Jennifer had an eating disorder, but Todd really didn't think that was likely. After all, Jennifer didn't look like a skeleton, and he was pretty sure she never made herself throw up or anything. When he mentioned his concerns to Jennifer, she said she was fine and just trying to get in shape. But then in nutrition class Todd's professor discussed something called disordered eating. She mentioned that people who look normal can still have serious eating problems. How can Todd determine for certain whether Jennifer has an eating disorder? What advice would you give Todd about how best to approach Jennifer about getting help?

Popular misconceptions state that eating disorders always involve starving oneself or throwing up after meals. Although these practices are certainly symptomatic of a disorder, they represent a mere fraction of the various behaviors and attitudes that health professionals regard as disordered eating. In fact, disordered eating behaviors and attitudes range on a continuum from being unhappy with one's shape or weight to clinical diagnoses of **anorexia nervosa** and **bulimia nervosa** (depicted in Figure 15.1). The continuum includes frequent dieting, binge eating, the use of unhealthy weight-loss methods such as vomiting and restricting food, meeting some but not all of the criteria for a diagnosable condition, and, of course, the clinical diagnoses. The entire continuum falls under the umbrella term **disordered eating.**

## How Do We Define Eating Disorders?

In order to be diagnosed with an eating disorder, a patient must be assessed by a physician or psychologist to determine whether he or she meets the strict criteria set forth in the *Diagnostic and Statistical Manual, Fourth Edition (DSM-IV)*. The *DSM* is a comprehensive manual that lists the symptoms and criteria of the various psychological disorders. Before making a diagnosis, physicians and psychologists use the *DSM* to determine whether a patient meets the criteria for a specific disorder. Figure 15.2 lists the criteria and symptoms for eating disorders as listed in the *DSM-IV*.

### Anorexia Nervosa

The diagnostic criteria for anorexia nervosa are listed in Figure 15.2. They include an unwillingness to maintain normal body weight, intense fear of weight gain, distorted body image, and **amenorrhea** (missing three consecutive menstrual periods). Many have, perhaps incorrectly, described anorexics as stubborn, vain, spoiled, skinny girls who just need a good meal. However, anorexia is much more than an out-of-control diet. It is a complex problem without an easy solution. It is a coping mechanism used as an escape from emotional pain, from growing up, and from certain feelings. The disorder is typically associated with an intense fear of weight gain that allows the sufferer to overpower his or her physical hunger and his or her body's desire to survive.

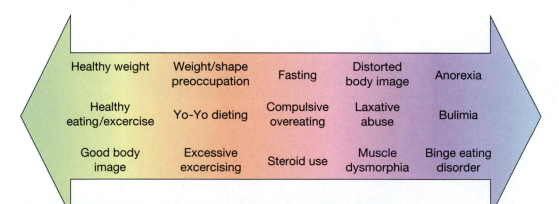

**Figure 15.1** Eating disorders occur on a continuum, with diagnosable eating disorders on one end and healthy eating on the other.

**Figure 15.2** Diagnostic Criteria for Eating Disorders

**Anorexia Nervosa**

A. Refusal to maintain body weight at or above a minimally normal weight for age and height (e.g., weight loss leading to maintenance of body weight less than 85 percent of that expected; or failure to make expected weight gain during period of growth, leading to body weight less than 85 percent of that expected).

B. Intense fear of gaining weight or becoming fat, even though underweight.

C. Disturbance in the way in which one's body weight or shape is experienced, undue influence of body weight or shape on self-evaluation, or denial of the seriousness of the current low body weight.

D. In postmenarcheal females, amenorrhea, i.e., the absence of at least three consecutive menstrual cycles. (A woman is considered to have amenorrhea if her periods occur only following hormone, e.g., estrogen, administration.)

*Specify type:*

**Restricting type:** During the current episode of anorexia nervosa, the person has not regularly engaged in binge-eating or purging behavior (i.e., self-induced vomiting or the misuse of laxatives, diuretics, or enemas).

**Binge-eating/purging type:** During the current episode of anorexia nervosa, the person has regularly engaged in binge-eating or purging behavior (i.e., self-induced vomiting or the misuse of laxatives, diuretics, or enemas).

**Bulimia Nervosa**

A. Recurrent episodes of binge eating. An episode of binge eating is characterized by both of the following:

1. Eating, in a discrete period of time (e.g., within any 2-hour period), an amount of food that is definitely larger than most people would eat during a similar period of time and under similar circumstances.

2. A sense of lack of control over eating during the episode (e.g., a feeling that one cannot stop eating or control what or how much one is eating).

B. Recurrent inappropriate compensatory behavior in order to prevent weight gain, such as self-induced vomiting; misuse of laxatives, diuretics, enemas, or other medications; fasting; or excessive exercise.

C. The binge eating and inappropriate compensatory behaviors both occur, on average, at least twice a week for three months.

D. Self-evaluation is unduly influenced by body shape and weight.

E. The disturbance does not occur exclusively during episodes of anorexia nervosa.

*Specify type:*

**Purging type:** During the current episode of bulimia nervosa, the person has regularly engaged in self-induced vomiting or the misuse of laxatives, diuretics, or enemas.

**Nonpurging type:** During the current episode of bulimia nervosa, the person has used other inappropriate compensatory behaviors, such as fasting or excessive exercise, but has not regularly engaged in self-induced vomiting or the misuse of laxatives, diuretics, or enemas.

**Eating Disorder Not Otherwise Specified**

The *eating disorder not otherwise specified* category is for disorders of eating that do not meet the criteria for any specific eating disorder.

*Source:* Reprinted with permission from the *Diagnostic and Statistical Manual of Mental Disorders.* 4th ed., text revision, (Copyright 2000). American Psychiatric Association.

Anorexia has two subtypes: restricting and binge-purging. Individuals with **restricting anorexia** lose weight by reducing food and overall caloric intake through fasting or very strict dieting. This type of anorexia may or may not be associated with extreme overexercising. Those with **binge-purging anorexia** combine restrictive dieting with frequent binge-and-purge episodes. During the binge-purge episodes, they consume what they consider to be large amounts of foods in a short time and then attempt to purge or get rid of the calories by self-induced vomiting, laxative use, excessive exercise, diuretic use, or any combination of these methods. Regardless of type, anorexia typically begins in adolescence but can begin at any age from preadolescence to middle-age. According to the latest data, it affects as many as 2 percent of young women and 1 percent of men.

## Bulimia Nervosa

The diagnostic criteria for bulimia nervosa are listed in Figure 15.2. They include recurrent binge-eating episodes characterized by abnormal amounts of food intake and a feeling of loss of control over that intake, consistent and pro-longed inappropriate weight compensation behaviors, and body image distortion. Subtypes include **purging bulimia** (by means of laxatives, diuretics, or vomiting) and **nonpurging bulimia** (excessive exercise or dieting).

Although the most recognizable symptoms of bulimia are related to food behaviors, bulimia can be thought of as a coping mechanism—a way to deal with distress and emotional pain. For some, bingeing provides a temporary escape from feelings of unhappiness and is an attempt to self-medicate. Purging provides a feeling of control and safety and often seems a release from the stress and guilt experienced after the binge. Many bulimics report feeling a tremendous sense of relief and relaxation immediately following a purge. The purging can be thought of as symbolic—a way to expel that which the sufferer considers bad or negative.

Many celebrities have struggled with eating disorders. Mary Kate Olsen has been reported to have anorexia nervosa.

**Want to know more?** To review a discussion of eating disorders specific to ethnicity, go to the text website at http://webcom8.grtxle.com/nutrition and click on the Chapters button. Select Chapter 15.

## Eating Disorders Not Otherwise Specified (EDNOS)

**Eating disorders not otherwise specified (EDNOS)** include anorexic and bulimic behaviors but do not meet the specific criteria of either diagnosis. For example, someone who starves himself or herself but is not below 85 percent of ideal body weight (thereby not meeting the criteria for anorexia nervosa) might be diagnosed with EDNOS. Someone who binges but does not purge might fall under EDNOS as well. Many experts refer to the partial syndromes as **borderline anorexia.**

**Binge-eating disorder (BED)** is classified in the *DSM-IV* under EDNOS and listed in an appendix as a diagnosis requiring additional study. BED is characterized by recurrent episodes of binge eating that occur without regular purging behaviors intended to prevent weight gain. The prevalence of BED among the general population is approximately 1–2 percent. However, the rate of BED is difficult to estimate because it often goes unreported and may be higher among obese individuals, thus making BED one of the more common eating disorders.

Another eating disorder classified under EDNOS is **night-eating syndrome (NES).** According to several published research studies, NES appears to be distinctly different from anorexia nervosa, bulimia nervosa, or binge-eating disorder. Night-eating syndrome is associated with loss of appetite in the morning, overeating in the evening, and sleep problems. Night eating is thought to be brought on by stress and is believed to affect about 2 percent of the general population, about 9 percent of obese patients, and about 27 percent of severely obese individuals.

## Eating Disorders Affect People of All Ages and Ethnicities

It was previously thought that eating disorders occurred only in wealthy Caucasian American teenage girls, but that is not the case. Eating disorders occur in men and women of all ethnicities and regions of the world.

Based on media coverage, eating disorders and their associated problems may seem to begin in adolescence and affect mainly teens. Although disordered eating behaviors often become most obvious during adolescence, with the appearance of physical side effects, the feelings associated with disordered eating and the dieting mentality may take root as early as age 7. Many adolescents report that they began dieting when they were only 8 to 10 years old. Even children as young as age 5 display a motivation to avoid becoming obese and describe dieting as a strategy for staying thin.

The feelings associated with disordered eating, including the motivation to avoid obesity, can begin in children as young as 5 of both genders and all ethnicities.

Although the number of adolescent girls with diagnosable eating disorders may be relatively small (2–15 percent for anorexia and 6–16 percent for bulimia), the number of young girls reporting disturbed self-image, dieting, overexercising, vomiting, and laxative use is alarmingly high. Eating disorders not meeting clear *DSM* diagnostic criteria affect a much larger segment of the adolescent population, with prevalence estimates as high as 15 percent. Furthermore, the Youth Risk Behavior Surveillance System (YRBSS) found that more than 11 percent of high school girls and 7 percent of high school boys in the United States reported taking diet pills, powders, or liquids to lose weight. Eight percent of girls and close to 4 percent of boys reported vomiting or taking laxatives to lose weight within the past month.

Eating disorders do not affect only teenagers and college students. Older people can be affected as well. Some women in their forties, fifties, and sixties develop eating disorders in response to a devastating loss or trauma, such as the death of a loved one, divorce, or a life-threatening disease. Other women have struggled with an eating disorder for years but perhaps were able to maintain enough health to remain undiagnosed or untreated. Regardless of the circumstances, more and more older women are developing eating disorders. Some experts say that the cultural emphasis on a young, thin body has caused the increase in this age group.

### ■ Make It a Practice

*How to tell whether someone has an eating disorder*

It is not always easy to tell whether someone has an eating disorder simply by looking at him or her. Many people with an eating disorder are of normal body weight and appear outwardly healthy to family and friends.

An obsession with food and exercise is often seen as evidence of remarkable self-discipline or as an appropriate mindset for achieving a healthy, lean physique. Thus, an eating disorder may go unrecognized until the individual develops a diagnosable condition. However, several warning signs and clues indicate that someone may have a problem.

In the case of eating disorders, warning signs are more like symptoms of a particular disease. Several of these common signs of an eating disorder are as follows:

- Constantly weighing oneself
- Excessive intake of caffeine

**APPLICATION TIP**

If a child close to you expresses a desire to diet to lose weight or avoid becoming obese, try to discourage dieting as an option. Help him or her make healthier choices. Discuss the concepts of the importance of a balanced diet and exercise covered in this text. MyPyramid.gov has a section dedicated to helping kids learn about healthier eating. Most importantly, be a positive role model for kids. Don't diet or criticize yourself or others based on appearance.

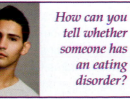

*How can you tell whether someone has an eating disorder?*

Many people who suffer from eating disorders may look normal and healthy to friends and family.

- Self-critical attitude
- Marked increase or decrease in weight not related to a medical condition
- Sudden change in eating habits, such as eliminating food groups from the diet
- Development of abnormal habits, such as ritualized behavior at meals
- Severe dieting and restricting food, even when not overweight
- Withdrawal from social situations to exercise or to skip meals
- An intense preoccupation with weight and body image
- Compulsive or excessive exercising
- Isolation, depression, irritability, tiredness
- Increased use of supplements, diuretics, laxatives
- Trips to the bathroom after meals
- Complaints of light-headedness or weakness
- Appearing preoccupied with eating habits of others—may even prepare elaborate meals for others
- Thinning or very dry hair
- Often complains of bloating or stomach pain after eating
- Constantly complains of being cold ■

If you are concerned about a friend or family member's attitudes about food or his or her health, it is okay to let the person know that you are concerned. However, be sure to do so in a nonconfrontational manner, expressing your concerns in a loving and supportive way, not in a tone that may sound like criticism or condemnation (Figure 15.3).

Before you express your concern to your friend or loved one, it is advisable to have a list of resources available where he or she can seek help. You can contact any of the treatment centers listed on the text website or obtain resources from the websites suggested in Figure 15.4.

As noted previously, you need to be honest and respect your friend's feelings and privacy, but not at the expense of his or her health and well-being. Be prepared for the possibility that your friend won't listen. He or she may be in denial that a problem exists. If so, you must accept this choice and emphasize that you will assist them in seeking the help he or she needs and deserves. Remember that the support of family and friends is one of the most valuable treatment tools available. Try not to police your friend's behavior or attempt to feed him or her in order to make things better. Remember, this is not an issue about food, but one of coping and dealing with emotions. So, rather than playing the role of food police, listen and express to your friend that you love him or her regardless of behavior or appearance. At the same time, be sure that you are not being manipulated or lied to. Let your friend know that although you support his or her efforts to get well, you will not support destructive behaviors such as stealing money to buy food for binges. Try not to take your friend's actions personally, but do not sacrifice yourself either. Be prepared to disengage or let go to take care of yourself. Finally, accept that your friend or loved one has a problem that requires a lengthy recovery process that does not happen instantly. Be patient and help him or her be patient as well.

*What should you do if you think someone you know has an eating disorder?*

**APPLICATION TIP**

If you think someone you know has an eating disorder, you should, if at all possible, seek professional advice. However, if you are unable to contact a qualified professional, many websites and support organizations (see Figure 15.4) offer advice and support for those with eating disorders and disordered eating, as well as their loved ones. *Internet resources are not meant to be a substitute for professional advice,* but they can help you find a professional in your area while providing information and general suggestions.

**Figure 15.3** What to Do if You Think a Friend Has an Eating Disorder

**Do:**

Tell her you want to help.

Let her know you care, but do so sincerely and without criticism or judgment.

Pick the right time and place to express your concerns free of distractions.

Encourage her to seek professional help from a psychologist, a mental health professional, or an RD.

Try to learn what you can about eating disorders

Be prepared for her to deny that she has a problem.

Reassure her there is no shame or embarrassment.

Remember that the **eating disorder is not about food,** but a substitute for dealing with pain and feelings.

Be patient.

Show your concern by listening and attempting to understand her feelings.

Watch for signs of deteriorating physical health and refer her to a health professional as needed.

Take any signs of suicide seriously.

Refuse to debate and argue.

Consider your own prejudice about thin or fat people.

Evaluate the messages you give about your own body.

**Don't:**

Try to solve his problem on your own.

Make comments about his weight or body in any way.

Get involved in discussions about healthy eating or weight.

Compare him to others.

Make him eat or force food on him.

Try to analyze his behavior.

Agree to keep his eating disorder a secret from significant others or health professionals when his health is impaired.

Take his actions or responses personally.

Enable the disorder.

Gossip about him to others.

**Figure 15.4** Selected Web Resources Regarding Eating Disorders

**The Renfrew Center**

A nationally recognized treatment center with a good website that contains resources, information, and links to treatment centers, professionals, and support groups.

**Gürze Books**

Offers a selection of books and resources on eating disorders and related topics.

**Alliance for Eating Disorders Awareness**

Provides educational information for parents and caregivers about the warning signs, dangers, and consequences of anorexia, bulimia, and other related disorders.

*(Continued)*

**Figure 15.4** Selected Web Resources Regarding Eating Disorders (*Continued*)

### National Association for Anorexia Nervosa and Associated Eating Disorders

The National Association for Anorexia Nervosa and Associated Disorders, Inc. is a nonprofit corporation that seeks to alleviate the problems of eating disorders, especially anorexia nervosa and bulimia nervosa.

### Something Fishy

Dedicated to raising awareness and to providing support to people with eating disorders and their loved ones.

### Anorexia Nervosa and Related Eating Disorders, Inc.

Supplies information about anorexia nervosa, bulimia nervosa, binge-eating disorder, and other less well-known food and weight disorders. Material includes self-help tips and information about recovery and prevention.

### Body Positive

Promotes body acceptance of all sizes with helpful articles, links, activism, and support.

### BodyImageHealth.org

Includes tools for preventing body image, eating, fitness, and weight problems before they start. Based on a program called the Model for Healthy Body Image by Kathy Kater.

### Eating Disorders Anonymous

A fellowship of individuals who share their experiences, strengths, and hopes that they may solve their common problems and help others recover from their eating disorders. Includes articles, discussion, and tools for recovery.

### EDEN—Eating Disorders & Education Network

Provides information and lists of treatment centers and professionals that specialize in treatment of eating disorders.

### Largely Positive

Promotes health and self-esteem for people of all sizes.

### National Association to Advance Fat Acceptance

A nonprofit human rights organization dedicated to improving the quality of life for overweight and obese people. NAAFA works to eliminate discrimination based on body size and to provide overweight and obese people with the tools for self-empowerment through public education, advocacy, and member support.

### National Eating Disorders Association

Information on eating disorders and helpful links to treatment centers and professionals.

### Eating Disorder Referral and Information Center

Provides referrals to health professionals who specialize in eating disorders and those who work with insurance companies. Also provides information on eating disorders.

---

**Before you go on . . .**

1. What are the diagnostic criteria for anorexia nervosa and bulimia nervosa?
2. What does it mean to say that eating disorders occur on a continuum?
3. What is the first thing you should do if you suspect a friend has an eating disorder?
4. What behaviors are included in the continuum of disordered eating?
5. Define *EDNOS* and give two examples.

# Risk Factors

It is important to recognize the complexity of eating disorders. They are not caused by any one thing, and they are different in each individual. However, a number of common traits and behaviors have been identified in people with eating disorders. These characteristics and behaviors are called risk factors. **Risk factors** are characteristics or behaviors that increase the likelihood that you will develop a disease, though they do not necessarily cause the disease. The identification of risk factors, or triggers, for the development of eating disorders is important for prevention, early diagnosis, and intervention. Identifying certain groups at risk may also help increase awareness and identify target groups for intervention. Although many experts have suggested individual risk factors that may lead to the development of an eating disorder, it would be unwise to assume there is a single or simple cause in the development of eating disorders. What causes someone to develop an eating disorder is complex and most likely involves a unique combination of factors in each person. The following risk factors have been identified as increasing one's risk of developing an eating disorder.

Studies show that dieting is a common weight management strategy for female college students. Interestingly, weight has little if any bearing on whether they *engage* in dieting. In one large study, there was no difference in the prevalence of dieting among overweight, obese and normal weight females. Eighty percent of female students whose weight was classified as *normal* reported dieting.

## Dieting

You may wonder why dieting would be included in a discussion about eating disorders. Everywhere you look, some health expert or group is citing statistics about our increasingly overweight population. A new diet plan seems to come along every week, and now even fast-food restaurants claim to offer "diet foods." Dieting has become a multi-billion-dollar industry, but if it's the answer to the obesity epidemic in this country, shouldn't the problem be solved by now?

Clearly, dieting is not the answer. As discussed in Chapter 7, diets do not work. But more than that, they may actually be a major aspect of the problem, contributing to obesity and other health issues. Although dieting may seem harmless, it has many potentially harmful consequences such as fatigue, anxiety, depression, low self-esteem, disturbed body image, amenorrhea, mental sluggishness, impaired performance in school, nutrient deficiencies, and impaired growth. Dieting can lead to vitamin deficiencies and impaired growth and development in children and teens, osteoporosis, impaired immune system function, and infertility. In addition, dieting for weight loss is strongly associated with later development of clinical eating disorders.

Beyond the physical consequences of dieting (and the associated disordered eating behaviors) are the psychological ones. Similar to the effects of diagnosable eating disorders, people with disordered eating experience low self-esteem, high self-criticism, perfectionism, depression, anxiety, and social isolation. Perhaps the most tragic consequence is that dieting robs those who regularly engage in it of joy, spontaneity, and the ability to embrace their own individuality both inside and out.

## Cultural Pressure

Few people would question the assumption that the current culture in the United States of "thinness at any cost" is linked to an increase in eating disorders. It is

### APPLICATION TIP

Have you ever been on a diet? Are you on one right now? Instead of chronically dieting, try to develop a balanced lifestyle and attitude that includes acceptance of all body types. Start by focusing on exercise for health and disease prevention, not for the sole purpose of burning calories. Try to adopt a healthful way of eating that incorporates all foods with the purpose of balancing caloric intake with energy expenditure. Try to avoid using food as reward or punishment, to help make the purpose of food nourishment and enjoyment.

**Want to know more?**
How has our body image changed over time? You can get the answer by visiting the text website at http://webcom8.grtxle.com/nutrition and clicking on the Chapters button. Select Chapter 15.

now considered "normal" for women and adolescent girls to have a certain level of body dissatisfaction and to diet frequently, even when they are at a healthy weight. Certainly, marketers and the media, as a reflection of the culture, play a role in pressuring people to be thin. But they are not the only culprit.

Historically, women have tried to change their bodies to conform to a given era's image of beauty. The portrayal of female body ideals through the decades—in movies, magazines, and books—says it all. For example, in the past, female plumpness was associated with fertility. Until the seventeenth century, Western culture favored the round tummy and what we would now consider a "plump" figure. This reproductive type was later replaced by the hourglass figure—narrow waist, full bosom, and round bottom. This ideal has been replaced yet again by the slightly emaciated figures idealized today. There has always been a female ideal and pressure to attain it. What makes today's culture different is that the media have become much more powerful. According to one study, children exposed to excessive media (TV viewing, magazines, and movies) were at a greater risk for becoming obese. Similarly, adults who watch an extraordinary amount of television were 50 percent more likely to become overweight. However, it appears that the type of exposure, not the amount, is correlated with negative body image. Specifically, rates of exposure to soap operas, movies, and music videos were associated with the highest rates of body dissatisfaction and motivation to become thin.

## ■ What's Hot

### The reality of extreme makeovers

Has a national preoccupation with appearance crossed over into an illness? Or is the current focus on plastic surgery and extreme makeovers simply a result of recent advances in reconstructive surgery? The reality TV show craze has merged with our cultural obsession with appearance, and an onslaught of plastic surgery shows has emerged. These shows and the media attention surrounding them, combined with the lower cost of plastic surgery, have brought the concept of surgical appearance enhancement to the mainstream public. Altering one's appearance to attain the ideal is no longer a privilege of the rich and famous. Although most TV shows and media attention have focused on the success and perceived happiness that can be achieved by going from an "ugly duckling" to a "swan," several have presented the unhealthy sides of the surgical transformations. One such aspect that has been brought into the limelight is the psychological condition **body dysmorphic disorder (BDD).** People with BDD are preoccupied with the thought that some aspect of their appearance is unattractive, deformed, or "not right" in some way. Many avoid social situations, often miss work, and even attempt suicide because of their perceived deformity. It is similar to eating and body image disorders, except that the focus is not only on body size and shape, but on any feature including the nose, face, chin, lips, and so on. Treatment often includes psychological counseling and medications such as serotonin uptake inhibitors. The success of the medications indicates that BDD may occur as a result of brain chemistry imbalances.

In the past, those with BDD often felt there was no hope for changing their appearance. But now, plastic surgery offers a seemingly perfect escape from their obsession. However, most people with BDD who have plastic surgery are not satisfied with the results and undergo

Heidi Montag has said that she is addicted to plastic surgery. Notice how she looked in 2006 (left) compared to 2010, after undergoing many procedures.

multiple subsequent operations without achieving satisfaction. We have witnessed this phenomenon in many high-profile celebrities who have obviously crossed the line from looking slightly better to looking rather like a mannequin, or worse.

It would be easy to assume that the national preoccupation with appearance and the growing popularity of plastic surgery have combined to create BDD. However, the disease is not newly recognized in the psychological literature; it was first written about more than 100 years ago. Furthermore, little research is conducted to establish prevalence data, and there are no data from the past for comparison. Perhaps mainstream access to plastic surgery and the ensuing media attention have simply brought new attention to an established condition. Perhaps this new attention will create funding for research to establish prevalence, to define risk factors, and to develop prevention programs. Hopefully it will raise cultural awareness of the realities of using modern medical advances to attain an unrealistic appearance.

If you think someone you care about has BDD, avoid reassurances that he or she looks fine, but refer the person to a mental health professional. ■

The index of an ideal body image for women has generally stabilized at 13–19 percent below healthy weight—an interesting observation, given that a body weight more than 15 percent below ideal weight is one of the *DSM* criteria for anorexia nervosa. A greater difference between actual and ideal body weight has been associated with an increased risk in developing an eating disorder or in participating in pathological weight-loss methods.

Research has revealed an increase in the number of weight-reduction articles over a period of thirty years (Figure 15.5). Interestingly, in eight years within this period the number of exercise articles surpassed the number of diet

**Figure 15.5** Weight loss articles appear in many magazines.

**Want to know more?**

To learn more about the connection between the media and eating disorders, go to the text website at http://webcom8 .grtxle.com/nutrition and click on the Chapters button. Select Chapter 15.

People who have a poor body image or body dissatisfaction may see themselves as fat even when they are very thin.

articles. This development is seen as somewhat encouraging as long as the exercise regime being promoted is not extreme. Recall that overexercising is listed as a method of purging in the *DSM*.

The media tend to equate thinness with beauty, which is in turn equated with success. This focus on beauty and thinness in women as their most important assets for success can influence children at a very young age. How to reverse or successfully resist this cultural pressure to achieve a healthier, less pathogenic ideal is a complex problem. If it were simply this unrealistic and unattainable ideal that leads people down such a destructive path, everyone exposed to it would be victims—but not all are. Science has not yet determined exactly what separates those who fall victim to it from those who don't.

### ■ You Decide

*Should there be limits for models' BMI?*

In September 2006 the Madrid regional government in Spain passed a ruling to establish a minimum BMI of 18 for all who participate as models in their annual fashion week. Any model who had a BMI *below* the standard would be banned from participating in events. The average BMI of top models is 16.3, according to data from the National Eating Disorders Association. The intent of the Spanish regulation is to promote a healthier body image. Many in the fashion industry have responded positively and have called for limits in other countries and across the industry. Others have criticized the ban, saying that it discriminates against models who are naturally thin. Some think it is not the government's right to pass such laws and that the fashion industry should be permitted to portray whatever images and ideals it chooses. Some also believe that it is the consumer's responsibility to think critically about what messages are being communicated. What do you think? Should the government get involved and why? Is it likely that the fashion industry will regulate itself? Is it solely the responsibility of the consumer to decide whether the body image of models is positive or negative? ■

## Body Dissatisfaction

**Body dissatisfaction**, or a poor body image, is a strong risk factor for developing disordered eating behavior. **Body image** is difficult to define, but basically it is how we picture ourselves or how we "feel" about how we look. It can change from day to day and from situation to situation. It is what many people are expressing when they say they "feel fat." According to www. edreferral.com, "Body image involves our perception, imagination, emotions, and physical sensations of and about our bodies. It's not static—but ever-changing; sensitive to changes in mood, environment, and physical experience. It is not based on fact. It is psychological in nature, and much more influenced by self-esteem than by actual physical attractiveness as judged by others. It is not inborn, but learned. This learning occurs in the family and among peers, and by what is learned and expected culturally."

It has become almost a standard for women in our culture to hate their bodies and to criticize their appearance. You might be surprised, however, to learn that many men are equally dissatisfied with their bodies.

### ■ Nutrition and Culture
#### Men and eating disorders

Men account for approximately 10–20 percent of reported cases of anorexia nervosa. Male cases of bulimia are very uncommon. Because they indicate reported cases, however, these data may be misleading. In reality, many more men may suffer from eating disorders. They either are misdiagnosed or do not seek treatment because of the shame and stigma of suffering from a perceived "female disease."

In Western cultures, men do not experience the same extreme social pressure to be as thin as women. Instead, men experience pressure to conform to the current male ideal of a V-shaped upper body, well-defined abdominal muscles, and virtually no fat. This trend is apparent in male action figures and male models.

When men diet, it is usually related to sports, obesity, gender-identity conflicts, or fear of future health problems rather than as a consequence of cultural pressure to be thin. Risk factors are similar in men and women, except that men are more likely than females to experience substance abuse. Puberty does not appear to be as significant a risk factor in boys as in girls. This is because the secondary sexual characteristics and social adjustments experienced by boys during puberty are considered more socially acceptable and therefore less stressful.

Medical complications of eating disorders are similar in men and women, except that men appear to experience a greater loss of bone density than women do. In addition, when compared to their healthy peers, men recovering from anorexia nervosa have a higher incidence of testicular abnormalities due to testosterone suppression.

Although disordered eating is more prevalent in women, men and women are equally dissatisfied with their bodies. Studies have shown that as many as 70 percent of college men are dissatisfied with their bodies and would prefer to be more muscular. This body dissatisfaction and

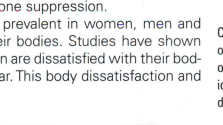

Changes in male action figures over time reflect the pressure on males to attain the current ideal of the *V*-shaped physique displayed by top male models.

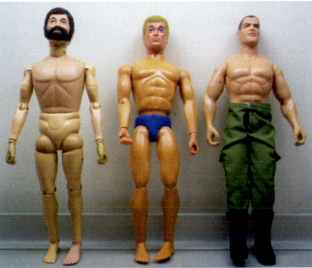

Men suffering from muscle dysmorphia believe themselves to be out of shape or too thin even when they are very muscular. People who have body dysmorphic disorder are preoccupied with the thought that one aspect of their appearance is very unattractive.

desire to gain muscle begins at a young age; 23 percent of third-grade boys surveyed reported a desire to gain weight and to become more muscular. Concerns about body image may show up in young men as compulsive overexercising or in the use of anabolic steroids rather than the unhealthy weight-loss behaviors seen in young women with body image concerns.

Men may feel pressured to emulate the strong, muscular physique of the ideal male in much the same way that women feel pressured to emulate the thin, lean, almost skeletal female ideal. This pressure can lead to **muscle dysmorphia.** Men with this condition perceive themselves to be thin even when they are very muscular. ■

*Muscle dysmorphia* is a specific type of body dysmorphic disorder (BDD) that is classified in the *DSM* as a type of delusional disorder. As mentioned previously, people with BDD are preoccupied with the thought that some aspect of their appearance is unattractive, deformed, or "not right" in some way. Individuals with muscle dysmorphia focus on their muscularity and never think they are big enough. They often seek cosmetic surgery or anabolic steroids to resolve their perceived flaws, sometimes undergoing multiple operations with no satisfaction. Muscle dysmorphia is often associated with low self-esteem, shame, embarrassment, fear of rejection, and obsessive-compulsive behavior, such as constantly checking one's appearance in the mirror. It has been estimated that 51 percent of those with BDD are men. It is not clear exactly how many of those specifically have muscle dysmorphia. Few studies have been done to assess the impact of body image dissatisfaction and media pressure on young men and their diet, exercise, and use of anabolic steroids.

## ■ To Supplement or Not

### Anabolic steroids—a vicious cycle

Those with muscle dysmorphia are at risk for taking anabolic-androgenic steroids (AAS). They quickly become impatient with the gradual muscle gains that occur with training and a balanced diet. They never feel big enough and therefore are drawn to the quick and unnatural gains in muscle that occur with AAS use. AAS are manufactured hormones that are related to male sex hormones. They were developed in the 1930s for medical purposes. In the 1950s, athletes began using AAS to enhance strength and muscle mass as well as to increase the intensity of their training. AAS are illegal to possess without a prescription and have been banned from most competitive sports.

Despite this ban, more athletes than ever are using steroids. And it is not just athletes; many non-athletes have discovered the body-enhancing properties of AAS as well. Although prevalence data vary because of the illegal nature of the drugs, the usage rate of AAS among high school students has been reported as 2–18 percent of those surveyed. Most students who admit having used the drugs indicate that they began before age 16. Many claim that when they started taking the steroids, they intended to use them for only a short time. However,

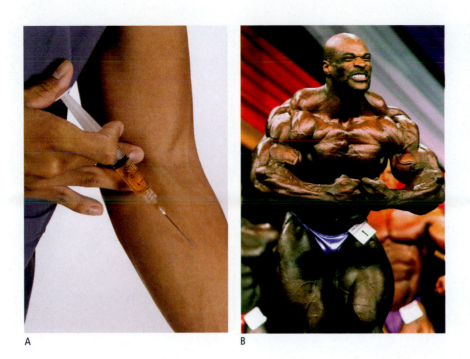

(A) Steroid use is common among athletes and nonathletes; (B) Former Mr. Olympia Ronnie Coleman showcases the typical modern bodybuilder physique.

A   B

when they went off steroids and lost the strength and size that had gained, they could not resist the lure of doing them again, thus developing a form of addiction. Because these drugs are illegal, many were reluctant to seek help when they wanted to stop taking them.

While the benefits of AAS are well known, many users are not aware of their potential physiological and psychological side effects and other dangers—such as the increased risk for HIV that comes with sharing needles. Several prevention programs have been designed and implemented in an attempt to decrease the use of AAS, but few have resulted in a decline. Prevention efforts may be challenged by the fact that AAS work. Simply informing adolescents of the dangerous side effects may be insufficient to deter use, and may in fact encourage it. In addition, the negative health consequences of AAS are often not immediate, and when they do occur, they can be difficult to link to the use of the drugs.

An additional challenge to prevention efforts is the well-publicized use of steroids among famous athletes.

Users and potential users see the performance benefits, the appearance benefits, and the numerous accolades that their role models receive as a result of taking AAS, but they see few obvious negative consequences. The challenge becomes preventing the use of something that works and that many athletic role models are using. How do we inform people of the side effects when many who admit using them do not appear to immediately suffer from these consequences? Better yet, how do we teach men and boys that many different body types are healthy and attractive and that they do not need to take harmful substances to attain an unrealistic ideal? Perhaps adoption of a true no-tolerance policy by the governing agencies in sports, the media, and the public is a place to start. ■

After pro wrestler Chris Benoit killed his wife, his son, and himself, speculation immediately turned to what role steroids may have played in Benoit's behavior. DEA agents raided the office of his personal physician, who acknowledged prescribing testosterone to Benoit.

As Barry Bonds chased and passed Hank Aaron as the leader in career home runs in major league baseball, fans and advertisers alike shunned him due to his alleged steroid use. Many see the change in his appearance during his rookie year (left) and now (right) as evidence of his steroid use.

When it comes to dieting, perceiving oneself as overweight is clearly more important than actually being overweight. A study to define characteristics of dieters discovered that what distinguishes them from nondieters is a personal experience of perceiving themselves to be overweight at any stage of life. The best predictor of the development of an eating disorder in adolescent girls is the presence of weight concerns, which encompasses fear of weight gain, worry over body weight and/or shape, and perceived fatness.

## Teasing

Teasing is also a major risk factor for disordered eating. The association between a history of being teased by peers and/or family members about physical appearance and the occurrence of both body image and eating disturbances has been well documented. Teasing words can be absorbed into a child's identity and developing sense of self, particularly if the cultural environment supports the comments. For example, a teasing remark made about a child's body shape may interact with his or her self-assessment of having a body that deviates from the cultural ideal. Teasing about body shape may lead children to evaluate their self-worth based predominantly on body appearance. In addition, teasing has been associated with low self-esteem, which has been identified as a risk factor for many problems. For example, teasing and bullying have recently received a lot of attention in the media in connection with the marked increases in violence and school shootings.

The teasing voices one may hear as a child become an unshakeable voice of self-doubt as an adult. Perhaps acceptance for diverse body shapes needs to be incorporated into the diversity-education programs already in place to teach acceptance for different races, religions, and cultures.

It is not just children who are subject to teasing; adults experience it as well. Many overweight adults feel shame and report being subject to societal prejudice. Have you ever judged someone or made assumptions about him or her based on physical size?

### ■ Self-Assessment

*Examine your fat prejudice*

How many times have you remarked to a friend about another person's weight gain? How many times have you praised someone for losing weight? How many times have you made negative comments about your own weight or body size? Every time that you do any of these things, you are exhibiting a fat prejudice, which is equally damaging and hurtful as an ethnic or gender prejudice. You are helping perpetuate the cultural pressure that may contribute to another person's eating disorder. Through your responses to the following questionnaire you can examine your own behavior and make sure you are part of the solution, not part of the problem.

This behavior assessment can be used to evaluate your support for the health and well-being of large people. Use the following scale to indicate the frequency of each behavior.

1—Never   2—Rarely   3—Occasionally   4—Frequently   5—Daily

Behaviors 1–28 are unhelpful or harmful. Look over areas that need improvement and strive to avoid these behaviors in the future. Behaviors 29–39 help support size acceptance. Reread items 29–39 that you marked *Never* or *Rarely*. Make a list of realistic goals for increasing supportive behavior.

| How often do you: | Never . . . . . . . . . . daily | | | | |
|---|---|---|---|---|---|
| 1. Make negative comments about your own fatness | 1 | 2 | 3 | 4 | 5 |
| 2. Make negative comments about someone else's fatness | 1 | 2 | 3 | 4 | 5 |
| 3. Directly or indirectly support the assumption that no one should be fat | 1 | 2 | 3 | 4 | 5 |
| 4. Disapprove of fatness (in general) | 1 | 2 | 3 | 4 | 5 |
| 5. Say or assume that someone is "looking good" because he or she has lost weight | 1 | 2 | 3 | 4 | 5 |
| 6. Say something that presumes that fat people want to lose weight | 1 | 2 | 3 | 4 | 5 |
| 7. Say something that presumes that fat people should lose weight | 1 | 2 | 3 | 4 | 5 |
| 8. Say something that presumes that fat people eat too much | 1 | 2 | 3 | 4 | 5 |
| 9. Admire or approve of someone for losing weight | 1 | 2 | 3 | 4 | 5 |
| 10. Disapprove of someone for gaining weight | 1 | 2 | 3 | 4 | 5 |
| 11. Assume that something is "wrong" when someone gains weight | 1 | 2 | 3 | 4 | 5 |
| 12. Admire weight-loss dieting | 1 | 2 | 3 | 4 | 5 |
| 13. Admire rigidly controlled eating | 1 | 2 | 3 | 4 | 5 |
| 14. Admire compulsive or excessive exercising | 1 | 2 | 3 | 4 | 5 |
| 15. Tease or admonish someone about his or her eating (habits or choices) | 1 | 2 | 3 | 4 | 5 |
| 16. Criticize someone's eating to a third person ("so-and-so eats way too much junk") | 1 | 2 | 3 | 4 | 5 |
| 17. Discuss food in terms of "good/bad" | 1 | 2 | 3 | 4 | 5 |
| 18. Talk about "being good" and "being bad" in reference to eating behavior | 1 | 2 | 3 | 4 | 5 |
| 19. Talk about calories (in the usual dieter's fashion) | 1 | 2 | 3 | 4 | 5 |
| 20. Say something that presumes that being thin is better (or more attractive) than being fat | 1 | 2 | 3 | 4 | 5 |
| 21. Comment that you don't wear a certain style because "it makes you look fat" | 1 | 2 | 3 | 4 | 5 |

*(Continued)*

| | | | | | |
|---|---|---|---|---|---|
| 22. Comment that you love certain clothing because "it makes you look thin" | 1 | 2 | 3 | 4 | 5 |
| 23. Say something that presumes that fatness is unattractive | 1 | 2 | 3 | 4 | 5 |
| 24. Participate in a "fat joke" by telling one or laughing/smiling at one | 1 | 2 | 3 | 4 | 5 |
| 25. Support the diet industry by buying its services and/or products | 1 | 2 | 3 | 4 | 5 |
| 26. Undereat and/or exercise obsessively to maintain an unnaturally low weight | 1 | 2 | 3 | 4 | 5 |
| 27. Say something that presumes that being fat is unhealthy | 1 | 2 | 3 | 4 | 5 |
| 28. Say something that presumes that being thin is healthy | 1 | 2 | 3 | 4 | 5 |
| 29. Encourage someone to let go of guilt | 1 | 2 | 3 | 4 | 5 |
| 30. Encourage or admire self-acceptance and self-appreciation/love | 1 | 2 | 3 | 4 | 5 |
| 31. Encourage someone to feel good about his or her body as is | 1 | 2 | 3 | 4 | 5 |
| 32. Openly admire a fat person's appearance | 1 | 2 | 3 | 4 | 5 |
| 33. Openly admire a fat person's character, personality, or actions | 1 | 2 | 3 | 4 | 5 |
| 34. Oppose/challenge fattism verbally | 1 | 2 | 3 | 4 | 5 |
| 35. Oppose/challenge fattism in writing | 1 | 2 | 3 | 4 | 5 |
| 36. Challenge or voice disapproval of a "fat joke" | 1 | 2 | 3 | 4 | 5 |
| 37. Challenge myths about fatness and eating | 1 | 2 | 3 | 4 | 5 |
| 38. Compliment ideas, behavior, character, and so on more often than appearance | 1 | 2 | 3 | 4 | 5 |
| 39. Support organizations that advance fat acceptance (with your time or money) | 1 | 2 | 3 | 4 | 5 |

*Source: Making Peace with Food: Freeing Yourself from the Diet Weight Obsession by Susan Kano, 1989, Harper and Row, New York. Reprinted from the NAAFA with permission.* ■

## Self-Esteem

People with anorexia and bulimia typically have lower self-esteem than their non-eating-disordered peers. In addition, their self-esteem appears to be unduly connected to body size. Most are highly self-critical and perceive themselves as inadequate in most areas of social and personal functioning. In addition to being self-critical, people with anorexia tend to be highly reliant on external feedback either from others or from numbers on the scale. This external reliance makes them extremely vulnerable to media messages. Lack of self-esteem typically occurs despite above-average performance in academics and/or athletics. Nothing, including their weight, ever seems good enough.

### ■ Self-Assessment
*How do you feel about your own body?*
Are the following statements true or false?

1. You seldom speak in a negative way about your body.
2. You don't feel the need to step on the scale more often than once a week.
3. You would exercise the same as you do presently even if society didn't focus on appearance.
4. Comparing your looks or body to others is rarely something you do.
5. Eating a high-fat food seldom makes you feel nervous or guilty.
6. When someone compliments your appearance, you accept it.
7. You would NOT do something unhealthy (take laxatives, vomit, or fast) to change your weight.

8. At this point in time, you feel mostly satisfied and happy with your life.

9. If you were to gain a few pounds, it wouldn't cause you anxiety.

10. Overall, you are content with your present body shape and size.

Count the number of true statements you have and see the results below:

8-10    You are content with your body.

4-7    You are a bit on the self-critical side of things.

0-3    You appear to be having a difficult time. It may be beneficial to seek help. ■

# Puberty

Body image may be affected by personal responses to puberty as well as the attitudes of family members and peers toward appropriate body size and shape. Additionally, new evidence suggests that puberty may also trigger any genetic predispositions to developing eating disorders. Research conducted at Michigan State University suggests that 50 percent of the increased risk of developing an eating disorder that emerges during puberty can be attributed to genetics. Adolescents who mature either earlier or later than others may be subject to teasing and therefore to body dissatisfaction. Boys who develop later than their peers, so-called late bloomers, may be more prone to body image disorders and therefore at greater risk for muscle dysmorphia. Puberty may be a greater risk factor for girls than boys. They may be poorly informed about the normal biological changes of puberty and about appropriate expectations for body shape and size. In a society in which a prepubescent female body is socially desirable, many girls perceive the increase in fat deposition that comes with normal puberty as unwanted weight gain and may begin dieting. Accordingly, girls who are more physically mature are more likely to display symptoms of disordered eating.

The onset of puberty may not be a risk factor by itself. Rather, it may be that so much happens at one time. It has been suggested that puberty is more traumatic for girls than for boys because so many social changes occur at the same time. Dating, increased academic pressure, and increased social expectations commonly occur during ages 11 to 14, which is the average age of onset for puberty in girls (boys tend to mature a bit later). This is the age range when females typically begin to show an increased awareness and dissatisfaction with their appearance, body shape, and body fat. For many girls, dieting seems to be part of an adjustment to the fat increase associated with menarche (the beginning of the menstrual cycle) and to the demands of dating attractiveness. The body fat changes that occur during puberty create an increasing discrepancy between their actual bodies and the cultural ideal of a near-prepubescent body. The confusion and uncertainty that many girls feel during puberty can be communicated through their feelings about their changing bodies. In other words, their new bodies are connected to their new experiences, and dieting can become their means of expression and control. Saying that one "feels fat" becomes a socially acceptable way of expressing many feelings. These issues are very age-specific and would not be relevant to a younger or older person struggling with the same disorder. Therefore, it has been suggested that any efforts to prevent or to understand the development of eating disorders be age and life-cycle sensitive.

## Family

No evidence indicates that family problems are the primary or only cause of an eating disorder. However, families of people with anorexia appear to interact more dysfunctionally than the families of non-eating-disordered individuals. Some common characteristics in families of people with anorexia have been identified: not accepting individuality, overprotectiveness, inflexibility in rules, lack of ability to solve conflicts, inadequate boundaries, rejection of communication or expression of feelings, and overinvolvement of the anorexic child in parental conflicts. Women who are part of such families may turn to eating disorders or substances such as alcohol and drugs to cope with the family problems. The family connection to eating disorder risk may also be genetic. Many of the first-degree relatives of eating-disordered women are either eating-disordered or have associated disorders.

Initial genetic studies using primarily twins found a genetic link for both anorexia nervosa and, to a lesser extent, bulimia nervosa. Recently, genetic studies based on families with two or more individuals with an eating disorder (anorexia nervosa or bulimia nervosa) revealed a genetic link for both disorders, but more so for anorexia. It is difficult to determine the role genetics plays in the development of eating disorders. As mentioned previously, they are complex diseases that are different in every person and therefore caused by different factors. The important thing to point out is that people with eating disorders have a psychological problem that they do not choose. Yes, they can learn how to manage the disorder, but they can't control its onset.

**Want to know more?**

How strong is the genetic connection to eating disorders? To explore the answer to this question, go to the text website at http://webcom8.grtxle.com/nutrition and click on the Chapters button. Select Chapter 15.

## Athletes

Does being an athlete increase one's risk of developing an eating disorder? The answer is that being an athlete in general may not increase one's risk, but participation in certain sports may. Athletes of any sport, from recreational exercisers to elite athletes, can have this condition. However, endurance athletes and athletes in appearance-based sports (such as gymnastics, ballet, figure skating, and diving,) are particularly prone to disordered eating and its associated health risks. Recognition of the increased risk in female athletes of developing disorders led to the coining of the term **female athlete triad** (Figure 15.6), which has been assigned to a serious health problem encompassing three interrelated health issues: disordered eating, amenorrhea, and osteoporosis.

This phenomenon and the potential deficiencies and long-term health problems that may result have a serious impact on the athlete's performance and overall health. Many who have this condition engage in disordered eating behavior, which may include severe dietary restriction. This creates the potential for deficiency in any nutrient, depending on the severity of restriction and the types of foods restricted or omitted from the diet. The extreme demands of training and competing may increase the nutrient needs of many athletes and thus put them at an even greater risk of deficiency and long-term health problems than a restricting non-athlete.

Of particular concern is the fact that many female athletes restrict their intake of the most nutrient-dense source

**Figure 15.6** The female athlete triad.

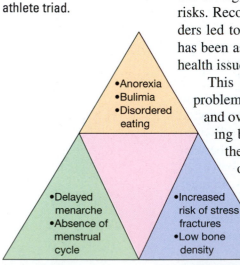

• Anorexia
• Bulimia
• Disordered eating

• Delayed menarche
• Absence of menstrual cycle

• Increased risk of stress fractures
• Low bone density

Amenorrhea                    Osteoporosis

Female athletes involved in all sports are at risk for developing disordered eating; however, athletes in appearance-based sports such as gymnastics may be at even greater risk.

of calcium—dairy products. An inadequate intake of calcium is one of the major risk factors for osteoporosis. Compared to non-athletes, athletes with disordered eating are at an increased risk for osteoporosis, and they are more likely to have the confounding risk factor of *amenorrhea,* or loss of their menstrual cycle, for more than three months in a row. Amenorrhea is not a normal consequence of training and should be recognized as a serious health problem. Amenorrhea is accompanied by low blood estrogen levels. **Estrogen**, the predominant female sex hormone, is also important in the development and formation of bone. When estrogen levels are decreased, as during amenorrhea, bone development is impaired. The longer the amenorrhea lasts or the more frequently it occurs, the greater the risk. Low estrogen levels can negate the benefits of physical activity for the formation of bone. In many athletes, low levels of estrogen result from a delayed onset of menses. This delay is sometimes intentional in sports where a female physique may not be considered optimal for performance, such as gymnastics. Athletes participating in these sports may be at an increased risk for disordered eating and other associated problems. Inadequate calcium intake and amenorrhea may prevent the young athlete from ever reaching peak bone mass, which puts her at greater risk for both developing osteoporosis in general, and for developing the disease at an earlier age. Most women don't lose a significant amount of bone mass until about age 50–60, when estrogen levels decrease at **menopause**. If a woman never reaches her peak bone density, she will be starting at a disadvantage and may see a more rapid decline. Although the long-term effects of inadequate calcium intake are potentially severe, the acute effects on performance are negligible because blood calcium levels are tightly maintained. This means that most people do not realize they have a problem until it is too late and they have already developed osteoporosis.

The female athlete triad can lead to more than a decrease in performance. It may also impair the long-term health of the athlete. The most effective way of addressing this problem is through prevention and education. Athletes, coaches, and parents need to be aware of the serious health problems associated with restricting calories, amenorrhea, and delaying menses. The concepts of healthy, balanced nutrition and the risks of dieting should be taught to parents and athletes at an early age to establish positive, well-informed, healthy attitudes and the practices that go along with them. Coaches need to encourage healthy eating and discourage severe restricting and weight loss. Any disordered eating should be addressed to prevent the development of a serious eating disorder in the future.

Although the preceding discussion focused on the onset of the triad of health conditions in athletes, the associated conditions can also occur in non-athletes with disordered eating.

**Before you go on . . .**

1. What are some warning signs that someone may have an eating disorder?
2. Identify the primary risk factors for developing an eating disorder.
3. What is body dissatisfaction, and what role does it play in the development of an eating disorder?
4. How does dieting increase the potential risk of developing an eating disorder?

# Medical Complications, Treatment, and Prevention of Eating Disorders

## Medical Complications

Anorexia nervosa, bulimia, and disordered eating are associated with many medical complications, even death. Death often results from complications associated with starvation. This section provides detailed listings of potential complications that can result from cases of anorexia and bulimia.

### Anorexia Nervosa

Anorexia nervosa has a multitude of medical complications ranging from mild to severe. In fact, 5 to 20 percent of people with anorexia die, usually from complications associated with self-starvation, such as heart, kidney, or multiple organ failure, or illnesses such as pneumonia, which may be due to an inability to fight infection. Other complications are as follows:

- Heart problems
- Gastrointestinal issues
- Cease in menstruation in females; decreased testicular function in males
- Anemia
- Profound tiredness
- Tendency to bruise
- Dental problems
- Decreased immune system functioning
- Dizzy spells and fainting
- Dry skin, hair and nails; yellow skin
- Water retention

- Insomnia
- Kidney and liver damage
- Growth of fine hair on the body in an attempt to keep warm due to low body temperature; but hair loss on head
- Hyperactivity
- Hypoglycemia
- Pancreatitits
- Muscle cramps and weakness
- Light and sound sensitivity

### Bulimia

Medical complications that may result from bulimia include, but are not limited to, the following:

- Stomach rupture
- Heart failure due to loss of vital minerals, such as potassium, caused by purging
- Less deadly but serious problems caused by vomiting, including the following:
  The acid in vomit wears down the outer layer of the teeth
  The backs of the hands are scarred when the fingers are pushed down the throat to induce vomiting
  The esophagus becomes inflamed
  Glands near the cheeks become swollen
- Irregular menstrual periods
- Diminished libido (sex drive)
- Addictions and/or compulsive behavior
- Clinical depression, anxiety, obsessive-compulsive disorder, and other psychiatric illnesses
- Increased risk for suicidal behavior

## Treatment

Considering the serious medical complications and life-threatening nature of eating disorders, rapid and successful treatment seems crucial. Unfortunately, success rates in the treatment of anorexia nervosa and bulimia are among the worst in the practice of psychological medicine.

A definition of what constitutes successful treatment has not been clearly established, making it difficult to measure. In other words, is treatment a success when the behavior stops, or when the thoughts and feelings leading to the behavior cease? Few controlled-outcome studies have been done to evaluate the success of different behavioral/psychological treatments for people with eating disorders or disordered eating. Nevertheless, according to the Society for Adolescent Medicine, it has been recognized for some time that children and adolescents with eating disorders require management by an interdisciplinary team consisting of physicians, nurses, dietitians, and mental health professionals.

Treatment goals for anorexia and other eating disorders are established on an individual basis. Goals are gradual and focus on stopping harmful behaviors, understanding the thoughts and feelings associated with those behaviors, and learning new ways to deal with the related emotions. For patients with anorexia, the first goal is to make sure that the patient is medically stable. This may be done in a physician's office or in the hospital; the evaluation typically includes close monitoring of electrolytes, fluid balance and other blood levels, and weight

# Real People, Other Voices

**Student:**

## Terry Wilson

Pima Community College

Todd's recurring suspicions show that he believes Jennifer has an eating disorder. Jennifer's mood swings, her sudden disinterest in food, her rapid weight loss, and her newfound enjoyment in lots of exercise have fueled Todd's suspicions and overshadowed Jennifer's insistence that she's just getting into shape. I think Todd should continue to listen to what Jennifer says, but he should also watch how she behaves with regard to diet and exercise. Her behavior and her appearance will provide the truest indication of whether she is "fine" or not.

Research has shown that people often are very secretive about eating disorders until they realize they have a problem. This puts Todd in an uncomfortable position. If he appears overly interested in Jennifer's exercise and diet, she'll likely become more secretive about her habits and will not change them. She might also decide that Todd is too nosy—that he no longer is the boyfriend she wants. She is changing and he'll need to decide whether to respond, ignore, or resist the new behaviors that could affect their relationship.

My advice to Todd is to tell Jennifer that he is concerned about her, and that he is there to help her. He should listen to her and be a good friend. But if the joy in the relationship dissolves over time, Todd will need to move on.

**Instructor:**

## Tammy J. Stephenson, PhD

University of Kentucky

Jennifer is very lucky to have a boyfriend and friend who are concerned about her well-being and health. It does seem as though Jennifer is experiencing some form of disordered eating. Many people think that all people suffering from eating disorders are very thin, pale, and fragile looking. But the reality is that a person can be at a perfectly normal or even above-normal weight and suffer from disordered eating. I am very concerned about Jennifer's skipping meals, exercising twice a day, losing weight rapidly, and experiencing moodiness. All of these behaviors are warning signs of an eating disorder.

The good news is that most college campuses have resources available to students and these services tend to be free. I suggest that Todd contact the student health service on campus to see what is available. It is likely that a team of professionals, including a physician, Registered Dietitian, and psychologist, can help Jennifer. If Todd feels comfortable doing so, I would encourage him to let Jennifer know he is concerned. He sounds like a loving boyfriend who will be supportive and nonconfrontational. Todd should not try to solve Jennifer's problems or force her to eat. Rather, he should tell her about the resources he has found on campus, and perhaps on the Internet, and should walk Jennifer over to the student health service to schedule an appointment.

Todd's support and patience will be important to Jennifer's wellness and health in the future.

**Registered Dietitian:**

## Kandi S. Perazzo, RD, LDN

Allentown, PA

Todd can get an idea of whether Jennifer really has an eating disorder by looking at the diagnostic criteria for anorexia and bulimia. If Jennifer meets these criteria, she may have a full-blown eating disorder and she should get help immediately. If, however, Jennifer does not meet the diagnostic criteria for an eating disorder, she may still be suffering from disordered eating, and Todd can offer some assistance.

Todd can contact some of the resources listed in this chapter, such as the Renfrew Center, for advice on how to help Jennifer. Most importantly, he should reassure her that he cares for her no matter what issues she may be dealing with, and that he supports her. He should not try to force her to change or make any judgments about her. He can approach her and mention that he realizes she may be going through some tough times, and he could suggest that she talk to someone about her feelings.

There are mental health professionals and dietitians who specialize in eating disorders. As the chapter mentioned, disordered eating is not easy to diagnose or treat, so a multidisciplinary approach is best. The website www.eatright. org can direct Todd and Jennifer to a Registered Dietitian who specializes in eating disorders and who can help her. If Jennifer wants to change and gets help, she can recover successfully and learn to have a positive relationship with food and her body.

regain. After medical stabilization, patients typically progress to either an inpatient or outpatient treatment center. Several centers across the United States have varying philosophies and approaches to treatment. Most embrace the **multidisciplinary treatment** approach and therefore use a variety of behavioral/psychological treatments, including individual counseling, group counseling, family therapy, behavior modification, and cognitive/behavioral therapy. Many also use complementary therapeutic approaches such as art, movement, music, nutrition, yoga, meditation, and exercise. In addition, medications have played a role in treatment and have benefited many patients, especially those who also have depression and anxiety. Others seek outpatient care through a mental health professional who specializes in working with people with eating disorders. These professionals will still most likely use a multidisciplinary approach whenever possible.

Unfortunately, for many with eating disorders, treatment is difficult to obtain. Either patients have no medical insurance or the insurance they do have does not cover eating disorders or offers minimal coverage. According to Jeanine Cogan, PhD, director of the Eating Disorders Coalition for Research Policy and Action, data show that health insurers provide an average of ten to fifteen sessions for people with eating disorders when at least forty may be needed. Patients who cannot afford a treatment center can inquire about outpatient services or obtain local references at any of the treatment centers.

Despite weight gain and improvement of physical complications, struggles with social interactions and family relationships, as well as a continuation of pathologic eating behaviors, occur in more than half the patients undergoing treatment. Successful treatment is less likely when the patient begins treatment at a very low body weight or after a long-established low weight. The prognosis is also worse when other factors such as anxiety, depression, alcoholism, and an unsupportive family environment are involved. Follow-up evaluation at two years indicates that most patients can maintain a job but that psychological problems remain in one-third to one-half of patients with anorexia. Therefore, preventing the development of eating disorders is critical.

## Prevention

Considering the prevalence of eating disorders, the broad range of people affected, the short- and long-term health consequences, the lack of success in treatment, and the years of personal suffering, there is a clear justification for increased attention to primary prevention of eating disorders.

Many primary prevention interventions have been developed for middle schools, high schools, and colleges. School-based primary preventive interventions have focused on one or more of the following areas related to eating disorders: knowledge, attitudes, behavior, and weight. The few interventions that have been evaluated have had a modest effect on knowledge but little apparent impact on attitudes, behavior, or weight change. Any reported changes typically disappear within six months after the program is completed. School-based eating disorder prevention programs may even be counterproductive in the long run by suggesting disordered behavior to those who may not have thought of it prior to the program.

In light of the consistent failure of middle and high school prevention programs, there is a strong argument for beginning eating disorder prevention programs at the elementary school level. Many findings suggest the advisability of age-appropriate intervention for younger children. Although there is evidence

**Want to know more?**
To review up-to-date lists of eating disorder treatment centers and professionals, go to the text website at http://webcom8.grtxle.com/nutrition and click on the Chapters button. Select Chapter 15.

**Want to know more?**
Do most health insurers cover eating disorders? You can explore this issue by visiting the text website at http://webcom8.grtxle.com/nutrition and clicking on the Chapters button. Select Chapter 15.

of dieting, fear of fat, and negative body image among elementary age children, these attitudes and behaviors are neither as interconnected nor as ingrained as they are in adolescents. In elementary school, attitudes concerning the meaning of body fat in self-identity or social success may not be integrated with other information, such as the malleability of body weight and shape. When these ideas and attitudes do become integrated, they become what is referred to as the "thinness schema." This schema then provides a thought process through which all messages and information about body shape and weight are organized. These then develop into attitudes, beliefs, and eventually behaviors. If this schema and its related factors are not developed fully in elementary school children, then early intervention may prevent the incorporation of this schema into attitudes, beliefs, and behaviors that may develop further into eating disorders if not prevented. Furthermore, the increase in body dissatisfaction in girls following onset of puberty and the intensification of body-targeted teasing, harassment, and violation following puberty may further suggest the importance of introducing prevention programs before and during puberty.

The few programs that have been conducted with this age group have been successful at improving knowledge of MyPyramid, teaching the concept that no foods are forbidden, pointing out the negative effects of dieting, and explaining the role of genetics and puberty on body fat. In addition, negative attitudes toward obese people decreased. However, the programs did not change other attitudes, such as body esteem. Furthermore, no behaviors (e.g., dieting) were improved over the course of the programs. Perhaps the reason for the limited success is that the programs are too short and too isolated from the many influences the children have that may contribute to their risk for developing an eating disorder.

Perhaps the prevention efforts need to be more culturally integrated, like the efforts to stop smoking or drinking and driving. Additionally, there is something we can all do and that is to ask ourselves, do we contribute to another's eating disorder?

Considering the prevalence of eating disorders, the broad range of people affected, the short- and long-term health consequences, the lack of success in treatment, and the years of personal suffering, there is clear justification for increasing attention to the primary prevention of eating disorders. Many organizations such as the National Eating Disorders Association have launched large-scale annual campaigns to raise awareness and promote the prevention of eating disorders. Each year they provide a strong message of self-acceptance and prevention.

## ■ Make It a Practice

### *What you can do to prevent eating disorders*

The following things may contribute to the development of an eating disorder in you or someone else. Do you find yourself doing any of the following?

- Praising or glorifying another's appearance based on body size or attractiveness.
- Complimenting someone when he or she loses weight or diets.
- Encouraging someone to lose weight.
- Talking negatively about your own body.
- Asking a person "how" he or she lost weight.
- Discussing measurements, weight, or clothing sizes.
- Thinking of and labeling foods as "good" or "bad."
- Making fun of another person's eating habits or food choices.
- Criticizing a person's eating habits or even your own eating habits.
- Criticizing your own weight or physical appearance.
- Considering a person's weight important as to who he or she is as a human being.
- Saying someone is "healthy" or "well" because he or she is thin.
- Expecting perfection in yourself or others.
- Participating in more exercise than is healthy.

- Assuming that a large person wants or needs to lose weight.
- Allowing the media to dictate what body type is "in."

So what should you do to prevent eating disorders?

- Compliment others on attributes other than size.
- Decrease diet and weight talk.
- Do not joke about size.
- Discourage dieting and weight-loss fads and encourage a wellness lifestyle.
- Do not equate thinness with happiness.
- Accept that beautiful bodies come in all sizes.
- Throw out scales.
- Decrease time in front of the mirror.
- Avoid labeling food as "good" or "bad."
- Respect diversity in weight and shape just as you would diversity in race, gender, and ethnicity.
- Do not buy magazines or endorse any form of media that promotes unrealistic body types or that focuses on dieting.
- Be a good role model.
- Do not criticize yourself. ■

Other organizations and student groups have provided their own prevention based slogans, such as this one from Murray State University.

**Before you go on . . .**

1. Why is treatment of eating disorders so difficult to measure?
2. Define the multidisciplinary approach to treating eating disorders.
3. On what areas have school-based primary preventive interventions focused, and how successful have they been?
4. List at least five things you can do to prevent eating disorders.

## Real People, Real Strategies

Todd followed the recommendations that his professor provided in class. He first found out what services were provided on campus for eating disorders. He discovered that the counseling center had a counselor who specialized in eating disorders. Todd made an appointment with her to discuss the problem and to get her advice as to exactly what he should say to Jennifer. He really wanted to understand what she was going through. After speaking with the counselor Todd knew that he had to approach Jennifer the right way. The first thing he did was educate himself more thoroughly about eating disorders by visiting some of the websites the counselor suggested (see Figure 15.4). He was surprised to read that eating disorders are not about food, but rather one's ability to cope with his or her self-image, emotions, and stress. He learned that he should approach Jennifer without coming across in an accusatory way, or as if he were judging her. He realized that one of the most important things he should do was tell her how much he cared about her and that he was there to support her. He learned that he should not try to monitor what she does and does not eat. The websites told him that she may continue to deny the problem's existence and even get angry at him for bringing up the topic. That possibility was okay because he knew that he was the only person close enough to her to say anything, and he had to let her know he was concerned. All the sites indicated that she, and she alone, would have to decide to get help and that recovery could be a very long process.

Todd still wasn't sure he really understood what this was all about or what she was going through, but he felt compelled to try. He found some personal accounts online that helped. Perhaps the best explanation of why someone develops an eating disorder comes from an individual who has had the disease. The following quote was taken from www.anorexicweb.com.

In the eating disordered, image is a big component. It is no accident either that if we feel unable to share our pain verbally that we might try to share it physically. For example, if a daughter feels silenced by the family and overbearing sibling, perhaps the daughter will starve herself to look as small as she feels. Smart, in a way, but it doesn't end up working. Instead of being seen for who she is by the family, she will now be seen as the "crazy one" and that won't help at all. Likewise, if a man feels he is not good enough for his work and fears he doesn't have what it takes, maybe he will (unconsciously) grow larger and gain weight, in an effort to "take up space" in the world and appear to be someone to contend with (in actuality he feels as small as the anorexic girl). Instead of feeling more powerful, however, society jumps on his biggest fear (not being good enough) and teases him for his weight. This adds to his depression and already low self-esteem.

**Want to know more?**
To read more personal stories from people with eating disorders, go to the text website at http://webcom8.grtxle .com/nutrition and click on the Chapters button. Select Chapter 15.

# Chapter Summary

- Disordered eating occurs on a continuum from being unhappy with one's weight or body shape to having a clinical eating disorder such as anorexia nervosa or bulimia nervosa, both of which have specific diagnostic criteria. Many more individuals have disordered eating than diagnosable eating disorders.
- The feelings, attitudes, and behaviors associated with eating disorders and disordered eating begin as early as age 7. The media can influence children at a young age and give the message that thinness equals beauty or success.
- Eating disorders are more about escaping emotional pain than they are about food. Diagnostic criteria for anorexia, bulimia, and eating disorders not otherwise specified (EDNOS) are set forth in the *Diagnostic and Statistical Manual, Fourth Edition (DSM-IV)*.
- There are two subtypes of anorexia nervosa.
  - Restricting-type anorexia describes an individual who restricts intake of food without purging.
  - Binge-eating/purging-type anorexia describes an individual who cycles between restricting and binge eating with purging.
- There are two subtypes of bulimia.
  - In purging-type bulimia, an individual engages in self-induced vomiting and uses laxatives, enemas, or diuretics following a binge.
  - In nonpurging bulimia, a person engages in behaviors such as fasting or excessive exercise after bingeing, but does not regularly engage in self-induced vomiting or use of laxatives, enemas, or diuretics.
- Eating disorders that do not fit the strict criteria for anorexia or bulimia are diagnosed as eating disorders not otherwise specified (EDNOS).
- The cause of an eating disorder is always complex.
- Risk factors can help identify individuals who may be prone to developing an eating disorder.
- Risk factors include dieting, cultural pressure, body dissatisfaction, teasing, body fatness experienced by teen girls at puberty, dysfunctional family dynamics, genetics, and gender. Each one of these risk factors is complex; together, they make the prevention and treatment of eating disorders a daunting task.
- Anorexia, bulimia, and disordered eating are associated with many medical complications ranging from mild to severe. These disorders are among the most difficult psychological conditions to treat. Successful treatment requires the attention of an interdisciplinary team of healthcare experts. A registered dietitian is an important member of this team. He or she will teach the patient how to reconnect with food in a healthy way.
- Eating disorders are often associated with other disorders such as depression, anxiety, and substance abuse. The link between substance abuse and eating disorders may be a mood disorder such as depression, or the presence of an addictive personality type that relates to food and drugs in the same way.
- Female athletes who restrict calories may develop deficiencies in nutrients that are critical to performance and overall health.

- Female athletes may be at increased risk for developing eating disorders and may experience the female athlete triad—disordered eating, amenorrhea, and osteoporosis.
- Although eating disorders are thought to be a woman's condition, men also have issues with body image and self-esteem.
- Males account for 10–20 percent of reported cases of anorexia. Men are more susceptible than women to body dysmorphic disorder.
- There is cultural pressure for males to attain a V-shaped muscular physique. Some men resort to steroid drugs to attain this ideal.

# Key Terms

**amenorrhea** (ay-men-uh-REE-uh) Loss of menstrual flow for at least three consecutive cycles. (p. 474)

**anorexia nervosa** (an-uh-REX-ee-uh ner-VOH-sa) An eating disorder characterized by refusal to maintain a healthy body weight, an intense fear of weight gain, distorted body image and loss of menstrual periods. (p. 474)

**binge-eating disorder (BED)** An eating disorder characterized by recurrent episodes of binge eating that occur without regular compensatory or purging behaviors intended to prevent weight gain. (p. 476)

**binge-purging anorexia** The *DSM-IV* diagnosis for individuals diagnosed with anorexia who combine periodic restrictive dieting with frequent binge-and-purge episodes. (p. 475)

**body dissatisfaction** A poor body image; being unhappy with one's body. (p. 484)

**body dysmorphic disorder (BDD)** (bah-dee dis-MOR-fic dis-OR-der) A psychological disorder in which an individual is preoccupied with the thought that some aspect of his or her appearance is unattractive, deformed, or "not right" in some way. (p. 482)

**body image** A multifaceted psychological concept that refers to a person's perceptions, attitudes, and experiences about the appearance of his or her body. (p. 484)

**borderline anorexia** The partial syndromes of anorexia and bulimia; an unofficial term that describes individuals who are thin but may not appear malnourished or emaciated. (p. 476)

**bulimia nervosa** (boo-LEE-mee-uh ner-VOH-sa) An eating disorder characterized by recurrent episodes of abnormal food

intake, loss of sense of control over that intake, persistent and prolonged weight compensation behaviors, and body image disturbance. (p. 474)

**disordered eating** The general term covering a range of eating disorders or behaviors that are not severe enough to be medically diagnosed as an eating disorder (such as anorexia nervosa). (p. 474)

**eating disorders not otherwise specified (EDNOS)** Eating disorders that encompass anorexic and bulimic behaviors but do not include all of the specific criteria. (p. 476)

**estrogen** (ESS-tro-jen) The predominate female sex hormone, which is also important for the development and formation of bone. (p. 493)

**female athlete triad** A serious health problem among female athletes that encompasses three interrelated health issues: disordered eating, amenorrhea, and osteoporosis. (p. 492)

**menopause** A female life stage during which, prompted by hormonal changes, ovulation and menstruation cease. (p. 493)

**multidisciplinary treatment** Approach that incorporates health professionals from many different areas and therefore uses a variety of behavioral, psychological, and physical treatment philosophies; such teams can include physicians, psychiatrists, psychologists, registered dietitians, nurses, physical therapists, movement therapists, art therapists and exercise physiologists. (p. 497)

**muscle dysmorphia** (MUSS-el dis-MOR-fee-uh) A form of body dysmorphic disorder characterized by a preoccupation with the idea that one is thin when he is actually very muscular. (p. 486)

**night-eating syndrome (NES)** An eating disorder associated with loss of appetite in the morning, overeating in the evening, and sleep problems. (p. 476)

**nonpurging bulimia** The *DSM-IV* diagnosis for individuals with bulimia who have used compensatory behaviors such as fasting or excessive exercise, but have not regularly engaged in self-induced vomiting or the misuse of laxatives, diuretics, or enemas. (p. 476)

**purging bulimia** The *DSM-IV* diagnosis for individuals diagnosed with bulimia who have

regularly engaged in a purging method such as self-induced vomiting or the abuse of laxatives, diuretics, or enemas. (p. 476)

**restricting anorexia** The *DSM-IV* designation for individuals diagnosed with anorexia who lose weight by reducing food and overall caloric intake by fasting or very strict dieting. (p. 475)

**risk factors** Characteristics, situations, or triggers that identify individuals or groups as being at risk for developing eating disorders. (p. 481)

# Chapter Quiz

1. What does it mean to say eating disorders occur on a continuum?

   a. Eating disorders continue to develop.

   b. Eating disorders can range from being unhappy with one's shape or weight to a clinical diagnosis.

   c. Eating disorders range from bulimia to anorexia.

   d. Anorexia and bulimia are the only eating disorders.

2. What is disordered eating?

   a. a term that defines anorexia and bulimia

   b. eating too fast

   c. the behavior of people who diet frequently, binge eat, and use unhealthy methods to lose weight such as vomiting and restricting food, and people who meet some but not all of the criteria for a medically diagnosable condition

   d. compulsive overeating

3. EDNOS is a term used for

   a. anorexic and/or bulimic behaviors that do not meet the specific criteria for those diagnoses

   b. binge-eating disorder

   c. dieting

   d. both a and b

4. Night-eating syndrome is associated with

   a. eating while sleepwalking

   b. eating very little during the day but overeating at night

   c. eating too much before bed

   d. eating a lot all day and very little at night

5. Eating disorders can occur in what age groups?

   a. only teenagers and people of college age

   b. only people who are underweight or overweight

   c. at any age

   d. only teenage girls

6. Which of the following statements is true when determining whether someone has an eating disorder?

   a. People who have eating disorders are always very thin.

   b. People with eating disorders always eat less than half of their food.

   c. Many people with eating disorders are of normal body weight.

   d. People with eating disorders have tremendous self-discipline.

7. If you are concerned about a friend or family member's attitudes about food or his or her body, you should

   a. Tell him or her that you are concerned.

   b. You tell the person's friends and family and then confront him or her as a group.

   c. Tell the person that her or she is not fat.

   d. Tell him or her that a friend of yours has an eating disorder.

8. What can be said about body dissatisfaction in adults?

   a. Men and women are equally dissatisfied with their bodies.

   b. Men are more dissatisfied with their bodies than women.

   c. Women are more dissatisfied with their bodies than men.

   d. Men do not have issues with body dissatisfaction.

9. Why is prevention of eating disorders critical?

   a. Eating disorders cannot be treated.

   b. Eating disorders are difficult to treat.

   c. Eating disorder treatments rarely succeed.

   d. none of the above

10. Which of the following ethnic groups is most likely to have eating disorders?

   a. Caucasian

   b. African American

   c. Hispanic

   d. People of all ethnicities can have eating disorders

# CHAPTER 16

# Pregnancy, Breastfeeding, and Infant Feeding

## The Foundations of a Healthy Future

## < Here's Where You've Been

*The following topics were introduced in preceding chapters and are related to concepts we'll discuss in Chapter 16. Be certain that you're familiar with them before proceeding.*

- Gestational diabetes is a type of diabetes that can occur during pregnancy. (Chapter 3)
- It is recommended that all women of childbearing age consume 400 mcg of folate daily to prevent neural tube defects. (Chapter 9)
- Vitamins and minerals are not required in the diet in large amounts or stored in the body in large quantities. If they are consumed in inadequate amounts, deficiencies can occur, resulting in significant health consequences. (Chapters 9 and 10)
- Iron-deficiency anemia is the second most prevalent nutrition problem in the United States. (Chapter 10)

## Here's Where You're Going >

*The following topics and concepts are the ones we'll emphasize in Chapter 16.*

- Nutritionally, a potentially healthy pregnancy begins before conception.
- Nutrient demands during pregnancy increase and should be met by consuming nutrient-dense foods.
- Breast-feeding has many health benefits.
- Breast-feeding is recommended exclusively for the first six months and, along with the addition of appropriate complementary foods, until at least the first twelve months of an infant's life.
- Little research supports a single order of progression when introducing solid foods to infants. Waiting until they are four to six months old and adding foods gradually is a wise approach to avoiding food allergies.

## Real People, Real Choices

Sarah and Stephen Beckerman met during their junior year in college. They are now married and live in New York City. As young working professionals living in a large, fast-paced urban environment, they have a hectic and stress-filled lifestyle. They are both now 26 years old and ready to start a family. They realize that undertaking this step will entail some major changes for each of them. The first thing they want to make sure of is that they are prepared for the baby in as many ways as they can identify. They began by researching and selecting both an obstetrician and a pediatrician. They also consulted a financial planner about the costs of raising a child and the best way to save for the baby's education. Additionally, they knew that at some point they would need to ensure that their condominium is "baby-proofed" to eliminate any household elements or hazards such as chemicals that could harm a baby.

When they discussed their decision and plans to begin a family with their best friends, Camille and Sean, one of the major topics of conversation centered on their current health. Camille asked Sarah whether she had thought about what she would need to eat during pregnancy and whether she planned to breast-feed the baby. They also asked Sarah and Stephen if they knew about how and what to feed a baby. Sarah and Stephen realized that in all their planning they had forgotten perhaps the most important part of ensuring a healthy pregnancy and future for their baby: nutrition. Their friends gave them several books to read, but in going through them Sarah and Stephen discovered some conflicting information, so they were hesitant to follow any of them. Stephen thought that Sarah would probably need to drink lots of milk and eat more fruits and vegetables and less fast food. Sarah thought that eating a healthy diet would be the least challenging thing when she became pregnant. After all, she would be eating for two. Before conception, do you think that what Stephen eats could make a difference? What do you think will be their best approach to nutrition during pregnancy? Should they seek professional advice? If they should, what recommendations do you think the RD will give them for eating, both before and during pregnancy?

You may be surprised to hear that a healthy pregnancy starts before a woman even becomes pregnant. Ensuring a healthy pregnancy involves both the mother and the father and can include the entire family. Even if you are a cousin, aunt, uncle, or friend, you can help by being a positive role model to the child through living a healthy life and pursuing balanced nutrition.

Approximately 6 million pregnancies occur each year in the United States. Most of these pregnancies result in a happy and healthy outcome for both the parents and baby. Deaths and complications from pregnancy in the United States have declined over the last 100 years, but too many women and infants still die of pregnancy-related complications each day. In fact, according to the Save the Child Research Fund, American babies are three times as likely to die in the first month following birth as are children born in Japan (see Figure 16.1). According to the Centers for Disease Control and Prevention (CDC), the newborn mortality rate in the United States was 6.37 deaths per 1,000 births in 2004. That is 2.5 times the rate in Finland, Iceland, or Norway. The rate is even higher for minority and impoverished women, reaching 13.6 per 1,000 for non-Hispanic black women. Experts think the United States trails behind other developed countries most likely because of a lack of access to quality prenatal care for minorities and those without health insurance.

According to an article published in the December 2005 issue of *Obstetrics and Gynecology*, the overall maternal mortality rate in the United States is not

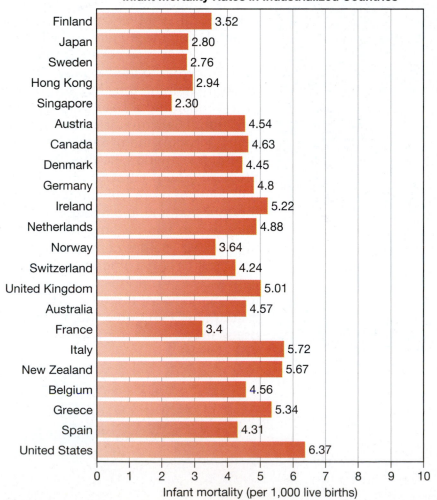

**Figure 16.1** Infant mortality rates in industrialized nations. The Unites States ranks among the highest because of disparities in health care.

*Source:* CIA World Factbook 2007 https://www.cia.gov/library/publications/the-world-factbook/

as low as it could be. Worldwide, complications of pregnancy are a major source of mortality among women. Although the United States observed a 99 percent reduction in maternal deaths during the twentieth century, twenty-nine developed nations still had lower maternal mortality rates than the United States.

Although maternal death is the most extreme adverse pregnancy outcome, a much greater number of women are affected by pregnancy-related complications, such as bleeding, pregnancy-induced high blood pressure, infection, and depression after delivery. As many as half of all deaths and complications from pregnancy could be prevented if women had better access to health care before, during, and after pregnancy; received better quality of care; and made changes in their health and lifestyle habits.

The time to start making positive lifestyle changes is before pregnancy. This is especially true when you consider that one of the most crucial times when health behaviors such as nutrition can influence fetal development is in the very beginning of pregnancy, before most women even know they are pregnant.

# Stages of Pregnancy

Pregnancy lasts for thirty-eight to forty-two weeks and is usually divided into three stages of about thirteen weeks each. These stages mark different phases of development for the fetus (see Figure 16.2) and therefore may be associated with different health implications and different physical sensations for the woman.

## First Trimester (Weeks 1–13)

The first trimester is when the sperm fertilizes the egg and rapid development occurs, leading to the development of an embryo. After about eight weeks of growth, organs are formed and the embryo becomes a fetus. In the initial stages of development, the embryo obtains nutrients from the lining of the uterus. After the first weeks, the **placenta** forms as a connection between the mother's and fetus's blood vessels (see Figure 16.3). This is how the developing fetus receives nutrients from the mother and rids itself of waste products. The placenta delivers these nutrients to the fetus through the **umbilical cord** connected to the fetus through the navel (or belly button). When you consider that the developing fetus is connected to the mother's blood supply, it makes sense that any substances that appear in the mother's body will also influence the very sensitive, rapidly developing fetus before a woman even knows she is pregnant. This is the time when the fetus is perhaps most vulnerable to inadequate nutrition and harmful substances such as drugs and alcohol in the mother. That is why it is critical to ensure adequate nutrient intake and to consider any medications or supplements if there is even a chance you could get pregnant.

## Second Trimester (Weeks 14–27)

During the entire second trimester, a fetus gains only about 1 kg (roughly 2 lbs.). The mother usually begins gaining about 0.5 kg (about a pound) per week at this point; by the end of the second trimester she weighs roughly 7 kg (16 lbs.) more than her prepregnancy weight. Much of this weight gain is due to the 30 percent increase in blood volume that occurs with pregnancy. The fetus can begin to hear sounds and to respond to light during this time.

**Figure 16.2** The first trimester is when the sperm fertilizes the egg and rapid development occurs, leading to the development of an embryo.

**Figure 16.3** A placenta moments after birth. The umbilical cord extends upward in this picture. It connects the developing fetus to the placenta. Note the dense concentration of capillaries supplying the placenta with blood and nutrients from the mother. The side facing down connects the placenta to the uterus.

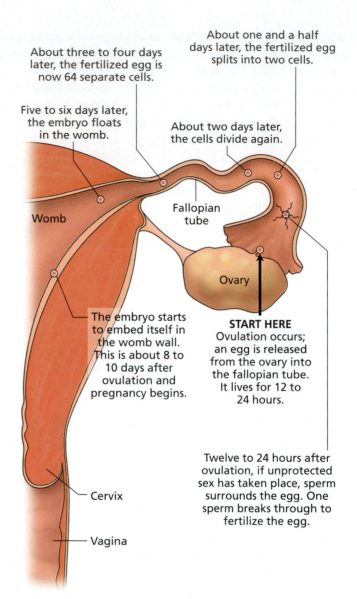

About three to four days later, the fertilized egg is now 64 separate cells.

About one and a half days later, the fertilized egg splits into two cells.

Five to six days later, the embryo floats in the womb.

About two days later, the cells divide again.

Womb

Fallopian tube

Ovary

The embryo starts to embed itself in the womb wall. This is about 8 to 10 days after ovulation and pregnancy begins.

**START HERE** Ovulation occurs; an egg is released from the ovary into the fallopian tube. It lives for 12 to 24 hours.

Twelve to 24 hours after ovulation, if unprotected sex has taken place, sperm surrounds the egg. One sperm breaks through to fertilize the egg.

Cervix

Vagina

**Figure 16.4** Timeline of fetal development.
*Source:* National Institutes of Health.

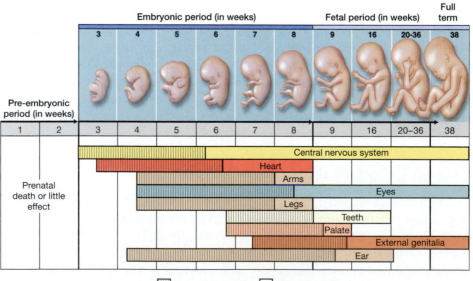

Embryonic period (in weeks)   Fetal period (in weeks)   Full term

Pre-embryonic period (in weeks)

Prenatal death or little effect

Central nervous system
Heart
Arms
Eyes
Legs
Teeth
Palate
External genitalia
Ear

▦ Major birth defects   ▢ Minor birth defects

## Third Trimester (Week 28 to Birth)

Although it is possible (with months of medical assistance) for a baby to survive after just two trimesters *in utero,* the third trimester fully equips the fetus for survival outside the womb. Growth and development is dramatic for the fetus during this period. Toward the end of pregnancy the fetus gains about 250 g (about half a pound) per week, so that the baby is typically born weighing 3–4 kg (7–9 lbs.). The fetus's skin, lungs, and suck-and-swallow reflex mature, and the fetus accumulates vital fat and nutrient stores. The baby triggers the onset of labor; once the fetus is fully developed, the fetus sends the mother a chemical cue—thought to be produced by the now fully-developed lungs—signaling to the mother's body that the baby is mature enough for labor to begin.

By the end of pregnancy, a woman will typically have gained 11–16 kg (25–35 lbs.) over her prepregnancy weight. The mother carrying twins or triplets will, of course, gain considerably more weight—about 23 kg (50 lbs.) for triplets.

## Low-Birthweight Newborns

An undernourished mother is likely to give birth to a smaller baby. An infant that weighs less than 5.5 lbs. is considered **low birthweight**. Low birthweight babies are at risk for several problems such as infection, lung problems, learning disabilities, insufficient physical growth, and death. Of course, other factors can cause a baby to be low in birth weight besides nutrition, but the impact of nutrition cannot be ignored.

> **Before you go on . . .**
> 1. Why is it important to start a healthy diet before pregnancy?
> 2. Describe the development of the fetus during the three stages of pregnancy.
> 3. Define *low birthweight* and list four potential health implications from this condition.

**Want to know more?**
If you would like to explore the various stages of fetal growth and development in greater detail, go to the text website at http://webcom8.grtxle .com/nutrition and click on the Chapters button. Select Chapter 16.

# Nutritional Needs During Pregnancy

The best approach to meeting the nutritional needs of pregnancy is to maintain a healthy diet and healthy weight before, during, and after pregnancy. Before pregnancy, this need for good nutrition applies to both parents. Increasing evidence suggests that the overall health and nutritional intake of the father is very important at the time of conception. Men who do not eat the recommended amount of fruits and vegetables tend to have the lowest sperm counts and the highest levels of inactive sperm.

## Weight Gain

Pregnant women are frequently concerned about gaining too much weight. Keep in mind that the mother's diet is the main source of energy for the baby and that weight gain is necessary for the development of a healthy baby. Also, not all weight gain during pregnancy is fat (see Table 16.1). How much weight a woman gains during pregnancy should depend on her weight before pregnancy. Expected weight gains should be individualized. They are typically based on prepregnancy

**Table 16.1**  **Where Does the Weight Come From?**

| | |
|---|---|
| Baby | 7½ pounds |
| Amniotic fluid | 2 pounds |
| Placenta | 1½ pounds |
| Uterus | 2 pounds |
| Breasts | 2 pounds |
| Body fluids | 4 pounds |
| Blood | 4 pounds |
| Maternal stores of fat, protein, and other nutrients | 7 pounds |

*Source:* American College of Obstetricians and Gynecologists. *Your Pregnancy and Birth,* 5th ed. Washington, DC: ACOG, 2010.

**Table 16.2**  **Recommended Weight Gain for Pregnant Women by Prepregnancy Body Mass Index (BMI)\***

| Weight-for-Height Category | Recommended Total Weight Gain | |
|---|---|---|
| | **(kg)** | **(lb.)** |
| Underweight (BMI < 19.8) | 12.5–18 | 28–40 |
| Normal weight (BMI 19.8 to 25) | 11.5–16 | 25–35 |
| Overweight (BMI 26 to 29) | 7–11.5 | 15–25 |
| Obese (BMI > 29) | 7 | No more than 15 |
| Twin gestation (any BMI) | 16–20 | 35–45 |
| Triplet Gestation (any BMI) | 23 | 50 |

Note: Women at greater risk for delivering low-birthweight babies, including adolescents, African American women, and others, should be monitored for optimal weight gain and dietary quality throughout pregnancy.

\*Body mass index, or BMI, is an indicator of nutritional status based on two common measurements, height and weight. Because it reflects body composition such as body fat and lean body mass, BMI is considered a more accurate indicator than height/weight tables.

BMI in this table is based on metric calculations, using the following formula:
  $BMI = wt/ht^2$ *(metric) = body weight in kilograms/height in meters squared*

A health care professional can help in calculating body mass index.

*Source:* Reprinted with permission of the National Academies Press, Copyright © 1990, National Academy of Sciences.

weight. Current recommendations suggest that a woman who is of a healthy weight before pregnancy should gain 25–35 lbs. If a woman is overweight, she should gain less, but some weight gain is normal. If she is underweight, she should gain more. Despite these guidelines, only 10–40 percent of women in the United States gain the recommended amount of weight (see Table 16.2).

## Meeting Increased Nutrient Needs

Nutritional needs are increased during pregnancy and must be met by eating many nutrient-dense foods. Calorie needs increase by only about 250–300 calories a day from prepregnant calorie requirements (or by 500 calories in adolescents). This may be less for some women, especially those who are extremely inactive.

The need will be slightly higher during the second and third trimesters compared to the first. Therefore, appetite and progression of weight gain are better indicators than just calorie intake of whether the pregnant woman is meeting her energy needs. The American Dietetic Association states that according to the *Dietary Guidelines*, women should consume a variety of foods (with cultural food practices considered) to meet energy and nutrient needs and gain the recommended amount of weight.

The need for some nutrients increases significantly, making nutrient density the main focus of nutrition goals during pregnancy (see Chapter 1 for more on nutrient density). This is also not a time to diet or to restrict any one food group, because it is important to gain weight during pregnancy. No specific diet needs to be followed; in fact, eating a nutrient-dense balanced diet during pregnancy is a good way to establish healthy eating habits for life. It is a good idea to limit intake of "empty calories" or "junk" foods and instead eat lots of nutrient-dense vegetables, whole grains, and lean proteins.

In order to meet the increased nutrient needs during pregnancy, it is important to consume nutrient-dense foods rather than a lot of extra calories.

## Protein

As discussed in Chapter 5, protein is important for building body tissues—exactly what pregnancy is all about. Protein needs during pregnancy increase by 25 g per day. Many American women already consume this amount of protein. However, women who are vegetarians may need to pay close attention to their protein intake. Some vegetarian women may add meat, eggs, and/or dairy to their diet during pregnancy and return to a vegetarian diet later. They can, however, attain adequate protein intake without animal products by adding protein sources such as tofu, legumes, nuts, and grains. Women who follow a strict vegan diet (no meat, eggs, or dairy) may need to consider supplemental vitamin $B_{12}$, because meat is the primary source of $B_{12}$.

## Carbohydrates

The main source of extra energy for a pregnant woman is carbohydrates. A pregnant woman should consume at least 175 g per day. Fiber is also very important, as it helps prevent constipation and hemorrhoids, which are often a problem during pregnancy. In addition, it is helpful to decrease intake of simple sugars or empty calories in order to meet the increased nutrient needs (see Chapter 3 for more information on carbohydrates).

A well-planned vegetarian diet can supply the nutrient needs of pregnancy.

## Fats

Although the recommended intake level does not change during pregnancy, fats are an important source of energy, and during the third trimester the fetus will store fat for energy use as a newborn. Therefore, the mother should consume adequate fat for her own health as well as for the health of the fetus. To ensure an adequate supply of essential fatty acids, intake should focus on the polyunsaturated fat found in nuts, oils, and whole grains (see Chapter 4 for more on fats).

It is important to consume adequate folate even before you become pregnant.

**Want to know more?**
To read more about folate and to make sure that you are consuming enough in your diet, go to the text website at http://webcom8.grtxle.com/nutrition and click on the Chapters button. Select Chapter 16.

## Vitamins and Minerals

Generally, a woman's need for vitamins and minerals increases by about 30 percent during pregnancy. Folate needs increase by about 50 percent, and vitamin $B_6$ needs by almost as much. Folate and $B_{12}$ are used in red blood cell and DNA manufacture; vitamin $B_6$ is used in amino acid metabolism.

### Folate

Folate, naturally occurring in many dark green leafy vegetables, beans, citrus fruits, whole grains, poultry, pork, and shellfish, may not be adequately available in modern Western diets, as indicated in Chapter 9. In the 1970s, a deficiency in dietary folate became clearly linked to *neural tube defects*. The neural tube develops into the brain and spinal cord during the first twenty-eight days after conception. Without adequate folate the tube may not close completely. One possible outcome of this incomplete closing is known as *spina bifida*, in which the lower end of the spinal cord may be exposed. Paralysis or weakness of the legs, bowel, or bladder can result. The U.S. Public Health Service and the March of Dimes recommend that all women of childbearing age consume 400 mcg of folate per day. This recommendation is made for all women because adequate intake is so crucial in the first twenty-eight days of pregnancy, which typically passes before most women know they are pregnant. In addition, low folate levels in the mother increase the risk of a preterm delivery, a low-birthweight baby, and slow fetal growth rate (see Chapter 9 for more information on neural tube defects).

### Iron

The DRI for iron increases from 18 mg per day to 27 mg per day during pregnancy. Because a pregnant woman is no longer losing blood and iron through menstruation, more iron is available for fetal use. But an increased iron intake helps ensure that the mother's own iron status does not suffer while she provides for her fetus. Many physicians recommend iron supplements for their pregnant patients because it may be difficult for some women to get adequate amounts from the diet alone. Iron is important for building red blood cells in the fetus and for the oxygen-carrying capacity of blood in both the mother and fetus. In addition, maternal iron-deficiency anemia is associated with an increased risk of giving birth prematurely, as well as low birthweight and low iron stores in the infant. It is important that the newborn have adequate iron stores because breast milk is a poor source of iron, and the infant will need those stores to last until iron-rich foods can be provided at four to six months of age.

### Calcium

An increase in calcium intake is needed during pregnancy both to promote proper development of bones and teeth in the fetus and to maintain strength in the bones of the mother. This need increases as much as 30 mg a day during the last trimester. The AI for calcium does not increase during pregnancy, because absorption increases. However, many women do not get enough calcium; therefore, it is very important to ensure adequate calcium intake through consumption of low-fat dairy products or fortified products such as soy products and juice.

## Zinc

DNA and RNA synthesis in the body depend on zinc and, therefore it is a critical mineral for the developing fetus. Inadequate zinc intake can lead to birth defects, poor cognitive development after birth, premature delivery, and prolonged labor. Table 16.3 lists the DRI for various vitamins and minerals during pregnancy. See Chapters 8, 9, and 10 for a review of the food sources of these nutrients.

## Prenatal Vitamin and Mineral Supplements

Eating a nutrient-dense diet to meet the slightly increased energy demands of pregnancy combined with the naturally increased absorption of nutrients that occurs during pregnancy is usually adequate to meet nutrient needs. Of course, even when a woman is not pregnant, it is always best to meet increased nutrient needs by consuming nutrient-dense foods. Supplements should not be used in place of a well-balanced diet whether a women is pregnant or not. After all, recall that the definition of the word *supplement* means "in addition to," not "instead of." That being said, supplements are often prescribed for pregnant women and women who wish to become pregnant as a precautionary measure.

A woman should always check with her physician or midwife before taking any supplements, whether over-the-counter or prescribed. Supplements should provide no more than 100 percent of the DRI for pregnant women and include 30 mg of iron and 600 mcg of folic acid daily. Folic acid supplementation should begin one month before conception if at all possible. Vegans, women under age 25, and those who choose to avoid milk products also are advised to take calcium supplements (600 mg per day). As noted previously, any woman of childbearing age who might become pregnant should consume 400 mcg of folic acid daily. This is the amount found in most multivitamins.

Vitamin/mineral supplements are also recommended for women who may be at a nutritional risk. This includes women who are vegans, are breast-feeding, follow restrictive diets, smoke cigarettes, abuse alcohol, or are carrying twins or triplets. For vegans, vitamin $B_{12}$ supplements (and perhaps vitamin D and zinc) are recommended. Vitamin D and zinc are typically low in vegan diets.

**Table 16.3    Changes in Nutrient Recommendations with Pregnancy for Adult Women**

| Micronutrient | Prepregnancy | Pregnancy | % Increase |
|---|---|---|---|
| Folate | 400 µg/day | 600 µg/day | 50 |
| Vitamin $B_{12}$ | 2.4 µg/day | 2.6 µg/day | 8 |
| Vitamin C | 75 mg/day | 85 mg/day | 13 |
| Vitamin A | 700 µg/day | 770 µg/day | 10 |
| Vitamin D | 5 µg/day | 5 µg/day | 0 |
| Calcium | 1000 mg/day | 1000 mg/day | 0 |
| Iron | 18 mg/day | 27 mg/day | 50 |
| Zinc | 8 mg/day | 11 mg/day | 38 |
| Sodium | 1500 mg/day | 1500 mg/day | 0 |
| Iodine | 150 µg/day | 220 µg/day | 47 |

*Source:* Adapted from Germann W., and Stanfield, C., *Principles of Human Physiology*, 2/e, Fig. 22–21, Pearson Benjamin Cummings.

A deficiency in vitamin B$_{12}$ can cause neural tube defects. This deficiency can be masked and occur independent of folate levels and folic acid supplementation. Because a higher level of iron can interfere with the absorption of zinc and copper, women who are taking more than 30 mg of iron per day should also take a supplement containing 15 mg of zinc and 2 mg of copper. This is the amount found in most prenatal vitamins; therefore, there is no need to take individual supplements. Because excessive levels of vitamin A can be toxic to the fetus, and adequate levels are available through a balanced diet, vitamin A supplementation is not recommended during pregnancy except at low levels.

### ■ To Supplement or Not

*Should pregnant women take herbal and botanical supplements?*

Because most medication cannot be taken during pregnancy, many women consider taking herbal and botanical products to treat various symptoms, thinking they are a natural and healthy alternative to medications. For example, many women take ginger to treat the symptoms of nausea often experienced during the first trimester. One study reported no adverse effects, but there is concern that it could increase bleeding. No formal studies have reported on other supplements commonly taken for nausea, such as red raspberry and wild yam. The same caution should be applied to herbal and botanical supplements as to medications and other supplements. Pregnant women should always check with their physician or midwife first. There is very little research regarding the safe use of most herbal and botanical supplements during pregnancy. Table 16.4 provides a list of some that may *not* be safe for consumption during pregnancy. ■

## Hydration

General fluid needs increase during pregnancy in order to support fetal circulation, amniotic fluid, and a higher blood volume. Adequate fluid intake can also

**Want to know more?** Would you like to more thoroughly investigate the use of herbal and botanical supplements during pregnancy? For an up-to-date list of current research on the safety of herbals and botanicals during pregnancy, go to the text website at http://webcom8 .grtxle.com/nutrition and click on the Chapters button. Select Chapter 16.

| **Table 16.4** | **Herbal and Botanical Supplements That May Not Be Safe during Pregnancy** |
|---|---|
| **Herb** | **Why You Should Avoid It** |
| Aloe (taken internally) | Causes severe diarrhea |
| Black cohosh | Can cause premature contractions |
| Chamomile oil | A uterine stimulant |
| Cinnamon | A uterine stimulant in high doses; safe as a culinary herb; avoid the essential oil completely |
| Fennel | Uterine stimulant in high doses, but OK as a culinary herb |
| Korean ginseng | High doses may lead to the development of an androgynous baby |
| Lavender | High doses can be a uterine stimulant |
| Licorice | High doses can exacerbate high blood pressure |
| Peppermint oil | Avoid completely; it can be a uterine stimulant |
| Tea, black | Limit to two cups a day, as excess can lead to palpitations and increased heart rate |

*Source:* Courtesy of the U.S. Department of Agriculture.

help prevent constipation by keeping food wastes moving through the intestines. Individuals generally need 1–1.5 mL of water for each calorie consumed (e.g., a person eating a 2,000-calorie diet would need 2,000–3,000 mL (about 64 oz. or 8–10 c.) of fluid each day). Most pregnant women are advised to increase their caloric consumption by about 300 calories, beginning in the second trimester. Therefore, they would need at least 300 mL of additional fluid intake.

> ## Before you go on . . .
> 1. What is the best way to meet the increased nutritional needs of pregnancy?
> 2. How many additional calories per day are needed and how many pounds should a woman of healthy weight gain during pregnancy?
> 3. Why is it so important to make sure all women of childbearing age consume adequate folate?
> 4. What is the best indication that a woman is meeting her nutritional needs during pregnancy?

# Factors That Can Affect Nutritional Intake and Pregnancy Outcome

What exactly is a "successful pregnancy"? The CDC refers to it as "Safe Motherhood" and states, "Safe motherhood begins before conception with proper nutrition and a healthy lifestyle and continues with appropriate prenatal care, the prevention of complications when possible, and the early and effective treatment of complications. The ideal result is a pregnancy at term without unnecessary interventions, the delivery of a healthy infant, and a healthy postpartum period in a positive environment that supports the physical and emotional needs of the woman, infant, and family." Additionally, success is often measured by the birth weight of the baby, as mentioned previously. Many factors can influence whether a pregnancy is successful; the influence of nutritional intake during pregnancy is perhaps one of the greatest. Let's begin by first discussing some of the factors that can affect nutritional intake and pregnancy outcome.

## Exercise and Pregnancy

Current research, although limited, consistently shows that women who exercised before pregnancy can continue to do so once pregnant. Moderate-intensity aerobic exercise has been shown to be safe in pregnancy. Many studies indicate that trained athletes may be able to exercise at a higher level than is currently recommended by the American College of Obstetricians and Gynecologists, but pregnant women in this category should consult their health care professional before doing so.

Compared to women who are inactive, those who exercise during pregnancy are reported to have an approximately 50 percent reduction in the risk for gestational diabetes and an approximately 40 percent reduction in the risk of developing high blood pressure. It was initially thought that exercising during pregnancy leads to an increased risk of neural tube defects if overheating occurs. This belief came from animal studies, but today the risk is no longer thought to be as great in humans because our bodies get rid of heat differently and more

**Want to know more?**
Although nutrition before and during pregnancy is critical to the health of the mother and the baby, there is more to prenatal care than nutrition. It should include regular visits to a health care provider. According to the March of Dimes, "Women who see a health care provider regularly during pregnancy have healthier babies, are less likely to deliver prematurely, and are less likely to have other serious problems related to pregnancy." For guidelines on when to seek prenatal care and for a list of benefits, go to the text website at http://webcom8.grtxle .com/nutrition and click on the Chapters button. Select Chapter 16.

It is important for pregnant women to remain hydrated by drinking 8 to 10 cups of fluids a day.

*What about exercise and weight training during pregnancy?*

Women who exercised before pregnancy can continue during pregnancy.

efficiently than animals. Nonetheless, because overheating does occur in humans, extra care should be taken to maintain adequate hydration during exercise and to avoid extreme temperatures. Experiencing a body temperature of 102°F or higher during the first six weeks of pregnancy has been shown to cause an increased risk of neural tube defects. Research suggests that moderate exercise may enhance birth weight, while intense or frequent exercise, maintained into the third trimester, may result in lower-birthweight babies. Therefore, strenuous exercise such as sprinting or any exercise that may involve impact such as martial arts should be avoided. Studies of pregnant women engaging in moderate resistance training while avoiding maximal lifts have reported no negative outcomes. Exercise is not recommended for women with complications during pregnancy or with a history of complications.

Breast-feeding mothers can exercise safely as long as they consume enough calories to compensate for the calorie needs of exercise and lactation. All exercise should be cleared with a health care practitioner.

## Morning Sickness

Although not a big threat to pregnancy outcome, morning sickness can make it difficult to consume all of the needed nutrients at the outset of pregnancy (first trimester), when it is so crucial. For some women this feeling of nausea occurs throughout pregnancy, but for most it subsides by the second trimester. "*Morning*" *sickness* is perhaps not the best term for this condition, as many pregnant women experience nausea at various times of day. It is most commonly experienced in the morning because long periods without food can trigger it. To help alleviate this feeling on wakening, many women keep crackers or dry cereal at their bedside so they can eat something before getting out of bed. Smaller, more frequent meals can also help, along with avoiding strong smells that appear to trigger the nausea. Some women find that somewhat acidic foods are tolerated especially well. Pickles, citrus fruits, apples, and even salsa may taste unexpectedly good. That preference for tart and sour tastes, combined with a rising desire for calories and a tendency to prefer cold to hot foods, may be the source of the old "pickles and ice cream" jokes about pregnancy cravings.

The following are some ideas to help alleviate the symptoms of morning sickness:

- Keep a little something in your stomach at all times by nibbling and sipping frequently.
- Start with bland food and go slowly. Think about lining your stomach with a stomach-friendly food before adding anything substantial to it.
- Drink water. Mild fruits, frozen fruit bars, sorbet, and low-fat yogurts all help prevent dehydration.
- Think salt. Potato chips, pretzels, crackers, and pickles may stay down when other foods do not.
- Try ginger as an herb or garnish for food. Ginger ale, ginger tea, or ginger candies may also help calm the stomach.
- Make your food count. Eat nutrient-dense foods when you can, to cover the times when you can't.

- Take prenatal vitamins with food, not on an empty stomach.
- Eat, even if you don't want to. Getting a little food into your stomach will help, but take it slowly.
- Beyond food: Try driving the car instead of riding in it, take naps, prop your bed up, sleep on your left side, and relieve stress.
- Call your doctor if you can't keep any food or drink down for twenty-four hours, if your urine decreases or becomes dark, or if you feel increasingly weak or sick.
- Hang in there; for most women morning sickness passes after the first trimester.

*I've heard that women often crave weird foods during pregnancy. Is that true?*

## Food Cravings

Some women do experience specific food cravings during pregnancy. Typically these preferences are for sweet or salty foods, such as that old cliché of pickles and ice cream. These cravings are harmless and can easily be fulfilled. They are, however, typically not associated with the body's need for a certain nutrient, as was once thought.

Occasionally, cravings can be harmful, particularly when they involve something other than food—clay, chalk, or even dirt. This behavior is called **pica** and generally refers to the compulsive eating of nonfood substances. It has been suggested that women with pica have been exposed at some time in their lives to lead or other environmental toxins. Pica can lead to iron deficiency in the mother and a smaller head circumference in the infant. It can also lead to inadequate weight gain, intestinal blockages, diarrhea, vomiting, infections, and other health complications. Therefore, any woman experiencing these cravings should consult a health care professional to discuss strategies to address the issue as soon as possible.

## Gastrointestinal Issues

Some of the hormones produced by the body during pregnancy cause muscle and ligament relaxation that will ultimately make labor easier. In the meantime, however, these same hormones can lead to constipation. Exercising, emphasizing whole grains and high-fiber foods such as prunes, and staying well hydrated will all help and may prevent the development of hemorrhoids. Hormonal changes can also relax the stomach's upper sphincter, letting stomach acids rise to the esophagus and causing heartburn. It may help to eat smaller meals and avoid anything that seems to cause heartburn, such as spicy foods and chocolate. It may also help to use an extra pillow at night and to sleep on the left side.

## Health Conditions

### Pregnancy-Induced Hypertension

**Pregnancy-induced hypertension** occurs when there is a rapid rise in blood pressure, with readings above the normal limits of 140 (systolic) and 90 (diastolic). As a woman's blood volume increases, her blood pressure also increases somewhat, but it should not increase rapidly. This rapid increase in blood pressure occurs in 5–10 percent of all pregnancies. It is closely related to **pre-eclampsia**, a condition characterized by high blood pressure, edema, and protein in the urine. **Eclampsia** is a manifestation of the same syndrome. Eclampsia can result in convulsions, puts the mother at risk for stroke, and can lead to maternal or fetal death. More women die from pre-eclampsia than eclampsia but one is not necessarily more serious than the other. Pre-eclampsia usually occurs after twenty weeks' gestation (in the late second or third trimester or middle to late pregnancy), though it can occur earlier. It is usually associated with swelling, sudden weight gain, headaches, and changes in vision, but there may also be no symptoms. Pre-eclampsia and other hypertensive disorders of pregnancy are a leading global cause of maternal and infant illness and death. According to the Preeclampsia Foundation, these disorders are responsible for 76,000 deaths each year. If untreated, it can become a serious complication of pregnancy. It causes impaired blood flow to the placenta, decreased fetal growth, and low birthweight. Bed rest, adequate calcium, magnesium sulfate, hypertension medications, and early delivery of the baby may help. However, because the causes of pregnancy-induced hypertension are poorly understood, there is no single clearly effective approach to treatment. Mothers who are overweight or obese are at greater risk for this disorder. Genetics and age (being younger than 19 or older than 40) are also risk factors. It tends to resolve with the birth of the baby.

### Edema

Edema is characterized by fluid retention that typically results in swelling of the hands, feet, and ankles. It can occur as a woman's blood volume increases and is generally a problem only if it is accompanied by symptoms of pregnancy-induced hypertension. Edema normally reverses quickly with the birth of the baby. Some believe that restricting sodium will decrease edema, but this is not necessarily true, and restricting sodium intake is not advised for pregnant women unless it is recommended by a physician.

### ■ Nutrition and Disease
#### *Gestational diabetes*

*Gestational diabetes* refers to any form of glucose intolerance that is diagnosed during pregnancy in a woman who did not have the condition before becoming pregnant. To meet the increased energy demands of her growing fetus, the mother's blood glucose levels also increase. A pregnant woman whose blood glucose is above normal is considered to have gestational diabetes. This occurs in about 7 percent of all pregnant women in the United States, and it usually goes away once the baby is born. Most women can control the condition through diet and exercise, but some need insulin. If controlled, gestational diabetes does not harm either the baby or the mother. If uncontrolled, high blood pressure in the mother can result from it. It can also result in a baby that is very large because of all the excess glucose it received during fetal development. Women diagnosed with gestational diabetes may be at higher risk for diabetes later in life. Testing for gestational diabetes is performed between twenty-four and twenty-eight weeks' gestation. ■

## Health Precautions During Pregnancy

To decrease the risk of complications during pregnancy and to minimize occurrence of some of the issues discussed previously, certain things should be avoided or limited.

### Extremes in Weight

As previously mentioned, the weight of the mother is a critical factor in terms of the outcome of pregnancy. Being overweight or underweight carries risks for both the mother and fetus. Thirty-eight percent of pregnancies in the United States occur in women who are overweight. An obese woman is more likely to experience gestational diabetes, hypertension, and other complications during pregnancy and labor. An infant born to an overweight mother is more likely to have congenital defects, be extremely large at birth, and be obese as a child. Despite these risks, pregnancy is not the time to lose weight or to diet, and women attempting to do so can put their baby at risk. It is best to lose the weight in a healthy way before becoming pregnant. This will ensure a healthier pregnancy for both mother and baby.

Of course, being underweight is not healthy either. An underweight woman increases her risk of having a premature birth and a low-birthweight baby, which in turn can increase the child's later susceptibility to cardiovascular disease, diabetes, and stroke.

## Caffeine

Some studies have suggested that drinking more than two or three cups of coffee daily (the equivalent of approximately eight cups of tea or nine cans of caffeinated soft drinks) when pregnant increases the chances of miscarriage or having a low-birthweight baby. Other studies have disagreed. However, caffeine can travel through the placenta and affect the heart rate and breathing of the fetus. Therefore, it is wise to consume caffeine in moderation and to discuss it with a physician. Breast milk can also transfer caffeine from mother to baby. Very high caffeine intake in nursing mothers may make babies irritable. A woman planning a pregnancy or who is pregnant should either avoid caffeine or limit her daily caffeine intake to no more than 300 mg per day. (There are roughly 136 mg in 8 oz. of coffee, 48 mg in 8 oz. of tea, and 35 mg in a 12-oz. soda).

**Figure 16.5** A pregnant woman should limit her daily caffeine intake to no more than 300 mg per day.

## Alcohol

Even moderate alcohol intake of one drink per day or one episode of binge drinking has been linked to impaired fetal growth and lower health outcomes of the baby at birth (see Chapter 12 for more on alcohol). The first trimester is a particularly vulnerable time; however, during any part of pregnancy, periods of heavy drinking are especially harmful. In fact, no truly safe level has ever been determined, and because damage can occur before a woman even realizes that she is pregnant, it is strongly recommended that pregnant women and women who believe that they might become pregnant avoid alcohol altogether. The visible effects of **fetal alcohol syndrome (FAS)**, a disorder characterized by growth retardation, facial abnormalities, and central nervous system (CNS) dysfunction caused by alcohol intake during pregnancy. Other abnormalities include reduced birth weight, heart defects, irritability and a short attention span, mental retardation, hyperactivity, and vision and hearing deficits. These reflect some degree of permanent brain damage that could have been avoided. Alcohol can impair cell division in an embryo and fetus, and can reduce the flow of oxygen and nutrients across the placenta. (See also the Nutrition and Lifestages feature in Chapter 12.)

## Drugs

It is important to make sure that any medicine or supplement you take during pregnancy is safe for the developing fetus. Any drug or even herbal supplement, no matter how insignificant it may seem, can have a negative impact. Even

*What if people around a pregnant woman are smoking, like her partner or the people she works with?*

a drug that may have minimal effects on the mother can alter how her baby develops. In fact, many drugs approved by the FDA for adults have never been tested on pregnant women or developing fetuses. So be aware that adequate scientifically based information may not be available on many medications. An example of this occurred in the early 1960s, when a drug called thalidomide was used to treat morning sickness in parts of Europe. It was discovered too late that thalidomide also inhibits the development of arms and legs in the fetus.

## Smoking

One of the worst things people can do to their health is to smoke, as smoking has many negative health implications beyond the scope of this chapter. Therefore, one can assume that when a pregnant mother smokes, it will have a severe negative impact on her developing baby. In fact, smoking is associated with increased risks for many complications, including miscarriages, below-average fetal growth, and preterm delivery. Mothers who smoke have smaller placentas, thereby limiting nutrient delivery and removal of wastes produced. During development, smoking may impair blood flow to the fetus and therefore decrease nutrient and oxygen delivery. Infants born to women who smoke during pregnancy have a lower average birthweight than infants born to women who do not smoke. Once they are born, children of mothers who smoke are more likely to have asthma and upper respiratory conditions than children of nonsmoking mothers.

Exposure to environmental tobacco smoke can also be very dangerous to the developing fetus. It has been associated with lower birthweight, increased risk of behavioral problems in childhood, and an increased incidence of respiratory problems such as bronchitis and asthma. Therefore, women who are pregnant should limit their exposure to tobacco smoke as much as possible.

## Food-Borne Illness and Toxins

Pregnant women are at an increased risk for food-borne illness. During pregnancy a woman's immune system is weakened and the fetus's is not fully developed, which makes it harder for their bodies to fight off harmful food-borne microorganisms. Two food-borne microorganisms are of greatest concern: listeria and toxoplasma. Listeria is a bacteria that can be found in uncooked meats and vegetables, unpasteurized milk, and ready to eat foods such as hot dogs and deli meats. Toxoplasmosis is caused by a parasite found in undercooked meat, eating from utensils contaminated by the meat or from cat litter. Pregnant women and people with weakened immune systems are particularly susceptible to this. Following the safe food handling guidelines provided in chapter 13 can greatly decrease your chances of exposure.

According to the March of Dimes, our everyday environment contains more than 400 million toxins, and little information is available about the risks of exposure to these toxins on a developing fetus. However, pregnant women can take some precautions to avoid exposure to harmful toxins. These toxins include lead, usually found in the paint of old buildings, and mercury, which is mostly found in fish. Mercury is most concentrated in large fish at the top of the food chain—those that eat other fish, such as swordfish, shark, king mackerel, and tilefish. Accordingly, pregnant women should not eat these fish. In addition, consumption of tuna, especially albacore, should be limited. Fish such as salmon and crustaceans (lobster, crab, and shrimp) have lower levels of mercury depending on the area where they were caught or farmed. Because fish may also be contaminated with other industrial pollutants such as PCBs (polychlorinated biphenyls), pregnant women or women who could become pregnant should not consume any fish without checking with their state or local health department or the EPA.

 **Want to know more?** If you would like to review additional information regarding food-borne illness, environmental toxins, and their implications for pregnant women and developing fetuses, go to the text website at http://webcom8.grtxle.com/nutrition and click on the Chapters button. Select Chapter 16.

**Before you go on . . .**
1. What are the exercise limitations for pregnant women?
2. What are some things that women should avoid or limit during pregnancy to prevent potential health problems for themselves and their baby?
3. What are the risks of being overweight during pregnancy?
4. Name two food-borne illnesses pregnant women are at an increased risk for and explain why.

# Breast-Feeding

Most health professionals and organizations recommend breast-feeding as the preferred method of feeding for newborns and infants. The American Dietetic Association states, "Exclusive breast-feeding provides optimal nutrition and health protection for the first 6 months of life, and breast-feeding with complementary foods is the ideal feeding pattern for infants." Although exclusive breast-feeding is ideal, even some breast-feeding appears to be beneficial. Breast-feeding can help protect babies against a number of childhood illnesses, including diarrhea, respiratory infections, some childhood cancers and autoimmune diseases, and obesity. Furthermore, mothers who breast-feed may lose weight faster, experience less stress during the postpartum period, build stronger bonds with their babies, and have a decreased risk of breast and ovarian cancer.

## Benefits of Breast-Feeding

Breast milk is recommended for the infant as it has all the necessary nutrients for the baby and some added benefits as well (see Table 16.5). According to

Breast-feeding offers many benefits for the mother and the baby. Initiatives to support and encourage it are available throughout the world.

| Table 16.5 | Comparison of Nutrient Content of Human Milk to Infant Formula | |
| --- | --- | --- |
| **Nutrient (per 100 mL or 3.4 oz.)** | **Human Milk** | **Infant Formula** |
| Kcal | 70 | 67 |
| Protein (g) | 0.9 | 1.5 |
| Total fat (g) | 4.2 | 3.5 |
| Iron (μg) | 40 | 1,000–1,200 |
| Vitamin A (μg) | 47 | 60 |
| Vitamin D (μg) | 0.04 | 1.0 |
| Folic acid (μg) | 5.2 | 10 |
| Alpha-lactalbumin (mg)* | 161 | None |
| Lactoferrin (mg)* | 167 | None |
| IgA (mg)* | 142 | None |

*Provides important immune functions.
*Source:* Adapted from American Academy of Pediatrics, *Pediatric Nutrition Handbook,* 5th ed. Elk Grove, IL: American Academy of Pediatrics, 2004, Appendix E.

the American Academy of Pediatrics and the American Dietetic Association, newborns who are breast-fed are less likely to experience the following:

- Allergies and intolerances
- Ear infections (otitis media)
- Vomiting
- Diarrhea
- Pneumonia, wheezing, and other respiratory diseases
- Meningitis
- Sudden infant death syndrome (SIDS)

**Other reasons why human milk is good for the infant:**

- It provides optimal nutrition for the infant.
- It enhances the baby's immune system.
- It improves cognitive function (the longer the duration of breast-feeding, the greater the benefit).
- It may decrease the baby's chance of becoming obese as a child.
- It is easier for babies to digest.
- It does not need to be prepared.
- It is good for the environment, because there are no bottles, cans, or boxes to put in the garbage.
- It provides physical contact, warmth, and closeness, which help create a special bond between a mother and her baby.

**Breast-feeding also provides many health benefits for the mother:**

- It burns more calories and in some cases helps the mother get back to her prepregnancy weight more quickly.
- It reduces the risk of ovarian cancer and breast cancer.
- It builds bone strength to protect against bone fractures in older age.
- It helps the uterus return to its normal size more quickly.

At first glance it may appear that formula provides more nutrients than human milk and is therefore superior. However, the benefits to the immune system of the infant cannot be underestimated. Furthermore, human milk is designed to meet the nutrient needs of the infant; exceeding these needs is not necessarily beneficial.

## ■ What's Hot?

*Are breast-fed infants less likely to become overweight?*

Recent studies have suggested that infants who are breast-fed have less risk of becoming obese as adults compared to their formula-fed counterparts. Although the research is not conclusive, in one study children who had been breast-fed were 21–34 percent less likely to be overweight than formula-fed babies. Some, but not all, of the studies suggest that the benefits increase the longer the child is exclusively breast-fed. Several factors may contribute to this difference. One possibility is that breast-fed infants may learn to self-regulate their food intake better than formula-fed infants. In other words, the mother is not as aware of how much a breast-fed baby is consuming and may be less likely to force or encourage consumption. Conversely, parents may be more likely to force a bottle-fed baby to finish the bottle even though the baby is full. Signs the baby is full include spitting out the nipple, turning the head away, or paying more attention to other things. More research is needed to determine whether these differences in self-regulation really exist between breast and formula-fed infants and, if they do, what influence they exert on self-regulation later in life.

Another possible explanation for this difference in adult weight is that early methods of feeding may affect hormone levels and therefore have implications for appetite, fat deposition, and weight gain later in life. Much more research is needed in this area. The causes of obesity are complex and are most likely due to the interactions of many factors. However, breast-feeding does appear to play a role in decreasing the risk of being overweight later in life, and therefore the role of breast-feeding is important to consider in efforts to prevent overweight and obesity. ■

Despite the known health benefits to infants and mothers, only about 71 percent of U.S. women ever start breast-feeding (see Figure 16.6). Less than one third continue breast-feeding until the baby is six months old, and even fewer breast-feed throughout the first year. African Americans and socioeconomically disadvantaged groups have even lower breast-feeding rates. This is not the case worldwide. Although breast-feeding rates vary by country, around the world breast-feeding is much more common than in the United States.

## ■ Global Nutrition

*Breast-feeding—a cultural thing*

Family and culture can have the greatest impact on the decisions of whether to breast-feed, for how long, and even when and what to start feeding the infant. In many instances family and culture have a far greater impact than the advice of a health care practitioner, recommendations from major health organizations, or scientific information. Female relatives, particularly grandmothers, are looked on to provide support and advice regarding breast-feeding and infant feeding. In order to effectively communicate recent recommendations and guidelines regarding breast-feeding and infant feeding to a multicultural population, it is both relevant and necessary to understand and appreciate the breast-feeding

**Figure 16.6** Percent of women in the U.S. who are breast-feeding at various stages of infant development.

*Source:* 2004 National Immunization Survey, Centers for Disease Control and Prevention, Department of Health and Human Services.

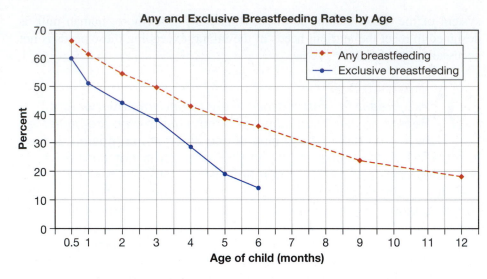

**Any and Exclusive Breastfeeding Rates by Age**

- - ◆ - - Any breastfeeding
——●—— Exclusive breastfeeding

Percent / Age of child (months)

**Want to know more?** To explore the topic of breast-feeding rates in different countries, go to the text website at http://webcom8.grtxle.com/nutrition and click on the Chapters button. Select Chapter 16.

**Want to know more?** You can learn more about cultured influences on breast-feeding and infant feeding, by going to the text website at http://webcom8.grtxle.com/nutrition and clicking on the Chapters button. Select Chapter 16.

practices of different cultures so as to deliver this information in a culturally sensitive manner.

Most women abandon the traditions of their culture of origin and adapt the breast-feeding practices of North America when they immigrate to the United States or Canada. There are many reasons for this. One is simply that they may not have family members close by to offer support and to reinforce the cultural practice of their native country. This is particularly true of the many cultures that believe that women need to stay at home for the first month after giving birth. For example, in traditional Vietnamese, Chinese, and Cambodian cultures, in the first month after giving birth women may follow a series of customs called "doing the month." The practices are based on the belief that giving birth depletes a woman of heat, blood, and vital breath. During this time women are thought to be very vulnerable to cold, wind, and magic. In order to correct this, women are expected to stay at home, avoid drafts, avoid bathing, dress warmly, and, if getting out of bed is necessary, take very small steps. This is generally a time when the new mother is pampered by relatives. Foods classified as "hot" are favored, while "cold" foods are avoided. The use of alcohol, including rice wine and brandy, is also avoided. Prescribed foods include chicken, pork, ginger, salt, black pepper, boiled rice, and Chinese tea. Foods to avoid include raw and cold vegetables and fruits, specifically spinach, mung beans, melon, lemon, and bananas, as well as deep-fried and fatty foods. Soup with cabbage, carrots, cauliflower, and potatoes is thought to increase the mother's supply of breast milk. Avoidance of "cold" foods in the mother's diet is also thought to protect the baby from diarrhea, coughs, and colds, as properties are thought to be transferred directly through the breast milk. This traditional month of rest and help from relatives supports exclusive breast-feeding of the infant. This is of course not always practiced by modern women, as demands of the workplace may make it difficult to follow.

In many countries the percentage of mothers who breast-feed is dictated by location or finances. For example, in rural areas of Vietnam, Cambodia, and Laos, most children are breast-fed for more than a year. Formula is considered too expensive or may not be available. In urban areas of Vietnam and Cambodia, infants are more likely to be formula-fed. Many women in urban areas indicate that they switched to formula because they think they have an insufficient milk supply. In addition, formula feeding is associated with fat babies, who are more likely to survive. Another reason many give for choosing formula is that they think breast-feeding will leave them drained and too skinny. This is in contrast to the belief in North America that the weight loss often associated with breast-feeding is desirable and a reason not to feed with formula.

In some cultures **colostrum** (the milk secreted by the mother for a few days after childbirth) is seen as "old milk" and is often discarded. Infants in many Asian cultures are fed either ginseng tea, herbal-root tea, or boiled sugar water for the first two to three days of life until the "milk comes in." This practice, however, is not recommended by health professionals, as the colostrum contains antibodies that help protect the infant from disease. Milk is commonly supplemented with chewed rice paste or rice-and-sugar porridge. A thin gruel of boiled rice flour *(bot)* followed by porridges are introduced into the baby's diet at around six months of age. Similar to these Asian cultures, many Latin American cultures also discard colostrum and give their infants herbal teas, olive oil, or castor oil in its place. The introduction of infant cereals and mashed fruit often occurs before the baby is six weeks old. This practice is also not recommended, as it may be too early for the baby's digestive system to handle solid food. *Weaning foods* (foods designed to replace the mother's milk) also include *sopa de frijol* (the juice of cooked beans), mashed sweet potatoes, and *agua de panela* (brown-sugar water). Sugar, cornstarch, or corn syrup is often added to the baby's bottle. This can lead to tooth decay in the newly forming teeth. It also adds empty calories that make the baby full and keeps him or her from consuming the more nutrient-dense breast milk or formula.

Exploring cultural differences and similarities in breast-feeding and infant feeding beliefs and practices offers an opportunity for those involved to both communicate health information more effectively and better understand and appreciate the deep impact tradition has on such behaviors. ■

Until about six months of age, breast milk and/or formula is the only nutrition that most infants need, and exclusive breast-feeding is recommended by most major health organizations.

## Recommendations by Government Organizations

In the 1980s, the World Health Organization (WHO) and the United Nations Children's Fund (UNICEF) reviewed falling breast-feeding rates worldwide. They found that breast-feeding was well protected in midwife-assisted home births around the world, but that modern hospital births often resulted in formula feeding. As a result of their findings, WHO and UNICEF began the Baby-Friendly Hospital Initiative (BFHI). Its cornerstone is the Ten Steps to Successful Breastfeeding. The Baby-Friendly Hospital Initiative does not decide for a mother how she will feed her baby. Rather, it helps ensure that she receives accurate information and that the facility in which she gives birth will give her skilled help with breast-feeding or formula feeding.

In addition to hospital initiatives, the U.S. Department of Health and Human Services Healthy People 2020 campaign sets high goals for breast-feeding,

 **Want to know more?**
To explore the Baby-Friendly Hospital Initiative and other campaigns to promote breast-feeding more thoroughly worldwide, go to the text website at http://webcom8.grtxle.com/nutrition and click on the Chapters button. Select Chapter 16.

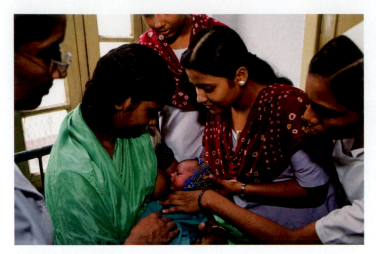

Although it is a very natural phenomenon, new mothers should be taught how to breast-feed properly. Lactation failure, which can harm the infant and even prove fatal in severe cases, is frequently the result of incorrect feeding techniques.

**Want to know more?**
Several reputable groups, such as La Leche League International, offer support and suggestions for mothers having difficulty breast-feeding. For information regarding these support groups, go to the text website at http://webcom8.grtxle.com/nutrition and click on the Chapters button. Select Chapter 16.

**APPLICATION TIP**

The type of fat a mother consumes during breast-feeding may affect the baby's immunity. Consuming adequate amounts of omega-3 fatty acids while breast-feeding accelerates the development of the baby's immune system, which leads to benefits that can last even after breast-feeding is discontinued.

aiming to increase initiation rates to 75 percent and prolonged breast-feeding rates to 50 percent and 25 percent at six and twelve months, respectively.

## Breast-Feeding in the First Days Following Birth

A baby's stomach is tiny at the start; most of his or her early meals from the breast are no more than 2–20 mL (1/2 tsp. to slightly over a tablespoon). As noted earlier, *colostrum* is the first milk produced after birth and is of a thinner consistency and has a slightly yellowish color. Frequent, small meals of colostrum in the first few days coat the baby's digestive tract and help prevent invasion by pathogens and foreign substances. High in protein, colostrum contains maternal antibodies and serves as a laxative to clear *meconium* (feces that accumulated during fetal development) from the baby's intestines. Over the next few days, the color and consistency of colostrum changes to the bluish color of human milk.

## Breast-Feeding After Six Months

Babies should be exclusively breast-fed for the first six months, with continued breast-feeding for up to two years. Thereafter, while breast-feeding continues, the World Health Organization, the American Academy of Pediatrics, and most experts agree that solids should be offered around six months of age. Breast-feeding is still a baby's main source of calories for some months, even after beginning solids. Slowly, at a rate that varies greatly from child to child, solids become the main food source and the contribution of breast milk to the daily calorie intake gradually diminishes.

## Nutritional Needs of the Breast-Feeding Mother

Women who exclusively breast-feed their infants during the first six months will typically need around 640 additional calories per day above their prepregnancy calorie requirement. Because some of these extra calories can come from fat stores established during pregnancy, the recommended increase in caloric intake for these mothers is at least 500 calories per day. In contrast, the mother's demand for certain nutrients, such as iron, is considerably less during lactation than during pregnancy.

Many women may be concerned about the weight gained during pregnancy and therefore attempt to restrict their caloric intake following birth. Caloric restriction should be avoided, as it will result in decreased milk production. Adding moderate exercise slowly may be all that is needed to lose weight, and many mothers gradually lose weight during breast-feeding without exercise or dieting.

A mother's need for complex carbohydrates during breast-feeding increases by 80 g from prepregnancy requirements. Good sources of dietary fiber—both soluble and insoluble—should also be emphasized in the mother's diet. Protein needs increase by 15–20 g above prepregnancy requirements. Both the types and amounts of fat mothers produce in their milk vary according to the kinds of fat they consume. An extremely low-fat diet during breast-feeding is not recommended, as it can reduce the needed amount of fat in the mother's milk. Mothers should aim for a diet that is not more than 30–35 percent fat with at least 10 percent from monounsaturated sources, about the same amount from polyunsaturated sources, and not more than 10 percent from saturated (animal) sources. Intake of vitamins A, C, E, and $B_{12}$ and many B vitamins should increase during lactation.

## Foods to Avoid

Lactating mothers should avoid both caffeine and alcohol, especially in the early stages of breast-feeding. Small amounts may be tolerated as the baby grows, but daily intake beyond a cup of coffee or one drink containing alcohol are not recommended.

About 20 percent of all newborns experience **colic**. Colic is extended crying in babies that are otherwise healthy and well nourished. In the past it was thought to be caused by digestive system symptoms such as painful gas. It is now believed to have more to do with an immature nervous system. Some studies among colicky breast-fed infants suggest that it may help to remove certain foods from the mother's diet that have been considered high-allergy foods; the results of these studies are inconclusive. Exactly how these foods (or their antigens) may cause colic is not known. However, antigens from cow's milk, peanuts, eggs, and wheat have been found in human milk. Therefore, eliminating these foods in the mother's diet may help alleviate symptoms of colic in the infant.

Babies who cry excessively may be suffering from colic.

## What Are the Alternatives to Breast-Feeding?

A mother may choose not to breast-feed for many reasons. These could be cultural, personal, or medical, or simply that the mother cannot physically do so.

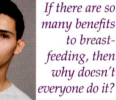

*If there are so many benefits to breast-feeding, then why doesn't everyone do it?*

Mothers who have HIV, smoke, or consume alcohol may be advised not to breast-feed. Regardless of the reason, a mother who does not breast-feed should not feel ashamed or inadequate in any way. Many mothers who cannot breast-feed do feel embarrassed when presented with the information regarding its benefits. This is unfortunate, as these recommendations are not meant to shame or alienate women who are unable or choose not to breast-feed. Moreover, bottle feeding is preferred and offers advantages in some cirumstances. It can offer more freedom and flexibility for the mother and can be helpful if someone other than the mother is caring for the baby. Because babies digest formula more slowly than breast milk, a baby who is getting formula may need fewer feedings than one who breast-feeds. Formula feeding also can make it easier to feed the infant in public, and it allows the father and other family members to help feed the baby, which can enhance bonding.

Not every mother can or should breast-feed. Many mothers simply cannot produce enough milk. Experts also agree that a mother should not breast-feed in certain situations. These include when a baby has galactosemia (a rare condition in which the baby cannot convert the monosaccharide galactose found in milk to glucose), mothers exposed to radioactive materials, mothers undergoing chemotherapy, mothers with active untreated tuberculosis, those who use street drugs, those with herpes simplex lesions on a breast (nursing on the other breast

Feeding a baby formula or breast milk through a bottle offers an opportunity for the father and other family members to participate in feeding and bonding with the baby.

*What is wrong with using infant formula?*

Infants under one year should never be given cow's milk, goat's milk, soy milk, or any product not specially formulated to match the nutrient needs of an infant.

is okay), and mothers infected with HIV. For mothers who cannot or who choose not to breast-feed, iron-fortified infant formulas represent a reasonable alternative to breast milk, and they provide babies with adequate nutrition for normal growth and development.

The World Health Organization recognizes four acceptable foods for infants. They are, in order of preference:

1. *Breast-feeding.*
2. *The mother's own milk, expressed (usually with a breast pump) and given to the baby through a bottle.* Some mothers who decide not to breast-feed are willing to express their milk, at least partially or at least for a while. Even a little breast milk makes a difference. Milk can be stored frozen up to two weeks and used as needed.
3. *Milk from another human mother.* Just as there are blood banks, there are also milk banks. In fact, unlike blood from a blood bank, milk from a milk bank is pasteurized, and is therefore considered completely safe. With donor milk as an option, a baby can be supplemented with human milk if the mother does not want to use formula. A list of the current human milk banks of North America is available at www.Hmbana.org.
4. *Commercial formulas.* There are numerous types of iron-fortified commercial formulas. Homemade formulas are not advised. Combining human milk and formula and beginning formula after a period of breast-feeding are both preferable to exclusive formula feeding from birth.

The simple answer is—nothing is wrong with infant formula. When human milk is not available, commercial formulas support acceptable growth and development. In addition, many mothers choose to feed their babies a combination of bottle and breast milk. Regardless of the circumstance, infant formulas can provide a healthy alternative.

Commercial infant formulas are designed to support the baby's growth and development. Formulas come in both powder and liquid forms and are typically made from the following:

*Cow's-milk formula.* Most infant formula is made with cow's milk that has been altered to closely resemble breast milk. The alteration gives the formula the right amount of carbohydrates and the right percentages of protein and fat. The alteration also makes the formula easier to digest. Remember that regular cow's milk isn't a substitute for infant formula. In fact, regular cow's milk should not be given to an infant until after he or she is a year old. Pasteurized goat's milk and evaporated milk are not acceptable alternatives.

*Soy-based formula.* Soy formula is an alternative for babies who are allergic to the proteins in the formula made from cow's milk or those who can't tolerate lactose, a sugar naturally present in cow's milk. If you choose to use soy products, be sure to use a soy-based infant formula—*not* soy milk.

*Protein hydrolysate formula.* Protein hydrolysate formula is meant for babies who have a family history of milk allergies. It's easier to digest and less likely to cause allergic reactions than standard cow's-milk formula because the proteins it contains are broken down in a process that mimics digestion.

More specialized infant formulas are available for premature infants and babies who have specific medical conditions.

**Want to know more?**
You can investigate and review more detailed information on different infant formulas by visiting the text website at http://webcom8.grtxle.com/nutrition and clicking on the Chapters button. Select Chapter 16.

[
**Before you go on . . .**
1. What are the benefits of breast-feeding?
2. Define *colostrum* and explain its benefits for a newborn.
3. Describe the nutritional needs of the breast-feeding mother.
4. What are the advantages of bottle feeding?
]

# The Nutritional Needs of Infants Beyond Milk

Infants need about 40–50 calories per pound of body weight per day. They need more in the first month of life and less as they approach twelve months of age, when the rapid growth of infancy begins to slow (see Figure 16.7).

Infants younger than age 2 need more fat than children beyond that age. About 50–60 percent of their caloric intake should come from fat. They need this extra fat to support the rapid growth and development experienced during these first years.

Protein is also important for growth, but the immature kidneys of infants are unable to process too much of it. Accordingly, no more than 20 percent of their calories should come from this source. Carbohydrates can provide the remaining calories. As infants begin to consume solid foods, whole-grain sources of carbohydrates should become an important part of their daily intake.

**APPLICATION TIP**

Children ages 1–2 should be given whole milk to provide the extra fat they need. Once they reach age 2, they can be switched to skim milk and should begin eating the same balanced diet the rest of the family is eating.

## Hydration

Infants are at an increased risk for dehydration. Because of their size they lose more water via evaporation, and their kidneys are not completely developed. Babies need about one third cup of fluid per pound of body weight up to 18 lb. At heavier weights, fluid needs by body weight are smaller. A 12-lb. baby, for example, needs about 4 cups (1 qt.) of fluid a day. Most of this should come from breast milk or formula. Breast milk or formula will meet the fluid needs of an

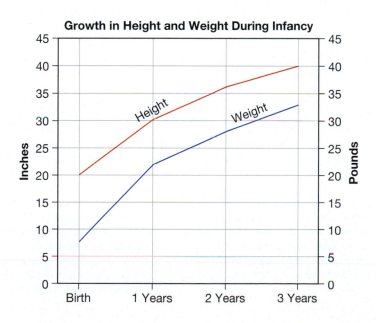

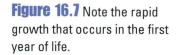
**Figure 16.7** Note the rapid growth that occurs in the first year of life.

# Real People, Other Voices

**Student:**
## Julie Gascoyne,
Butte Community College

Sarah and Stephen are definitely headed in the right direction, guaranteeing a well-planned lifestyle for their baby and themselves. They are both well educated, although not well informed, in the area of nutrition, which makes me think that a dietitian would be of great help to them. A dietitian can guide them with regard to their individual dietary needs before and during the pregnancy, stressing that eating nutrient-dense foods is key.

Before pregnancy, Sarah would ensure a healthier pregnancy for herself and the child by eating foods high in folate, iron, calcium, and zinc, as well as consuming adequate amounts of water. Stephen's food intake before and during pregnancy is also important. By eating nutrient-dense foods, he will build healthy eating habits; and studies have shown that men who eat adequate amounts of fruit and vegetables have a higher active sperm count.

When Sarah becomes pregnant, her nutrient needs will increase, but not as much as she may expect. In reality, her calorie needs will increase by only 250 to 300 a day for the first two trimesters. Sarah's vitamin needs will increase, so it would be best for her to take a prenatal vitamin for extra protection against birth problems. It is important for her to incorporate the following foods into her diet: dark green leafy vegetables, beans, whole grains, nuts, certain kinds of seafood, fortified breakfast cereals, and dairy products.

With the help of a dietitian, Sarah and Stephen will be able to develop a dietary plan they can follow while continuing to lead their busy lifestyle.

**Instructor:**
## Melissa Chabot
University at Buffalo

Sarah and Stephen have already made some wise choices by preplanning for their pregnancy. Their preplanning will enable them to make appropriate weight and diet changes to support a healthy pregnancy. We know that the nutritional status of both mother and father prior to conception is important.

I suggest that Sarah and Stephen seek the advice of a Registered Dietitian, who would explain the diet changes necessary to support a healthy pregnancy. An RD would describe the importance of getting adequate sources of folate (green leafy vegetables, orange juice) early in the pregnancy in order to prevent neural tube defects. The dietitian would also encourage Sarah to avoid alcohol and certain types of fish, and to limit her caffeine consumption. An RD would stress the importance of Sarah's consuming sufficient iron (meat, enriched bread) and calcium (dairy products, fortified orange juice) through her diet. He or she may recommend that Sarah start taking a prenatal vitamin to ensure that she gets all the proper nutrients needed for a successful pregnancy. The RD would explain that only an additional 300 calories are needed during the first two trimesters of pregnancy. She or he would also review the many benefits of breastfeeding (such as providing optimal nutrition for the infant and enhancing the baby's immune system) to Sarah and Stephen.

Stephen is correct in thinking that Sarah does need to focus on nutrient-dense foods such as milk, fruit, and vegetables, and limit the intake of empty-calorie foods such as fast food. These nutrition tips would also be helpful for Stephen to adopt prior to conception.

**Registered dietitian:**
## Helen Curhan, RD
Santa Barbara, CA

My first recommendation is that the Beckermans seek out a Registered Dietitian early on, when preparing for a successful pregnancy. I also recommend the pregnancy books on the market that contain a chapter on nutrition written by a licensed, trained professional with RD or MS (master of science) credentials.

A dietitian would stress the immense importance of healthy eating before conception, and would explain how to maintain a high level of healthy eating during and after the pregnancy. Diet during pregnancy involves more than merely eating for two. Intake of certain nutrients, vitamins, and minerals needs to be increased. For example, males need a balanced diet for adequate sperm production. Females, who bear most of the pregnancy responsibility, should have good nutrition stores before conception because their health will impact fetal development and assure that the mother is not placed at risk. Nothing new should be added to the pregnancy diet without the approval of a qualified health professional.

The mother's diet is the primary source of energy. Everything taken by mouth will critically affect the birth outcome. Pregnancy is not the time to diet, drink alcohol, smoke, or consume excessive caffeine; drink raw milk or eat cheese or fish with high mercury levels; or consume foods that have been contaminated with industrial pollutants. It is crucial to increase intake of certain nutrients, vitamins, and minerals—for example, folic acid and iron.

Proper nutrition before and during pregnancy ensures a higher percentage of thriving birth outcomes.

infant unless the infant is vomiting, has diarrhea, or is exposed to extreme heat. It is not advisable to dilute formula with water, as too much water dilutes the sodium in their blood, causing water intoxication, which can lead to seizures, coma, and death.

## Vitamins and Minerals

Breast milk and commercial formulas contain adequate amounts of vitamins and minerals for normal infants. Although breast milk and formula contain very small amounts of vitamin C, it is enough to meet a baby's needs. Giving the baby extra vitamins and minerals is probably unnecessary under normal conditions and can be dangerous if excessive amounts are given. Supplementation may be justified in some circumstances under the advice of the baby's pediatrician. Vitamin K shots are given to all babies born in hospitals in the United States at birth. The bacteria in the intestine produce vitamin K in adults, but babies do not have enough bacteria to provide adequate vitamin K until they are about a month old. As you may recall from Chapter 9, vitamin K plays an important role in blood clotting. Some infants, particularly those who are dark skinned or who are not exposed to adequate sunlight, may require a vitamin D supplement to support bone development, as breast milk is low in vitamin D. Exclusively breast-fed infants need iron at four to six months of age; iron can be provided in fortified cereal. Breast-fed infants over six months of age may need fluoride supplements, particularly if they are consuming unfluoridated water. Babies who are breast-fed by mothers who follow a vegan diet may need $B_{12}$ supplements. Formula-fed infants who are healthy do not require supplementation. Of course, a sick baby may need further supplementation depending on the specific condition.

## Starting Solid Foods

When it comes to starting solid foods, the single most important word is *wait*. Both the American Academy of Pediatrics and the World Health Organization recommend waiting until six months of age before introducing anything but breast milk (or, if necessary, commercial formula) to a normal baby's diet. This is because the iron and zinc content of human milk decreases rapidly after about three months, and the baby's stores from birth will typically be used within the first six months.

**Complementary foods** are the solids and liquids that join breast-feeding in the normal progression toward adult eating patterns. There is no evidence that a normal, thriving baby benefits from complementary foods before six months of age. In fact, feeding solids to infants too early can lead to serious health problems. Iron-fortified cereal, our culture's traditional first food, is a starch that requires an enzyme for digestion that many babies do not produce in sufficient amounts until about six months of age. Two recent studies suggest that if cereal is introduced before four months of age, a child's risk of diabetes later in life may be increased. The introduction of fruits and vegetables before about six months of age is also a problem; the existing iron within the infant's system may

Solids may be introduced to babies 4 to 6 months of age in the form of iron-fortified cereals in addition to breast milk.

It is important to allow the baby to progress to solid foods at his own pace. Part of the exploration of new foods includes touching, smelling and tasting new foods.

bind preferentially with these solids, increasing the risk of anemia. Chunky foods offered to a baby who can't yet use his or her tongue and jaws well can result in choking. And research indicates that early solids can increase the risk of obesity in later life.

Breast-fed babies must be given complementary foods that are high in iron and zinc at six months of age. This is the time when they will have depleted most of the mineral stores they were born with and, as noted previously, human breast milk does not provide the baby with adequate amounts of zinc and iron, especially by the time he or she reaches six months of age. Therefore, improving the quality of complementary foods may be one of the most cost-effective strategies for improving health and reducing illness and death in young children. Iron-fortified cereals are often the first foods introduced. Nutrients that have been identified as problematic for breast-fed infants after six months of age are iron, zinc, vitamin A, and vitamin B$_6$. These nutrients are not as great a concern for formula-fed babies because formulas will be fortified with them.

Physical signs that the baby is ready for solid foods are perhaps the best indicator that it is time to start introducing them. By six months of age, most babies have lost the tongue-thrusting reflex, or **extrusion reflex**, that protected them from early solids. They are capable of sitting on their own or with minor support and have probably become intrigued with the sight of a spoon, fork, or cup going to their parents' mouths. Most important, a six-month-old is generally capable of bringing an interesting item to his or her mouth, investigating it with his or her lips and tongue, chewing and swallowing it if it turns out to be food, and deciding to reach for more if he or she liked the experience. Using a baby-led approach to solids—offering them only when a baby clearly has the skills to manage the experience on his or her own—is safer, simpler, and far easier than starting too soon.

Even after solids are started, human milk or infant formula remains the cornerstone of a baby's diet until about twelve months of age. No single food or combination of foods equals breast milk in its comprehensive nutritional value. However, complementary foods still need to be nutrient-dense. As an example, it has been suggested that complementary foods need to provide more than 90 percent of the recommended intake of zinc for 9- to 11-month-old babies.

## The Importance of Nutrient-Dense Foods

Until recently, discussions of nutrient needs for infants have focused primarily on iron. Iron-enriched baby cereals are traditionally used for this reason, but baby cereal offers no nutrients of importance besides the iron and vitamins that have been added. Other approaches include favoring foods that are naturally iron-rich in a child's early diet, adding prescribed iron drops, or simply monitoring the baby's iron status during regular visits to the pediatrician. There is growing awareness that many infants beyond six months of age are zinc deficient, particularly in developing countries. Low zinc levels have also been reported in the United States in babies that are exclusively breast-fed. Therefore, many cereals are now fortified with zinc. In addition, many major organizations such as the World Health Organization and the Pan American Health Organization have published guidelines suggesting that "meat, poultry, fish or eggs (eggs only after 12 months) should be eaten daily or as often as possible." These guidelines go on to say that plant-based foods such as the cereals and gruels often given to infants in developing countries, when consumed alone, are inadequate in providing the baby's nutrient needs unless fortified or supplemented. Recent recommendations in the United States have also suggested puréed meats, such as those found in jarred baby foods, as an alternative or complement to iron-fortified cereal. In fact, the Institute of Medicine's report on the foods provided for children as part of our federal government's program for Women, Infants, and Children (WIC) suggested that meats be provided as part of the foods for breast-fed infants at six months of age. These recommendations are supported by the Centers for Disease Control and Prevention (CDC) and the American Academy of Pediatrics. However, they have not yet been widely accepted or practiced. In fact, in the United States meats are often not introduced as a complementary food until at least eight months of age and sometimes even as late as eleven months. One survey of more than 3,000 caregivers in the United States reported that only 3 percent of 7- to 8-month-old infants and 8 percent of 9- to 11-month-old infants were consuming meats daily.

## Vegetarianism

### *Are vegan and vegetarian diets safe for infants?*

A lot of controversy surrounds the issue of feeding vegetarian or vegan diets to infants and young children. Some parents believe that consuming animal products is immoral and unhealthy for children. Many others think that by restricting animal products you are denying a child nutrients necessary for growth. Still others go as far as to say that denying infants meat and other animal products constitutes abuse. There are documented cases of children becoming malnourished on vegan diets. However, in most cases the diets were very extreme and the parents misinformed. Well-informed parents who plan carefully can provide their children with all the necessary nutrients. This position is well supported by major health organizations. The American Dietetic Association Position on vegetarian diets states, "Well-planned vegan, lacto-vegetarian, and lacto ovo-vegetarian diets are appropriate for all stages of the life cycle including pregnancy, lactation, infancy and childhood." They caution that extremely restrictive diets such as a raw-foods diet or a fruitarian diet (eating only fruit) are inadequate in nutrients needed for growth and therefore are *not* recommended for infants and children.

Guidelines for the introduction of solid foods are similar, but when it is time to provide meats, vegetarian infants should receive mashed tofu and legumes. At twelve months of age, eggs and milk, yogurt, and cheese (from soy or cow's milk) can be introduced. Eventually, meat substitutes such as veggie burgers can be provided. If dairy or other products that are fortified with $B_{12}$ are not consumed, a supplement should be considered. Vegetarian infants and children may have slightly higher protein needs than nonvegetarian children because of differences in protein digestibility and the amino acid content of plant-based protein sources. Special care should be taken to ensure adequate intake of good sources of calcium, iron, and zinc. Vegan and vegetarian diets can provide children with all the nutrients necessary for growth, and they may even provide lifelong health benefits. The keys are well-informed parents and planning. ■

**Want to know more?**

Several government-funded programs are designed to provide adequate nutrition to pregnant and lactating women, infants, and children. One such initiative is WIC, the Special Supplemental Nutrition Program for Women, Infants, and Children. WIC attempts to safeguard the health of low-income women, infants, and children up to age 5 who are at nutritional risk by providing nutritious foods to supplement diets, information on healthy eating, and referrals to health care. For more information on WIC, go to the text website at http://webcom8.grtxle.com/nutrition and click on the Chapters button. Select Chapter 16.

**Want to know more?**

For more information on the various food sources of iron, zinc, vitamin $B_{12}$, and so on for infants and toddlers, visit the text website at http://webcom8.grtxle.com/nutrition and click on the Chapters button. Select Chapter 16.

**APPLICATION TIP**

The American Academy of Pediatrics recommends that children younger than 2 years old be discouraged from watching television, and encouraged to participate in more interactive activities that will promote proper brain development, such as talking, playing, singing, and reading together. This may also help to encourage exercise and non-sedentary activities.

# Sequencing Solid Foods

The traditional recommendations regarding the order for introducing foods are based on preventing allergies rather than on scientifically based evidence. Introducing one food at a time and then waiting to introduce another makes it easier to identify whether the infant has a food allergy as well as which food is causing the allergic reaction. The typical order of introduction of foods in the United States is iron-fortified cereal, then fruits and vegetables, and finally meats.

A simple first food is a lightly mashed bit of ripe banana. It is soft enough for a baby without teeth to manage and is unlikely to cause an allergic reaction. Iron-fortified rice cereals are often recommended because rice is better utilized and less likely to cause allergic reactions. Other easy early foods are listed here, along with some to be avoided. A tablespoon once or twice a day makes a fine start for a first food, gradually increasing the volume according to the baby's pace and growth.

**Some Starting Foods**

- Ripe banana
- Avocado
- Cooked yam or sweet potato
- Grated or cooked apple or pear
- Chopped cooked prune
- Iron-fortified rice cereal
- Chopped or ground beef (in the form of baby food or puréed)
- Small slivers of chicken (moistened if needed)
- Whole-grain breads (toasted or stale)

**By Nine Months of Age, Most Babies Can Enjoy:**

- Peas, perhaps cooked and squeezed from their skins to improve digestibility
- Easy-to-handle pasta
- Soft-cooked vegetable pieces
- Soft-cooked fruits except citrus and pineapple
- Cubed soft foods
- Fish (Note: allergic families may want to avoid during the first year)
- Tofu (Note: allergic families may want to avoid during the first year)
- Products from cow's milk such as cheese and yogurt in small amounts (Note: allergic families may want to avoid during the first year or more)
- Bread and toast

 **Want to know more?**

With recent cases of contaminated additives and tainted imported foods, many people are considering making their own baby foods by pureeing or finely mashing fresh whole foods. For tips and ideas for making baby food at home, go to the text website at http://webcom8.grtxle.com/nutrition and click on the Chapters button. Select Chapter 16.

### It Is Best to Wait for a Year Before Introducing:

- Honey (toxins from botulism, readily handled by adults, can be fatal for babies)
- Cow's milk (the most common food allergen for young children)
- Eggs, especially egg whites (another common allergen)
- Peanuts (allergic families may want to avoid during the first three years)
- Citrus fruits and tomato, especially raw (also common allergens)
- Dried fruits (sticky on teeth and a possible choking risk)
- Fried foods (high-calorie with low nutritional value)
- Foods with added sugar or salt (why encourage poor habits?)

Most allergies are outgrown within the first few years. Because peanut allergies can be extreme and long lasting, peanut products are not recommended for children in highly allergic families before age 3.

### Foods That May Cause Choking in the Early Years:

- Nuts
- Whole grapes
- Popcorn
- Hot dog pieces
- Any large chunks of raw foods that must be thoroughly chewed (carrots, celery, apple)
- Small candies (be careful of dishes that contain small candies such as M&Ms and mints—these are tempting to infants and are choking hazards)
- Cherries and some dried fruits

It is best not to introduce more than one new food every few days at first, to be sure there are no allergic reactions such as rash, hives, congestion, or digestive upsets. Any foods already shown to be safe and accepted can be combined as desired. When the baby or toddler seems interested in any appropriate food that adults are eating, a small amount can be offered for him or her to investigate. In the progression of introducing solids, many people start with baby food or puréed food. Babies tend to tolerate the mashed-up consistency much better. Many people choose to make their own baby food by puréeing the foods the rest of the family is eating. Breast-feeding continues as before, and solids—if the child chooses to eat any—simply work their way in around his or her accustomed routine.

Some babies are pleased just to be part of the family circle at mealtime, and do little more than finger-paint with food for several months. Others consume solid foods with actual shouts of glee. Most babies are somewhere in the middle, slowly working their way from small samples to true meals. Although adults may want to help here and there, they should remember that starting solids is primarily the baby's job. The baby will undertake it at his or her own pace, with gradually increasing skill and interest. At six or seven months of age the need for extra food is usually so small that it can be ignored on trips or in restaurants, and there is no need to offer snacks. By twelve months of age, meals and snacks have usually become a significant part of the child's intake, and many babies are done breast-feeding.

## Bottle-Mouth Syndrome

Infants or toddlers who go to bed with a bottle or sippy cup of milk or juice are at risk for developing **bottle-mouth syndrome**. The fluid tends to pool around

---

**APPLICATION TIP**

What is the best way to make sure that your toddler doesn't become overweight? Be a good role model. Studies show that this is more what you do than what you say. Model healthy eating and exercise habits without ever saying a word!

**Want to know more?**
To explore the topic of nutrition for infants more extensively, go to the text website at http://webcom8.grtxle.com/nutrition and click on the Chapters button. Select Chapter 16.

Putting babies to bed with a bottle can lead to bottle-mouth syndrome or decaying teeth.

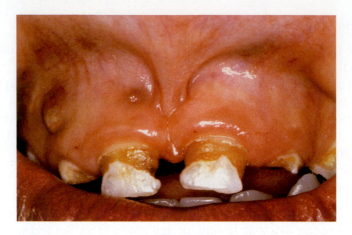

the front teeth and provides a breeding ground for decay-causing bacteria. However, some children have teeth that are more susceptible to damage than others, and some strains of mouth bacteria are more likely to cause decay. All small children should have their teeth wiped carefully at least once a day; practicing with a damp washcloth should be part of the nighttime routine even before the first tooth emerges.

Regardless of the choices and preferences you may have regarding the feeding of your infant, making well-informed decisions under the direction of your health care practitioner is the best way to ensure that your baby has a proper start to a long and healthy life.

## Before you go on . . .

1. Identify the first four foods that are recommended for infants.
2. When should solid foods be introduced to an infant and why?
3. Are vegan and vegetarian diets safe for infants?
4. Why should you introduce solid foods gradually?

## Real People, Real Strategies

In order to obtain credible information, Sarah and Stephen decided to speak with Sarah's doctor. Her doctor recommended that they attend a class for expectant parents at their local hospital and that they visit the websites of reputable organizations such as La Leche League International and the March of Dimes. The doctor also referred them to a Registered Dietitian.

Sarah and Stephen expected the RD to give them advice on what Sarah should eat while she was pregnant and what to feed the new baby. They were surprised when he began by asking questions about their prepregnancy diet. Stephen was very surprised to hear that what he ate could actually have an impact on how easy it would be for them to conceive and potentially on the health of the baby. Sarah learned that she needed to consume more folic acid by adding more fruits and vegetables such as broccoli, asparagus, and peas. The RD also pointed out that this would also help during pregnancy, when her folate needs increased even more. He also emphasized that she really shouldn't approach eating during pregnancy as if she is "eating for two." He told her she would not need to increase her calories significantly during pregnancy, but rather would need to increase her intake of nutrient-dense foods. He assured Sarah and Stephen that by adhering to a healthy diet before, during, and after pregnancy, they would be doing the best thing they could to make sure that their baby had a healthy start. He cautioned them about the multitude of conflicting advice they might receive from well-meaning friends and family members and even from books and websites. He suggested that the best available recommendations were provided by major health organizations such as the American Dietetic Association and the American Academy of Pediatrics. Sarah asked if she should continue attending her yoga classes after she became pregnant, and he said that as long as her physician cleared it, continuing would be a good idea, but she has to be careful of overheating. Sarah and Stephen agreed to come back once she became pregnant to discuss breast-feeding and to get other feeding information.

## Chapter Summary

- The rate of mortality in newborns is higher in the United States than in almost all other developed countries, most likely because of socio-economic disparities in health care for pregnant women.
- The best approach to meeting the nutritional needs of pregnancy is to maintain a healthy diet and a healthy weight before, during, and after pregnancy.
- Pregnancy lasts for thirty-eight to forty-two weeks and is usually divided into three phases of about thirteen weeks called trimesters.
- The first trimester is the time when the fetus is most vulnerable to inadequate nutrition and harmful substances such as drugs and alcohol in the mother. That is why it is critical to ensure adequate nutrient intake and to consider any medications or supplements if there is even a chance you could get pregnant.

- An infant who weighs less than 5.5 lb. is considered low-birthweight. Low-birthweight babies are at risk for illness, infection, lung problems, learning disabilities, insufficient physical growth, and death.
- Current recommendations suggest that a woman who is of normal weight before pregnancy should gain 25–35 lb. If a woman is overweight, she should gain less, but some weight gain is normal. If she is underweight, she should gain more.
- Pregnancy is a time when the nutritional needs are increased and must be met by eating many nutrient-dense foods.
- All women of childbearing age should consume 400 mcg of folate per day. The recommendation is made for all women because adequate intake is crucial in the first twenty-eight days of pregnancy, before many women even know that they are pregnant.
- Pregnancy-induced hypertension is diagnosed when there is a rapid rise in blood pressure above 140/90; it is related to pre-eclampsia and eclampsia, which can lead to death.
- Obese and overweight mothers and their babies are at higher risk for complications.
- Caffeine, alcohol, drugs, and smoking should be avoided during pregnancy.
- Because fish may be contaminated with industrial pollutants such as PCBs (polychlorinated biphenyls), pregnant women or women who could become pregnant should not consume any fish without checking with their state or local health department or the EPA.
- Most health professionals and organizations recommend exclusive breast-feeding for newborns and infants up to six months of age.
- Breast-feeding can help protect babies against a number of childhood illnesses, including diarrhea, respiratory infections, some childhood cancers and autoimmune diseases, and obesity.
- A mother may choose not to breast-feed for many reasons. These reasons could be cultural, personal, or medical, or the mother may simply not be able to physically do so. Regardless of the reason a mother does not breast-feed, she should not feel shamed or inadequate for not doing so.
- Formulas offer an adequate substitute to breast milk.
- After an infant reaches six months of age, most experts agree that solids should be offered while breast-feeding continues.
- The World Health Organization recognizes four acceptable liquid foods for consumption by infants less than six months old: breast-feeding, mother's milk given via a bottle, milk from another human mother, and commercial formula.
- Infant formulas are made from cow's-milk, soy-based, or protein hydrolysate formula.
- Infants need about 40–50 calories per pound of body weight per day. They need more in the first months and less as they approach twelve months of age as the rapid growth of infancy slows down. Infants younger than age 2 need more fat than children over age 2.
- Infants are at risk for dehydration but can usually meet fluid needs through breast milk or formula.
- Complementary foods can be given at six months of age.

- Iron-fortified cereals or similar foods should be given to breast-fed infants at four to six months of age to avoid anemia.
- Foods should be introduced gradually and one at a time to avoid allergies.
- Infants should not be given cow's milk, goat's milk, or honey during their first twelve months.

## Key Terms

**bottle-mouth syndrome** Tooth decay in infants caused by bacteria-producing fluids (milk, fruit juice, etc.) that pool around the front teeth. (p. 537)

**colic** A condition with unknown causes that is characterized by extended crying in babies that are otherwise healthy and well nourished. (p. 529)

**colostrum** (co-LOSS-trum) The breast milk produced by mothers in the first few days following birth. It has a thinner consistency than subsequent breast milk, has a slightly yellowish color, and is rich in antibodies. (p. 527)

**complementary foods** Solids and liquid foods that join breast-feeding in the normal progression toward adult eating patterns. (p. 533)

**eclampsia** (ee-CLAMP-see-uh) A manifestation of pre-eclampsia that can result in convulsions, puts the mother at risk for stroke, and can lead to maternal or fetal death. (p. 519)

**extrusion reflex** The tongue-thrusting reflex that exists at birth but is usually gone by six months of age. (p. 534)

**fetal alcohol syndrome (FAS)** A disorder in infants caused by alcohol intake during pregnancy and characterized by growth retardation, facial abnormalities, and central nervous system (CNS) dysfunction. (p. 521)

**low birthweight** A birth weight of less than 5.5 lb. (p. 511)

**pica** (PIKE-uh) Compulsive eating by pregnant women of nonfood substances such as clay, chalk, or dirt. (p. 519)

**placenta** The organ formed in the uterus and that provides for nourishment of the fetus and elimination of waste products. (p. 509)

**pre-eclampsia** (pre-ee-CLAMP-see-uh) A condition that occurs during pregnancy and is characterized by high blood pressure, edema, and protein in the urine. (p. 519)

**pregnancy-induced hypertension** A condition in a pregnant woman characterized by a rapid rise in blood pressure, with readings above the normal limits of 140 (systolic) and 90 (diastolic). (p. 519)

**umbilical cord** (um-BILL-ik-ul cord) A cord full of arteries and veins that connects the baby to the mother through the placenta. (p. 509)

## Chapter Quiz

1. Folate deficiency in the very beginning of pregnancy has been linked to which of the following?

   a. autism

   b. neural tube defects

   c. anemia

   d. low birthweight

2. At what time during pregnancy is a fetus *most* vulnerable to inadequate nutrition, drugs, alcohol, and toxins?

   a. at conception

   b. during the first trimester

   c. during the second trimester

   d. during the third trimester

3. Weight gain during pregnancy is best determined by which of the following?

    a. how much fat the woman has gained.

    b. how much exercise she does

    c. her prepregnancy weight

    d. the size of the fetus

4. Which of the following is the most important approach to meeting nutrient needs during pregnancy?

    a. eating extra calories

    b. eating to meet food cravings

    c. eating for two

    d. eating a nutrient-dense diet

5. Which of the following is not a health benefit of breast-feeding?

    a. The infant may have a lower chance of obesity later in life.

    b. It enhances the infant's immune system.

    c. It prevents anemia.

    d. It helps decrease the likelihood of allergies in infants.

6. When should solids be introduced to the infant?

    a. around six months of age

    b. as soon as the infant accepts them

    c. not until twelve months of age

    d. no specific time

7. Which of the following is true regarding the recommendations for fat intake for infants?

    a. Infants need the same amount of fat as adults.

    b. Infants need less fat than adults.

    c. Infants need more fat than adults.

    d. Infants can follow low-fat diets.

8. One of the best first foods to introduce to an infant is

    a. iron-fortified cereals.

    b. any cereal.

    c. cow's milk.

    d. cherries.

9. At six months of age, what nutrients have been identified as being inadequate for infants who are exclusively breast-fed?

    a. thiamin and niacin

    b. iron, zinc, $B_6$, and vitamin A

    c. copper and magnesium

    d. protein

10. Why should you not give cow's milk to a baby until twelve months of age?

    a. It will cause food poisoning.

    b. It may cause allergies.

    c. The baby will not like the taste.

    d. The baby can't absorb it.

Chapter Quiz Answer Key

1. b; 2. b; 3. c; 4. d; 5. c; 6. a; 7. c; 8. a; 9. b; 10. b

# As We Grow

## Nutrition for Children, Adolescents, and Older Adults

## < Here's Where You've Been

*The following topics were introduced in preceding chapters and are related to concepts we'll discuss in Chapter 17. Be certain that you're familiar with them before proceeding.*

- Food choices are determined by many factors, including culture, the taste appeal of the food item, age, media advertising, convenience, finances, and family. (Chapter 1)
- Several government guidelines have been developed regarding the necessary intake of nutrients to maintain health, including the DRIs and MyPyramid.gov. (Chapter 2)
- Energy balance to maintain a healthy weight is one of the most challenging nutrition problems facing our society. (Chapters 1, 3, 4, and 7)
- Micronutrient deficiencies occur worldwide, and a lack of iron in the United States continues to be a major public health nutrition problem. (Chapters 9 and 10)
- On a per-weight basis, infants have greater nutrient requirements than any other age group. (Chapter 16)

## Here's Where You're Going >

*The following topics and concepts are the ones we'll emphasize in Chapter 17.*

- Food habits develop at a very early age, with the environment playing a major role in what children and adolescents will eat.
- The major health concerns of children include obesity or overweight, iron-deficiency anemia, lead toxicity, food allergies and intolerances, and dental decay.
- Many adolescents develop dietary habits that can lead to chronic diseases when they become older.
- Older adults do not have the substantial energy needs of children or adolescents, but are faced with the challenge of incorporating all of the essential nutrients in their diets without consuming excess calories.
- Government programs have been developed to ensure adequate nutrition for children, teens, and older adults.

## Real People, Real Choices

Natalie Huang is a 73-year-old retired schoolteacher who lives in Orlando, Florida. About a year ago she lost her husband of forty years. She has three children, two of whom live out of state. Her youngest daughter, Jill, lives in Tampa, about a forty-five-minute drive from her. Natalie has been retired for several years.

Despite the demands of her teaching career, Natalie always managed to prepare and serve evening meals for her family as the children were growing up. During retirement, she continued her routine of cooking for both herself and her late husband. Now that she is by herself, Natalie continues to live on her own, look after herself, prepare her own meals, and do routine housecleaning. The yard work is done by a local boy. In essence, she is still trying to maintain some semblance of how things were before her husband passed away. One thing she has realized is how difficult it is to cook for only one person. On the positive side, though, she occasionally is inspired to prepare a creative meal and then freeze the leftovers for later use. However, in recent months she has become increasingly passive about cooking and, consequently, has started skipping some meals. She especially tends to forgo dinner. On some days, she justs snacks or eats only what is available in her refrigerator, or has something from the pantry that is heat-and-serve. She has also stopped walking on a daily basis—her only form of exercise.

Natalie prefers to live independently, but her daughter Jill is concerned about her mother's change of behavior and knows that her health will start to decline if her nutrition doesn't improve. What advice would you give Natalie to address her nutritional problem? What could she do to improve her appetite and motivation to cook?

The example of Natalie's skipping meals or not having a desire to eat is typical of older adults. However, there are other times or ages in life when people may not seem to have an appetite compared to just a few months before. Parents and relatives often become frustrated with the eating habits of children and teenagers. Adult children of older adults become concerned when they see their parents not eating or not having an appetite that they know was once there. The extent to which food acceptance is biological or sociological depends on the circumstances. A young child going through a growth spurt may have a huge appetite and then suddenly reduce the volume of his or her food consumption as growth slows. On the other hand, when an older adult ceases to eat, this is typically cause for concern and may indicate a sociological, psychological, or biological problem. In this chapter, we will learn that nutrient requirements differ by age and life stage. The nutrient needs of an infant on a per-weight basis are very high, because growth requires more of everything in the diet. Young children and teenagers also continue to have high nutrient requirements because of growth. On the other hand, this requirement in adulthood shifts to maintenance. In older adults, the focus is not only on maintenance, but on how to support and adapt to physiological and physical changes that affect nutrient requirements. In older adults, more emphasis is placed on consumption of sufficient essential nutrients without oversupplying calories, because their physical activity is typically less.

## Nutrition During Childhood

The time between being a toddler and becoming a child is a period of tremendous change, both physically and emotionally. *Toddlers* are ages twelve to twenty-four months, and most people define *childhood* as the time that spans from the second birthday until prepuberty. The rate of growth from infancy through the end of childhood drops and levels off (Figure 17.1). The rate increases during the growth spurt as puberty begins. The childhood years with their steady and gradual growth are a great time to store nutrients for the adolescent years, when growth is so rapid that nutrient needs cannot always be met with diet.

The child transitions from infant to adult foods in a short time and begins to develop food preferences as a toddler. As the child grows, he or she becomes more independent in thought, expression, and food preference but still has high nutrient requirements for growth and maintenance. During childhood, the development of eating habits and nutrition practices typically has profound and lifelong consequences.

### Rapid Development Change in Childhood

Early and middle childhood is characterized by slow and steady growth. The child's growth rate after age 1 is slow relative to what it was during the first year of life. Appetite and food preferences vary as children go though a period of *food jags,* in which they may eat only one type of food for a while and then switch to another food preference. As noted earlier, children normally consume more food when they are in a growth phase and then decrease their food intake when the growth phase slows or ceases.

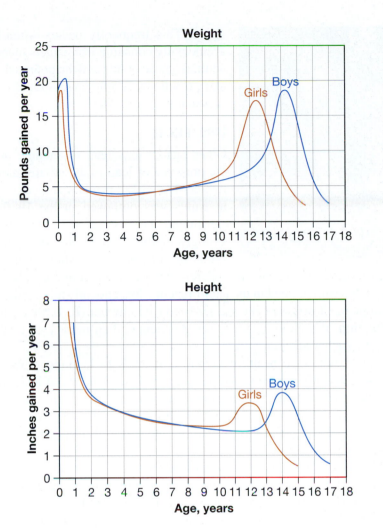

**Figure 17.1** A comparison of the rate of growth in both height and weight. The rate for both slows down at about 2 years of age. Note that the growth spurt begins earlier for girls than for boys.

## Health Concerns of Childhood

Throughout childhood and adolescence, numerous nutritionally related conditions can affect growth, development, and general health. Some of the more common ones are listed here.

### Iron-Deficiency Anemia

Iron-deficiency anemia is often a problem among children, particularly in low-income families. In fact, it remains the number one problem in terms of nutrient deficiency in the United States today. Iron deficiency may influence one's mood and attention span because less oxygen is being carried to tissues, including the brain. In addition to these physical limitations, children with anemia score lower on standardized exams. It is important that children be screened for anemia. Good sources of iron for children include more than just meat, although iron from meat sources is more absorbable. Peanut butter, which many children love, is also a good source of iron. Flour tortillas, fortified cereals, beans, sunflower seeds, farina cereal, fortified dry cereals, rice noodles, green peas, dried peaches and apricots, chicken, eggs, nuts, and potato skins are some of the other foods that kids may enjoy and that have a good level of iron.

Although iron deficiency is a problem in children, iron toxicity can also be an issue. Iron toxicity is a leading cause of poisoning among children under

Despite years of education and the outlawing of lead-based paint, lead poisoning as a result of children eating old paint chips remains a problem in the United States and elsewhere. Even toys with lead-based paint were imported from China and sold in the U.S. as recently as 2007.

age 6. This frequently occurs when children accidentally consume iron tablets meant for an adult. Because of this and the potential for other toxic reactions, supplements should always be locked away from children.

## Lead Toxicity

Other factors may lead to anemia, one being the presence of lead in the environment. Paint in older homes is a primary source (use of lead in paints was outlawed in the 1980s). Lead can inhibit the absorption of iron, but it also strongly inhibits an enzyme that helps in the synthesis of hemoglobin. Many times a child is thought to have anemia because of iron deficiency when in fact this condition is due to exposure to lead in the environment. Consequently, giving the child an iron supplement does not reverse lead-induced anemia. To further complicate this situation, if a child also has iron deficiency, then more lead is absorbed, leading to greater anemia.

Lead toxicity is a health concern, as it leads to learning problems. The developing brain is very sensitive to even the lowest levels of lead, and early exposure can lead to lifelong learning disabilities. Damage to the brain from lead can be severe, and medical treatment does not guarantee reversal. Impaired perception, the lack of ability to reason, and lowered academic performance may remain.

Children can become exposed to lead from a variety of means. Children often chew on chips from peeling paint, if they are available, that contain lead. This is especially true in areas where the child does not have enough food and consumes other substances. Low-income families tend to live in older homes that used lead paint. The United States has banned not only the use of lead-based paints but also leaded gasoline because of its toxic effects. Lead pipes used in plumbing can also be a problem, and many areas have switched to other types of piping material to provide a safer water supply. Soldering (the process of fusing metals) typically involves lead and has been used in manufacturing plumbing fixtures. Some eating utensils, such as mugs, clay pots, and imported plates and cups, may contain lead because of the production method used. Candies from Mexico have also been reported to contain lead. As recently as 2007, RC2 Corporation recalled toy trains it manufactured because they contained a lead-based paint. The toys were made in China and imported to the United States. Clearly, lead in the environment and certain products remains a current and relevant problem.

Not all nations have followed the United States in imposing these bans. Poor Hispanic infants and children may immigrate to the United States from countries where they have already been exposed to high levels of lead, either as a fetus (from the mother) or during infancy and childhood.

## Obesity and Overweight

One of the most significant problems among children is that of obesity. The incidence in the United States has more than tripled since the early 1960s, when only 5 percent of children were considered overweight or obese, to about 18 percent and growing (Figure 17.2). Physical inactivity, video games, television, excessive snacking on nutrient-poor foods, large portion sizes, overconsumption of

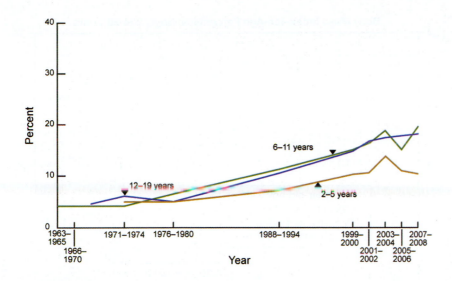

**Figure 17.2** Obesity in children and adolescents has grown at an alarming rate since the mid-1970s.

*Source:* Reprinted from the Centers for Disease Control.

calories, saturation of food advertising directed to children, vending machines in the school system, widespread availability of food, and the use of food as a reward to motivate positive behaviors are all reasons advanced as causes. Children are clearly affected by food advertisements; they consume sugared soda and may order "super-size" meals when eating out. Emotional and psychological factors are also responsible causes.

How do you know whether a child or even a teenager is overweight or obese? We don't use the terms *overweight* and *obesity* as we do for adults. The body mass index, discussed in Chapter 7, is needed. The Centers for Disease Control and Prevention has developed BMI charts for children through teens of each sex from age 2 to 20 in which percentile growth curves can be used (Figure 17.3). If a child or teen's BMI is at the 85th percentile or greater, the individual is "at risk for being overweight." If the BMI for age and sex is at the 95th percentile, the individual is "overweight."

### ■ What's Hot
*Fast food—excess calories for children*

Should children eat at fast-food restaurants, given the large and rapid increase in obesity and the negative nutrition value associated with fast-food menus? Although we do not need to avoid fast-food restaurants altogether, for either ourselves or children, we do need to practice sensible nutrition. One-third of children in the United States eat a fast-food meal daily, and in doing so they tend to consume more than the recommended number of calories. If you are ordering at a fast-food establishment, there are some fundamental principles to follow. Here are some healthy food items to choose from (not all items will be available at all fast-food restaurants):

- Grilled chicken or grilled fish sandwich (watch the sauces, though)
- Whole-wheat rolls
- Fruit or fruit and yogurt
- Baked potato (with vegetable toppings instead of cheese, butter, or sour cream)
- Salad with dressing on the side or fat-free salad dressing
- Single hamburger (regular or children's size)
- Low-fat deli sandwiches on pita or wheat bread

**Figure 17.3** Interpreting a BMI chart. This is an example of a hypothetical 10-year-old boy with different BMI values. Above the 95th percentile for the BMI he is considered overweight; between the 85th and 95th percentile, he is at risk of being overweight. On the other extreme, a BMI below the 5th percentile is considered underweight. BMIs between the 5th and 85th percentiles are considered desirable or normal.

*Source:* Reprinted from the Centers for Disease Control and Prevention.

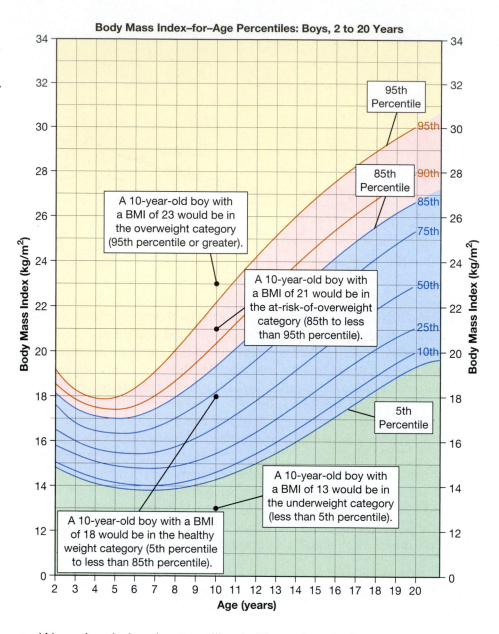

**Body Mass Index–for–Age Percentiles: Boys, 2 to 20 Years**

- Wraps in whole-wheat tortillas (without dressing)
- Fat-free/low-fat milk or water

The added ingredients in a fast-food meal can transform an otherwise healthy food into the opposite. For example, when sour cream, bacon, and cheese are added to a baked potato, the increase in the number of calories and introduction of saturated fat makes it unhealthy. A plain hamburger with tomato, onion, lettuce, and/or ketchup and mustard can satisfy and provide significant nutrients. When cheese, bacon, mayo, or "special sauce" is added, the calories and fat can double with little or no addition of vitamins or minerals. To combat this problem, ask for substitutions and avoid the following items:

- Cheese sauce
- Most "special sauces"
- Tartar sauce
- Sour cream
- Gravy

You may wish to purchase child-size portions of some food items. Beverage choices can also make a significant difference. Limit your intake of milkshakes and sodas containing sugar. Instead, drink low-fat milk, fruit juice, or diet soda. Limit things that are high in fat such as fried foods, chicken nuggets, croissant breakfast sandwiches, fried fish or fried chicken sandwiches, fried chicken, large and "super-sized" fries, and onion rings. Many other fast-food menu items are filled with hidden fat, cholesterol, sodium, and calories. To make healthy choices, take the time to review the nutrition facts before buying. Most fast-food establishments provide nutrition facts on their websites. ■

## Dental Decay

The water in many communities in the United States has naturally occurring or added fluoride, which has decreased the incidence of tooth decay. In California, however, just under half of all communities have fluoride in their water. Fluoridation of water has remained a controversial issue in some locales; if it is not naturally occurring, its addition to water is determined by voters in a community or by a public health agency (see Chapter 10). Besides fluoridation, avoiding sweet, sticky foods (e.g., caramel and taffy) and practicing good oral hygiene are important. Sticky foods such as candies allow bacteria to attach to the tooth. Acid is secreted by bacteria feeding on the sugar of the sticky surface, thereby eating away at the tooth's enamel (Figure 17.4). As discussed in Chapter 16, a poor practice that can contribute to severe dental decay in toddlers is the bottle feeding of juice and milk, especially at bedtime. Bedtime bottle feeding allows the sugar in the juice or milk to react longer with the bacteria and dissolve the enamel on the teeth to produce cavities.

## Food Allergies and Food Intolerance

**Food allergies** in children are a major concern of parents. A food allergy is a condition in which the body produces antibodies against particular food molecules and physical symptoms result. The reactions can involve difficulty in breathing, skin rashes, or intestinal upset including diarrhea and vomiting. Food may cause an allergic reaction almost immediately, or it may take as much as twenty-four hours after ingestion of the suspected item to produce a reaction. One can avoid a specific allergic reaction by removing the offending food item from the diet. Items such as wheat, eggs, chocolate, seafoods (shellfish), tree nuts, peanuts, and milk are some foods that are notable for producing allergic reactions. Many food allergies, except peanuts, are outgrown. Peanuts are especially notorious for causing allergic reactions, not only in children but in people of all ages. People who are allergic to peanuts can experience breathing difficulties and **anaphylactic shock**, a condition in which blood pressure is very low and breathing is shallow. If medical attention is not sought immediately, death can result. Occasionally, the allergy is so severe that even breathing the food particles can trigger the allergic response. Peanuts are a prime example of this; some schools have banned peanuts and peanut butter as ingredients in their lunch programs. Most airlines have banned the use of peanuts as snacks on flights because of the risk of severe allergic reactions. A food allergy is different from **food intolerance**. Food intolerance is an adverse reaction to a food or a food additive

**Figure 17.4** Various factors in the micro-environment of the mouth interact and lead to the production of dental cavities.

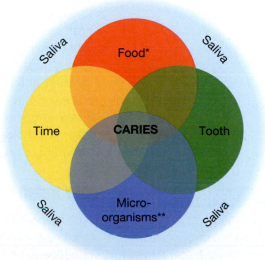

\* Fermentable carbohydrate
\*\* Particularly *streptococcus mutans*

without producing antibodies from allergic reactions. A good example is lactose intolerance, as discussed in Chapter 3.

## Food and Behavior in Children

*Do certain foods cause hyperactivity in children?*

Parents often ask whether certain foods cause hyperactivity in children. Is there any evidence to support this? The basic answer is no; however, it is not uncommon for people to believe that sugar and food additives can lead to behavior problems in children. Despite these suspicions, carefully controlled studies do not support this notion. The cause of attention deficit disorder and behavioral problems is an issue of brain chemistry. In order for food to have an impact, it would have to alter brain chemistry. Drug therapy can sometimes control hyperactivity in children. Any effect the elimination of certain foods appears to have on hyperactivity is most likely a placebo effect. Although eating breakfast can improve the attention span in children, no evidence exists that specific food items such as sugar cause hyperactivity.

Stimulants such as caffeine and products that contain caffeine can be a problem in children just as in adults. Sodas and chocolate contain caffeine, and parents should be aware of this. Caffeine content is often found on the ingredients part of the food label, not on the Nutrition Facts Panel. Caffeine can cause sleeplessness and irritability. Children are less able to break down caffeine compared to adults, and thus its stimulating effect is much greater. It may actually be the caffeine in the soda and candy that increases a child's activity and not the sugar content. Although caffeine can increase activity, it is not a cause of hyperactivity in children.

### ■ Nutrition and Lifestages

*Does breakfast for children improve brain function?*

There has been a growing trend for children to go to school without having breakfast. This is despite mounting evidence that they can concentrate and learn better if they have eaten something. Therefore, many schools now offer breakfast at no cost or reduced cost. Most studies have revealed that going to school without breakfast results in lower memory, decreased arithmetic scores, decreased problem-solving ability, and other deficits in cognitive abilities. Providing a breakfast appears to reverse many of these problems. Studies have also reported that the type of food consumed at breakfast may affect performance. Children who consume a breakfast that provides foods with a low glycemic index (see Chapter 3 for more information) demonstrate better cognitive ability than children who consume a breakfast with a high glycemic index. For example, a cereal such as oatmeal has a low-to-moderate glycemic index and most ready-to-eat cereals have a high glycemic index. Therefore, good old-fashioned oatmeal may be a better investment for schools providing a reduced-cost breakfast than ready-to-eat cereals would be. ■

### APPLICATION TIP

When your kids see you eating and enjoying healthy foods in the proper amounts, they will too. Talk with them about what you like and why.

## The Nutritional Needs and Eating Habits of Children

A child's need for calories depends on body size, activity, and growth rate. A lack of calories will slow the growth of a child. The number of calories needed per kilogram of weight is greater in childhood, but it decreases as we go through adolescence, leveling off as we become adults. As growth occurs, the total amount of calories required increases, because the energy must support a greater body weight. Table 17.1 gives energy recommendations assuming an active pattern of physical activity. The energy requirement is lower for sedentary children and adults. These recommendations are based on a reference weight, height, age, and physical activity level. The U.S. Department of Agriculture has developed a customized MyPyramid for children, shown in Figure 17.5.

Protein requirements are based on weight and are higher for children than adults. However, there is no distinction based on sex. Later we will see that during the teen years, boys require more energy and protein than girls. On a per-weight basis, adults need less protein than children do. Adults need about 0.8 g/kg/day, whereas 2- to 3-year-olds need 1.05 g/kg/day and 4- to 8-year-olds need 0.95 g/kg/day. This is about 13 g and 19 g of protein per day for each age

| Table 17.1 | **Energy and Protein Recommendations for Active Children Compared to Adults** | | | |
|---|---|---|---|---|
| | **Boys** | | **Girls** | |
| | **Energy** | | | |
| **Age** | **kcal/kg/day** | **kcal/day** | **kcal/kg/day** | **kcal/day** |
| 2–3 | 87 | 1,046 | 83 | 992 |
| 4–8 | 87 | 1,742 | 82 | 1,642 |
| Adult | 44 | 3,067 | 42 | 2,403 |
| | **Protein** | | | |
| | **g/kg/day** | **g/day** | **g/kg/day** | **g/day** |
| 2–3 | 1.05 | 13 | 1.05 | 13 |
| 4–8 | 0.95 | 19 | 0.95 | 19 |
| Adult | 0.8 | 56 | 0.8 | 46 |

*Note:* kcal/kg/day for adults was calculated by dividing kcal/day by the reference weights of 70kg and 57kg for males and females, respectively.

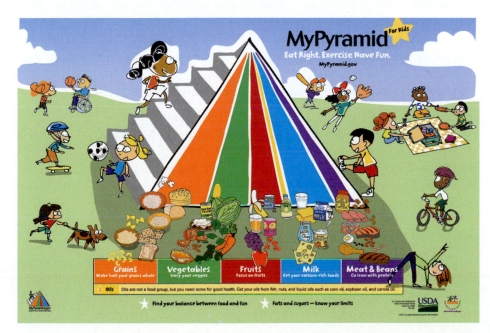

**Figure 17.5** MyPyramid for children who are physically active.

**Want to know more?**
To explore ways to increase physical activity in children, go to the text website at http://webcom8.grtxle.com/nutrition and click on the Chapters button. Select Chapter 17.

group, respectively, regardless of sex. A very good source of protein for children is milk.

## What Children Like to Eat and Why

As children become older, their diet should become more varied to help ensure adequate nutritional intake. Many parents become upset when their children will not eat or when they will not eat what the parents consider the "right foods." Ellyn Satter is a dietitian and authority on childhood eating and feeding. She states that "the parent is responsible for the what, when and where of feeding. The child is responsible for how much." She offers some useful tips and solutions to eating issues common in childhood and stresses the importance of having structured family meals whenever possible. See www.ellynsatter.com for more information.

As children get older and spend more time eating meals away from home, the parents need to provide guidance with flexibility. It is advisable to allow children to play a more active role in meal planning and perhaps even in meal preparation. Allow older children to make more choices while maintaining guidance. For example, ask the child what kind of cereal he or she would like for breakfast. You have made the guiding choice that he or she will eat cereal, and you have purchased the different types to guide the choice, but the child will ultimately feel that he or she has decided what to eat for breakfast.

What causes a child to accept certain foods? The acceptance of a particular food item by a child may depend on several factors, although it is important to remember not to overgeneralize. Children may be afraid to try something new, and some foods may need to be offered to them as many as eight to ten times before they will accept them. Children react to such things as color, flavor, texture, temperature, serving size, and even the attitude of the server/preparer and the atmosphere in which the food is presented. Most children like foods that are soft. Typically, they do not like dry, tough parts or foods that are too thick. They may prefer thin instead of thick pudding, or prefer lukewarm to either cold or hot foods. For instance, children often wait for their ice cream to melt because they dislike extreme coldness. Children also respond to what others in their family unit consume. This may be the most significant factor. If they observe a parent or sibling eating a food item, children are more likely to try it. Likewise, if they hear a negative comment about a food, they will be less likely to try that food item.

Food preferences of children include the following:

- Temperature of the food: lukewarm, not too cold
- Foods crisp in texture (versus soggy); soft textures, not tough
- Foods to hold: finger foods
- Flavor: foods that are not bitter like broccoli; foods that are bland
- Color: a variety of colors of food on a plate
- Small serving sizes
- Relaxed, fun atmosphere
- Helping to prepare food

Children have the greatest number of taste buds during the preschool period. As a consequence, preschoolers tend to dislike strongly flavored food, such as cooked vegetables, spicy foods, and temperature extremes. As taste buds are lost throughout life, they are not replaced. Therefore, adults can usually tolerate a broader array of flavors in foods than younger people, who taste more acutely.

The serving size presented to a child normally affects what they will eat. The quantity of food should be less than what the parent expects the child will eat. It is preferred that they ask for seconds. A study at a day care center, for instance, noticed a great deal of food wasted. In an experiment, a very small serving size of food was presented to each child. When the children had smaller portion sizes, they tended to ask for more servings. As a result, the child care center ended up with an extraordinarily high food bill and very little waste! A good rule of thumb for serving size is a tablespoon of each item for each year of age up to age 5. For instance, 2 Tbsp. of corn for a 2-year-old would be an appropriate serving size. Table 17.2 presents serving sizes by food groups for children of different ages.

Children are more receptive to trying new foods if they are able to help with the meal preparation.

## Snacking

Given the rapid growth in obese and overweight children in the United States, allowing snacks has become controversial. On the other hand, young children have smaller stomachs and need to eat five to six times a day in order to meet their energy and growth needs. Snacks are okay if well chosen, because frequent eating at these ages is essential for proper growth and development. Research has demonstrated that frequent smaller meals are used in the body so as to limit formation of fat tissue. This may help prevent overweight children. This eating pattern in childhood could prevent the propensity for obesity later in life. Fruit and 100 percent fruit juices should be encouraged. However, fruit juices that are not 100 percent juice may provide too many calories in the form of simple sugar as well as lack other nutrients found in natural fruit. In either case, fruit juice should be limited because many children like the sweet taste and tend to overconsume it. See the brief list on the next page for some nutritionally healthy snacks that offer positive alternatives to the fat-laden products many children are given.

*Is it okay for kids to snack?*

| Table 17.2 | Serving Sizes per day of Foods within Food Groups by a Child's Age and Assuming Less Than 30 Minutes of Activity per Day | | | | |
|---|---|---|---|---|---|
| **Age (years)** | **Milk, Cheese Yogurt** | **Meat, Fish, Poultry, Beans, Nuts, Eggs** | **Vegetables** | **Fruit** | **Pasta, Cereal, Rice, Bread** |
| | | | Girls | | |
| 2–3 | 2 c. | 2 oz. | 1 c. | 1 c. | 3 oz. |
| | | | Boys | | |
| | 2 c. | 3 oz. | 1-1/2 c. | 1 c. | 4 oz. |
| | | | Girls | | |
| 4–8 | 2 c. | 3 oz. | 1 c. | 1-1/2 c. | 4 oz. |
| | | | Boys | | |
| | 2 c. | 4 oz. | 1-1/2 c. | 1-1/2 c. | 5 oz. |

*Source:* United States Department of Agriculture.

**APPLICATION TIP**

To promote awareness of proper nutrition, school-age children should be involved in preparing their school lunchbox and in making meals at home.

- Apples and cheese
- Graham crackers and low-fat milk
- Crackers and cheese
- Oatmeal cookies and low-fat milk
- Fresh fruit
- Raisins
- Celery sticks with peanut butter
- Cauliflower, broccoli, celery, cucumber, and carrot sticks with low-fat dip
- Fruit and yogurt
- Low-sugar cereal and low-fat milk
- Baked chips with cheddar cheese and boiled/drained whole beans

**Before you go on . . .**

1. What is the number one nutritional deficiency among children in the United States?
2. How do health professionals define a child who is at risk for being overweight? An overweight child?
3. What is the basic difference between food intolerance and a food allergy?
4. What are some important factors in determining what a child will eat?
5. Why are smaller, more frequent meals a good thing for young children?

## Nutrition During the Adolescent Years

As in childhood, significant bodily changes continue to occur throughout the teen years. Some of these changes are as dramatic as in the first year of life, and many hormone changes contribute to overall body growth and development during this period. Figure 17.6 shows how the proportions of our bodies change from birth to young adulthood. Note that the head is relatively larger in infancy and decreases thereafter, whereas the relative size of the legs increases.

Let's explore these changes and how nutrition can affect them.

**Figure 17.6** Human development from infancy to young adult.

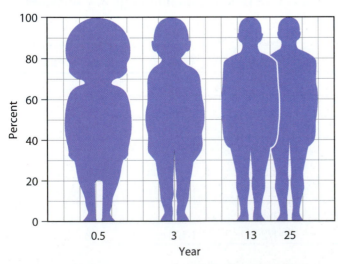

### Rapid Growth

The growth spurt for girls occurs before that for boys. In girls it occurs around age 10–11, and in boys around 12–13. The timing of the growth spurt depends on the child's attaining a certain critical weight. This can vary by parts of the world. In the United States, it is generally about 30 kg or 66 lbs. and when body fat is 10 percent. The rate of growth is an interaction between heredity and the environment, with nutrition playing a big role in achieving genetic potential.

### Puberty

**Puberty** is the period of sexual maturation that occurs until sexual reproduction is possible.

Sex hormones are produced and have a profound effect on the physical changes experienced at this time. Boys, because of the male sex hormone, **testosterone**, gain proportionately more lean tissue than fat. They tend to develop heavier skeletons and have more red blood cells than girls. Even in the preschool period, girls tend to have more body fat than boys, and the difference becomes even greater during adolescence. This means that boys have greater nutrient and energy needs than girls, but overall needs increase for both sexes during the teen years.

The onset of a girl's first menstrual cycle occurs up to three years after the growth spurt has begun. Her weight reaches 47 kg (approximately 100 lbs.) and fat stores have doubled to 20–24 percent. Adequate body fat and nutrition are needed for girls and women to maintain a normal menstrual cycle. This may mean that naturally thin girls may have delayed onset of menstruation. The delayed onset of menstruation means that increased production of *estrogen* (the female sex hormone) is also delayed. Because estrogen plays an important role in bone development, a delayed onset of menstruation can then lead to an increased risk of osteoporosis. On the other hand, delayed onset of menstruation also decreases the risk for breast cancer, because estrogen is correlated with this disease. Obese or overweight girls often have their first menstrual cycle earlier than their normal-weight counterparts. The onset of *menarche,* the establishment of menstruation, slows the growth spurt or the total height gained. Therefore, an overweight or obese teen may have a shorter adult height if menarche occurs earlier.

## What Are Some of the Major Health Concerns of Adolescents?

### Obesity

Clearly obesity is one of the biggest problems for teens today, and the percentage of adolescents who experience it continues to grow at an alarming rate. In the early 1960s the percentage of overweight and obese teens was around 5–6 percent. Today it is close to 18 percent. Girls tend to have this problem more than boys do, and African-American girls in particular. However, obese teenage girls tend to become obese adults more so than boys. In many cases these obese teens may not eat more than their leaner counterparts, but are less physically active. Teenage girls who are overweight or obese tend to adopt quick weight-loss

More U.S. children and teens are overweight than ever before.

fad diets. Because adolescent growth and development requires a higher intake of nutrients, nutrition experts advise overweight and obese teens to become more physically active to lose weight, rather than to "diet" or severely restrict caloric intake. Mild caloric restriction is okay as long as nutrient-dense foods are increased and poor snacking habits are decreased. Because of the desire to fit in and achieve an ideal body, eating disorders are also prevalent during this age period.

**Want to know more?**
To investigate the use of drugs in the treatment of overweight adolescents, go to the text website at http://webcom8 .grtxle.com/nutrition and click on the Chapters button. Select Chapter 17.

### APPLICATION TIP

When eating in fast-food restaurants, order off the children's menu when possible. Avoid "super-sizing" and "value meals."

## Anemia

The form of anemia caused by a lack of dietary iron remains a problem among teenagers, and girls are particularly vulnerable during this time period. Not only may iron intake be inadequate, but iron requirements increase because of the monthly menstrual cycle. During menstruation, blood is lost, which is a major route of iron loss. Adolescent girls may consume less meat and often diet, excluding many foods that are rich in nutrients.

## Dental Decay

As in childhood, dental decay in adolescence is also a problem, but because of the fluoridation of our drinking water the incidence has declined dramatically. However, the increase in sugar consumption via soft drinks is likely to have a negative future impact on the dental health of teens. In the 1970s adolescents consumed more milk than soft drinks, but in the 1990s that trend reversed.

## Adolescent Eating Patterns and Disease Risks

During adolescence, we see a transition from dependence on adults to independence, and this includes eating behavior and patterns. Teenagers often eat alone and frequently prepare their own food. Because the incidence of overweight and obesity has increased in this age group and the rate of increase has been accelerating, numerous intervention programs have been developed to help both children and teenagers eat more nutritiously and to improve their nutrition knowledge and practices. With obesity, we begin to note increased levels of cholesterol, which can lead to an early onset of heart disease such as atherosclerosis. Additionally, we are witnessing a rapid increase in Type 2 diabetes among children and adolescents, and this is also linked to obesity. High blood pressure is also becoming more common among adolescents. Those who have abnormally high blood pressure during their teen years are more likely to be hypertensive as adults, and there is a strong relationship between being overweight at this early age and developing hypertension. Losing weight is a good step in the direction of correcting this problem. In summary, good food habits at this age are critical to ensuring continued healthy food habits during adulthood.

### ■ Nutrition and Disease

*Are adolescents at risk for diabetes?*

Diabetes can and does occur in adolescents. In Chapter 3 we discussed diabetes in detail. As you may recall, diabetes in children or teens who fail to produce pancreatic insulin is called Type 1 or insulin-dependent diabetes. This form of diabetes can occur at later ages as well. People with Type 1 diabetes fail to produce the hormone insulin, which breaks down glucose; they are often thin and at high risk for heart disease. The other form of diabetes, known as Type 2 diabetes (formerly known

A culture of fast food and its ready availability leads to overconsumption of food and calories among many adolescents. The teen at left has chosen to eat a healthy apple instead.

as *adult-onset diabetes*), is associated with increased insulin secretion, which in many cases occurs when the insulin the body is producing fails to function correctly. Historically, those most vulnerable were women over age 40 who were overweight and white, but today minority groups are affected at a higher rate. Weight loss, controlled diet, and exercise are among the methods used to mitigate the effects of the disease.

Recently the number of adolescents developing Type 2 diabetes has increased. Teens most likely to develop Type 2 diabetes are those who are overweight or obese. The rise in Type 2 diabetes in both children and adults has paralleled the increased rate of obesity. Teenagers who have Type 2 diabetes should know that later in life they are at an increased risk for heart disease, limb amputation, blindness, and kidney failure. For those with Type 2 diabetes, an increase in physical activity can help immediately lower blood sugar as well as help reverse obesity. Controlling calorie intake with nutrient-dense food choices can help lower body fat and diabetes over the longer term. ■

## Alcohol, Drugs, and Smoking

Alcohol, discussed in Chapter 12, is the most frequently used drug among adolescents. Alcohol is a diuretic, and its use can result in a loss of B vitamins, which in turn results in undernutrition. Many of these vitamins are critical for extracting energy from the foods we consume. In some individuals alcohol often takes the place of other foods, causing malnutrition, and with prolonged use it damages the liver. The nutritional and social issues of alcohol abuse are significant, as discussed in Chapter 12.

Drugs may have several effects on nutrition. Smoking marijuana may alter taste perception. Because of brain chemistry changes, there is increased appetite, but this effect is short-lived. On the other hand, other drugs such as cocaine result in the loss of appetite along with other very serious physiological consequences. Smell and taste perception are often altered and somewhat decreased because of cocaine use. Drug abusers often spend less on food and more on illicit drugs. They lose interest in food and decrease their regularity in eating. Many develop liver and other infectious diseases, which can greatly impair nutrient utilization as well as cause permanent, irreversible damage to vital organs.

Use of Ecstasy has become more common in teens. This drug affects the mood of users and can impair memory because of nerve damage. Ecstasy affects serotonin levels in the brain, and many abusers tend to lose weight. Use of Ecstasy results in a surge of energy, with increased body temperature and water loss being common. The thirst center of the brain may temporarily be impaired, but users may also experience water intoxication in response to the thirst that becomes apparent after the drug has worn off.

Methamphetamine suppresses the appetite and inhibits sleep. With its sustained use, severe and rapid weight loss usually occurs. Substance abusers often quickly become malnourished. *Meth mouth* is a term applied to the poor oral health of methamphetamine users. Meth has many corrosive acids and when smoked can irritate and burn the oral lining of the mouth, causing infections. Meth users may have teeth eroded to the gum line. Also, because of anxiety, they frequently grind their teeth, resulting in cracking.

Cigarette smoking reduces hunger, and smokers may weigh less than nonsmokers, but the risks that smoking poses to your health far outweigh this benefit. Smokers are known to have lower vitamin C levels as compared to nonsmokers,

**Table 17.3** **Energy and Protein Recommendations for Active Adolescents Compared to Adults**

| | Boys | | Girls | |
|---|---|---|---|---|
| | **Energy** | | | |
| **Age** | **kcal/kg/day** | **kcal/day** | **kcal/kg/day** | **kcal/day** |
| 9–13 | 63 | 2,279 | 56 | 2,071 |
| 14–18 | 52 | 3,152 | 44 | 2,368 |
| Adult | 44 | 3,067 | 42 | 2,403 |
| | **Protein** | | | |
| | **g/kg/day** | **g/day** | **g/kg/day** | **g/day** |
| 9–13 | 0.95 | 34 | 0.95 | 34 |
| 14–18 | 0.85 | 52 | 0.85 | 46 |
| Adult | 0.80 | 56 | 0.80 | 46 |

*Note:* kcal/kg/day for adults was calculated by dividing kcal/day by the reference weights of 70kg and 57kg for males and females, respectively.

and other nutrient levels may also be altered because of smoking. Tobacco is a known carcinogen and should be avoided, even as secondhand smoke.

## Nutrient Needs of Adolescents

In general, adolescents need more energy and easily absorb more calories to meet this need. However, these calories are useful only if the vitamins, minerals, and protein needed for lean growth are available. If an adolescent consumes calories, but not other nutrients, the calories will be stored as fat and result in teen-onset obesity.

Boys have a greater energy requirement than most girls. The daily calorie needs for teens, assuming an active level of physical activity, is shown in Table 17.3. As we discussed earlier with respect to children, if a teen is sedentary, fewer calories will be needed daily. Note that on a per-weight basis, the energy requirements decrease for higher age groups.

The protein requirement for 9- to 13-year-olds is 0.95 g/kg/day; and for the 14- to 18-year-olds it is 0.85 g/kg/day. For adults, it drops to 0.8 g/kg/day.

Most surveys report that the levels of iron, calcium, and vitamin A consumed in these age groups are not adequate. Iron is one of the most critical needs of teenage girls. Table 17.4 shows the greater need for girls compared to boys. However, because boys have more muscle tissue, their iron needs are also important.

**Table 17.4** **Iron RDAs for Teenage Boys and Girls by Age and Adults**

| Age (years) | Boys | Girls |
|---|---|---|
| 9–13 | 8 mg/day | 8 mg/day |
| 14–18 | 11 mg/day | 15 mg/day |
| Adult | 8 mg/day | 18 mg/day |

Calcium deposits into bone mass during the teenage years, and calcium needs are higher during this period than at any time in the entire lifespan. For boys and girls ages 9–18, the DRI is 1,300 mg per day. For an adult, it is 1,000 mg per day. During adolescence it is important to obtain the greatest level of bone mass, because bone loss increases as one ages.

### ■ To Supplement or Not
*Should teenage girls take a calcium supplement?*

As noted earlier, to prevent osteoporosis we need to accrue as much bone mass as possible during adolescence and early adulthood. This peak bone mass is generated in both men and women primarily during adolescence, with maximum levels normally achieved in the mid-to-late twenties. After age 30, gradual bone loss becomes a simple fact of life. The more dense the bone to begin with, the less likely there will be complications from osteoporosis later in life.

Dairy products, such as milk, are the best form of calcium in most diets. Unfortunately, many teens, especially girls, may not want to consume as much calcium from dairy foods (or other food sources) as recommended. Consumption of soda and other beverages displaces milk. Therefore, the question arises as to whether calcium supplements are appropriate. Many nutritionists, but not all, suggest that taking calcium supplements during this age period can help achieve greater bone mass.

Many calcium supplements come as calcium carbonate, calcium citrate, calcium gluconate, or calcium phosphate. Calcium citrate malate is another popular calcium supplement with good absorption, and it may be the best choice of those available. Supplements may also include vitamin D, which helps absorption. Other supplements are made with oyster shells and bone meal. These forms may contain lead and are not recommended. Another note of caution is needed: in susceptible individuals, excess intake of calcium supplements has been linked to the development of kidney stones. The upper limit for calcium intake from all sources is 2,500 mg per day.

How much calcium should one take from a supplement? The more you take, the less you absorb. It is suggested that no more than 500 mg of calcium at one time is best and that you take it between meals in order to obtain better absorption. Use of calcium supplements by adolescents can make them more vulnerable to iron-deficiency anemia, because of calcium's ability to inhibit iron absorption. Also, be aware that labels can be misleading. Some state that they contain 300 mg of calcium carbonate, but only 40 percent (120 mg) is calcium. ■

## Food Habits of Adolescents

Adolescents normally become more independent as they age. Young girls who tend to be concerned about their health are usually emotionally stable and are products of stable home environments. These girls typically choose better diets than those affected more by group status, and they have greater independence from their parents. Many adolescent girls are sensitive to criticism about their appearance, and weight comments can result in skipped meals or other eating disorders. Anorexia and bulimia have a high incidence among teenage girls, and perhaps more boys than once thought. Many of these individuals have a distorted image of themselves, believing they are overweight or fat. Parents should continue to encourage their adolescent children to participate in family meals for the purposes of promoting better nutrition and communication.

Nutritionists have observed seasonal variation in the selection of more nutritious meals by adolescents. In the winter months, better food choices are made, perhaps because of a less hectic or more regular schedule. Also, the more meals teens consume away from home, the more likely they are to eat foods that do not provide adequate nutrient content. Some of the most common poor food habits picked up by teens are as follows:

- Failure to eat breakfast or some other meal
- Lack of time or companionship for regular meals
- Not drinking milk or not consuming other calcium-rich foods
- Nutrient-poor food selection in meals eaten away from home
- An overriding fear of obesity, especially among girls, which leads to dieting
- Use of bodybuilding supplements among boys to increase muscle mass
- Avoiding certain foods that they think will aggravate adolescent acne
- Excessive intake of convenience foods and fast foods

Adolescents tend to skip breakfast at a higher rate than any other age group. Having a healthy breakfast has two major advantages:

1. It generally provides nutrients, especially vitamin C, calcium, and riboflavin (vitamin $B_2$). These particular nutrients are best supplied by breakfast foods such as milk, cereals, juices, and fresh fruit.
2. The availability of a readily usable carbohydrate results in a rapid increase in blood glucose levels. This improves or maintains performance level, reduces accidents, and enhances attention span.

Those who omit breakfast reduce their intakes of calcium and vitamin C by about 40 percent. Intakes of iron and vitamin $B_1$ (thiamin) are reduced by about 10 percent. Many schools now offer a low-cost (sometimes free) breakfast to students. Studies have demonstrated that having breakfast leads to an improved attention span, better performance (especially in math), and fewer behavior problems. Typically, adolescent boys eat breakfast more frequently and include more nutritious foods than do girls.

Breakfast need not be the usual fruit, cereal, toast, and beverage pattern. It can be a combination of foods, either liquid or solid, that provides at least 300 kcal and sufficient protein and fat and a sense of satiety (satisfaction) with a reasonable contribution of nutrients. Examples include a sandwich, a fruit-and-yogurt smoothie, yogurt with granola, whole-wheat toast with peanut butter, cereal with milk and fruit, low-fat granola, a bagel with cream cheese, and leftovers from the night before.

## ■ Myths and Legends

### Do certain foods cause or contribute to acne?

It is not uncommon to see a story about how the foods you eat during adolescence can cause acne. Foods such as potato chips, soda, chocolate, and sugar-filled food items have been blamed for causing acne in teenagers. To date, no evidence suggests that things you eat cause or even aggravate acne. Acne is an inflammation of the sebaceous glands of the skin and is normally caused by physiological changes that accompany becoming an adult. Testosterone stimulates the secretion of these glands, and estrogen can reduce it. Mechanical irritation of the skin from clothing friction and the use of oil-based cosmetics can also aggravate or cause an eruption of acne.

Some misconceptions about food and acne may arise from the knowledge that several nutrients play a role in maintaining the health of the skin. For instance, vitamins A, E, and C along with the trace element zinc have a role in skin health. The drug Accutane is a vitamin A derivative that can improve the skin with respect to cystic acne, but it should not be taken for more than six months at a time and must not be taken during pregnancy, because it has been shown to cause birth defects. However, young people need to be aware that taking massive doses of vitamin A will not have a beneficial effect on acne, as it differs from the drug Accutane. Good hygiene is far more important than diet in preventing acne. ■

> ### Before you go on . . .
>
> 1. How does the percentage of body fat in girls relate to both the growth spurt and puberty?
> 2. What percentage of today's teens are overweight and obese?
> 3. What are some major differences between sexes in the nutrient requirements of adolescents?
> 4. What are some advantages to beginning the day with breakfast?

## Nutrition for Older Adults

The average age of Americans is becoming much older, with more than one-fifth of the population over age 65. This is double the number in 1950. We are living much longer, healthier lives today. A 70-year-old today is much more youthful physiologically than 70-year-olds several generations ago. An increasing number of people are *octogenarians* (living to age 80 or older), and it's no longer rare for more someone to live past age 100. In fact, the number of people living past age 100 has doubled in the last decade. Clearly, better medical care, better methods of treating infectious diseases, and better nutrition have all contributed to our increased longevity. Much of our emphasis in nutrition is devoted to enhancing the quality of the remaining years of the older adult. The baby boomers are retiring, and as a generation they are very health conscious. They want to look young and remain active, and they demand better health care and nutrition to improve their lives.

What age are we referring to when we discuss the "older adult"? Surprisingly, given our increased life expectancy, the National Research Council defines anyone age 50 or older as an older adult. In setting nutrition requirements and DRIs, a separate category for people over age 50 is listed. However, there is no distinction in the recommendations for those who are age 55 versus age 75, although there are separate recommendations by sex. This does not mean that there are no differences in these age groups beyond age 50 with respect to several nutrient requirements. It is likely that a consensus among the scientific community has yet to emerge and a separate category for those age 70 or older may be appropriate.

It is important for older adults to stay active in order to maintain quality of life and promote health.

## Social and Psychological Aspects of Aging

The psychological and social aspects of aging have as profound an impact on nutrition as do the biological aspects. These are generalities and may not apply to all older adults.

Depression is common among older adults, and it can affect food intake, resulting in malnutrition.

### Living Alone

People who live alone frequently lack the motivation to cook regular meals, which may lead to the consumption of less-healthy snack foods at irregular times. Normally people eat better when they have companionship. Community eating centers are usually helpful in getting older adults to socialize and eat healthier as a result of the food served to them in a social environment.

### Depression

Older adults may be more vulnerable because of sociological and biological changes. This condition frequently affects food intake, as either overeating or undereating.

### Anxiety

People who are anxious or concerned frequently report a loss of appetite. Anxious people often have changes in hormones and other nervous system chemicals. These changes affect how much digestive juice the body releases. Many times the anxious person releases less digestive juice. This results in a decreased ability to digest and absorb nutrients from the food consumed.

### Long-Standing Food Habits

Food preferences and patterns among older people are often the result of lifelong food habits. The grocery store today is much different than that of the 1950s and 1960s, when there was much less variety. People who are 70 and 80 years old may have established their food habits fifty or sixty years ago. They may regard fruits and vegetables as seasonal items, consuming them only when they are "in season" as they did when they were younger.

Older adults may have learned to consume fruits and vegetables only during certain times of the year, when in season. Today fresh fruits and vegetables are made available year-round in many places.

Older adults may consume foods they associate with pleasant memories, often referred to as "comfort foods." Some of these foods may be high in fat, calories, and sodium. They also may harbor misconceptions about certain foods, such as that cheese is constipating, or that milk is only for younger people or infants.

### Economic Considerations

Many older adults are on fixed incomes and therefore need to live in inexpensive housing. This cheaper housing frequently lacks adequate cooking and refrigeration facilities, which in many cases contributes to the poor nutrition habits of its senior occupants.

Older adults living on fixed incomes typically cannot purchase more costly food items. High-carbohydrate foods, such as breads and grain products, which are relatively inexpensive, tend to be purchased more often. Expensive products such as meat, fish, and fresh fruits and vegetables are more likely to be avoided.

In the United States, health care and medication costs are high. As a result, many older adults do not seek needed care or fill prescriptions. Older adults may resort to other modes of therapy in an attempt to save money, making them more vulnerable to fad diets or products designed as anti-aging products. They also may be tempted to consume large quantities of supplements or buy those that are unproven and sometimes dangerous. Although supplements within the DRI recommendations are safe, they are not a substitute for good food selection and balanced nutrition. Worse, the expense of supplements may contribute to a lack of funds for purchasing adequate, nutrient-dense foods.

### ■ Make It a Practice
*Community food programs*

Community food programs are very important to the nutritional well-being of many older adults. Not only do adults benefit from having a balanced meal, they benefit from companionship. It is often difficult to cook for one person, and many older adults prefer not to cook for themselves. This causes them to snack instead of consuming nutritious meals. Meals served at senior citizen sites are available in many communities. Home delivered meals, such as the *Meals on Wheels* program, offer nutritious meals but lack the social interaction older adults often need. The *Elderly Nutrition Program* is an initiative of the federal government designed to improve the nutritional well-being of older adults, prevent medical problems, and help them stay in their community rather than being institutionalized. Low-cost, nutritious meals are offered. Shopping assistance, counseling and referral to social services, and help with transportation are also available. Many older adults benefit from federally sponsored food stamps, but others refuse to accept and use them. Some choose not to use them out of pride, whereas others simply lack the knowledge regarding eligibility. Today, use of a card instead of the old traditional stamps has helped minimize the negative stereotype or embarrassment in the checkout line.

By law, the Elderly Nutrition Program must provide at least one-third of the RDA for nutrients. All adults older than age 60 are eligible to receive meals from these programs regardless of how much money they have, although priority is given to those who are economically disadvantaged. Throughout the country the county extension agent for family and consumer sciences can be contacted to provide information regarding these programs. ■

Many communities offer meals at senior citizen centers. The availability of companionship, as well as having someone else prepare meals, helps to assure better nutrition.

## Physical and Physiological Factors

As we reach older adulthood, many organs of the body decline in function. All parts of the body are eventually affected (see Figure 17.7). We discuss some of these changes below.

### Loss of Teeth

Many older adults did not have the benefits of good dental care early in life, or now. Fifty percent of adults over age 65 and 65 percent of adults over

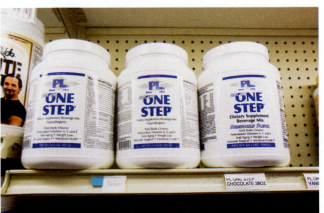

Because of their susceptibility to health claims, many older adults are more likely to consume supplements. Unfortunately, many of these claims are not supported by science.

**Figure 17.7** Parts of the body that change as we age.

Organs                    Tissues

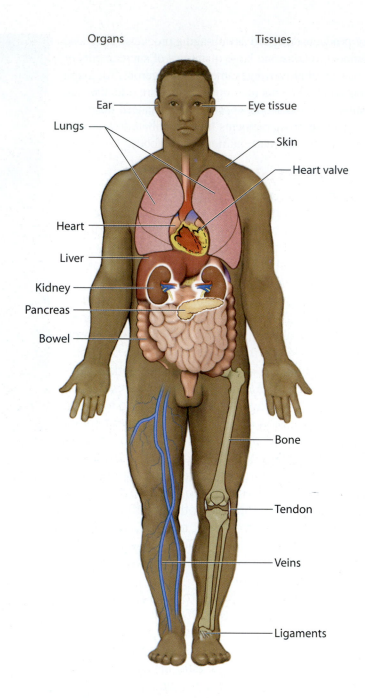

Ear
Lungs
Heart
Liver
Kidney
Pancreas
Bowel

Eye tissue
Skin
Heart valve

Bone
Tendon
Veins
Ligaments

age 75 have experienced tooth loss to varying degrees. Almost 80 percent of these individuals either fail to replace their teeth with dentures or use poorly fitting ones. Some of the dental problems older adults experience may also be due to the loss of the supporting bone from periodontal disease. Loss of teeth can be caused by low dietary calcium and vitamin D intake as well as poor dental hygiene and/or lack of dental care.

Because of these dental problems, chewing food is much more difficult and often results in swallowing difficulties. Accordingly, many older people replace nutritious foods with less-nutritious choices that require less chewing. Plant foods are tougher to chew, and therefore fruits and vegetables may be limited or omitted from the diet, or softened by prolonged cooking. This reduction in the consumption of fruits and vegetables or excessive cooking can result in decreased fiber that leads to lower *motility* (the ability to move food along) in the gastrointestinal tract and constipation. However, canned fruits and vegetables are much easier to eat and can be consumed by people with poor teeth because they are easier to chew. Meat is difficult to chew, but omitting it from the diet can lead to low intakes of iron and zinc. Even foods such as seeds, nuts, salads, and popcorn, all good sources of nutrients, are difficult to eat if there are dental problems.

## Loss of Neuromuscular Coordination

Older adults may develop tremors from a wide variety of disorders, including Parkinson's disease. This makes handling food items and utensils more difficult. Rather than risk the embarrassment that would come with spilled food or the inability to cut meat or eat soup, older people are likely to avoid such food items. They may fear working with boiling water on stoves and thus may choose foods that do not need to be cooked. In the grocery store, they may not wish to reach for food items on the upper or lower shelves because of lack of strength or flexibility or increased back pain. Overall, these restrictions result in a decrease in the variety of foods selected.

## Impaired Hearing and Vision

An individual who cannot read labels or identify foods that are not at eye level has a greatly reduced basis for selecting foods in a grocery store. An inability to see clearly makes it difficult for older adults to remain independent. Also, poor hearing can result in older customers being timid about asking questions of store personnel.

**Age-related macular degeneration** is a vision disease with a nutrition connection. This condition affects a specific region of the retina known as the macular region and is a cause of blindness in older adults. It is believed that free radicals cause this disease, but exposure to sunlight and perhaps genetic factors may also contribute. However, research suggests that the plant pigments related to β-carotene, such as lutein, along with the trace element zinc may help prevent this condition. There is also evidence that the omega-3 fatty acids found in fish oils have protective properties.

As we age, cloudiness of the lens of the eye can lead to **cataracts**. Elevated blood glucose present in uncontrolled diabetes can increase the risk of cataract formation. Untreated, this disease can lead to blindness. Surgical removal of the lens and replacement is the treatment; otherwise, blindness will result. As with age-related macular degeneration, antioxidant nutrients may be helpful in prevention. Although this condition may also be caused by free-radical damage to the lens, there is often a genetic basis.

## Physical Discomfort

Older adults may experience discomfort after consuming certain foods. This happens in almost all age groups, but is more of an issue in older adults. Some foods may be more likely to cause heartburn, indigestion, and gastric discomfort. Some of this is due to incomplete food digestion. People may again refrain from eating particular food items, reducing their variety, in order to avoid the discomfort.

Soy-based products tend to be more difficult to digest in older adults. High-fat foods may lead to heartburn. Carbonated beverages, caffeinated beverages,

**APPLICATION TIP**

If you or others in your family have trouble chewing, try the following: cooking vegetables instead of eating them raw; choosing more tender cuts of meat; grinding nuts and seeds before adding them to recipes; removing the skin from fruits and vegetables; and drinking lots of water or fluids with meals.

This image reflects the limited vision experienced by an individual with age-related macular degeneration.

spices, green peppers, onions, and garlic are food items that may not be tolerated in some older adults.

## Loss of Muscle Mass

The loss of muscle mass in older adults is a major problem. This is often referred to as **sarcopenia**. With less muscle mass, strength is diminished and limited. Remember, muscle requires more calories to maintain. Consequently, the basal metabolism is lower in older adults because they have less muscle. Muscle mass can be better maintained if exercise such as daily walks, hiking, yoga, and low-impact aerobics is part of the older adult's daily activities.

## Arthritis

Arthritis affects the joints of our bodies. The type of arthritis that leads to the deterioration of cartilage and loss of lubrication of the joints is **osteoarthritis**. Contrary to popular belief, walking and weight-bearing exercise will not make the condition worse, but may in fact help. Many older adults have turned to supplements in the belief that arthritis symptoms can be controlled, but scientific evidence is lacking. Those who are overweight can easily correct some of the pain associated with this disease by losing weight.

A much different form of this disease is **rheumatoid arthritis**, which is thought to be a malfunction of the autoimmune system. Rheumatoid arthritis occurs when the immune system attacks the bone joints, leading to inflammation. Rheumatoid arthritis can cause hand and finger deformities to the point at which a person cannot pick up eating utensils or a cup because of pain. Some foods may actually reduce the inflammation. Again, omega-3 fatty acids from fish oils may be helpful. Foods high in vitamin C and E as well as vitamin C and E supplements may also help, as these are also potent antioxidant vitamins. However, keep in mind that any time you use supplements, it is important not to exceed the DRI.

## Diminished Sense of Taste and Smell

Our senses of taste and smell decrease as we age. By the time we are 70 years old, we have lost 36 percent of our taste buds compared to when we were 30. Smell is connected to taste. Ever notice that you cannot taste something when you have nasal congestion from a cold? Loss of taste normally results in decreased eating pleasure and decreased intake. Loss of salt and sweet tastes are most notable for many older adults, who then add a lot of extra salt and sugar to compensate. Older adults may also have a greater intake of medications that can affect their senses, particularly taste. Not only is there a decrease in taste, but the sense of

CT scans of the thighs of a young adult woman (right) and an older adult woman (left) that demonstrates the change in muscle and fat. The yellow area is muscle and the red area is fat. Notice how much more fat the older adult woman has compared to the younger adult.

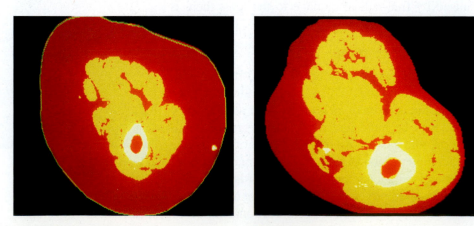

taste may be negatively altered. Some drugs can cause high-protein foods, such as meat, to taste bitter.

### Anorexia

As discussed in Chapter 15, this condition is characterized by a lack of interest in eating, which results in a decreased intake of food. Age-related anorexia is different from anorexia nervosa. At one time, many experts thought anorexia could be the result of a micronutrient deficiency. Deficiencies in vitamin $B_1$ (thiamin) and zinc can cause a decrease in taste and appetite. However, in older adults, most cases may actually be psychological, resulting from loneliness, anxiety, or being unhappy. Older adults become more aware of their own mortality. Loved ones and close friends begin to die. As they age, a change in brain chemistry can result in a decrease in appetite or make them feel full sooner when eating similar amounts of food. Typically, older adults are less physically active, which can tend to make them feel less hungry.

Two suggestions to aid in overcoming anorexia are the consumption of smaller, more frequent meals or snacks and eating with companions. Many older adults prefer smaller portions. Food they once liked when they were younger and associate with happy memories may be useful, so some knowledge about the person's past is typically beneficial.

### ■ Nutrition and Disease

*Is aging really a disease?*

Is aging a disease that can be classified, as heart disease and cancer are? Some individuals appear to have been born with a gene that accelerates the aging process. By their early teens, these individuals have fragile skeletons, muscle loss, hair loss, and aging of the face. One such disease is *progeria*, but it's rare. What about aging in other parts of the population? Are there other theories on what causes aging?

Some scientists believe that in a theoretical sense, humankind can live forever. Another theory is that after we have performed our job of reproduction, we are "programmed" to grow old and die. Is there a way to slow aging and extend life? The quick answer is yes. We know that we can extend the life of an animal in the laboratory by restricting how much food it consumes on a daily basis. For example, if we restrict the amount of calories fed to a rat by 40 percent, it can live almost another year! Under normal conditions a rat's life span is 1½ to 2 years, so a rat that lives 2–3 years is very old! Although this evidence exists with respect to rats, whether caloric restriction of this magnitude will extend the life of a human has never been scientifically tested. Another theory suggests that aging is caused by free radicals and that antioxidants, such as

In Ogimi, Okinawa, a 96-year-old woman eats lunch in a "longevity restaurant"—an eatery claiming to serve food that will make you live longer. Among the foods on the menu are silver sprat fish, bitter grass with creamy tofu, daikon, seaweed, tapioca with purple potato and potato leaves, and pork cooked in limes. Do you think longevity restaurants would be successful in the United States?

many of the nutrients we've discussed in this book, can slow the aging process. Remember that fruits and vegetables are high in antioxidants.

Another question scientists would like to answer is whether the environment can be modified to allow our cells to live forever. Certain types of cells can live indefinitely in the laboratory. Cancer cells are one example; they not only live forever in a laboratory but continue dividing as well. However, healthy normal cells cannot do this; they divide only so many times before dying off. Some scientists believe that if we can improve the quality of our environment, improve the sources and purity of the food we consume, and cure many of the diseases associated with aging such as heart disease and cancer, we may be able to extend the human life span to as much as 120 years. So does eating healthy throughout life mean you will live longer? Although science cannot yet provide a definitive answer to this question, we can say that by balancing a healthy diet with regular physical activity you can decrease your risk of many of the diseases that lead to death and in the process improve your quality of life, regardless of how long you live. ■

**Before you go on . . .**

1. List the social and psychological factors that may influence nutrition habits in older adults.
2. What nutrients may prevent the onset of age-related macular degeneration?
3. How would loss of neuromuscular coordination and impaired hearing and vision affect food selection in older adults?

## Major Nutrition-Related Issues and Older Adults

Some nutrition issues are common to all age groups—for example, obesity and anemia. However, as we will discuss, many age-related changes alter nutrient requirements. For example, the use of certain prescription drugs, which can interfere with nutrient absorption and utilization, to treat many conditions and diseases is just one of many issues that can have a significant nutritional impact on older adults. Other issues include the following:

- Obesity
- Anemia
- Undernutrition
- Osteoporosis
- Drug-nutrient interaction
- Food-induced malnutrition
- Alzheimer's disease
- Hypertension
- Type 2 diabetes
- Hyperlipidemia

### The Most Common Issues

#### Obesity

In the United States, one out of four individuals over age 50 is obese, and this percentage is increasing. Of those who are older than 50 and obese, 75 percent

# Real People, Other Voices

**Student:**

**Dawn Riden**

University of Central Oklahoma

Natalie's loss of her husband has been life altering. When her children moved out, she still had her husband, which allowed her to keep up her routines. Now, without her husband, she lacks the companionship and drive to continue those routines. These circumstances have led to a decline in her nutritional health.

A beneficial change would be for Natalie to attend a senior congregate meal site. Not only would this provide a nutritious meal that gives her one-third of the RDA for nutrients, but her daily attendance would help Natalie to start a new routine, during which she would make new friends and also get more exercise by traveling to the site. She could learn new ways to prepare meals for herself by sharing ideas with the other seniors. Having one meal cooked by someone else would also give Natalie more energy and motivation to cook dinner.

Additionally, I would tell Natalie that she would benefit greatly from increased communication with her children. It can be difficult for her out-of-town children to come over for dinner, but Natalie could call them during the week to see how they are doing. She could also invite Jill, who lives nearer, to drive over for dinner on the weekends, during which time they could create individual meals to freeze for the following week.

Adding a daily multivitamin, in addition to the changes mentioned, could also help Natalie avoid any nutritional deficiencies she might be developing.

**Instructor:**

**Maggi Dorsett**

Butte College

Natalie is lucky that she can still live independently. However, not preparing meals for herself may soon harm her health. Natalie may be more motivated to cook if she were sharing a meal with someone. Perhaps she could get together with friends to take turns preparing meals or going out to eat. Jill can help her mother to plan meals and maybe spend one day each month batch-cooking extra portions and freezing them individually. Healthier types of packaged frozen dinners (lower fat and reduced sodium) can be coupled with a salad, vegetable, or fruit. Grocery deli sections also have pre-prepared foods that can be used for an occasional meal.

Natalie can learn to cook certain items that could be used for several meals. For example, she could roast a turkey breast or a chicken. Some of the meat could be used for dinner and the rest for sandwiches, tortillas, burritos, or salads. The scraps can be used in a soup. This strategy also works with lean hamburger and kidney or black beans.

Jill can help her mother stock the kitchen with healthy snacks. When Natalie doesn't feel like cooking, she should snack on nuts, dried fruit, whole-grain cereals, energy bars, smoothies or instant breakfast drinks, low-fat cottage cheese and fruit, or hard-boiled eggs.

**Registered Dietitian:**

**Libby Watanabe**, MPA, RD, LD

Sitka, AK

I would suggest that Natalie consider finding out whether her community offers a nutrition program for seniors that serves meals in a group setting. Such an arrangement may help to stimulate her appetite and her desire to eat meals on a regular basis. Participation would increase the regularity of meal consumption, especially dinner, and it would increase the quantity and variety of foods consumed. This would reduce or eliminate the risk for iron-deficiency anemia, osteoporosis, loss of teeth, and constipation. Reducing the risk for these nutrition-related problems could greatly enhance Natalie's quality of health and life.

If a community group nutrition program is not available, I'd recommend applying for Meals on Wheels so that Natalie could have dinner prepared and delivered to her. If that program provides only lunch, I'd still recommend that Natalie apply for the meals and receive lunch, refrigerating leftovers and reheating them for dinner. Dinner seems to be the most problematic meal, and having a meal prepared and delivered would alleviate many of her concerns.

Another helpful activity would be a walking program for elderly people. Since Natalie used to walk every day, she may be willing to begin walking again, and this may improve her mood and sense of well-being. Many cities have group walking programs that meet in malls before they open, and this option may be appealing to Natalie.

Finally, Natalie should drink eight cups of water daily to stay well hydrated.

of them are age 50–69. After age 70, the ratio drops to 17 percent. Rates are higher for those with lower incomes and with less education, and obesity is also more common in older women than men. Body mass index (BMI), one indicator of obesity, starts to decrease at age 60. However, this statistic may be misleading because many of those who were extremely obese may have died. Also, sarcopenia may partly explain this observation.

One of the reasons for obesity in older adults is lowered metabolism due to decreased muscle mass. Older adults are less physically active, and lack of activity leads to muscle atrophy (wasting). The combination of a lower basal metabolism and less physical activity means less energy required. Another factor that can lead to decreased basal metabolism may be less thyroxin secretion (Chapter 10). Hormones produced in the thyroid gland normally increase basal metabolism. However, as the body reaches an advanced age, fewer hormones are secreted, including thyroxin, which results in a lower metabolism.

## Anemia

In other stages of life, such as pregnancy, infancy, and adolescence, iron-deficiency anemia remains a large problem. However, in older adults, particularly postmenopausal women, iron requirements decrease. Consequently, iron-deficiency anemia is not as major a problem for this age group compared to others.

Anemia observed in older adults is more likely due to other causes than failing to consume enough dietary iron. Many times, issues such as gastric ulcers and other related ailments lead to blood loss over time, which results in anemia. Vitamin $B_{12}$ deficiency causes large-cell anemia (Chapter 9), which can happen if there is insufficient stomach acid or not enough intrinsic factor needed for absorption. The DRI committee recommends cereals that are fortified with vitamin $B_{12}$ or supplements for older adults. Megadoses of vitamin $B_{12}$ force absorption of the vitamin and can prevent a deficiency. Alternatively, vitamin $B_{12}$ injections can be an option to treat a vitamin $B_{12}$ deficiency for those with reduced absorption.

## Undernutrition

As noted, fewer people over age 70 are obese. Older adults who are hospitalized are often malnourished. Forty percent of hospitalized older adults show some form of undernutrition. This percentage may be even higher in nursing homes. A principal type of undernutrition is protein-energy malnutrition, and another form is characteristically the result of micronutrient deficiencies. The following circumstances and conditions typically account for undernutrition in older adults:

- Little or no appetite
- Problems with chewing or swallowing
- Consuming inadequate amounts of nutrients
- Eating fewer than two meals a day

Of course, many other economic, physiological, social, and psychological factors can contribute to undernutrition.

## Osteoporosis

We discussed this disease in Chapter 9. Osteoporosis is typically apparent in older adulthood. Although it is more of a problem in women, more attention is being directed to older men, who also have a higher incidence than men of a younger age. Osteoporosis is not simply lack of calcium. So taking more calcium at this stage will not reverse it, but having sufficient nutrients, including calcium and vitamin D, along with doing weight-bearing exercise, can slow the process. Older adults are at risk for low vitamin D because the ability to synthesize it through ultraviolet light exposure decreases by up to 75 percent. Also, they may not have as much sun exposure compared to younger people.

Older adults can fall and break a hip, or they can first break a hip with the slightest of force and then fall. When someone breaks a hip, it is much more serious than just bone healing. Nearly 15 percent of older adults who fall and break a hip die within a year from complications: loss of lean body mass, limited mobility, pneumonia, and general malnutrition. Collapse of the spinal column (which can occur in osteoporosis) causes severe and chronic pain. The best way to treat osteoporosis is to prevent it from occurring in the first place. As we've noted, the best means to accomplish this is by maximizing peak bone mass in the adolescent and early adult years.

### Drug-Nutrient Interaction

Extensive use of prescription drugs by older adults has significant nutritional implications. Some drugs cause a lack of appetite. Others interfere with absorption of some nutrients. This may lead to weight loss and/or inadequate intake of many nutrients. Oral diuretics to control blood pressure and other ailments can cause the excretion of water-soluble vitamins and minerals. Some drugs lead to depletion of zinc stores, which can result in a loss of appetite and taste. Others taken to neutralize stomach acidity can interfere with vitamin D absorption.

Antibiotics are well known to have nutritional risks. They can interact with the intestinal mucosa, leading to malabsorption of nutrients and incomplete digestion. Vitamin K is produced by intestinal bacteria, and prolonged use of antibiotics at any age can lead to low vitamin K levels.

Some older adults practice *polypharmacy,* which is the consumption of multiple medications for an illness or illnesses. In some cases this may be warranted. However, multiple side effects and interactions with nutrient utilization, absorption, excretion, and appetite can occur simultaneously, leaving the patient malnourished. However, when patients visit multiple physicians and don't disclose their prescription history, unwarranted duplication of drugs can occur. Individuals often visit multiple doctors if they believe their current treatment is failing, and doing so can lead to polypharmacy. Polypharmacy is not limited to prescription medications, but can include over-the-counter medications (laxatives, pain medications) and herbs as well.

The rate of drug metabolism and detoxification in the liver is much slower in older individuals. Consequently, drugs remain in the body longer and have a longer time to affect nutrients. In some cases, nutrients may interfere with drugs. Some vitamins such as folic acid and vitamin $B_6$ can interfere with the action of anticonvulsants.

### Food-Induced Malnutrition

Long-term intake of particular foods sometimes interferes with absorption of other nutrients. For example, consuming tea in large amounts increases the need for thiamin, because tea contains an enzyme that breaks down thiamin. A large intake of phytic acid from tea and even oatmeal may reduce the body's absorption of iron and zinc. The intake of foods high in phosphorus, such as soft drinks, can lead to an imbalance of calcium to phosphorus, which contributes to bone loss.

**APPLICATION TIP**

Increase water intake to help the body break down and excrete drugs efficiently.

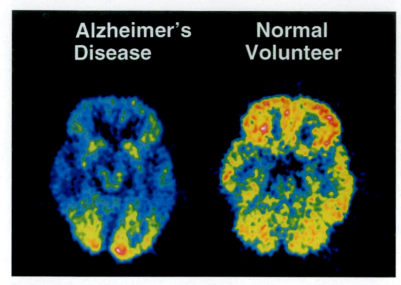

Brain scans of normal brain (right) and Alzheimer's brain (left).

**Want to know more?**
To explore recent developments in the role of diet and Alzheimer's disease, go to the text website at http://webcom8 .grtxle.com/nutrition and click on the Chapters button. Select Chapter 17.

## Alzheimer's Disease

Alzheimer's disease has received much public attention in recent years. This disease has a slow and steady onset. When diagnosed, most patients are past age 70. Initially, it is characterized by frequent loss of memory for things such as names, past events, the locations of items such as keys or glasses, and simple things. Unfortunately, the advanced state of this disease results in being unable to communicate and perhaps even walk. Those with clinical signs of the disease cannot care for themselves, including preparation of meals, driving, or using the telephone. Consequently, without supervised care, people with Alzheimer's disease are at serious risk for malnutrition. In order to assure adequate calorie intake, caregivers need to provide balanced meals featuring foods that the person finds appealing.

### ■ Make it a practice
*A diet to grow old with.*

Chances are that as they retire, baby boomers and generations after them will have health issues that previous generations never experienced. Chances are, they will be more obese and will experience a higher incidence of chronic diseases such as heart disease, diabetes and cancer. In fact, in the past people typically lost weight as they got past 50 years of age, but they didn't live as long either. Generations of today are faced with a longer-living, increasingly obese aging population with a myriad of chronic diseases. To address these issues it is important to look at lifestyle behaviors throughout the lifespan, but it is equally important to recognize that it is never too late to make effective lifestyle changes. As we age, we usually need fewer calories, but we still require a nutrient-dense diet. Therefore, we actually need more vitamins and minerals per calorie. For instance, calcium is important to protect against bone loss. Remember that the DRI for calcium is 1,200 mg a day, up by 200 mg from the recommendation for adults less than 70 years old. To help prevent heart disease, older adults should consume more omega-3 fatty acids and monounsaturated fats such as olive oil. High blood pressure increases with age, and thus avoiding a high-salt diet becomes more important. Diet, exercise and weight loss are important for helping to prevent and manage type 2 diabetes. These same nutrition and lifestyle choices also contribute to preventing cancers of various types such as colon cancer, esophageal cancer, breast cancer and others. Diet can also help to decrease and prevent joint problems associated with osteoarthritis. Specifically, a diet high in omega-6 fatty acids can increase inflammation of the joints and thus should be consumed in limited quantities. Foods that are fried or prepared with corn or soybean oil may be high in omega-6 fatty acids. Finally, as we age, our memory can be impaired. Studies have revealed that a nutrient-dense diet such as the Mediterranean diet can help to prevent your chances of developing dementia. Altogether, it would appear that the components of a healthy diet that we have discussed throughout this book are all the more important as we age. ■

# Factors Affecting Nutrient Use

As we age, our physiological functions change. Often our gastrointestinal system and other vital organs are less efficient in performing the jobs required. This circumstance has a significant impact on our ability to use nutrients. What are some of these changes?

- Decreased digestive secretions and inability to break down foods
- Lower gastric motility, leading to constipation and swallowing disorders
- Deterioration in kidney function
- Nutrient malabsorption due to degenerative changes of the intestinal mucosa
- Decreased output of hormones such as insulin, thyroxin, and estrogen

**Want to know more?**
To learn more about factors affecting nutrient use in older adults, go to the text website at http://webcom8.grtxle.com/nutrition and click on the Chapters button. Select Chapter 17.

# Nutrient Requirements of Older Adults

Older adult's especially need a nutrient-dense diet. This means that they should consume foods high in vitamins, minerals, and high-quality protein, but with limited calories. Meats, vegetables, fruits, milk, eggs, and even cheese are good examples of nutrient-dense foods. At the same time, sweets and fats need to be restricted.

Energy recommendations decrease for men and women over age 50. The recommended energy intake for both sexes is 2,000–2,200 kcal per day. This is lower than the recommendations for adult men and women who are younger than 50. Some experts suggest a range of 1,600–1,800 kcal per day, especially for those with sedentary behavior. Further reductions are recommended for those older than age 75 because people in this age group normally engage in less physical activity and have less lean body mass.

The needed high-quality protein should be obtained from lean meats, fish, poultry, low-fat or skim milk, and legumes. Here again, older adults should select protein foods with little fat and less refined or simple sugars, because their caloric needs are decreased. If the older adult is underweight or malnourished, then snacking between meals or the use of nutritional liquid supplements may be necessary to meet the body's needs.

Proper water intake is another nutrition issue about which older adults should be aware. As we age, we do not recognize thirst as easily or quickly as we do when we were younger, and as a result dehydration is frequently a problem. In some cases, those who have lost some bladder control may be reluctant to consume liquids, thereby worsening the risk for dehydration. Water is also important to help older adults better tolerate fevers. Older adults should consume at least 6 c. of fluids each day in order to stay properly hydrated.

Inadequate intake of certain other nutrients is common among older adults. Specifically, many older adults fail to consume adequate quantities of vitamin D, folate, vitamin $B_6$ and $B_{12}$, calcium, zinc, magnesium, and iron. In order to address this issue, they must exercise extra care to select foods that provide these nutrients. Calcium requirements increase from 1,000 mg per day to 1,200 mg per day for women after age 50. For both men and women greater than 70 years of age the DRI is 1,200 mg per day. In order to minimize or reduce the rate of bone loss, especially among postmenopausal women, daily requirements of calcium and vitamin D need to be met. The DRI for vitamin D increases from 15 mcg per day to 20 mcg per day for both men and women greater than 70 years of age. Inadequate levels of vitamin $B_6$ are of concern in older adults because of the body's inability to maintain sufficient stores as we age. And because older adults have difficulty absorbing vitamin $B_{12}$, they need to consciously increase their intake.

## ■ You Decide

*Should older adults use vitamin and mineral supplements?*
In order to maintain a healthy weight, older people need to make sure they consume a diet that is nutrient dense, meaning that it provides adequate vitamins and minerals without supplying excess calories. However, what about the use of supplements to get your vitamins and minerals? As we become older, many will turn to supplements to obtain the needed vitamins and minerals. In fact, older adults tend to be big users of supplements of various types. Is there a chance that older adults who supplement may get too much of a good thing? The answer could be "yes." A study has suggested that some who supplement may exceed the upper tolerable limit for the DRIs for calcium, vitamin C, and magnesium. On the other hand, this is not the case for potassium, where those who were users and non-users of supplements continued to have diets low in potassium. (Remember that fruits are good sources of potassium.) Another study suggested that older adults who supplemented exceeded the Upper Tolerable Limit for vitamin $B_3$, folic acid, and vitamin A. Consistent with the new USDA dietary guidelines, the use of supplements may not be the best solution to obtain these micronutrients as we age. Consuming nutrient-dense foods may be the best advice for middle aged and older adults. What do you think of older adults using supplements? ■

## ■ To Supplement or Not

*Are fiber supplements needed to prevent constipation?*
It has long been recognized that the higher rate of constipation that is common in many Western societies is linked to low fiber intake. Constipation tends to occur more frequently in older adults. Studies show that older adults average around 14 g of fiber intake per day. Many nutritionists suggest that the targeted level of consumption should be placed much higher, at 25–30 g of fiber per day.

Do older people need to use fiber supplements to prevent constipation? The answer is no. Most nutritionists strongly recommend that we obtain our required fiber intake from food. Here again, eating fruits, vegetables, legumes, and whole-grain cereals and breads is recommended as the best way to accomplish this. You can also add wheat germ to yogurt or hot cereal, or even to the batter when you make pancakes and waffles. You can obtain sufficient fiber from your diet if you choose foods carefully. However, be mindful of the need for adequate fluid intake, which is a common problem in this age group. If fiber is added to the diet without adequate fluid intake, intestinal blockages can occur.

Is there any harm in the older adult consuming a fiber supplement? Some fiber supplements sold in a capsule or pill form do not appear to dissolve when placed in water. How they behave in the GI tract is not always clear. Moreover, taking fiber supplements on a regular basis may lead to mineral imbalance, because fiber can bind up certain minerals and make them unavailable for absorption. This is a problem in cases in which the intake of iron and zinc may be marginal. Consuming fiber supplements on a regular basis can also lead to dependence on them for bowel movements. However, studies have suggested that adding fiber supplements to food tends to significantly increase the number of bowel movements per day in older adults. Getting fiber from foods also gives you other nutrients that you do not get from fiber supplements. Finally, a remedy from previous generations that can help is the consumption of prunes or dried plums. The bottom line has been and continues to be that it is best to get your fiber from food, but use of a fiber supplement is not unreasonable. ∎

### Before you go on ...

1. List at least five nutrition issues/diseases older adults may experience and explain their causes.
2. List the primary reasons for lower energy requirements in older adults.
3. Besides iron-deficiency anemia, what other nutrient factor can most likely cause anemia in older adults?
4. Discuss the pros and cons of older adults using a fiber supplement.

## Real People, Real Strategies

Natalie's youngest daughter, Jill, who lives in Tampa, came to visit her and noticed that she was skipping meals. She discussed this with her mother and realized that Natalie's appetite was not the primary issue, but rather loneliness. Jill is aware that depression and loneliness often occur together. She therefore suggested to her mother that she join a senior citizens' club, or at least begin going to the daily luncheons at the local center for seniors. She also obtained information regarding the local Meals on Wheels program for use by her mother on days when she is unable to go out. Jill also reviewed the medications and vitamin and mineral supplements Natalie was taking. She sent the list to Natalie's doctor for review and asked him for updated recommendations. In order to increase Natalie's motivation to resume cooking at home, she decided that she would try to visit her for dinner at least once a week, and during these visits she plans to take her for a walk. Finally, Jill contacted a friend of her mother's and asked that she take her to the neighborhood seniors' club the next time she went. On Natalie's first visit she found the companionship rewarding and the food better than she expected. Within a month she and her friend were going to the club at least three days a week. She made several new friends, her appetite improved, and her outlook on living alone is much more positive.

## Chapter Summary

- Throughout the stages of the life cycle, nutrient requirements change. Children and teenagers are growing rapidly and therefore need high levels of nutrients.
- Children adjust their food intake in accordance with their rate of growth. At the same time they are developing food preferences and go through "food jags" during which they may change their preferences.
- Iron-deficiency anemia and obesity are the top health concerns of children. However, other health issues such as lead toxicity, dental decay, food intolerance, and allergies are common, and steps can be taken to prevent them.
- Food preferences of children can be due to factors such as food temperature, textures, flavors, and serving sizes. A major factor in getting a child to accept new food is seeing the parents consume it.
- Compared to children, adolescents have both similar and different health concerns. Changes in hormonal secretions by sex result in large differences in body composition and nutrient requirements. Another major health concern for adolescents is the lack of parental supervision in food selection as the teen becomes more independent and eats away from home more frequently. Poor food habits such as skipping breakfast and not drinking milk become apparent.
- Older adults are less active, are not growing, and use nutrients less efficiently. This means they require less energy, but still need a balanced and adequate supply of other nutrients.
- Older adults have many nutrition concerns that are affected by sociological, psychological, and economic factors. Living alone,

depression, anxiety, long-standing food habits, and financial considerations may negatively affect their nutrition.

- Drug-nutrient interactions are common in older adults. The practice of polypharmacy can affect nutrient utilization, absorption, and excretion, and may negatively impact appetite. Polypharmacy can result in a malnourished older adult.

- Physical and physiological changes in older adults occur and must be taken into account in order to provide them with adequate nutrition. Difficulty in chewing, loss of neuromuscular coordination, impaired hearing and taste, and the physical discomfort generated by certain foods can all negatively affect their eating choices.

- Older adults should consume foods that are nutrient-dense and contain adequate levels of protein, vitamins, and minerals, while monitoring caloric intake so as to avoid obesity.

## Key Terms

**age-related macular degeneration** A condition that affects a specific region of the retina known as the macular region and is a cause of blindness in older adults. (p. 567)

**anaphylactic shock** (an-uh-fil-Ak-tik shok) A condition in which blood pressure is very low and breathing is shallow. If medical attention is not sought immediately, death can result. (p. 551)

**cataracts** (CAT-uh-raktz) Cloudiness of the lens of the eye that can lead to blindness. (p. 567)

**food allergy** A condition in which the body produces antibodies against particular food molecules and physical symptoms result. (p. 551)

**food intolerance** An adverse reaction to a food or a food additive without producing antibodies. (p. 551)

**osteoarthritis** (ahs-tee-oh-ar-THRY-tis) A type of arthritis that leads to the deterioration of cartilage and loss of lubrication of the joints. (p. 568)

**puberty** The period of sexual maturation that occurs until sexual reproduction is possible. (p. 556)

**rheumatoid arthritis** (ROO-muh-toyd ar-THRY-tis) A specific type of arthritis that occurs when the immune system attacks the bone joints, leading to inflammation. (p. 568)

**sarcopenia** (sar-ko-PEE-nee-uh) The loss of muscle mass, strength, and function in older adults. (p. 568)

**testosterone** (tes-TAHS-ter-own) The male sex hormone. (p. 557)

## Chapter Quiz

1. Anemia in older adults is most likely due to
   a. a lack of dietary iron.
   b. a lack of vitamin C.
   c. inability to absorb vitamin $B_{12}$.
   d. decreased muscle mass.

2. In children, the most accepted definition of overweight is
   a. 25 lbs. or more overweight for one's age.
   b. a BMI of greater than 25.

   c. having a BMI at or above the 95th percentile for age.
   d. having a BMI at or above the 85th percentile for height.

3. Among the following factors that may influence what a child will eat, what is the *most* significant?
   a. the serving size
   b. the food's appearance

c. the food's temperature

d. seeing a parent or family member eat the food item

4. Which of the following individuals probably needs the most dietary iron?

a. a 2-year-old toddler

b. a teenage girl

c. an 8-year-old boy who is physically active

d. an older adult woman

5. A food allergy differs from a food intolerance in that a food allergy

a. can occur only in young children.

b. always results in difficult breathing.

c. can be medically treated.

d. involves the production of antibodies.

6. In older adults, which of the following factors is *least* likely to affect food selection?

a. loss of neuromuscular coordination

b. difficulty in reading food labels

c. type of cooking and food storage facilities

d. osteoporosis

7. On a per-weight basis, the amount of protein needed daily as age progresses from infancy to adulthood

a. stays the same.

b. decreases.

c. increases.

d. is based on iron requirements.

8. Which percentage is closest to the proportion of adolescents in the United States who are overweight and/or obese today?

a. 4–5 percent

b. 10 percent

c. 15–18 percent

d. 30 percent

9. A health condition in older adults that may be linked to an inadequate intake of carotenoids from plants is

a. cataracts.

b. rheumatoid arthritis.

c. age-related macular degeneration.

d. sarcopenia.

10. Of the following age groups, which one needs the most nutrient-dense diet?

a. toddlers age 2–3

b. children age 5–8

c. a teenage male football player

d. a retired women over age 70.

Chapter Quiz Answer Key:
1. c; 2. c; 3. d; 4. b; 5. d; 6. d; 7. b; 8. c; 9. c; 10. d

# Glossary

**absorption:** The movement of the smaller products of digestion across the lining of the intestinal tract, into our bodies, and ultimately into our cells.

**Acceptable Macronutrient Distribution Range (AMDR):** A recommended range of requirements for carbohydrates, fats, and proteins based on the total daily calorie needs and balance of nutrients that are associated with a decreased risk of chronic disease.

**acetaldehyde (a-she-tal-de-hide):** A toxic compound resulting from the conversion of ethanol in the liver.

**acetic acid:** The converted form of ethanol; it is nontoxic and can be metabolized by the body for energy or used to make fat.

**acetyl CoA:** A molecule produced in aero-bic metabolism that is part of the first steps of the Krebs cycle, produced when fat, car-bohydrate, or protein is broken down.

**acid group:** One of four chemical groups that make up an amino acid.

**acid-base balance:** The mechanisms the body uses to keep its fluids close to neutral pH (that is, neither basic nor acidic) so that the body can function normally.

**acidosis:** A buildup of acids in body fluids such as blood.

**adenosine triphosphate (ATP) (uh-DEN-oh-zeen try-FOSS-fate):** A high-energy molecule that can be broken down to a usable form of energy.

**Adequate Intake (AI):** The value assigned to a nutrient if some scientific evidence is available, but not quite enough to establish a recommendation with certainty.

**adjustable gastric band procedure:** Performed laproscopically. Most of the stomach is removed and a vertical sleeve or tube is fashioned from the remaining stomach. Because the stomach is so much smaller, patients are forced to eat less.

**aerobic:** Requiring oxygen.

**aerobic metabolism (air-OH-bic meh-TAB-oh-lizm):** *Aerobic* means "with oxygen"; the term refers to all pathways of metabolism that use oxygen.

**age-predicted maximum heart rate:** The maximum heart rate you can achieve while exercising; it is calculated by subtracting your age from 220.

**age-related macular degeneration:** A condition that affects a specific region of the retina known as the macular region and is a cause of blindness in older adults.

**agribusiness:** Farming and related food processing operated as a large-scale industry.

**agua de panela:** A weaning food that is made from brown sugar water.

**albumin:** A protein that constitutes 60 percent of the body's *plasma* (the watery part of blood) proteins. Among albumin's many functions, it transports drugs and thyroid hormones and carries fatty acids from adipose tissue to the muscle cells for use as energy.

**alcohol:** A nonnutrient that has 7 kcal per gram.

**alcohol dehydrogenase:** A liver enzyme that converts ethanol to the toxic acetaldehyde.

**aldehyde dehydrogenase 2 (AL-de-hide dee-hi-DRAH-jen-ase):** A liver enzyme that converts toxic acetaldehyde to nontoxic acetic acid in the breakdown of ethanol.

**aldosterone:** Hormone produced by the adrenal glands above the kidneys. It induces the kidneys to retain more sodium and, consequently, more water.

**alkaline bicarbonate (bicarb):** A substance released from the pancreas into the small intestine to neutralize the acidic contents from the stomach.

**allium:** A vegetable family that includes onions, garlic, ginger, scallions, leeks, and chives.

**amenorrhea (ay-men-uh-REE-uh):** Loss of menstrual flow for at least three consecutive cycles.

**amine group:** One of the four groups that make up an amino acid; the group that contains nitrogen.

**amino acid pool:** Short-term storage of amino acids found in cellular fluids.

**amino acids:** The building blocks of protein. They contain nitrogen and link together to form proteins.

**anabolism (an-AB-oh-lizm):** Any metabolic reaction that builds molecules, such as protein synthesis needed for growth.

**anaerobic:** Without oxygen.

**anaerobic metabolism (AN-air-oh-bic meh-TAB-oh-lizm):** *Anaerobic* means "without oxygen"; the term refers to all pathways of metabolism that do not use oxygen.

**anaphylactic shock (an-uh-fil-Ak-tik shok):** A condition in which blood pressure is very low and breathing is shallow. If medical attention is not sought immediately, death can result.

**android (An-droyd):** A pattern of body fat distribution in which most body fat is carried in the abdomen; the "apple" shape.

**anemia (uh-NEE-mee-uh):** A condition characterized by below-normal levels of red blood cells, hemoglobin, or both.

**angina pectoris:** A type of heart disease with symptoms of pain in the chest, shoulder, or arms; it is typically caused by insufficient blood flow to the heart.

**anion (AN-eye-on):** A mineral that is negatively charged.

**anomalies:** Deviations from the norm.

**anorexia nervosa (an-uh-REX-ee-uh ner-VOH-sa):** An eating disorder characterized by refusal to maintain a healthy body weight, an intense fear of weight gain, distorted body image and loss of menstrual periods.

**antibodies:** The proteins the immune system produces as a defense against antigens.

**antidiuretic hormone:** Hormone released by the pituitary gland in the brain to signal the kidneys to retain water.

**antigens:** Any foreign substances that threaten a body's health.

**antioxidant nutrient:** A nutrient that fights against free radicals.

**appetite:** The psychological mechanisms that determine how much we eat.

**arginine (AR-jin-een):** A conditionally essential amino acid. Supplementation appears most beneficial for people who have heart disease, are recovering from trauma, or have a compromised immune function.

**ascorbic acid (uh-SCOR-bick AS-id):** Another name for vitamin C.

**aseptic packaging (ay-SEP-tic):** A method in which food is sterilized and then placed in previously sterilized containers, which are then sealed in a sterile environment; used for liquid foods such as concentrated milk and soups.

**aspartic acid or aspartate (uh-SPAR-tick AS-id; AS-par-tate):** A non-essential amino acid used to make urea, proteins, glycogen, and energy.

**atherosclerosis (ath-er-oh-skler-O-sis):** The process in which deposits of fatty substances, cholesterol, cellular waste products, calcium, and other substances (referred to as plaque) build up in the inner lining of an artery.

**autism:** A complex, pervasive developmental disorder that involves the functioning of the brain; it is a neurological disability and not simply a psychiatric disorder, even though typical characteristics include problems with social relationships and emotional communication, as well as stereotyped patterns of interests, activities, and behaviors.

**balance:** Incorporating foods from all food groups into your daily eating plan.

**basal metabolic rate (BMR):** The rate at which basal metabolism occurs; it is more precisely defined as

the REE measured after waking in the morning, at least twelve hours after the last meal.

**basal metabolism (BAY-zul meh-TAB-uh-lizm):** Body processes involving involuntary activities only, such as heartbeat, breathing, and chemical reactions.

**beriberi:** The result of thiamin deficiency.

**"best before":** A date that appears on food labels and refers to the relationship between the shelf life and the quality of the product.

**beta-carotene:** A precursor of vitamin A found in plants.

**beta-oxidation:** The pathway that breaks down fatty acids.

**bifidobacterium:** A common bacteriafound in probiotic products.

**bile:** A substance made in the liver; it is stored in the gallbladder and released into the small intestine to help with fat digestion.

**binge-eating disorder (BED):** An eating disorder characterized by recurrent episodes of binge eating that occur without regular compensatory or purging behaviors intended to prevent weight gain.

**binge-purging anorexia:** The *DSM-IV* diagnosis for individuals diagnosed with anorexia who combine periodic restrictive dieting with frequent binge-and-purge episodes.

**bioelectrical impedance analysis (BIA):** A method of measuring body composition based on the fact that lean tissue, with high water content, conducts electricity relatively well while fat tissue, with low water content, conducts electricity poorly. When a mild electric current is passed through the body, the body's impedance, or resistance to current, indirectly indicates the amount of lean tissue and the amount of fat.

**bipolar disorder:** A mental disorder characterized by episodes of mania and depression.

**bitot spots:** Small, grayish, foamy, and triangular deposits on the eye as a result of a vitamin A deficiency.

**black cohosh:** A member of the buttercup family that is also called black snakeroot, macrotys, bugbane,

bugwort, rattleroot, and rattleweed. It has a history of use for rheumatism (arthritis and muscle pain), but it has been used more recently to treat postmenopausal symptoms.

**blood alcohol concentration (BAC):** The percentage of alcohol present in the blood. It is used to measure the amount of intake and to predict correlations with physiological effects.

**body dissatisfaction:** A poor body image; being unhappy with one's body.

**body dysmorphic disorder (BDD) (bah-dee dis-MOR-fic dis-OR-der):** A psychological disorder in which an individual is preoccupied with the thought that some aspect of his or her appearance is unattractive, deformed, or "not right" in some way.

**body image:** A multifaceted psychological concept that refers to a person's perceptions, attitudes, and experiences about the appearance of his or her body.

**body mass index (BMI):** A height-weight relationship used to assess obesity; it equals (weight in kilograms)/(height in meters squared), or (weight in pounds × 704.5)/(height in inches squared).

**bolus:** The form that food is in before it is swallowed.

**borderline anorexia:** The partial syndromes of anorexia and bulimia; an unofficial term that describes individuals who are thin but may not appear malnourished or emaciated.

**boron:** A trace element found in foods such as avocados, peanut butter, peanuts, prune and grape juice, chocolate powder, wine, pecans, and raisin bran cereals.

**bottle-mouth syndrome:** Tooth decay in infants caused by bacteria-producing fluids (milk, fruit juice, etc.) that pool around the front teeth.

**branched-chain amino acids (BCAAs):** The essential amino acids—leucine, isoleucine, and valine—that are different from other amino acids because they can be used for energy directly in the muscle, without having to go to the liver to be broken down during exercise.

**bulimia nervosa (boo-LEE-mee-uh ner-VOH-sa):** An eating disorder characterized by recurrent episodes of abnormal food intake, loss of sense of control over that intake, persistent and prolonged weight compensation behaviors, and body image disturbance.

**cage-free:** Describes eggs from chickens that are uncaged inside barns or warehouses, but generally do not have access to the outdoors.

**calbindin:** A calcium-binding protein that increases calcium absorption.

**calorie:** A scientific unit of energy; the calories used to measure food energy are actually *kilocalories* (kcal). One kilocalorie, or food calorie, equals 1,000 calories.

**carbohydrate:** A category of macronutrients that includes energy-yielding nutrients such as starches and sugars, as well as non-energy-yielding nutrients such as fiber.

**carbohydrate loading:** A method of manipulating training and diet for several days before an event in order to maximize glycogen stores.

**carboxyl group:** It is represented by COOH and allows fatty acids to mix with water.

**cardiomyopathy:** Weakening of the heart muscle.

**cardiovascular diseases:** The collective term for myocardial infarct, heart attack, and stroke.

**carnitine (CAR-nih-teen):** The substance that transports long-chain fatty acids into the mitochondria for metabolism. Carnitine supplementation is said to enhance fat burning, but it appears to be ineffective.

**carotenoids (kuh-ROT-en-oyds):** The recognizable form of coloring pigment in plants such as carrots and sweet potatoes. The carotenoid family includes molecules such as alpha-, beta-, and gamma-carotene; lutein; zeaxanthin; lycopene; cryptoxanthin; vioaxanthin; and bixin. As many as 450 different carotenoids may exist.

**carpal tunnel syndrome:** A compression or swelling of the nerves that run from the forearm to the hand.

**catabolism:** Any metabolic reaction that breaks down molecules, such as glycolysis, which breaks down glucose.

**cataracts (CAT-uh-raktz):** Cloudiness of the lens of the eye that can lead to blindness.

**catechin (KA-teh-kin):** A polyphenol found in grapes and other plants that protects against free radical damage.

**cation (CAT-eye-on):** A mineral that is positively charged.

**cell differentiation:** The process by which specialized cells develop that are capable of performing specific functions.

**chemical energy:** Energy contained in a molecule that has not yet been released; it is also called *potential energy*.

**chitosan:** A fiberlike compound derived from the shells of crustaceans such as shrimp and crab.

**cholecalciferol:** Another term for vitamin D.

**chromium:** A trace mineral that is widely distributed in the food supply, though most foods provide only small amounts (less than 2 micrograms per serving). Meat and whole-grain products, as well as some fruits, vegetables, and spices, are relatively good sources.

**chronic diseases:** Diseases of long continuance, or that progress slowly, in distinction from acute diseases, which speedily terminate

**chylomicrons (kye-loh-MY-kronz):** Lipoproteins formed in the cells lining the small intestine following absorption of fats. They are made in the small intestinal cells and transport dietary lipids to the liver.

**chyme:** The substance that results after the stomach mixes and liquefies food.

**ciquatoxin poisoning:** An illness caused by eating certain types of contaminated tropical reef fish.

**cirrhosis (sir-ROH-sis):** A disease resulting in the hardening and scarring of the liver.

*cis:* The common arrangement of hydrogen bonded to a carbon.

***Clostridium botulinum:*** A bacterium found in honey that can lead to botulism.

**coenzyme Q$_{10}$ (ubiquinone):** A fat-soluble vitamin-like substance made in the body. It is an antioxidant and a coenzyme for several of the key enzymatic steps in the production of energy within the cell.

**coenzymes:** Molecules that combine with an enzyme to increase its activity.

**cofactors:** Substances that act with or aid other factors in causing disease.

**colic:** A condition with unknown causes that is characterized by extended crying in babies that are otherwise healthy and well nourished.

**collagen (COLL-uh-jen):** A protein that forms connective tissues such as tendons, bone, teeth, and skin.

**colostrum (co-LOSS-trum):** The breast milk produced by mothers in the first few days following birth. It has a thinner consistency than subsequent breast milk, has a slightly yellowish color, and is rich in antibodies.

**complementary foods:** Solids and liquid foods that join breast-feeding in the normal progression toward adult eating patterns.

**complementary proteins:** Two or more foods whose amino acid content, when combined, provides all of the essential amino acids.

**complete protein:** A protein that provides all of the essential amino acids in the amount that the body needs and is easy to digest and absorb. Also called a *high-quality protein*.

**conditionally essential amino acids:** Essential amino acids that under certain circumstances cannot be made in sufficient quantity by the body and therefore must be consumed in the diet.

**control group:** The participants in an experiment or research study who do not receive the treatment or substance being studied. A control group provides an "untreated" basis of comparison with the *experimental group*.

**cornea:** The transparent outer layer of the eye that covers the iris and pupil.

**cortisol:** An example of a stress hormone and sterol.

**creatine (KREE-uh-teen):** Part of creatine phosphate, the key component of the immediate energy system used primarily during sporting events lasting thirty seconds or less. It is made in the body and can be consumed in the diet, mostly from meat and fish.

**cretinism (CREE-tin-izm):** The mental and physical retardation of children whose mothers were iodine deficient during pregnancy.

**critical control points (CCPs):** Points in the food production process where the potential hazards could occur and can be prevented and/or controlled.

**Crohn's disease:** Chronic ileitis that typically involves the distal portion of the ileum; often spreads to the colon; and is characterized by diarrhea, cramping, and loss of appetite and weight with local abscesses and scarring.

**cross-contamination:** The transfer of a substance that can cause illness from one food to another, usually on a utensil or a surface such as a cutting board or plate.

**Daily Values:** The nutrient standards used on food labels; they are based on a 2,000-calorie diet.

**danger zone:** The temperature range (40° F to 140° F) at which microbial growth is most likely to occur.

**DASH (Dietary Approaches to Stop Hypertension):** A tool to help individuals lower sodium intake and implement the *Dietary Guidelines*.

**deamination:** The removal of the nitrogen group during the breakdown of amino acids.

**dehydration:** Excessive water loss in the body.

**dehydroepiandrosterone (DHEA) (dee-hy-droh-ep-ee-ann-DRAHS-ter-own):** A steroid hormone that is synthesized and secreted by the adrenal glands.

**denaturation (dee-nay-chur-AY-shun):** A process in which a protein's structure and function are changed by heat, acid, enzymes, agitation, or alcohol.

**depression:** A mental state characterized by a pessimistic sense of inadequacy and a despondent lack of activity.

**diabetes mellitus:** The inability of the body to regulate blood glucose levels within normal limits.

*Diagnostic and Statistical Manual, Fourth Edition (DSM-IV):* A comprehensive manual that lists the symptoms and criteria of the various psychological disorders.

**diastolic blood pressure:** When the heart relaxes and blood pressure falls; the lowest blood pressure reading during cardiac relaxation.

**Dietary Approaches to Stop Hypertension (DASH):** A diet advocated to reduce the incidence of high blood pressure.

**dietary fiber:** A carbohydrate composed of repeating units of glucose and other monosaccharides that cannot be digested by human enzymes and thus cannot be absorbed and used by the body.

**dietary folate equivalent:** A unit of measure used to represent the conversion of folic acid to folate.

*Dietary Guidelines for Americans:* A summary of science-based advice to promote health through diet and physical activity and to reduce the risk for major chronic diseases in people over age 2.

**Dietary Reference Intakes (DRIs):** Guidelines designed for healthy people, established to replace the original RDAs in the United States and the Recommended Nutrient Intakes (RNIs) in Canada.

**dietary standards:** Recommended intakes for specific nutrients. They can be used to plan diets for individuals and groups.

**dietary supplement:** A product (other than tobacco) that is intended to supplement the diet and that contains one or more of the following dietary ingredients: a vitamin; a mineral; an herb or other botanical; an amino acid; a dietary substance used to supplement the diet by increasing the total daily intake; or a concentrate, metabolite, constituent, extract, or combination of these ingredients.

**Dietary Supplement Health and Education Act of 1994 (DSHEA):** A federal law that significantly changed the role the FDA plays in supplement regulation and further expanded the formal definition of "dietary supplement."

**diffusion:** The movement of electrolytes from an area of greater concentration to an area of lesser concentration.

**digestion:** The first step in the process of converting food to energy; it is a complex series of chemical reactions and interactions combined with muscular movements that break the food down into smaller compounds.

**discretionary calories:** The calories you can consume after you meet all your nutrient needs, without going over your total calorie target for the day.

**disordered eating:** The general term covering a range of eating disorders or behaviors that are not severe enough to be medically diagnosed as an eating disorder (such as anorexia nervosa).

**diuretic:** A compound that, when consumed, causes you to urinate more and can lead to dehydration.

**docosahexaenoic acid (DHA):** An important omega-3 fatty acid that is abundant in coldwater fish.

**double-blind study:** A study in which the participating subjects and the scientists conducting the experiment do not know who is receiving which treatment.

**dual-energy X-ray absorptiometry (DEXA) (Doo-ul EN-er-jee EKS-ray ab-ZORP-tee-om-eh-tree):** The most reliable technique in estimating body composition; it uses two X-ray energies to measure body fat, muscle, and bone mineral.

**duodenum (doo-oh-DEE-num):** The top part of the small intestine, extending about 25 cm from the pyloric sphincter.

**eating disorders not otherwise specified (EDNOS):** Eating disorders that encompass anorexic and bulimic behaviors but do not include all of the specific criteria.

**echinacea (ek-ih-NAYSH-uh):** A plant with tall stems, single pink or purple flowers, and a central cone that is usually purplish-brown in color. It is believed to reduce the symptoms and duration of a cold.

**eclampsia (ee-CLAMP-see-uh):** A manifestation of pre-eclampsia that can result in convulsions, puts the mother at risk for stroke, and can lead to maternal or fetal death.

**edema:** A condition in which fluid accumulates in the tissues of the body and results in swelling.

**eicosanoids (eye-koh-sah-noydz):** Metabolically active chemicals synthesized from fatty acids. These chemicals have powerful physiological effects, including relaxing blood vessels and promoting blood clotting.

**eicosapentaenoic acid (EPA):** An important omega-3 fatty acid abundant in coldwater fish.

**Elderly Nutrition Program:** A federal government program designed to improve the nutritional well-being of older adults, prevent medical problems, and help them stay in their community rather than in institutions.

**electrolytes (ee-LEK-tro-lyetz):** Minerals such as sodium, potassium, and chlorine that assume a charge when dissolved in water.

**electrons:** Negatively charged particles that are part of atoms; in metabolic pathways they are associated with the hydrogen atoms that are transferred in pathways used to break down and build energy.

**electron transport chain:** The primary site in the cell where ATP is made; it is used only for aerobic metabolism because oxygen is final acceptor of hydrogen in this chain.

**emerging pathogen:** Microorganisms previously not recognized as human pathogens, or those unexpectedly found in particular foods.

**empty calories:** Calories with little or no nutrient content.

**emulsification:** The act of combining two or more liquids that do not typically mix together well, such as oil and water; the function of bile in fat digestion.

**endocrine organ:** An organ that secretes hormones.

**endosperm:** The middle portion of a grain kernel, which is high in starch.

**enriched foods:** Foods that have had nutrients added back that were removed during processing. For example, enriched white rice has had some nutrients added back that were present before the outer brown husk was removed.

**enrichment:** The restoration of micronutrients that were originally present in the food but were lost during processing.

**ephedra (ef-ED-ruh):** An herbal stimulant used for respiratory illnesses such as asthma because it helps open the airways. It has also been marketed for weight loss and performance enhancement. Side effects include high blood pressure, heart irregularities, and nausea.

**epinephrine:** A hormone produced by the adrenal gland, also known as adrenalin, which is released by the body to raise blood glucose levels.

**epithelial:** The cells found in the skin and lungs as well as the lining of the gastrointestinal tract.

**ergogenic aids:** Any substances that can potentially enhance athletic performance.

**essential amino acids:** Amino acids that cannot be made in the body, so we must obtain them from the food we eat.

**essential body fat:** The amount of fat required for normal physiological functioning; it consists of the fat needed for the body's organs, central nervous system, muscles, and bone marrow.

**essential fatty acids:** Fatty acids that cannot be made by the body and can be provided only by the diet.

**essential hypertension:** High blood pressure that is due to an unknown cause.

**essential nutrient:** A compound that must be in the diet and is considered essential for life of the organism; the body cannot make it at all or produces insufficient amounts.

**Estimated Average Requirement (EAR):** The value assigned to a nutrient that would meet the needs of 50 percent of the people of a specific age or gender. It is used only by federal agencies for research and policy making.

**Estimated Energy Requirement (EER):** A general recommendation for energy needs.

**estrogen (ESS-tro-jen):** The predominate female sex hormone, which is also important for the development and formation of bone.

**Expanded Food and Nutrition Education Program (EFNEP):** A government program to help people of limited financial means enhance their food and nutrient intake.

**experimental group:** The participants in an experiment or research study who receive the treatment or substance being studied to determine whether it has an anticipated outcome.

**extracellular:** Outside a cell.

**extrusion reflex:** The tongue-thrusting reflex that exists at birth but is usually gone by six months of age.

**FAD:** A carrier for electrons through the electron transport chain that is made from riboflavin.

**fat:** An energy-yielding nutrient that is insoluble in water; it provides more than twice as much energy as carbohydrate or protein.

**fat-based:** Describes products made from lipids.

**fat-soluble vitamins:** Vitamins that are insoluble in water, can be stored in the body for long periods of time, and do not need to be consumed daily.

**Federal Trade Commission:** The federal agency that has the responsibility for monitoring the accuracy of the advertising and labeling of supplements.

**female athlete triad:** A serious health problem among female athletes that encompasses three interrelated health issues: disordered eating, amenorrhea, and osteoporosis.

**ferritin (FAIR-uh-tin):** A protein that binds iron for storage and is a good indicator of iron status.

**fetal alcohol syndrome (FAS):** A set of birth abnormalities in babies born to mothers who consume alcohol during pregnancy, characterized by abnormal facial features, abnormal arms and legs, and lower-than-normal intelligence.

**fibrin:** A protein that forms blood clots.

**fibrinogen:** A protein present in blood plasma; it converts to fibrin when blood clots.

**first in, first out (FIFO):** A practice followed by many restaurants and retail establishments in which older items are placed in front of newer items and therefore used first.

**fitness:** The ability to perform moderate-to-vigorous levels of physical activity without undue fatigue, and the capability of maintaining this capacity throughout life.

**flatus:** Intestinal gas.

**flavonoids:** A group of plant compounds that have potent antioxidant properties and give bright pigments to foods such as cranberries, blueberries, and strawberries.

**fluorosis (flor-OH-sis):** Fluoride toxicity that causes discoloration and mottling of the teeth.

**folic acid:** The synthetic form of folate that is used in dietary supplements and enriched foods.

**food allergy:** A condition in which the body produces antibodies against particular food molecules and physical symptoms result.

**food intolerance:** An adverse reaction to a food or a food additive without producing antibodies.

**food irradiation (food ir-ray-dee-AY-shun):** Exposure of food to low-level radiation to prolong shelf life and eliminate pathogens.

**food jags:** A period of time when children prefer only one type of food.

**food-borne illness:** Diseases, usually either infectious or toxic in nature, caused by agents that enter the body through the ingestion of food.

**fortification:** The addition of vitamins and minerals to foods that are not naturally present in those foods.

**fortified foods:** Foods with nutrients added to them that were not originally present. An example is orange juice fortified with calcium.

**free radicals:** Unstable compounds with an unpaired electron that attack other molecules and break them down.

**free-range:** There are no USDA standards in "free-range" egg production. Typically, free-range egg-laying hens are uncaged inside barns or warehouses and have some degree of outdoor access. They can engage in many natural behaviors such as nesting and foraging. However, there is no information on stocking density, the frequency or duration of outdoor access, or the quality of the land accessible to the birds.

**free-roaming:** Also known as "free-range," the USDA has defined this claim for some poultry products, but there are no standards in "free-roaming" egg production. This essentially means the hens are cage-free.

**French paradox:** The low incidence of heart disease among the French despite their consumption of a diet relatively high in fat and cholesterol.

**fructose:** A monosaccharide that has a simple ring structure. It is the sugar found abundantly in fruit, honey, and also some vegetables such as beets, sweet potatoes, parsnips, and onions. It is the sweetest sugar.

**functional food:** Foods that when added or present in a diet provide a health benefit beyond normal nutrition.

**galactose:** A monosaccharide that is consumed as a part of the disaccharide lactose found in milk; it is a basic component of other, more complex carbohydrates.

**gallbladder:** An accessory organ for digestion that releases bile.

**gastric emptying:** Movement of food from the stomach to the small intestine.

**gastrointestinal (GI) tract:** A series of organs with many complex outer layers of muscles and an inner mucosal layer of glands and absorptive cells.

**gestational diabetes (jes-TAY-shun-ul die-uh-BEE-tees):** Diabetes that occurs in some women during pregnancy.

**ginkgo biloba (GINK-go bye-LOBE-uh):** An extract of the leaves of the maidenhair tree that has long been used in China to treat many diseases and conditions. Ginkgo is thought to increase blood flow by dilating blood vessels and decreasing blood thickness, as well as modifying neurotransmitter systems and decreasing oxygen free radicals.

**ginseng:** The root of the Asian ginseng plant; it is said to improve overall health and well-being.

**glucagon:** A hormone produced by the pancreas and released when blood sugar levels fall to raise blood glucose levels in the body.

**gluconeogenesis (gloo-coh-nee-oh-JEN-eh-sis):** Synthesis of new glucose from noncarbohydrate sources.

**glucosamine chondroitin (gloo-KOSE-uh-meen kon-DROIT-in):** Glucosamine is thought to stimulate the production and repair of cartilage; chondroitin is a cartilage component that is thought to promote water retention and elasticity and to inhibit the enzymes that break down cartilage. The combination is marketed to help with symptoms of osteoarthritis.

**glucose:** The monosaccharide that circulates in the blood and is often referred to as *blood sugar*. It is the main source of energy for the body.

**glutamine (GLOO-tuh-meen):** A nonessential amino acid that is abundant in the body. Supplementation may enhance immune system function and recovery after exhaustive exercise, surgery, or trauma.

**glutathione peroxidase:** An antioxidant enzyme that contains selenium.

**glycemic index:** A measure of how fast blood glucose increases when a person ingests a particular food, compared to ingestion of glucose.

**glycemic load:** A mathematical tool used to account for the total carbohydrate contained in a food.

**glycerol:** An organic compound that is part of triacylglycerols (triglycerides or fats) and phospholipids. It is also used as a sweetener in syrups, liquors, and some foods. Glycerol combined with water intake has been suggested to help prevent dehydration in endurance athletes who exercise in hot, humid environments.

**glycogen:** The storage form of starch found in the liver and muscle of animals.

**glycolysis (gly-COLL-ih-sis):** The metabolic process that breaks down glucose to a usable form of energy.

**goiter:** An enlarged thyroid gland due to an iodine deficiency.

**gram:** A metric unit of weight equal to one thousandth of a kilogram.

**gynoid (GUY-noyd):** A pattern of body fat distribution in which most body fat is carried on the hips and thighs; the "pear" shape.

**hard water:** Water that contains elevated levels of calcium and magnesium.

**Hazard Analysis Critical Control Point (HACCP) system:** Guidelines established to promote food safety at every step of food production; the farm, storage, retail stores, restaurants and consumers. It provides a detailed manual of educational materials and training workshops for organizations and individuals to follow.

**health claims:** Statements made about a product that link it or some of its ingredients to a reduced risk of disease, such as a claim that consuming fiber reduces your risk of heart disease.

**Healthy People 2020:** A list of health objectives for the nation to achieve by 2020. It is designed to identify the most significant preventable threats to health and to establish national goals to reduce these threats.

**heart attack:** Episodes of chest pains under the left arm caused by a completely blocked artery.

**heartburn:** A burning sensation that occurs in the chest when substances from the stomach leak back into the esophagus..

***helicobacter pylori* or *H. pylori* (HEL-ih-coh-bak-ter-pie-LOR-ee):** A bacterium that can invade the stomach lining and cause peptic ulcers.

**hemachromatosis:** A genetic disorder that causes iron toxicity.

**hematocrit:** The percentage of blood that is composed of red blood cells.

**heme iron (HEEM EYE-rn):** An organic form of iron that is still part of the complex ring structure that makes up hemoglobin.

**hemoglobin (HEE-moh-gloh-bin):** A protein contained in the red blood cells that carries oxygen throughout the body.

**hemophilia:** A disease that results in excessive bleeding and bruising from minor injuries.

**hepatitis:** Inflammation of the liver.

**herbs and botanicals:** Supplements that contain extracts or active ingredients from the roots, berries, seeds, stems, leaves, buds, or flowers of plants.

**high intensity:** A level of activity in which you exceed 70 percent of your age-predicted maximum heart rate. To reach this level requires intense exercise for twenty minutes or longer.

**high-density lipoproteins (HDLs):** Lipoproteins that are made mostly in the liver, but in the small intestine as well; they decrease heart disease risk by removing excess cholesterol from cells and blood vessels and returning it to the liver for breakdown and elimination.

**high-fructose corn syrup:** A carbohydrate derived from cornstarch and converted to fructose using enzymes through food processing. In essence, cornstarch is made into a syrup that is about half fructose and half glucose.

**high-quality protein:** A protein that provides all of the essential amino acids in the amount that the body needs and is easy to digest and absorb. Also called a *complete protein*.

**highly susceptible population:** People who are more likely than other people in the general population to develop food-borne illness.

**"hitting the wall" or "bonking":** Slang terms used by endurance athletes to describe a condition in which glycogen stores in the liver and muscles are depleted, resulting in a major performance drop.

**HMB (beta-hydroxy beta-methyl-butyrate):** A product of the breakdown of the essential amino acid leucine. It is synthesized naturally in humans and is also available in some foods (such as citrus fruits and catfish). It is marketed to prevent muscle breakdown associated with resistance training, to enhance strength, and to decrease body fat.

**homocysteine:** An amino acid that is found in human cells and blood.

**hunger:** The physiological mechanisms that determine how much and when we eat.

**hydrochloric acid (HCl):** A substance secreted in the stomach to denature protein.

**hydrogenation:** A process that adds hydrogen bonds to unsaturated fatty acids, thus turning a liquid into a solid.

**hydrophilic:** Describes the part of the carbon chain that allows fatty acids to mix with water.

**hydrophobic:** Describes the part of the carbon chain that does not like to be mixed with water.

**hydroxyapatite (hi-DROX-ee-ap-uh-tite):** The large and complex crystal in bone that contains calcium and gives bone its strength.

**hyperglycemia:** An elevated blood glucose level.

**hypertension:** High blood pressure.

**hyperthermia:** Increased body temperature.

**hypervitaminosis:** Vitamin toxicity, with symptoms such as headache, abdominal pain, skin rashes, liver damage, diarrhea, nausea, hair loss, and joint pain.

**hyponatremia (high-poh-na-TREE-mee-uh):** Low blood sodium.

**hypokalemia:** Low potassium levels due to excessive sweating with inadequate electrolyte replacement.

**ileum (ILL-ee-um):** The bottom part of the small intestine.

**immediate energy system:** Also called the ATP-PC system; the body uses this system in the first ten seconds or so of any exercise. We also rely on it for very short-duration maximal efforts, such as power lifting, kicking a soccer ball, or short sprints.

**incomplete proteins:** Foods that do not contain all of the essential amino acids in the amount needed by the body. They include beans, legumes, grains, vegetables.

**inorganic:** Describes a substance that does not contain carbon.

**insensible water loss:** Water lost through daily sweating, exhalation of air, and other mechanisms.

**insoluble fiber:** A type of fiber that is mainly composed of plant cell walls. It cannot be dissolved in water and resists human digestive enzymes. It is composed of cellulose, hemicellulose, and lignin.

**insulin:** A hormone released from the pancreas that allows glucose to enter cells to be used for energy.

**insulin-dependent diabetes mellitus:** A disease that occurs when the pancreas is unable to produce insulin; it was formerly known as juvenile-onset diabetes mellitus because of its frequent diagnosis in children and adolescents.

**insulin resistance:** A condition in which an individual may be able to produce insulin but the cells do not respond to it; often observed in people with Type 2 diabetes.

**International Units (IU):** A standard measurement that was once used for several vitamins.

**interstitial fluid:** The water between tissue cells.

**intracellular:** Inside a cell.

**intrinsic factor:** A protein produced by stomach cells that binds to vitamin $B_{12}$ and protects it from degradation until it can be absorbed.

**ischemia (iss-KEE-mee-ah):** A restriction in blood supply to the heart, generally due to factors in the blood vessels with resultant damage or dysfunction of tissue.

**isoflavonoids:** A group of compounds found in plants that have been shown to have health benefits.

**jaundice:** A condition in which the liver is inflamed and the skin may appear yellow.

**jejunum (jeh-JOO-num):** The middle part of the small intestine.

**keratin:** A type of protein that is hard and tough, similar to fingernails.

**ketone bodies:** Acidic fat derivatives that arise from the incomplete breakdown of fat.

**ketosis:** A condition that occurs due to high levels of ketone bodies caused by insufficient carbohydrate intake or from incomplete fat breakdown; it can be found in people who have diabetes or are on a low-carbohydrate diet and leads to damage of the acid-base balance of blood, altered kidney function, and dehydration.

**Krebs cycle or tricarboxylic acid (TCA) cycle:** A complex series of reactions following glycolysis that converts carbohydrates, fats, and proteins into ATP.

**kwashiorkor (kwah-she-OR-kor):** A form of protein energy malnutrition (PEM) characterized by a swollen

appearance, especially in the abdomen, caused by a lack of protein.

**lactase:** An enzyme that breaks down the disaccharide lactose found in milk.

**lactic acid:** A three-carbon molecule formed from pyruvate in glycolysis during anaerobic exercise; also called *lactate*.

**lactobacillus:** A bacterium commonly found in probiotic products.

**lacto-vegetarians:** People who consume milk and dairy products, such as cheese and yogurt, but avoid eggs, seafood, and meat.

**lacto-ovo vegetarians:** People who consume eggs and dairy products, but no meat or seafood.

**lactose:** A disaccharide, commonly known as milk sugar, that is composed of glucose and galactose.

**lactose intolerance:** A congenital disorder consisting of an inability to digest milk and milk products; absence or deficiency of lactase results in an inability to hydrolyze lactose.

**lecithin:** An emulsifier commonly found in egg yolks.

**leptin:** A hormone produced by fat cells that plays a role in body weight regulation.

**lignin:** The component of dietary fiber that is not a carbohydrate.

**limiting amino acid:** An essential amino acid that is not present in sufficient amounts through dietary protein.

**linoleic acid:** An omega-6 essential fatty acid.

**linolenic acid:** An omega-3 essential fatty acid.

**lipase:** An enzyme that breaks down fats.

**lipogenesis:** The pathway that produces fats.

**lipoproteins:** Molecules in the blood that help transport cholesterol and fatty acids to tissues.

**low birthweight:** A birth weight of less than 5.5 lb.

**low intensity:** A level of activity in which you stay below 55 percent of your age-predicted maximum heart rate.

**low-density lipoproteins (LDLs):** Remnants of the breakdown of VLDLs. They deliver cholesterol to other tissues, including blood vessels.

**lower esophageal sphincter:** After food travels down the esophagus, it passes through this muscle into the stomach.

**lutein:** A carotenoid that may protect the eye.

**lymph system:** The tissues and organs, including the bone marrow, spleen, thymus, and lymph nodes, that produce and store cells that fight infection and disease. The channels that carry lymph are also part of this system.

**macrobiotic vegetarians:** People who consume mostly whole grains, especially brown rice, in their diets along with vegetables, soy, legumes, fruits, and sometimes whitefish.

**macrocytic anemia:** Anemia characterized by enlarged, immature red blood cells that are fewer in number than normal cells.

**macromineral:** A mineral required by the body in excess of 100 mg per day; also called a *major element*.

**macronutrients:** Nutrients needed in large amounts, such as carbohydrates, proteins, fats, and water.

**macula:** The center portion of the retina that makes basic visual acuity possible.

**macular degenerative disease:** A group of eye disorders characterized by the breakdown of the macula, the center portion of the retina that makes basic visual acuity possible.

**malnutrition:** Lack of proper nutrition resulting from deficient or excessive food or nutrient intake.

**maltase:** An enzyme that breaks down the disaccharide maltose.

**maltose:** A disaccharide that is composed of two glucose units.

**marasmus (ma-RAZZ-muss):** A form of protein energy malnutrition (PEM) characterized by emaciation, or a skeletal appearance due to inadequate intake of protein and calories.

**Meals on Wheels:** A program that delivers nutritious meals to older people's homes.

**meat, fish, and poultry factor (MFP):** A factor in these foods that enhances the absorption of elemental iron.

**meconium:** Feces that accumulates during fetal development.

**megaloblasts (MEG-uh-low-blasts):** Immature, enlarged red blood cells.

**menopause:** A female life stage during which, prompted by hormonal changes, ovulation and menstruation cease.

**metabolic pathways:** A series of chemical steps or reactions that either break down or build compounds in the body.

**metabolic rate:** The number of calories burned per body weight each day.

**metabolic water:** Water that is produced during the breakdown of carbohydrate, fats, and protein.

**metabolism (mu-TAE-bu-lizm):** The biochemical activity that occurs in cells, releasing energy from nutrients or using energy to create other substances such as proteins.

**meth mouth:** The poor oral health resulting from methamphetamine use.

**methionine:** An essential amino acid.

**methyl group:** The opposite end of a fatty acid chain; it is represented as CH3 and is hydrophobic.

**micromineral:** A mineral required by the body in an amount less than 100 mg per day.

**micronutrients:** Nutrients needed in small amounts, such as vitamins and numerals.

**microvilli (MIKE-roh-vil-ee):** Tiny hairlike projections extending from the villi into the inside of the small intestine to assist absorption and secrete digestive enzymes.

**mitochondria (my-toh-KON-dree-uh):** The part of the cell where most of the energy-producing pathways occur.

**moderate intensity:** A level of activity that increases your heart rate to 55–70 percent of your age-predicted maximum heart rate.

**moderation:** Avoiding overconsumption of any one food or food group.

**monosaccharides:** Simple sugars.

**monounsaturated fatty acid:** A fatty acid that contains only one double bond.

**multidisciplinary treatment:** Approach that incorporates health professionals from many different areas and therefore uses a variety of behavioral, psychological, and physical treatment philosophies; such teams can include physicians, psychiatrists, psychologists, registered dietitians, nurses, physical therapists, movement therapists, art therapists and exercise physiologists.

**muscle dysmorphia (MUSS-el dis-MOR-fee-uh):** A form of body dysmorphic disorder characterized by a preoccupation with the idea that one is thin when he is actually very muscular.

**myelin sheath (My-uh-lin):** An insulating sheath for nerve fibers that enhances conduction.

**myocardial infarct:** A heart attack; the complete blockage of an artery.

**MyPyramid:** An interactive website and program that can be used to translate the concepts of balance, moderation, and variety, along with the information from the *Dietary Guidelines* and the Dietary Reference Intakes, into a usable diet plan.

**NAD:** A carrier for electrons through the electron transport chain; derived from niacin.

**negative nitrogen balance:** A situation in which the body is breaking down more protein than it is producing, such as during a time of illness or injury.

**nephrons:** Microscopic structures in the kidneys that control the composition of urine and blood.

**neural tube defect:** The result of a dietary folate deficiency during pregnancy that affects the neural tube, which develops into the brain and spinal cord within the first twenty-eight days after conception.

**neurons:** Excitable cells found in nerves.

**night-eating syndrome (NES):** An eating disorder associated with loss of appetite in the morning, overeating in the evening, and sleep problems.

**nitrates and nitrites:** Salts used in the curing and smoking process that

have been used for centuries to preserve meats.

**nitrogen:** A chemical element found in protein.

**nitrogen balance techniques:** A technique based on nitrogen excretion during amino acid breakdown; it helps measure nitrogen in the protein consumed and nitrogen excreted in the urine, feces, skin, hair, and other body fluids.

**nonessential amino acids:** Amino acids that can be made in the body by transferring the amine group, or nitrogen, from an essential amino acid to another compound containing a carbon, an acid group, a hydrogen, and an R group.

**non-essential nutrient:** A compound that the body can make in sufficient amounts.

**nonheme iron:** The elemental form of iron that is not a part of hemoglobin.

**non-insulin-dependent diabetes mellitus:** Type 2 or adult-onset diabetes.

**nonnutritive sweeteners:** Products that are sometimes referred to as alternative sweeteners or sugar substitutes. They are synthetic and do not provide food energy.

**nonpurging bulimia:** The *DSM-IV* diagnosis for individuals with bulimia who have used compensatory behaviors such as fasting or excessive exercise, but have not regularly engaged in self-induced vomiting or the misuse of laxatives, diuretics, or enemas.

**nonstarch polysaccharide:** Dietary fiber.

**nutrient:** A substance that the body needs for energy, growth, and development.

**nutrigenomics:** An integrated science that attempts to understand a genetic and molecular connection for how dietary compounds alter the expression and/or structure of an individual's genetic makeup, thus affecting their health and risk of disease.

**Nutrition Facts label:** Part of the required information on a food label that provides the nutritional content of the product.

**nutritive sweeteners:** Sweeteners that can be digested and yield calories.

**obesity:** The condition of having a BMI of 30 or greater.

**octogenarians:** People who live to age 80 or older.

**omega-3:** An essential fatty acid with nutritional significance found in cold-water fish and flax; it comprises the cell membranes and helps prevent tissue inflammation, heart disease, and the formation of blood clots.

**omega-6:** An essential fatty acid with nutritional significance that comprises the cell membranes and is a precursor to biological compounds that play roles in reproduction and blood flow.

**organic:** Descrbes a substance that contains carbon.

**orthomolecular psychiatry:** A field of inquiry that advocates the treatment of some mental illnesses with megadoses of certain vitamins.

**osmosis:** The movement of water across a membrane from an area where there are fewer particles to an area where there are more particles in order to equalize the concentration.

**osteoarthritis (ahs-tee-oh-ar-THRY-tis):** A type of arthritis that leads to the deterioration of cartilage and loss of lubrication of the joints.

**osteomalacia (os-tee-oh-ma-LAY-she-uh):** A softening of the bones in adults that results from vitamin D deficiency.

**osteoporosis (oss-tee-oh-por-OH-sis):** A condition that affects older women in particular and is characterized by a decrease in bone mass and density and an enlargement of bone spaces, producing porosity and brittleness.

**overhydrated:** The condition of someone who has consumed too much water, therefore diluting the blood of electrolytes.

**overnutrition:** A type of malnutrition characterized by too much of a specific nutrient; it is generally associated with excess energy intake and results in overweight or obesity.

**overweight:** The condition of having a BMI of 25 or greater.

**oxalate (ox-uh-late):** A compound with negative charges that binds calcium and other minerals that have positive charges.

**oxaloacetate:** An intermediate of the Krebs cycle derived from pyruvate.

**pancreas:** A large lobulated gland of vertebrates that secretes digestive enzymes and the hormones insulin and glucagon.

**pancreatic amylase:** An enzyme released from the pancreas that breaks carbohydrates into smaller chains of glucose.

**pancreatic lipase:** An enzyme that acts on fat molecules to break them down into smaller molecules of fatty acid and glycerols.

**parasite:** An organism that derives nourishment and protection from another living organism known as the *host*.

**parathyroid hormone:** A hormone produced by the parathyroid glands located next to the thyroid glands in the neck; it is released if blood calcium levels decrease.

**partial hydrogenation:** The process of making an unsaturated fat more saturated, thus creating trans fats.

**pasteurization (pass-chur-ih-ZAY-shun):** The process of heating food to temperatures below the boiling point to kill harmful organisms while still maintaining its quality. The process is usually associated with milk and was named after its inventor, the French scientist Louis Pasteur.

**pathogens:** Microorganisms or infectious agents such as bacteria, viruses, fungi, mold, and parasites that can be transmitted in food and cause illness.

**peer-review system:** A system in which analyzed data is submitted to a science journal to be reviewed, judged, and commented on by other experts.

**pellagra (puh-LAG-ruh):** A disease caused by a niacin deficiency.

**pepsin:** An enzyme that breaks bonds in proteins into smaller units.

**pepsinogen:** The inactive form of pepsin; it is released from the wall of the stomach and converted to its active form, pepsin, to activate protein digestion.

**peptide bonds:** Very strong bonds that link amino acids together to make proteins. The bond is formed between the acid group of one amino acid and the amine group of another.

**peristalsis (pair-ih-STALL-sis):** A muscular movement that propels food through the digestive tract.

**pernicious anemia (per-NISH-us uh-NEE-mee-uh):** Anemia that results from a vitamin $B_{12}$ deficiency because of a lack of intrinsic factor.

**pH:** A numerical scale that measures and reflects acid-base balance.

**phenylalanine:** An essential amino acid.

**phenylketonuria:** An inherited disease in which the enzyme that breaks down the amino acid phenylalanine is not produced.

**phospholipid (fos-fo-LIP-id):** A lipid that has a three-carbon glycerol backbone; the first two carbons of the glycerol molecule have fatty acids bound to them, and the third carbon has a phosphate group bonded to it.

**photosynthesis:** The process in which carbon dioxide from the atmosphere, water from the soil, and energy from the sun interact in a biochemical reaction in plant cells to produce glucose.

**phytate (FYE-tate):** A substance that looks like a sugar molecule and is found inside the husk of whole grains and cereals; it binds certain minerals—calcium and zinc in particular—making them unavailable to cells.

**phytochemicals (FIE-toe-KEM-i-kulz):** Chemical compounds in plants that have various effects on body functions; they are not nutrients in the classical sense.

**phytoestrogens:** Compounds found in plants, such as soy, that may help prevent symptoms of menopause and osteoporosis in postmenopausal women.

**pica (PIKE-uh):** Compulsive eating by pregnant women of nonfood substances such as clay, chalk, or dirt.

**placebo (pluh-SEE-boh):** In an experiment or research study, an inert substance or treatment given to subjects in the control group instead of the actual substance or treatment being studied.

**placenta:** The organ formed in the uterus and that provides for nourishment of the fetus and elimination of waste products.

**plaque:** The calcification of cholesterol-laden cells that narrow blood vessels, cutting off the blood flow to the heart.

**plasma:** The watery part of blood.

**polypharmacy:** Consumption of multiple medications for an illness or illnesses.

**polysaccharide (pahl-ee-SAK-er-ide):** A carbohydrate composed of a chain with thousands of glucose molecules linked together.

**polyunsaturated fatty acid:** A fatty acid that contains two or more double bonds.

**positive nitrogen balance:** A situation in which protein intake exceeds what is excreted, such as during periods of growth, recovery from illness, and pregnancy.

**post-marketing surveillance:** Restricting a substance after it has been sold and used, only if it poses a "significant and unreasonable" risk.

**potentially hazardous foods:** Foods that support the rapid growth of disease-causing microorganisms—usually proteins or carbohydrates with high moisture content and low acidity.

**pound:** A unit now in general use among English-speaking peoples equal to 16 ounces.

**pre-eclampsia (pre-ee-CLAMP-see-uh):** A serious blood disorder in pregnancy characterized by headache, fatigue, protein in the urine, and high blood pressure.

**pregnancy-induced hypertension:** A condition in a pregnant woman characterized by a rapid rise in blood pressure, with readings above the normal limits of 140 (systolic) and 90 (diastolic).

**premenstrual syndrome:** A varying group of symptoms experienced by some women before menstruation that may include emotional instability, irritability, insomnia, fatigue, anxiety, depression, headache, edema, and abdominal pain; also called PMS.

**prevalence:** The number or proportion of cases of a condition in a given population.

**probiotics:** Live microbial food products and supplements that improve the health and microbial balance of the intestine; most contain *Lactobacillus* and *Bifidobacterium*.

**protein:** An energy-yielding nutrient that contains nitrogen; its primary purpose is to support growth, maintenance, and repair of tissues.

**protein breakdown:** A process in which proteins in the body are broken down into individual amino acids.

**Protein Digestibility–Corrected Amino Acid Score (PDCAAS):** A value assigned to proteins that accounts for their protein quality (amino acid content) and their digestibility.

**protein energy malnutrition (PEM):** A disorder that occurs when a person does not consume adequate amounts of protein, calories, or both.

**protein synthesis:** A process in which amino acids are linked together to make proteins.

**protein turnover:** The balance of protein synthesis and protein breakdown.

**prothrombin:** A plasma protein produced in the liver in the presence of vitamin K and converted into thrombin by the action of various activators (as thromboplastin) in the clotting of blood.

**provitamins:** Substances that need to be converted in order to have vitamin-like activity in the body.

**puberty:** The period of sexual maturation that occurs until sexual reproduction is possible.

**purging bulimia:** The *DSM-IV* diagnosis for individuals diagnosed with bulimia who have regularly engaged in a purging method such as self-induced vomiting or the abuse of laxatives, diuretics, or enemas.

**pyruvate:** A molecule produced during glucose metabolism.

**Recommended Dietary Allowances (RDAs):** The recommended nutrient intake required to meet the known nutrient needs of the healthy population.

**Recommended Nutrient Intakes (RNIs):** In Canada, the original standards that were established to prevent diseases caused by nutrient deficiencies.

**Registered Dietitian (RD):** A professional who has the education and clinical training to make dietary recommendations and to counsel patients.

**resistant starch:** a starch that escapes the digestion in the small intestine.

**resting energy expenditure (REE):** The energy expended by the body for heartbeat, breathing, nerve impulse transmission, kidney function, growth and repair, and other basic functions.

**restricting anorexia:** The *DSM-IV* designation for individuals diagnosed with anorexia who lose weight by reducing food and overall caloric intake by fasting or very strict dieting.

**resveratrol (rez-VIR-uh-trol):** A polyphenol found in grapes and other plants that protects against free radical damage.

**retinol activity equivalents or RAE:** The units in which carotenoids are measured.

**rheumatoid arthritis (ROO-muh-toyd ar-THRY-tis):** A specific type of arthritis that occurs when the immune system attacks the bone joints, leading to inflammation.

**rhizome:** A rootlike plant stem; an example is ginger.

**rickets:** A softening and deformity of long bones that results from vitamin D deficiency in children.

**risk factors:** Characteristics, situations, or triggers that identify individuals or groups as being at risk for developing eating disorders.

**Roux-en-Y gastric bypass:** The most commonly performed bariatric surgery in the United States. In this procedure, stapling creates a small stomach pouch. The remainder of the stomach is not removed, but is completely stapled shut and divided from the stomach pouch. The outlet from this newly formed pouch empties directly into the lower portion of the jejunum (part of the small intestine), thus creating some malabsorption as well as limiting intake.

**salivary amylase:** An enzyme in the saliva that breaks carbohydrates into smaller glucose links.

**salmonella:** A group of related bacteria that can cause illnesses in humans and animals.

**salt sensitive:** Describes people whose blood pressure declines as a result of a low-sodium diet or increases as a result of a high-sodium diet.

**sarcopenia (sar-ko-PEE-nee-uh):** The loss of muscle mass, strength, and function in older adults.

**satiety (suh-TYE-eh-tee):** The feeling of being satisfied after consuming food.

**saturated fatty acid:** Fatty acid that contains no double bonds.

**schizophrenia:** A psychotic disorder characterized by loss of contact with the environment, noticeable deterioration in the level of functioning in everyday life, and disintegration of personality expressed as disorders of feeling, thought (as in delusions), perception (as in hallucinations), and behavior.

**scientific method:** An approach to generate information through research under rigorous controls and methods.

**scorbutic rosary:** An abnormal formation on the rib cage in which the ribs appear beaded because of a vitamin C deficiency.

**second-messenger role:** The process of hormone regulation with calcium.

**scurvy:** A disease caused by vitamin C deficiency.

**"sell by":** A date that appears on food labels and tells the store how long to display a food product.

**semivegetarians:** People who occasionally eat meat and seafood, yet predominately practice a vegetarian diet.

**serotonin:** An organic compound found in animal and human tissue that acts as a neurotransmitter.

**set point theory:** A theory that states that the body is programmed to gravitate toward a particular weight; the metabolism may adjust upward or downward to ensure that weight is neither lost nor gained.

**short-chain fatty acids:** Fatty acids composed of six carbons or fewer; they can be made from plant material by bacteria in our large intestine.

**sickle-cell anemia:** A form of anemia that occurs when a person inherits two abnormal genes (one from each parent) that cause one amino acid to be missing in the sequence for the protein hemoglobin. The missing amino acid causes the shape of the cell to be more sickle shaped rather than disc shaped. The sickle-shaped cells do not allow for complete bonding of hemoglobin and oxygen and can easily stick together.

**side chain or R group:** One of four chemical groups that make up amino acids and give them their unique functions.

**skinfold calipers:** A tool used to measure the thickness of the fat layer under the skin in several locations on the body to estimate the percentage of body fat.

**soluble fiber:** Fiber that can dissolve in water. It is composed of many repeating monosaccharides that are acid derivatives of galactose. It is a jellylike material that acts as a cement in plants.

*sopa de frijol:* An example of a weaning food; it is made from the juice of cooked beans.

**Special Supplemental Nutrition Program for Women, Infants, and Children (WIC):** A nutrition program run by the U.S. Department of Agriculture that is designed to improve the nutrition of pregnant and breastfeeding mothers, infants, and children up to age 5.

**sphincters (SFINK-terz):** Circular muscles located throughout the digestive system that work like one-way doors to control the movement of its contents from one part to another.

**spina bifida (SPY-nuh BIF-ih-duh):** A birth defect that results from the failure of the spine to close properly during the first month of pregnancy.

**St. John's wort:** The extract of a plant with yellow flowers called *Hypericum perforatum;* it has been used for centuries to treat mental disorders such as depression as well as nerve pain.

**starch:** The storage form of carbohydrate found in plants.

**storage fat:** Fat that comes from adipose tissue, lies under the skin, or pads essential organs.

**stroke:** A condition that occurs when the blood supply to the brain is suddenly interrupted by a blood clot, hemorrhage, or other cause.

**subcutaneous fat (sub-kyoo-TAY-nee-us fat):** Body fat stored over the muscle and under the skin.

**sucrose:** A disaccharide commonly known as table sugar; it is composed of one glucose molecule and one fructose molecule.

**systolic blood pressure:** The peak pressure generated when the heart contracts and forces blood to move because of an increase in pressure from the pumping action.

**testosterone (tes-TAHS-ter-own):** The male sex hormone.

**thermic effect of food (TEF):** The energy expended by the body in digesting, absorbing, transporting, storing, metabolizing and otherwise processing food; it amounts to about 10 percent of calories consumed.

**thrombin:** An enzyme that converts fibrinogen to fibrin.

**thyroid hormone or thyroxine:** A hormone that controls the basal metabolic rate and heat production in our bodies.

**tocopherols (toe-COFF-er-alls):** A group of compounds with vitamin E activity.

**Tolerable Upper Intake Level (UL):** The highest level of daily nutrient intake that poses little risk of adverse health effects to individuals in a specific age or gender group.

**total energy expenditure (TEE):** The sum of REE, physical activity, and TEF.

**total parenteral nutrition (TPN):** A technique used to deliver calories and nutrients through a central vein.

**trans fatty acid:** An unhealthy fatty acid produced through the addition of hydrogen atoms to double bonds of fatty acids, which causes the molecule to assume an unnatural shape.

*trans:* The arrangement of hydrogens bonded to a carbon.

**transamination (tranz-am-in-AY-shun):** Transference of the amine group (the nitrogen-containing part) from one molecule to another to make an amino an acid.

**transferrin:** A blood protein that carries iron to organs.

**transit time:** The period of time it takes food to travel the length of the digestive tract.

**triglyceride:** A form of fat found in food and in the body; chemically, it is composed of a three-carbon compound called glycerol in which fatty acids are bonded to each of the carbons.

**tryptophan:** An essential amino acid that is converted to niacin.

**Type 1 diabetes:** A disease that occurs when the pancreas is unable to produce insulin. It was formerly known as juvenile-onset diabetes or insulin-dependent diabetes mellitus (IDDM), because of its frequent diagnosis in children or adolescents.

**Type 2 diabetes:** A disease that occurs when the insulin produced by the pancreas does not appear to function. It was formerly known as adult-onset diabetes or non-insulin-dependent diabetes mellitus (NIDDM).

**tyrosine:** A conditionally essential amino acid.

**ulcer:** Also called a peptic ulcer; an erosion that occurs in the lining of the stomach or the upper part of the small intestine.

**ultra high temperature (UHT):** A sterilization process that raises the temperature of milk even higher than in ultrapasteurization, and the milk is then rapidly cooled and aseptically packaged so it can remain on the shelf without refrigeration.

**ultrapasteurization (UP):** A process similar to traditional pasteurization that uses slightly different equipment, higher temperatures, and longer processing times.

**umbilical cord (um-BILL-ik-ul cord):** A cord full of arteries and veins that connects the baby to the mother through the placenta.

**undernutrition:** A type of malnutrition characterized by lack of specific nutrients.

**underwater weighing:** A technique for estimating body composition by comparing weight on land to underwater weight and the volume of water displaced by the body.

**underweight:** The condition of being 10 percent below what is considered a healthy weight for your height and build, associated with inadequate nutritional intake.

**"use by":** A date that is placed on a food package voluntarily by the manufacturer and suggests when the product will start to lose peak quality.

**valerian:** A plant native to Europe and Asia that has been grown in North America; it has been used as a treatment for insomnia.

**vanadium (vuh-NAY-dee-um):** A trace mineral found in mushrooms, shellfish, black pepper, parsley, dill seed, and some processed foods.

**variety:** Eating different types of foods within each food group.

**vegan (VEE-gun):** A person who consumes no meat, seafood, eggs, or dairy products.

**vegetarians:** People who do not consume animal flesh but may eat eggs and dairy products.

**vertical sleeve gastrectomy:** Type of bariatric surgery that uses an adjustable band that fits around the upper part of the stomach. The band divides the upper portion of the stomach into a pouch and separates it from the lower. This limits food intake. The band can be adjusted to allow more or less food to pass through to individualize weight loss.

**very low-density lipoproteins (VLDLs):** Lipoproteins that are synthesized in the liver and contain both triglycerides and cholesterol. They function to deliver triglycerides to other tissues.

**villi:** Fingerlike projections in the small intestine that increase the surface area to maximize absorption.

**visceral fat:** Body fat stored under the abdominal muscle.

**vitamins:** A group of nutrients that contain carbon and are required in small amounts to maintain normal body function.

**waist-to-hip ratio:** A measure of the health risks associated with android obesity.

**water intoxication:** A condition caused by excess water consumption that results in dilution of blood electrolytes, particularly sodium.

**water-soluble vitamins:** Vitamins that dissolve in water, are not stored in the body to any extent, and are excreted mostly through the urine.

**weaning foods:** Foods designed to replace a mother's milk.

**Wernicke-Korsakoff syndrome:** The symptoms that result from the loss of water soluble vitamins, particularly thiamine, from excess alcohol consumption over time.

**whey:** A by-product of cheese making that is used as a source of protein in many protein supplements.

**xerophthalmia (zeer-off-THAL-mee-uh):** Irreversible damage to the eye caused by vitamin A deficiency.

**yohimbine (yoh-HIM-been):** An extract of the bark of the West African tree *Pausinystalia yohimbe* that is best known as an aphrodisiac. It has also been used to treat sexual side effects caused by some antidepressants, to increase female sex drive, and to treat very low blood pressure and dry mouth.

**zeoxanthin:** Irreversible damage to the eye caused by a vitamin A deficiency that can lead to permanent loss of vision.

# References

Able, T., Knechtle B, Perret C, Eser P, von Arx P, Knecht H. (2005) Influence of chronic supplementation of arginine aspartate in endurance athletes on performance and substrate metabolism—a randomized, double-blind, placebo-controlled study. *Int J Sports Med* 26:344–349.

Ables AZ, Simon I, Melton ER. (2007) Update on *Helicobacter pylori* treatment. *Am Fam Physician* 75:351–358.

Adams JS, Hewison M. (2010). An update on vitamin D. *J Clin Endocrinol metab.* 95:471–478.

Agnew T, Gilmore J, Sullivan P. (1997) A multicultural perspective of breast-feeding in Canada. Health Canada. www.phac-aspc.gc.ca/dca-dea/publications/pdf/multi-cultural_bf_e.pdf

Agras WS. (2001) The consequences and costs of the eating disorders. *Psychiatr Clin North Am* 24:371–379.

Albanes D, Heinonen OP, Taylor PR, Virtamo J, Edwards BK, Rautalahti M, Hartman AM, Palmgren J, Freedman LS, Haapakoski J, Barrett MJ, Pietinen P, Malila N, Tala E, Lippo K, Salomaa ER, Tangrea JA, Teppo L, Askin FB, Taskinen E, Erozan Y, Greenwald P, Huttunen JK. (1996) Alpha-tocopherol and beta-carotene supplement and lung cancer incidence in the alpha-tocopherol, beta-carotene cancer prevention study: effects of base-line characteristics and study compliance. *J Natl Cancer Inst* 88:1560–1570.

Alfman L, Muller M. (2006). Nutrigenomics: from molecular nutrition to prevention of disease. *J Am Diet Assoc.* 106:569–576.

American Academy of Pediatrics, Work Group on Breast-Feeding. (2005) Breast-feeding and the use of human milk. *Pediatrics* 115: 496–506.

American Academy of Pediatrics. (2004) *Pediatrician Nutrition Handbook.* 5th ed. Washington, DC: American Academy of Pediatrics.

American College of Sports Medicine, American Dietetics Association, and Dietitians of Canada (2000). Joint position statement: nutrition and athletic performance. *Med Sci Sports Exerc* 32:2130–2145.

American College of Sports Medicine, American Dietetics Association, and Dietitians of Canada (2000). Joint Position Statement: nutrition and athletic performance. *Medicine Science Sports Exerc.* 32:2130–2145.

American College of Sports Medicine, Sawka MN, Burke LM, Eichner ER, Maughan RJ, Montain SJ, Stachenfeld NS. (2007) American College of Sports Medicine position stand. Exercise and fluid replacement. *Med Sci Sports Exerc* 39:377–390.

American Dietetic Association (2003) Position of the American Dietetic Association: vegetarian diets. *J Am Diet Assoc* 103:748–765.

American Dietetic Association. (2004). Position of the American Dietetic Association: Dietary Guidance for Healthy Children Ages 2 to 11 years. *J Am Diet Assoc.* 104:660–677.

American Dietetic Association (2006) Position of the American Dietetic Association: Food Security and Hunger in the United States. *J Am Diet Assoc* 106:446–458.

American Psychiatric Association, Task Force on DSM-IV. (2000) *Diagnostic and Statistical Manual of Mental Disorders: DSM-IV-TR.* 4th ed. Washington, DC: American Psychiatric Association.

Andersen A, Cohn L, Holbrook T. (2000) *Making Weight: Men's Conflicts with Food, Weight, Shape, and Appearance.* Carlsbad, CA: Gürze.

Armstrong LE, Case DJ, Maresh CM, Ganio MS. (2007) Caffeine, fluidelectrolyte balance, temperature regulation, and exercise-heat tolerance. *Exerc Sport Sci Rev* 35:135–140.

Bachman CM, Baranowski T, Nicklas TA. (2006) Is there an association between sweetened beverages and adiposity? *Nutr Rev* 64:153–174.

Baines S, Powers J, Brown WJ (2007) How does the health and wellbeing of young Australian vegetarian and semi-vegetarian women compare with non-vegetarians? *Public Health Nutr* 10: 436–442.

Bandini LG, Must A, Phillips SM, Naumova EN, Dietz WH. (2004) Relation of body mass index and body fatness to energy expenditure: longitudinal changes from pre-adolescence through adolescence. *Am J Clin Nutr.* 80:1262–1269.

Barr SI, Rideout CA. (2004) Nutritional considerations for vegetarian athletes. *Nutrition* 20:696–703.

Barr SI. (2006) Applications of Dietary Reference Intakes in dietary assessment and planning. *Applied physiology, nutrition, and metabolism,* pubs.nrc-cnrc.gc.ca

Barrett S. (2003) Gastrointestinal quackery: colonics, laxatives, and more. www.quackwatch.org/01QuackeryRelatedTopics/gastro.html

Bates CJ, Benton D, Biesalski HK, Staehelin HB, van Staveren W, Stehle P, Suter PM, Wolfram G. (2002) Nutrition and aging: a consensus statement. *J Nutr Health Aging.* 6:103–116.

Baum MK, Shor-Posner G, Lai S, Zhang G, Lai H, Fletcher MA, et al. (1997) High risk of HIV-related mortality is associated with selenium deficiency. *J Acquir Immune Defic Syndr Hum Retrovirol.* 15:370–374.

Baumer JH. (2007) Obesity and overweight: its prevention, identification, assessment and management. *Arch Dis Child Educ Pract Ed* 92:92–96.

Beals KA, Meyer NL. (2007) Female athlete triad update. *Clin Sports Med* 26:69–89.

Beard J, Dawson H, Pinero DJ. (1996) Iron metabolism: a comprehensive review. *Nutr Rev* 54:295–317.

Beck TJ, Looker AC, Mourtada F, Daphtary MM, Ruff CB. (2006). Age trends in femur stresses from a simulated fall on the hip among men and women: evidence of homeostatic adaptation underlying the decline in hip BMD. *J Bone Miner Res.* 21:1425–1432.

Berdanier CD. (1998) *Advanced nutrition: micronutrients.* Boca Raton, FL: CRC Press.

Berkow SE, Barnard N. (2006) Vegetarian diets and weight status. *Nutr Rev.* Apr;64(4):175–88.

Bertuccio P, Edefonti V, Bravi F, Ferraroni M, Pelucchi C, Negri E. (2009). Nutrient dietary patterns and gastric cancer risk in Italy. *Cancer Epidemiol Biomarkers Prev.* 18:2882–2886.

Bilsborough S, Mann N. (2006) A review of issues of dietary protein intake in humans. *Int J Sport Nutr Exerc Metab* 16:129–152.

Birks J,Grimley Evans J. (2002) Ginkgo biloba for cognitive impairment and dementia. *Cochrane Database Syst Rev* (4):CD003120.

Black HS. (2010). Interaction of ascorbic acid and tocopherol on beta-carotene modulated carcinogenesis. *Hemoglobin.* 34:284–290.

Black M, Medeiros DM, Brunnett E, Welke RA. (1988). Zinc supplements and serum lipids in young adult white males. *Am J Clin Nutr.* 47:970–975.

Blomstrand E. (2006) A role for branched chain amino acids in reducing central fatigue. *J Nutr* 136:544S–547S.

Bonakdar, RA, Guarneri, E. (2005) Coenzyme Q10. *Am Fam Physician* 72:1065–1070.

Borsheim E. (2005). Enhancing muscle anabolism through nutrient composition and timing of intake. *SCAN's Pulse: a publication of the ADA.* 24(3):1–5.

Bourre JM. (2006) Effects of nutrients (in food) on the structure and function of the nervous system: update on dietary requirements for brain: Part1: Micronutrients. *J Nutr Health Aging.* 10(5):377–385.

Brand-Miller JC. (2003) Glycemic load and chronic disease. *Nutr Rev* 61:S49–S55.

Brannon C. (2005) Dietetic diversity [continuing education course]. Ashland, OR: Nutrition Dimension.

Bray GA, Ryan DH, Harsha DW. (2003). Diet, weight loss, and cardiovascular disease prevention. *Curr Treat Options Cardiovasc Med.* 5: 259–269.

Bray GA, Ryan DH. (2007) Drug treatment of the overweight patient. *Gastroenterology* 132: 2239–2252.

Breslow RA, Guenther PM, Juan W, Graubard BI. (2010). Alcoholic beverage consumption, nutrient intakes, and diet quality in the US adult population, 1999–2006. *J Am Diet Assoc.* Apr; 110(4):551–562.

Bronner F. (1994). Calcium and osteoporosis. *Am J Clin Nutr.* 60:831–836.

Broyles S, Katzmarzyk PT, Srinivasan SR, Chen W, Bouchard C, Freedman DS, et al. (2010). The pediatric obesity epidemic continues unabated in Bogalusa, Louisiana. *Pediatrics.* 125:900–905.

Burd L, Roberts D, Olson M, Odendaal H. (2007) Ethanol and the placenta: A review. *J Matern Fetal Neonatal Med* 20:361–375.

Burge SK, Schneider FD. (1999). Alcohol related problems: recognition and intervention. *Am Fam Phys.* 59: 361–380.

Burke L. (2007). Practical sports nutrition (p. 530). Champaign, IL: Human Kinetics.

Burke LM, Kiens B, Ivy JL. (2004) Carbohydrate and fat for training and recovery. *J Sports Sci* 22:15–30.

Burke LM, Loucks AB, Broad N. (2006) Energy and carbohydrate for training and recovery. *J Sports Sci* 24:675–685.

Burke LM. (2007) Nutrition strategies for the marathon: Fuel for training and racing. *Sports Med* 37: 344–347.

Burnett-Hartman AN, Fitzpatrick AL, Gao K, Jackson SA, Schreiner PJ. (2009) Supplement use contributes to meeting recommended dietary intakes for calcium, magnesium, and vitamin C in four ethnicities of middle-aged and older Americans: the Multi-Ethnic Study of Atherosclerosis. *J Am Diet Assoc.* 109:422–429.

Burt BA. (2006). The use of sorbitol- and xylitol-sweetened gum in caries control. *J Am Dent Assoc.* 137:190–196.

Butterworth CE. (1974). The skeleton in the hospital closet. *Nutr Today.* 9:4–8.

Callamaro CJ. (2000) Infant nutrition in the first year of life: tradition or science? *Pediatric Nursing* 26: 211–215.

Campa A, Shor-Posner G, Indacoche F, Zhang G, Lai H, Asthana D, et al. (1999). Mortality risk in selenium-deficient HIV-positive children. *J Acquir Immune Defic Syndr Hum Retrovirol.* 15:508–513.

Campbell WW, Joseph LJO, Davey SL, Cyr-Camobell D, Anderson RA, Evans WJ. (1999). Effects of resistance training and chromium picolinate on body composition and skeletal muscle in older men. *J Appl Physiol.* 86:29–39.

Campos FG, Logullo Waitzberg AG, Kiss DR, Waitzberg DL, Habr-Gama A, Gama-Rodrigues J. (2005). Diet and colorectal cancer: current evidence for etiology and prevention. *Nutr Hosp.* 20:18–25.

Carr AC, Frei B. (1999). Toward a new recommended dietary allowance for vitamin C based on antioxidant and health effects in humans. *Am J Clin Nutr.* 69:1086–1107.

Castro GD, de Castro CR,Maciel ME, Fanelli SL, de Ferreyra EC, Gomez MI, Castro JA. (2006) Ethanol-induced oxidative stress and acetaldehyde formation in rat mammary tissue: Potential factors involved in alcohol drinking promotion of breast cancer. *Toxicology* 219:208–219.

Catenacci VA, Wyatt HR. (2007) The role of physical activity in producing and maintaining weight loss. *Nat Clin Pract Endocrinol Metab* 3:518–529.

Centers for Disease Control and Prevention (CDC). (2003) Prevalence of physical activity, including lifestyle activities among adults—United States, 2000–2001. *MMWR Morb Mortal Wkly Rep* 52:764–769.

Centers for Disease Control and Prevention (CDC). (2005) *Behavioral Risk Factor Surveillance System Survey Data.* Atlanta, GA: U.S. Department of Health and Human Services, Centers for Disease Control and Prevention.

Centers for Disease Control and Prevention (CDC). (2007) How Active Do Adults Need to Be to Gain Some Benefit? www.cdc.gov/nccdphp/dnpa/physical/recommendations/adults.htm

Centers for Disease Control and Prevention (CDC). (2007) Youth exposure to alcohol advertising in magazines, United States, 2001–2005. *MMWR Morb Mortal Wkly Rep* 56:673–676.

Centers for Disease Control and Prevention. (2000) Surveillance for foodborne disease outbreaks—United States, 1993–1997. *MMWR Surv Summ* 49(SS01):1–51.

Centers for Disease Control and Prevention. (2002) State-Specific prevalence of obesity among adults with disability: eight states and the District of Columbia. *MMWR Morb Mortal Wkly Rep* (36):805.

Chagan L, Ioselovich A, Asherova L, Cheng JW. (2002) Use of alternative pharmacotherapy in management of cardiovascular diseases. *Am J Manag Care* 8:270–285; quiz 286–288. www.ajmc.com/files/articlefiles/AJMC-2002mrChaganCE270–288.pdf

Chapin RE, Robbins WA, Schieve LA, et al. (2004) Off to a good start: The influence of pre- and periconceptional exposures, parental fertility, and nutrition on children's health. *Environ Health Persp* 112:69–78.

Chin, ed. (2000) *Control of Communicable Diseases in Man.* 17th ed. Washington, DC: American Public Health Association.

Chiuve SE, Rimm EB, Manson JE, Whang W, Mozaffarian D, Stampfer MJ, et al. (2009). Intake of total trans, trans-18:1, and trans-18:2 fatty acids and risk of sudden cardiac death in women. *Am Heart J.* 158: 761–767.

Clark N. (2003) *Nancy Clark's Sports Nutrition Guidebook.* 3rd ed. Champaign, IL: Human Kinetics.

Clegg DO, Reda DJ, Harris CL Klein MA, O'Dell JR, Hooper MM, Bradley JD, Bingham CO, Weisman MH, Jackson CG, Lane NE, Cush JJ, Moreland LW, Schumacher HR Jr., Oddis CV, Wolfe F, Molitor JA, Yokum DE, Schnitzer TJ, Furst DE, Sawitzke AD, Shi H, Brandt KD, Moskowitz RW, Williams HJ. (2006) Glucosamine, chondroitin sulfate, and the two in combination for painful knee osteoarthritis. *N Eng J Med* 354:795–808.

Cody MM, Hogue MA. (2003) Results of the Home Food Safety—It's in Your Hands 2002 Survey: Comparisons to the 1999 benchmark survey and Healthy People 2010 food safety behaviors objective. *J Am Diet Assoc* 103:1115–1125.

Coyle EF. (2004). Fluid and fuel intake during exercise. *J Sports Sci.* 22:39–55.

Crabb DW, Matsumoto M, Chang D, You M. (2004). Overview of the role of alcohol dehydrogenase and aldehyde dehydrogenase and their variants in the genesis of alcohol-related pathology. *Proceedings of the Nutrition Society.* 63:49–63.

Craddick SR, Elmer PJ, Obarzanek E, Vollmer WM, Svetkey LP, Swain MC. (2003). The DASH diet and blood pressure. *Curr Atheroscler Rep.* 5:484–91.

Cranenburg EC, Schurgers LI, Vermeer C. (2007) Vitamin K: the coagulation vitamin that became omnipotent. *Thromb Haemost* 98:120–125.

Croissant AE, Washburn SP, Dean LL, Drake MA. (2007). Chemical properties and consumer perception of fluid milk from conventional and pasture based production methods. *J Dairy Sci.* 90;4942–4953.

Cui R, Iso H, Date C, Kikuchi S, Tamakoshi A; Japan Collaborative Cohort Study Group (2010). Dietary folate and vitamin B6 and B12 intake in relation to mortality from cardiovascular diseases: Japan collaborative cohort study. *Stroke.* (6):1285–1289.

Cummings S, Parharn ES, Strain GW. (2002) Position of the American Dietetic Association: weight management. *J Am Diet Assoc* 102:1145–1155.

Cunningham CC, Van Horn CG. (2003). Energy availability and alcohol-related liver pathology. *Alcohol Res Health.* 27: 291–299.

Dachs R. (2007) Exercise is an effective intervention in overweight and obese patients. *Am Fam Physician* 75:1333–1335.

De Lorgeril M, Salen P. (2005). The Mediterranean-style diet for the prevention of cardiovascular diseases. *Public Health Nutr.* 9:118–123.

DeMaria EJ. (2007) Bariatric surgery for morbid obesity. *N Engl J Med* 356:2176–2183.

Deng R, Chow TJ. (2010). Hypolipidemic, antioxidant, and antiinflammatory activities of microalgae Spirulina. *Cardiovasc Ther.* 28(4):e33–e45.

Denic S, Agarwal MM. (2007) Nutritional iron deficiency: an evolutionary perspective. *Nutrition* 23:603–614.

Deshmukh-Taskar PR, Nicklas TA, O'Neil CE, Keast DR, Radcliffe JD, Cho S. (2010). The relationship of breakfast skipping and type of breakfast consumption with nutrient intake and weight status in children and adolescents: the National Health and Nutrition Examination Survey 1999–2006. *J Am Diet Assoc.* 110:869–878.

Deurenberg-Yap M, Schmidt G, van Staveren WA, Deurenberg B. (2000) The paradox of low body mass index and high body fat percentage among Chinese, Malays and Indians in Singapore. *Int J Obes Relat Metab Disord* 24:1011–1017.

DeWals P, Tairou F, Van Allen MI, Uh SH, Lowry RB, Sibbald B, Evans IA,Van den Hof MC, Zimmer P, Crowley M, Fernandez B, Lee NS, Niyonsenga T. (2007) Reduction in neural-tube defects after folic acid fortification in Canada. *N Engl J Med* 357:135–142.

Dewey K, (2002) Pan American health organizations guiding principles for complementary feeding of the breast-fed child. www.paho.org/English/AD/FCH/NU/GuidingPrinciplesCF.htm

Dewey KG (2003) Is breast-feeding protective against childhood obesity? *J Hum Lact* 19:9–18.

Dhar R, Stout CW, Link MS, Homoud MK, Weinstock J, Estes NA. (2005) Cardiovascular toxicities of performance-enhancing substances in sports. *Mayo Clin Proc* 80:1307–1315.

Dietary Guidelines for Americans. (2005). US Department of Health and Human Services and US Department of Agriculture. HHS Publication Number HHS-ODPHP-2005-01-DGA-A and USDA Publication number: Home and Garden Bulletin No. 232. http://www.health.gov/dietaryguidelines/dga2005/document/pdf/DGA2005.pdf

Dietz WH Jr, Gortmaker SL. (1985). Do we fatten our children at the television set? Obesity and television viewing in children and adolescents. *Pediatrics.* 75(5):807–812.

Dietz WH, Bellizzi MC. (1999) Introduction: the use of body mass index to assess obesity in children. *Am J Clin Nutr.* 70(suppl):123S–125S.

Donatelle RJ. (2005) *Health: The Basics.* 6th ed. San Francisco: Pearson Education.

Dresne S, Siegel S, Pollock D. (1982) *The Jewish Dietary Laws.* New York: United Synagogue.

Drewnowski A, Shultz JM. (2001). Impact of aging on eating behaviors, food choices, nutrition, and health status. *J Nutr Health Aging.* 5:75–79.

Dwyer J, Picciano MF, Raiten DJ. (2003). Estimation of usual intakes: what we eat in America-NHANES. *J Nutr.* 133:609s–623s.

Eastwood M, Kritchevsky D. (2005). Dietary fiber: how did we get where we are? *Annu Rev Nutr.* 25:1–8.

Edefonti V, Bravi F, La Vecchia C, Randi G, Ferraroni M, Garavello W, et al. (2010). Nutrient-based dietary patterns and the risk of oral and pharyngeal cancer. *Oral Oncol.* 46:343–348.

Eichholzer M, Tonz O, Zimmermann R. (2006). Folic acid: a public health challenge. *The Lancet.* 367:1352–1361.

Eisenstein J, Roberts SB, Dallal G, Saltzman E. (2002) High-protein weight-loss diets: Are they safe and do they work? A review of the experimental and epidemiologic data. *Nutr Rev* 60:189–200.

Elder KA, Wolfe BM. (2007) Bariatric surgery: a review of procedures and outcomes. *Gastroenterology* 132:2253–2271.

Ellickson PL, Collins RL, Hambarsoomians K, McCaffrey DF. (2005). Does alcohol advertising promote adolescent drinking? Results from a longitudinal assessment. *Addiction.* 100:235–246.

Ellwood, K. (2006) What are qualified health claims? *Nutrition Today* 41: 56–61.

Engler MM, Engler MB. (2006). Omega-3 fatty acids: role in cardiovascular health and disease. *J Cardiovasc Nurs.* 21:17–24.

Erkkila AT, Lichtenstein AH. (2006). Fiber and cardiovascular disease risk: how strong is the evidence? *J Cardiovasc Nurs.* 21:3–8.

Ervin RB. (2006). Prevalence of functional limitations among adults 60 years of age and over: United States, 1999–2002. *Adv Data.* 23:1–7.

European Food Safety Authority. (2005) Opinion of the AHAN Panel related to the welfare aspects of various systems of keeping laying hens. EFSA-Q-2003–92. Final report for the European Commission. www.efsa.eu.int/science/ahaw/ahaw_opinions/831_en.html

Evans WJ. (2004) Protein, nutrition, exercise and aging. *J Am Coll Nutr* 23:601S-609S.

Expert Panel on Detection, Evaluation, and Treatment of High Blood Cholesterol in Adults. (1994). Second report. *Circulation.* 89:1329–1445.

Expert Panel Review. (1998). Fat replacers. Scientific status summary. Institute of Food Technologists. *Food Technology.* 52:47–52.

Fairfield KM, Fletcher RH. (2002) Vitamins for chronic disease prevention in adults: scientific review. *JAMA* 287:3116–3126.

Farooqi S,O'Rahilly S. (2005) Monogenic obesity in humans. *Annu Rev Med* 56:443–458.

Faure P, Barclay D, Joyeux-Faure M, Halimi S. (2007) Comparison of the effects of zinc alone and zinc associated with selenium and vitamin E on insulin sensitivity and oxidative stress in high-fructose-fed rats. *J Trace Elem Med Biol* 21:113–119.

Ferdowsian HR, Barnard ND. (2009). Effects of plant based diets on plasma lipids. *Am J cardiol.* 1;104(7):947–956.

Fewtrell MS, Morgan JB, Duggan C, Gunnlaugsson G, Hibberd PL, Lucas A, Kleinman RE. (2007). Optimal duration of exclusive breast-feeding: What is the evidence to support current recommendations? *Am J Clin Nutr* 85:635S–638S.

Fischer-Posovszky P, Wabitch M, Hochberg Z. (2007) Endocrinology of adipose tissue—an update. *Horm Metab Res* 39:341–321.

Flegal KM, Carroll MD, Ogden CL, Johnson CL. (2002) Prevalence and trends in obesity among US adults, 1999–2000. *JAMA* 288:1723–1727.

Fleming-Morn M, Thiagarajah K. (2005) Behavioral interventions and the role of television in the growing epidemic of adolescent obesity—data from the 2001 youth risk behavioral survey. *Methods Inf Med* 44:303–309.

Folts JD. (2002). Potential health benefits from the flavenoids in grape products on vascular disease. *Adv Exp Med Biol.* 505:95–111.

Food and Agriculture Organization and World Health Organization. (1996) *Preparation and use of food-based dietary guidelines.* Geneva: World Health Organization.

Food and Agriculture Organization of the United Nations and World Health Organization. (1998) Carbohydrates in human nutrition. FAO Food and Nutrition Paper No. 66.www.fao.org/docrep/W8079E/w8079e00.HTM.

Food and Nutrition Board. (1997) *Dietary Reference Intakes for Calcium, Phosphorus, Magnesium, Vitamin D, and Fluoride.* Washington, DC: National Academies Press.

Food and Nutrition Board. (2000) *Dietary Reference Intakes for Energy, Carbohydrate, Fiber, Fat, Fatty Acids, Cholesterol, Protein, and Amino Acids (Macronutrients).* Washington, DC: National Academies Press.

Food and Nutrition Board. (2002/2005) *Dietary Reference Intakes for Energy, Carbohydrate, Fiber, Fat, Fatty Acids, Cholesterol, Protein, and Amino Acids (Macronutrients).*Washington, DC: National Academies Press.

Food Facts Asia. (1998) It's a small world after all: Dietary guidelines around the world. www.afic.org

Fox MK, Pac S, Devaney B, Jankowski L. (2004) Feeding infants and toddlers study: What foods are infants and toddlers eating? *J Am Diet Assoc* 104:22–30.

Fraser GE. (2009). Vegetarian diets: what we do know of their effects on chronic diseases. *Am J Clin Nutr.* 89(5):1607s–1612s.

Freis ED. (1992) The role of salt in hypertension. *Blood Press* 1:196–200.

Freis ED. (1992). The role of salt in hypertension. *Blood Pressure.* 1:196–200.

Fugh-Berman A. (2003) Echinacea for the prevention and treatment of upper respiratory infections. *Seminars in Integrative Medicine* 1:106–111.

Gades MD, Stern JS. (2002) Chitosan supplementation does not affect fat absorption in healthy males fed a high fat diet, a pilot study. *Internal J Obes* 26:119–122.

Gao X, Wilde PE, Lichtenstein AH, Tucker KL. (2006) The 2005 USDA Food Guide Pyramid is associated with more adequate nutrient intakes within energy constraints than the 1992 Pyramid. *J Nutr*136:1341–1346.

Garrett WS, Gordon JI, Glimcher LH. (2010). Homeostasis and inflammation in the intestine. *Cell.* 1409(6): 859–870.

Gatzke-Kopp LM, Beauchaine TP. (2007) Direct and passive prenatal nicotine exposure and the development of externalizing psychopathology. *Child Psychiatry Hum Dev* (May 23). Epub ahead of print; PMID 17520361.

Gibala MJ, Hargreaves M, Tipton KD. (2000). Amino acids protein and exercise performance. *Sports Sci Exchange Roundtable.* 42.11(4):1–4. http://www.gssi-web.com

Gibala MJ. (2002). Dietary protein, amino acids supplements and recovery from exercise. *Sports Sci Exchange.* 15(4):1–4.

Gidding SS, Dennison BA, Birch LL, Daniels SR, Gilman MW, Lichtenstein AH, et al. (2005). Dietary recommendations for children and adolescents: a guide for practitioners: consensus statement from the American Heart Association. *Circulation.* 112:2061–2075.

Gleeson M. (2006) Immune system adaptation in elite athletes. *Curr Opin Clin Nutr Metab Care* 9:659–665.

Goldenberg RL, Culhane JF. (2007) Low birth weight in the United States. *Am J Clin Nutr* 85:584S–590S.

Goodwin DK, Knol LL, Eddy JM, Fitzhugh EC, Kendrick OW, Donahue D. (2006) The relationship between self-rated health status and the overall quality of dietary intake of US adolescents. *J Am Diet Assoc.* 106:1450–1453.

Gowers S, Bryant-Waugh R. (2004) Management of child and adolescent eating disorders: the current evidence base and future directions. *J Child Psychl Psychiatry* 45:63–83.

Grieve FG. (2007) A conceptual model of factors contributing to the development of muscle dysmorphia. *Eat Disord* 15:63–80.

Grummer-Strawn LM, Mei Z. (2004) Does breast-feeding protect against pediatric overweight? Analysis of the longitudinal data from the Centers for Disease Control and Prevention Pediatrics Nutrition Surveillance System. *Pediatrics* 113:81–86.

Grunbaum JA, Kann L, Kinchen S, Ross I, Hawkins I, Lowry R, Harris WA, McManus T, Chyen D, Collins I. (2004) Youth risk behavior surveillance—United States, 2003. *Morb Mortal Wkly Rep Surveill Summ* 53:1–29.

Gunter MJ, Leitzmann MF. (2006). Obesity and colorectal cancer: epidemiology, mechanisms and candidate genes. *J Nutr Biochem.* 17:145–156.

Haines J, Neumark-Sztainer D. (2006) Prevention of obesity and eating disorders: A consideration of shared risk factors. *Health Educ Res* 21:770–782.

Hambidge KM, Miller LV, Westcott JE, Sheng X, Krebs NF. (2010). Zinc bioavailability and homeostasis. *Am J Clin Nutr.* 91:1478S–1483S.

Hargreaves M, Hawley JA, Jeukendrup A. (2004) Pre-exercise carbohydrate and fat ingestion: Effects on metabolism and performance. *J Sports Sci* 22:31–38.

Harvard School of Public Health. (2006). *Protein moving closer to center stage.* http://hsph.harvard.edu/nutritionsource/protein.html

Hawley JA, Tipton KD, Millard-Stafford ML. (2006) Promoting training adaptations through nutritional interventions. *J Sports Sci* 24:709–721.

Heaney RP, Layman DK. (2008). Amount and type of protein influences bone health. *Am J Clin Nutr.* 87(5):1567s–1570s.

*Heart Disease and Stroke Statistics—2003 Update.* American Heart Association. (2002) Publication no. 55–0567.

Heckman MA, Sherry K, Gonzalez de Majia. (2010). Energy drinks: an assessment of their market size, consumer demographics, ingredient profile, functionality, and regulations in the United States. *Comp Rev Food Sci Food Safety.* 9:303–317.

Heird WC. (2007) Progress in promoting breast-feeding combating malnutrition and composition of infant formula, 1981–2006. *J Nutr* 137:499s–502s.

Heller MC, Keoleian GA. (2000) *Life Cycle–Based Sustainability Indicators for Assessment of the U.S. Food System.* Ann Arbor, MI: Center for Sustainable Systems, University of Michigan, p. 40.

Hensrud DD, Klein S. (2006) Extreme obesity: A new medical crisis in the United States. *Mayo Clin Proc* 81:S5–S10.

Hines DA, Straus MA. (2007) Binge drinking and violence against dating partners: The mediating effect of antisocial traits and behaviors in a multinational perspective. *Aggress Behav* 33:441–457.

Hitz MF, Jensen JE, Eskildsen PC. (2007) Bone mineral density and bone markers in patients with a recent low-energy fracture: Effect of 1 y of treatment with calcium and vitamin D. *Am J Clin Nutr* 86:251–259.

Hochberg MC. (2006) Nutritional supplements for knee osteoarthritis—still no resolution. *N Engl J Med* 354:848–850.

Holick MF. (2004) Sunlight and vitamin D for bone health and prevention of autoimmune diseases, cancers, and cardiovascular disease. *Am J Clin Nutr* 80:1678S–1688S.

Holick MF. (2006) Vitamin D. In *Biochemical, Physiological, and Molecular Aspects of Human Nutrition*, 2nd ed. (ed. MH Stipanuk) pp. 863–883. St. Louis, MO: Saunders Elsevier.

http://catholicism.about.com/cs/lent/f/whynomeat04.htm

http://www.aolnews.com/gulf-oil-spill/article/gulf-seafood-after-the-oil-spill-who-decides-how-safe-is-safe/19534995

http://www.fda.gov/Food/FoodSafety/Product-SpecificInformation/Seafood/ucm210970.htm

http://www.healthsystem.virginia.edu/internet/chaplaincy/hindu.cfm

http://www.jamiat.org.za/hguideline.html

http://www.vegetarian-diet.info/

Humane Society of the United States. (2006) An HSUS report: Human health implications of cage and cage-free egg production—a review of food safety. www.hsus.org/farm/resources/research/pubhealth/food_safety_eggs.html

Humane Society of the United States. (2006) An HSUS report: The economic consequences of adopting alternative production systems to battery cages. www.hsus.org/farm/resources/research/economics/battery_cages_econ.html

International Food Information Council (IFIC) and U.S. Food and Drug Administration. (November 2004). *Food Ingredients and Colors* [brochure]. www.cfsan.fda.gov/~dms/foodic.html

Janssen I, Katzmarzyk PT, Ross R. (2002) Body mass index, waist circumference, and health risk: Evidence in support of current National Institutes of Health guidelines. *Arch Intern Med* 162:2074–2079.

Jay M. (2000) *Modern Food Microbiology.* 6th ed. Gaithersburg, MD: Aspen.

Jeukendrup A, Gleeson M. (2004) *Sport Nutrition: An Introduction to Energy Production and Performance.* Champaign IL: Human Kinetics.

Johnston LD, O'Malley PM, Bachman JG. (2001) *Monitoring the Future: National Survey Results on Drug Use, 1975–2000.* Vol. 1 *Secondary School Students.* NIH Pub.No. 014924. Bethesda, MD: National Institute on Drug Abuse.

Kalra EK. (2003) Nutraceutical—definition and introduction. *AAPS PharmSci.* 5:article 25. DOI: 10.1208/ps050225.

Kant AK, Graubard BI. (2006). Secular trends in patterns of self-reported food consumption of adult Americans: NHANES 1971–1975 to NHANES 1999–2002. *Am J Clin Nutr.* 84(5):1215–1223.

Kaufman DW, Kelly JP, Rosenberg L, Anderson TE, Mitchell AA. (2002) Recent patterns of medication use in the ambulatory adult population of the United States: the Slone survey. *JAMA* 287:337–344.

Keel PK, Brown TA. (2010). Update on course and outcome in eating disorders. *Int J Eat Disord.* Apr;43(3):195–204.

Keith SW, Redden DT, Katzmarzyk PT, Boggiano MM, Hanlon EC, Benca RM, et al. (2006). Putative contributors to the secular increase in obesity: exploring roads less traveled. *Int J Obes.* 11:1585–1594.

Kelly JP, Kaufman DW, Kelley K, Rosenberg L, Anderson TE, Mitchell AA. (2005) Recent trends in use of herbal and other natural products. *Arch Int Med* 165:281–286.

Kennedy E, Meyers L. (2005). Dietary reference intakes: development and uses of micronutrient status of women—a global perspective. *Am J Clin Nutr.* 81:1194S–1197S.

Kern M. (2006). Dietary intake of adolescent athletes and nonathletes. *J Am Diet Assoc.* 6:717–718.

Key TJ, Appleby PN, Rosell MS. (2006). Health effects of vegetarian and vegan diets. *Proc Nutr Soc.* 65(1):35–41.

King DE. (2005). Dietary fiber, inflammation, and cardiovascular disease. *Mol Nutr Food Res.* 49:594–600.

Kjelsas E, Bjornstrom C, Gotestam KG. (2004) Prevalence of eating disorders in female and male adolescents (14–15 years). *Eat Behav* 5:13–25.

Klein S. (2004) Clinical trial experience with fat-restricted vs. carbohydrate-restricted weight-loss diets. *Obes Res* 12:141S–144S.

Klump KL, Perkins PS, Alexandra Burt S, McGue M, Iacono WG. (2007) Puberty moderates genetic influences on disordered eating. *Psychol Med* 37:627–634.

Kongi A, Bousan C, Cohen JT, Conner WE, Kris-Etherton PM, Gray GM, et al. (2005). A quantitative analysis of fish consumption and coronary heart disease mortality. *Am J Prev Med.* 29:335–346.

Kramer MS, Kakuma R. (2002) Optimal duration of exclusive breastfeeding. *Cochrane Data Base System Rev* (1):CD003517.

Krebs N. (2007) Food choices to meet nutritional needs of breast-fed infants and toddlers on mixed diets. *J Nutr* 137:511s–517s.

Krebs NF, Hambidge KM. (2007) Complementary feeding: clinically relevant factors affecting timing and composition. *Am J Clin Nutr* 85:639s–645s.

Krebs-Smith SM, Kris-Etherton P. (2007) How does MyPyramid compare to other population-based recommendations for controlling chronic disease? *J Am Diet Assoc* 107:803–837.

Kris-Etherton PM, Taylor DS, Yu-Poth S, Huth P, Moriarty K, Fishell V, et al. (2000). Polyunsaturated fatty acids in the food chain in the United States. *Am J Clin Nutr.* 71(suppl):179S–188S.

Krukowski RA, Harvey-Berino J, Kolodinsky J, Narsana RT, Desisto TP. (2006) Consumers may not use or understand calorie labeling in restaurants. *J Am Diet Assoc* 106:917–920.

Lawlor DA, Martin RM, Gunnell D, Galobardes B, Ebrahim S, Sandhu J, Ben-Shlomo Y, McCarron P, Davey Smith G. (2006) Association of body mass index measured in childhood, adolescence, and young adulthood with risk of ischemic heart disease and stroke: Findings from 3 historical cohort studies. *Am J Clin Nutr* 83: 767–773.

Lawlor DA, Martin RM, Gunnell D, Galobardes B, Ebrahim S, Sandhu J, et al. (2006) Association of body mass index measured in childhood, adolescence, and young adulthood with risk of ischemic heart disease and stroke: findings from 3 historical cohort studies. *Am J Clin Nutr.* 83:767–773.

Le Grange D, Lock J. (2005) The dearth of psychological treatment studies for anorexia nervosa. *Int J Eat Dis* 37:79–91.

Lee CM, Geisner IM, Patrick ME, Neighbors C. (2010). The social norms of alcohol-related negative consequences. *Psychol Addict Behav.* 24:342–348.

Leitzman C. (2003). Nutrition ecology: the contribution of vegetarian diets. *Am J Clin Nutr* 78:657S–659S.

Leshner, AI. (2000) Anabolic Steroid Abuse. *National Institute on Drug Abuse Research Report Series*, 1–8.

Leurs LJ, Schouten LJ, Mons MN, Goldbohm RA, van den Brandt PA. (2010). Relationship between tap water hardness, magnesium, and calcium concentration and mortality due to ischemic heart disease or stroke in the Netherlands. *Environ. Health Perspect.* 118:414–420.

Levine HG. (1992) Temperance cultures: Alcohol as a problem in Nordic and English-speaking cultures. In *The Nature of Alcohol and Drug-Related Problems*, (eds. M Lader, G Edwards, C Drummond), pp. 16–36.New York: Oxford University Press.

Levine HG. (1992). Temperance cultures: alcohol as a problem in Nordic and English-speaking cultures. In: *The nature of alcohol and drug-related problems.* pp. 16–36, Lader M, Edwards G, Drummond C (Eds.), New York: Oxford University Press.

Levine M, Padayatty SJ, Wang Y, Corpe CP, Lee J, Wang J, Chen Q, Zhang L. (2006) Vitamin C. In: *Biochemical, physiological, molecular aspects of human nutrition.* Pp. 760–796, Martha H. Stipanuk (Ed.), 2nd edition, St. Louis, MO: Saunders Elsevier.

Lewis MA, Rees M, Logan DE, Kaysen DL, Kilmer JR. (2010). Use of drinking protective behavioral strategies in association to sex-related alcohol negative consequences: the mediating role of alcohol consumption. *Psychol Addict Behav.* 24:229–238.

Light KE, Hakkak R. (2003). Alcohol and nutrition. In: *Handbook of food-drug interactions.* Pp. 168–189, McCabe BJ, Wolfe JJ, Frankel EH, (Eds.), Boca Raton, FL: CRC Press.

Lin PH, Aickin M, Champagne C, Craddick S, Sacks FM, McCarron P, et al. (2003). Food group sources of nutrients in the dietary patterns of the DASH-Sodium trial. *J Am Diet Assoc.* 103:488–496.

Linde K, Barrett B, Wolkart K, Bauer R, Melchart D. (2006) Echinacea for preventing and treating the common cold. *Cochrane Database Syst Rev* (1):CD000530.

Littarru GP, Tiano L. (2010). Clinical aspects of coenzyme Q10: an update. *Nutrition.* 26(3):250–254.

Lu C, Barr DB, Pearson MA, Waller LA. (2008). Dietary intake and its contribution to longitudinal organophosphorous pesticide exposure in urban/suburban children. *Environ Health Perspect.* April;116(4).

Lukaski HC. (1999). Chromium as a supplement. *Ann Rev Nutr.* 19:279–302.

MacLean CH, Newberry SJ, Mohica WA, Khanna P, Issa AM, Suttorp MJ, et al. (2006). Effects of omega-3 fatty acids on cancer risk: a systematic review. *JAMA.* 295:403–415.

Mahan LK, Escott-Stump S. (2000) *Food, Nutrition, and Diet Therapy*. 10th ed. Philadelphia: Saunders.

Mahoney CR, Taylor HA, Kanarek RB, Samuel P. (2005). Effect of breakfast composition on cognitive processes in elementary school children. *Physiol Behav.* 85:635–645.

Manore M, Thompson JA. (2000) *Sport Nutrition for Health and Performance*. Champaign, IL: Human Kinetics.

March of Dimes. (2000) *Nutrition Today Matters Tomorrow: A Report from the March of Dimes Task Force on Nutrition and Optimal Human Development.* www.marchofdimes.com/professionals/14480_1926.asp

Marriott BM, Campbell L, Hirsch E, Wilson D. (2007) Preliminary data from demographic and health surveys on infant feeding in 20 developing countries. *J Nutr* 137:518s–523s.

Martinez MF. (2005). Primary prevention of colorectal cancer: lifestyle, nutrition, exercise. *Recent Results Cancer Res.* 166:177–211.

Matsuzaki T. (1992). Longevity, diet, and nutrition in Japan: epidemiological studies. *Nutrition Rev.* 50:355–359.

Matthiessen J, Fagt S, Biltoft-Jensen A, Beck AM, Ovesen L. (2003) Size makes a difference. *Public Health Nutr* 6:65–72.

Maughan R. (2002) The athlete's diet: nutritional goals and dietary strategies. *Proc Nutr Soc* 61:87–96.

Mayo Clinic. (2005) Colon cleansing: is it helpful or harmful? www.mayoclinic.com/health/colon-cleansing/AN00065

McArdle WD, Katch FI, Katch VL. (2007) Human energy expenditure during rest and physical activity. In *Exercise Physiology: Energy, Nutrition, and Human Performance*, 6th ed. Malvern, PA: Lea and Febiger.

McCabe MP, Ricciardelli LA. (2004) Body image dissatisfaction among males across the lifespan: a review of past literature. *J Psychosom Res* 56:675–685.

McCormick DB. (2006) Niacin, riboflavin, and thiamin. In *Biochemical, Physiological, and Molecular Aspects of Human Nutrition*, 2nd ed. (ed. MH Stipanuk), pp. 665–692. St. Louis, MO: Saunders Elsevier.

McCullough ML, Willett WC. (2006). Evaluating adherence to recommended diets in adults: the Alternate Healthy Eating Index. *Public Health Nutr.* 9(1A):152–157.

McDaniel SM, O'Neill C, Mertz RP, Tarbutton E, Stacewicz-Sapuntzakis M, Heimendinger I, Wolfe P, Thompson H, Schedin P. (2007) Wholefood sources of vitamin A more effectively inhibit female rat sexual maturation, mammary gland development, and mammary carcinogenesis than retinyl palmitate. *J Nutr* 137:1415–1422.

McDowell MA, Fryar CD, Hirsch R, Ogden CL. (2005) Anthropometric reference data for children and adults: U.S. population, 1999–2002. *Advance Data for Vital and Health Statistics*, no. 361. Hyattsville, MD: National Center for Health Statistics.

McSwane D, Rue N, Linton R. (2003) *Essentials of Food Safety and Sanitation,* 3rd ed. Upper Saddle River, NJ: Prentice Hall.

Medeiros DM, Hampton M. (2007) Olive oil and health benefits. In *Handbook of Nutraceuticals and Functional Foods* (ed. REC Wildman), pp. 297–307. Boca Raton, FL: CRC Press.

Medeiros DM, Wildman R. (1997). New findings on a unified perspective of copper restriction and cardiomyopathy. *Proc. Soc. Exp. Biol. Med.* 215:299–313.

Messina V, Vessanto M, Mangels AR. (2003). A new food guide for north American vegetarians. *Can Diet Pract Res.* 64:82–86.

Millard-Stafford ML, Cureton KJ, Wingo JE, Trilk J, Warren GL, Buyckx M. (2007) Hydration during exercise in warm, humid conditions: effect of a caffeinated sports drink. *Int J Sport Nutr Exerc Metab* 17:163–177.

Millen AE, Dodd KW, Subar AF. (2004) Use of vitamin, mineral, nonvitamin, and nonmineral supplements in the United States: The 1987, 1992, and 2000 National Health Interview Survey results. *J Am Diet Assoc* 104:942–950.

Millen BE, Quatromoni PA, Pencina M, Kimokoti R, Nam BH, Corbin S, et al. (2005). Unique dietary patterns and chronic disease risk profiles of adult men: the Framingham nutrition studies. *J Am Diet Assoc.* 105:1723–1734.

Montgomery, KS. (2002) Nutrition column: An update on water needs during pregnancy and beyond. *J Perinat Educ* 11:40–42.

Mooney KM, Cromwell CL. (1997). Efficacy of chromium picolinate and chromium chloride as potential carcass modifiers in swine. *J Anim Sci.* 75:2661–2671.

Mozaffarian D, Katan MB, Alberto Ascherio A, Stampfer MJ, Willet WC. (2006) Trans fatty acids and cardiovascular disease. *N Engl J Med* 354:1601–1613.

Muise AM, Stein DG, Arbess G. (2003) Eating disorders in adolescent boys: A review of the adolescent and young adult literature. *J Adolesc Health* 33:427–435.

Muller O, Krawinkel M. (2005) Malnutrition and health in developing countries. *CMAJ* 173:279–286.

Murphy S, Poos M. (2002) Dietary Reference Intakes: Summary of applications in dietary assessment. *Public Health Nutrition* 5:843–849.

Murphy SP, Barr SI. (2007) Food guides reflect similarities and differences in dietary guidance in three countries (Japan, Canada, and the United States). *Nutr Rev* 65:141–148.

National Academy of Sciences. (1997). *Dietary reference intakes for calcium, phosphorus, magnesium, vitamin D, and fluoride.* Washington, DC: National Academies Press.

National Academy of Sciences. (2000). *Dietary reference intakes for Vitamin A, Vitamin K, arsenic, boron, chromium, copper, iodine, iron, manganese, molybdenum, nickel, silicon, vanadium, and zinc.* Washington DC: National Academies Press.

National Center for Health Statistics. Prevalence of overweight and obesity among adults United States 2003–2004. www.cdc.gov/nchs/products/pubs/pubd/hestats/overweight/overweight_adult.03.htm

National Digestive Diseases Information Clearinghouse. (2004) *H. pylori* and peptic ulcer. NIH Publication No. 05–4225. http://digestive.niddk.nih.gov/ddiseases/pubs/hpylori/

National Heart Lung and Blood Institute. (2007) Keep an Eye on Portion Size. http://hp2010.nhlbihin.net/portion/keep.htm

National Institute on Drug Abuse. (1991) *National Household Survey on Drug Abuse: Main Findings 1990.* DHHS Pub. No. (ADM) 91–1788.Washington, DC: U.S. Government Printing Office.

Naylor R, Steinfeld H, Falcon W, Galloway J, Smil V, Bradford E, et al. (2005). *Science.* 310:1621–1622.

NCAA issues notice about nutritional supplement provision (2005, May 25) The NCAA News Online NCAA.

Neumark-Sztainer D. (2006) Eating among teens: Do family mealtimes make a difference for adolescents' nutrition? *New Dir Child Adolesc Dev* 111:91–105.

Newberry H, Beerman K, Duncan S, McGuire M, Hillers V. (2001) Use of nonvitamin, nonmineral supplements among college students. *J Am Coll Health* 50:123–127.

Nguyen DM. (2010). The epidemiology of obesity. *Gastroenterolgy.* 39(1):1–7.

Nord M, Andrews M, Carlson S. (2004) *Household Food Security in the United States*. Washington, DC: Economic Research Service, U.S. Department of Agriculture.

Nord M, Andrews M, Carlson S. (2004). Household food security in the United States. Economic Research Service, United States Department of Agriculture.

Nowson CA, Morgan TO, Gibbons C. (2003). Decreasing dietary sodium while following a self-selected potassium-rich diet reduces blood pressure. *J Nutr.* 133:4118–4123.

Noy N. (2006) Vitamin A. In *Biochemical, Physiological, and Molecular Aspects of Human Nutrition,* 2nd ed. (ed. MH Stipanuk ), pp. 835–862, St. Louis, MO: Saunders Elsevier.

Obarzanek E, Proschan MA, Vollmer WM, Moore TJ, Sacks FM, Appel LJ. (2003). Individual blood pressure responses to changes in salt intake: results from the DASH-Sodium trial. *Hypertension.* 42:457–458.

O'Connor TM, Yang SJ, Nicklas TA. (2006). Beverage intake among preschool children and its effect on weight status. *Pediatrics.* 118: e1010–e1018.

Ogden CL, Flegal KM, Carroll MD, Johnson CL. (2002) Prevalence and trends in overweight among US children and adolescents, 1999–2000. *JAMA* 228:1728–1732.

Ogden CL, Yanovski SZ, Carroll MD, Flegal KM. (2007) The epidemiology of obesity. *Gastroenterology* 132: 2087–2102.

Ohtani M, Sugita M, Maruyama K. (2006) Amino acid mixture improves training efficiency in athletes. *J Nutr* 136:538S–543S.

O'Mahony L, McCarthy J, Kelly P, Hurley G, Luo F, Chen K, O'Sullivan GC, Kiely B, Collins JK, Shanahan F, Quigley EMM. (2005) *Lactobacillus* and *bifidobacterium* in irritable bowel syndrome: Symptom responses and

relationship to cytokine profiles. *Gastroenterology* 128:783–785.

Paddon-Jones D, Borsheim E, Wolfe RR. (2004) Potential ergogenic effects of arginine and creatine supplementation. *J Nutr* 134:2888S–2894S.

Parker RS. (2006) Vitamin E. In *Biochemical, Physiological, and Molecular Aspects of Human Nutrition.* 2nd ed. (ed. MH Stipanuk), pp. 819–834. St. Louis, MO: Saunders Elsevier.

Peele S. (1993). The conflict between public health goals and the temperance mentality. *Am J Pub Health.* 83:805–810.

Peele S. (1997). Utilizing culture and behavior in epidemiological models of alcohol consumption and consequences for Western nations. *Alcohol & Alcoholism.* 32:51–64.

Philips SM. (2004) Protein requirements and supplementation in strength sports. *Nutrition* 20:689–695.

Philips SM. (2006) Dietary protein for athletes: from requirements to metabolic advantage. *Appl Physiol Nutr Metab* 31:647–654.

Phung OJ, Quercia RA, Keating K, Baker WL, Bell JL, White CM, et al. (2010). Improved glucose control associated with I.V. chromium administration in two patients receiving enteral nutrition. *Am J Health Syst Pharm.* 67:535–541.

Pihl RO, Paylan SS, Gentes-Hawn A, Hoaken PNS. (2003). Alcohol affects executive cognitive functioning differentially on the ascending versus descending limb of the blood alcohol concentration curve. *Alcsm Clin Exp Res.* 27:773–779.

Pipher M. (1994) *Reviving Ophelia: Saving the Selves of Adolescent Girls.* New York: Ballantine.

Piran N, Levine MP, Steiner-Adair C. (1999) *Preventing Eating Disorders.* Ann Arbor, MI: Edwards Brothers.

Pitkanen HT, Nykanen T, Knuutinen J, Lahti K, Keinanen O, Alen M, Komi PV, Mero AA. (2003) Free amino acid pool and muscle protein balance after resistance exercise. *Med Sci Sports Exerc* 35:784–792.

Pope HG, Gruber A, Mangweth B, Bureau B, DeCol C, Jouvent R, Hudson JI. (2000) Body image perception among men in three countries. *Am J Psychiatry* 157:1297–1301.

Pope HG, Lalonde JK, Pindyck LJ, Walsh T, Bulik CM, Crow SJ, McElroy SL, Rosenthal N, Hudson JI. (2006) Binge eating disorder: A stable syndrome. *Am J Psychiatry* 163:2181–2184.

Poschl G, Seitz HK. (2004) Alcohol and cancer. *Alcohol* 39:155–165.

Position of the American Dietetic Association: Dietary guidance for healthy children ages 2 to 11 years. (2004) *J Am Diet Assoc* 104:660–677.

Position of the American Dietetics Association and Dietitians of Canada: Vegetarian diets. (2003) *J Am Diet Assoc* 103:748–765.

Position of the American Dietetics Association: Nutrition and lifestyle for a healthy pregnancy outcome. (2002) *J Am Diet Assoc* 102:1479–1490.

Position of the American Dietetics Association: Promoting and supporting breast-feeding. (2005) *J Am Diet Assoc* 105:810–818.

Prentice AM, Jebb SA. (1995). Obesity in Britain: gluttony or sloth? *BMJ.* 311(7002):437–439.

Pryor WA, Stahl W, Rock CL. (2000) Beta carotene: from biochemistry to clinical trials. *Nutr Rev.* 58:39–53.

Puhl R, Brownell KD. (2001) Bias, discrimination and obesity. *Obes Res* 9:768–805.

Pynaert I, Delangthe J, Temmerman M, De Henauw S. (2007) Iron intake in relation to diet and iron status of young adult women. *Ann Nutr Metab* 51:172–181.

Qian M, Wang D, Watkins WE, Gebski V, Yan YQ, Li M, et al. (2005) The effect of iodine on intelligence in children: a meta-analysis of studies conducted in China. *Asia Pac J Clin Nutr.* 14:32–42.

Quinconzes-Santos A, Andreazza, AC, Mardin P, Funchal C, Concalves CA, Gottfried C. (2007) Resverastrol attenuates oxidative-induced DNA damage in C6 Glioma cells. *Neurotoxicology* 28:886–891.

Radimer K, Bindewald B, Hughes J, Ervin B, Swanson C, Picciano MF. (2004) Dietary supplement use by U.S. adults: Data from the National Health and Nutrition Examination Survey, 1999–2000. *Am J Epidemiol* 160:339–349. DOI: 10.1093/aje/kwh207.

Raiten DJ, Kalhan SC, Hay WW. (2007) Maternal nutrition and optimal infant feeding practices: Executive summary. *Am J Clin Nutr* 85: 577S–583S.

Rampersaud GC, Pereira MA, Girard BL, Adams J, Metzl JD. (2005). Breakfast habits, nutritional status, body weight, and academic performance in children and adolescents. *J Am Diet Assoc.* 105:743–760.

Rantala A. (2001) Risk factors and carotid atherosclerosis in hypertensive and control subjects [academic dissertation]. Department of Internal Medicine, University of Oulu, Finland. http://herkules.oulu.fi/isbn9514264657

Redlich CA, Blaner WS, Van Bennekum AM, Chung JS, Clever SL, Holm CT, et al. (1998). Effect of supplementation with beta-carotene and vitamin A on lung nutrient levels. *Cancer Epidemiol Biomarkers Prev.* 7:211–214.

Reger B, Wootan MG, Booth-Butterfield S. (2000) A comparison of different approaches to promote community-wide dietary change. *Am J Prev Med* 18:271–275.

Reid G. (2002) Regulatory and clinical aspects of dairy probiotics. FAO/WHO expert consultation on the evaluation of health and nutritional properties of powdered milk with live lactic acid bacteria. Cordoba, Argentina, Oct 1–4, 2001.

Rice S, Whitehead SA. (2006) Phytoestrogens and breast cancer—promoters or protectors? *Endocr Relat Cancer* 13:995–1015.

Rivera L, Moron R, Zarzuelo A, Galisteo M. (2009). Long term resveratrol administration reduces metabolic disturbances and lowers blood pressure in obese Zucker rats. *Biochem Pharm.* 77(6):1053–1063.

Ronnenberg AG, Venners SA, Xu X, Chen C, Wang L, Guang W, Huang A, Wang X. (2007) Preconception B-vitamin and homocysteine status, conception, and early pregnancy loss. *Am J Epidemiol* 166:304–312.

Rowlands DS, Thomson JS. (2009). Effects of beta-hydroxy-beta-methylbutyrate supplementation during resistance training on strength, body composition, and muscle damage in trained and untrained young men: a meta-analysis. *J Strength and Cond.* 23(3):836–846.

Rowlands JC, Hoadley JE. (2006) FDA perspectives on health claims for food labels. *Toxicology* (2006) 221:35–43. Epub 2006 Feb 9.

Ruffolo JS, Phillips KA, Menard W, Fay C, Weisberg RB. (2006) Comorbidity of body dysmorphic disorder and eating disorder: Severity of psychopathology and body image disturbance. *Int J Eat Dis* 39:11–19.

Ruowei LI, Rock VJ, Grummer-Strawn L. (2007) Changes in public attitudes toward breast-feeding in the United States, 1999–2003. *J Am Diet Assoc* 107:122–127.

Sacks FM, Bray GA, Carey VJ, Smith SR, Ryan DH, Anton SD, et al. (2009). Comparison of weight-loss diets with different compositions of fat, protein and carbohydrates. *New Engl J of Med.* 360(9):859–873.

Saladin KS. (2007) *Anatomy and physiology: The unity of form and function* 4th ed. New York: McGraw-Hill.

Satter E. (1987). *How to get your child to eat . . . but not too much.* Palo Alto, CA: Bull Publishing Co.

Satter E. (2000). *Child of mine.* Palo Alto, CA: Bull Publishing Co.

Saunders JB, Aasland OG, Babor TF, de al Fuente JR, Grant M. (1993). Development of the Alcohol Use Disorders Identification Test (AUDIT): WHO Collaborative Project On Early Detection Of Persons With Harmful Alcohol Consumption—II. *Addiction.* 88:791–804.

Savaiano DA, Boushey CJ, McCabe GP. (2006). Lactose intolerance symptoms assessed by meta-analysis: a grain of truth that leads to exaggeration. *J Nutr.* 136:1107–1113.

Sawitzke AD, Shi H, Finco MF, Dunlop DD, Harris CL, Singer NG, et al. (2010) Clinical efficacy and safety of glucosamine, chondroitin sulfate, their combination, calecoxib or placebo taken to treat osteoarthritis of the knee: 2 year results from GAIT. *Ann Rheum Dis.* Aug;69(8):1459–1464.

Sawka MN, Burke LM, Eichner ER, Maughan RJ, Montain SJ, Stachenfeld NS. (2007) Exercise and fluid replacement. Position stand of the American College of Sports Medicine. *Med Sci Sports Exer* 39:377–390.

Saxelin M, Tynkkynen S, Matilla-Sandholm T, de Vos WM. (2005) Probiotic and other functional microbes: from markets to mechanisms. *Curr Opin Biotechnol* 16:204–211.

Schack-Nileson L, Michaelson KF. (2007) Advances in our understanding of the biology of human milk and its effects on the offspring. *J Nutr* 137:503s–510s.

Scheeman B, Trumbo P, Ellwood K, Satchell F. (2006) The regulatory process to revise nutrition labeling relative to the dietary reference intakes. *Am J Clin Nutr* 83:1228S–1230S.

Schnirring L. (2003) New hydration recommendations: risk of hyponatremia plays a big role. *Phys Sportsmed* 31:1145–1155.

Schwartz MB, Chambliss HO, Brownell KD, Blair SN, Billington C. (2003) Weight bias among health professionals specializing in obesity. *Obes Res* 11:1033–1039.

Scornik H. (2007) Changing the American diet. *Pediatrics in Review* 28:4.

Seal CJ. (2006). Whole grains and CVD risk. *Proc Nutr Soc.* 65:24–34.

Shane B. (2006) Folic acid, vitamins B12, and vitamin B6. In *Biochemical, Physiological, and Molecular Aspects of Human Nutrition*, 2nd ed. (ed. MH Stipanuk), pp. 693–732. St. Louis, MO: Saunders Elsevier.

Shetty P. (2005) Energy requirements of adults. *Public Health Nutr* 8:994–1009.

Shils ME, Olson JA, Shine M, Ross AC. (1999) *Modern Nutrition in Health and Disease.* 9th ed. Philadelphia: Lippincott.

Shirreffs SM, Armstrong LE, Cheuvront SN. 2004. Fluid and electrolyte needs for preparation and recovery from training and competition. *J Sports Sci.* 22:57–63.

Sikorska H, Cianciara J, Wiercinska-Drapalo A. (2010). Physiological functions of L-ornithine and L-aspartate in the body and the efficacy of administration of L-ornithine–L-aspartate in conditions of relative deficiency. *Pol Merkur Lekarski.* 28(168):490495.

Small L, Anderson D, Melnyk BM. (2007) Prevention and early treatment of overweight and obesity in young children: A critical review and appraisal of the evidence. *Pediatr Nurs* 33:149–152, 155–161, 127.

Smitasiri S, Uauy R. (2007) Beyond recommendations: implementing food-based dietary guidelines for healthier populations. *Food Nutr Bull* 28:S141–151.

Smith SM, Mathews Oliver SA, Zwart SR, Kala G, Kelly PA, Goodwin JS, et al. (2006). Nutritional status is altered in the self-neglecting elderly. *J Nutr.* 136:2534–2541.

Snyder LB, Milici FF, Slater M, Sun H, Strizhakova Y. (2006). Effects of alcohol advertising exposure on drinking among youth. *Arch Pediatr Adolesc Med.* 160:18–24.

Song GJ, Norkus EP, Lewis V. (2006) Relationship between seminal ascorbic acid and sperm DNA integrity in infertile men. *Int J Androl* 29:569–575.

Soory M. (2009). Relevance of nutritional antioxidants in metabolic syndrome, ageing and cancer: potential for therapeutic targeting. *Infect Disord Drug Targets.* 9(4):400–414.

Speakman JR. (2004) Obesity: the integrated role of environment and genetics. *J Nutr* 134:2090S–2105S.

Stacy AW, Zogg JB, Unger JB, Dent CW. (2004). Exposure to televised alcohol ads and subsequent adolescent alcohol use. *Am J Health Behav.* 28:498–509.

Stewart ML, Nikhanj SD, Timm DA, Thomas W, Slavin JL. (2010). Evaluation of the effect of four fibers on laxation, gastrointestinal tolerance and serum markers in healthy humans. *Ann Nutr Metab.* 56:91–98.

Stipanuk MH. (2000). *Biochemical and physiological aspects of human nutrition.* Philadelphia, PA: W.B. Saunders.

St-Onge MP, Keller KL, Heymsfield SB. (2003). Changes in childhood food consumption patterns: a cause for concern in light of increasing body weights. *Am J Clin Nutr.* 78:1068–1103.

Storey ML, Forshee RA, Andersen PA. (2006). Beverage consumption in the US population. *J Am Diet Assoc.* 106:1992–2000.

Strasburger VC, Jordan AB, Donnerstein E. (2010). Health effects of media on children and adolescents. *Pediatrics.* Apr;125(4):756–767.

Stratton K, Howe C, Battaglia F, eds. (1996) *Fetal Alcohol Syndrome: Diagnosis, Epidemiology, Prevention, and Treatment.* Washington, DC: National Academies Press.

Striegel-Moore RH, Dohm F, Hook JM, Schreiber GB, Crawford PB, Daniels SR. (2005) Night eating syndrome in young adult women: prevalence and correlates. *Int J Eat Dis* 37:200–206.

Sullivan A, Nord CE. (2005) Review: Probiotics and gastrointestinal diseases. *J Intern Med* 257:78–92.

Sullivan L. (1997). Fetal alcohol syndrome and other effects of alcohol on pregnancy outcome. In: *Alcohol and health: 7th report to the US Congress.* pp. 139–162. Darby, PA: Diane Publishing Co. http://www.fda.gov/Food/ResourcesForYou/Consumers/ucm079516.htm

Tarnopolsky M. (2004) Protein requirements for endurance athletes. *Nutrition* 20:662–668.

Ting JH, Wallis DH. (2007) Medical management of the athlete: evaluation and treatment of important issues in sports medicine. *Clin Podiatr Med Surg* 24:127–158.

Tipton KD, Rasmussen BB, Miller SL, Wolf SE, Owens-Stovall SK, Petrini BE, et al. (2001). Timing of amino acid carbohydrate ingestion alters anabolic response of muscle to resistance exercise. *Am J Physiol Endocrinol Metab.* 281:E197–E206.

Tipton KD, Witard OC. (2007) Protein requirements and recommendations for athletes: Relevance of ivory tower arguments for practical recommendations. *Clin Sports Med* 26:17–36.

Tipton KD, Wolfe RR. (2004) Protein and amino acids for athletes. *J Sports Sci* 22:65–79.

Tran N, Barraj L. (2010). Contribution of specific dietary factors to CHD in US females. *Public Health Nutr.* 13:152–162.

Tsintsifa E, Faxantidis P, Tsiligkriroglou-Fachanidon A, Deligianis A. (2006). Interactions among habitual physical activity, eating patterns, and diet composition. *Angiology.* 57:205–209.

Tucker KL. (2009). Osteoporosis prevention and nutrition. *Curr Osteoporos Rep.* 7:111–117.

Tucker ON, Szomstein S, Rosenthal RJ. (2007) Nutritional consequences of weight-loss surgery. *Med Clin North Am* 91:499–514, xii.

U.S. Department of Health and Human Services and U.S. Department of Agriculture. (2005) *Dietary Guidelines for Americans.* HHS Publication No. HHS-ODPHP-2005–01-DGA-A. USDA Home and Garden Bulletin No. 232. www.health.gov/dietaryguidelines/dga2005/document/pdf/DGA2005.pdf

U.S. Department of Health and Human Services. (2002) Physical activity fundamental to preventing disease. http://aspe.hhs.gov/health/reports/physicalactivity

U.S. Department of Health and Human Services. (2007) FDA announces new tools for the nutrition facts label *FDA. Consum* 41:33.

U.S. Food and Drug Administration (2001) *FDA 2001 Food Code.* Washington, DC: U.S. Public Health Service.

U.S. Food and Drug Administration. (1998) *Managing Food Safety: A HACCP Principles Guide for Operators of Food Establishments at the Retail Level: Regulatory Applications in Retail Food Establishments.* Washington, DC: Center for Food Safety and Applied Nutrition.

van Rosendal SP, Osborne MA, Fassett RG, Coombes JS. (2010). Guidelines for glycerol use in hyperhydration and rehydration associated with exercise. *Sports Med.* 40(2):113–129.

Venderley AM, Campbell WW. (2006) Vegetarian diets: nutritional considerations for athletes. *Sports Med* 36:293–305.

Wadden TA, Butryn ML, Wilson C. (2007) Lifestyle modification for the management of obesity. *Gastroenterology* 132:2226–2238.

Walley AJ, Blakemore AI, Froguel P. (2006) Genetics of obesity and the prediction of risks for health. *Hum Mol Genet* 15:R124–130.

Wallin R, Hutson SM. (2006) Vitamin K. In: *Biochemical, Physiological, and Molecular Aspects of Human Nutrition.* 2nd ed. (ed. MH Stipanuk), pp. 797–818. St. Louis, MO: Saunders Elsevier.

Wang Y, Zhang Q. (2006). Are American children and adolescents of low socioeconomic status at increased risk of obesity? Changes in the association between overweight and family income between 1971 and 2002. *Am J Clin Nutr.* 84:707–716.

Ward C, Lewis S, Coleman T. (2007) Prevalence of maternal smoking and environmental tobacco smoke exposure during pregnancy and impact on birth weight: retrospective study using Millennium Cohort. *BMC Public Health 7* (May 16): 81.

Weeden A, Remig V, Holcomb CA, Herald TJ, Baybutt RC. (2010). Vitamin and mineral supplements have a nutritionally significant impact on micronutrient intakes of older adults attending senior centers. *J Nutr Elder.* 29:241–254.

Weichselbaum E. (2010). Potential benefits of probiotics—main findings of an in-depth review. *Br J Community Nurs.* 15(3):110–114.

Whitlock G, Lewington S. (2002) Surprising evidence about associations between body mass index and risks of coronary heart disease and stroke. *Arch Intern Med* 162:2490–2491.

Wildman REC, Medeiros DM. (2000) *Advanced Human Nutrition.* Boca Raton, FL: CRC Press.

Wildman REC, Miller BS. (2004) *Sports and Fitness Nutrition.* Belmont, CA: Wadsworth/Thomson Learning.

Wildman REC. (2002) *The Nutritionist: Food, Nutrition, and Optimal Health.* New York: Haworth Press.

Willett, WC. (2001). *Eat, Drink, and Be Healthy: The Harvard Medical School Guide to Healthy Eating.* New York: Simon and Schuster.

Wilson KM. (2006). Use of complementary medicine and dietary supplements among U.S. adolescents. *J Adolesc Health* 38:385–394.

Wolsko PM, Slondz DK, Phillips RS, Shachter SC, Eisenberg DM. (2005). Lack of herbal supplement characterization in published randomized controlled trials. *Am J Med* 118:1087–1093.

World Health Organization, Food and Agriculture Organization. (2003) *Diet, Nutrition and the Prevention of Chronic Diseases.* Geneva: WHO. www.who.int/hpr/NPH/docs/who_fao_expert_report.pdf

World Health Organization. (2001) *Fifty-Fourth World Health Assembly Global Strategy for Infant and Young Child Feeding: The Optimal Duration of Exclusive Breast-Feeding.* Geneva: World Health Organization.

World Health Organization. (2002) *WHO Global Database on Child Growth and Malnutrition.* Geneva: WHO.

World Health Organization/Food and Agriculture Organization Expert Consultation on Diet, Nutrition and the Prevention of Chronic Diseases (2003). http://www.who.int/hpr/NPH/docs/who_fao_expert_report.pdf

Wu G, Bazer FW, Davis TA, Kim SW, Li P, Rhoads M, Satterfield MC, Smith SB, Spencer TE, Yin Y. (2009). *Amino Acids.* 37(1):153–168.

Yang CY. (1998). Calcium and magnesium in drinking water and risk of death from cerebrovascular disease. *Stroke.* 29:411–414.

Yates AA. (2006) Dietary references intakes: concepts and approaches underlying protein and energy requirements. *Nestle Nutr Workshop Ser Pediatr Program* 58 :79–90; discussion 90–4.

Young LR, Nestle M. (2002). The contribution of expanding portion sizes to the U.S. obesity epidemic. *Am J Public Health* 92:246–248.

Zemel MB, Thompson W, Milstead A, Morris K, Campbell B. (2004). Calcium and dairy acceleration of weight and fat loss during energy restriction in obese adults. *Obesity Res.* 12:582–590.

Zemel MB. (2002). Regulation of adiposity and obesity risk by dietary calcium: mechanisms and implications. *J. Am Coll Nutr.* 21:146S–151S.

Zhang S, Hunter DJ, Forman MR, Rosner BA, Speizer FE, Colditz GA, et al. (1999). Dietary carotenoids and vitamins A, C, E and risk of breast cancer. *J Natl Cancer Inst.* 91:547–556.

Zimmerman E, Wylie-Rosett J. (2003). Nutrition therapy for hypertension. *Curr Diab Rep.* 3: 404–411.

Zlotkowska R, Zejda JE. (2005) Fetal and postnatal exposure to tobacco smoke and respiratory health in children. *Eur J of Epidemiol* 20:719–727.

# WEBSITES

About.com

Christianity/Catholicismhttp//:catholicism.about.com

The Bad Bug Book

www.cfsan.fda.gov/~mow/intro.html

Centers for Disease Control and Prevention, Division of Bacterial and Mycotic Diseases *Helicobacter pylori* infections (*H. pylori*)

www.cdc.gov/ulcer/

Coffee: filtering the facts

www.xterraplanet.com/training/dsp_content.cfm?id=90

CSPI's Guide to Food Additives

www.cspinet.org/reports/chemcuisine.htm

Dietary and Herbal Supplements

http://nccam.nih.gov/health/supplements.htm

Dietary Supplements—Warnings and Safety Information

www.cfsan.fda.gov/~dms/ds-warn.html

FDA Issues Draft Documents on the Safety of Animal Clones

www.fda.gov/bbs/topics/NEWS/2006/NEW01541.html

Florida Department of Agriculture and Consumer Services, Division of Food Safety: From Farm to Table

www.doacs.state.fl.us/fs/safety.html

Food Additives: What Are They?

www.extension.iastate.edu/Publications/NCR438.pdf

Food Pyramids: What Should You Really Eat?

www.hsph.harvard.edu/nutritionsource/pyramids.html

Gatorade Sport Science Institute

www.gssiweb.com

A Guide to Dietary Supplements

www.extension.iastate.edu/nutrition/supplements/supplement_list.php

HACCP Questions and Answers

http://haccpalliance.org/alliance/haccpqa.html

Halal Guidelines for a Muslim Diet

www.jamiat.org.za/hguideline.html

Harvard Medical School Family Health Guide. (2005) Health benefits of taking probiotics.

www.health.harvard.edu/fhg/updates/update0905c.shtml

Harvard School of Public Health. (2006) Protein moving closer to center stage.

http://hsph.harvard.edu/nutritionsource/protein.html.

Hindu Beliefs and Practices Affecting Health Care

www.healthsystem.virginia.edu/internet/chaplaincy/hindu.cfm

How to Know What Is Safe: Choosing and Using Dietary Supplements

www.cancer.org/docroot/ETO/content/ETO_5_3x_How_to_Know_

How to Understand and Use the Nutrition Facts Label

www.cfsan.fda.gov/~dms/foodlab.html

Infant Formula: The Next Best Thing to Breast Feeding

www.cnn.com/HEALTH/library/PR/00058/html

The Issues: Fossil Fuel and Energy Use

www.sustainabletable.org/issues/energy/

Mercury Contamination in Fish

www.nrdc.org/health/effects/mercury/index.asp?gclid=CJ7Eusjp3owCFReQgQodzIV82Q

My Pyramid.gov Dietary Guidelines

www.MyPyramid.gov/guidelines/index.html

National Digestive Disease Information Clearinghouse (NDDIC): What I need to know about Irritable Bowel Syndrome

http://digestiveniddk.nih.gov/ddiseases/pubs/ibs_ez/

National Institutes of Health, Office of Dietary Supplements

http://dietary-supplement.info.nih.gov/health_information/health_information.aspx

Natural Medicines Comprehensive Database

www.naturaldatabase.com

Oldways

www.oldwayspt.org

The Preeclampsia Foundation

www.preeclampsia.org

Red Bull in Suspected Link to Deaths

http://news.bbc.co.uk/1/health/1435409.stm

A Risk-Based Approach to Evaluate Animal Clones and Their Progeny Draft

www.fda.gov/cvm/CloneRiskAssessment.htm

University of Florida, Institute of Food and Agriculture Science http://edis.ifas.ufl.edu.

Usprobiotics.org

www.usprobiotics.org

Vegetarian Nutrition Resource List

www.nal.usda.gov/fnic/pubs/bibs/gen/vegetarian.htm

Vegetarian Resource

Groupwww.vrg.org

What You Need to Know about Mercury in Fish and Shellfish

www.cfsan.fda.gov/~dms/admehg3.html

What_Is_Safe_Choosing_and_Using_Dietary_Supplements .asp

The Worlds of David Darling: Small Intestine

www.daviddarling.info/encyclopedia/S/small_intestine .html

# Photo Credits

## Chapter 1

p. 2 top: © 2011 Graeme Dawes. Used under license from Shutterstock, Inc., bottom: © 2011 Bogdan Wankowicz. Used under license from Shutterstock, Inc.

p. 3 © 2011 crolique. Used under license from Shutterstock, Inc.

p. 4 M. Deioma/PhotoEdit Inc.

p. 5 © 2011 Serg64. Used under license from Shutterstock, Inc.

p. 6 © 2011 keko64. Used under license from Shutterstock, Inc.

p. 7 Copyright © Teri Stratford/Six-Cats Research, Inc. Reprinted by permission.

p. 8 © 2011 Shutterstock, Inc.

p. 10 © Peter Menzel/menzelphoto.com; beans and rice: © 2011 Hemera. Used under license from Shutterstock, Inc.

p. 11 © 2011 Shutterstock, Inc.; strawberries © 2011 Adisa. Used under license from Shutterstock, Inc.; corn © 2011 Sandra Caldwell. Used under license from Shutterstock, Inc.; pears © 2011 Valentyn Volkov. Used under license from Shutterstock, Inc.

p. 13 © 2011 Darren Brode. Used under license from Shutterstock, Inc.

p. 14 Getty Images/Antonio Mo; shrimp: © 2011 Michael C. Gray. Used under license from Shutterstock, Inc.

p. 15 © 2011 Cheryl E. Davis. Used under license from Shutterstock, Inc.

p. 16 Copyright © Teri Stratford/Six-Cats Research, Inc. Reprinted by permission.

p. 17 © 2011 Shutterstock, Inc.

p. 18 bottom: © 2011 Shutterstock, Inc.

p. 20 © 2011 Shutterstock, Inc.

p. 21 top: © Keith Dannemiller/Corbis; bottom: © 2011 iStockphoto.

p. 22 © 2011 Shutterstock, Inc.

p. 24 © Jerry Arcieri/Corbis

p. 25 top left: Copyright © Teri Stratford/Six-Cats Research, Inc. Reprinted by permission.; top right: Copyright © Teri Stratford/Six-Cats Research, Inc. Reprinted by permission.; peppers © 2011 Yellowj. Used under license from Shutterstock, Inc.

## Chapter 2

p. 30 top: © 2011 Kevin Britland. Used under license from Shutterstock, Inc.; bottom: © 2011 Morgan Lane Photography. Used under license from Shutterstock, Inc.

p. 31 © 2011 Africa Studio. Used under license from Shutterstock, Inc.

p. 32 © 2011 Yuri Arcurs. Used under license from Shutterstock, Inc.

p. 33 left: © 2011 Denis Pepin. Used under license from Shutterstock, Inc.; right: PhotoEdit Inc/David Young Wolff

p. 36 © Peter Menzel/menzelphoto.com

p. 45 Copyright © Teri Stratford/Six-Cats Research, Inc. Reprinted by permission.

p. 49 baseball © 2011 Joyce Michaud. Used under license from Shutterstock, Inc.; rice: © 2011 Blaj Gabriel. Used under license from Shutterstock, Inc.

p. 50 © 2011 Enrico Jose. Used under license from Shutterstock, Inc.

p. 52 Courtesy of Egglands Best, Inc.

p. 59 Jennifer Bruno, The Augusta Chronicle

p. 60 pots © 2011 Ivonne Wierink. Used under license from Shutterstock, Inc.; measuring spoons © 2011 tacar. Used under license from Shutterstock, Inc.

p. 62 © 2011 discpicture. Used under license from Shutterstock, Inc.

p. 63 © 2011 msheldrake. Used under license from Shutterstock, Inc.

p. 64 © 2011 Magone. Used under license from Shutterstock, Inc.

p. 65 top: © 2011 tomas24. Used under license from Shutterstock, Inc.

p. 65 bottom: © 2011 keko64. Used under license from Shutterstock, Inc.

p. 66 top: © 2011 Gemenacom. Used under license from Shutterstock, Inc.; bottom: © 2011 Josh Resnick. Used under license from Shutterstock, Inc.

p. 67 © 2011 Hannamariah. Used under license from Shutterstock, Inc.

p. 69 © 2011 svry. Used under license from Shutterstock, Inc.

## Chapter 3

p. 70 top: © 2011 Aaron Amat. Used under license from Shutterstock, Inc.; bottom: © 2011 ultimathule. Used under license from Shutterstock, Inc.

p. 71 © 2011 Marie C. Fields. Used under license from Shutterstock, Inc.

p. 73 wheat © 2011 Mark Kuipers. Used under license from Shutterstock, Inc., rice © 2011 Ambient Ideas. Used under license from Shutterstock, Inc., cassava © 2011 Jakub Pavlinec. Used under license from Shutterstock, Inc., corn © 2011 keren-seg. Used under license from Shutterstock, Inc.

p. 75 © 2011 Ljupco Smokovski. Used under license from Shutterstock, Inc.

p. 78 Whole Grains Council

p. 79 © 2011 sahua d. Used under license from Shutterstock, Inc.

p. 82 © 2011 Yanas. Used under license from Shutterstock, Inc.

p. 84 © 2011 Bochkarev Photography. Used under license from Shutterstock, Inc.

p. 86 © 2011 monticello. Used under license from Shutterstock, Inc.

p. 89 © 2011 Christy Thompson. Used under license from Shutterstock, Inc.

p. 92 © Kim Kulish/Corbis

p. 93 © Lester Bergman/Corbis/Lester Bergman

p. 97 Copyright © Teri Stratford/Six-Cats Research, Inc. Reprinted by permission.

## Chapter 4

p. 102 top: © 2011 Cheryl E. Davis. Used under license from Shutterstock, Inc., bottom: © 2011 Dmitry Rukhlenko. Used under license from Shutterstock, Inc.

p. 103 © 2011 DUSAN ZIDAR. Used under license from Shutterstock, Inc.

p. 104 © 2011 Shutterstock, Inc.

p. 108 © 2011 Gordon Swanson. Used under license from Shutterstock, Inc.

p. 110 Copyright © Teri Stratford/Six-Cats Research, Inc. Reprinted by permission.

p. 116 © 2011 Joao Virissimo. Used under license from Shutterstock, Inc.

p. 118 © 2011 Shutterstock, Inc.

p. 120 top: From CP Kelco. Copyright © by CP Kelco. Reprinted by permission.; bottom: Copyright © Teri Stratford/Six-Cats Research, Inc. Reprinted by permission.

p. 122 top left: © Robert Llewellyn/Corbis; top right: Copyright © Teri Stratford/Six-Cats Research, Inc. Reprinted by permission.; bottom left: © 2011 llepet. Used under license from Shutterstock, Inc., bottom right: © 2011 Elena Elisseeva. Used under license from Shutterstock, Inc.

p. 123 © 2011 Mats. Used under license from Shutterstock, Inc.

p. 124 © 2011 Elena Elisseeva. Used under license from Shutterstock, Inc.

p. 129 top left: © Robert Llewellyn/Corbis; top right: Phototake NYC

p. 131 © 2011 eleana. Used under license from Shutterstock, Inc.

p. 132 © Olinchuk. Used under license from Shutterstock, Inc.

p. 133: © Peter Menzel/menzelphoto.com

## Chapter 5

p. 138 top: © 2011 bluefox. Used under license from Shutterstock, Inc., bottom: © 2011 omkar.a.v. Used under license from Shutterstock, Inc.

p. 139 © 2011 Gregory Gerber. Used under license from Shutterstock, Inc.

p. 140 Copyright © Teri Stratford/Six-Cats Research, Inc. Reprinted by permission.

p. 143 Photo Researchers/Oliver Meckes & Nicole Ottawa

p. 144 All images © 2011 Shutterstock, Inc. Used under license from Shutterstock, Inc.

p. 145 Phototake NYC/Bart's Medical Library

p. 147 © 2011 Shutterstock, Inc. Used under license from Shutterstock, Inc.

p. 148 PhotoEdit/Richard Hutchings

p. 150 left: © 2011 Shutterstock, Inc. Used under license from Shutterstock, Inc., right: Copyright © Teri Stratford/Six-Cats Research, Inc. Reprinted by permission.

p. 152 Copyright © Teri Stratford/Six-Cats Research, Inc. Reprinted by permission.

p. 152 AP/Wide World

p. 153 © 2011 Shutterstock, Inc. Used under license from Shutterstock, Inc.

p. 154 © 2011 JinYoung Lee. Used under license from Shutterstock, Inc.

p. 155 © Peter Menzel/menzelphoto.com

p. 156 © 2011 Shutterstock, Inc. Used under license from Shutterstock, Inc.

p. 157 Vegetarian Society

p. 159 top: © 2011 Shutterstock, Inc. Used under license from Shutterstock, Inc., bottom: © 2011 Shutterstock, Inc. Used under license from Shutterstock, Inc.

p. 160 left: © Corbis/Paul Almasy; right: © Corbis/Shepard Sherbell

p. 161: AP/Wide World/Evan Vucci

## Chapter 6

p. 170 top: © 2011 Mircea BEZERGHEANU. Used under license from Shutterstock, Inc., bottom: © 2011 Tischenko Irina. Used under license from Shutterstock, Inc.

p. 171 © 2011 Liv friis-larsen. Used under license from Shutterstock, Inc.

p. 172 From Dorling Kindersley/Kevin Jones. Reprinted with permission.

p. 173 From Dorling Kindersley. Reprinted with permission.

p. 175 top: Photo Researchers/Dr. KFR Schiller; bottom: From Dorling Kindersley. Reprinted with permission.

p. 176 From Dorling Kindersley. Reprinted with permission.

p. 177 Photo Researchers, Inc.

p. 179 (a) From Dorling Kindersley. Reprinted with permission.; (b) Photo Researchers/Innerspace Imaging; (c) Photo Researchers/Dr. KFR Schiller

p. 181 Photo Researchers/Cordella Molloy

p. 182 © 2011 Shutterstock, Inc. Used under license from Shutterstock, Inc.

p. 184 © 2011 Monkey Business Images. Used under license from Shutterstock, Inc.

p. 185 © 2011 Sergey Peterman. Used under license from Shutterstock, Inc.

p. 186 © 2011 Darren Baker. Used under license from Shutterstock, Inc.

p. 187 © 2011 Chubykin Arkady. Used under license from Shutterstock, Inc.

p. 190 © 2011 Kiselev Andrey Valerevich. Used under license from Shutterstock, Inc.

p. 191 left: © 2011 Ondrej Schaumann. Used under license from Shutterstock, Inc., center: © 2011 Monkey Business Images. Used under license from Shutterstock, Inc., right: © 2011 Kiselev Andrey Valerevich. Used under license from Shutterstock, Inc.

p. 193 © 2011 maribell. Used under license from Shutterstock, Inc.

## Chapter 7

p. 200 top: © 2011 Loskutnikov. Used under license from Shutterstock, Inc., bottom: © 2011 debr22pics. Used under license from Shutterstock, Inc.

p. 201 © 2011 GalaxyPhoto. Used under license from Shutterstock, Inc.

p. 202 top: © 2011 Givaga. Used under license from Shutterstock, Inc., bottom left: © 2011 planet5D LLC. Used under license from Shutterstock, Inc.

p. 203 Copyright © Teri Stratford/Six-Cats Research, Inc. Reprinted by permission.

p. 204 © 2011 DUSAN ZIDAR. Used under license from Shutterstock, Inc.

p. 205 (a) © 2011 Branislav Senic. Used under license from Shutterstock, Inc., (b) © 2011 Galayko Sergey. Used under license from Shutterstock, Inc., (c) © 2011 PhotoEdit/Tony Freeman.

p. 206 © 2011 Monkey Business Images. Used under license from Shutterstock, Inc.

p. 214 © 2011 Gabi Moisa. Used under license from Shutterstock, Inc.

p. 215 left: Photo by David Madison/Photographer's Choice/Getty Images; right: © 2011 jcpjr. Used under license from Shutterstock, Inc.

p. 216 top © 2011 Robert Asento. Used under license from Shutterstock, Inc., bottom: Photo Edit/David Young-Wolff

p. 217 left © 2011 Wendy Nero. Used under license from Shutterstock, Inc., right © 2011 Hannamariah. Used under license from Shutterstock, Inc., center

© 2011 Andrey_Popov. Used under license from Shutterstock, Inc.

p. 220 © Peter Menzel/menzelphoto.com

p. 221 © 2011 Igor S. Srdanovic. Used under license from Shutterstock, Inc.

p. 224 © 2011 Losevsky Pavel. Used under license from Shutterstock, Inc.

p. 226 Laboratory for the Study of Human Ingestive Behavior, Penn State University

p. 227 © Jerry Arcieri/Corbis

p. 231 Copyright © Teri Stratford/Six-Cats Research, Inc. Reprinted by permission.

p. 232 © 2011 Thinkstock.com

p. 234 (a) Phototake/Kevin Somerville; (b) Phototake/BSIP; (c) © 2011 hkannn. Used under license from Shutterstock, Inc.

p. 236 © 2011 Roman Sigaev. Used under license from Shutterstock, Inc.

## Chapter 8

p. 242 top: © 2011 Anelina. Used under license from Shutterstock, Inc., bottom: © 2011 Hannamariah. Used under license from Shutterstock, Inc.;

p. 243 © 2011 Sergey Peterman. Used under license from Shutterstock, Inc.

p. 244 © 2011 oksana.perkins. Used under license from Shutterstock, Inc.

p. 246 bottom left: Copyright © Teri Stratford/Six-Cats Research, Inc. Reprinted by permission. bottom right: © 2011 Yuriy Kulyk. Used under license from Shutterstock, Inc.

p. 247 © 2007 Danylchenko Iaroslav. Used under license from Shutterstock, Inc.

p. 248 © 2011 Sergey Peterman. Used under license from Shutterstock, Inc.

p. 250 © 2011 Joyce Michaud. Used under license from Shutterstock, Inc.

p. 252 From Dorling Kindersley. Reprinted with permission.

p. 253 © 2011 Aaron Amat. Used under license from Shutterstock, Inc.

p. 255 © 2011 All photos from Shutterstock, Inc.

p. 256 © 2011 OtnaYdur. Used under license from Shutterstock, Inc.

p. 258 © 2011 Jag_cz. Used under license from Shutterstock, Inc.

## Chapter 9

p. 268 top: © 2011 Serg64. Used under license from Shutterstock, Inc., bottom: © 2011 Marie C. Fields. Used under license from Shutterstock, Inc.

p. 269 © 2011 Anna Hoychuk. Used under license from Shutterstock, Inc.

p. 273 top: ImageSmythe/David Farr; bottom: Centers for Disease Control and Prevention (CDC)

## Chapter 10

## Chapter 11

p. 370 bottom left: © 2011 Vitaly Korovin. Used under license from Shutterstock, Inc.

p. 371 ginger: © 2011 LianeM. Used under license from Shutterstock, Inc., ginseng: © 2011 Sidorovich V. Used under license from Shutterstock, Inc., ginkgo: © 2011 Alexander Raths. Used under license from Shutterstock, Inc.

p. 372 © 2011 Vasilieva Tatiana. Used under license from Shutterstock, Inc.

## Chapter 12

p. 380 top: © 2011 cmfotoworks. Used under license from Shutterstock, Inc., bottom: © 2011 El Choclo. Used under license from Shutterstock, Inc.

p. 381 © 2011 alex saberi. Used under license from Shutterstock, Inc.

p. 382 © 2011 Carlos Caetano. Used under license from Shutterstock, Inc.

p. 383 © 2011 Jakub Pavlinec. Used under license from Shutterstock, Inc.

p. 384: © Robert Wallis/Corbis

p. 384 bottom: © 2011 Lisa F. Young. Used under license from Shutterstock, Inc.

p. 386 © 2011 Anton Prado PHOTO. Used under license from Shutterstock, Inc.

p. 387 © 2011 Andresr. Used under license from Shutterstock, Inc.

p. 388: Copyright © Teri Stratford/Six-Cats Research, Inc. Reprinted by permission.

p. 389 left: Visuals Unlimited/L. Bassett, right: Photo Edit

p. 392: Copyright ©Ellen Senisi

p. 394 © 2011 ostill. Used under license from Shutterstock, Inc.

p. 395 © 2011 bikeriderlondon. Used under license from Shutterstock, Inc.

p. 398 © 2011 Rachell Coe. Used under license from Shutterstock, Inc.

p. 399 © 2011 Ryan Carter. Used under license from Shutterstock, Inc.

## Chapter 13

p. 404 top: © 2011 Inga Nielsen. Used under license from Shutterstock, Inc., bottom: © 2011 vlad_star. Used under license from Shutterstock, Inc.

p. 405 © 2011 TFoxFoto. Used under license from Shutterstock, Inc.

p. 406 carrot field: © 2011 Niv Koren. Used under license from Shutterstock, Inc., pick carrots: © 2011 Tish1. Used under license from Shutterstock, Inc., planting: © 2011 EMJAY SMITH. Used under license from Shutterstock, Inc., processing: © 2011 Richard Thornton. Used under license from Shutterstock, Inc., buy carrots: © 2011 Radu Razvan. Used under license from Shutterstock, Inc., prepare carrots: © 2011 Juriah Mosin. Used under license

from Shutterstock, Inc., eating carrots © 2011 Monkey Business Images. Used under license from Shutterstock, Inc.

p. 407 © 2011 VR Photos. Used under license from Shutterstock, Inc.

p. 408 Slow Food USA

p. 409 © 2011 Anna Dickie. Used under license from Shutterstock, Inc.

p. 411 © 2011 Gary James Calder. Used under license from Shutterstock, Inc.

p. 415 top left: © 2011 marco mayer. Used under license from Shutterstock, Inc., top right: © 2011 Kiselev Andrey Valerevich. Used under license from Shutterstock, Inc., bottom right: © 2011 Ragne Kabanova. Used under license from Shutterstock, Inc.; bottom: © 2011 Picsfive. Used under license from Shutterstock, Inc.

p. 418 left © 2011 Orientaly. Used under license from Shutterstock, Inc., right: © 2011 auremar. Used under license from Shutterstock, Inc.

p. 420 © BRENDAN MCDERMID/Reuters/Corbis

p. 421 © Ted Soqui/Corbis

p. 423 © 2011 Jean Frooms. Used under license from Shutterstock, Inc.

p. 425 © 2011 Flashon Studio. Used under license from Shutterstock, Inc.

p. 427 © 2011 Mona Makela. Used under license from Shutterstock, Inc.

p. 428 © 2011 iofoto. Used under license from Shutterstock, Inc.

p. 431 left: © 2011 Voronin76. Used under license from Shutterstock, Inc., right: © 2011 deepspacedave. Used under license from Shutterstock, Inc.

p. 432 top: © 2011 Simone van den Berg. Used under license from Shutterstock, Inc.; bottom: © 2011 Carlos Yudica. Used under license from Shutterstock, Inc.

## Chapter 14

p. 440 top: © 2011 Roxana Bashyrova. Carlos Yudica. Used under license from Shutterstock, Inc., bottom: © 2011 Fotocrisis. Carlos Yudica. Used under license from Shutterstock, Inc.

p. 441 © 2011 matka_Wariatka. Carlos Yudica. Used under license from Shutterstock, Inc.

p. 442 sprinter: © 2011 Pete Saloutos. Used under license from Shutterstock, Inc., swimmer: © 2011 Schmid Christophe. Used under license from Shutterstock, Inc., marathon runner: © 2011 Phase4Photography. Used under license from Shutterstock, Inc.

p. 446 top left: 101 Degrees West Photography, top right: © 2011 GWImages. Used under license from Shutterstock, Inc., bottom PhotoEdit/Tom Prettyman

p. 450 © 2011 Nicholas Rjabow. Used under license from Shutterstock, Inc.

p. 450: © John Springer Collection/CORBIS

p. 452 © 2011 Monkey Business Images. Used under license from Shutterstock, Inc.

p. 453 Courtesy of Hammer Nutrition

p. 455 © 2011 ARENA Creative. Used under license from Shutterstock, Inc.

p. 457 Getty Images/Robyn Beck

p. 461 © 2011 auremar. Used under license from Shutterstock, Inc.

p. 462 © 2011 Vaclav Volrab. Used under license from Shutterstock, Inc.

p. 464 © 2011 BEPictured. Used under license from Shutterstock, Inc.

p. 465 © 2011 BIGCHEN. Used under license from Shutterstock, Inc.

## Chapter 15

p. 472 top: © 2011 Daniel Gilbey Photography. Used under license from Shutterstock, Inc., bottom: © 2011 Dumitrescu Ciprian-Florin. Used under license from Shutterstock, Inc.

p. 473 © 2011 Mark Stout Photography. Used under license from Shutterstock, Inc.

p. 476 © Edward Le Poulin/Corbis

p. 477 © 2011 Monkey Business Images. Used under license from Shutterstock, Inc.

p. 478 © 2011 Jaimie Duplass. Used under license from Shutterstock, Inc.

p. 481 © 2011 Andresr. Used under license from Shutterstock, Inc.

p. 483 top left:© Gina James/Retna Ltd., top right: © RD/Kabik/Retna Ltd./Corbis, bottom: Photoedit/Bill Aaron

p. 484 top: © WWD/Condé Nast/Corbis, bottom: © 2011 dodorema. Used under license from Shutterstock, Inc.

p. 485 left: © Reuters/CORBIS, right: © 2011 Vladimir Wrangel. Used under license from Shutterstock, Inc.

p. 486 © 2011 Andresr. Used under license from Shutterstock, Inc.

p. 487 top left: © 2011 Phil Date. Used under license from Shutterstock, Inc.; top right: Phototake/J.D. Talasek; bottom: Photo by Kevin Mazur/Wire Image/Getty Images

p. 488: left© Bettmann/CORBIS, right: © John A. Angelillo/Corbis

p. 493 skater: © 2011 André Klaassen. Used under license from Shutterstock, Inc., runner: © 2011 Pete Saloutos. Used under license from Shutterstock, Inc., gymnast: © 2011 John Lumb. Used under license from Shutterstock, Inc.

p. 498: From National Eating Disorders Association.

p. 499: From Mind on the Media. Reprinted with permission.

## Chapter 16

p. 506 top: © 2011 Iakov Kalinin. Used under license from Shutterstock, Inc., bottom: © 2011 stoupa. Used under license from Shutterstock, Inc.

p. 507 © 2011 Teresa Kasprzycka. Used under license from Shutterstock, Inc.

p. 510: Visuals Unlimited

p. 513 top: © 2011 Baevskiy Dmitry. Used under license from Shutterstock, Inc., bottom: © 2011 Junial Enterprises. Used under license from Shutterstock, Inc.

p. 514 top: © 2011 MAGDALENA SZACHOWSKA. Used under license from Shutterstock, Inc.

bottom: © 2011 Robyn Mackenzie. Used under license from Shutterstock, Inc.

p. 517 © 2011 Diego Cervo. Used under license from Shutterstock, Inc.

p. 518 © 2011 Diego Cervo. Used under license from Shutterstock, Inc.

p. 521 © 2011 Bostjan Uran. Used under license from Shutterstock, Inc.

p. 523: left © Liba Taylor/CORBIS, right: © 2011 Torsten Schon. Used under license from Shutterstock, Inc.

p. 528: © Liba Taylor/Corbis

p. 529 © 2011 Golden Pixels LLC. Used under license from Shutterstock, Inc.

p. 530 © 2011 afitz. Used under license from Shutterstock, Inc.

p. 533 © 2011 Vivid Pixels. Used under license from Shutterstock, Inc.

p. 534 top: © 2011 PeterG. Used under license from Shutterstock, Inc., bottom: © 2011 Jack.Qi. Used under license from Shutterstock, Inc.

p. 536 © 2011 Alex Valent. Used under license from Shutterstock, Inc.

p. 538 Custom Medical Stock/Edward Gill

## Chapter 17

p. 544 top: © 2011 Raymond Kasprzak. Used under license from Shutterstock, Inc., bottom: © 2011 Heather L Harris. Used under license from Shutterstock, Inc.

p. 545 © 2011 Magone. Used under license from Shutterstock, Inc.

p. 546 © 2011 VladGavriloff. Used under license from Shutterstock, Inc.

p. 547 © 2011 Thomas M Perkins. Used under license from Shutterstock, Inc.

p. 548 Getty Images/Spencer Platt

p. 555 © 2011 Monkey Business Images. Used under license from Shutterstock, Inc.

p. 557 © Karen Kasmauski/Corbis

p. 558 left: © 2011 holbox. Used under license from Shutterstock, Inc.

# Index

Note: Italic page numbers refer to photographs, figures, and tables.